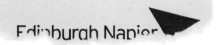

Dynamics of Leadership in Public Service

Dynamics of Leadership in Public Service

Theory and Practice

SECOND EDITION

Montgomery Van Wart

M.E.Sharpe
Armonk, New York
London, England

Copyright © 2011 by M.E. Sharpe, Inc.

Library of Congress Cataloging-in-Publication Data

Van Wart, Montgomery, 1951–
  Dynamics of leadership in public service : theory and practice / by Montgomery Van Wart.
2nd ed.
    p. cm.
  Includes bibliographical references and index.
  ISBN 978-0-7656-2365-2 (hardcover : alk. paper)
  1. Leadership—Handbooks, manuals, etc. 2. Public administration—Handbooks,
manuals, etc. I. Title.

  JF1525.L4V35 2011
  352.3′9—dc22   2010040048

Printed in the United States of America

The paper used in this publication meets the minimum requirements of
American National Standard for Information Sciences
Permanence of Paper for Printed Library Materials,
ANSI Z 39.48-1984.

EB (c)   10   9   8   7   6   5   4   3   2   1

Contents

Preface to the Second Edition

This book addresses leadership in public organizations from two perspectives. First, it examines—in detail—the competencies that organizational leaders at all levels need. Second, it offers a comparative review of the theoretical literature on leadership from a public sector perspective. Both of these elements have received remarkably little attention, despite the abundance of materials available for the private sector.

The book is written for scholars, instructors, students, and practitioners. Academics should appreciate that all discussions have a solid foundation in social science research. Although this study includes a thorough review of the literature, the author has also relied on his own studies (provided as appendixes) and extensive experience as a management trainer. Several of the analyses are original to this book. The applied model used as the basis in Part II is the most articulated action research model in the literature to date. The review of styles provides a coherent, state-of-the-art discussion that is innovative and should provide a useful advancement for an area that has become confused and fragmented. The comparative analysis of all the major schools of thought, including the new "shared leadership" school and integrated leadership theories, is also unprecedented.

Faculty seeking not only to teach practical management and leadership skills but also to relate the analytic and theoretical aspects should find this book particularly useful. The book lays out the theories of leadership in Part I and then proceeds to a pragmatic review of competencies in Part II. In some cases, instructors may find it helpful to change the order and introduce concrete competencies first, especially in practice-oriented classes. With seventeen chapters, the book fits well within a semester format as a primary or secondary text, and provides enough material from which instructors may readily pick and choose.

Trainers using the book as a resource for substantial leadership development programs will be able to provide the detailed feedback necessary for improvement plans. The competencies in this study can easily be keyed to the leadership elements in all the major leadership assessment instruments.

Practitioners and students will find the plan of the book simple to follow in that a leadership action cycle provides a single heuristic model of the leadership process. The model breaks leadership down into five major elements (with seventy subelements overall), including thirty-seven specific leadership competencies (leader characteristics and leader behaviors). The competencies are straightforward. Readers can use the assessment form in Appendix A for self-analysis as well as for distribution.

Reviewers have been unanimous in their praise of the book's illustrative materials.

I have made an effort to provide a wide variety of examples, stories, and data for this enormously broad subject. In addition, I have blended a good deal of ancient, folk, and literary wisdom about leadership with the empirical analysis. Modern scholars in most fields including leadership like to ignore nonempirical knowledge, no matter how wise and respected. Yet, many of these ancient insights are no less true for being old, and readers will find such pearls and insights succinctly expressed and refreshing compared to drier, empirical analysis. For the most part, I do not use standard citation format for quotations from nonacademic sources. Most of these allusions come from Bartlett's *Familiar Quotations*, Van Ekeren's *Words for all Occasions*, and Sherrin's *The Oxford Dictionary of Humorous Quotations*.

CHANGES IN THE SECOND EDITION

The changes in the second edition are extensive. Some of the changes are improvements or attempts to fill in oversights in the first edition, while others cover the enormous research productivity and advances that have occurred since the first edition was sent out for review. The more important ones will be identified here.

The format of the book has also been changed. The theoretical chapters now precede the chapters discussing competency clusters. This is a more traditional organization and is in line with feedback received from those using the first edition.

Chapter 1 now includes an extensive discussion of postmodernism as it relates to leadership studies. Topics such as collaboration, horizontal leadership, and complexity theory are more fully discussed and much better situated in the contemporary intellectual and philosophical climate. A discussion of types of leadership (e.g., political vs. administrative) was also moved from the preface to this chapter.

Chapter 2 includes the substitution of one generic style with two, more specific, styles. That is, while the first edition discussed external leadership as a broad category, this edition follows the literature more closely and uses strategic and collaborative styles as analytically distinct and pragmatically quite different categories. While both have an external focus, the thrust of one focuses on competition and comparative position. The thrust of the other focuses on cooperation and the benefits of sharing. To some degree, they parallel the more internally focused achievement-oriented and inspirational styles.

The section on distributed leadership has been expanded to a chapter titled "Horizontal and Distributed Models of Leadership." Added to discussions in the first edition of superleadership, substitutes theory, self-leadership, and team theory are discussions of informal leadership, followership, and network leadership theory. The latter two areas have seen an explosive growth of interest and research recently. Shared leadership theory, as essentially an overarching model, was moved to be with other integrated theories.

The section on ethics and leadership was also expanded into a full chapter. That chapter now discusses five perspectives. It first lays out a model generally assumed by nearly all theories, a basic integrity model that emphasizes virtue. Four other models extend the normative assumptions or responsibilities of leaders beyond basic virtue. The moral manager approach emphasizes the fostering of appropriate organizational and legal compliance. Authentic leadership focuses on self-awareness and development as a means of grounding oneself to make ethically balanced decisions. Spiritual or servant leadership celebrates the "other" focus of great leaders who epitomize compassion, empathy, and inclusiveness. It is also related to affective leadership and emotional labor. Finally, there is the ethical perspective that leaders are transforming agents for the common good in the vein of Burns (1978, 2003) and Heifetz (1994).

The chapter on specialized approaches still includes the topics of power and gender. Sections on leadership and world cultures, primarily based on the Globe studies, were added. It also includes the domestic parallel: a section on subcultures, diversity, and leadership.

The section on integrative theories was expanded to a full chapter with a much more robust discussion. Added to the array of integrative theories considered are shared leadership (moved from another chapter), strategic theory, social change theory, and complexity leadership theory. All of the chapters on applied leadership competencies have been updated and have additional contemporary examples.

The final chapter has a completely new and substantial discussion evaluating the public leadership research literature. It covers defining the boundaries of types of leadership, fundamental shifts in the field, advances in traditional research approaches, research gaps in leadership studies, and the status of public sector leadership research in general.

Overall, while the book still has a special focus on organizational leadership from an individual perspective, it has followed the field to give much more emphasis to collaboration, networking, diversity, citizen input, and the like. These perspectives do not so much replace authoritarian, hierarchical approaches that have been out of vogue for managers for decades, as add to the important complement of necessary perspectives for today's leaders (Uhl-Bien, Marion, and McKelvey 2007; Raffel, Leisink, and Middlebrooks 2009). Ultimately, leadership for individuals is somewhat more challenging, no matter whether one is looking at managerial competencies (Van Wart and Berman 1999) or current inclusive leadership patterns. Although the focus of the theoretical review is still on the individual perspective, substantially more attention is now given to the process perspective as well.

ACKNOWLEDGMENTS

The help of many along the way has been indispensable. Any work of intellectual value stands on the shoulders of other major scholars. I am particularly indebted to the fine integrative work of Bernard Bass, Gary Yukl, Jerry Hunt, Mary Uhl-Bien, John Bryson and Barbara Crosby, and Jay Conger, among others. I am also indebted to the research of the U.S. Office of Personnel Management, which I have used extensively throughout this text. I wish to thank the managers in Arizona, Iowa, Texas, Florida, and California with whom I have worked; they have shared their experiences with me, and in some cases I have actually used them as examples. And, of course, I have special thanks for my editor at M.E. Sharpe, Harry Briggs, who adopted this project and has been very patient during its development and refinement.

I am personally most indebted to Paul Suino. He has read and reread the book and he has patiently critiqued and proofed it. He also provided the encouragement necessary to complete such an ambitious task, while I was attempting to lead in my own organizations.

Dynamics of Leadership in Public Service

1

Introduction

Those wishing to study leadership in an effort to improve their effectiveness need to be aware of three related facts:

- leadership is a complex phenomenon;
- those embarking on a study must be willing to consider more sophisticated intellectual and applied models if more than platitudes are desired; and
- ultimately, leadership is such a vast subject that one must focus on the particular domain of leadership (e.g., leadership of organizations versus social movements) that one is interested in to provide concrete insights (Bass 1990).

The complexity of the subject becomes apparent when trying to specify a focus or perspective on leadership. For example, is it only about political, social, and business leaders who change the world, or does it include those in charge who simply run things well? Are those who change the world for the worse nonetheless leaders? Does it have to be about executives exclusively, or can it include managers, supervisors, frontline workers, soldiers, or even volunteers? And when we have settled on an operational definition of leadership, do we want our theory to explain the best styles and behaviors to use in an "average" situation? In preparing for a controversial change or responding to a crisis? Do we want to explain how some leaders accomplish things by employing charisma while others do so with a quiet, life-long passion devoid of significant charm? Do we explain the totality of leadership or do we address certain traits, such as decisiveness, only when they appear to make a difference?

Because of the complexity of leadership, simplistic models have limited utility for those wanting useful intellectual or practical insights. Streamlined, overarching theoretical models of leadership certainly have the virtue of elegance. However, they also invariably fall prey to three problems. First, they can overgeneralize, meaning that occasionally good advice may be wrong in a given situation. Second, they can be incomplete, meaning that the advice may be detailed and accurate enough in a few areas but many critical elements of leadership are ignored. Finally, they can lack applicability, meaning that even if the principle is broad enough to be right, it falls short on advice about how to use it. An overview of schools of thought about leadership is provided in this chapter, with theoretical perspectives covered extensively in Part I of this book.

At the applied level, leadership is complex. It involves, among other things, an array of assessment skills, a series of characteristics (traits and skills) that the leader brings to a particular setting, and a wide variety of behavioral competencies. Furthermore, the leadership skills needed in the same position may vary over time as the organization's environment and life cycle change. An applied model distilled from the theoretical and applied literature is provided in Part II. A leadership assessment instrument in the appendix of this book is keyed to this applied model. Part III looks at issues related to leadership development and evaluation.

Finally, types of leadership vary substantially, even though elements of leadership have some commonality at the most global level. For example, the followers of a general differ markedly from those of a religious leader. Likewise, the head of a successful accounting firm will need skills very different from those needed by the head of a troubled manufac-turing firm whose bottom line is being undermined by international competition.

This chapter sets the stage for the theoretical, practical, and developmental analyses of leadership. It first defines the scope of study with a review of leadership types. It next reviews the leadership literature by focusing on traditional and contemporary themes, and follows up by contrasting the mainstream and public sector literatures. The chapter then concentrates on the perennial debates that weave throughout the mainstream leader-ship literature and again contrasts them with those in the public sector literature. Finally, some of the important nomenclature (terms) used in leadership studies are defined and discussed. It is from these discussions that one working operational definition of leader-ship (among many possible) is offered.

TYPES OF LEADERSHIP

An important distinction to make when discussing leadership is to decide what type is involved. While types of leadership inevitably have some similarities, they have important differences, too. Consider organizational leaders, political executives, legislators, community leaders, and the range of opinion leaders. The organizational leader has a large number of defined followers (generally paid) and concrete services or products to produce. Rather than employees, the followers of a political execu-tive tend to be an electorate, producing public policy and ensuring implementation compliance. Legislators are certainly leaders, but their followers are exclusively the electorate, and their major product is legislation. Local level community leaders (e.g., parent–teacher association presidents, volunteer fire chiefs, small nonprofit advisory board chairs), depending on their exact role, often have characteristics that coincide with those of political leaders and organizational leaders. They are often trying to influence policy, but just as often they are a part of the service delivery system, too, if only as volunteers. Opinion leaders (e.g., religious leaders, inventors, and ideological leaders without formal positions) are generally an entirely different sort; they lead others who are not accountable to them, and they affect policies or social trends that are not their direct responsibility. See Exhibit 1.1 for an analysis of the "followers" among different types of leaders.

The primary topic of this book is organizational leadership. Special attention is given to public- and nonprofit-sector settings. Generally, organizational leaders have been de-livered authoritative assessments about which problems to address. This is particularly

Exhibit 1.1

A Simplified View of Different Types of Leaders

		Types of work		
		Execution	Policy	New ideas
Types of followers	Employees	Managers	Executives with policy responsibilties	Transformational leaders
	Constituents	Community leaders of volunteer groups	Legislators and advisory board members	Lobbyists and policy entrepreneurs
	Adherents	Small group leaders	Leaders of social movements	Philosophical zealots and social trendsetters

true in the public sector. Their concern is how to deliver services or products through their organization. Thus, organizational leaders will spend the bulk of their time assessing internal capacities such as task skills, role clarity, and other attributes that are of marginal interest to political leaders. Because of the mission orientation infused in public and nonprofit leadership, the book also includes community-change leadership. Although community-change leadership can have political ramifications, it is a reality for senior and midlevel public sector organizational leaders.

Even narrowing the focus to organizational leadership leaves a broad array of perspectives to consider. Some important distinctions include: leadership exercised at various levels of the organization (executive, management, supervisory, or even frontline employee), line leadership versus staff leadership, leaders in small or large organizations, leaders in old or new organizations, leaders in resource-rich environments versus those in poor environments, and leaders in relatively static organizational environments versus those in relatively dynamic environments.

HISTORY OF THE LITERATURE ON LEADERSHIP IN THE MAINSTREAM AND PUBLIC SECTORS

A brief historical overview of the massive leadership literature is provided as an initial introduction to the subject. It begins with the traditionally dominant themes and then follows up with contemporary themes since the 1990s. Next, the discussion contrasts the distinctly different tones and emphases assumed in the public- versus the private-sector leadership literature.

Dominant Themes in the Modern Leadership Mainstream Through the 1990s

It is certainly impossible to pigeonhole all the mainstream leadership literature[1] into distinct eras with clear demarcations; however, it is possible to capture themes and interests for a heuristic overview. An excellent, exhaustive review can be found in *The Bass Handbook of Leadership* (Bass 2008) for those interested in a detailed history and more complex analysis.

The nineteenth century was dominated by the notion of the "great man" thesis. Particular great men (women were invariably overlooked despite great leaders in history such as Joan of Arc, Elizabeth I, and Clara Barton) somehow move history forward due to their exceptional characteristics as leaders. The stronger version of this theory holds that history is handmaiden to men; great men actually change the shape and direction of history. Philosophers such as Friedrich Nietzsche and William James firmly asserted that history would be different if a great man were suddenly incapacitated. Thomas Carlyle's 1841 essay on heroes and hero worship is an early popular version of this, as was Galton's 1869 study of hereditary genius (cited in Bass 1990, 37–38). Such theories generally have an implicit class bias. A milder version of the theory is that as history proceeds in its irrevocable course, a few men will move history forward substantially and dramatically because of their greatness, especially in moments of crisis or social need. This sentiment was expressed by Hegel, who thought that the great man was an expression of his times, as did Herbert Spencer. Economic determinists such as Karl Marx and Friedrich Engels, although not theorizing about leadership per se, imply that great men overcome obstacles of history more effectively and quickly than do lesser individuals.[2] Although these lines of thinking have more sophisticated echoes later in the trait and situational leadership periods, "hero worship" is certainly alive and well in popular culture and in biographies and autobiographies. It has as its core a belief that there are only a few, very rare individuals in any society at any time that have the unique characteristics to shape or express history. Although this thesis may serve sufficiently for case studies (essentially biographies), it is effectively nonrefutable and therefore unusable as a scientific theory, and it is equally unsatisfying as a primary leadership teaching tool.

The scientific mood of the early twentieth century fostered the development of a more focused search for the basis of leadership. What traits and characteristics do leaders seem to share in common? Researchers developed personality tests and compared the results of average individuals with those perceived to be leaders. By the 1940s, researchers had amassed very long lists of traits from numerous psychologically oriented studies (Bird 1940; Jenkins 1947). This tactic involved two problems. First, the lists became longer and longer as research continued. Second, and more important, the traits and characteristics identified were not powerful predictors across situations. For example, leaders have to be decisive but they must also be flexible and inclusive. Without situational specificity, the endless list of traits offers little prescriptive assistance and descriptively becomes nothing more than a long laundry list. In 1948, Ralph Stogdill published a devastating critique of pure trait theory, which subsequently fell into disfavor as being too unidimensional to account for the complexity of leadership (Stogdill 1948).

The next major thrust looked at the situational contexts that affect leaders, and attempted to find meaningful patterns for theory building and useful advice. One early example was the work that came out of the Ohio State Leadership Studies (Shartle 1950; Hempill 1950; Hempill and Coons 1957). These studies began by testing 1,800 statements related to leadership behavior. By continually distilling the behaviors,

Exhibit 1.2

The Administrator as Leader

"If administration is to be leadership and not command, then it were well that the high echelons of hierarchy were Escoffiers or Rembrandts, sensitive to the flavor and shades of coloring in the group relationships. Such leadership requires not just an understanding of the organizational interrelationships of the hierarchy. It requires some knowledge of the psychological dynamics of group behavior, of belief systems, of status values, and of the learning process itself. The administrator who is a leader must also be a teacher. For such leadership he requires not only formal education in administration but also apprenticeship and on-the-job training."

Source: Marshall (1953, 13).

researchers arrived at two underlying factors: consideration and the initiation of structure. Consideration describes a variety of behaviors related to the development, inclusion, and good feelings of subordinates. The initiation of structure describes a variety of behaviors related to defining roles, control mechanisms, task focus, and work coordination both inside and outside the unit. Coupled with the humanist/human relations revolution that was occurring in the 1950s and 1960s, these (and similar studies) spawned a series of useful, if often simplistic and largely bimodal, theories. Arygris's maturity theory (1957), Likert's motivational approach (1959), and McGregor's Theory X and Theory Y (1960) all implicitly encourage more consideration in all leadership behavior. Maslow's (1967) eupsychian management recommends that leadership be assigned based on the needs of the situation so that authoritarian tendencies (excessive structure) can be curbed. This line of thinking was further advanced and empirically tested by Fiedler (1967), who developed a contingency theory and related leader-match theory (Fiedler, Chemers, and Mahar 1976). Blake and Mouton's (1964, 1965) managerial grid recommends leaders be highly skilled in both task behaviors (initiating structure) and people-oriented behaviors (consideration). Hersey and Blanchard's life-cycle theory (1969, 1972) relates the maturity of the followers (both in terms of expertise and attitude) to the ideal leader behavior—telling (directing), selling (consulting), participating, and delegating. (For an early example of this insight, see Exhibit 1.2.)

These early situational theories were certainly useful for several reasons. First, they were useful as an antidote to the excessively hierarchical, authoritarian styles that had developed in the first half of the twentieth century with the rise and dominance of large organizations in both the private and public sectors. Second, they were useful as teaching tools for incipient and practicing managers who appreciated the elegant constructs even though they were descriptively simplistic. As a class, however, these theories generally failed to meet scientific standards because they tried to explain too much with too few variables. Of the major theories, only Vroom's normative-decision model broke out of this pattern because it self-consciously focused on a single dimension of leadership style—the role of participation—and identified seven problem attributes and two classes of cases (group and individual) (Vroom and Yetton 1973; Vroom and Jago 1988). Although the situational perspective still forms the basis of most leadership theories today, it has largely done so either in a strictly managerial context (i.e., a narrow level of analysis) on a factor-by-factor basis or it has been subsumed in more comprehensive approaches to leadership at the macro level.

While ethical dimensions were occasionally mentioned in the mainstream litera- ture, the coverage was invariably peripheral because of the avoidance of normative (value-laden) issues by social scientists. The first major text devoted to ethical issues was Robert Greenleaf's book, *Servant Leadership* (1977). He was ignored by main- stream theorists who were dominated by positivists, despite his affiliation with the Massachusetts Institute of Technology, Harvard, Dartmouth, and the University of Virginia, and he ultimately founded the Center for Applied Ethics.[3] In contrast, James Macgregor Burns's book on leadership burst onto the scene in 1978 and had unusually heavy ethical overtones.[4] However, it was not the ethical dimension that catapulted it to prominence but its transformational theme, which is discussed below. Both Green- leaf (a former business executive) and Burns (a political scientist) were outside the usual leadership academic circles whose members came primarily from business and psychology backgrounds. A number of contemporary mainstream leadership theorists, both popular and academic, such as DePree (1989), Gardner (1989), Rost (1990), Block (1993), Bennis, Parikh, and Lessem (1994, in contrast with Bennis's other work), and Zand (1997), continue in this tradition, to one degree or another. For an example of the profound difference this one element can make, however, see Exhibit 1.3. This theme was covered earlier and more frequently (at least in terms of ethical uses of discretion) in the public sector literature, but that was not part of the mainstream literature and will be discussed separately.

Until 1978, the primary focus of the mainstream literature was on leadership at lower levels, which was amenable to small-group and experimental methods with simpli- fied variable models, while executive leadership (with its external demands) and more amorphous abilities to induce large-scale change were largely ignored.[5] Burns's book on leadership dramatically changed that interest by introducing the notion that transac- tional leadership was what was largely being studied and that the other highly important arena—transformational leadership—was largely being ignored.[6] This struck an especially responsive chord in the nonexperimental camp, which had already been explicitly stating that nationally there was a surfeit of managers (who use a "transactional" mode) and a serious deficit of leaders (who use a "transformational" mode) (Zaleznik 1977). Overall, this school agreed that leaders have special responsibility for understanding a changing environment, that they facilitate more dramatic changes, and that they often can energize followers far beyond what traditional exchange theory would suggest.

Overstating for clarity, three subschools emerged that emphasized different aspects of these "larger-than-life" leaders.[7] The transformational school emphasized vision and overarching organizational change (e.g., Burns 1978; Bass 1985; Bennis and Nanus 1985; and Tichy and Devanna 1986). The charismatic school focused on the influence processes of individuals and the specific behaviors used to arouse inspiration and higher levels of action in followers (e.g., House 1977; Meindl 1990; Conger and Kanungo 1998).

Exhibit 1.3

Two Great Visionary and Entrepreneurial Leaders in the Public Sector—With One Big Difference

Great cities must occasionally reinvent themselves, or else they get stuck in the notions and needs of past ages. The city of Paris is the most famous example. An ancient medieval city, Paris by the nineteenth century had become a ramble of narrow, winding streets. Napoleon III, none too graciously, commanded the redesign of the city to install major boulevards to ease traffic problems. Not only did this provide modern traffic flow and infrastructure, but in the minds of many it also established Paris as the most beautiful city in the world. New York City was another such example in the twentieth century. Despite its bedrock base for skyscrapers, a brilliant harbor, and financial preeminence, by the early twentieth century it had become a candidate for decline as an island city outgrowing its own infrastructure. Two public servants—Austin Tobin and Robert Moses—thoroughly reinvented the city to make it the greatest city (at least in terms of population, wealth, and power) on earth in the latter part of the century.

Austin Tobin (1903–1971) joined the Port Authority of New York (later called the Port Authority of New York and New Jersey) not long after its creation in 1921 and became its executive director in 1942. Although a lawyer by training, he mastered the internal and technical dynamics of leading a large organization. He inherited an agency that was largely independent because it was self-funding through fees; he was able to expand his legal purview over the years through his political connections and knowledge of the law; and he was able to use the variety of projects and responsibilities of the Authority as a great source of power. During his tenure as executive director, Tobin was responsible for the inclusion of all three major airports in his agency—Newark, LaGuardia, and Idlewild (now Kennedy)—added the Newark seaport, created the Elizabeth seaport, added terminals in Brooklyn, two tubes to the Lincoln Tunnel, and a second tier to the George Washington Bridge, built the largest bus terminal in the world, and set the stage for the building of the World Trade Center. His vision of New York as the leading commercial center in the world was not diminished by the extraordinary challenges of managing across the various jurisdictions of many mayors, borough presidents, and two very powerful governors. His entrepreneurial flare helped him create massive projects that were brilliantly executed and stood the test of time.

Robert Moses (1888–1981) had no less impact on New York than his sometimes rival, Tobin. Moses became the city parks commissioner in 1934 as well as chairman of most of the major bridge and tunnel authorities in New York (which ultimately included the Triborough Bridge, Brooklyn Battery Tunnel, and the Verrazano-Narrows Bridge with their immense revenue base). He further added to his power later by becoming the city construction coordinator and a member of the City Planning Commission. During his career he masterminded and built the immensely successful Jones Beach State Park, the East Side highway (FDR Drive), the crucial Cross-Bronx Expressway, the 1964 World's Fair, and many of the modern port facilities. Just as Tobin's vision was New York as a commercial powerhouse, Moses's vision was New York as a great metropolis of fluid movement and great parks. A genius of detail and the creation of timeless projects, he was a virtuoso of power, able to defy mayors and governors with relative ease.

Plutarch noted that "the most glorious exploits do not always furnish us with the clearest signs of virtue or vice in men; sometimes a matter of less moment informs us better of their character and inclinations." So it can be argued about these two "great" men. Tobin was known for his stand on diversity in an age when such notions were not popular and had no legal weight. He promoted Jews and women in the mid-1940s (over opposition) and fought extremely hard for the integration of the trade unions in the 1960s. He provided internal development programs, had a widespread reputation for equitable treatment of the rank-and-file employees, and inspired great loyalty despite his toughness and occasional rigidity. Finally, his tenant relocation programs were considered models of compassion and integrity. On the other hand, Moses was a thoroughgoing

(continued)

Exhibit 1.3 *(continued)*

elitist in the worst sense. His staff was as ethnically pure and male dominated as any other of his age. He worked with the white-dominated labor unions to keep Puerto Ricans and African Americans out. Lastly, his tenant relocation programs—affecting tens of thousands of citizens over the years—were legendary uses of brutal state force that provided no state assistance, even in an era of severe housing shortages.

So we are left with a question about the greatness, and perhaps even about the leadership, of these two extraordinary men. Both were technically brilliant, entrepreneurial geniuses; both had great visions that they were able to execute. Both transformed the New York City miniregion into a leading world commercial and community center. Yet, Tobin's "underside" reveals a caring for employees, a sense of social fairness, and a compassion for those affected by his projects that is totally lacking in Robert Moses. It is unlikely that anyone would argue that Austin Tobin was not a great leader, but do you consider Moses a great leader, just a leader, or neither?

Less articulated in terms of leadership theory was an entrepreneurial school that urged leaders to make practical process and cultural changes that would dramatically improve quality or productivity; it shared a change emphasis with the transformational school and an internal focus with the charismatic school (Peters and Austin 1985; Hammer and Champy 1993; and Champy 1995).

The infusion of the transformational leadership school(s) led to a reinvigoration of academic and nonacademic studies of leadership as well as to a good deal of initial confusion and ultimately to multifaceted approaches by the 1990s. Was the more transactional leadership that the situationalists had so assiduously studied really just mundane management? Or was the new transformational leadership just an extension of basic skills that its adherents were poorly equipped to explain with conventional scientific methodologies? Even before the 1980s some work had been done to create more integrative models that tried to explain the many aspects of leadership (Yukl 1971; Winter 1979). Yet, it was not until the 1980s that work began in earnest and conventional models incorporated transactional and transformational elements rather routinely. Bass's work is a good example in this regard. Even his original work on transformational leadership (1985) has strong transactional elements (transformational leaders being those who not only master transactional skills but also are able to capitalize on transformational skills),[8] that were further strengthened in later work (Bass and Avolio 1990; Bass 1996). In the third edition of *Bass & Stogdill's Handbook of Leadership*, Bass was able to assert that the field "has broken out of its normal confinement to the study of [leader group] behaviors" to more studies on executives, more inclusion of perspectives from political science, and more cross fertilization among schools of thought (Bass 1990, xi).

From the 1990s, three major themes developed. First, there has been an interest in integrating the proliferation of perspectives to the degree possible. Second, there has been a better appreciation of horizontal leadership, for example, team leadership. Third, there have been arrays of postmodern perspectives that have challenged the dominance of leader-centric and even organization-centric leadership perspectives.

Contemporary Theme 1: Integrated or Comprehensive Leadership Models

The urge for integrative theories in the popular literature has been relatively constant and has tended to lead to prescriptive, normative, universalistic, and relatively simplistic models. Though they may be inspiring and provide numerous useful tips, they are not generally particularly rigorous, especially from a contextual perspective. The most rigorous and relatively elegant integrative model from the scientific community is generally considered to be Bass's "full range" leadership model (1985), which merges both transactional and transformational approaches. It has found wide support and has been reported to include up to 70 percent of the variance of leadership factors in some studies. Essentially it says that one starts with good management in which employees are monitored and incentivized at the transactional level. Performance exceeds expectations, however, at the transformational level with personal/group consideration, the ability to inspire the transcending of self-interest, leadership that has vision and promotes creativity, and leaders who are themselves somewhat charismatic. As powerful as this may be at a macro level, it is still highly universalistic (noncontextual) and simplistic (it does not account for numerous factors not in the model nor does it predict the proportion of emphasis of the various factors in different situations).

Recently there has been a call from the traditional empiricist perspective for better, descriptively precise theories, as well as a call from the newer postmodern theorists for more complex and relational theories. Avolio (2007) suggests that integrative theories must contain five elements: cognitive elements of leaders and followers, individual and group behaviors, the historical context, the proximal or internal context, and the distal or environmental context. This is a tall order because it involves so many simultaneous spheres, each with numerous factors, that it is nearly impossible to represent in more than a descriptive framework. Some examples of such models from the mainstream are Yukl's flexible leadership theory model (2008), Hunt's extended multiple organizational level model (1996), Boal and Hooijberg's integrated strategic leadership model (2001), Pearce and Conger's shared leadership model (2003a and b; Pearce, Conger and Locke 2008), Chemers's integrative model (1997), and Uhl-Bien, Marion, and McKelvey's complexity adaptive systems theory (2007).

One of the great challenges in organizing leadership research as well as teaching it to practitioners is the enormous situational variety related to different sectors, organizing structures, levels of analysis, and focus of analysis. Even narrowing the focus to organizational leadership, is one addressing the private or public sector with their different emphases on profit maximization and competition versus the public good and governance, examining a hierarchical or a team-based organization, distinguishing among the competencies for a frontline supervisor or an agency head, or focusing on managing-for-results versus the effects of gender, power, or ethics on leadership? While normal science and deep understanding is built upon individual cases, ultimately classes of cases are aligned into categories and types and midlevel theories, which are further aggregated into macro-level theories. While mainstream leadership research has been strong at the empirical and midlevels, leadership research has had difficulty agreeing to frameworks in order to incorporate the disparate theories referenced earlier (i.e., transactional, transformational, distributed, servant, etc.). As mentioned earlier, the most successful broad approach is probably Bass's widely cited full range theory, which is relatively successful at integrating transactional and transformational leadership theory (Bass 1985, 1996).

Starting with a community leadership basis, Crosby and others have provided a wide variety of publications related to integrative leadership (Crosby and Bryson 2005; Crosby and Kiedrowski 2008). Integrative leadership focuses on cross-boundary problem solving that elevates the community in the tradition established by Burns (1978) of "transforming" leadership (raising the consciousness of followers to solve problems through enlightenment as much as self-interest) rather than merely transformational (i.e., change-oriented) leadership. It tends to be executive, policy, and ideologically oriented.

Van Wart (2004) frames leadership from an individual and organizational perspective using a "leadership action cycle" to integrate transactional, transformational, and distributed approaches with particular reference to public sector settings. His model includes five major leader domains—assessments, characteristics, styles, behaviors, and evaluation/development—which ultimately incorporate seventy factors. His framework aims to be useful as a tool for relating research studies to an overarching context and as a teaching matrix of concrete leadership and management mechanics.

Matthew Fairholm (2004; Fairholm and Fairholm 2009) follows in the tradition of Gilbert Fairholm (1991) in framing leadership more broadly from a public values perspective. He emphasizes "five leadership perspectives (ranging from leadership as equivalent to scientific management, to leadership being a whole-soul or spiritual endeavor) held by public managers and discusses their implications for public administration" (Fairholm 2004, 577). In doing so, he provides a classical apology for administrative leadership. Fernandez (2005) looks at the critical factors leading to superintendent success (educational performance) using an integrative framework and a large data set of Texas school districts. He found that over half of the variance in organizational performance could be explained by six variables: community support, task difficulty, experience, promotion of change, choice of style, and internal management. While community support had a direct, positive relationship with performance, in other cases variables had nonlinear effects, such as task difficulty, which moderated the choice of style and internal management emphasis, and promotion of change, which had a short-term negative effect because of disruption. Fernandez and Pitts (2007) followed up with a study of leadership change using the same data set. These and other comprehensive perspectives are elaborated in chapter 7.

Contemporary Theme 2: Distributed Leadership

Even as the focus on the role of "big picture" and change leadership was being emphasized by transformational leadership following the 1980s, contemporary trends forced many organizations to rethink overreliance on strong leaders. Of course an acknowledgment of followers has been a theme of leadership since its inception, with approaches such as early attribution theory, which studied leaders' power and effectiveness as affected by followers' perceptions, and Hollander's (1958) idiosyncratic credit theory, which noted that leaders build up and lose psychological support that they use in their initiatives.

However, the traits of leaders, their daily practices (transactions), and the ability to inspire change have tended to be center stage.

Contemporary trends have increasingly placed followers in their various guises in an equal light, and have given them far more research attention. Pearce and Conger's (2003a) important work, *Shared Leadership: Reframing the Hows and Whys of Leadership*, crystallized the new rethinking about non–leader-centric forms of leadership by incorporating elements of vertical leadership with horizontal leadership (i.e., self, self-managed teams, and various types of empowering leadership). Horizontal leadership is often called distributed leadership; *Leadership Quarterly* devoted a special issue to it in 2006, as well as one that included followers in 2001. Examples in the follower-distributed vein are numerous; a few noteworthy ones are Kellerman's book on followership (2008), Drath and associates' call for an "increasingly peer-like and collaborative" framework (2008), and Van Vugt, Hogan, and Kaiser's (2008, 182) historical-evolutionary analysis for why leadership research "tends to ignore the central role of followers." Calls for more emphasis on followers and collective action in public sector settings have become more common around the globe (Dunoon 2002; Alimo-Metcalfe and Alban-Metcalfe 2005; Lawler 2008; Lemay 2009).

Teams started to become important in the 1980s (e.g., Scholtes 1988), but research lagged until the 1990s as did leadership functions in particular (Burke et al. 2006). The different types of teams (senior management, functional, cross-functional, self-managed, etc.) with their different emphases on regular production, communication, and innovation, as well as vertical versus horizontal (distributed) modalities have made research in this area complex. Today, with the increased importance of distributed leadership, leadership in teams has become an important topic (Day, Gronn, and Salas 2006). Transformational leadership effects have been formally studied (Schaubroeck, Lam, and Cha 2007; Purvanova and Bono 2009), and transformational approaches have been encouraged in the popular literature as well (Logan, King, and Fischer-Wright 2008). Significant work has been done on different types of teams such as senior management teams (Wageman et al. 2008), comparing the importance of vertical and shared leadership elements (Ensley, Hmieleski, and Pearce 2006; Pearce, Conger, and Locke 2008), the role of empowerment (Chin et al. 2007), representative teams and organizational democracy (Clarke 2006), and the effects of formal leadership roles on individual performance (Day, Sin, and Chen 2004), among other topics. Distributed-leadership theory is discussed more fully in chapter 5.

Contemporary Theme 3: Postmodern Perspectives on Leadership

A third trend has been an attempt to provide a paradigm shift from the modernist approach, which has tended to be relatively uncritical of leaders, power systems, and the methods of traditional social science at "discovering knowledge." By critiquing or refuting modernist assumptions, it offers fresh perspectives. It will be discussed more fully here because its subtle but profound effects are discussed in numerous chapters (especially chapters 5, 6, and 7).

Several characteristics have tended to dominate the mainstream regarding the overall approach. First, until recently, leadership research followed "modern" trends regarding the emphasis on empiricism, rationalism, positivism, and reductionism. Empiricism holds that all knowledge comes from the senses, and that the metaphysical is not an interest of science. Rationalism asserts that the mind organizes knowledge of the external world by observation and contemplation. Positivism (built on empiricism and rationalism) holds that science is testable, cumulative, and neutral, and that things are ultimately measurable. Reductionism attempts to reduce complexity to the fewest elements or variables, and to explain science at the most fundamental level (e.g., reducing classical genetics to molecular biology, Sarkar 1992).

Second, and flowing from the first, the study of leadership (overall) has tended to be objectivist, leader-centric, and status-quo-oriented. The objectivist trend was manifested by the effort to break leadership down into its constituent parts (traits, skills, behaviors, attitudes, etc.) and analyze the empirical relationship among them, with the hope that increasingly abstract general rules could be interpolated from microlevel studies. Research tended to be leader-centric because the leader in the leadership process has tended to be the major object of study. How does the leader relate to follower? How does the leader maintain order, control, and productivity? How does the leader use different styles in different situations to achieve what ends? How does the leader use her/his values, or change the organization's values? Finally, leadership studies have tended to assume that leadership forms are inherent and that individuals and organizations need to discover and master those forms (sometimes called realism).

Incipient challenges to some of the tenets of modernist research began as early as the late 1970s with the work of people like Burns (1978) with the introduction of social values and Greenleaf (1977) with the introduction of individual values and a denial of instrumentalism. The two earliest journals on leadership, the *Journal of Leadership and Organizational Studies* (started in 1980) and *Leadership Quarterly* (started in 1990), both hoped to promote more positivist (and thus modernist) research, although they allowed eclectic approaches. Since 2000, leadership studies have been increasingly affected by calls for approaches that reflect postmodern research trends. The newer journals of *Integral Leadership* (2000) and *Leadership* (2005) reverse the modernist emphasis by appeals for more eclectic, relational, and holistic approaches.

While the tenets underlying modern research will not be abandoned, they are likely to be overtaken by a radically different perspective from many leading researchers in the longer term. Postmodern thought asserts that science is not neutral, science is not necessarily cumulative, sensory knowledge is only one form of knowledge and nonsensory knowledge can be studied, and that the structure of knowledge is a form of power, and thus accepting that structure is to reify the status quo. An alternative way of knowing and perceiving is constructionism (aka constructivism), which challenges the supremacy of empiricism, rationalism, positivism, and reductionism. It holds that all knowledge is constructed, truth is relative to our purposes (i.e., based on intersubjectivity), the notion of "progress" is largely a myth, and that far from being a neutral observer of "facts," scientists are active participants in creating reality or distorting it for our (generally unintentional) ends. It also points out that differences are often as or more important than similarities.

Postmodernists assert that the myth of neutrality allows personal assumptions to go unchallenged; it is better to state one's values and incorporate them in the research endeavor explicitly than to purport to be unbiased. The scientific theory underlying postmodernism is complexity and chaos systems theory to the degree that it emphasizes the importance of understanding the whole as much or more than the dissected parts, the prospect for external perturbations, and the unexpected effects of seemingly tiny incidents (e.g., tipping points and butterfly effects). Examples of research reflecting strong elements of postmodernism in leadership research are identified below related to discourse (aka discursive) theory, gender and ethnic studies, complexity and relational theory, integral leadership studies, organizational learning and time. Some public sector examples of these trends follow.

Discourse theory has its roots in Foucault (1970, 1972), who examined the reification of social structures through language and extended usage. For example, calling guerilla military activists in another country either "freedom fighters" or "terrorists" entirely changes the terms of debate. In leadership studies in particular, an interest in discourse theory "began with a more general dissatisfaction with the results and lack of coherence in trait and style based psychological research" (Kelly 2008, 764). Those with a discourse theory perspective tend to question traditional definitions of leadership (Barker 1997, 2001), question and challenge traditional leadership studies as excessively involved in the psychology of leaders (Fairhurst 2007), emphasize the importance of studying followers in context (Gronn 2002; Alvesson and Sveningsson 2003; Collinson 2005, 2006), and ask for longer ethnographic studies (Kelly 2008). L. Chen (2008, 547) notes that the more traditional positivist research tradition of leadership psychology and more constructionist discursive leadership "appear to have little in common." Nonetheless, she "finds ample room for coexistence . . . when one takes into consideration the enormous complexity of the subject matter, coupled with the multiplicity of perspectives for study" (L. Chen 2008, 549).

Gender theory in leadership is loosely aligned with discourse theory. Gender theory has used a variety of critiques to understand the glass ceiling, but discourse theory is particularly powerful at describing and studying the subtle structures of power that do not necessarily block women from power in the contemporary world, but tend to create amorphous cultural challenges for women to reach the highest levels (Eagly and Carli [2007] use the labyrinth metaphor). Other critiques exploring the difficulty of women as leaders include work by Chin et al. (2007), Heilman (2001), Heilman and Okimoto (2007), Powell, Butterfield, and Parent (2002), and Powell and Graves (2003). Hogue and Lord use complexity theory (2007) to understand gender bias.

Uhl-Bien, Marion, and McKelvey (2007, 298) suggest that "leadership models of the last century have been products of top-down, bureaucratic paradigms. These models are eminently effective for an economy premised on physical production but are not well suited for a more knowledge-oriented economy. Complexity science suggests a different paradigm for leadership—one that frames leadership as a complex interactive dynamic from which adaptive outcomes (e.g., learning, innovation, and adaptability) emerge." Unlike the rather monolithic general systems theory that underlies most of modern social science, complexity theory is a type of general systems theory that appreciates the massive complexity and interconnectedness of all phenomena, particularly in human social processes such as leadership. Because of this complexity, it points out that the most successful organizations are often ones that have evolving structures that bubble up from below and percolate in from the environment—often called complex adaptive systems (Schneider and Somers 2006; Osborn and Hunt 2007). Complexity theory is very good for studying the multidirectional relational nature of leadership (Uhl-Bien 2006), and the emergence of new organizational and leadership forms (Lichtenstein and Plowman 2009). This approach has reached the popular literature in many subtle and not-so-subtle ways. For example, in defining leadership, Goffee and Jones (2009) say—to lay audiences—it is relational, nonhierarchical, and contextual, a far cry from many earlier definitions focusing on leaders' influence, power to change for better or worse, leader traits, and so on.

Integral leadership tends to focus on leadership as a community process, democratizing and decentralizing leadership as much as possible. This is the focus of the *Integral Leadership Review*. One example is McCrimmon (2007, 1), who asserts that "leadership needs to be reframed for a digital, postmodern age. The world is losing its stable and hierarchical character. Life is now more dynamic, chaotic; final authorities have vanished." Edwards (2009) is another good example of this emphasis, as illustrated in the title of his essay, "Seeing Integral Leadership Through Three Important Lenses: Developmental, Ecological, and Governance," which incorporates a focus on followers, the environment, and community. Integral leadership themes are common in the popular literature because of the concern for corporate social responsibility among leaders and private organizations, as well as in the public administration literature because of its focus on serving the community and doing good.

As Gary Yukl (2009, 49) points out, "organizational learning is an important determinant of long-term performance and survival, but many companies seem unable to master the learning process." Yet as Waldman, Berson, and Keller (2009, 1) note, despite the obvious overlap, "there has not been much work attempting to specifically link leadership and organizational learning phenomena." The seminal work in connecting the literatures was Vera and Crossan (2004), who explore the relationship of organizational learning in terms of transactional and transformational styles. They propose that a transformational leadership style will be particularly critical in creating the right environment for the creation and diffusion of useful knowledge. Yukl (2009) is more inclined to think that organizational learning can be enhanced through multiple styles, including transactional ones properly utilized.

Certainly all of these themes have been expressed in the literature regarding public sector organizations, but in many cases the theoretical or ideological specification has been substantially more muted and related trends are intermingled more freely. An excellent example of discourse (and gender bias) theory is by Ford (2006, 77), who "examines contemporary discourses of leadership and their complex inter-relations with gender and identity in the UK public sector. . . . Accordingly, this article questions dominant hegemonic and stereotypical notions of subjectivity that assume a simple, unitary identity and perpetuate andocentric depictions of organizational life." Crosby and Kiedrowski (2008) provide four levels of integral leadership spanning the individual, group, organization, and society. Schweigert (2007, 325) provides a concrete example in a community setting in which "leadership is rooted in the authority of the followers" and further asserts that "leadership development must focus less on the qualities of individual leaders and more on the social settings, processes, and needs that require and facilitate authoritative action." Critique of the limits of hierarchy and measurement have suggested more integrated and values-oriented public sector leadership models (Loveday 2008). Some analysts examining the overarching models of leadership with a public sector context have found that they are excessively managerial and pay too little attention to appropriate values (Fairholm 2004), and lack an agenda defining public sector distinctiveness (Van Slyke and Alexander 2006). Some work has been done in trying to provide more specified models (Fernandez 2005; Thach and Thompson 2007).

The interconnectedness of problems, the regionalization and globalization of solutions, and the decrease in government resources have emphasized the need to move increasingly from government to governance and from hierarchy to networks (Maak and Pless 2006). This requires that leaders have a new worldview, different competencies, and additional tools. Several sets of literature have evolved that overlap with organizational leadership, which is our primary focus here. One important example relates to a special issue on collaborative management in *Public Administration Review* in 2006. The symposium editors provide two helpful definitions. "Collaborative public management is a concept that describes the process of facilitating and operating in multiorganizational arrangements to solve problems that cannot (readily) be solved by single organizations. Collaborative means to colabor, to cooperate to achieve common goals, working across boundaries in multisector relationships. Cooperation is based on the value of reciprocity" (O'Leary, Gerard, and Bingham 2006, 7). They further note that "participatory governance is the active involvement of citizens in government decision making. Governance means to steer the process that influences decisions and actions within the private, public, and civic sectors." Don Kettl (2006, 10) discusses the historical importance of boundaries and how the contemporary imperative is to collaborate. He notes: "Working effectively at these boundaries requires new strategies of collaboration and new skills for public managers. Failure to develop these strategies—or an instinct to approach boundaries primarily as political symbolism—worsens the performance of the administrative system." Thompson and Perry (2006) dissect collaboration into five variable dimensions that leaders have to understand and master for maximum effectiveness: governance, administration, organizational autonomy, mutuality, and norms of trust and reciprocity. Researchers even point out when collaboration is less than ideal (McGuire 2006). Sometimes these issues are looked at through the lens of networks, as analyzed in a symposium in *Public Performance and Management Review* that looks at a "myriad of cross-agency networks, partnerships, consortia, alliances, joint ventures, contracts and other collaborative ventures" (Agranoff 2008b, 315). What are the most critical aspects for networks to function successfully? In his empirical study, B. Chen (2008) suggests that the answer is resource sharing and trust. Excellent case studies of collaboration and citizen involvement are common in the field (e.g., Callahan 2007), as are theoretical pieces that probe and challenge the limits of collaboration (Bevir 2006).

(See Exhibit 1.4 for a summary of the eras of mainstream leadership theory and research.) This cursory review cannot cover the full range of perspectives on specific leadership topics such as the types of leaders, leader styles, the types and effects of followers, and the relevance of societal and organizational cultures on leadership, but most of these topics will be covered throughout the text.

The Public Sector Literature on Leadership Theory and Research

Although the literature on leadership with a public sector focus is a fraction of that with a private-sector focus, it has nevertheless been substantial, albeit relatively unfocused. One way to begin a brief review is to look at the track record of *Public Administrative Review* (*PAR*). In the course of an informal content analysis of the journal since its inception, and using a rather loose definition of leadership that includes the broader management topics, most executive topics, much of the explicit discretion literature, and the part of the organizational change literature that has a strong leadership component, the author found 110 articles relating to the topic, published over sixty-one years. However, using a stricter criterion, namely, that leadership was an explicit focus of the article, only about twenty-five articles qualified, or about four per decade on average (see Van Wart [2003] for a full discussion of this study and the literature).

In the 1940s, articles by Finer (1941) and Leys (1943) defined the administrative discretion debate—how much discretion should public administrators have and under what conditions?—which was taken up again so vigorously in the 1990s. Donald Stone's 1945 "Notes on the Government Executive: His Role and His Methods" is as good an equivalent to Follett's "The Essentials of Leadership" (1933/1996) or Barnard's *The Functions of the Executive* (1938/1987) as ever appeared in the journal.

There was a trickle of high-quality pieces with a generalist and nonscientific approach in the 1950s (Lawton 1954; Dimock 1958). A piece based exclusively on empirical evidence was published in this period, which brought together the literature on small groups in public sector settings (Golembiewski 1959).

In the 1960s, only one empirical study examined the variation in the motivation of public and private leaders (Guyot 1962). One commentator observed that federal managers had wholly inadequate management training (Fisher 1962). The editor in chief of *PAR*, James Fesler (1960), provided a superb editorial comment on the importance of studying leadership and its many contexts. Other topics addressed were influence and social power (Altshular 1965; Lundstedt 1965).

No important articles appeared in the 1970s, which reflects the low profile of leadership publications in the popular literature. Yet, the lacuna is made up by the resurgence of interest in leadership topics in the 1980s. DiIulio (1989) reasserted the importance of both leadership and the management component. Probably the three best articles on the training and development of leaders were written during this time (Likert 1981; Flanders and Utterback 1985; and Faerman, Quinn, and Thompson 1987). Stone (1981) and Dimock (1986) wrote essays regarding how important it is for leaders to nurture innovation and creativity in organizations. Empirical pieces also

Exhibit 1.4

Eras of Orthodox Leadership Theory and Research

Era	Major time frame	Major characteristics/examples of proponents
Great Man	Pre-1900; continues to be popular in biographies	• Emphasis on emergence of a great figure such as a Napoleon, George Washington, or Martin Luther who has substantial effect on society • Era influenced by notions of rational social change by uniquely talented and insightful individuals
Trait	1900–1948; resurgence of recognition of importance of natural talents	• Emphasis on the individual traits (physical, personal, motivational, aptitudinal) and skills (communication and ability to influence) that leaders bring to all leadership tasks • Era influenced by scientific methodologies in general (especially industrial measurement) and scientific management in particular (e.g., the definition of roles and assignment of competencies to those roles)
Contingency	1948 to the 1980s; continues as basis of most rigorous models but with vastly expanded situational repertoire	• Emphasis on the situational variables with which leaders must deal, especially performance and follower variables. Shift from traits and skills to behaviors (e.g., informing and analytic skills versus consulting and motivating). Dominated by bimodal models in its heyday • Era influenced by the rise of human relations theory, behavioral science (in areas such as motivation theory), and the use of small-group experimental designs in psychology • Examples emphasizing bimodal models include Ohio State, Michigan, Hersey-Blanchard, managerial grid, leadership theory involving maximal levels of participation (generally with three to seven major variables) includes Fiedler, House, Vroom
Transformational	1978 to present	• Emphasis on leaders who create change in deep structures, major processes, or overall culture. Leader mechanisms may be compelling vision, brilliant technical insight, and/or charismatic quality • Era influenced by the loss of American dominance in business, finance, and science, and the need to reenergize various industries that had slipped into complacency • Examples (academic and popular) include Burns, House, Bennis, Iacocca, Kouzes and Posner, Senge, Tichy and Devanna, Bass and Conger
Servant	1977 to present	• Emphasis on ethical responsibilities to followers, stakeholders, and society. Business theorists tend to emphasize service to followers; political theorists emphasize citizens; public-administration analysts tend to emphasize legal compliance and/or citizens • Era influenced by social sensitivities raised in the 1960s and 1970s • Early proponents include Greenleaf and Burns. Contemporary and popular proponents include DuPree, Covey, Rost, Autry, Vaill, Gardner
Multifaceted approaches	1990s to present	• Integrated models with emphasis on search for relatively sophisticated comprehensive models within organizational leadership (Hunt, Yukl, Chemers) • Distributed leadership with emphasis on understanding leadership as a horizontal process involving teams, follower empowerment, and development of leaders (Manz, Pearce and Conger) • Postmodern perspective with emphasis on critique of status quo leadership structures, positivist methodologies, progressive assumptions, and reductionism (Wheatley, Uhl-Bien, Kiel)

appeared on followership (Gilbert and Hyde 1988) and leader action planning (Young and Norris 1988).

Because leadership is so highly related to reform, and because of the debate regarding the appropriate reforms to make that occurred throughout the decade, leadership is discussed at least indirectly in nearly every issue of *PAR* after 1992. This is particularly true of the debate about administrative discretion, which largely pitted an "entrepreneurial" camp against a "stewardship" camp. Although they cannot do justice to the full range of topics in these two idealized perspectives, good examples are provided in Bellone and Goerl's "Reconciling Public Entrepreneurship and Democracy" (1992) and Terry's "Administrative Leadership, Neo-Managerialism, and the Public Management Movement" (1998). Some of the best and most focused empirically based studies in *PAR* have appeared since the 1990s (Hennessey 1998; Moon 1999; Considine and Lewis 1999; Borins 2000; Javidan and Waldman 2003; Trottier, Van Wart, and Wang 2008).

Using generalization about the leadership literature in *PAR* as one barometer of the field, the following observations can be made. First, until the past decade, leadership was considered largely an executive phenomenon, and thus when small group and lower-level leadership were the focus of the mainstream leadership literature in the 1960s and 1970s, leadership topics were lightly covered. Second, there was only a handful of empirical pieces on leadership in the first fifty years of the journal. Finally, in terms of the "thoughtful essay" tradition, many of the best examples occur in book reviews; Donald Stone, John Corson, and Paul Appleby were frequent contributors. Though important, *PAR* is but one source; what other contributions were being made to a distinctively public sector leadership literature?

In the first half of the century during the trait period, public sector sites were frequently examined, although no distinctive public sector perspective emerged (Jenkins 1947). The first in an important genre of executive studies was done by Macmahon and Millett, in this case regarding federal administrators (1939). The tradition of biographies and autobiographies of important administrative leaders was also established (e.g., Pinchot 1947). In the 1950s, a series of good leadership studies in the administrative realm was produced, most notably by Bernstein (1958). However, Selznick's 1957 classic, *Leadership in Administration*, is probably the single best overall treatment of the subject in terms of timelessness. The tradition of examining administrative leaders was sustained in the 1960s (e.g., Graubard and Holton 1962; Corson and Shale 1966). Downs's (1967) well-known book on bureaucracy is notable for its popular, if negative, typology of leaders. Again, the 1970s produced little of special note with the exceptions of the administrative role in iron-triangle politics (Heclo 1977) and several good studies of military and quasi-military leadership (Winter 1979; Jermier and Berkes 1979).

The resurgence of more general interest in leadership with the introduction of the transformational and charismatic literatures in the 1980s was mirrored in the administrative leadership literature as well. The concept of the administrative leader as entrepreneur was introduced by Eugene Lewis (1980) and expanded upon by Doig and Hargrove (1987). Kaufman provided a definitive executive study (1981); Cleveland (1985) and Gardner (1989) provided masterfully well-rounded essays in the Selznick tradition. The more specialized studies on public sector leadership continued to be primarily for the military (Taylor and Rosenback 1984; Van Fleet and Yukl 1986).

The volume of materials produced since the 1990s requires more selectivity for the present purpose. Many public sector leadership books have elements that are applicable for administrative leaders, but really focus on local and national policymakers (such as councils, mayors, state legislators, etc.) and civic leaders (Chrislip and Larson 1994; Heifetz 1994; Svara 1994; Henton, Melville, and Walesh 1997; Luke 1998). Some emphasize specific elements of leadership such as planning (Bryson and Crosby 1992), complexity (Kiel 1994), problem focus (Terry 1993), public service values (Rost 1990; Fairholm 1991; Riccucci 1995), and frontline leaders (Vinzant and Crothers 1998). Larry Terry (1995) provided a full-length argument supporting leadership as stewardship (which he calls "conservatorship"). Much of the more narrowly focused leadership literature continued to be for the military (e.g., Hunt, Dodge, and Wong 1999). The *International Journal of Public Administration* sponsored a symposium on transformational leadership in 1996 that was edited by the distinguished leadership expert Bernard Bass. In 2001, Rusaw provided the first book that was designed as an overarching textbook with a review of the literature, which has since been followed by Van Wart (with Suino 2008; Van Wart and Dicke 2007) and the Fairholms with a universal organizational perspective (Fairholm and Fairholm 2009). Morse and his colleagues have provided excellent books on leadership theory with a public sector thrust (Morse, Buss, and Kinghorn 2007) and development (Morse and Buss 2008).

PERENNIAL DEBATES IN LEADERSHIP THEORY

Another way to analyze the leadership literature is to examine the major debates that have shaped both leadership paradigms and research agendas. For simplicity, only four of the broadest are discussed here: What should leaders focus on? Does leadership make a difference? Are leaders born or made? What is the best style to use?

What Should Leaders Focus on? Technical Performance, Development of People, or Organizational Alignment?

We expect leaders to "get things done," to maintain good systems, to provide the resources and training for production, to maintain efficiency and effectiveness through various controls, to make sure that technical problems are handled correctly, and to coordinate functional operations. These and other more technical aspects of production are one level of leadership focus. This focus is implicit in much of the management literature from scientific management and classical management, the productivity literature, and the contemporary measurement and benchmark literature. It is also one of two explicit elements of most of the situational literature with its focus on task (initiating structure) and people (consideration). It is particularly relevant for leadership at the lower levels of the organization closest to production.

Another perspective is that leaders do not do the work; they depend on followers to actually do the work. Therefore, followers' training, motivation, maturation and continued development, and overall satisfaction are critical to production and organizational effectiveness. This insight is not new. As Lao Tzu said 2,500 years ago: "A good leader, one who talks little and listens much, when his work is done and his aim fulfilled, they will all say, we did this ourselves." Popular writers today echo these thoughts: "The signs of outstanding leadership appear primarily among the followers" (DePree 1989, 12). Indeed, as stated by foremost researchers studying the stumbling blocks for leaders: "Many studies of managerial performance have found that the most critical skill for beginning managers, and one most often lacking, is interpersonal competence, or the ability to deal with 'people problems'" (McCall, Lombardo, and Morrison 1988, 19). While this train of thought was present (if underrepresented) in the first half of the century among commentators like Follett (1933/1996) and Barnard (1938/1987), it blossomed during the humanist era, starting with Maslow in the 1940s and peaking during the 1960s with writers like Argyris, McGregor, and Likert. In the situational leadership research of the 1970s and 1980s, the other half of the task-people dualism was studied (particular schools of thought are reviewed more fully below in the literature section). It is still very popular today, especially in team leadership literature (Katzenbach and Smith 1993), excellence literature (Peters 1994), and charismatic elements of the transformational leadership literature.

The emergence of the transformational leadership paradigm in the 1980s brought the idea that "the essential function of leadership [is] to produce adaptive or useful change" (Kotter 1990, ix). (This notion was, in reality, resurrected from the great man theories in political science and Weberian charismatic theory in sociology.) Similarly, Edgar Schein asserted that *the only thing of real importance that leaders do is to create and manage culture* (1985, 2, emphasis in original). Indeed, it was popular to assert that "true" leaders delegated management issues and focused squarely on the "big picture" and big changes. By the end of the millennium the shrillness of the more extreme perspective that management was not an important element of leadership subsided, but it has not disappeared as a perspective.

Certainly not a major theme in the mainstream, if not altogether absent, was the additional notion that leadership is service to the people, end consumers, society, and the public interest (rather than followers per se). While it is common for biographies of religious and social leaders to advance this most strongly, exemplars in public service do so nearly as strongly (e.g., Cooper and Wright 1992; Riccucci 1995). This notion does not displace technical performance, follower development, or organizational alignment, but often largely downplays these dimensions as "givens." Although much less common in the mainstream until the emergence of the postmodern perspective, it has long been a prominent element of scholarly discussion in the public administration literature.

Lastly and logically, leadership can be seen as a composite of several or all of these notions. When we think of great leaders, we typically think of people who contribute in all domains. Alexander the Great not only reinvented warfare and realigned the world, but his men happily followed him as he conquered previously unknown lands. Napoleon, whose empire building was ultimately unsuccessful despite extraordinary popularity among the French, nonetheless rebuilt the modern administrative state. George Washington, a technically talented general and a capable president, was trusted and beloved by soldiers and fellow statesmen alike, and, undoubtedly, a dedicated servant to his society. Such a composite perspective has both logical and emotional appeal. Leaders typically are called upon to do and be all these things—perform, develop followers, align their organizations, and foster the common good. Yet it also sidesteps the problem to some degree. Most leaders must make difficult choices about what to focus on and what they themselves should glean from the act of leadership. What is the appropriate balance and who determines it? Such normative questions loom large when reckoning the merits of the checkered histories of administrative leaders such as Robert Moses (Caro 1974), J. Edgar Hoover (Powers 1987), and more recently, Robert Citrone (the unwise public treasurer of Orange County, California). For an array of possible definitions related to administrative leadership, see Exhibit 1.5.

To What Degree Does Leadership Make a Difference?

Burns (1978, 265) tells the cynical story of a Frenchman sitting in a café who hears a disturbance, runs to the window, and cries: "There goes the mob. I am their leader. I must follow them!" Such a story suggests that, at a minimum, we may place too great an emphasis on the effect that leaders have. The question, "Do leaders make a difference?" is essentially philosophical at its loftiest level because we are unable to provide meaningful control groups to define what leadership means other than in operational terms. Yet, no matter whether it is great man or transformational theorists comparing Hitlers to Chamberlains or situational theorists working with small groups comparing the results of finite solution problems, the answer is generally yes, leaders do make a difference (Kaiser, Hogan, and Craig 2008; Trottier, Van Wart, and Wang 2008). Nonetheless, it is important to remember that leaders do not act in a vacuum; they are a part of the flow of history and set in a culture with an environment filled with crises, opportunities, and even dumb luck. In practical terms, however, the question about whether leaders make (any) difference gets translated into the questions of how much difference and when.

In its various permutations, the question of how much difference leaders make takes up the largest part of the literature, especially when the question relates to the effect of specific behaviors, traits, and skills or their clusters. At a more global level, the transformational and "great man" devotees generally assert that great leaders can make a great difference. Some of the best practical writers, however, caution that leaders' effects are modest only because of the great constraints and inertia they face (e.g., Barnard 1938/1987; Gardner 1989). Stories about how Truman pitied the incoming Eisenhower because his orders would not be followed as they were in the army, and about how Kennedy ordered the missiles out of Turkey only to find out during the Cuban crisis that they were still there, reflect this perspective. It is also likely that this wisdom is directed largely at the excessive reliance on formal authority and insulated rationalistic thinking that some inexperienced or weaker leaders exhibit.

At the level of the discrete effects of individual or clustered behaviors, the compari-

Exhibit 1.5

Possible Definitions of Leadership in an Administrative Context

Leadership can focus strictly on the ends, for example, getting things done (technical performance) and the means by which things get done, for example, the followers (their motivation and development), or on aligning the organization with external needs and opportunities (which can result in substantive change). A definition of leadership can also emphasize the spirit with which leadership is conducted: In the public sector this is invariably a public service commitment. Of course, generally, definitions are a blend of several of these elements but with different emphases. One's definition tends to vary based on normative preferences and one's concrete situation and experience.

Administrative leadership is the process of providing the results required by authorized systems in an efficient, effective, and legal manner.
(This narrower definition might apply well to a frontline supervisor and would tend to be preferred by those endorsing strict political accountability.)

Administrative leadership is the process of developing/supporting followers who provide the results.
(Because all leaders have followers and because it is the followers who actually perform the work and provide its quality, it is better to focus on them than on the direct service/product. This is a common view in service industries with mottoes such as "Our Employees Are Our Number One Priority.")

Administrative leadership is the process of aligning the organization with its environment, especially the necessary macro-level changes, and realigning the culture as appropriate.
(This definition tends to better fit executive leadership and emphasizes the "big picture." Many public sector analysts are concerned about the application of this definition because of a breakdown in democratic accountability.)

The key element to administrative leadership is its service focus.
(Although leadership functions and foci may vary, administrative leaders need to be responsive, open, aware of competing interests, dedicated to the common good, and so forth, so that they create a sense of public trust for their stewardship roles.)

Leadership is a composite of providing technical performance, internal direction to followers, and external organizational direction—all with a public service orientation.
(This definition implicitly recognizes the complex and demanding challenge to leaders; however, it eschews the tough decision about defining the proper emphasis or focus that leaders may need to—and operationally do—make.)

sons are easier for social scientists. For example, how much difference does monitoring followers make, versus scanning the environment, and, of course, in what situational contexts? One important variant line of research examines the substitutes of leadership (Kerr and Jermier 1978). That is, some organizations over time acquire positive features that diminish the need for leadership in some task and interpersonal situations. When a leader has inherited or created an organization with good training, a highly competent workforce, clear task structures with feedback flowing directly from the task, innately satisfying work, group cohesiveness, and well-functioning rules, the need for strong leadership is less, at least in the short term.

Another particularly important dimension of the question about the effect of leadership relates to the levels at which leadership occurs. At the extreme, some theorists empha-size leadership that is almost exclusively equivalent to grand change (Zaleznik 1977), while minimizing and even denigrating the notion that leadership occurs throughout the organization. On the contrary, the small-group research of the 1950s through the 1970s suggests that leadership is fundamentally similar at any level. Some research, especially the customer service and excellence literature, emphasizes the importance of frontline supervisors (Peters 1994; Buckingham and Coffman 1999). The more comprehensive models tend to emphasize the idea that there are different types of leadership required at different levels, especially because of the increasing levels of discretion allowed as one moves higher in the organization (Hunt 1996). Different levels simply require different types of skills (Katz 1955).

Are Leaders Born or Made?

An implicit assumption of the great man theories is that leaders (invariably the heads of state and of major businesses such as banks and mercantile houses) are essentially born, probably allowing for some significant early training as well.[9] That is, you either have the "stuff" or you do not, and most do not. Of course, in an age when leadership gener-ally required either membership in the privileged classes (i.e., the "right stuff" included education, wealth, connections, and senior appointments) or, in rare instances, extraor-dinary brilliance (such as Napoleon's) in a time of crisis,[10] there was more than a little truth to this. In a more democratic era, such factors have less force, especially insofar as leadership is generally conceived so much more broadly in terms of position.

The behavioral geneticists have weighed in with rather compelling empirical data in recent years. In several studies with differing populations, Arvey and his colleagues have found that 30–32 percent of the variance in the leadership role could be accounted for by genetic factors (Arvey et al. 2006, 2007). That is an important role for genetics, to be sure, but leaves the even larger role for development.

Today the question is generally framed as one of degree, rather than as a strict dichotomy (Bennis 2007). To what degree can leaders be "made" and how? The developmental por-tion actually has two major components according to most researchers and thoughtful practitioners. While part of leadership is the result of formal training, this may actually be the smaller component. Experience is likely the more important teacher. In the extreme, this position states that while leadership cannot be taught, it can be learned. As Nietzsche noted, "a man has no ears for that which experience has given him no access." Of course, random career paths might or might not provide a useful string of experiences, and a mentor might or might not be present to help the learner to extract significant lessons from both the challenges and failures that experience provides. Ideally, high-potential leaders-in-the-making get appropriate rotational assignments. Certainly, this has been a major strategy of the armed services and major businesses for a long time. It does mean that early decisions are made about which individuals to groom because of their exceptional potential. Such assignments, it is commonly suggested, should broaden the protégé by including new experiences (horizontal experiences before vertical advancement), should be moderately challenging, and should include visible role models and opportunities for interaction with them (Kotter 1990, 154).

More formal training is not without its virtues, too, providing technical skills and credibility, management knowledge, external awareness, coaching, and encouragement toward reflection. Leaders must have (or in some instances acquire) the basic technical knowledge of the organization, often more for credibility than for the executive function itself; formal training can assist greatly here. Management is a different profession altogether from doing line work; again, training can greatly facilitate the learning process, especially for new managers. Formal leadership training, when properly done, is excellent for providing an awareness of different models of managing and leading for different situations, often outside one's own industry. Because mentors are hard to find, and *good* mentors are downright rare, formal training often plays this role, giving attendees a chance to process their experiences with instructors and fellow participants. Finally, good leaders more often than not are people of action, which means that opportunities for reflection are often even more important for leadership improvement; formal training structures opportunities for reflection, forcing doers to alternate thinking for action. Yet, while virtually no one would deny that formal training is useful, data to prove that it is of significant assistance are modest if one excludes studies of those promoting their own training agendas. Thus, while the black-and-white debate about leaders being made or born is largely considered sophomoric, the more sophisticated debate about the *relative* importance of innate abilities, experience (unplanned or rotational), and formal training is alive and well.

What Is the Best Style to Use?

Although leader style is really just an aggregation of a specific pattern of traits, skills, and behaviors, it has been an extremely popular topic of research and debate in its own right. One of the most significant issues has been definitional: What is leader style? Although leader style can be thought of as the cumulative effect of *all* traits, skills, and behaviors, it is generally used to describe what is perceived as the key, or at least a prominent, aspect of the universal set of leader characteristics. Examples include: follower participation, such as command, consign, consult, and concur styles (as discussed by Zand 1997, 43); change styles, such as risk-averse or risk-accepting; and personality styles, such as those based on the Myers-Briggs Type Indicator. Other leader style definitions involve communication, individual versus group approaches to leadership, value orientations—especially involving integrity—and power and influence typologies.

A slightly different approach to the issue of style examines it in relation to function. Much of the situational literature addresses the style issue in this light. Leaders have to get work done ("initiate structure") and work through people ("consideration"). How they are perceived to balance these factors can be operationally defined as their style. A somewhat different but very useful insight into functional style preference has to do with the type of situation that the leader prefers or excels in: a maintenance situation, a project or task force situation, a line versus function situation, a "start-up," or turning a business around (McCall, Lombardo, and Morrison 1988). In the next chapter of this book a taxonomy of nine distinct styles is discussed. Chapters 3 through 8 compare the styles implicit in all major schools of thought.

Another important set of issues regarding style has to do with whether, and to what degree, style can be changed in adults.[11] Not many have taken the hard line that changing style is nearly impossible. Fiedler (1967; Fiedler, Chemers, and Mahar 1976) is probably most prominent in this regard, largely advising that it is better to figure out the situation first, and find the appropriate leader second. Yet, even assuming that change in style is possible, most serious researchers warn against excessive expectations of dramatic change, although radical style-change anecdotes do pepper the popular literature. If style can be changed, then how it can be accomplished is the important issue that emerges (and this becomes largely an applied training issue). Hersey and Blanchard (1969, 1972) have been the most popular in this vein, teaching people to compare their style preference (defined as allowing worker participation in decision making) with the style needs of various situations (primarily follower maturity). In addition to style need (situational demands), style preference, and style range (a leader's repertoire of different styles) is the issue of style quality. For example, just because a situation seems to call for consultation, and this is among the style sets of the leader, it does not mean that she will do it well. Each style requires an extensive set of skills that must be artfully integrated into an evolving situation, but that may be beyond the abilities of a particular neophyte manager or inept leader (Lynn 1996).

Debates and Discussions in Administrative Leadership Theory

Although these debates have strong echoes in the public sector literature, the differences in the debate structures are as important as the similarities. Of the four major questions, only the first regarding the proper focus is discussed as robustly in the public sector literature as it is in the mainstream; indeed, from a normative philosophical basis, the administrative leadership literature probably argues this issue even more thoroughly. However, the question of proper focus is translated into the discretion debate, which has taken numerous forms affecting the proper role of administrative leaders. For the sake of simplicity, the first era (1883 to the 1940s) can be conceptualized as the time when a dichotomy between the political world of policy decisions and the world of technical and neutral implementation was the overarching ideal. It was generally argued that good administrative leaders made many technical decisions but referred policy decisions to their political superiors. The role of discretion was largely ignored or downplayed. The second era (the 1940s to the 1980s), adopting a less idealistic model, recognized that the interplay of the political and administrative worlds is far more intertwined than a simple dichotomy would explain. The dominant model during this period was one of administrative responsibility, that is, the appropriate and modest use of significant discretion. The recent era (from the 1990s), driven by a worldwide governmental reform agenda, has interjected entrepreneurial uses of discretion for public administrators. The debate about what to reform in government (e.g., the size, the cost, the processes, the structures, the accountability mechanisms) and how to reform it has stirred huge controversies in the scholarly community. To the degree that it is embraced, the newest model encourages creative and robust uses of discretion and diffuses authority among more stakeholders and control mechanisms.

The discretion debate has shaped the proper-focus debate primarily in terms of a management orientation (transactional) versus a change orientation (transformational). If leaders should not exercise significant discretion or be too activist, then they should *not* play a substantial change role but should focus more on management issues. In a contrasting position, many in the New Public Management[12] school echo the strains of the mainstream school of the 1980s in asserting that public administrators are uniquely qualified to play a large role that will otherwise leave a critical leadership lacuna. Another element in the "proper focus" discussion that is robust in the public sector literature adds, or sometimes substitutes altogether, the issue of inclusion of customers/clients/citizens and the public good more generally. Although the different schools disagree rather caustically about the way to frame these notions and the proper terms to use, there is nevertheless impressive agreement that external constituencies and the common good are a fundamental focus of public sector administrators that is not to be taken for granted.

The debate about the importance of leadership is much more muted and underdeveloped. Although some argue from the perspective of democratic theory that administrative leaders should *not* be important from a strictly political perspective, most public administration scholars and almost all practitioners simply assume or assert the importance of public administrators. Unfortunately, there is a great tendency to treat all the situations in which leadership is important as a single monolith, rather than to explore the ramifications of different types of leadership in different contexts with varying missions, organizational structures, accountability mechanisms, environmental constraints, and so on. This means that the issues of the technology of leadership are much less articulated in the public sector than they are in the private sector. Attempts at scholarly syntheses that reflect sophisticated multifunctional, multilevel, and multisituational models that were in evidence in the mainstream by the 1990s (e.g., Hunt 1996; Chemers 1997; Yukl 1998) were largely lacking in either monographs or journal literature in the public sector until recently (e.g., Van Wart 2004; Fairholm and Fairholm 2009).

Part of the weakness of the literature resides in its nonintegrated character, with the ironic exception of many surprisingly good chapter overviews on leadership in general public administration and public management textbooks. The serious debate about the best style to use is separated into many parts and is rarely as explicitly or holistically discussed as in the mainstream leadership literature. Fragments of this literature are found in management topics such as total quality management, motivation, and routine problem solving in publications such as *Public Productivity and Management Review*, and part of the literature is found in executive topics such as strategic planning and organizational change and development in journals such as *Public Administration Quarterly*. The ethics-values literature, for all its normative robustness, generally offers few concrete recommendations on this score, beyond general admonitions to be responsive, trustworthy, honest, courageous, prudent, and so forth.

The debate about whether leaders are born or made is also not particularly well-developed from a theoretical perspective. In the 1960s, the situational models presented relatively elementary task-people matrices. Both task and people skills could be taught, and a more humanistic approach that was less reliant on directive styles was encouraged. This was generally adopted in the public sector literature. In the 1980s, when the mainstream field was searching for a more comprehensive and complex model, some good examples of sophisticated training models did emerge on the public sector side (Flanders and Utterback 1985; Faerman, Quinn, and Thompson 1987) and saw a resurgence in the 2000s (e.g., Parks 2005; Morse and Buss 2008). The "born" side of the argument recognizes the importance of recruitment and selection of exceptional individuals. Such discussions have been relatively common in the human resource context, especially in reports recommending ways to strengthen the public sector (e.g., the "Volcker" Commission 1990, and the "Winter" Commission 1993), but have not been integrated in an explicit leadership discussion.

A DISCUSSION OF SOME IMPORTANT TERMS AND CONCEPTS

A major challenge in leadership studies is the specialized language used for concepts that often have a lay usage or are used in contradictory ways by different researchers. Some of the more important terms and concepts are defined or described in this book.

Levels of Leadership Action

One of the most important distinctions has to do with the level of analysis used for leadership actions, which varies from specific activities to overarching classifications used to simplify the welter of leader responsibilities. The narrowest level of analysis is generally tasks, which are the discrete functions common to many jobs. Examples of tasks are "conduct briefings or other meetings" or "serve as agency representative in outside meetings or activities" (U.S. OPM 1997). Typically, studies that define job tasks for leaders and managers list more than 100 tasks and some, more than 1,000, at which point they are generally considered microtasks.

Behaviors, traits, and skills are at the next level of analysis. Behaviors are observable patterns of leader activities, primarily used to link related tasks. All leader behavior is typically broken down into ten to thirty behaviors, which, according to most theories, are the elemental building blocks. For example, Howard and Bray (1988) identify organizing and planning as a behavior whereas Yukl, Wall, and Lepsinger (1990) break this area into planning and organizing, monitoring operations and the environment, and clarifying roles and objectives. (This book will identify twenty-one behaviors as the backbone of its analysis.) Another way of looking at this level of analysis is with traits and skills. Traits and skills are innate aptitudes and learned abilities that affect the quality of behaviors. They are generally indirectly observed through the quality with which behaviors are performed. Examples include energy, flexibility, communication skills, and analytic ability. One directly performs a behavior such as (operations) planning, but one uses analytic ability to improve its quality. Environmental scanning is a behavior but flexibility is a trait/skill that enhances scanning by enriching the means with which it is done. Frequently, "behavioral" taxonomies are a combination of both behaviors and traits and skills. In this case, the term competency is often used to apply to both.

The next level of analysis is style. A style is a moderate-sized cluster of leader behaviors, primarily used to describe or prescribe actual or ideal leader patterns. For example, Vroom and Yetton (1973) discuss a delegative leadership style in the context of decision making that emphasizes the behaviors of delegating (assigning responsibilities to others and providing minimal oversight), problem solving (examining operational problems), and managing innovation and creativity. On the other hand, Hersey and Blanchard (1969, 1972) discuss delegating in the context of follower maturity, and thus refer to the behaviors of delegating, clarifying roles and objectives, informing, and developing staff. The two operational definitions clearly are quite similar, but a behavioral analysis demonstrates that they are not identical. The use of styles as the primary unit of analysis is very popular with researchers, trainers, and lay practitioners. Note that some leadership theories focus on only a portion of all possible leader behaviors in their analysis of styles, such as those solely incorporating followers.

The highest level of analysis is metacategories. A metacategory is a very large cluster of behaviors used primarily to analyze the universe of leader functions. Typically, such taxonomies include from two to five elements. A famous example derived from the Ohio State University leadership studies in the 1950s. After analyzing more than 1,500 tasks, the researchers distilled two overarching leadership metacategories: consideration and initiating structure. Another famous taxonomy is the division of leader functions into technical, interpersonal, and conceptual categories (Katz 1955). The purpose of metacategories is conceptual elegance; that is, they are meant to explain how many different tasks or behaviors can be rolled into a few for purposes of conceptual simplicity and clarity. Styles, on the other hand, generally have a more applied focus and less elegance. Exhibit 1.6 summarizes these terms.

Level of Organizational Conceptualization

Another way to think about leadership is to focus on where it occurs (Yammarino et al. 2005; Yammarino and Dansereau 2008). If the focus is between specific leaders and followers, it is generally called dyadic. That is, the leadership occurs between two people—a dyad—in which one might consider the effects of the leader's behaviors on a follower, or a follower's attributions of a leader. Often, all followers of a leader are conceptualized as a single entity. Another increasingly common focus is the group level of analysis. How does leadership emerge from an unstructured group? What are the leadership dynamics with different types of followers in the same group? How do leaders transform low-performing groups into high-performing or self-managed teams? A still higher level of analysis is the organization. What type of leadership does an organization need in a time of crisis as opposed to a time of effectively implemented innovation? What are the competency differences between a frontline supervisor and a chief executive officer?

Exhibit 1.6

A Hierarchy of Terms Related to Types of Leader Activities

Type of activity	Typical range of activities	Definition of activities	Examples of types of activities
Metacategories	2 to 5	A large cluster of leader behaviors, used primarily to analyze the universe of leader functions	Consideration and initiating structure (Ohio State studies); task oriented, relations oriented, participative leadership (Michigan studies); technical, interpersonal, conceptual (Katz 1955)
Styles	3 to 12	A moderate-sized cluster of leader behaviors, used primarily to describe or prescribe actual or ideal leader patterns	Impoverished, authority compliance, country club, team (Blake and Mouton 1965); directive, supportive, participative, achievement oriented (House and Mitchell 1974)
Behaviors	10 to 30	Observable patterns of leader activities, used primarily to link related tasks	Short-term planning, clarifying task objectives and roles, monitor operations, provide support, provide recognition, develop member skill and confidence, consult with members, empower members to take initiative in problem solving, monitor the environment, propose innovative strategies, think innovatively, take appropriate risks to promote change (Yukl 2002)
Traits and skills	5 to 25	Innate aptitudes and learned abilities that affect the quality of behaviors; they are generally indirectly observed through the quality with which behaviors are performed; sometimes lumped with behaviors	Adaptable, alert to social environment, ambitious, assertive, cooperative, decisive, dependable, dominant, energetic, persistent, self-confident, stress tolerant, willing to assume responsibility, skilled analytically, creative, diplomatic, persuasive, knowledgeable about work, organized (Stogdill 1974)
Tasks	100 plus	Discrete functions common to many jobs	Implement programs to meet objectives, make decisions for the agency, recruit, integrate client expectations into the delivery process, evaluate performance and project accomplishments to assess overall program effectiveness, motivate subordinates and peers toward future goals, provide career growth opportunities for staff, conduct selection interview during the selection process (U.S. OPM 1997)

Leadership Versus Management

A heated debate about the meanings of and relationship between leadership and management emerged in the late 1970s (Zaleznik 1977) and is unlikely to ever be fully settled. First, what do these terms mean? Is leadership about interacting with followers only (Mintzberg 1973), or is it about everything that a leader does (Bass 1985), or does it imply a special obligation to change the organizational direction or culture? Is management about basic task and general management functions (human resources, finances, etc.), everything that an executive does, or does it simply imply the maintenance of ongoing operational activities? Zaleznik and others (Bennis and Nanus 1985; Kotter 1990) have suggested that leadership is about producing change and movement and thus focuses on vision, strategizing, aligning people, and inspiring, and that management is about order and consistency, and thus emphasizes planning, organizing, controlling, staffing, and budgeting. They then assert that leaders are both more important and in short supply. Mintzberg, on the other hand, has asserted that managing many things is what executives do, and only one of those things is leading followers. This text will follow the convention common to leadership studies that leaders do many things, including leading people, leading production, and leading change. (The operational definition below will elaborate.) The terms "leaders" and "managers" will be used interchangeably, in the sense that managers (at any level) rarely have the luxury of focusing only on maintenance or change, or focusing only on followers or tasks or organizational alignment. Rather, all good managers must occasionally be leaders (in any of the narrower meanings), and all good leaders had better be good managers (even in the most prosaic sense) at least some of the time if they are not to be brought down by technical snafus or organizational messiness. Indeed, one of the enormous challenges of great leadership is the seamless blending of the more operational-managerial dimensions with the visionary leadership functions.

Descriptive Versus Prescriptive

Descriptive studies attempt to define and describe leadership processes, typical behaviors, and contingency factors. Descriptive studies include case studies, experimental studies in laboratory settings, experimental studies in the field, factor analysis of survey feedback instruments, unobtrusive observation of leaders, interviews, and so forth. They essentially form the basic science of leadership studies in which evidence for relationships is established. Prescriptive studies attempt to make applied recommendations from descriptive findings: What must leaders do to be more effective and under what conditions? For example, the following might be asserted: "Research shows that it is hard to perform many other supportive activities unless consultation has occurred first; therefore, consult with employees early and regularly." Prescriptions can be very useful when the average behavior varies substantially from the most effective behavior. Because prescriptions not only involve many theoretical assumptions but also often include value preferences (normative assumptions), it is wise to examine them critically. Many studies include both descriptive and prescriptive elements, and the line is not always very clear. Nonetheless, it is a useful distinction to keep in mind.

Universal Versus Contingency Approaches

A universal approach to leadership assumes that at some level there is an ideal pattern of leadership behavior that fits nearly all situations. A contingency approach to leadership assumes that the situations in which leaders find themselves are crucial to determining the appropriate behavior and style. Early trait theory sought a universal approach but failed to achieve one, and thus universal approaches have been somewhat discredited. However, at a high level of abstraction, they are still attractive. For example, Blake and Mouton's leadership grid (1965, 1985) is still popular, even though it ultimately recommends a single style across situations (the "team" approach), and more recent transformational leadership theories are largely universalist in their approaches, too. However, contingency approaches are generally more powerful for defining the concrete relationships of tasks and behaviors to effectiveness, and for more detailed prescriptions.

Formal Versus Informal Leadership

Formal leadership stems from occupying a defined position (legitimacy). With their authority and resources, formal leaders generally have some ability to reward and coerce members. They augment their formal or position power with personal power that comes from expertise, wisdom, trust, and likability. Informal leaders, on the other hand, have little or no position power and therefore must rely nearly exclusively on personal power. Examples of informal leadership occur when a group convenes but there is no assigned chair, and one person emerges as the leader. (Informal leadership is generally called emergent leadership.) When leaders emerge from ill-defined social movements, they do so as informal leaders; however, over time they may acquire formal positions. Sometimes a follower may be so well liked and crucial to operations that he or she has more power than the formal leader.

Vertical Versus Horizontal Leadership

Vertical leadership is commonly expressed in hierarchical relationships when the bulk of the power is with the formal leader. Leaders can express their vertical leadership not only by being directive but also by largely limiting participation to input only. Horizontal leadership occurs when hierarchy is reduced or eliminated. It emphasizes employee/follower empowerment and delegation as well as partnering relationships. Vertical leadership tends to provide tighter accountability chains and efficiency. It is also prone to corrupt the leadership process for the needs and preferences of the leader. Horizontal leadership tends to provide greater input, participation, adaptability, and creativity. It is also prone to loose accountability and inefficiency. Contemporary organizations tend to use both forms of leadership, and much organizational design is concerned with getting an optimum balance of the two.

Leaders Versus Leadership

Because of the importance of individualism in Western culture, it is easy to exaggerate the role of the leader (Graen 2007; Kort 2008) and to confuse leaders with leadership. Eastern culture tends to be more sensitive to the roles of culture, tradition, and the group. Although much leadership research focuses on an individual leader's perspective, leadership is a process that includes not only leaders, but followers and the environment as well. For example, in contexts in which leaders inhabit networks, a collaborative mindset may be far more optimal than a more leader-centric one (Weber and Khademain 2008).

AN OPERATIONAL DEFINITION OF LEADERSHIP FOR INDIVIDUALS

Definitions of leadership abound. They can be oriented toward whole systems, organizations, or individuals. The bias of the following definition is an individual or practitioner orientation.

Leadership is a complex process involving numerous fundamentally different types of acts. Leadership is technical competence and achieving results. It is working with and through people. It is making sure that the organization is in alignment with the environment in terms of resources, services and products, structures and processes, and so forth. And it is also being sure that the organization's norms are appropriate and consistently adhered to, and that a healthy dynamic organization culture is maintained.

Leadership involves assessing one's environment and one's leadership constraints. Leaders cannot get somewhere (achieve goals) if they do not know from where they are starting. A rigorous assessment process requires looking at the major processes of organizational effectiveness with a highly critical eye. It also requires a realistic assessment of one's own constraints, so that excessive frustrations, missteps, and underachievement are minimized.

Leadership involves developing numerous leadership traits and skills. Before the leader ever acts, he or she needs to utilize and develop natural talents and to refine more acquired skills into a coherent set of leadership characteristics. Such traits include self-confidence, energy, flexibility, a need for achievement, integrity, and emotional maturity. Skills include the abilities to continually learn, influence and negotiate, and communicate. This partial list is challenging in its length. In this book, ten traits and six skills are highlighted and discussed in chapters 11 and 12.

Leaders must refine and modify their style for different situations. Whether refining their preferred style for a narrower set of situational factors or modifying it to handle situations of considerable variety, leaders must be in command of their style. In other words, even if a leader chooses not to personally change his or her style for a new situation, an effective leader will be aware of the ideal style for the situation and be able to make a practical judgment about whether to modify that style or provide an alternative (such as having someone else with a more appropriate style handle the situation). Further, mastering even a single style is a challenging endeavor that takes a great deal of conscientious study and practice.

Exhibit 1.7

An Operational Definition of Leadership

Leadership is a complex process involving the acts of:

1. assessing one's environment and one's leadership constraints;
2. developing the numerous necessary leadership traits and skills (such as integrity, self-confidence, a drive for excellence, and skill in communications and influencing people);
3. refining and modifying one's style for different situations;
4. achieving predetermined goals; and
5. continually self-evaluating one's performance and developing one's potential.

Leaders achieve predetermined goals. Leaders' assessments, characteristics, and styles are only the tools or means to acting. The actions of effective leaders result in goal accomplishment. Actions are the actual activities that fill up the days of leaders and include monitoring task processes, informing, motivating, building and managing teams, scanning the environment, networking and partnering, and decision making, among many others. Yet, actions are themselves only a means to an end: goal achievement.

Leaders continually self-evaluate their own performance. Just as effective organizational and environmental assessment is necessary for effective leadership, continual self-evaluation is critical too. Otherwise, it is easy to rest on old laurels and successes and slide into complacency, or worse, incompetence and dysfunctionality. Bringing all these factors together is a tall order, but it explains why consistently high leadership performance is relatively uncommon. A compilation of this leadership profile, an operational definition, is provided in Exhibit 1.7.

CONCLUSION

The leadership process is often treated as a simple phenomenon, but in reality it is not. This is why relatively few people excel at it, especially in contexts that are demanding. Simplistic explanations of leadership are elegant and fine for limited purposes such as providing an inspirational speech or identifying an important principle. However, simplistic explanations also tend to fall prey to overgeneralization, lack of completeness, and lack of applicability. Therefore, the genuine study of leadership requires an appreciation of the subtlety (complexity) of the leadership process, the need for more sophisticated models to explain how it operates in various circumstances, and the fact that there are fundamentally different types of leadership.

References to leadership are as old as written language. The more serious study began in the nineteenth century in which the "great man" thesis prevailed. Leaders were endowed with the gift of leadership by a combination of innate talents and early training and education. The first half of the twentieth century was dominated by the trait perspective, a belief that select traits and skills caused leadership. The contingency perspective pointed out that without situational contexts, the traits and skills made little sense. Early contingency theories tended to be simplistic models balancing task- and people-oriented perspectives. The charismatic and transformational schools of thought reiterated the importance of the leader's force of character and ability to affect change. Servant leadership reinforced the ethical dimensions of leadership, asserting the fundamental responsibility to serve those one is leading. More contemporary emphases in leadership research include enhanced efforts to find integrative models, the reexamination of horizontal or distributed leadership, and the postmodern rethinking and critique of the meaning of leadership itself. The literature on public sector leadership was mixed with the mainstream and did not emerge as a distinct subfield until quite recently.

Although the perennial debates in leadership cannot be authoritatively answered, they provide a dialectic that informs the reader of the competing issues involved in this dynamic subject. One debate is about what leaders should focus on in terms of achievement, people, or change. Another debate is about just how important leaders really are, a debate that becomes convoluted in the context of administrative leaders in a political system. A third debate is about whether leaders are born or made—the nature versus nurture debate found in other social sciences as well. It is often transformed into a discussion about the relative importance of inherited talents versus education, training, and experience. Finally, there is the debate about the best style to use, no matter whether it is about the amount of inclusiveness such as directive versus participative styles or the amount of focus on individual needs (i.e., an achievement-oriented style) versus group needs (i.e., an inspirational style).

Various terms and concepts were reviewed. Leadership can be analyzed with different levels of action, from tiny tasks to overarching metacategories. Leadership occurs at different organizational levels, from supervisors to executives. Leadership and management can be defined as functionally so overlapping as to be largely synonymous, or with management being a maintenance function and leadership being the change function. Descriptive studies focus on empirical facts and testable theories and prescriptive studies focus on normative and ethical issues. Universal approaches emphasize the generalizability of theories across all situations and contingency approaches emphasize the context variables affecting leadership success. Formal leadership stems from position and authority whereas informal leadership arises nearly solely from personal power and expertise. Finally, while leadership is often studied with a focus on the role of the individual leader and the skills s/he must employ to be successful, leaders are embedded in groups and are a part of a process.

The chapter concluded with an operational definition of leadership at an individual level. Leadership is a complex process involving numerous fundamentally different types of acts. It involves assessing one's environment and constraints, developing numerous leadership traits and skills, modifying one's style for different situations, achieving predetermined goals, and evaluating one's performance. Ultimately, every individual, whether student or researcher, must define leadership for his/her own purpose. Indeed, individuals may redefine leadership for different purposes, which is fine, as long as their reasons for doing so are explicit and their assumptions are transparent. This book should help readers to clarify their specific purposes and thus their personal definitions of leadership.

NOTES

1. By the term "mainstream" I refer to the literature that self-consciously labels itself as a part of the leadership literature and addresses itself to relatively broad audiences. I exclude literatures that are primarily meant for the consumption of a single discipline with specialized interests and terms. Thus, while many of the studies of public sector administration are to be found in the mainstream, many of the issues and materials are not. Needless to say, as with all distinctions regarding large bodies of work, such differentiations are more for general insight and convenience than for use as rigorous taxonomies.

2. Later examples and reviews include Wiggam (1931), Hook (1943), Murphy (1941), and Jennings (1960).

3. For example, Greenleaf is not among the 7,500 citations in Bass (1990).

4. For example, Burns states that "moral leadership emerges from and always returns to, the fundamental wants and needs of followers" (1978, 4), and he later adds that "transforming leadership ultimately becomes moral in that it raises the level of human conduct and ethical aspiration of both the leader and the led, and thus it has a transforming effect on both" (20).

5. Of course, Weber (1922/1963) had introduced the notion of charismatic leadership quite clearly, and it had been used by those influenced by sociology and political science such as Willner (1968), Dow (1969), and Downton (1973). Even Freud had made it clear that leadership involved more than simple exchange processes implicit in most situational theories.

6. Although part of this avoidance may have been due to a proexperimental or positivist perspective, part of it may have been an eschewal of the "great-man school" (which clearly has transformational trappings) that was disdained as antiscientific.

7. Because the overlap is so extensive for the subschools, these distinctions are more for analytic insight than articulation of groups that would necessarily self-identify with these monikers.

8. For example, Bass notes: "We find that leaders will exhibit a variety of patterns of transformational and transactional leadership. Most leaders do both but in different amounts" (1985, 22).

9. This is a variation on the nature-nurture debate found in some form in most of the social sciences.

10. The time-of-crisis motif is prominent in the change literature, for example, Kanter, Stein, and Jick (1992) and also in the leadership literature. Transformationalists have reminded us that there are exceptional leadership opportunities, which may or may not be filled, when: there is a dramatic crisis or a leadership turnover, and/or at select stages of the organizational life cycle (especially the birth-to-growth and the maturity-to-decline phases).

11. This debate is related to the made-born argument above but with a critical difference. While the made-born argument is about whether a leader can learn any style, the style debate focuses on whether a leader can learn styles other than his/her native or preferred style.

12. The New Public Management school of thought is a term that was invented by the British but refers to trends across the English-speaking world starting in the 1990s. In the United States it emphasizes customer focus, worker empowerment, work streamlining, cross-sector collaboration, and performance management. It also emphasizes greater results accountability and deemphasizes employee tenure rights. Proponents welcome the new style of accountability, which has market overtones; critics are concerned about the slippery slope to a new age of spoils.

PART I

LEADERSHIP THEORIES

2

Theoretical Building Blocks:
Contingency Factors and Leader Styles

A deeper understanding of leadership requires an analysis of the competing theories and frameworks that have been advanced in the field and that provide a variety of perspectives for this complex topic. Narrower models help explain why the individual concepts or elements of leadership function as they do singly, and broader theories explain the complex relationships among numerous elements.

The scientific model of social science works by asserting various relationships or correlations that then can be tested across broad classes of situations. The most common research question is generally framed: What do leaders do to be effective (and how can we prove the reply)? Concepts are defined in specific, observable ways—operational definitions. Concepts that are being tested under different conditions are called variables; independent variables are those that are changed to examine the effects on others, which are the dependent variables. Hypotheses are formulated and tested concerning the relationships of specific variables, say, leader intelligence on decision quality. The notion of theory building is normally reserved for the explanation of how numerous concepts function together in interrelated causal chains, generally called a model. For example, decision quality is affected not only by leader intelligence but also by problem ambiguity, follower sophistication, and so forth; combining all these relationships into a model constitutes a theory. Looser models in which concepts are difficult to measure or in which causality is unclear because of the complexity of relationships are often called frameworks.

We now return to the theoretical aspects of leadership, which were briefly alluded to in chapter 1. The most common format involves the question: What contingency factors affect which ideal leader styles that in turn will increase the likelihood of leader and organizational effectiveness? The four common specific research questions are: What are the most important contingency factors? What are the predominant leader styles? What is the correlation between contingency variables and styles? What is the correlation between styles and leader effectiveness? (See Exhibit 2.1.) This chapter addresses the first and second questions; chapters 3 through 8 examine the third and fourth questions.

Contingency factors are all the different types of variables that affect the style or behavior of leaders as they seek to be effective. Here the term is used very broadly. Styles are the generalized patterns of behaviors exhibited by leaders. Leader effectiveness must be operationally defined in terms of a specific outcome: productivity, worker develop-

---

Exhibit 2.1

Major Variables Considered by Prominent Leadership Theories

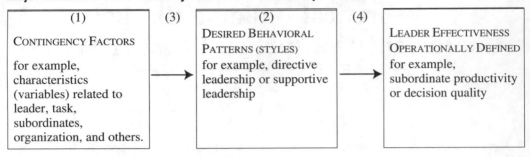

Major theoretical questions asked:

(1) What are the most important contingency factors?
(2) What are the predominant leader styles?
(3) What is the correlation between contingency variables and styles?
(4) What is the correlation between styles and effectiveness?

---

ment, worker involvement and cohesion, effective problem solving and decision making, successful organizational change, or a combination of these factors. An example of the correspondence between a grounded/applied perspective (represented by the leadership action cycle explicated later in this book) and the empirical model of most leadership theories is illustrated in Exhibit 2.2.

The two approaches differ markedly in purpose. The applied approach is descriptive; the theoretical approach is explanatory. The applied approach assumes relationships and generally seeks to affect practice; the theoretical approach tests relationships. Because of the different purposes, they tend to use different formats and terminology. Nonetheless, there is a fundamental comparability of the two approaches, as is highlighted in Exhibit 2.2.

Prior to analyzing some of the major theories of leadership, it is useful to examine the principal elements common to most theories: (1) contingency factors, (2) dimensions of style, and (3) types of leader styles.

This chapter first examines five clusters of contingency factors (fourteen in all) commonly considered in major leadership theories. Some theories consider many contingencies and some just a few. In studies of leadership, contingency factors are most commonly used as two types of variables: intervening and moderating. Intervening variables affect which behavior/style is/should be selected to enhance the desired outcome. For example, problem structure is an intervening variable in some theories because a structured problem might lead to one style while an ambiguous problem might lead to another. Moderating variables affect the strength, quality, or success of a behavior/style. For example, a common moderating variable is leader expertise in a specific behavior or style. A leader can use the right style but minimize its effectiveness because of poor execution.

Next, the chapter examines the dimensions most commonly associated with styles.

Exhibit 2.2

Correspondence Between Theoretical Issues and an Applied Perspective

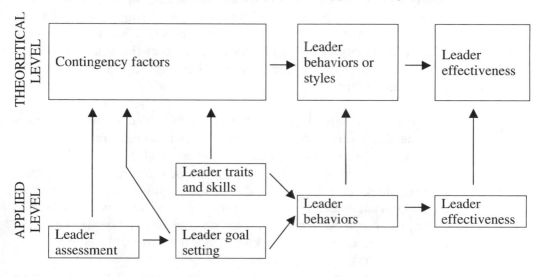

Because leader style is a higher-level concept, it can be defined in many ways. The discussion of style dimensions will help us understand some of the major ways in which the concept can be defined.

Finally, the chapter extrapolates nine overall styles identified and/or recommended by the various theories that will be covered in the following chapters. Of course, different theories use different numbers of styles to explain leadership effectiveness and they define each style in significantly different ways. The taxonomy of styles presented here is more comprehensive than the one found in most theories, which often have a narrower focus. With these theoretical "building blocks" in place, the following chapters examine specific theories in more detail.

CONTINGENCY FACTORS

As should be evident from these discussions, an immense number of factors affect the leader's preferred modes of action (exhibited as styles) and the degree of effectiveness of those actions. What does the leader think the overall goals should be? What are the task skills of the followers? What is subordinate effort like? How good is the organization of the work and how does this align with performance strategies? What types of constraints do leaders have to incorporate, including their own abilities such as traits, skills, and behavioral competencies? The social scientist studying leadership wants to know not only which contingencies are important but also exactly how important each factor is. In other words, how much explanatory power does each factor provide in different classes of situations? For example, a social scientist may test the often-held assumption that emergencies (one type of task contingency) require a directive mode of leadership (one type of leadership style). Ideally, the researcher can examine situations in which identical emergencies are handled with and without a directive style. Further, the researcher would compare different types of emergencies using experimental and control groups.

It is easier to understand the effects of contingencies on leadership styles when only one or a few contingencies dominate. (More typically, of course, combinations of contingencies call for a combination of styles.) Below are a series of situations provided as examples in which the specific contingencies would generally call for relatively pure leadership styles (in parentheses).

- Sam is a new general manager who has been assigned a troubled division with many problems: financial overruns, some highly inappropriate administrative practices, low productivity, lack of a customer focus, poor morale, and sloppy administrative procedures. All these problems will need to be addressed over time, but all cannot be dealt with simultaneously. He has decided that the first issues to tackle are improved fiduciary oversight and dealing with rule violations. In some areas, such as administrative procedures that must be carefully redesigned and implemented, his style will only be to observe and gather insights for now, so that he is prepared to improve them at a later date (laissez faire).
- Nydia, a frontline supervisor, has an employee who has become increasingly schizophrenic in the past six months. The worker refuses to acknowledge the problem, which is probably due to a biochemical imbalance, and is becoming highly disruptive due to extreme paranoia and mood shifts (directive).
- Susan, also a frontline supervisor, has a new employee who has tremendous potential but who is a slow learner and highly insecure. The employee has the right social skills and disposition for the job, but is currently overwhelmed by the extensive technical demands of certifying clients and denying benefits (supportive).
- Steve is the director of information technology (IT) *not* because he is a technical expert but because he has first-rate management skills. The last three directors all failed because of their general lack of management skills and tendencies toward autocratic micromanagement. His small agency has to change its backbone information system. Although each of Steve's subordinates has an opinion about the best system to use, they do not agree on the same system. Steve is also aware that no one has consulted with the other departments, such as finance and human resources, that would be major users of the system (participative).
- Sylvia is the director of the agency. Because of her position, she receives many legitimate, routine requests that must be channeled to departments to handle (delegative).
- Sean is a manager in charge of a group of lawyers. To keep productivity up, he must appeal to their sense of personal accomplishment and provide benchmark standards that they can customize to their specialized jobs (achievement oriented).
- Shelly is in charge of fleet maintenance for a state university that is under intense pressure to reduce costs. The large fleet maintained by the university provides convenience and control for the institution, but currently at a premium price. If fleet maintenance is not to be privatized, she believes that she will need to dramatically

change the business model, work routines, and performance standards. Her employees are only vaguely aware of the threat and are likely to become less motivated if they are not convinced that a positive change is likely and can be attractive to the group (inspirational).

- Demetrius is the director of parks for a midsized suburban city. The city has experienced a home and park building boom for seven years. A recession has recently hit the private sector, and the downturn in the public sector is only a matter of time. In the past, in order to maintain public safety, cuts to parks have doubled. Although authorized to do so, Demetrius is not filling vacancies and, where he has discretion, is simplifying some of the project designs. He is also considering some selective service cuts (strategic).
- Helena is the division director for support services in a sheriff's department. Although busy with her operational duties, she finds time to do several outside activities. First, she serves as the liaison for the sheriff on the regional crisis response board bringing together public safety, various governments, the private sector, and nonprofits, which become a major responsibility for her when there are emergency response exercises. She also serves on the regional law enforcement roundtable, and this year is serving as the chair of the group (collaborative).

Although the range of contingency factors is very extensive, the factors commonly used can be grouped into five major types: leadership characteristics, task characteristics, subordinate characteristics, organizational characteristics, and other characteristics. Leadership theories in the first half of the twentieth century tended to emphasize leader characteristics; task and subordinate characteristics were most heavily emphasized in the 1950s through the 1970s; and organizational and other characteristics were more emphasized from the 1980s to the present.[1]

Leadership Characteristics

Three of the more common leadership characteristics are traits and skills, leader behaviors, and leader attributions of followers. Much research examines leadership characteristics at the microanalytic level. However, leader characteristics are often assumed in mid- and macrolevel theories of leadership. For example, while the study of self-confidence as a contingency yields useful microlevel data about this important leadership trait, it is often assumed or subsumed in leadership theories as a part of the leader's general competence in broader styles such as directiveness or supportiveness.

Trait and Skill Characteristics

Trait and skill characteristics include inherent and early learned proclivities, such as resilience, and talents, such as social skills. They include generalized abilities to cope in common leadership situations as well as the personality characteristics, motivations, and values of leaders that tend to promote success. In given traits and skills of specific leaders, what leadership situations should they be placed in, what situations will they excel at, and what biases might they have? Leadership characteristics are an especially important contingency to consider when the interest is in leader selection.

Behavior Characteristics

Behavior characteristics are more affected by education, training, and experience than traits and generalized skills. They include task-, people-, or organization-oriented elements such as operations planning, motivating, and budgeting. One primary virtue of considering behavioral characteristics as contingency variables is that they can be used for developmental purposes in more applied settings. What specific behaviors are well or poorly exhibited and what are the ramifications for effectiveness with specific leaders or classes of leaders? Factor analysis approaches use behaviors as a contingency for modeling purposes. That is, in research contexts they tend to distill the most important patterns from the survey data of a large number of leaders.

Leader Attributions of Followers

Leader attributions include a leader's estimation of followers—their competence, dedication, and loyalty. A few theories focus on what leaders think of their followers as a contingency, especially as a potentiality or preconceived notion. Attributions can be a very positive factor leading to improved performance because of the Pygmalion effect (i.e., expressions of confidence in followers leading to improved self-confidence and higher expectations leading to higher follower standards). They can also be a negative factor when leaders assume that followers are inherently lazy, personally disloyal, generally less competent or simply incompetent, and so forth.

Task Characteristics

Task and subordinate characteristics are the primary focus of leadership theories from the 1950s through the 1970s. Although still very important, most broad-based leadership theories now include additional contingency factors.

Role, Task, and Organizational Clarity

This characteristic reflects followers' perceived clarity of what their job is, how to do various required tasks, and how to work within the organization. This variable is highly linked to the concept originally called "initiating structure" because of the need of workers to know what to do, how to do it, and how to contribute in the organizational setting in accordance with rules and regulations, in accessing resources, and so on. Often, lack of follower clarity leads to recommendations of a directive style because followers need direction in the form of information, instructions, and training, or to a participative style in order to redefine roles interactively.

Task Clarity and Complexity

Task clarity and task complexity are somewhat different but related. Generally, tasks are clear when the leader has knowledge of how to do a job or solve a problem and can easily share this knowledge with the follower if s/he chooses to do so. For example, a supervisor may clarify how to use a specialized client claim form that an employee has never used before. Tasks are ambiguous when the leader may be unable to predict an exact solution or may not even know the correct answer her/himself. For example, an employee may be assigned to redesign a client form for which the general parameters of change are known but the exact solution is not, or an employee could be assigned to investigate the reasons for an error increase in which the solution is currently unknown but the cause is most likely due to a single factor. Tasks become complex when there are multiple elements to coordinate in task completion or the solutions to problems are intricate. For example, problems become complex when there are multiple causal factors necessitating an analysis of comparative importance and different strategies for each major factor. Assuming competent followers, ambiguity and complexity generally lead to a variety of styles emphasizing increased worker decision inclusion/independence or enhanced worker motivation so that the worker can "rise to the challenge" of a problem or meet a new productivity standard. Task ambiguity and complexity lead to directive styles only if followers are untrained or might be overwhelmed.

Task Interdependence

Task interdependence is the need to share work among followers and to work in teams. Initially, task interdependence was considered largely in terms of the need to specialize and coordinate. Directive behaviors might be quite suitable under these limited conditions. Later, the increasing need for group decision models due to a more complex and faster changing work environment added the possibility of more collaborative forms of leadership. The most recent iterations of task interdependence emphasize the need for group creativity and team self-management, which in turn tend to lead to prescriptions for more facilitative or achievement-oriented styles of leadership.

Subordinate Characteristics

Because a primary function of leadership involves followers, the characteristics of subordinates are important. Just which characteristics are most critical to consider when deciding on a leadership style?

Follower Traits and Skills

One aspect of follower traits has to do with their competence. What is their level of innate ability, their training and education, and their experience? A second related area is follower self-confidence. Those who have higher self-assurance about their job abilities are often hypothesized to be more productive and capable of more independent work, and therefore amenable to a different leadership style. Generally speaking, most macrolevel theories hypothesize that those with less ability and self-confidence are better targets of a directive style, whereas more "mature" workers are better suited to styles highlighting worker independence. Another type of trait that is sometimes examined is followers' personality structures. For example, regardless of worker maturity, some followers prefer highly structured settings with relatively directive styles, while other followers bristle at directive styles even when they are new at a job and have achieved little task expertise or confidence; they prefer to learn on their own and make their own mistakes. Still another important subordinate personality trait is the need for affiliation.

Task Commitment

The connection between task commitment and work effort is very significant, and is thus another commonly included variable. It may be expressed in terms of innate commitment such as job satisfaction, shared goals, or a professional orientation. Innate commitment may also be expressed in negative terms such as boredom with the job, perhaps because of the repetitive nature of the job or perhaps because of a lack of interest in the type of work. For example, leaders must sometimes contend with worker burnout, even for the most interesting jobs. Generally speaking, the lower the innate commitment, the more a directive style is recommended; the higher the innate commitment, the more other styles are recommended such as participative, delegative, or achievement oriented. Another important aspect of task commitment is external motivation, stemming from follower perceptions of rewards and punishments. Do rewards for good performance and disincentives for poor performance exist, and how much are those rewards valued and disincentives heeded? Problems with rewards may have style implications related to followers. For example, a high-performing employee may need to be rewarded with increased independence (e.g., as exhibited by a delegative style), but a very poor employee may need a more directive (authoritarian) style. However, some reward problems have more to do with the inadequacy of reward systems than with the followers themselves.

Follower Attributions of the Leader

What the followers think of the leader will affect their commitment, productivity, and overall organizational effectiveness. While some theories emphasize how to increase follower commitment, most general style theories simply point out the differences among levels of leader acceptance. Moderate levels of leader acceptance by followers stem from legitimate authority and basic competence. Slightly higher levels stem from belief in leader expertise, trust, and general likeability. High levels of leader acceptance stem from a belief in great wisdom or exceptional talent to lead. When perceptions of competence are coupled with high levels of likability, it is generally called charisma. Moderate and high levels of leader acceptance are generally necessary for certain types of styles such as achievement oriented or inspirational to be effective.

Organizational Characteristics

The characteristics of organizations that affect leadership are some of the most interesting but some of the most nebulous to study and quantify. Many leadership theories (e.g., transactional theories) ignore them entirely in order to focus on internal aspects related to tasks and followers. While organizational characteristics are important at all levels of leadership, they are generally more important at executive levels, and thus these characteristics are more prominently featured in theories emphasizing the roles of senior managers and chief executives.

Power Relationships and Organizational Design

Organizational design can have a major effect on the types of power relationships available to leaders. It will also affect the concrete influence strategies typically used. For example, if a leader has the ability to provide substantial rewards and punishments, when should it affect their style? If a leader does not have much reward and coercive power (more typical of the public sector), how should it affect their style? Does excessive formal power corrupt style? How important is personal power (expert and referent) for participative, achievement-oriented, and inspirational styles? When a leader has a lot of legitimate authority and substantial organizational change seems necessary, how should it affect style? For example, should a powerful leader sensing the need for major organizational change implement a top-down approach, as is often advocated by change consultants, or a participative change process as advocated by the quality-management literature?

External Connectedness

External connectedness has to do with the organizational need for external information, influence, and negotiation. For instance, how do/should the ideal styles of leaders at agencies with large discretionary budgets, such as the National Aeronautics and Space Administration and the National Endowment for the Arts, vary from those with highly fixed and stable budgets such as the U.S. Treasury and the Social Security Administration? This variable may also examine the specific role requirements of leaders whose external foci may vary enormously. For example, how does the style of a frontline supervisor with many subordinates and a major training function differ from a legislative liaison working with the legislature on a regular basis?

Environmental Uncertainty

Related to, but different from, external connectedness are environmental uncertainty and risk. Organizations have different needs for change based on type, speed, breadth, and acceptability (Dawson 2003). How do the needs for narrow process change, slow incremental change, or dramatic downsizing affect the style to be used? How risk averse or risk taking should a leader be and under what circumstances? For example, consider the enormously different leadership demands on post office executives in 1944 versus those in 1971; that is, in a period of intense process refinement and a period when re-organization from a department to a government corporation was required by Congress (for additional information, see Exhibit 9.5 on page 221). Most transactional leadership theories exclude this from consideration, while transformational theories emphasize this factor, although they sometimes accept it as a given rather than treating it as a true variable. Generally speaking, the prescription is that the greater the uncertainty and risk, the more the leader must emphasize an external style, which itself includes a number of substyles most commonly associated with change.

Other Characteristics

There are innumerable variables that can be considered in conjunction with leadership styles. However, two of the more well-known ones are ethics and gender.

Ethics

Ethics is related to doing the right thing. In leadership, it relates strongly to paying attention to the needs of others, especially followers. In public sector settings, paying attention to and balancing various types of public needs (e.g., the needs of a narrow constituency versus the common good) are also much emphasized. This type of inquiry goes back to Aristotle, who argued for certain types of leader styles based on the need for quality public leadership and an ethical perspective (i.e., the philosopher king). In modern times, Burns (1978), Greenleaf (1977), Heifetz (1994), and Block (1993), among others, have grappled with the ethical dimensions of leadership as they analyzed leadership behaviors. More often than not, however, the ethical dimensions have been considered as either present or absent. Often, prescriptions from this research emphasize participative and inclusive styles. The exemplary leader literature looks at the differences between leaders of "good" character and those of "high" character. Those of good character recognize, reflect on, and integrate ethical issues. Those of high character demonstrate these characteristics but also make substantial contributions to the community and are willing to display courage and make personal sacrifices on behalf of the public good. Not surprisingly, such examinations lead to somewhat different formulations of style than do other aspects of the leadership literature. There is also a practical element of ethics as a variable that is more conceptually aligned with conventional style taxonomies. Trust is invariably among the top considerations of follower importance in leader abilities. Although trust is partially based on competence, it is equally founded on a sense of leader honesty and fairness—ethical competencies. Trusted leaders typically have followers with higher task commitment and commitment to the common good.

Gender

Gender has often been used as a direct or indirect situational variable in leadership studies. Numerous trait studies have included masculinity as a specific characteristic (see the review by Mann [1959] and the meta-analysis by Lord, DeVader, and Alliger [1986]); others

Exhibit 2.3

Factors Commonly Included in Major Leadership Theories

A. Leadership characteristics
    1.   Trait and skill characteristics
    2.   Behavior characteristics
    3.   Leader attributions of followers
B. Task characteristics
    4.   Role, task, and organizational clarity
    5.   Task clarity and complexity
    6.   Task interdependence
C. Subordinate characteristics
    7.   Follower traits and skills
    8.   Task commitment
    9.   Follower attributions of the leader
D. Organizational characteristics
    10. Power relationships and organizational design
    11. External connectedness
    12. Environmental uncertainty
E. Other characteristics
    13. Ethics
    14. Gender
    15. Other

have used a situational variable—for example, "dominance"—as a proxy for masculinity. Sometimes the question has been whether or not (or to what degree) men and women have different styles and what their impact is on effectiveness (Donnell and Hall 1980; Dobbins and Platz 1986; Rosener 1990; Powell 1993). At other times the research question has focused on the strengths and weaknesses of women's styles, often thought to be more participative, inclusive, and supportive (e.g., Eagly and Johnson 1990). Some studies looked at women and power, especially with regard to problems of the glass ceiling and penetration into certain professions (Mainiero 1994). See Exhibit 2.3 for a summary of contingency factors.

DIMENSIONS OF STYLES

Not all styles seek to emphasize the same aspect of leadership, and therefore the styles that theorists have proposed have different dimensions. Some of the common dimensions include how much control the leader needs to have in terms of providing direction and making unilateral or joint decisions, the types of goals and performance expectations, the type of motivation used, and the focus of the leader's attention. Many other dimensions are possible (but not discussed here) such as the amount of risk the leader is willing to assume, the type of communication the leader uses, and the leader's orientation toward change. Nonetheless, the dimensions discussed will provide readers with ample evidence of why it is so difficult to capture all the nuances of leadership in a few styles if a relatively comprehensive style taxonomy is proposed. The styles that are alluded to in this section will be more fully described in the next.

Leader Control

How much control does a leader need or exhibit, and under what conditions? Control can be exhibited as level of monitoring, or level of inclusion in problem solving and work decisions. A high level of control is generally reflective of a directive leadership style. As with all leader styles, the style is appropriate only to the degree that the situation merits it. A directive style might be effective when there are new and untrained employees who are prone to numerous or critical errors, or when long-term employees need retraining. Of course, there are also many situations in which a directive style may be inappropriate, such as with longtime, well-trained employees. A medium level of control is often reflected in participative and achievement-oriented styles. The leader may either include others in decision making or use an interactive method of determining unit goals. Finally, it is possible that a leader may exhibit a low amount of control, as is seen in delegative and laissez-faire styles. Highly competent employees with a strong professional background and good internal standards of performance might be good candidates for a delegative style. Other factors encouraging delegation include decentralization, unique roles, high group norms, and provision of developmental opportunities for those equipped to handle new challenges. However, low control may not be appropriate for employees who have little or poor training, weak work standards, poor time management or project management skills, or who are not ready for self-managed projects. When leaders are not paying attention to the situational demands and delegate primarily based on convenience, they may be exhibiting a laissez-faire style.

Goals and Performance Expectations

Although there are many structural elements that affect productivity, leader behaviors and style clearly can have an enormous impact. Because low-level goals and expectations of performance invariably indicate poor leader effectiveness, this condition generally indicates a laissez-faire style in which the leader has not bothered to exert an effort toward higher performance standards, or simply does not want to bother doing so. However, many styles indirectly permit an average or moderate level of performance. After all, by definition not everyone can be above average or perform at a high level. Excessive expectations may lead to disappointment or burnout. Styles that generally accommodate an average performance level, and hopefully at least set the stage for a high performance level, include directive, supportive, participative, and delegative styles. Yet, some styles explicitly strive for challenging goals and high levels of performance. Those would include achievement-oriented and inspirational styles.

Type of Motivation Used

Styles vary remarkably in the types of motivation that they assume or use to encourage follower performance. If the leader does not try to motivate workers and is indifferent to their motivational needs, it generally indicates a laissez-faire approach. The leader may primarily use his/her legitimate authority as leader, and use rewards and punishment for compliance and noncompliance. This indicates a directive style. Leaders may emphasize workers' concerns, need for affiliation, and desire for compassion and sympathy. This would be reflected in a supportive style. Leaders may also emphasize workers' interests in being involved and appreciated as members of the work unit or team. This is most reflected in a participative style. Or leaders may emphasize some workers' interest in being independent, self-managed, and recognized for their professional mastery. This would fit a delegative style most closely. If leaders want to emphasize the achievements of individuals, then an achievement-oriented style is likely; however, group goal achievement is emphasized with an inspirational style. The complexity and subtlety of this dimension, which is oversimplified for clarity in this discussion, should highlight the difficulty of providing clear and absolute style prescriptions in any but relatively narrow instances. Human beings are highly complex and have a large array of motivational needs, a number of which are likely operating at any given time, thus the number and complexity of recommendations for leaders can become highly complex.

Focus of Leader's Attention

All of the dimensions discussed so far have largely related to followers. However, leaders have responsibilities quite apart from followers, and in some cases attention to followers may legitimately be a small part of the leader role. For example, a university chancellor may be nearly exclusively oriented toward fund-raising, working with university regents and the state legislature, and public relations as compared to a provost who is normally described as the chief operating officer. Sometimes, then, the focus of attention is on internal production and followers. This might be indicated by directive, supportive, participative, delegative, or achievement-oriented styles. Sometimes the focus of leader attention is on external alignment of the organization with the environment and relations with outside groups and entities. This is typified by an external style. The style that emphasizes bringing the external needs of the environment back to the organization and changing it accordingly (an integrated style) is best captured by the transformational style. Exhibit 2.4 summarizes the discussion of leadership style dimensions.

TYPES OF LEADER STYLES

This section directly examines the second of four research questions posed earlier in this chapter: What are the predominant leader styles? Not surprisingly, different theories have somewhat different answers. Many use similar concepts but provide different names. Some use the same name for different concepts. And many theories do not try to comprehensively capture all aspects of the major leader functions. This analysis aims to provide an overview of "generic" styles as discussed in the literature. The nine styles identified are distinct enough to be separate categories and are relatively comprehensive of all leader functions. Nonetheless, three caveats are in order. First, the nine styles identified do overlap considerably. Second, few leaders use a single style all the time; most

Exhibit 2.4

Five Common Style Dimensions

Dimension	Range of variance	Examples of styles affected by the dimension and variable
Leader control	• High • Medium • Low	Directive Participative, achievement oriented Delegative, laissez faire
Goals and performance expectations	• Low • Average • High	Laissez faire Directive, supportive, participative, delegative Achievement oriented, inspirational, strategic, collaborative
Type of motivation used	• None • Reward, coercion, legitimate power • Human compassion • Appreciation • Independence, recognition of professional mastery • Individual achievement • Group achievement	Laissez faire Directive Supportive Participative Delegative Achievement oriented Inspirational, strategic, collaborative
Focus of leader's attention	• Internal production and followers • External alignment of organization with environment	Directive, supportive, participative, delegative, achievement oriented Strategic, collaborative

leaders vary their styles with different situations or contingencies. Third, some "ideal" styles that are recommended by researchers are really fusions of two or more of the nine styles; these conglomerates are called combined styles for this taxonomy.

Laissez-faire Style

The laissez-faire style occurs when the leader exhibits passivity or indifference about tasks and subordinates or purposely neglects areas of responsibility. It can be considered a hands-off style, a nonstyle, or on occasion, a conscious strategy when competing demands necessitate overlooking some areas of responsibility. It tends to be identified as a style in universal approaches that have a hierarchical approach to leadership. The laissez-faire style is often identified as the bottom or worst style (although it can also be considered a style with functional and dysfunctional uses like all other styles). Bass (1985) uses this term, but Blake and Mouton (1964, 1965) call it an impoverished style. Most contingency approaches do not discuss a laissez-faire style. However, this does not mean they do not assume that such a style exists. That is, because contingency theories focus on the most effective styles of leadership, rather than a survey of all leader styles, they simply do not address suboptimal styles.

The laissez-faire style has the most in common with the delegative style because both tend to result in minimal intervention. However, the delegative style assumes that minimalist intervention is done (1) after careful analysis, (2) only in select circumstances, and (3) for the good of the followers and organization. Those using a laissez-faire style (badly), however, generally do not bother to analyze the situation, tend to use it indiscriminately (but not necessarily uniformly), and for their own good, especially to conserve their own time and energy.

This is the only style identified that is nearly always poor. However, all leaders occasionally resort to a laissez-faire style when overwhelmed by excessive job demands that cannot be simultaneously met. For example, a leader may consciously neglect a low-priority responsibility for a year or more while attending to other, more pressing concerns. As a practical reality, then, when a laissez-faire style is consciously and appropriately used to defer exercising leadership, it is a type of prioritization in terms of putting off less critical issues, or sometimes a timing strategy to let an issue "ripen" as more data and results provide better perspective in handling situations.

A laissez-faire style is often typified by theorists as providing low leader control, low leader goals and performance expectations, and little or no motivational stimulation for followers. It can mean that the leader is not focusing on either the internal or external aspects of the organization, or it is possible that the leader's focus on external matters leads to a laissez-faire style internally.

It is not uncommon for those with a laissez-faire style to experience a significant problem, crisis, or scandal from time to time. Laissez-faire style leaders often consider their only job to be fixing problems, crises, and scandals after subordinates have failed to properly carry out their duties; therefore, when such negative events occur, such leaders are often quite unapologetic, spring to action, and take decisive and frequently firm steps to correct others' failings. In many instances an inattentive laissez-faire leader can appear to be the hero by seizing the initiative, fixing the problem, and punishing the innocent. That is, inattentive leaders can fail to do their job in preventing problems by properly monitoring and then blame others as they belatedly fix a "mess" of their own making.

Directive Style

A directive style is exhibited when a leader lets subordinates know what they are expected to do, gives directions and guidance, asks subordinates to follow rules and procedures, and schedules and coordinates work activities. Behaviorally, it emphasizes task skills such as monitoring, operations planning, clarifying roles, informing, and delegating in relation to the assignment of work projects. At the organizational level, it also involves general management functions, such as human resource management, as an extension of coordinating and scheduling functions. A directive style assumes high leader control, average (or above) performance expectations, a formalistic notion of motivation based on legitimacy of command, reward, and punishments, and an internal focus.

A directive style is probably the most commonly identified style. It is also known as task-oriented (Fiedler 1967; Fiedler, Chemers, and Mahar 1976), authority-compliance

(Blake and Mouton 1965), autocratic decision making (Vroom and Yetton 1973; Vroom and Jago 1988), strongman (Manz and Sims 1989, 1991), top-down leadership (Locke 2003), and the one-best-way in scientific management (Taylor 1911), among others. This approach to leadership is commonly identified in the classical management literature (Gulick 1937; Mooney and Reiley 1939; Fayol 1949), although it can still be seen as an important element in some contemporary management literature, for example, with respect to reengineering (Hammer and Champy 1993) with its top-down, analytic approach.

A variety of subtypes can be identified that have distinctly different connotations. Several of the prominent subtypes point to the fundamental importance of the leader's making sure that the work of the organization is done properly. An instructive style emphasizes the telling, informing, and clarifying aspects of directing. Followers need instruction on what they do not know how to do, what they are doing improperly, or what will be done differently because of changes in mandate or technology. They also need to know what the rules are, what rule infractions mean, when exceptions are allowable, and how to interact with others. Finally, they need help with their questions and problems. Followers who do not get this task support may be untrained, error prone, frustrated, and so forth. A related subtype is structuring. Structuring means that work activities are arranged in advance, work schedules are coordinated, and contingency plans have been developed. There is always much behind-the-scenes work that managers and leaders must do to make sure that operational problems do not occur and that resources are properly received and allocated. Structuring also includes a good deal of task monitoring, whether that is reading reports, analyzing data trends, or managing by walking around. The absence of good structuring can mean a substantially higher incidence of problems and crises.

A directive style often has negative connotations, which is generally identified with a term like "authoritarian." Telling becomes commanding or being bossy, informing becomes dictating, clarifying becomes threatening, and planning becomes micromanagement. At its worst, this substyle is typified by rigidity, complete lack of input from others, leader centeredness, and the treatment of subordinates as replaceable parts. A strong directive style was more common and accepted in the first half of the twentieth century. Since then, it has become less and less popular or acceptable. Nonetheless, in times of crisis or when major change is imperative, people often expect a stronger style and then an authoritarian style may be considered appropriate as a short-term approach. Even here, the general rule of thumb is that time must also be crucial for this substyle to suit the circumstances and gain a minimum of acceptance.

Supportive Style

A supportive style is demonstrated by showing consideration toward followers, displaying concern for their needs, and creating a friendly work environment for each worker individually. It focuses exclusively on people-oriented behaviors: consulting (especially the listening modality), coordinating personnel, developing staff, motivating, and, to a lesser degree, building and managing teams and managing conflict. Remember that planning and coordinating personnel is different from operations planning; it refers to matching the talents, interests, and preferences of people to the work, rather than vice versa. A supportive style does not directly imply a lack of leader control if a leader can both direct and support at the same time. However, if doing so distracts a leader, then it implies low leader control. Supportive behavior assumes at least average performance, and many researchers assert that its absence negates the prospect of high performance. In terms of motivation, this style emphasizes human compassion and dignity, and was originally highly influenced by the human relations school (e.g., Argyris 1957; McGregor 1960). It assumes an internal approach to the organization that specifically focuses on followers.

A supportive style (House 1971; House and Mitchell 1974) is also known as consideration in the Ohio studies (Hemphill and Coons 1957), individualized consideration (Bass 1985), relationship oriented (Likert 1961, 1967; Fiedler 1967), coaching (Hersey and Blanchard 1969, 1972), and consultation (Vroom and Yetton 1973, especially substyle CI).

The predominant subtype is a caring model. Leaders first make sure that subordinates or followers feel socially connected and that they are part of a group. This may be demonstrated by a cheerful tone of voice, friendly body language, and inclusiveness in the social aspects of work. This also means that leaders work at making sure that followers feel both good about themselves and valued in the work context. This is often exhibited by providing individual attention, soliciting information, and offering praise. Second, supportive leaders are attuned to followers' personal and career needs. This may be exhibited by adjusting a schedule for the parent of a newborn or recommending a management training class for an employee who wants to advance. These behaviors should lead to an atmosphere of trust in the workplace (because the employees' interests are considered along with work interests) and increased liking and respect of the leader. A negative subtype also exists when a supportive style squeezes out proportionate concerns for production. Blake and Mouton (1964) call this the country club style (a 1, 9 style in their grid approach). In this style the emphasis on personal satisfaction, interpersonal relations, and personal development becomes overweening, while the tougher demands of trying to achieve high standards, fix short-term problems, and confront vexing long-term issues are overlooked.

Participative Style

Leaders using a participative style consult with subordinates and take their opinions into account, provide suggestions and advice rather than direction, and establish a friendly and creative work environment for the team as a whole. Behaviors include consulting (in the discussion mode), coordinating personnel, developing staff, motivating, building and managing teams, managing conflict (especially as it arises out of constructive disagreements and creative tensions), and managing personnel change by including followers in change decisions. It also includes a modest amount of delegation in the task domain. Supportive and participative styles are similar; however, supportive styles emphasize listening and empathy, whereas participative styles emphasize discussion and inclusiveness in work decisions and problem solving. The participative style assumes only moderate control, at least average performance goals, appreciation of competence and involvement as motivators, and an internal focus.

The participative style (House 1971; House and Mitchell 1974; Likert 1961, 1967) is also known as consultation (Vroom and Yetton 1973, primarily CII in their scheme), shared leadership (Locke 2003), and superleadership (Manz and Sims 1989, 1991). In the Hersey and Blanchard typology, the participative style is most similar to their support- ive style, which they call facilitative in a decision mode and which is the third quadrant in their matrix (high support and low direction). This style is highly affiliated with the team literature that emerged in the 1970s but blossomed in the 1990s, as well as with the learning organization literature. A specialized variant is called co-leadership, in which two leaders share or split executive responsibilities, such as a chief executive officer and a chief operating officer (Hennan and Bennis 1999).

One subtype is an inclusive style of leadership. The leader seeks to discuss issues with individuals to surface problems and get a broad base of information and input, coordinates the needs of the group such that individual needs are not neglected, and motivates by providing a robust inclusiveness. A second subtype is a self-conscious team approach. The leader facilitates team discussions, provides relatively wide decision parameters, and tends to implement team decisions as recommended, given the range of decision making that the leader has established for the group. This subtype focuses on interactive meetings, group learning, and managing complex group processes. There is not really a negative subtype of participative leadership per se. However, contingency approaches point out that a participative style is only one of several and that circumstances may not be ideal for this mode much of the time. Leaders who are always in a participative mode may be inefficient a good deal of the time even though they are blessed with a good team when, for example, an executive mode (i.e., a directive style) would be more effective in some cases, and a delegative style would better conserve group resources in others. Stated differently, sometimes the group wants the leader to handle business unilaterally because it does not want to be bogged down by details, and at other times the assignment of a problem to an individual makes better sense than a more time-consuming group process.

Delegative Style

A delegative style is defined as one that allows subordinates relative freedom for deci- sion making and from daily monitoring and short-term reviews. The main behavior of this style is delegation, which involves designation of responsibility and allocation of authority. Providing additional responsibility is similar to job enlargement. Allocation of authority means greater decision-making independence and thus is a form of power. It is the latter element that is considered especially critical to true delegation. Additional behaviors involved in this style include developing staff and motivating. A delegative style assumes low leader control and at least moderate performance goals. The motivational assumption is that followers seek independence as a form of self-fulfillment. In addi- tion, they often perceive delegation as recognition of professional mastery and superior competence. The style does not necessarily assume either an internal or external focus on the part of the leader. Delegation should free up the leader's time for other activities, which can include other production-people issues, public relations, strategic issues, or even personal pursuits.

A separate delegative style is not always included in style taxonomies that sometimes fuse participative and delegative styles together as a range of empowerment options (Fiedler 1967; House and Mitchell 1974; House 1996). Those who do identify a separate delegative style include Hersey and Blanchard (1969, 1972), who call it delegating; Bowers and Seashore (1966), who call it peer leadership; Locke (2003), who calls it bottom-up leadership; and Vroom and Yetton (1973), who call it joint decision making even though the decision locus shifts to the followers.

Theory on leadership substitutes also indirectly but powerfully addresses the delegative style (Kerr and Jermier 1978). It essentially asks the question: When can you reduce leadership functions? It identifies primary situations in which leadership can be reduced:

- Followers have ample education, training, or experience in their jobs.
- Followers have a professional orientation and have internalized work standards and ethical norms.
- The work itself is somewhat structured, so that relatively few substantial issues arise. The roles and procedures are clear.
- Feedback is provided as a part of the job.
- The work is intrinsically satisfying—which is, of course, a self-referential perception.
- The work group is cohesive, so that there is more support for peer training and intermember routine problem solving.

In other words, when these types of situations exist, less leadership or more delegation is a realistic option to explore, assuming that other factors do not contravene—and complicate—the leadership situation.

There are two forms of delegating, as alluded to previously. The first is when subordinates are given additional duties, functions, or tasks to perform. The leader maintains the same level of monitoring, clarifying, and review. The second form is when subordinates are given additional decision-making power over processes, problems, exceptions, and the like. This authority is closer to what is generally considered true delegation and is often referred to as empowerment. Under the right conditions, such as those specified by the leadership substitutes theory, empowerment can be helpful to the efficiency of both the subordinate and the leader, and for enhancing motivation. However, with greater empowerment must also go greater accountability and—generally—shifts in types of accountability. Thus, the subordinate who receives a project (responsibility), and the ability to handle it in whatever way seems most appropriate without prior approval (authority), must be accountable for the quality of the decisions made under the circumstances. Greater empowerment and authority generally mean that accountability shifts from a prior-approval approach using an item-by-item method to a post-performance review on an aggregate basis, perhaps for an entire project or series of projects. Greater empowerment

Exhibit 2.5

The President as Delegator

The president of the United States is a busy person. Of course, he is in charge of the famous fifteen—the cabinet departments—including old departments such as State and Treasury and newer departments such as Education and Homeland Security. The president has varying levels of responsibility for over sixty independent agencies and government corporations including the United States Agency for International Development, the Central Intelligence Agency, the Environmental Protection Agency, the Federal Emergency Management Agency, the General Services Administration, the National Aeronautics and Space Administration, the Office of Personnel Management, the Securities and Exchange Commission, and the U.S. Postal Service. His personal office—the Executive Office of the President—includes over a dozen major divisions and councils, including the Office of Management and Budget (OMB), the Council of Economic Advisers, the Office of the U.S. Trade Representative, and the Office of the Vice President. Just selecting the top appointees is a major job, with approximately 1,200 requiring Senate approval and another 2,000 not requiring it. It is not uncommon for the heads of smaller agencies never to meet with their boss in a one-on-one meeting! The president must delegate by the nature of his overextended span of control, which ultimately includes nearly 2.5 million civilians and approximately as many in the armed forces.

The president's delegation rarely reflects a true laissez-faire style, however.* Agency heads and their deputies are expected to have or acquire the professional capacity to run their agencies effectively with the help of career executives. The delegated control of staff agencies such as the OMB and the Government Accountability Office will point out agency faults. If found wanting by the president, replacement is a real option which is exercised from time to time. While delegation is the president's major style vis-à-vis the federal bureaucracy, he can and does use other styles from time to time. For example, the president frequently sends directives through senior staffers, and less frequently through executive orders. Agency heads are invited to add to the policy mix with other key players. Given that Congress sets many bureaucratic policies including pay, agency staffing levels, agency structure, personnel rules, benefits guidelines, and others, the president's delegation is not really unreasonable. Presidents who have become more involved in administrative affairs such as Franklin Delano Roosevelt, Jimmy Carter, and Bill Clinton (through Vice President Al Gore) have primarily become involved in structural reforms rather than daily operations.

*Notable exceptions might be presidents Warren Harding and Ronald Reagan. While Harding appointed some exemplary officials to lead the government, his choices for Veterans Affairs, the Attorney General, and the Interior brought on separate scandals that later became known collectively as the Teapot Dome (one of the sites where oilmen secured government leases through bribing Albert Fall, secretary of the Interior). Reagan's appointments in the Department of Housing and Urban Development (under the Pierce administration) cost $2 billion in fraud and mismanagement, his appointees in the savings and loan debacle made a bad situation much worse, and his misplaced trust in Oliver North was the only reason that he ever slipped from exceptional popularity.

and authority also generally signals a shift to more "internalized" control mechanisms such as professional norms and a sense of virtue or character regarding the organization's interests. (See Exhibit 2.5 for an example of the president as delegator.)

Achievement-Oriented Style

In an achievement-oriented style a leader sets challenging task goals, seeks task improvements, emphasizes excellence in follower performance, and shows confidence that followers will perform well. The primary behaviors involve a combination of both people and task domain types. In terms of task focus, it includes clarifying roles, informing, delegating, problem solving, and managing innovation and creativity. In terms of people focus, it includes consulting, developing staff, and building and managing teams. It assumes a medium level of leader control and an internal organizational focus on the part of the leader. The achievement-oriented and inspirational styles (discussed next) are the only two styles that specifically focus on challenging goals and high expectations. The primary motivational base is individual achievement, which will be contrasted with inspirational style, a more group-achievement approach.

Although identified here and by some theorists as a separate style, it clearly overlaps to some degree with other styles. It is similar to the directive style in its task orientation and "getting the job done" but an achievement-oriented style involves and challenges people to task accomplishment rather than informing, instructing, or even demanding task completion. Its inclusion of people in setting goals makes it similar to the participative style, but the participative style is much more focused on group process, mutual education, and consensus than on the overriding quest for higher productivity typical of the achievement-oriented style. Also an achievement-oriented style almost always has a competitive, individualistic element that is lacking in the participative style, which emphasizes equality. As mentioned above, the achievement-oriented and inspirational approaches diverge in their motivation as well as in leader focus, insofar as an inspirational approach relies more heavily on organizational behaviors and an external focus.

The theoretical basis for this style is anchored in the social-exchange literature that emerged in the 1950s (Homans 1958), which emphasized the transactional basis of most social behavior. The achievement factor was much advanced by McClelland (1965, 1985), who studied the trait more than the style, but whose insights are nonetheless useful (see the discussion of achievement in chapter 11). In particular, he points out the limitations of an achievement-oriented approach in terms of the excesses to which it is prone and the potential problems with overly obsessed and selfish leaders and followers who feel exploited and distrustful. Although House did not include it in his original formulation of path-goal theory (1971), he did include it in his later formulation (House and Mitchell 1974). Bass (1985) discusses what is essentially an achievement-oriented style as contingent reward, which is then contrasted with elements of an inspirational approach. That is, normally in an achievement-oriented style there are specific, individual payoffs (contingent rewards) for high achievement levels. Mintzberg's (1973) entrepreneurial function also implies an achievement style; similarly, the style has loose ties to the excellence and goal-setting literatures. Management by objectives strongly encourages an achievement style, although it allows for a more directive or participative approach as situations demand. Manz and Sims (1989, 1991) call it a transactor style, which is discussed below.

Because it is wedged in fairly tightly among other styles, there really are no subtypes of achievement-oriented style other than the negative version. As McClelland's (1965, 1985) research indicated, excesses of competition that are not well integrated can lead to self-serving behaviors, egotism, and insensitivity. Manz and Sims (1989, 1991) discuss the dynamics of this style: interactive goal setting, contingent personal reward, contingent material reward, and contingent reprimand. However, they point out that the result can be followers who are "calculators." The followers can quickly become accustomed to relying on motivation external to themselves (the what's-in-it-for-me syndrome), and when that motivation does not exist, they may become obstinately passive. Another aspect of this problem is the divisibility and immediacy of rewards implied by this style. While a highly reward-driven style may work well most of the time in sales and mass-production jobs because of the narrow task range and ability to tie results to individuals, it works well less frequently in professional jobs and when there is a group product.

Inspirational Style

An inspirational style uses intellectual stimulation in order to produce new ideas or to gain their acceptance for new approaches, and to arouse contagious enthusiasm for the achievement of group goals. It relies heavily on acceptance of the leader's wisdom and/ or integrity by followers, and it draws on many behaviors. In the task domain, it includes managing innovation at the operational level. In the people domain, it includes managing personnel change because the style often implies significant attitudinal changes in followers. At the organizational level, it includes scanning the environment, strategic planning, vision articulation, networking and partnering, decision making, and managing organizational change. Note this style's emphasis on rising to the challenges of all types of change. The style generally assumes high goal levels, but, as often as not, the goal is a "change" goal as opposed to a strictly quantitative performance objective more common to the achievement-oriented style. The degree of leader control varies tremendously among the substyles. The leader's focus is largely divided between an internal focus on tasks and people and external needs for new structures and production reconfiguration. The motivational base focuses on group achievement through acculturation ("oneness" with the group), intellectual engagement, and trust of and excitation by the leader.

The inspirational style was introduced as a style employing a distinctive approach with the transformational-charismatic school of thought, which itself covers a wide array of perspectives. The overall style is sometimes called transformational (Burns 1978; Tichy and Devanna 1986) and sometimes charismatic (Conger 1989; Bryman 1992; Shamir, House, and Arthur 1993), but in reality is a combination or aggregation of styles, of which the inspirational style is but a single, if complex, element. That element is most clearly articulated by Bass (1985) and has already been identified in the definition of the style. House (1996) added six styles to his 1974 typology of styles, in which value-based leader behavior is extremely similar to an inspirational style.

Slightly different transformational models imply slightly different types of inspirational style. When the transformational approach is directed at the operational level, sometimes a process improvement approach is recommended and sometimes a reengineering approach. The former emphasizes change and innovation coming from the line and espouses a learning-organization environment; the latter encourages top-down analysis of dysfunctional processes in which significant improvements are possible, largely based on leader direction, if follower implemented (Hammer and Champy 1993). Transformational leadership often encourages organizational change, and thus vision, strategy, and mission articulation are featured. Again, it is possible for this to be an inclusive, evolving process with an egalitarian tone such as in a visioning process. It may also be driven by a strong-willed leader with a sharply defined vision, a crisp timeline, and a willingness to make some hard decisions. Overlapping with these different approaches is the charismatic aspect of change leadership. Charismatic leaders are viewed as having a "special gift," special insights or wisdom, and an especially appealing personality (at least to most people). Not all exceptional transformational leaders are charismatic (Bennis and Nanus 1985).

The leadership literature is also well attuned to the negative aspects of the inspirational style, especially the overreliance on charisma and overly powerful leaders. For example, Manz and Sims (1989, 1991) point out that the common, leader-driven transformational style encourages communication of the leader's vision, emphasis on the leader's values, exhortation, and inspirational persuasion. This type of leader, they assert, tends to create followers who are "enthusiastic sheep." The dark side of charisma is well known among researchers (Conger 1989; Sandowsky 1995; Bass and Steidlmeier 1999), and the general public is familiar with cult charismatics such as Adolf Hitler, David Koresh, and Jim Jones. Yukl points out some of the many problems that can occur with inspirational leaders: "Being in awe of the leader reduces good suggestions by the followers, desire for leader acceptance inhibits criticism by followers, adoration by followers creates delusions of infallibility, excessive confidence and optimism blind the leader to real dangers, denial of problems and failures reduces organizational learning, risky and grandiose projects are more likely to fail, taking complete credit for successes alienates some key followers" (Yukl 2002, 251).

Strategic Style

A strategic style focuses attention on organizational matters in the environmental context that contribute to organizational alignment, the ability to gain and retain resources, and the opportunity to gain comparative advantage in public settings and competitive advantage in private settings. It is based on the capacity to learn, change, and implement initiatives effectively (Boal and Hooijberg 2001; Pajunen 2006). Not surprisingly, it involves all the organizational behaviors but emphasizes environmental scanning, strategic planning, vision articulation, decision making, and managing organization change. Various other terms have significant overlap with strategic leadership as defined here: visionary (idea-based), ideological (principles-based), entrepreneurial (technical innovation-based), and charismatic (when change is accompanied by strong personality).

Much of the older leadership-style literature omits strategic style because of that literature's focus on unit and internal operations: people and tasks. Strategic leadership has certainly been much discussed in the older literature, if not always as a style per se. The strategic management literature addresses the issues that a leader in an external mode must consider. Some of the work that has brought leadership style to bear on this literature includes the evolution of the organization and its specific leadership needs (Tushman and Romanelli 1985; Lord and Maher 1991; Jaques 1989), leadership tenure (Hambrick and Fukutomi

1991), executive teams (Ancona and Nadler 1989), and leadership succession (Day and Lord 1988), among others. For example, an organization that has had a long period of stable leadership with an internally focused leader but is increasingly out of touch with its environment may seek an externally focused leader who can discover new opportunities and make strategic changes to prevent organizational decline. The transformational and charismatic approaches include strategic elements but do so by creating a far larger megastyle including aspects of supportiveness and participation (e.g., Kouzes and Posner 1987), achievement (e.g., Bass 1985), and inspiration (e.g., Conger and Kanungo 1987).

Two predominant substyles emerge from an examination of strategic leadership primarily related to the degree or magnitude of change involved. The "incremental improver" sees opportunities primarily but not exclusively from the external environment for technical updates, process redesign, client or market expansion, and refinement of mission and vision for clarity of performance objectives. The "radical reformer" perceives a major misalignment with the organizational environment and assists or forces the organization to take on major change initiatives involving such activities as restructuring, closing down or selling off major operations, starting new operations, slashing expenditures, and so on. This calls for a substantially revised vision generally and sometimes a significant change in the mission too.

The negative aspects of this style are largely centered on its misapplication. It is easy to misjudge the type of change required as well as to misdiagnose the level of change that would be ideal. The change process is quite challenging, so underestimating its difficulty can lead to a failure that can further jeopardize the organization. Finally, getting the timing right is critical but challenging (Bartunek and Necochea, 2000).

Collaborative Style

A collaborative style focuses on representation, external networking/partnering, goodwill, and "expanding the pie" (an external win–win perspective). The representative function provides an organizational presence; networking provides a sense of collegiality, contacts, and enhanced trust that comes from long-term interaction; and partnering engages in cooperative projects in which there is mutual gain. All of these activities tend to build goodwill while simultaneously providing long-term organizational and personal advantage (Kanter 1994). A collaborative style is also used when leaders engage in building professional or local communities (Chrislip and Larson 1994). Community building can be for mutual self-gain through expanding the capacity or reputation of a cluster of organizations, but it can also be based on ethical grounds such as the enhancement of the common good (Luke 1998). Philanthropic activities such as donations of time, resources, and money fall under this style as well. There are many terms that have substantial overlap with a collaborative style: community leadership (Schweigert 2007), integral leadership (McCrimmon 2007; Edwards 2009), global leadership (Goldsmith et al. 2003), facilitative leadership in groups (Schwarz 2002) and in local government political settings (Svara 1994), networking (Graen and Graen 2006, 2007), partnering (Segil, Goldsmith, and Belasco 2003), and shared power (Bryson and Crosby 1992; Crosby and Bryson 2005).

Both strategic and collaborative styles of leadership have an external focus, but the collaborative style is not competitive. It is also related to an inspirational style in encouraging group behaviors for unselfish purposes, but at the community level rather than within the organization. The subtypes include the "chairman," in terms of emphasizing representation in public functions (Mintzberg's figurehead and spokesman roles, 1973), the "partner," in terms of finding mutual benefits in working collaboratively, the "civic-minded colleague," in terms of participating in the community without specific payoffs in mind, and the "philanthropist," in terms of giving to charity and providing significant support to nonprofit community activities.

The negative version of this style is simply an excess of external issues to the neglect of internal issues. This is common among elected officials in executive capacities, who often have little interest in administrative affairs. Presidents, governors, and mayors may focus almost exclusively on select external issues (i.e., the politics of policy) and rarely notice internal operations except in terms of new appointments, which are generally concentrated into a short phase very early in their "administration." Frequently, both morale and administrative processes suffer when internal issues are neglected. If elected executives often overemphasize their external roles to the exclusion of internal roles, then midlevel managers often suffer from the reverse problem: a neglect of the collaborative style. It is easy for midlevel managers to ignore community concerns in favor of operations and their specific responsibilities, especially when those internal concerns are so evident and constantly demanding.

Combined Style

A combined style is the use of two or more styles simultaneously in a single fused style, for example, directive and supportive. The behaviors will vary according to the styles that are fused as will the dimensions of the combined style.

A variety of combined styles can be cited as examples. For example, many of the taxonomies in the literature that have fewer categories are simply combinations of various styles discussed here having similar characteristics. A directive style will not only include the narrower definition used here, but may also include aspects of delegative, achievement-oriented, and inspirational styles. A supportive style may implicitly include aspects of participative and inspirational styles. Thus, a combined style can simply be a cluster of styles with similarities.

However, some combined styles purposely integrate divergent elements or perspectives to achieve an overall balance. One of the most famous examples is team leadership as defined by Blake and Mouton (1964, 1965) in their grid leadership theory. Ideal leaders are both supportive and directive—two conceptually distinctive styles—simultaneously. Likert's System 4 style is similar in its approach (1981). Later iterations of leader-member exchange theory implicitly recommend a combined directive, supportive, and participative style (Graen and Uhl-Bien 1995). Locke (2003) calls a combined style "integrated," which is defined as elements of top-down, bottom-up, and shared styles that are blended as circumstances dictate. Lipman-Blumen (2000) calls a combined style "connective," although she envisions it as a variety of alternating styles that match organizational needs.

The most inclusive combined style is the transformational style. For example, Bass's (1985) highly articulated transformational style explicitly includes all of those discussed (although participative and delegative are implied rather than stated). In his hierarchy of leadership styles, leaders essentially begin by successfully employing directive behaviors (shedding a slothful laissez-faire style), next integrating achievement-oriented behaviors, and ultimately overlaying supportive and inspirational behaviors, informed by an external perspective. Such an approach to styles has many merits. When done well, as is the case with Bass, it has intuitive appeal. It is elegant in that it brings a great deal of style knowledge together in a single-style hierarchy. It implicitly acknowledges the complexity and artistry of using leadership style. The weaknesses are also substantial, however. Because of the breadth of the style, which ultimately becomes a universal approach, the advice for practicing managers becomes extremely abstract. Just when and how are various elements of a transformational style used in various concrete situations? To overcome this problem, Kouzes and Posner (1987) focus on inspirational behaviors (challenging the process, inspiring a shared vision, enabling others to act, modeling the way, and encouraging the heart), but then they are no longer really discussing transformational style with its style diversity, just some of the most critical elements. The transformational approach is also highly biased in favor of change and inspirational behaviors, when many times a more stable approach with a more "mundane" style may be appropriate.

This does raise the interesting question about whether a combined style is really a fused style or a series of rapidly alternating styles. It is easy to think of a supervisor who daily rotates a directive style in instructing and informing employees, concern and warmth in frequent consultations, participation in staff meetings and ad hoc problem discussions, and delegation with more senior employees. The gentle manner the supervisor uses leads his employees to label this a supportive style overall. On the other hand, a supervisor may have a recalcitrant employee in his office whom he must reprimand and direct (command performance improvement), while he simultaneously shows concern, empathy, and support (i.e., a truly fused style). Similarly, it is easy to imagine a transformational leader rotating direction, support, inspiration, external focus, and so forth as they proceed through their days and weeks. However, it is also possible to imagine a transformational leader commanding followers but nonetheless inspiring them and stimulating their own personal sense of achievement. Think of a general just before battle, commanding but exciting the troops with images of group success and individual valor and honor. More important than settling questions of style breadth or style average versus fusion are simply being able to analyze the different types of styles that are put forward by different researchers and being able to think of styles coherently as a practicing manager. See Exhibit 2.6 for a summary of leader styles. See Exhibit 2.7 for an example of style range.

CONCLUSION

This chapter provides the background to be able to understand and critique the major leadership theories. The scientific approach to leadership studies generally asks four questions: What are the most important contingency factors? What are the predominant

Exhibit 2.6

Styles Most Commonly Described by Leadership Theories

Leadership style	Narrative description	Behavioral competencies
Laissez-faire	Passive indifference about task and subordinates; essentially a nonstyle	—
Directive	Letting subordinates know what they are expected to do; giving specific guidance; asking subordinates to follow rules and procedures; scheduling and coordinating	Tasks: *monitor, plan operations clarify roles, inform, delegate* People: *manage conflict,* manage personnel change Organizational: general management functions
Supportive	Considering the needs of followers; displaying concern for their needs; creating a friendly work environment for each worker	People: *consult* (listen), *coordinate personnel, develop staff, motivate,* build and manage teams, manage conflict
Participative	Consulting with subordinates and taking their opinions into account; providing advice rather than direction; establishing a friendly and creative work environment for teams	Task: delegate People: *consult* (discuss), *coordinate personnel, develop staff, motivate, build and manage teams,* manage conflict, manage personnel change
Delegative	Allowing subordinates relative freedom for decision making and from daily monitoring and short-term review	Task: *delegate* People: develop staff, motivate
Achievement-oriented	Setting challenging task goals; seeking task improvements; emphasizing excellence in follower performance; showing confidence that followers will perform well	Tasks: *clarify roles (goals),* inform, delegate, *problem solve, manage innovation and creativity* People: *consult, plan and organize personnel, develop staff, motivate,* build and manage teams
Inspirational	Using intellectual stimulation (for new ideas or processes); expressing confidence in groups and the organization; enhancing group motivation goals; charisma	Tasks: manage innovation People: *motivate,* team building, *managing personnel change* Organization: scan the environment, strategic planning, *articulate vision, network and partner internally,* making decisions, *manage organization change*
Strategic	Focusing attention on organizational matters in the environmental context in order to align the organization with the external environment, to retain or gain resources, or to maintain comparative or competitive advantage	Organization: *scan the environment, strategic planning, vision articulation, decision making,* manage organization change

(continued)

Exhibit 2.6 *(continued)*

Leadership style	Narrative description	Behavioral competencies
Collaborative	Focusing on representation, external partnering, external networking in order to build up a positive image and create goodwill, and enhance the professional or local community	Task: *inform* internally and externally People: *consult* (externally) Organization: *network and partner*
Combined	Using of two or more styles simultaneously in a single fused style; for example, directive and supportive	—

Notes: (1) Behaviors in italics indicate a special emphasis or focus of the theory. (2) Styles are not mutually exclusive categories; substantial overlap exists. (3) Styles examined here are generally based on relatively holistic assessments. Leadership theories that examine "styles" from a relatively narrow perspective (e.g., risk aversion, change style, communication style, planning style, etc.) are not included.

leader styles? What are the correlations among contingency variables and styles? What are the correlations among styles and leader effectiveness? This chapter has provided a review of the first two questions, which are the building blocks of theory. However, the third and fourth questions are the heart of leadership theories, and will be covered in the following chapters.

The variables affecting leadership—the contingencies—are very extensive. Five clusters of commonly used contingencies have been discussed. One group has to do with leader characteristics. When leader characteristics vary, how do/should styles vary? Another group is task characteristics. Task clarity, project ambiguity, and task interdependence are issues that affect style substantially. Another group of characteristics is subordinate characteristics—their traits and skills, their commitment to task, and their attributions of leaders' ability and trustworthiness. Still another category of variables is organizational in nature. Power relationships, organizational design, external connectedness, and environmental uncertainty all affect the type of style that a leader uses. In addition, some miscellaneous variables have been mentioned that tend to lead to specialized approaches or subfields of leadership studies. The two examples cited here are leader ethics and leader gender.

Leader style is a level of analysis higher than leader competencies (behaviors, traits, and skills), but lower than leadership metacategories (see chapter 1 for a discussion of the hierarchy of concepts and terms). It is defined as a moderate-sized cluster of leader behaviors, primarily used to describe or prescribe ideal leader patterns. It is a very popular level of analysis for both the lay public and researchers because it offers more specificity than the highly abstract metacategories, but more elegance than behavioral and competency theories, which invariably include dozens of factors. Some of the problems with this level of analysis are that the styles must be defined in operational terms very carefully and these operational definitions often vary substantially. This leads to major

Exhibit 2.7

An Example of a Range of Styles

Few managers and leaders have a single style that they use all of the time. Rather, as circumstances vary, their styles will vary, too. Contingency theories of leadership emphasize the application of different styles. For example, Hersey and Blanchard (1969, 1972) discuss style in terms of style profile and style adaptability (capacity). Their terms are redefined slightly here to apply to all contingency leadership theories. Style profile indicates preferred and secondary styles as well as style range. That is, preferred style is the one that you use instinctively, and secondary styles are those that you feel comfortable using, even if you do so more consciously. Style range indicates the degree to which a leader is inclined to use different styles at some point as circumstances dictate. Style capacity is the degree to which a leader uses a style effectively and appropriately matches the readiness of the follower or other leadership contingencies. Even though someone has a preferred style, they may not use it well or in the right circumstances. For example, someone who prefers a directive style may use it in an annoying and demeaning way, and someone with a participative style may use it even though an executive decision would be more appropriate for a serious personnel action.

Our example of style range is Barbara. She has just been promoted from a supervisory position to a midlevel management position in a large social service agency where she has been employed for twenty-one years. Barbara has been a very good supervisor, which is a major reason for her promotion. She excels at training new employees, providing an excellent workflow in the unit, and maintaining agency standards (directing). Nonetheless, Barbara is very well liked by her employees who feel that she is attentive and caring (supporting). In recent years Barbara has learned to include more group decision making when special production problems have occurred (participating). In addition, Barbara would occasionally let one of the senior employees take on projects without constant oversight (delegating). As a long-time supervisor, Barbara is adept at combining styles as necessary. For example, she is able to firmly discipline an employee and yet communicate her caring and support at the same time.

Barbara has to adapt her leadership styles and add to her repertoire because now supervisors, not frontline employees, report to her. Although she knows she will quickly master the new scheduling and training aspects easily, she is very uncomfortable directing her former peers, some of whom she feels need significant improvement (directing). She is also unsure how to use her supportive style without being perceived as too "soft." Barbara is already using participative and delegative styles more, as they are styles that the supervisors expect most of the time.

Barbara will have to improve substantially in three styles if she wants to be completely well rounded as a leader. First, Barbara has not used an achievement-oriented style much as a supervisor because she likes to maintain a high degree of hands-on control. As a supervisor, she regularly reviewed case files and other work products to maintain quality control and to ensure concrete feedback. Now her task as manager has shifted more to efficiency and scale of production, which she does not directly supervise. Her challenge is to motivate supervisors to increase work efficiency and productivity. Because this requires effectively appealing to their individual sense of planning and accomplishment, she must learn to use an achievement-oriented style more often. Even more alien to Barbara are external and inspirational styles. No longer is Barbara simply implementing directives at the unit level. Now she must make more substantial decisions about allocation of resources, and she must anticipate organizational changes due to legislation or rule changes. Furthermore, Barbara's low-key, high-control style is suitable for supervision, but is not always ideal for leading change, in which a more dynamic approach is often necessary (inspirational). She is quite unaccustomed to talking about mission, vision, and organizational goals, or using symbolic language. Finally, because the agency is chronically underfunded and therefore understaffed, she will need to decide which areas she will tackle as major priorities, which she will merely monitor, and which she will ignore (essentially adopting

(continued)

Exhibit 2.7 (*continued*)

a laissez-faire style) unless brought to her attention, if she is not to burn out. Hopefully she can attend to some of these low-priority areas later.

Overall, then, Barbara has the potential to be a well-rounded leader. The combined directive-supportive style is her primary style, but increasingly participative and delegative styles are becoming second nature, too. She will have to work hard to be comfortable with other styles in order for them to be useful secondary styles. Her personality is detail oriented so an external style (except for the general management functions) is not natural to her. She prefers to think of people doing their duty, not challenging them to achieve personal goals at work. And she is not inclined to think in strategic terms, to network extensively in other divisions and outside the agency, or to use evocative language as is required in an inspirational style. Although Barbara may never excel at using these styles, she would like to include them in her repertoire as alternative styles for the broader array of management challenges that she now faces.

problems with nomenclature. Further, few theories attempt to be comprehensive, which may have the virtue of providing greater focus, but may make connecting them very difficult. To address some of the problems, this chapter has reviewed the most common dimensions of styles such as leader control, goals and performance expectations, types of motivation used, and focus of the leader's attention, as well as the most common styles identified in the literature.

Eight "true" styles have been identified, as well as a nonstyle and a combined style (ten in all). The laissez-faire style is one in which the leader exhibits passive indifference about tasks and subordinates. A directive style is exhibited when a leader lets subordinates know what they are expected to do, gives directions and guidance, asks subordinates to follow rules and procedures, and schedules and coordinates work activities. A supportive style is demonstrated by showing consideration toward followers, displaying concern for their needs, and creating a friendly work environment for each worker individually. Leaders using a participative style consult with subordinates and take their opinions into account, provide suggestions and advice rather than direction, and create a friendly and creative work environment for the team as a whole. A delegative style is defined as one allowing subordinates relative freedom for decision making and from daily monitoring and short-term reviews. In an achievement-oriented style a leader sets challenging task goals, seeks task improvements, emphasizes excellence in follower performance, and shows confidence that followers will perform well. An inspirational style uses intellectual stimulation in order to produce new ideas or to gain their acceptance for new approaches, inspirational motivation to achieve group goals, and heavy reliance on acceptance of the leader's wisdom and/or integrity by followers. A strategic style focuses leaders', especially executives', attention on the competitive environment and calls for the capacity to learn, change, and implement change wisely. A collaborative style is utilized when leaders participate in the external environment to represent, network, and partner in noncompetitive ways. A combined style is the use of two or more styles simultaneously in a single fused style, for example, directive and supportive. It has been argued that although these styles are not mutually exclusive, they are distinctive enough to be conceptually useful categories because of the patterns they imply and because of their utilization by researchers and popular writers of leadership.

The next chapters examine the ways that various theories explain the dynamics of leadership and assert that specific contingencies lead to a variety of style prescriptions.

NOTE

1. An especially notable exception to this trend was Mary Parker Follett who lectured and wrote extensively in the 1920s (Graham 1996). Follett discussed the "law of the situation" in which leaders needed to pay close attention to the situation in which they found themselves and let that situation, rather than rigid rules or formal authority, determine how to handle problems.

3

Leadership Theories: Early Managerial and Transactional Approaches

Because leadership is a large social phenomenon as well as highly complex, we should not be surprised that many theories have been advanced to explain it. Consider the famous fable of the ten blind Indian men who had never seen an elephant. Each was trying to discover the nature of the elephant by investigation. Going up to the elephant, each felt a different part and thus came to a different conclusion. After feeling the side of the animal, one blind man asserted that the elephant was like a wall and another blind man on the other side of the elephant agreed. However, these men were contradicted by another blind man who, after feeling the leg, stated that the elephant was really like a tree, and the three other men feeling the legs agreed with this wisdom. The blind man feeling the trunk corrected the overstatement of those feeling legs by stating that the elephant was more like a snake, while still another blind man scoffed at all of them, saying that the elephant was little more than a rope as he handled the tail. Still another blind man was amazed at the inaccuracy of all the others; the elephant was clearly like a spear, he said as he felt the tusk, and the blind man feeling the other tusk corroborated this perception. Not only could the blind men not agree on a simple description, but they had not yet begun to investigate the interesting questions of the elephant's strength, endurance, speed, or uses. Similar to our blind men, a bewildering number of theories have been advanced to explain a variety of aspects of leadership, each with its own partial wisdom or advantages. To appreciate these numerous theories, we will compare their contributions and liabilities.

In the previous chapter, the building blocks used in leadership theory were discussed. Nine generalized types of behaviors, or styles, common to most theories were reviewed. Chapter 2 also reviewed the types of contingencies that affect when these styles should be used and how effective they will be. Contingencies can be related to leader characteristics, task characteristics, subordinate characteristics, organizational characteristics, and other characteristics.

This and the next five chapters describe different approaches to leadership, often called schools of thought, and different theories (or models and frameworks) within each approach. The descriptions and analyses emphasize a comparative perspective. For each theory the following aspects will be briefly discussed:

- What is the background of the theory and what have researchers tried to explain?
- Which situational variables or contingencies does the theory emphasize?

- Which styles does the theory emphasize?
- What type of performance criteria does the theory emphasize?
- What are the strengths and weaknesses of the theory or approach?

This chapter covers major leadership theories from the turn of the twentieth century through the 1970s that focus on the leaders and followers in narrower organizational contexts. All of these theories are commonly taught in management and leadership classes, but only a few of them are actively used as research models today. The next chapters focus on leadership and change, distributed leadership, ethical theories, specialized theories, and integrated or comprehensive theories.

USE OF A CAUSAL-CHAIN MODEL TO COMPARE APPROACHES AND THEORIES

Theories of leadership certainly come in all shapes, sizes, and formats. Some attempt to be elegant; that is, they try to explain a good deal with as few variables as possible. Particularly notable for this type of analysis are universal theories. Such theories attempt to explain leadership in a uniform fashion regardless of the situation. Others pride themselves on being comprehensive; they try to consider all significant factors. Some theories try to explain a narrower aspect of leadership very well—say, the causes and effects of leader attribution processes on followers. Other theories try to explain a broader array of leadership functions simultaneously, so that not only production and worker satisfaction but also the need for external alignment and organizational change are addressed. Sometimes leadership styles are experimentally treated as independent variables, sometimes as dependent variables, and at other times as contingencies. In order to provide a consistent basis for comparison, however, all the theories will be discussed in terms of a similar causal-chain model.

The generic, causal-chain model of leadership that is used here incorporates four different types of variables: behavior, intervening, moderating, and performance variables. Because the list of behaviors is extensive, most theories discuss them in clusters or styles. Chapter 2 identified nine commonly used styles as well as a combined style for cases in which a relatively broad array of behaviors is expected simultaneously or in tight sequence. *Behaviors or styles* are at the beginning of the causal chain because they are the first demonstrable action toward followers, the organization, the environment, and so forth. They also lead the chain in terms of *practitioner* interest: What actions lead to what performance?

The next elements considered are the *intervening variables*. They were defined in the preceding chapter as variables that affect which behavior or style should be selected to enhance the desired outcome. Theories that recommend a variety of different styles based on the contingencies of the situation emphasize intervening variables. In the leadership literature, those theories that emphasize intervening variables are called either contingency or situational theories, although those names are sometimes applied to the specific theories of Fiedler (1967; Fiedler, Chemers, and Mahar 1976) and Hersey and Blanchard (1969, 1972), respectively.

Moderating variables are defined as those that affect the strength, quality, or success of a behavior or style. The most common types of moderating variables have to do with leader expertise in executing the desired style. The ideal behavior in a given situation may be supportive, and while the leader may demonstrate that behavior, it may be in a clumsy fashion that makes followers feel as if the attention they receive is micromanagement rather than helpfulness. Of course, many other factors can affect the success of a given behavioral strategy. For example, frontline supervisors use directive behaviors extensively, but their long-term effectiveness will be enhanced or diminished based on the supervisor's ability to provide extrinsic incentives. The effectiveness of an inspirational style will be moderated by the group's cohesiveness and the consistency of its goals.

Finally, there are *performance variables*. Originally, performance was seen almost exclusively from an organizational perspective as production efficiency or as organizational effectiveness in dividing work and coordinating business activities. (Relatedly, the power literature emphasizes the role of leader influence with the assumption that the leader is the principal representative of the agency's interests.) Later it was demonstrated that follower satisfaction and inclusion were important for maximum productivity, and still later it was shown that they were useful for short-term problem solving, long-term creativity, and also for nonhierarchical organizational management structures (see Kaplan and Norton 1996; Niven 2003). Because an organization may be efficient and effective in doing something, but no longer doing the right thing or using an outdated method, organizational alignment with the environment and organizational change become performance variables as well. Thus, performance variables can be narrow or extensive, including production efficiency, follower satisfaction and development, decision quality, external alignment, and organizational change, among others.

Exhibit 3.1 displays the causal chain-model that will be used throughout the following chapters. To review, how a leader behaves directly affects performance. That is, the behaviors or styles s/he uses affect how much is accomplished, how followers feel, how well the organization adapts, and so forth. However, important factors influence this relationship. Some factors (intervening variables) are so important that they determine what styles will work most effectively in a given situation. For example, in some cases a directive style is most effective and in others it may be dysfunctional while an inspirational style is best. Other factors (moderating variables) affect only the impact of a style. For example, a leader who correctly assesses that an inspirational style is called for and attempts to employ it, but who lacks the trust of his followers and who has weak motivational speaking skills, is likely to have limited success.

EARLY MANAGEMENT AND LEADERSHIP APPROACHES

Serious study of management and leadership began to develop around the turn of the twentieth century. Both fields developed mindsets or paradigms that guided researchers for nearly fifty years. Calls for a shift in the fields began to be heard in the late 1940s (Dahl 1947; Simon 1947; Stogdill 1948; Waldo 1948). Although work from this era is often characterized as either simplistic or wrong, a fairer assessment is to note that while

Exhibit 3.1

A Generic, Causal-Chain Model of Leadership

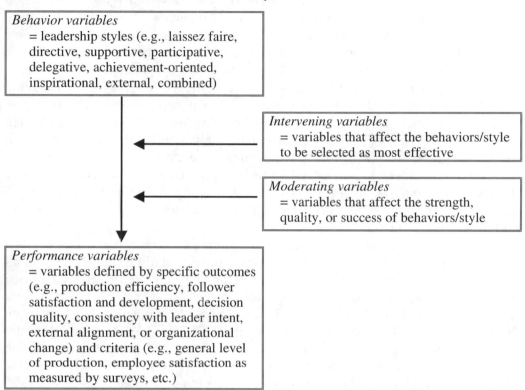

Behavior variables
    = leadership styles (e.g., laissez faire,
    directive, supportive, participative,
    delegative, achievement-oriented,
    inspirational, external, combined)

Intervening variables
    = variables that affect the behaviors/style
    to be selected as most effective

Moderating variables
    = variables that affect the strength,
    quality, or success of behaviors/style

Performance variables
    = variables defined by specific outcomes
    (e.g., production efficiency, follower
    satisfaction and development, decision
    quality, consistency with leader intent,
    external alignment, or organizational
    change) and criteria (e.g., general level
    of production, employee satisfaction as
    measured by surveys, etc.)

many of the insights of the era were very good, the frameworks proposed tended to be both narrower and more time specific than was acknowledged in their day. The natural progression of science requires these periodic scientific revolutions (Kuhn 1962) in which the overthrow of one era's research framework does not mean the next is not partially built on prior insights and failures. Rather, new perspectives require a new approach to better explain the gaps and anomalies of the previous era.

The fields of both management and leadership sought a universal prescription of ideal practices. Classical management purported to find it by proposing the centrality of analytic skills. Leadership theory searched in vain for a universal list of ideal traits. Although analytic skills and ideal traits are important elements of leadership, they are not sufficient to explain the entire phenomenon or to specify the conditions in which different skills and traits are necessary.

Classical Management Theory

The first half of the twentieth century is considered the classical management period and includes two approaches, so-called scientific management and management principles. In the United States the scientific management movement was a reaction to the major changes that had occurred in the American economy, which was just becoming an industrial power. Manufacturing and business operations—emerging from a period of cottage industries that were small and randomly ordered—were frequently poorly organized because they failed to change practices as their industries matured and new technologies emerged. Scientific management gurus such as Gantt (1916), Taylor (1911), and Gilbreth and Gilbreth (1917) *advocated the use of analytic tools to design management practices efficiently.* One powerful analytic tool was the time-and-motion study. Experts would study a process and the workers' patterns of activity to determine (1) the most efficient way of doing the work by individuals and (2) the most efficient way of coordinating people within the workplace. It was during this period that training became professionalized through standardization and work specialization resulted in enormous advances in assembly-line technology. Although the term "scientific management" is out of favor, the tools of scientific management and its focus on work analysis and efficiency at the worker and unit level are very much a part of good standard management practices today.

Even when managers have instructed workers in efficient protocols and have clarified best practices, they still have substantial responsibilities in staffing, planning, and communicating with superiors on productivity and planning issues. The principles approach emphasized the role of mid- and senior-level managers in organizing rationally at a higher level. Gulick and Urwick's (1937) summary of these practices has become an anagram famous in the management literature, POSDCoRB, which stands for planning, organizing, staffing, directing, coordinating, reporting, and budgeting. Just as scientific management focused on the study and efficient design of worker and unit systems, the principles approach *focused on the study and efficient design of entire organizations.* Important concepts such as span of control and unity of command emerged. Just as scientific management experts argued for expert analysis of line workers' job functions and unit coordination, advocates of the principles approach encouraged analysis of manager functions to ensure that responsibilities were reasonable and not excessively fragmented. Although some of the specific prescriptions that were relevant for their time are obsolete (such as reducing span of control and maintaining tight unity of command, which results in relatively steep hierarchies), the general ideas behind a principles approach are still valid. That is, management itself needs to be analyzed by experts and studied by its constituents, which requires self-conscious rationality and extensive training.

Although classical management theory did much to propel management into a science and profession by emphasizing careful analysis, planning, and implementation at all levels, the indirect contributions to leadership theory were much more modest. This approach assumes high leader control, high use of formal authority and extrinsic incentives, and an internal focus. The only style assumed is directive, and the only kinds of outcomes of interest are unit or organizational production and efficiency improvements. The only moderating variable is the use of analytic and management tools. This results in a simple causal model: The more that a directive style relying on analytic tools is

Exhibit 3.2

Causal-Chain Model Implicit in Classical Management Theory

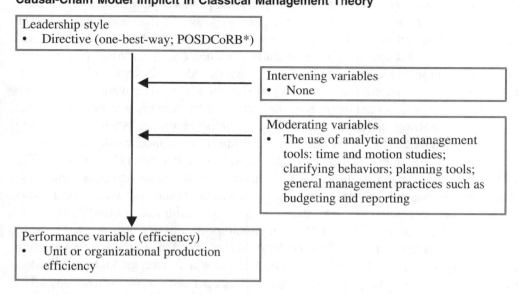

*POSDCoRB = planning, organizing, staffing, directing, coordinating, reporting, and budgeting.

used and used well, the better unit and organizational performance will be. The logic is summarized in Exhibit 3.2.

The value of this simplistic conceptualization of leadership is not without virtue. First, in its day it made a particularly important statement that the authoritarian management style so popular at the time was different from a directive style. The latter style uses analysis and rationality before implementing formal authority; the former uses formal authority based on personal impressions and traditions. Even today these simple truths are much violated in practice; some leaders are selected without experience or training, and those with experience too frequently rely on authority and past practice rather than disciplined data gathering and analysis. Second, classical-management theory helped establish crucial aspects of what has long been considered a pivotal style of successful leaders.

The weaknesses of classical management are also apparent. Its focus is very narrow, and thus it leaves a great deal out of both the management and leadership equations. There are styles other than directive, there are tools other than analytic and management-oriented ones that affect performance, and there are types of performance other than efficiency. The weaknesses of overextending the theory in the first half of the twentieth century were less noticeable in a climate in which organizations had simpler products and services and in which management experience was largely sufficient for all design and problem solving. As organizations have to accomplish increasingly complex tasks in greater numbers as well as to change products and services more frequently, an exclusively directive style becomes more dysfunctional because it prevents necessary worker contributions and frustrates the educated workforce who drive such services.

Trait Theory

The underlying assumption of trait theory was that *leaders have certain characteristics that are utilized across time to enhance organizational performance and leader prestige.* The notion was that traits affected behaviors and behaviors affected effectiveness. The hope was to identify a master list of traits (i.e., essentially a master style) that would prescribe the ideal candidate or ideal leader in action. The field examined a wide variety of leader traits that bore a positive correlation to leadership. It was found that "the average person who occupied a position of leadership exceeded the average member of his or her group, to some degree, in the following respects: (1) sociability, (2) initiative, (3) persistence, (4) knowing how to get things done, (5) self-confidence, (6) alertness to and insight into situations, (7) cooperativeness, (8) popularity, (9) adaptability, and (10) verbal facility" (Bass 1990, 75). However, Stogdill asserted two problems with this master-list approach to leadership. First, no traits were universally required for leadership. Second, leadership varied extensively according to the "characteristics, activities, and goals of the followers" (1948, 64).

In terms of leadership style, the underlying assumption was that a master list of traits would provide the indirect basis for a combined style. That is, even though traits are not actual behaviors, they guide activity (e.g., knowing how to get things done; sociability), and, as important, guide the qualities of behavior (e.g., persistence and adaptability). The above list is indeed a useful starting point for thinking about the types and qualities of behaviors that are typically significant (Zaccaro 2007). The weakness of this approach is that it does not tell us when select traits are critical or can be omitted without extensive situational analysis. In fact, two leaders can use different traits to achieve the same level of success, and, more important, the same leader could apply the same traits in two different situations, only to succeed in one and fail miserably in the other (Vroom and Jago 2007). The underlying causal model is provided in Exhibit 3.3.

TRANSACTIONAL APPROACHES

By the 1950s, some of the implicit leadership assumptions of the early management and trait theories were being consciously challenged by the basic research being conducted at Ohio State University, the University of Michigan, and in other settings. By the 1960s, theories of leadership began to develop in what later came to be called the transactional approach. The heyday of this approach was from the early 1960s to the early 1980s, although interest continues today. The closed-system perspective, emphasizing internal organizational needs, continued to dominate thinking in the transactional approach, as it had in the early management period. However, transactional approaches integrated the insights of the human relations school, which emphasized the importance of worker needs and motivations on productivity, retention, and decision making. In turn, this challenged the extreme reliance on a top-down managerial philosophy and a "worker-as-replaceable-part" mentality. Transactional approaches tend to include either more leader styles or more complex combined styles, all of which emphasize more worker inclusiveness. They also tend to include a development and learning-focused perspective.

Exhibit 3.3

Causal-Chain Model Implicit in Universal Trait Theory

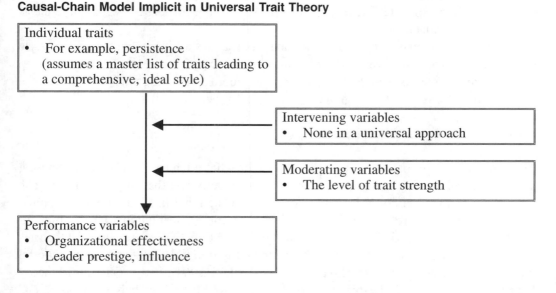

Human relations theory focuses on worker motivations. It argues that workers' motivations are not only complex, but legitimate and necessary considerations for managers to address. Maslow's hierarchy of needs suggests that humans have needs at five different levels: physiological, economic security, love and belonging, self-esteem, and self-actualization (1954). Generally speaking, humans seek out fulfillment of the most basic needs first and then go on to "higher" needs. However, because all needs exist concurrently, need fulfillment often overlaps. Furthermore, individuals have different levels of desire for fulfillment at different levels; some individuals have a great need for economic security while others may have almost none. A human relations approach has enormous implications for leaders who can no longer simply direct people based on analytic needs and management principles, but must also pay close attention to worker needs.

Another contributor to this shift in thinking toward including workers more in work processes was the rise of social exchange theory. Social exchange theory argued that all interaction is fundamentally an exchange of benefits or favors that can include not only tangible benefits such as work and money, but also psychological benefits such as recognition, loyalty, security, friendship, esteem, and so forth (Homans 1958; Thibaut and Kelley 1959). If the earlier management perspective had an exclusively organizational perspective, social exchange theory required leaders to take into account the rational self-interest of followers. Optimizing organizational efficiency and effectiveness, then, would require simultaneously optimizing a complex array of worker values. In an early sophisticated version of social exchange, Hollander (1958) proposed that leaders contribute competence to the social exchange while workers contribute loyalty. Leaders who contribute successful innovations and changes receive affirmations of loyalty and in the future an allowance for still larger deviations from past norms. Hollander called this store of goodwill and acceptance "idiosyncrasy credits"; highly successful leaders could propose bold solutions and act more unconventionally. Of course, failures have the reverse effect, so that some leaders may face resistance for relatively logical requests because of past mistakes.

In terms of leadership styles, transactional approaches all include a supportive style to complement the directive style. Some include participative, delegative, and achievement-oriented styles as well. Some transactional theories blend together several of these behavioral patterns into an integrated or combined style.

Blake and Mouton's Grid Theory

The trait theory approach relies on personality or what a leader "has." The behavioral approach emphasizes what a leader "does" and the activities that they undertake. The Ohio State and University of Michigan studies indicated that task- and people-oriented behaviors were the core leadership tasks. Task behaviors are critical to goal accomplishment while relationship behaviors are critical to motivation. One of the very first theories that tried to make sense of the new behavioral orientation to leadership, the managerial grid, was proposed by Robert Blake and Jane Mouton (1964). It was called grid theory because it locates five leadership styles on a grid constructed of two behavioral axes. *The managerial grid integrates task and supportive factors in a multiplicative fashion.*

Grid theory largely fits into a universal, rather than contingency, approach to leadership. While the authors acknowledge situational factors (Blake and Mouton 1982), they do not address them significantly in their model. Leaders should be aware of situational factors and should select ideal behaviors accordingly, always striving to achieve a combined style that they propose as ideal. The causal model implicit in Blake and Mouton's grid theory is illustrated in Exhibit 3.4.

Concern for results is the horizontal axis and concern for people is the vertical axis in grid theory. Each axis varies from 1 (low) to 9 (high). A 1.1 leader has little concern for either subordinates or production. This is called an "impoverished" management style. A 9,1 leader places great emphasis on efficiency and workers merely as vehicles of production. Because efficiency in operations is the exclusive concern, "human elements interfere to a minimum degree" (Blake and Mouton 1985, 12). This is called an "authority-compliance" management style. A 1.9 leader places great emphasis on people concerns which in turn leads to "a comfortable, friendly organization atmosphere and work tempo" (ibid.). This is called a "country club" management style. A 5.5 leader combines both concern for production and people, but not at optimal levels. It leads to "adequate organization performance." This is called "organization man" management. The ideal style is 9.9 leadership, which combines both elements at high levels. "Work accomplishment is from committed people; interdependence through a 'common stake' in organization purpose leads to relationships of trust and respect" (ibid.). It is called the "team" management style.

Team management, according to Blake and Mouton, calls for management objectives that are mutually determined, clarification of organizational goals in alignment with

Exhibit 3.4

Causal-Chain Model Implicit in Blake and Mouton's Grid Theory

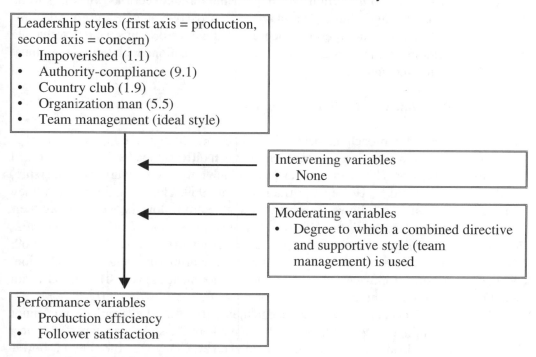

Source: Based on Blake and Mouton (1964).

worker needs, creative use of worker talents and skills, and is based on trust, respect, and openness. Many managers espouse this style but, when provided feedback on their actual style, find that their perceptions and those of their subordinates vary markedly (Blake and Mouton 1985).

Grid theory was the first highly popular theory of leadership that utilized the task-people duality. Part of this success was due to the elegance and directness of the theory and its appeal at an intuitive level. Therefore, it provided an excellent heuristic framework for training purposes as well as an overarching ideal of management behavior. Yet the theory also suffers from a variety of important deficiencies. First, as a universal theory it does not provide explanations about why behavior should vary from one situation to another, even though the authors acknowledge that leaders need to vary their behavior. This is because the primary strength of the theory—its elegance—is simultaneously its weakness—excessive simplicity. Not surprisingly, empirical support has been modest because of its lack of situational discrimination (e.g., Weed, Mitchell, and Moffitt 1976). Even more problematic is that the high-high or team management style does not always seem to be ideal. Even though a balance of directive and supportive behaviors may be preferable most of the time, it is not hard to imagine many situations in which a disproportionately directive or supportive style would be more appropriate (e.g., Miner

1982). A hardworking perfectionist subordinate who has just discovered her own error may need a great deal of support but no direction, while a highly selfish and destructive employee who is about to be terminated may misinterpret concern as weakness to be manipulated. Thus the high-high style as a one-best-way style may be a useful ideal for new managers, but it does not present much detailed advice or a mechanism to handle the many exceptions that leaders encounter in various situations with which they must deal daily (Yammarino and Dansereau 2008).

Hersey and Blanchard's Situational Leadership

Unlike the universal approach advocated by Blake and Mouton, a number of other re-searchers advocated a contingency approach in which different leadership styles hinged upon different factors. The most popular has undoubtedly been situational leadership, which was put forward by Hersey and Blanchard in 1969. The contingencies that they proposed were based on follower capacity. How able are followers and what are their levels of motivation? *Depending on these contingencies, situational leadership prescribes four different leadership styles: directing, coaching, supporting, and delegating* (1969, 1972). The performance variables that they assume are primarily related to production, but they do consider follower satisfaction and development as well. The causal-chain model is illustrated in Exhibit 3.5.

As Hersey and Blanchard have responded to their critics, they have varied some minor aspects of the contingencies that they use, but have kept the styles constant. In all ver-sions of situational leadership there is a combined contingency variable called follower maturity that is composed of two elements: job maturity and psychological maturity. Job maturity is composed of experience, education, and capacity. Is the follower able to do the task or not? The progression of competence or ability is relatively straightforward over time. Generally speaking, competence increases in a linear fashion, assuming good instruction and feedback.

The second element, which has varied slightly in different versions, is attitudinal. The focus is on willingness or commitment. In turn, willingness is based on motivation and confidence. It functions in a curvilinear manner over time. Willingness starts on a high level as new employees come to jobs full of excitement and enthusiasm. However, as the realities of the job and the challenges of reaching mastery sink in over time, motiva-tion sags. In the long term, however, as workers become highly competent and absorb professional values, their commitment increases again. The developmental aspect of situ-ational leadership largely depends on this pattern—high, low, high—being a relatively universal one. However, it is much disputed whether this is so or whether many other common attitudinal patterns also exist such as low, medium, high (especially as related to confidence) or even high, medium, low (as related to burnout).

Leader styles are a combination of directive and supportive behaviors. Directive behaviors include monitoring, giving directions, instruction, clarifications; goal-setting; establishing timelines; and so on. The emphasis is on one-way communication. Supportive behaviors include listening, various types and levels of inclusion, and encouragement.

Exhibit 3.5

Causal-Chain Model Implicit in Situational Leadership

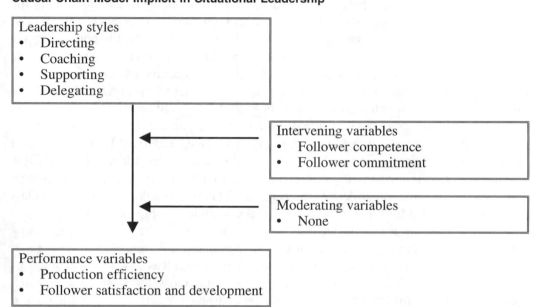

A directing style is composed of high directive behavior and low supportive behavior. A coaching style is composed of high directive and supportive behavior. A supporting style is composed of low directive and high supportive behavior. A delegating style is composed of low directive and supportive behavior.

Hersey and Blanchard explain that followers who are low in competence but high in commitment, such as new employees, are eager for instructions and structure but do not need much supportive behavior. These types of situations call for a directing style. Followers who are moderate in competence but low in commitment because of a lack of confidence generally continue to need a lot of both directive behavior and supportive behavior to encourage them. The coaching style encourages high engagement with subordinates, with the leader being highly engaged in terms of goals and supervision. As followers' competence continues to increase within the moderate range, and as they are increasingly able to handle problems and issues, leaders should provide low direction and high support. In the supporting style, leaders either emphasize joint participation in subordinate decision making or their availability for problem solving. Finally, highly mature followers need little direction or support. Followers seek out advice and technical support on an as-needed basis. Emotional needs tend to be much more subtle, such as occasional recognition of expertise rather than frequent praise. The delegating style assumes that relative worker independence is both a reward and an efficiency strategy.

The strengths of this theory are significant. The first is that various aspects of the model have intuitive appeal. The job maturity aspect has tremendous face validity because it uses a widely accepted developmental learning model. When people do not know how to do something, they need direction; as they learn, they need less and less direction. In similar fashion, supportive behavior should shift with types of needs and maturity of the followers. Hersey and Blanchard's explanation that moderately competent followers need the most supportive behaviors is plausible, as is the assertion that highly competent followers need the least. Because of its intuitive appeal, this model has been the most widely used in applied training settings. Moreover, the principles behind the model are easy to master because leadership style is based only on follower maturity. Further, the model is highly prescriptive, which provides clear diagnoses for practitioners who like answers more than rather abstract theories. Finally, the theory emphasizes leadership style range and adaptability. The instrument used (currently called the Leadership Effectiveness and Adaptability Description, or LEAD), formerly called the Leader Adaptability and Style Inventory, or LASI) does a good job of pointing out whether a person tends to use a single style most of the time, regardless of the situation. This is a valuable concept for leaders to grasp because leadership flexibility enhances overall leadership capacity.

The weaknesses of the model are also very substantial. First, the basis for determining the correct leadership style is quite narrow. Style is based only on subordinate competence and commitment, and excludes other contingencies such as task, organizational, or leader factors. As long as follower characteristics are the most important factors, which they frequently are for frontline supervisors, the contingency narrowness is not a major problem. However, when other factors become more important (Slocum 1984), additional leadership theories must be used and integrated with situational leadership. Second, the psychological maturity aspect of the theory is quite loose, and explanations have varied significantly about the pattern and connection to leadership style. Overall, the single, non-linear pattern proposed in different versions of situational leadership is unconvincing in a tougher analysis. Why should the first flush of commitment always decrease over time? Further, the psychological maturity element itself fuses some very different subfactors, such as motivation and confidence, that could merit rather different leader approaches. Imagine an employee who is unmotivated because of an inherent lack of interest in the job, and another employee who likes the job but is insecure because she has never been given the opportunity to exercise independent judgment. These problems have probably contributed to a third concern. Although some support has been provided (e.g., Hambleton and Gumpert 1982; Yun, Faraj, and Sims 2005), overall, the level of empirical support is quite low. Indeed, generally the research community has either responded with negative findings (e.g., Blake and Mouton 1982; Fernandez and Vecchio 1997; Graeff 1997) or concerns about the fundamental explanations of the theory. Later versions of the theory are not considered significant improvements (Thompson and Vecchio 2009).

Path-Goal Theory

Path-goal theory asserts that "leaders, to be effective, engage in behaviors that complement subordinates' environments and abilities in a manner that compensates for deficiencies and is instrumental to subordinate satisfaction and individual and work unit performance"

(House 1996, 323). In other words, *it is the leader's responsibility to align worker and organizational goals and then to ensure that the employee's path to goal attainment is clear.* The theoretical foundation of path-goal theory derives from both social exchange theory (Hollander 1958; Homans 1958) and expectancy theory (Vroom 1964). Path-goal theory assumes that workers and employers are in a mutually beneficial exchange relationship, and that it is a leader's job to enhance reciprocity and shared goals. This is conceptualized more fully in expectancy theory (discussed in chapter 14), which states that motivation is a multiplicative function of worker capacity, reward accessibility, and reward desirability. Worker capacity includes those elements that contribute to successful task completion, such as native ability, training, procedural clarity, resource and equipment support, motivational support, assistance with problems, and so forth. Reward accessibility includes those elements that contribute to reward attainment, such as ensuring that rewards are available, fairly distributed, and clearly understood. Reward desirability includes those elements that contribute to workers' actively seeking rewards, such as matching the rewards to worker preferences and ensuring that the level of the reward is significant from the worker's perspective.

Path-goal theory emphasizes the two types of contingencies found in transactional leadership models—task and subordinate characteristics—but does so comprehensively. Because the task and subordinate characteristics considered are numerous and ultimately open-ended, path-goal theory is really more a framework than a theory per se. The number of styles appropriate to most effectively deal with the contingencies identified is also open-ended and has increased over the years. The most commonly referenced path-goal articulation, by House and Mitchell (1974), has four styles and will form the basis of the current discussion.

Comparisons with grid and situational leadership are instructive. Because of their historical proximity, all three tend to emphasize task- and people-oriented contingencies and to omit organizational and leader factors. Grid theory and path-goal theory are the least alike because grid theory is based on a universal approach with a single comprehensive prescription whereas path-goal theory is a fully developed contingency approach. On the surface, situational leadership and path-goal theory have much in common. Both are dyadic contingency approaches employing four styles. Both emphasize subordinate needs. However, situational leadership seeks to explain only two subordinate factors (job and psychological maturity), whereas path-goal theory seeks to incorporate all substantial task and subordinate factors, of which there are many. Situational leadership envisions a single developmental path using a linear progression of leader styles, whereas path-goal assumes that numerous factors can provide countervailing influences and a blend of different styles. If situational leadership is rather narrow and rigid, then path-goal is rather complex and loose.

Another important contribution of the theory is its conceptualization of the need for leadership. Simply stated, leadership is not always needed. Rather, leadership supplies what is needed or missing for subordinates or their task environments. Under ideal conditions, well-trained, highly motivated, cooperative employees with ample supplies and incentives need very little "leadership." Because ideal conditions are rare, however, leadership is usually needed to improve and maintain those conditions. Path-goal theory examines the many contingencies that may be deficient and suggests the type of leadership that would remedy the specified need. This aspect of the theory was later expanded and refined in leadership substitutes theory, which will be examined in a later chapter.

Although theoretically the number of task-related contingencies is endless, the research on path-goal theory has identified five major types of variables. The first is task ambiguity. Ambiguity can be related to clarity of the job for the incumbent or the level of formalization present in the job. If the incumbent does not understand the job, it is ambiguous, and, if the job is highly routinized, it is not ambiguous. Low ambiguity generally requires less leadership and high ambiguity more. Task difficulty is another factor. Tasks can be difficult because they are complex, for example, requiring extensive information and problem solving or involving a great deal of variety. Another aspect of difficulty is the demand for change that is a function of the job. Low difficulty requires less leadership and high difficulty more. A third commonly considered element is the inherent quality of the job. Some jobs are more stressful, boring, or even dangerous, while others tend to be more inherently interesting. Path-goal generally asserts that low-quality jobs require more leadership. Another contingency is the degree of job interdependency. Highly interdependent jobs are more likely to need leadership because of the coordination required. Finally, path-goal often examines worker control over the job. Some jobs provide a good deal of autonomy and feedback that are built into the job itself for self-evaluation and correction. Such jobs provide high worker control and generally require less leadership.

Another class of contingencies involves subordinates. A very important one is the level of education, training, and experience of subordinates. Low levels of training and experience require higher levels of leadership. Work preferences also affect leader style. For example, some workers have a higher preference for structure and prefer an "authoritarian" or dogmatic style. They expect more leadership. Further, some followers prefer to control their work (i.e., an internal locus of control), whereas other employees feel more comfortable sharing the control or having the control exercised elsewhere. These preferences help shape the type of leadership used. Finally, path-goal theory has examined the degree to which subordinates prefer different types of fulfillment at any given time. Competing types of fulfillment include the desire for security, the need for affiliation, the craving for individual recognition, and the aspiration for group success. When each of these types of fulfillment dominate a follower, it will subtly affect the style of leadership he or she prefers to be exercised.

To attend to these contingent needs, directive and supportive styles were originally proposed (House 1971). Later, House and Mitchell (1974) added participative and achievement-oriented styles. "Directive path-goal clarifying leader behavior is behavior directed toward providing psychological structure for subordinates: letting subordinates know what they are expected to do, scheduling and coordinating work, giving specific guidance, and clarifying policies, rules, and procedures" (House 1996, 326). Such behavior is nonpunitive and nonauthoritarian. Such behavior helps to structure and clarify the work and provides extrinsic motivation where intrinsic motivation may be lacking.

"Supportive leader behavior is behavior directed toward the satisfaction of subordinates' needs and preferences, such as displaying concern for subordinates' welfare and creating a friendly and psychologically supportive work environment." It is a "source of self-confidence and social satisfaction and a source of stress reduction and alleviation of frustration" (House 1996, 326). Supportive behavior may also be exhibited as calming subordinates or providing them with a sense of significance and/or equality.

"Participative leader behavior is behavior directed toward encouragement of subordinate influence on decision making and work unit operations: consulting with subordinates and taking their opinions and suggestions into account when making decisions" (House 1996, 327). It has four effects. First, it clarifies the relationships among effort, goal attainment, and extrinsic rewards. Second, it increases worker and employer goal congruence through the influence process. Third, it increases worker effort and performance by having subordinates clarify intentions even as they act more autonomously. Finally, it increases both the involvement and commitment of peers as well as the social pressure that they can apply to enhance organizational performance.

"Achievement-oriented behavior is behavior directed toward encouraging performance excellence: setting challenging goals, seeking improvement, emphasizing excellence in performance, and showing confidence that subordinates will attain high standards of performance" (House 1996, 327). It also tends to encourage differentiating the levels of contingent reward more sharply, and to emphasize self-actualization through work goals. The causal-chain model of path-goal theory is provided in Exhibit 3.6.

Based on the contingencies present, different styles will supply what is "missing" according to path-goal theory. When job clarity and formalization are lacking, directive leadership supplies structure. When jobs are difficult because of complexity or change, participatory leader behaviors are helpful, as well as achievement-oriented behaviors when higher standards are required. Unpleasant jobs call for supportive leader behaviors. Highly interdependent jobs call for more participatory styles. When workers control their jobs more, achievement-oriented leader behaviors work better than directive ones. Lack of training and education commonly calls for a more directive style, as do situations in which subordinates have a preference for structure and order. However, when workers have a preference for high control over their work, a more participatory or achievement-oriented style tends to work better. When need for security is high, directive leadership is preferred, but when it is low, an achievement style may work better. High need for affiliation tends to call for supportive and/or participative behaviors, while directive and achievement-oriented styles become dysfunctional. Individuals with strong yearnings for individual recognition prefer supportive and achievement-oriented styles, while those interested in group success are more amenable to participatory styles (House 1996).

One of the strengths of path-goal theory is its focus on the connection between leadership and subordinate motivation in the context of the work environment. Followers are the ones who get the work done, and thus a primary responsibility of leaders is to ensure that they have the resources, direction, support, and opportunities for inclusion and success that will benefit both them and the organization. Expectancy theory, on which path-goal theory is based, is a well-respected model of the more transactional types of motivation that occur in the workplace. Thus, the face validity of the theory is

Exhibit 3.6

Causal-Chain Model Implicit in Path-Goal Theory (1974 version)

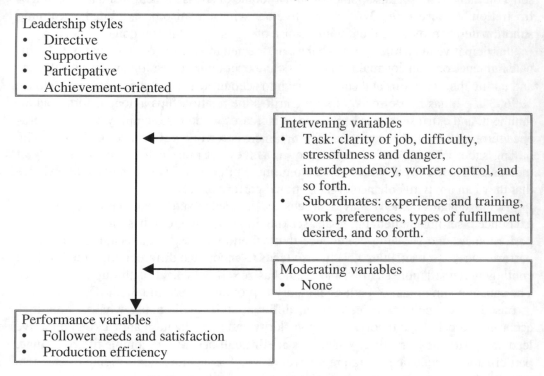

almost irrefutable. Furthermore, unlike grid and situational leadership models, path-goal
is more flexible because it is really a framework. As new relationships become established regarding the contingencies that subordinate experience and the styles leaders use,
they can easily be incorporated into path-goal theory. In 1996, House did just that, by
incorporating new hypotheses (a total of twenty-six) and new styles. Some of the styles
he suggested were a division of previous ones, but he also added entirely new styles,
such as value-based leadership, which would be similar to inspirational leadership in
the taxonomy presented in this book, or representation and networking behavior, which
would be similar to external leadership. Further, the theory does not preclude blended
leadership styles and assumes alternating styles as different subordinate needs evolve.
While the theory or framework has become increasingly complex, it can be argued that
leadership is simply a complex phenomenon and that simpler models are either much
narrower in what they explain, or extremely abstract and unspecific.

The inclusive nature of the path-goal theory has given rise to several weaknesses. First,
it is not an elegant theory. The propositions are widely scattered over the motivational
terrain, and thus must be learned one at a time. There is no reason that House's twenty-
six propositions could not double or that the styles could not be enumerated endlessly.
Not surprisingly, path-goal has not provided the basis of leadership training programs

because of its complexity. Ironically, for all of its complexity and sophistication, path-goal theory does not purport to be comprehensive. In its earlier versions, it completely excluded leader and organizational contingencies. House's reformulated 1996 version includes many organizational contingencies, but even so, path-goal should not be mistaken for a comprehensive leadership theory.

Leader-Member Exchange Theory

Leader-member exchange (LMX) theory focuses on the ongoing relationship that leaders and members of their group experience as they negotiate and exchange mutual perceptions, influence, types and amount of work, loyalty and perquisites, and so forth. Unlike the other exchange theory that was just examined, this theory examines the leader-member exchange as long-term interaction trends rather than discrete and unrelated events, as is the case in path-goal theory. Initially this theory described the nature of in-groups and out-groups in the workplace; later the theory looked more closely at the effects of the presence of in-groups and out-groups.

The initial version of the theory was called vertical dyad linkage theory (Graen and Cashman 1975). It separates followers into two member categories according to high- and low-exchange relationships. High-exchange relationship members tend to have expanded roles and negotiated responsibilities. Leaders perceive high-exchange relationship members as more competent, hardworking, and more likable. Such members tend to get more benefits, including desirable assignments, tangible rewards, better schedules, more praise, assistance with career advancement, and consultation in decision making. In turn, to have and maintain high-relationship status, members must be willing to take on more responsibilities or work such as administrative duties, must be loyal, and/or produce more. The advantages to the leader are a core group of committed people, loyalty, and backup for special and administrative functions. However, high-relationship members expect greater inclusion and support, and avoidance of coercive or authoritarian tactics. Low-relationship members tend to stay within their defined roles and do little more than what is required; that is, they "put in their time." Further, they are less committed to either the job or the leader. Leaders perceive low-exchange relationship members as less competent, hardworking, and/or loyal. Therefore, low-exchange relationship members are less likely to be provided extra benefits, professional or personal support, or to be consulted on organizational decisions.

A second version of LMX theory shifted from this descriptive approach to a more prescriptive one based on the assumption that good leaders create as many high-exchange relationships as possible. This assumption is based on research indicating that high-exchange members tend to have better attitudes, produce more, be more flexible, experience less turnover, advance more frequently, and be more willing to participate in and advance group goals. Implicitly, it proposes an ideal style: ideal leaders maintain numerous high-exchange relationships; poor leadership produces many low-exchange relationships (Graen and Uhl-Bien 1995).

This theory does not focus on situational or intervening variables. It does look at moderating variables—those that affect the strength of the ideal leader style. One important characteristic is the nature of influence. In low-exchange relationships, influence is one-way or directive (from the leader to the member), but in high-exchange relationships, influence is reciprocal. That is, in the latter relationship, followers can influence leaders by expressing their opinions and new ideas. Leaders are more likely to use participative or achievement-oriented behaviors. Another characteristic is the nature of the roles played by the member. In low-exchange relationships the roles are defined or scripted by procedures and protocols. In high-exchange relationships, the roles are more fluid and negotiated. Another characteristic is the amount of respect and trust that is shared by both leaders and members, which is quite limited or formalistic in low-exchange relationships. In high-exchange relationships, respect and trust are deep and relatively unconditional. This means that ideal leaders will more frequently incorporate supportive behaviors in order to build up goodwill. Finally, there is the nature of the focus on interests. In low-exchange relationships, member interests are nearly entirely self-serving (as are the interests of management), but in high-exchange relationships, interests of both leaders and members focus on those of the group, which realistically integrates individual and organizational needs. This tends to encourage better group and creative behaviors (Ilies, Nahrgang, and Morgeson 2007; Atwater and Carmeli 2009).

Styles range from the least desirable to the ideal style. The "stranger" style tends to be formal, directive, and distant. Leaders have low respect for and trust in their subordinates. The "acquaintance" style is less formal, directive, and distant, but is still cautious in monitoring and managing members. Leader confidence in members is moderate. The "partner" style is characterized by reciprocity, unconditional "favors," flexibility, high trust and confidence, and high support of member needs. The partner style is reminiscent of the ideals promoted in the team management style advocated by Blake and Mouton. The implicit causal chain-model is illustrated in Exhibit 3.7.

One of the major strengths of the theory is that it describes a commonly perceived reality—the presence of in-groups and out-groups, as well as high producers and low producers. In-group members get more "perks" but also are expected to be better, more loyal, and more flexible. The more recent version also recognizes that it is possible, but not as common, to have high-performing teams in which the out-group has been largely eliminated. All members are valued, make different types of contributions, and get different types of rewards. Competition is focused outside the unit, and internal cutthroat competition is discouraged.

Another strength of the theory is that it brings attention to the long-term relationship aspects of leadership. While not alone in this focus (Hollander 1958), it is in contrast to the theories that have been explored so far. Leadership is more than a series of discrete and unrelated episodes between leaders and members in which the calculus of exchange begins anew each time. Leaders and members have interacted many times in the past and know that they will interact a great deal in the future as well. Therefore, long-term sentiments and beliefs are substantial motivations for both parties. In high-exchange relationships, neither the leader nor the member needs to be concerned about who is

Exhibit 3.7

Causal-Chain Model Implicit in Leader-Member Exchange Theory

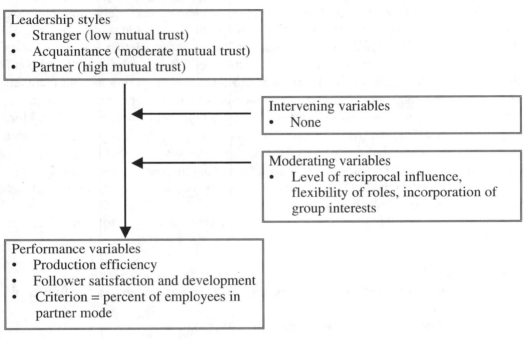

Leadership styles
- Stranger (low mutual trust)
- Acquaintance (moderate mutual trust)
- Partner (high mutual trust)

Intervening variables
- None

Moderating variables
- Level of reciprocal influence, flexibility of roles, incorporation of group interests

Performance variables
- Production efficiency
- Follower satisfaction and development
- Criterion = percent of employees in partner mode

Source: Graen and Uhl-Bien (1995).

getting what in the short term because there is trust that reciprocal interests will be fairly addressed over time.

Finally, the theory is practical in realizing that although the relationship is a shared one and the subordinate contributes to it, it still puts final responsibility for managing the relationship on the leader. Leaders frequently project their biases on followers or create/ maintain dysfunctional first impressions of members, which this theory blames squarely on leaders' shoulders.

A major weakness of the later, prescriptive version of LMX is that it falls prey to the problems of universal approaches. It tends to be simplistic and to ignore situational variables. For example, what do you do when a member is a sociopath, the unit has a history of intense self-serving behavior, or the unit has a lot of generally untalented and incompetent employees? While the ideals of the theory are exemplary, they do not always match the starker realities or the short-term demands of management.

The other major weakness of the theory is that it does not adequately explain how high and low relationships evolve. The incorporation of attribution theory would probably assist in this regard (Yukl 2002). Attribution theory posits that (1) leaders try to determine the reasons for effective and ineffective performance, and (2) leaders take the appropriate action according to their behavior/style. In determining the reasons for ineffective performance, external attribution places problems beyond a subordinate's control (e.g., lack of resources or unusual circumstances) while internal attribution defines the problem as lack of ability or lack of effort. When external attribution is made by a leader, his/her behavior is more likely to provide assistance or support, or to ignore the problem altogether. When internal attribution is made, the leader is more likely to monitor and instruct, set easier goals, counsel, or use a punishment. The problem in terms of LMX theory is what is often called fossilized behavior. It is very difficult to break out of the rut of being perceived as an in-group or out-group member. When performance is deficient, the tendency is for leaders to make external attributions to high-relationship members and internal attributions to low relationship members, regardless of the actual situation. Yet, sometimes high-relationship members may need to be held more accountable. More important, low-relationship members may be blamed for problems and get less assistance than they need and deserve because of the leader's stereotype. Furthermore, it sets up a cycle of resentment by low-exchange members about in-group members or favorites. Weak leaders tend to project internal attributions too quickly, rather than providing assistance and building on subordinate strengths.

Some of the strategies suggested to assist low performers with performance deficiencies are:

- Express a sincere desire to help and show confidence in the person.
- Gather information about problem performance prior to acting and carefully avoid attributional biases.
- Provide feedback quickly and do so in specific terms.
- When providing feedback, do so calmly and professionally by focusing on the behavior rather than the individual.
- Point out the adverse effect of the behavior.
- Mutually identify reasons for inadequate performance.
- Ask the person to suggest remedies and then mutually reach agreement on specific action steps.
- Summarize the discussion and verify agreement (adapted from Yukl 2002, 124).

Vroom's Normative-Decision Theory

One important model of leadership specifically focuses on decision making. One of the primary functions of a leader, but certainly not the only function, is to set the parameters for decision making in their organization or unit. In the narrower sense, decision inclusion issues are only three of the twenty-one functions identified earlier in this study: problem solving at the task level, conflict management at the people-oriented level, and decision making at the organizational level. However, in a broader sense it subtly affects nearly half of the leadership functions, which includes all planning and many implementation activities.

Vroom's basic theory proposes that four types of leadership should be used, under a variety of conditions, to attain a good decision in terms of quality, acceptance, timeliness, and cost, as well as to provide opportunities for employee development. The basic causal chain of the model is illustrated in Exhibit 3.8. The model has a rigorous research

Exhibit 3.8

Causal-Chain Model Implicit in Normative-Decision Theory

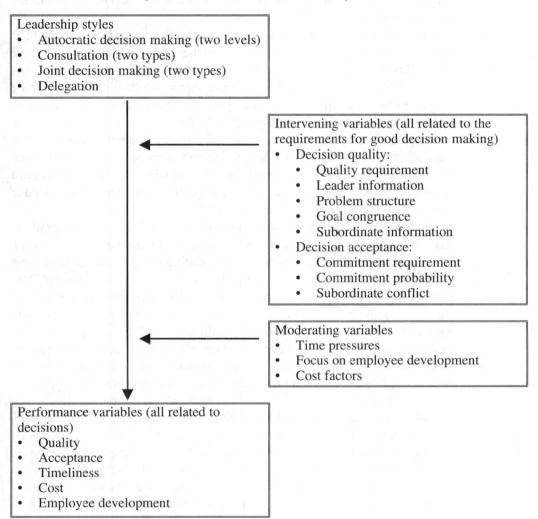

and theoretical foundation, but is relatively complex. It was originally proposed in 1973 (Vroom and Yetton) and refined in 1988 (Vroom and Jago). It is called the normative-decision model, because it prescribes what styles to use under what conditions for both groups and individuals. For simplicity, group and individual decision contexts will be combined in this discussion.

There are four different types of management decision methods (Vroom and Jago 1988, 33–35). AI and AII refer to authoritarian styles, CI and CII refer to consultative styles, GI and GII refer to joint decision-making or participation styles, and DI refers to a delegation style.

AI   You solve the problem or make the decision yourself using the information available to you at the present time.

AII   You obtain any necessary information from subordinates, then decide on a solution to the problem yourself.

CI   You share the problem with the relevant subordinates individually, getting their ideas and suggestions without bringing them together as a group. Then you make the decision. This decision may or may not reflect your subordinates' influences.

CII   You share the problem with your subordinates in a group meeting. In this meeting you obtain their ideas and suggestions. Then you make the decision, which may or may not reflect your subordinates' influence.

GI   You share the problem with one of your subordinates, and together you analyze the problem and arrive at a mutually satisfactory solution in an atmosphere of free and open exchange of information and ideas. You both contribute to the resolution of the problem with the relative contribution of each being dependent on knowledge rather than on formal authority.

GII   You share the problem with your subordinates as a group. Together you generate and evaluate alternatives and attempt to reach agreement (consensus) on a solution. Your role is much like that of chairperson, coordinating the discussion, keeping it focused on the problem, and making sure that the critical issues are discussed. You can provide the group with information or ideas that you have, but you do not try to press them to adopt your solution, and you are willing to accept and implement any solution that has the support of the entire group.

DI   You delegate the problem to one of your subordinates, providing the person with any relevant information that you possess, but giving the person full responsibility for solving the problem alone. Any solution that the person proposes will receive your support.[1]

There are two fundamental situational variables that are related to good decision making: decision quality and decision acceptance. Good decision quality depends on basing the decision on the best information possible, dealing with the problem structure adequately so that simple problems are handled efficiently and ambiguous problems are given more reflection, and ensuring that competing values and goals are adequately considered. Good decision acceptance is concerned with making sure that subordinate commitment is adequate for the type of decision made and that goal conflict does not impede the decision process.

Each of these situation demands is examined by looking at a variety of specific criteria. Vroom and Jago specify these problem attributes as a series of questions (1988, 217–228). For decision quality, the relevant questions are:

- How important is the technical quality of this decision?
- Do you have sufficient information to make a high-quality decision?
- Is the problem well structured?
- Do subordinates share the organizational goals to be attained in solving this problem?
- Do subordinates have sufficient information to make a high-quality decision?

For decision acceptance, the relevant questions are:

- How important is subordinate commitment to the decision?
- If you were to make the decision unilaterally by yourself, is it reasonably certain that your subordinates would be committed to the decision?
- Is conflict among subordinates over the preferred solution likely?

A number of features of these problem attributes are important to note. First, each of the attributes tends to indicate a direction from less to fuller inclusion by subordinates in decision making or vice versa. The basic model indicates a range of behaviors that is likely to be effective, called a feasible set. Second, the attributes may indicate contradictory levels of inclusion; the feasible set is based on balancing these factors, giving substantial rational consideration to problem demands.

Problem demands are further moderated by the decision maker's value judgment about the relative importance of time pressures, employee development, and cost factors. Depending on which of these three factors is most critical, the feasible set will be narrowed considerably. Time pressures and cost factors tend to move decisions toward more authoritarian styles; employee-development concerns tend to move decisions more toward a joint decision-making or delegation style. The relevant questions are:

- Does a critically severe time constraint limit your ability to involve subordinates?
- How important is it to you to maximize the opportunities for subordinate development?
- How important is it to you to minimize the time it takes to make the decision (to limit resource expenditure)?

Based on the problem attributes and moderating factors, leaders should analyze situations to determine the ideal level of inclusion with a decision tree. The normative decision model prescribes the following (Vroom and Jago, 1988, 134–158):

1. Move toward joint decision making and delegation when there is a *quality requirement*.
2. Avoid the use of an authoritarian style and move toward a joint decision style when *the leader lacks the necessary information*.
3. Avoid the use of authoritarian or consultative styles when the *problem is unstructured*.
4. Avoid the use of joint decision-making or delegation styles when *subordinates do not share the organizational goals;* move toward these styles when they do.
5. Avoid the use of joint decision-making or delegation styles when *the subordinates do not have the necessary information*.
6. Avoid the use of joint decision-making styles *when subordinate commitment is not required;* move toward this style when it is.

7. Avoid authoritarian styles when the *probability of subordinate commitment to unilateral decisions* is low.
8. Move toward a joint decision-making style when there is *conflict among subordinates* over preferred solutions, unless time or cost dimensions are particularly important.
9. Move toward authoritarian styles when *time pressures* exist.
10. Move toward joint decision making and delegation when *subordinate development* is a major consideration.
11. Move toward an authoritarian style if subordinates are dispersed or there is subordinate conflict over preferred solutions if *decision costs* are an important consideration.

The normative-decision theory has a number of important strengths. First, it consciously delimits the aspects of leadership it attempts to explain. Second, it does not attempt to oversimplify the conditions for a phenomenon as complex as decision making. Third, because of the relative narrowness of the theory and the breadth of the situational demands it considers, it has been a large body of empirical support and is generally highly regarded by the research community. Fourth, despite the sophistication of the model, its prescriptions remain useful and accessible to serious-minded practitioners.

The theory is not without its weaknesses, some of which are the obverse side of its strengths. First, normative-decision theory should not be mistaken for a comprehensive theory (which it does not purport to be). Other midlevel theories need to be combined with it for a comprehensive framework. Second, the number of factors to be considered for a decision is very extensive. Thus, although each aspect of the theory is easy to comprehend, the overall theory lacks parsimony and is difficult to master because of its complexity. It cannot be explained quickly or applied casually. Training sessions based on normative-decision theory are rarely brief. Additionally, some researchers have maintained that the model is excessively complex (Field 1979; Tjosvold, Wedley, and Field 1986). Third, because of the enormous number of stipulations, many of the specific assumptions have been challenged (e.g., Sinha and Chowdry 1981).

CONCLUSION

Two approaches and seven explicit or implied theories of leadership were explored in this chapter. All theories were compared according to four types of variables: leadership styles (behaviors), intervening, moderating, and performance variables.

Leader styles are related clusters of behaviors (see chapter 2). In early approaches, analysis of style was simplistic. Early management theory assumed a multipurpose directive style that was made effective by the analysis done by managers. Scientific management assumed that leaders would give orders based on job analysis, and classical management assumed that leaders would give orders based on organizational analysis. Of course, good direction does require expertise and accurate information. The trait approach assumes that leaders have a great set of qualities, mostly inborn, which result in a universal "heroic" style. However, the heroic style is indirect and ambiguous because

Exhibit 3.9

Comparison of the Leader Styles Implied by Early Management and Transactional Perspectives

Leadership style	Early management	Trait approach	Leadership theory				
			Grid (Blake and Mouton)	Situational (Hersey and Blanchard)	Path-goal (House 1974)	Leader-member exchange (Graen and Uhl-Bien 1995)	Normative-decision theory
Laissez faire			Impoverished				
Directive	One-best-way* POSDCoRB*		Authority-compliance	Directing	Directing	Stranger	Autocratic decision making (two styles)
Supportive			Country club	Coaching	Supporting	Acquaintance	Consultation (two styles)
Participative				Supporting	Participative		Joint decision making (two styles)
Delegative				Delegating			Delegative
Achievement-oriented					Achievement-oriented		
Inspirational							
Strategic							
Collaborative							
Combined		Heroic* (multiple styles implicit in multiple traits)	Team*			Partner*	

Notes: Many style equivalencies are only "best fit."
* Denotes a style recommendation considered superior.

traits are not the same as behaviors, and many of the traits recommended contradict or confound one another under different conditions. Transactional approaches added to the sophistication of style analysis by identifying three or four styles each. All include a directive style as well as a supportive style. A participative style is explicit in three of the transactional theories discussed (situational, path-goal, and normative-decision theory) and implied in the other two (grid and LMX). Only two of the theories discuss a delegative style (situational, and normative-decision theory). Only path-goal theory articulates an achievement style, and grid theory largely assumes it with its comparison between middle-of-the-road management and team management. Two offer a combined style (grid and LMX). However, almost none of the theories incorporate inspirational or external styles (except perhaps trait theory). A comparison of the styles identified in the theories in this chapter is provided in Exhibit 3.9. Note that different theories use different names for styles that are roughly equivalent.

Four of the theories do not provide intervening variables; the assumption is that a single style applies in all or most leadership situations. These universal theories include early management, trait, grid, and LMX. Three of the theories do provide intervening variables or contingencies. Situational leadership is based only on follower competence and commitment. Normative-decision theory is based only on decision quality and decision acceptance. However, path-goal theory is based on a potentially unlimited number of task and follower variables, such as role ambiguity, task ambiguity, subordinate skills, task commitment, and so on.

In six of the seven theories reviewed, those that do not provide *intervening* variables do provide or imply variables affecting the degree of success of a style. Generally speaking, it is the quality of the leader's ability to implement a style that *moderates* or controls its success. In the respective theories, it is the quality of the analytic skills, traits, a combined task-people orientation, and the ability to partner with subordinates. In normative-decision theory it is the leader's purpose that can moderate—differential interest in cost, timeliness, and employee development factors. Situational leadership and path-goal theory do not focus on moderating influences.

In terms of performance variables, scientific management focuses almost exclusively on efficiency, and classical management on effectiveness. In addition, the trait approach emphasizes leader prestige or influence. All of the transactional approaches include an efficiency/effectiveness element. In the case of normative-decision theory, it is decision quality, timeliness, and cost. They all also emphasize various types of follower outcomes, although the variance is significant in the subordinate needs versus satisfaction spectrums. Significantly, none of the theories address external alignment or organizational change as significant outcomes. This absence was dramatically addressed by the charismatic and transformational theories, which developed next and are the topic of the next chapter.

NOTE

1. Although Vroom specifies only delegation to individuals, there is no reason not to project a DII style for groups such as problem-solving teams. This type of delegation was not emphasized until the 1990s, after the Vroom model had been refined.

Leadership Theories: Charismatic and Transformational Approaches

In the 1980s, new theories of leadership emerged that diverged markedly from those that grew out of the Ohio State and University of Michigan studies. The U.S. economy had lost its preeminence by the late 1970s, and there was a swell of interest in strong leaders who could provide boldness, incisive strategies, wide appeal, and sweeping changes when necessary. It was widely felt that "the problem with many organizations, and especially the ones that are failing, is that they tend to be overmanaged and underled" (Bennis and Nanus 1985, 21). This view had been clearly articulated as early as 1977 in *Harvard Business Review* by Abraham Zaleznik in an article entitled, "Managers and Leaders: Are They Different?"

PRECURSORS TO CONTEMPORARY CHARISMATIC AND TRANSFORMATIONAL THEORIES

Three major studies preceded and prepared for the theories that emerged in the mid-1980s. An early and prominent one was by Max Weber, the brilliant German sociologist who analyzed the structure of large bureaucratic organizations, as well as political, economic, and religious systems (notable early English translations were produced in 1930 and 1947). One of Weber's insights had to do with the structure of charismatic leadership. He derived the meaning of the term from the Greek word "charisma," meaning to have the gift of God's grace, especially in religious contexts to suggest divinely inspired talents such as prophesizing. He adapted the term to suggest a heroic leader of exceptional abilities. He noted that power was most often based on traditional and/or formal (legal-rational) authority. However, in times of social and economic crisis, people yearn for new answers and are thus receptive to other sources of power. In such times, it is possible for a leader with radical ideas, a compelling personality, and an ability to show some early successes to provide an appealing alternative to the status quo. Charismatic leaders who are highly successful will reorganize societies or organizations during their lifetimes. However, inevitably the new structures must be institutionalized and charisma itself is routinized, becoming the new status quo. Although later leadership theorists have borrowed heavily from Weber's original conceptualization, they have also departed from it in significant ways (Yukl 2002).[1]

In 1977, Robert House published a book with a chapter titled "A 1976 Theory of

Charismatic Leadership." Conger and Kanungo describe the important contribution of the theory:

> House argued that charismatic leaders could be distinguished from others by their tendency to dominate, a strong conviction in their own beliefs and ideals, a need to influence others, and high self-confidence. Through emotionally appealing goals and the demonstration of behaviors that aroused followers' own needs for achievement, affiliation, and power, the charismatic leader was able to motivate high levels of task accomplishment. In addition, House theorized that these leaders simultaneously communicated high performance expectations as well as confidence in their followers' ability to meet such expectations. These actions, in turn, enhanced follower expectations that their efforts would lead to accomplishments. Through role-modeling, charismatic leaders demonstrated the values and beliefs they wished for followers to endorse so that the mission would be successful. (Conger and Kanungo 1998, 16)

Although House's theory was not fully articulated and had a number of weaknesses, it successfully "modernized" Weber's ideas about charismatic leadership, as well as suggested useful paths of inquiry for transformational leadership.

It was James McGregor Burns, however, who emphasized somewhat different aspects and popularized the term transformational leadership (1978). Writing from the political science tradition, Burns discusses various types of leadership, especially contrasting transactional leadership, which largely appeals to followers' self-interested motivations, with transformational leadership, which largely attempts to raise followers' consciousness to reform and improve institutions. Burns also points to a third type of leadership—bureaucratic leadership—which is based on legal-rational authority in the Weberian tradition. While Burns does not ignore the reality and even the importance of force of personality in leadership transformation, he was very interested in establishing a normative theory emphasizing the ethical use of power.

COMPARING TRANSACTIONAL AND TRANSFORMATIONAL APPROACHES TO LEADERSHIP

This sets the stage for a general analysis of the differing emphases exhibited by transactional and transformational-charismatic approaches. (Transformational will refer to both charismatic and transformation theories for brevity in this section.) Coming later in time, transformational theories often absorbed many aspects of transactional theories, creating a great deal of overlap. Exaggerating the fundamental differences for clarity, however, provides an opportunity to understand the major interest of the two major schools of thought. (Of course, the wide range of theories begs exceptions, which will not be noted in this brief analysis.) First, the theoretical emphasis of transactional leadership focuses on supervisors in a closed system. Researchers are interested in keeping variables limited and testable. Transformational researchers are more interested in executives, political leaders, and social leaders in relatively open systems. Such leaders function as the nexus between the external economic and political environment and the internal organizational environment, and have to adjust the latter to conform to the former. Because of the wider perspective that they seek to explain, they either use a larger number of variables or must be more abstract in their explanations.

Transactional leaders rely heavily on certain types of power: legitimate, reward, and punishment. As formal leaders they have the mantle of authority and the ability to administer and adjust incentives. Thus, researchers in this tradition tend to emphasize extrinsic influence at close range. Moreover, transactional researchers have largely assumed expert power and tended to ignore referent power. Transformational researchers, on the contrary, emphasize expert and referent power. To make a major impact, for good or ill, leaders have to be perceived as wise and brilliant, and they must have enough interpersonal appeal to sell their ideas and be trusted. Such leaders can use their power indirectly through emotional appeal and at a distance through ideological appeal.

Transactional researchers were originally highly influenced by economic perspectives, such as social exchange and expectancy theory. The basic self-interests and immediate needs of followers are the focus, ranging from pay to clear instructions to adequate resources and working conditions. Follower motivation in the leadership phenomenon is largely a rational-calculative process. On the other hand, transformational researchers emphasize stimulating individuals' interest in group productivity and organizational success. They also frequently examine followers' motivations in emulating or idolizing leaders for personal or ideological reasons. Follower motivation is much more of a symbolic process based on ideology, inspiration, and the intellectual belief that past patterns are no longer functional.

In transactional settings, organizational conditions are assumed to be stable. Problems in organizations involve adjustments, exceptions, or refinements in properly functioning systems. In transformational settings, the assumption is that change is inevitable, constant, and healthy. This is particularly true in the new economy in which the U.S. market must contend with vigorous—sometimes vicious—global competition. Of particular interest to transformational researchers are the roles of crisis, organizational collapse, and other dramatic forms of system deterioration.

Performance expectations in transactional theories tend to emphasize "good" performance. To be reasonable, efficient, effective, sustainable, and consistent, performance should be engineered by management with the substantial input of employees. Good performance is the goal in systems that have already been well designed. Transformational theories tend to assume that standards or quality has languished, or that extensive adaptation to new processes, technologies, or organizational structures is required. Exceptional performance is necessary for organizational success, whether that entails higher productivity levels, a greater contribution in adaptation and innovation, or effective organizational transformation.

Leader behaviors in transactional theories strongly emphasize the task and people-oriented domains. In particular, they emphasize monitoring, operations planning, clarifying roles, informing, delegating, problem solving, consulting, personnel planning, developing

Exhibit 4.1

A Rough Comparison of Transactional Theories and Transformational/Charismatic Theories

	Transactional	Transformational
Theoretical emphasis:	Supervisors Closed system Narrow range of variables	Executives Open system Broad range of variables
Leader's type of power:	Legitimate, reward, punishment Direct influence at close range	Expert, referent Indirect influence, includes influence at a distance
Follower motivation:	Self-interests such as pay; immediate needs such as resources, group compatibility	Group interests such as organizational success; psychic satisfaction such as emulation of leader
	Rational processes (calculative)	Symbolic processes based on ideology or breaking with the past
Facilitating conditions:	Stable; refinement of functioning systems	Unstable; need for change; crisis
Performance expectations:	Good performance	Exceptional performance either in terms of quantity or adaptation
Leader behaviors emphasized:	Monitoring, operations planning, clarifying roles, informing, delegating, problem solving, consulting, personnel planning, developing staff, and motivating	Environmental scanning, strategic planning, vision articulation, networking, decision making, managing organizational change, as well as informing, delegating (empowering), managing innovation, consulting, developing staff, motivating, building teams, and managing personnel change

Note: Because of the tremendous variety of transactional and transformational theories, there are some exceptions to these general trends.

staff, and motivating. Leader behaviors in transformational theories strongly emphasize organizational-oriented behaviors as well as people-oriented behaviors. They do not completely neglect, but certainly downplay, task-oriented behaviors in general. In particular, they emphasize environmental scanning, strategic planning, vision articulation, networking, decision making, and managing organizational change, as well as informing, delegating (empowering), managing technical innovation, consulting, developing staff, motivating, building teams, and managing personnel change. A rough comparison of these differences between transactional and transformational theories is displayed in Exhibit 4.1.

The relative importance of transactional versus transformational approaches varies according to a range of factors. First, the scope of the definitions is critical. For example, if supportive behavior is defined as transformational, then transactional behavior contributes significantly less to employee satisfaction and perceived performance improvements (Trottier, Van Wart, and Wang 2008). In the extreme, transactional leadership activities can be defined as nonleadership functions related to management, and therefore pertinent to "true" leadership. Second, the relative importance will vary according to sector and the organizational environment. Most third-party reviews note that both transactional and transformational leadership are important, if to somewhat varying degrees (e.g., Rowold and Heinitz 2007; O'Shea et al. 2009). This is also the general sentiment in public sector settings (Schrieshiem et al. 2006), with some emphasizing the relative importance of transactional (Vecchio, Justin, and Pearce 2008) versus transformational leadership (Wright and Pandey 2010).

CHARISMATIC AND TRANSFORMATIONAL APPROACHES

It is not inappropriate to group charismatic and transformational theories together because of their strong similarities in interests. However, they are distinctive enough for one to point out where they tend to diverge as well (Strange and Mumford 2005). Charismatic approaches have tended to focus on the personality of the leader and thus have shown much greater interest in leader traits, especially mystique, and cultural expectations. On the other hand, transformational theories have tended to focus on leaders leading change and the "triggers" of change. Charismatic researchers have also focused more on follower attributions of leaders, such as personal identification, value internalization, and even social contagion, that is, effecting excitation in individuals and groups or masses. Transformational researchers have been much more interested in the ethics of great leadership and the upholding of exemplary principles. Because of the sociological and psychological foundations of charismatic leadership, leader power and behavior have been much more thoroughly investigated whether leaders were considered good or evil. Examples of such topics include unconventional behavior, impression management, and utilization of follower dependence. Because of the ethical overtones of the transformational approach, these researchers tend to focus on the empowerment of followers. In sum, charismatic theory has been more descriptive and willing to examine the negative aspects of great, powerful, or influential leaders in topics such as narcissism. It has produced a real understanding of leadership gone wrong because of poor traits, misuse of power, self-serving behaviors, and weak followers. Transformational leadership has been more normative in its perspective, nearly always focusing on ideal behaviors of great leaders. Rather than comparing good and wicked leaders, it has generally compared transformational and transactional leaders. It has also been more prescriptive. As the major theories from the two approaches have been revised and expanded, they have tended to merge more and more into a single approach rather than the reverse.

The following sections examine five major theoretical frameworks by Conger and Kanungo (1998), other charismatic theorists such as Meindl (1990) and Kets de Vries (1988), Tichy and Devanna (1986), Bass (1985), and Kouzes and Posner (1987). It should be noted that these five major approaches were presented nearly simultaneously. The first reviewed is the conventional charismatic approach, followed by the extreme charismatic approach, and then followed by three different transformational approaches.

Conger and Kanungo's Charismatic Leadership Theory

In 1987, Conger and Kanungo proposed a theory of charismatic leadership, which they later refined in book-length treatments (1987, 1998). Their focus is on *how charisma is attributed to leaders*. What is it about the leader's context in conjunction with the leader's traits and behavior that produces the perception of charisma?

The context, according to Conger and Kanungo, has to be problematic in some way for the emergence of charismatic leadership. The more a sense of crisis or emergency exists, the more likely that charismatic leadership can emerge, and do so flamboyantly. "In some cases, contextual factors so overwhelmingly favor transformation that a leader can take advantage of them by advocating radical changes for the system. . . . [Yet] during periods of relative tranquility, charismatic leaders play a major role in fostering the need for change by creating the deficiencies or exaggerating existing minor ones" (Conger and Kanungo 1998, 52–53). Some negative charismatics may even create a sense of crisis or deficiencies for personal advancement, even though such problems do not exist. Thus, the situational demand for charismatic leadership is a moderating factor; long-term disappointments, outright failures, and debacles all substantially increase the chance for charismatic leadership but guarantee neither its emergence nor its success.

Even if the environment has major deficiencies or is in a state of crisis, followers are likely to attribute charismatic characteristics only to leaders who have certain traits and behave in certain ways. First, charismatic leaders are dissatisfied with the status quo and are interested in changing it. They have an idealized vision of the future that is highly discrepant from the current and projected state of affairs. Charismatic leaders are willing to articulate their bold notions of how things could be and are interested in leading others to a better future. Because of their opposition to the status quo, charismatic leaders are willing to be perceived by many (initially) as unconventional or proposing values different from those that have prevailed. Indeed, their advocacy is so passionate that they are willing to take personal risks or make personal sacrifices. As Conger and Kanungo note, "because of their emphasis on deficiencies in the system and their high levels of intolerance for them, charismatic leaders are always seen as organizational reformers or entrepreneurs" (1998, 53).

Many leaders respond to situations that allow or encourage charismatic behaviors, and in fact exhibit those behaviors, but are still not successful because their execution of them is flawed. In opposing the status quo, charismatic leaders must propose an alternate vision. That vision must be based on external assessments, such as the needs of constituents or the market, rather than the internal needs of the leader. It must also include a realistic assessment of the resources available to achieve the vision. Frequently, the environment shifts even as a plan or vision is being crafted; leaders who are inflexible about adapting to changing needs may doom their enterprise. Because changing cultures and traditions calls for unconventional behaviors and new values, they invariably create some opposition; if charismatic leaders create too much opposition at any one time, however, they are likely to fail or lose power. Charismatic leadership is also based on the leader's passion, confidence, and exceptional ability to persuade and sway people. But these same abilities may also predispose the leader toward a variety of dysfunctional behaviors over time: excessive egoism, contempt for superiors who do not agree with them, a tendency to turn nonsupporters into a hostile out-group, a propensity to turn supporters into sycophants, dismissal of contravening information, and encouragement of overreliance on the leader rather than an emphasis on subordinate development. Because such leaders enjoy not only position and expert power but also enormous personal power, opportunities to use their power in self-serving ways are enormous, and often unconscious, temptations. Conger and Kanungo describe the leader who is charismatic but in a negative way:

> Charismatic leaders can be prone to extreme narcissism that leads them to promote highly self-serving and grandiose aims. As a result, the leader's behaviors can become exaggerated, lose touch with reality, or become vehicles for pure personal gain. In turn, they may harm the leader, the followers, and the organization. An overpowering sense of self-importance and strong need to be at the center of attention can cause charismatic leaders to ignore the viewpoints of others and the development of leadership ability in followers. (1998, 211–239)

The causal chain implicit in charismatic leadership is outlined in Exhibit 4.2.

An enormous strength of charismatic leadership theory is that it is descriptive of the world around us. It acknowledges that there have been good leaders who are charismatic such as John F. Kennedy, Ronald Reagan, Margaret Thatcher, Charles DeGaulle, Nelson Mandela, and George Patton, as well as good leaders who are noncharismatic such as Dwight Eisenhower, Harry Truman, Mikhail Gorbachev, and Paul Volcker. It attempts to explain why this is so before prescribing an ideal set of principles for leaders to follow. In one recent study using a high-tech context, charismatic leadership contributed 15 percent to followers' organizational citizenship behavior, and 11 percent to managerial performance above transactional leadership alone (Sosik 2005). There is little doubt that charismatic leadership affects followers across sectors (Bono and Ilies 2006), but it clearly does so differentially (De Hoogh et al. 2005).

A second strength follows from the first one. It also recognizes that for every good charismatic, it is possible to have a negative charismatic as well. There have been Roosevelts and Hitlers, Mother Teresas and Jim Joneses, Mahatma Ghandis and Saddam Husseins. There can even be flawed charismatics such as Bill Clinton, Oliver North, or Mao. Whether leaders are in charge of countries or small organizational units, they have the opportunity to use their personality and personal vision to shape culture and affect group success, or to distort their authority to assuage their egos or bring personal benefit to themselves. It is important to understand the negative syndromes as well as the positive ones if one is to have a robust understanding of leadership.

Charismatic leadership theory is not without its problems, of course. It is certainly

Exhibit 4.2

Causal-Chain Model Implicit in Charismatic Leadership

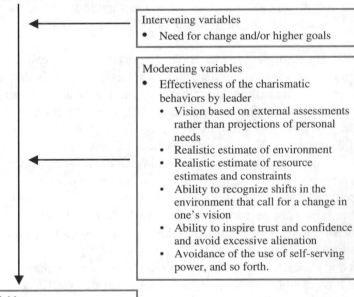

Leadership styles
- Noncharismatic (lack of charismatic style)
- Good charismatic (ideal style)
  - Opposes the status quo and strives to change it
  - Has idealized vision that is highly discrepant from the status quo
  - Articulates strong and/or inspirational future vision and has motivation to lead
  - Exhibits unconventional methods or counternormative values
  - Exercises passionate advocacy
  - Is willing to incur great personal risk and cost
- Bad charismatic (misuse of charismatic style)

Intervening variables
- Need for change and/or higher goals

Moderating variables
- Effectiveness of the charismatic behaviors by leader
  - Vision based on external assessments rather than projections of personal needs
  - Realistic estimate of environment
  - Realistic estimate of resource estimates and constraints
  - Ability to recognize shifts in the environment that call for a change in one's vision
  - Ability to inspire trust and confidence and avoid excessive alienation
  - Avoidance of the use of self-serving power, and so forth.

Performance variables
- Follower satisfaction with leader
- Follower trust in leader
- Group cohesion
- External alignment and organizational change

Note: Based on the model by Conger and Kanungo (1998).

not a comprehensive leadership theory inasmuch as it acknowledges but largely ignores noncharismatics and leadership situations that do not encourage change. If anything, it is moderately dismissive of noncharismatic leaders even though they may be more numerous and extremely necessary in the daily operations of organizations. This may be because charismatic leaders are "called upon" to do greater things, and their force of personality—derived from superb communication skills, excellent talent for drawing vivid images, and ability to persuade others—is relatively uncommon. Finally, the emphasis in charismatic leadership is essentially on personality-based leadership. Useful and important though this perspective may be, it does not give a full picture of leadership because of its emphasis on the heroic and despotic leadership types that it can spawn. Before turning to more normatively balanced types of change-oriented leadership, it is useful to examine the most extreme forms of charisma.

Extreme Charisma and Negative Leadership

Extreme charisma, the cultlike status achieved by certain leaders, invariably stimulates popular interest and has been the subject of a good deal of in-depth analysis. Although milder forms of charisma—for example, strong leader affiliation and respect and strong belief in leader wisdom—are not uncommon, extreme charisma is very rare (Bennis and Nanus 1985). For example, while many presidents of the United States have had charismatic qualities (House, Spangler, and Woycke 1991), only a handful might qualify as extreme charismatics. Why does extreme charisma get so much attention when it is so uncommon? There are at least three reasons. First, extreme charisma is interesting by definition. As a group, extreme charismatics are defined by their enormous referent power. People with exceptional referent power have a magnetic appeal fueled by eloquence, emotional expressiveness, unusual self-confidence, and belief in their own exceptional abilities, insights, or sources of divinity. This combination of factors creates a mystique that people find fascinating even when they dislike the charismatic leader. Second, extreme charismatics may not be common historically, but, for good or bad, they are the people who have most profoundly shaped history. They have founded new empires, religions, and organizations. They have also destroyed nations, led organizations to collapse, and brought catastrophe on groups. Finally, it is easy to identify extreme charisma with leadership. Leadership is often defined as having a compelling vision as well as the strength of character to convince others to "stay the course." Thus, all things being equal, leaders with extreme charisma are more likely to succeed than noncharismatic leaders. Of course, charisma has many potential liabilities, as were discussed with reference to Conger and Kanungo above, and these liabilities are only exacerbated by the presence of extreme charisma.

Extreme charismatics can exhibit an almost unlimited number of behaviors that contribute to their effectiveness as people who are perceived as extraordinary or as having an extraordinary role or vision. However, three characteristics seem nearly indispensable and will be discussed here. First, extreme charismatics have vast referent power. This personal power is born of an ability to charm, speak well, persuade, understand others, and project magnetism. It may also be aided by physical appearance, social grace, intellectual prowess, wealth, and other attributes leading to personal and social esteem.

Second, extreme charismatics are characterized by personal dominance. This is generally exhibited by strong beliefs about what is wrong with the current state of affairs, what needs to be done, and the correct actions to take. It also means that they have strong beliefs about how to act and what to believe. Because they are convinced of their own self-worth and correctness, it means that they will persevere in achieving their vision and plans at almost any cost to themselves or others. The ultimate insistence of extreme charismatics on personal dominance leads to heated discussions of the positive values and liabilities of such dominance. Many dictators have started as relatively idealistic extreme charismatics, only to metamorphose into murderous and avaricious despots when their power became absolute.

Third, extreme charismatics are characterized by unconventional behavior. Charismatic military leaders may use new technological tactics, or be able to inspire and even mesmerize soldiers into confidently disregarding severe military disadvantages. Religious charismatics may deviate from past dogma and assert different principles or an entirely new divine order. Political leaders may espouse views that are initially unpopular or go against common wisdom due to current political realities such as subservience to a strong colonial power. Extreme charismatics in organizations may introduce radical management practices or strike out on their own to create new organizations altogether.

Just a leader's desire to be charismatic, however, is not enough. A leader has to be perceived by a portion of the target population as charismatic. What is it about followers that predisposes them to extreme charismatic leadership? The psychodynamic school of thought explains followers' reactions in terms of regression and transference. When people regress, they psychologically return to earlier times in their lives—usually happier and more secure times. When people transfer, they psychologically associate the positive values of one person in the past to another in the future. Charismatic personalities are able to tap into the sense of security provided by traditional father figures or the sense of nurturance of traditional mother figures, regardless of whether these projections are from real people or human archetypes (Lindholm 1988). Other particularly powerful archetypes that charismatics often adopt are those of prophet, sage, or savant. Charismatics also often liken themselves to popular or powerful figures in history. When these positive images did not exist in the follower's personal past, the yearning for them may be even stronger because of the insecurities that their absence breeds. Numerous studies have shown that followers of charismatics tend to be more prone to feelings of helplessness, frustration, loneliness, anger, distrust, and uncertainty (Corsino 1982; Galanter 1982; Kets de Vries 1988). Such transference or fulfillment of needs leads to unusually strong personal identification. Personal identification is the follower's tendency to connect with leaders' beliefs and ideals, a desire to emulate the leader, and a desire to please the leader. Extreme personal identification results in the total and uncritical substitution of the leader's beliefs for one's own, slavish imitation of the leader, and unctuous adulation.

Sometimes the needs of followers stem from current social, economic, political, religious, or ideological perceptions of deprivation. Although noncharismatic leaders suggest solutions to problems, extreme charismatics become highly associated with the solution or even become the solution itself. This is intensified by the tendency to provide unconventional solutions that strike a chord in individuals who are disenchanted and then spread to other people. According to social contagion theory, a leader can articulate an unconventional belief that is consonant with some people's existent self-notion of how things should be. This gives the followers an external point of reference and support allowing them to be more local or visible in their beliefs. Others become caught up in the freshness and excitement of the new beliefs and adopt them, even though they did not formerly hold them (Meindl 1990). Social contagion is a two-edged sword. It can lead to healthy reform, for example, when a charismatic leader points out the self-dealing behavior of a particular social or political elite, or it can lead to demagoguery that turns minorities into scapegoats.

The presence of crisis or impending catastrophe enhances the likelihood of extreme charismatic leadership, but does not guarantee it. For example, numerous peasant revolts and "wildcat" union strikes have occurred despite an absence of any real leadership (Bass 1990). In other cases leaders may emerge in times of crisis but may not be charismatic, such as Stalin in early Soviet Russia or Robespierre in early revolutionary France. It is quite common, however, that crisis enhances the charismatic qualities of leaders who are deemed successful. Both Abraham Lincoln and Robert E. Lee were modest, contemplative men who would not have been widely emulated in their own time and memorialized in history were it not for the exceptional circumstances in which they found themselves.

Unlike other leadership theories, charismatic theories that examine the nature of the psychological attribution are not directly concerned with traditional leadership outcomes such as efficiency, effectiveness, external alignment, or successful organizational adaptation. They focus on leaders who successfully convince followers to be consistent with their ideas, voluntarily follow their plans, and be inspired by them. They seek to explain, not justify, charismatic leadership, especially in its extreme forms. This largely psychological view of leadership is illustrated in Exhibit 4.3.

In recent years there has been much research on negative leadership, variously called destructive, toxic, and narcissistic. For example, Schilling (2009) breaks down negative leadership into eight categories: insincere, despotic, exploitative, restrictive, failed, laissez-faire, and two types of avoidance leadership. Padilla, Hogan, and Kaiser (2007, 176) point out that destructive leadership occurs from a "confluence of destructive leaders, susceptible followers, and conducive environments." One review of destructive leadership defined it in terms of tyrannical, derailed, and supportive-disloyal behaviors (Einarsen, Aasland, and Skogstad 2007). The conducive-environments issue has gotten more interest with the string of financial and corporate scandals that have occurred since 2001, for example, leadership environment in the Enron debacle (Tourish and Vatcha 2005). The financial collapse of 2008 seems to beg for more study of the destructive elements identified by Padilla, Hogan, and Kaiser in both the private and public sector contexts.

Most of the strengths and weaknesses suggested by Conger and Kanungo's attributional theory can be applied to psychosocial theories of extreme charisma. The

Exhibit 4.3

Causal-Chain Model Implicit in Extreme Charisma

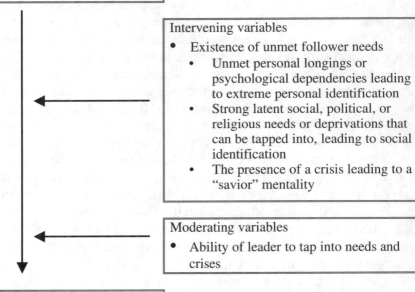

insights that analysis of extreme/narcissistic charisma provides are very valuable (Paunonen et al. 2006; Rosenthal and Pittinsky 2006). On the other hand, although this is an important and legitimate lens through which one can view the phenomenon of leadership, it is certainly not the only one, and for many purposes, it is not the best one. Transformational theories, which are discussed next, offer a more broad-based and normative approach.

Tichy and Devanna's Theory of Transformational Leaders

A model of leadership similar to Conger and Kanungo is provided by Tichy and Devanna (1986, 1990), except in a transformational mode. That is, rather than emphasizing the traits and behavioral mechanisms necessary for leadership success in a changing environment, they emphasize organizational needs first and examine the cascading behavioral needs second. They assert that "more than ever the key to global competitiveness will be widespread capability of institutions around the world to continuously transform" (1990, iv). In addition, "increasingly excellence is the condition not just for dominance but for survival" (ibid.). Therefore, "transformational leadership is about change, innovation, and entrepreneurship" (ibid., xii). *Their model also emphasizes the temporal phases of change* reminiscent of Lewin, who proposed that change requires unfreezing, changing, and refreezing the organization (1951). However, they use a three-act play as their metaphor, linking both organizational and individual needs to each of those acts.

They provide only two alternate styles: a managerial style and a transformational style. Following the Zaleznik (1977) tradition, Tichy and Devanna assert that managers are relatively commonplace but that transformational leaders are rarer and increasingly critical to organizational success. Managers are "individuals who maintain the balance of operations in an organization, relate to others according to their role, are detached, impersonal, seek solutions acceptable as a compromise among conflicting values, and identify totally with the organization" (1990, xiii). Leaders, that is, transformational-type leaders, are "individuals out to create new approaches and imagine new areas to explore; they relate to people in more intuitive and empathetic ways, seek risk where opportunity and reward are high, and project ideas into images to excite people" (ibid., xiii).

The transformational leader must change organizations and people in three successive stages. The first stage is recognizing the need for revitalization. Because of the competitive environment and the speed of responsiveness required in that environment, the need for revitalization is nearly ubiquitous. The challenges and problems at this stage include making sure that environmental needs are not ignored, overcoming the innate resistance to change, and avoiding the quick fix. Individuals must disengage from the past and deal with the disenchantment of giving up past successes and comforts.

The second stage is creating a new vision. New ways of doing business must be contemplated, refined, rehearsed, and widely articulated. Commitment to a new vision must be mobilized through involvement, strategic internal structuring, and excellent communication. Individuals must be encouraged to identify with the new vision, which is a combination of logical persuasion about the nature of a better future, and a leap of faith that the driving vision is accurate and realistic.

The third stage is institutionalizing change. As the new vision is understood and accepted, new structures, mechanisms, and incentives must be put in place. Workable elements from the old culture must be retained, while less viable ones must be changed. The natural tendency to adjust the easy elements must be resisted, so that a more coherent

Exhibit 4.4

Causal-Chain Model Implicit in Transformational Leadership as Change Master

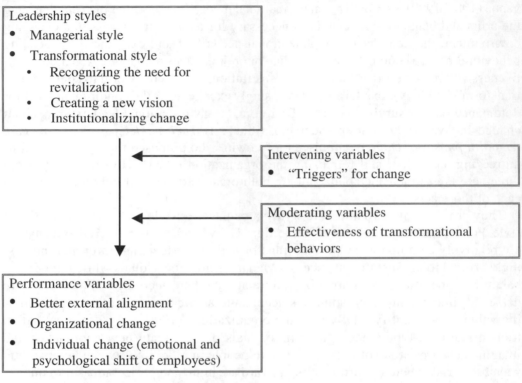

Source: Based on Tichy and Devanna (1986, 1990).

and fundamental change process can be embraced. This requires a creative destruction and reweaving of the social fabric of the organization. Keeping the motivation of individuals high remains key so that they continue their inner realignment and adaptation to new internal scripts. As this takes hold for individuals, they should find new energy and overcome the debilitating effects of change.

The variables in their causal chain are essentially the same as those of Conger and Kanungo. The "triggers" for change are the intervening variables; the moderating variables are the levels of leader effectiveness in behaviors leading to transformational change. Thus, like most transformational models, they are less interested in specifying the exact conditions under which the preferred style is useful than they are in articulating the general set of behaviors that has universal utility. While they freely acknowledge the critical adaptation process, interest here is in developing a high-level conceptual model of the relationship between change and leadership. Success is measured in terms of successful improvement of organizational alignment that requires constant change as well as individual change in both behaviors and attitudes. See Exhibit 4.4 for a review of Tichy and Devanna's transformational model.

Exhibit 4.5

Bass's Continuum of Leadership Styles ("Full Range Theory")

Source: Bass (1985).

Bass's Transformational Theory: "Full Range Theory" or Performance Beyond Expectations

If Tichy and Devanna excelled at providing a good articulation of transformational leadership as a process over time, Bass (1985) excelled at providing a good articulation of the continuum of factors, or closer to what we would call styles in this study, that make up leadership. *Bass conceives leadership as a single continuum. It progresses from nonleadership to transactional leadership to transformational leadership.* Nonleadership provides haphazard results at best; transactional leadership provides conventional results; but transformational leadership provides, as his book title indicates, "performance beyond expectations." The additive nature of his theory is portrayed in Exhibit 4.5.

Bass asserts that transformational leadership is a widespread phenomenon across levels of management, types of organizations, and around the globe. It is therefore a universal theory without real intervening variables. However, as with other transformational theories, it does assume that both the quality of the transformational factors executed and the number of styles/factors used will have a moderating effect on the performance. That is, there is a substantial additive effect of the styles.

Starting with an essentially nonleadership style, laissez-faire takes a hands-off approach to leadership. Laissez-faire leaders are largely uninvolved in operations, slipshod about details, resistant to participation in problem solving, lax in decision making, negligent in providing feedback, and indifferent to subordinate needs. Other than in leaders who are simply lazy, laissez-faire leadership is most likely to be seen in executives or senior managers who have an excessive external focus, or in longtime managers who are close to retirement and have already begun to "coast" in their positions.

Management-by-exception is a style that utilizes mistakes or deviations from standards as corrective opportunities, and that emphasizes negative feedback. In the more lax or passive form of management-by-exception, the manager intervenes or takes corrective action only after a mistake has been made or a problem has become obvious. For example, a manager who receives a number of complaints about an employee's customer relations skills, and who proceeds to reprimand the employee, is largely using a passive management-by-exception style if s/he had neither noted nor discussed the problem prior to this action. An active management-by-exception style simply indicates that the manager is monitoring more closely and intervening before problems go outside the unit. In the above case, the manager would closely monitor the employee, observe the deficient behavior, and take corrective action before the clients complain. Neither of these styles is necessarily bad in and of itself. Managers cannot be everywhere and spot everything in advance and sometimes can react only after the fact. Managers should monitor actions and production as carefully as possible to ensure quality control. And negative incentives are legitimate tools in the management arsenal because they represent consequences for those not appropriately meeting their responsibilities. However, Bass holds that it is generally an inferior style that should be used sparingly. Extensive use of this style creates fear and intimidation and discourages initiative and creativity.

The more progressive and positive half of transactional leadership is contingent reward. Managers using contingent reward find out what employees value and vary the incentives that they offer, accordingly. An employee willing to take on one assignment may be released from another. A high-performance employee may get a large raise or a promotion. A high-quality employee may get additional perks such as supplementary travel and training monies. Such leadership is at its best, generally, when the work and incentives are negotiated and mutually agreed upon in advance. Management-by-objectives is a sophisticated form of contingent reward. While contingent reward is a fundamental part of most organizational systems and represents a practical reality—we expect rewards for hard work—it does have its weaknesses. First, by itself, contingent reward systems can easily lead to extensive tit-for-tat systems in which only what is specifically rewarded gets done. Thus, all responsibilities must be carefully laid out, documented, and counted in order for there to be accurate rewards. This is especially difficult in systems in which responsibilities are rapidly shifting and end products are not easily counted. Second, contingent rewards are generally set up as individual reward systems, and thus do not directly account for group achievements. Although group contingent rewards are useful and laudable, they are generally much more difficult to implement because of the free-rider syndrome, overlapping responsibilities, and the political resistance of other managers and elected officials to group rewards for "doing one's job." Furthermore, an exclusive reliance on contingent rewards may leave many, perhaps most, managers and executives with few leadership options when resources are extremely scarce or diminishing and yet the organizational needs are critical or increasing. A manager with a cut in budget and an implicit threat of unit dissolution has little psychological leverage if s/he can rely only on contingent rewards.

One of the four factors designated as transformational by Bass and others in the transformational school is called "idealized consideration." However, consideration has a long and venerable tradition in the transactional literature as has already been extensively discussed. Whether it is the consideration factor identified in the Ohio State studies, Blake and Mouton's concern for people, the supportive style advocated by House in path-goal theory, or the supportive behavior identified in Hersey and Blanchard's developmental model, consideration is key to good leadership. Ultimately, whether consideration is a transactional or transformational characteristic is probably largely definitional and moot. The term has similar meaning for Bass: coaching, professional and personal support, individualized treatment based on specific needs, increased delegation as employees mature professionally, and so forth. In short, it boils down to respect and empathy.

Bass calls the next factor or style "idealized influence," which is very similar to the concept of charisma. Those who exhibit individualized influence function as powerful role models for their followers. Followers identify with leader goals and emulate their actions. This requires a perception by followers of a high level of integrity and wisdom. While the charismatic school emphasizes strong attachments based on ideological or psychological grounds, the transformational school tends to emphasize the ethical basis. Essentially, idealized influence translates to leader likability and trust.

"Intellectual stimulation" is the factor of leadership that encourages people to create new opportunities, to solve problems in new ways, and to envision a different future. Not only does it foster intellectual flexibility in followers, it also requires the ability to reexamine competing values. This style emphasizes techniques such as information sharing, brainstorming, vision articulation, and employee development targeted at specific organizational improvements. These types of leaders are often thought of as idea people or visionaries.

The final factor in Bass's taxonomy is "inspirational motivation"—in a sense, the most critical element of a transformational style. When leaders successfully use inspirational motivation, their followers are able to transcend their self-interests long enough to become passionate about organizational pride, group goals, and group achievements. Through enhanced "team" spirit, leaders are able to motivate followers to pursue higher standards or to make sacrifices, without reliance on extrinsic incentives. Although the greater good is expected to redound to followers at some point in the future, there is generally not an exact commitment or transaction contract because of the uncertainty or abstractness of the goals. The causal chain implied in Bass's model is illustrated in Exhibit 4.6.

All four transformational elements are generally present in concert in successful change initiatives, but that is not to say that the leader must supply all of them. Colleagues may supply their own consideration; low-key trust may successfully substitute for brassier charisma; young, highly motivated professionals in the group may provide the intellectual stimulation; and inspirational motivation may be largely the result of a rich and proud tradition as well as a professional indoctrination instilling strong ethical values.

Of all the transformational theories, Bass's is the most highly researched and has a good deal of positive support (Yammarino et al. 2005; Yammarino and Dansereau 2008). His additive approach is intuitively appealing as well as relatively elegant, considering the large number of styles that it incorporates. Further, one gets the sense that Bass's approach builds

Exhibit 4.6

Causal-Chain Model Implicit in Transformational Leadership as High Performance

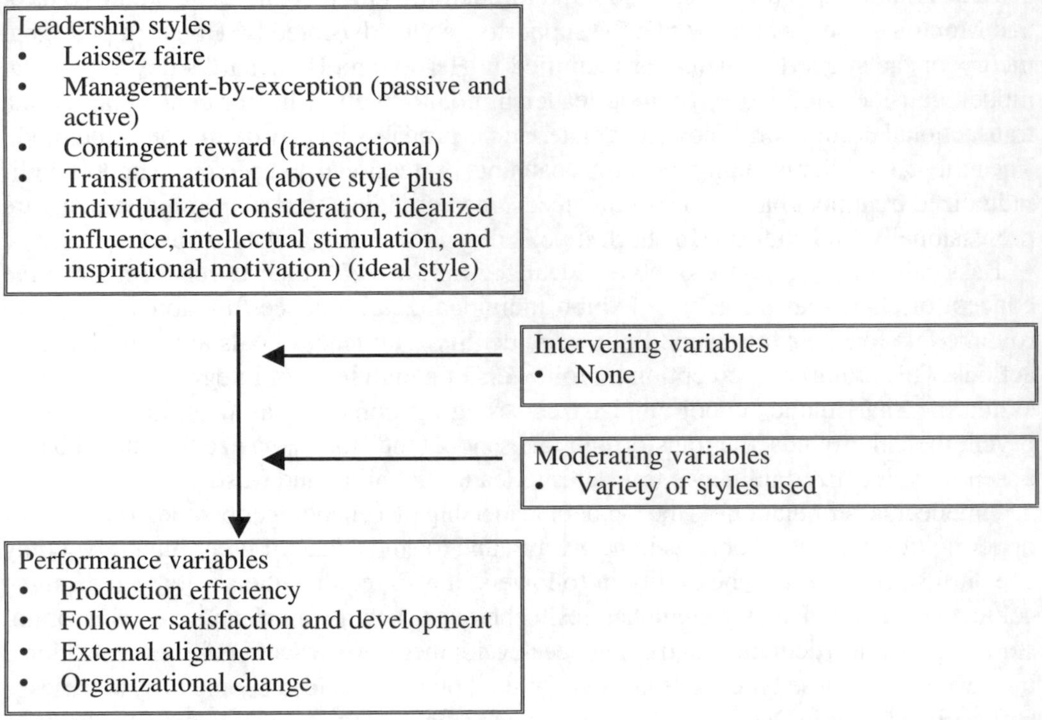

Leadership styles
- Laissez faire
- Management-by-exception (passive and active)
- Contingent reward (transactional)
- Transformational (above style plus individualized consideration, idealized influence, intellectual stimulation, and inspirational motivation) (ideal style)

Intervening variables
- None

Moderating variables
- Variety of styles used

Performance variables
- Production efficiency
- Follower satisfaction and development
- External alignment
- Organizational change

Source: Based on Bass (1985).

on earlier transactional theory, even though the earlier theory and concepts are somewhat downplayed. In terms of weaknesses, one of the most obvious is its universality, which in turn implies that transformational leadership is better in all leadership levels and situations. This would seem to fly in the face of the day-to-day reality of many leaders, especially those working at ground operational levels. Second, the overlap and fuzziness of the transformational concepts are problematic. Part of the problem is structural, however, because higher-level human motivations are abstract and related in extraordinarily complex ways. Additionally, the nomenclature of the concepts is not always easy to understand and remember. Even though his transformational factors have the mnemonic of all starting with "i," differences between concepts such as those between individualized consideration and idealized influence have to be explained and memorized.

Transformational Leadership as Ideal Practices

The leadership practices theory employed by Kouzes and Posner (1987) represents a third approach in the transformational school. Rather than starting with either a chronological approach, as did Tichy and Devanna, or a conceptual approach, as did Bass, they started with an empirical approach. They asked: *According to leaders themselves, what leads to excellent leadership based on their personal experiences?* They originally surveyed 1,330 individuals using a critical incident methodology focusing exclusively on "personal best" experiences. They assert that the five major practices they identified, each composed of two "commitments," described more than 70 percent of respondents' descriptions of personal best scenarios. Subsequently, they designed a leadership instrument called the Leadership Practices Inventory that has been highly popular in the training sphere, as have their writings. Both the instrument and their framework are pragmatic but largely atheoretical. That is, they are based on survey research about actual trends, but the explanation of how the practices all fit together is quite weak, even though each of the practices they advocate is consistent with research findings. They focus more narrowly on transformational leadership than the more comprehensive approach used by Bass. They omit (using this text's nomenclature) laissez-faire, directive, and achievement styles (for the most part), and they emphasize supportive, participative, and inspirational styles. While delegative and external styles are not directly covered, they are somewhat implied by the strong empowerment and change-oriented themes.

Like other transformational theorists, Kouzes and Posner use a universal approach. Their critical-incident methodology did not discriminate based on level of leadership or types of situations. The only moderating variable, then, is the quality of implementation of the practices themselves.

They assert that successful leaders must "challenge the process," a type of inspirational leadership similar to Bass's intellectual stimulation. In turn, the two supporting practices involve searching for opportunities and experimenting and taking risks. Successful leaders must be open to change and dedicated to finding better ways of doing things. They must be willing to upset the status quo and tradition. They must be receptive to the good ideas of others, because that is where most good ideas come from. "The leaders' primary contribution is in the recognition of good ideas, the support of those ideas, and the willingness to challenge the system in order to get new products, processes, and services adopted" (Kouzes and Posner 1987, 8). Yet, to challenge the status quo and to try new ideas, leaders must be willing to take appropriate risks and to learn from failures.

The second practice involves "inspiring a shared vision" composed of the commitment to envision the future and to enlist others in a common vision by appealing to their values, interests, hopes, and dreams. This is similar to Bass's inspirational motivation. Leaders essentially "see" the future first, and then how to get there. "Their clear image of the future pulls them forward" (Kouzes and Posner, 9). But just as important as having clear ideas about the range of ideas that will or will not work, is the act of including others. This means that leaders must incorporate both concrete ideas and the sentiments of followers into a common vision. Leaders "develop a deep understanding of the collective yearnings. They listen carefully for quiet whisperings in dark corners. They attend to the subtle cues. They get a sense of what people want, what they value, what they dream about" (Kouzes and Posner 1987, 115). Then they express this common vision with vivid language, personal appeal, and conviction.

This inclusion of others' ideas and dreams flows into the next practice, "enabling others to act," which is a type of participative style. It is composed of fostering collaboration and strengthening others. Kouzes and Posner assert that others found this to be the most important practice, and one that leaders themselves mentioned in 91 percent of the cases they studied (1987, 10). Leaders need to develop cooperative goals. While leadership can be constructive with external targets or groups, "creating competition within the team or between team members was never described in anyone's personal best as a way that got something extraordinary accomplished in their organization" (1987, 135). Instead, cooperation takes trust building based on integrating others' ideas and being sensitive to their needs.

The fourth practice involves "modeling the way," which consists of setting the example and planning small wins. It is roughly equivalent to Bass's idealized influence. Good leaders know what their philosophy is, state it, and stick by it. Sometimes this is a difficult challenge, but followers will notice when different standards apply to them or when there is unfair or inconsistent practice. Good leaders lead by example and in "moments of truth." If followers are being asked to make some sacrifices, good leaders are often the first to make painful changes. When confronted with pesky but significant details, leaders do not abandon high ideals with executive prerogative. Leaders build on their philosophical consistency by showing how it is done in ways that can be replicated and adapted. This usually requires experimenting continuously, dividing tasks into small chunks, reducing items to the essentials, and not rushing people into change. It also relies on obtaining commitment by giving people a sense of choice, making choices visible to others, and creating choices that are hard to revoke.

The final practice involves "encouraging the heart." It is a supportive style that consists of recognizing contributions and celebrating accomplishments. It is somewhat similar to Bass's individualized consideration. Kouzes and Posner point out that the "climb to the top is arduous and long. People become exhausted, frustrated, and disenchanted. They often are tempted to give up. Leaders must encourage the heart of their followers to carry on" (1987, 12). Recognizing contributions actually begins with high expectations so that accomplishments are real. And the rewards must also be real and varied. Perhaps the key reward is the celebration of accomplishment. This is not necessary all of the time but the cheering, publicness, and socialness of success must occasionally be visibly shared in order to generate passion, appreciation, and group commitment. The relationship of these five practices to Kouzes and Posner's leadership framework is provided in Exhibit 4.7.

Because it is based on real practices culled from more than 1,000 managers, the leadership practices approach has pragmatic appeal. What do we, as leaders, need to do to be excellent? Indeed, it is clear that Kouzes and Posner have identified and loosely amalgamated the more important inspirational, supportive, and participative styles. This has led to the popularity of the approach, which has been greatly enhanced by especially readable and dynamic books aimed largely at a nonscholarly audience. However, the weaknesses of the approach are also significant. Most important, the approach tells a persuasive and rational story, but does not really provide a true theory or even data from other studies for the most part. It does use a grounded approach to research, so it can be called applied

Exhibit 4.7

Causal-Chain Model Implicit in Leadership Practices

```
┌─────────────────────────────────────┐
│ Leadership styles                    │
│ •  Transformational (ideal style)    │
│    •  Challenging the process        │
│    •  Inspiring a shared vision      │
│    •  Enabling others to act         │
│    •  Modeling the way               │
│    •  Encouraging the heart          │
└─────────────────────────────────────┘
              │
              │  ◄──────────  ┌─────────────────────────────────┐
              │               │ Intervening variables           │
              │               │ •  None                         │
              │               └─────────────────────────────────┘
              │  ◄──────────  ┌─────────────────────────────────┐
              │               │ Moderating variables            │
              │               │ •  Ability to employ            │
              ▼               │    transformational practices   │
                              └─────────────────────────────────┘
┌─────────────────────────────────────┐
│ Performance variables                │
│ •  Production efficiency             │
│ •  Follower satisfaction and         │
│    development                       │
│ •  External alignment                │
│ •  Organizational change             │
└─────────────────────────────────────┘
```

Source: Based on Kouzes and Posner (1987).

theory, but it does not really give researchers a good basis for more rigid testing. Moreover, the theory should not be mistaken for a comprehensive theory of leadership. The more pragmatic aspects of leadership—largely managerial—are mostly lacking.

CONCLUSION

Two related approaches and five explicit or implicit theories of leadership were explored in this chapter. All theories were compared according to four types of variables: leadership styles (behaviors), intervening, moderating, and performance variables.

Unlike transactional approaches, both the charismatic and transformational approaches tend to emphasize inspirational and external styles. Charismatic theories emphasize the use of referent power, its utility in achievement and change, and its liabilities when abused for antisocial or unethical purposes. Prosocial or socialized charismatics balance the needs of others with the need for change and their own personal success and benefits. Personalized charismatics allow their own psychological, safety, personal, reputational, or other selfish interests to shape their use of formal and personal power. Transformational theories all emphasize inspiration and external styles and deemphasize the personalist aspects investigated in charismatic theories. Tichy and Devanna's transformational style sketches out the need for change management skills. Bass's high performance theory is by far the most articulated in terms of styles, with eight substyles identified. The ideal transformational style is a combination of all but the laissez-faire style. While two of the styles identified in this study—participative and delegative—were not explicitly covered, they are not antithetical to Bass's framework. Kouzes and Posner's leadership practices cover five of the eight distinct styles in the style taxonomy. Implied is a combined transformational style. It does not refer either to a directive style, which is perceived as nonempowering, or to an achievement-oriented style, which fosters too much internal competition. A comparison of the leader styles implied by charismatic and transformational perspectives is presented in Exhibit 4.8.

The intervening variables in Conger and Kanungo's charismatic theory emphasize the effectiveness of charismatic behaviors. If leaders cannot exhibit them effectively, they will be noncharismatic. In extreme charisma, the intervening variable is the existence of unmet follower needs; without such needs, there is no need for charisma. Of course this begs the question of needs created, hyped, or invented by unscrupulous individuals long on magnetism but shy on talent. Similar to Conger and Kanungo, Tichy and Devanna propose that the intervening variable is the effectiveness of transformational behaviors. Those who are not transformational are managers with largely directive-supportive behaviors. Bass and Kouzes and Posner propose a universal transformational style as ideal and therefore do not have intervening variables.

The degrees of success achieved in using the styles proposed—the moderating variables—differ as well. In charismatic theory, it is the need for change that will moderate success; the more that change is necessary, the more likely charisma is to appear. Extreme charisma is moderated by the ability of leaders to tap into followers' needs and desires. Change-master transformationalists are also aided by the degree of change needed by the group, society, or organization. High-performance transformationalists depend on the variety of styles that they can employ simultaneously just as the number of current practices used in Kouzes and Posner's theory moderate success.

Although the implied performance outcomes have a good deal of overlap, the range is still impressive. Extreme charisma theory is completely focused on the mechanisms of successful leader influence over followers (whether that influence is good or evil). Charismatic theory emphasizes group goals and change through the mechanism of leaders powerful with the infusion of referent power and related symbolic skills. Transformational theories emphasize a broader array of primary goals including external alignment, organizational change, high(er) performance, follower satisfaction, follower development, and follower trust in the leader. Tichy and Devanna and Bass give slight precedence to organizational needs, whereas Kouzes and Posner give priority to follower or empowerment needs.

All the charismatic and transformational theories discussed here are ultimately leader centered. Even the most follower-centered theory, that of Kouzes and Posner, ultimately involves the leader's supplying of power to followers. The next chapter examines the dynamics of leadership in terms of the various possible influence relationships, especially when followers have substantial power and share it among themselves, and the role of formal leaders is modest or nonexistent.

Exhibit 4.8

Comparison of the Leader Styles Implied by Charismatic and Transformational Perspectives

Leadership style	Leadership theory				
	Charismatic (Conger and Kanungo)	Extreme charisma	Change master (transformational; Tichy and Devanna)	High performance (transformational; Bass)	Leadership practices (transformational; Kouzes and Posner)
Laissez-faire				Laissez-faire	
Directive	Noncharismatic	Noncharismatic	Managerial	Management by exception: passive and active	
Supportive				Individualized consideration	Encouraging the heart
Participative					Enabling others to act
Delegative					
Achievement-oriented				Contingent reward	
Inspirational	Charismatic —good* —negative			Inspirational motivation; idealized influence	Challenging the process; modeling the way
Strategic	(Charismatic)		Visionary	Intellectual stimulation	Inspiring a shared vision
Collaborative	(Charismatic)				Inspiring a shared vision
Combined		Extreme charisma (primarily directive and inspirational)	Transformational* (focuses on change management skills and external style)	Transformational* (Combination of all styles except laissez-faire)	Transformational* (combining of non-management practices)

Sources: Based on models of Conger and Kanungo (1998); Tichy and Devanna (1986); Bass (1985); Kouzes and Posner (1987).
Notes: Many style equivalencies are only "best fit."
*Denotes a style recommendation considered superior.

NOTE

1. Weber's work is often interpreted out of context. It should be noted that Weber's theory of charisma is an "ideal type," a term that he invented. It suggests a description of a pattern functioning in its purest form, but does not suggest that the pattern is ethically or socially good or preferable. An ideal type is a useful heuristic device for scholars and teachers, but pure manifestations of ideal types are rare in social contexts. Weber does not suggest that charismatic leaders must appear during times of social/economic crisis, only that they are much more likely to do so. Nor does he suggest that they are either innately good or bad since the lexicon of famous charismatics is replete with both saints and demagogues.

5

Horizontal and Distributed
Models of Leadership

Because of the complexity of leadership, a significant number of approaches contribute to our understanding of it. Previous chapters have focused on early management, trait, transactional, and transformational approaches. Yet, the leadership phenomenon is so wide-ranging that these approaches can be usefully complemented by others in this and the next three chapters.

In this chapter we cover distributed leadership, so known because the leadership function is distributed more broadly than in hierarchical forms of vertical leadership, where the role of the leader in the leadership process is the focus. While this is an instructive perspective, it certainly does not represent the entire leadership process. Leadership as a process includes not only leaders but also followers in their various roles and guises, and a set of environmental conditions.

All approaches discussed to this point have essentially asked: How can formal leaders act to *maximize their roles* to enhance effectiveness under a variety of conditions? The distributed-leadership approach turns this implicit fundamental question on its head. In contrast, it asks: Under what conditions can formal leaders *minimize their roles* to enhance effectiveness? It then asks the question: How are the traditional functions of leadership (e.g., decision making, coordinating, feedback, support, etc.) accomplished if not by the formal leader?

DISTRIBUTED-LEADERSHIP APPROACHES

Distributed leadership emphasizes the sharing of leadership functions from different perspectives and through various mechanisms. It has been very slow to evolve into a clearly defined area of study with a standardized nomenclature and set of broadly accepted concepts (Conger and Pearce 2003). Even today, widely different terms are used for similar concepts, conceptual overlap is bewildering, and connections between types of distributed leadership and traditional leadership are weak (Pearce and Conger 2003a; Clarke 2006). The distributed-leadership approach has been divided into seven distinct theoretical frameworks: informal leadership, followership, superleadership, substitutes for leadership, self-leadership, team leadership, and network leadership. Exhibit 5.1 provides some examples to accompany the discussion of the various types of distributed leader.

Exhibit 5.1

Examples of Seven Types of Distributed Leadership

Distributed-leadership theory	Examples
Informal leadership	A subordinate reminds his boss of the union rules barring a specific practice in a group setting; a subordinate champions a productivity improvement, even though management is disinclined to adopt it at first.
Followership	A nearly unanimous faculty vote of no-confidence causes the replacement of the chair of the department, even though the vote is nonbinding on administration.
Superleadership	An executive grooms a likely successor; a manager creates a new committee for an important issue; a supervisor delegates a task, requiring a report only if there is a problem.
Substitutes for leadership	A new administrative protocol sets out unwritten policies clearly, reducing the need for leader monitoring and training; increased management training enables employees to solve more problems on their own.
Self-leadership	An employee develops her own plan for self-development; a worker reminds himself what he learned from a failure and resolves to try again; an employee reminds herself of all the positive aspects of her job in order to put some annoying features of it in context.
Team leadership	After a leader carefully selects a team that has complementary skills and provides a broad mandate, she allows them to refine their purpose, define their mutual accountability, and set their specific work schedule.
Network leadership	A manager meets with three other agencies that provide similar services to work a resource-sharing plan for emergencies when need spikes; an executive participates in a number of community organizations with largely common-good objectives where concrete return is nebulous but connections, goodwill, and trust are greatly enhanced over the long term.

It should be noted that there is a good deal of overlap in distributed-leadership models and theories. A theory that combines a number of these perspectives, shared leadership, is presented in chapter 8 with other integrated frameworks.

Informal Leadership Theory

It is a well-known truism that all who have positions of authority—formal leaders—are not necessarily "true" leaders, insofar as they may fail to lead well or at all. Similarly, it is well known that many who lack formal positions of power are nonetheless viewed as leaders. Although the informal organization has received a good deal of attention from

Barnard (1938/1987), the human relations school, and management researchers (e.g., the classic study of the grapevine by Davis 1953), informal leadership has been little studied (Pielstick 2000). Informal leaders are those who lack formal positions but who nonetheless influence others, whether they support formal leaders or not. Both formal leaders and informal leaders can draw on expertise and knowledge of various types and personal dynamism (alternatively known as charisma and referent power). Only formal leaders have substantial position or legitimate power, that is, rank and the ability to reward and punish. Nonetheless, history is famous for leaders who, even without any formal authority at all, rose to incredible levels of influence, from Spartacus in ancient Rome leading an enormous slave revolt that nearly toppled the empire, to various "leaderless" peasant revolts in Europe that reminded aristocratic masters that there is a limit to avarice (Bass 2008, 11). Further, it is important to remember that most modern workers have considerable legitimate power embedded in systems with civil service rights or strong unions. Such environments encourage informal leadership by limiting management capriciousness and managerial retaliation, and by providing either legal rights or the power of ready-made frontline solidarity to frontline workers. Thus the organizational environment tends to create or diminish the likelihood of informal leaders. However, the presence of strong-willed individuals who have the requisite skills is also critical for the development of strong informal leaders.

Informal leaders have the capacity to act as sources of influence that are separate from formal leaders. They can act in ways that passively or actively support formal leaders but they can also act in contravention to formal leaders from simple lack of support to active opposition (Wheelan and Johnston 1996). Informal leadership is particularly important at the beginning of new initiatives (Pescosolido 2001), in leadership transitions, and in times of crisis when formal leadership is weak or challenged by external conditions. Informal leaders can curb the corrosive effects of the power of formal leaders, provide fresh ideas, aid communication, and ensure that employee and alternative perspectives are properly considered (Van Vugt, Hogan, and Kaiser 2008). Because there are generally few informal leaders, some research asserts that they are actually rated by colleagues as more highly talented on average than formal leaders (Pielstick 2000). Just as formal leaders, informal leaders can be "bad." Informal leaders can use their "informal" power corruptly to enhance their self-serving interests rather than the interests of the group or vulnerable individuals, resist good ideas simply because they are new, distort and manipulate information, and create an adversarial atmosphere. The power associated with influential informal leaders tends to derive from good communication skills, including listening, expertise and credibility, and respect and trust of colleagues.

In terms of performance goals, informal leaders tend to focus on the interests and needs of lower-level employees or constituents. They often use their informal power to protect employee or client rights, sometimes using themselves as test cases. Informal leaders can seek to increase production by demanding process changes, better equipment, or the removal of ineffective managers. Frequently, informal leaders are unconcerned about productivity as efficiency at all because of the concern for employee needs and rights; occasionally, informal leaders will seek to diminish productivity to punish management and increase their power. Because informal leadership tends to become more important, for good or ill, in power-sharing arrangements, it is particularly important in teams with a lot of self-determination, and this is where it has been studied the most (often called emergent leadership). Informal leadership can and does sometimes occur within management itself, where junior leaders become influential with their managerial peers or because of their extreme popularity with employees or external stakeholders. While formal leaders ignore informal leaders at their own peril, they generally must be careful to maintain a balance of healthy respect for and independence from them (Barnard 1938/1987). When good formal and informal leaders are functioning ideally, there exists a type of coproduction in which informal leaders help humanize the organization, provide useful and early feedback, and enhance worker motivation by facilitating sense-making and engagement. See Exhibit 5.2 for causal chain implicit in informal leadership.

Followership Theory

Followership theory overlaps with informal leadership theory, but is analytically distinct enough to cover separately. (See Shamir et al. 2007 for a complete range of follower and informal leader perspectives.) While informal leadership tends to emphasize the separate basis of power of those who lack formal positions (regardless of the benefit or harm), followership tends to emphasize the importance of followers in critically and fairly evaluating formal leadership performance. Here we will focus on the work of Barbara Kellerman (2007, 2008), a prominent researcher in this area.

To be a part of the change process, especially in terms of resisting and changing leaders, followers must be engaged. Kellerman proposes five types of followers based on their level of engagement: isolates, bystanders, participants, activists, and diehards. Isolates are withdrawn and detached, and generally alienated from the organization and their peers. Bystanders passively support the status quo with their inaction and are a type of "free rider," depending on their self-interests. Participants are engaged enough to occasionally invest some of their time. Activists are very engaged and eager to express either their support of or opposition toward formal leaders. Diehards are exceptionally committed to ideological positions or select issues and are willing to fight enthusiastically for the success of their position even if it jeopardizes their own job. Those who have no or little engagement—isolates and bystanders—add little to the leadership process in any circumstance. Those with moderate to strong engagement can add a lot to the leadership process, but it is tempered by their willingness to make informed assessments rather than assessments based on snap judgments or selfish interests. Thus, good followers are both engaged and self-informed. Proponents of followership also emphasize the moral obligation of leaders to respect followers as a separate source of authority, wisdom, and expertise (Drath et al. 2008).

Followership theory draws a lot from political perspectives emphasizing the nature of representation mechanisms. For example, good voters are engaged and informed. While informal leaders are generally few in number, good followers are hopefully numerous and relatively cohesive in calling for leadership change when necessary. Like informal leaders,

Exhibit 5.2

Informal Leadership Causal Chain

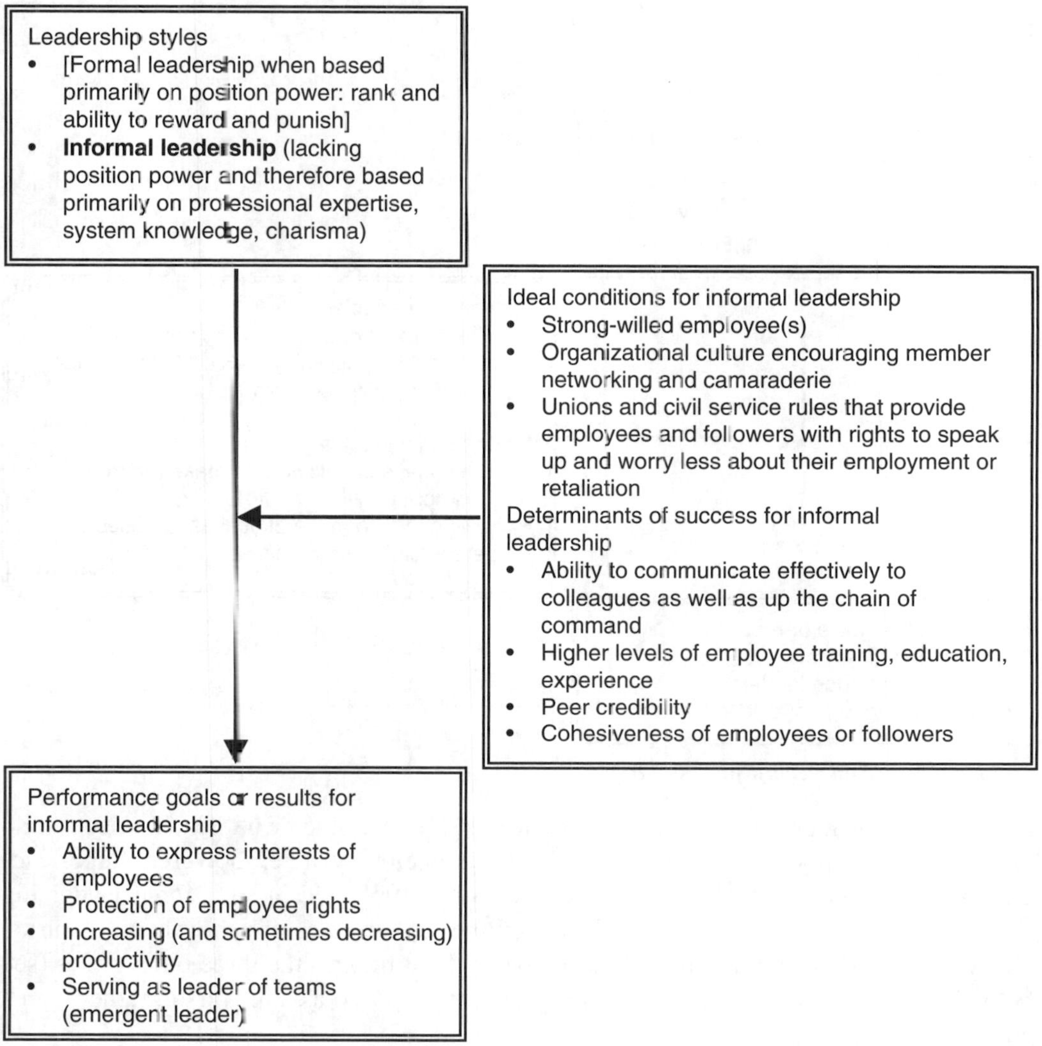

Leadership styles
- [Formal leadership when based primarily on position power: rank and ability to reward and punish]
- **Informal leadership** (lacking position power and therefore based primarily on professional expertise, system knowledge, charisma)

Ideal conditions for informal leadership
- Strong-willed employee(s)
- Organizational culture encouraging member networking and camaraderie
- Unions and civil service rules that provide employees and followers with rights to speak up and worry less about their employment or retaliation

Determinants of success for informal leadership
- Ability to communicate effectively to colleagues as well as up the chain of command
- Higher levels of employee training, education, experience
- Peer credibility
- Cohesiveness of employees or followers

Performance goals or results for informal leadership
- Ability to express interests of employees
- Protection of employee rights
- Increasing (and sometimes decreasing) productivity
- Serving as leader of teams (emergent leader)

followers are not limited to frontline employees; corporate boards are a type of institutionalized function to promote followers' interests in the case of stockholders (Pick 2009). See Exhibit 5.3 for the causal chain implicit in followership theory.

Superleadership Theory

Manz and Sims have been proponents of a process of "leading others to lead themselves," which they call superleadership (1987, 1989, 1991). Distributed leadership has ramifica-

Exhibit 5.3

Followership Causal Chain

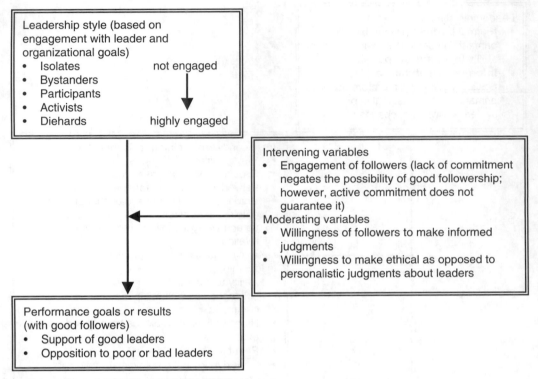

Leadership style (based on engagement with leader and organizational goals)
- Isolates   not engaged
- Bystanders
- Participants
- Activists
- Diehards   highly engaged

Intervening variables
- Engagement of followers (lack of commitment negates the possibility of good followership; however, active commitment does not guarantee it)

Moderating variables
- Willingness of followers to make informed judgments
- Willingness to make ethical as opposed to personalistic judgments about leaders

Performance goals or results (with good followers)
- Support of good leaders
- Opposition to poor or bad leaders

Source: Based on Kellerman (2007, 2008).

tions for both leaders and followers; superleadership examines what leaders need to do to prepare and support followers to be successful when they are empowered. Superleadership has similarities to Hersey and Blanchard's (1969, 1972) situational leadership theory, which advocated four styles based on the subvariables of subordinate maturity. However, superleadership omits the directive style, it merges the three other styles (see below) into a combined style, and it is essentially proposed as a universal, rather than a contingency, theory.

The combined style that Hersey and Blanchard recommend has three elements: supporting others, allowing participation in decision making, and delegating substantial responsibilities to subordinates. The supportive element that they advocate emphasizes development of staff, consultation, and psychological support. The participative element emphasizes consultation, listening, and increased inclusion in areas of responsibility. The delegation element focuses on creating relative worker autonomy and self-review by subordinates.

Superleadership is a universal theory because it recommends a single overarching style. Nonetheless, proponents do acknowledge that the theory assumes a long-term approach because short-term demands such as crises might temporarily make another style

Exhibit 5.4

Superleadership Causal Chain

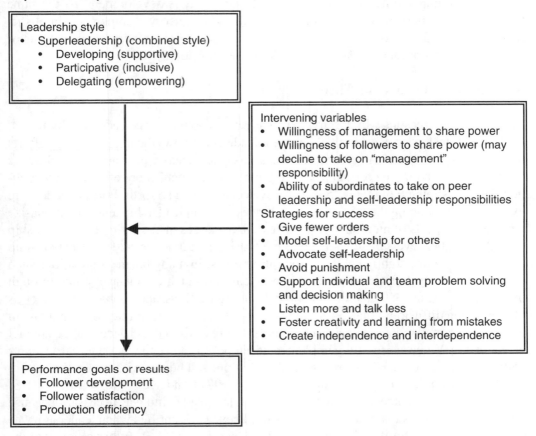

Leadership style
- Superleadership (combined style)
  - Developing (supportive)
  - Participative (inclusive)
  - Delegating (empowering)

Intervening variables
- Willingness of management to share power
- Willingness of followers to share power (may decline to take on "management" responsibility)
- Ability of subordinates to take on peer leadership and self-leadership responsibilities

Strategies for success
- Give fewer orders
- Model self-leadership for others
- Advocate self-leadership
- Avoid punishment
- Support individual and team problem solving and decision making
- Listen more and talk less
- Foster creativity and learning from mistakes
- Create independence and interdependence

Performance goals or results
- Follower development
- Follower satisfaction
- Production efficiency

more effective (Houghton, Neck, and Manz 2003, 134–135). The quality with which the necessary strategies are applied moderates their effectiveness. Such strategies include giving fewer orders, supporting individual and team problem solving and decision making, modeling self-leadership, advocating self-leadership, avoiding punishment, listening more and talking less, fostering creativity, encouraging others to learn from mistakes, and creating independence and interdependence among workers where possible. The primary performance variable is follower development and empowerment. Secondary performance variables include follower satisfaction and production efficiency. The causal chain implicit in superleadership is provided in Exhibit 5.4.

Superleadership helped to provide a theoretical basis for the "empowerment" literature that evolved in the late 1980s. It provided a clearer picture of aspects of empowerment as a style and as a series of concrete strategies. Furthermore, superleadership reminds us that shared leadership begins with the active role of the formal leader in preparing, recognizing, and "letting go of" followers. If followers are not ready for self- and team leadership over time, then it is because of a deficiency in the formal leader. Finally, given the importance of flattened and fast-moving organizations today, superleadership emphasizes that the major function of an effective leader today is development. At the same time, the term superleadership is rather jingoistic and the theory is somewhat simplistic. In addition, the theory is not really a new one, but a more contemporary repackaging of older theories emphasizing leadership as "follower development."

Substitutes for Leadership Theory

There are many reasons why it might be an advantage to have less leadership by formal leaders. Formal leaders have limited time; less leadership allows them to focus their efforts more narrowly and thus enhance effectiveness in critical areas. For example, if followers need little leadership, the formal leader might be able to focus more effectively on public relations, strategic planning, resource development, and so forth. Formal leaders are expensive, so reducing their number saves money. Formal leadership tends to emphasize the external aspects of monitoring and the external sources of creativity. Less leadership can allow higher levels of self- or group monitoring and innovation. Formal leadership tends to restrict and tightly control information flows. In many business situations such restrictions are dysfunctional because good ideas and much enthusiasm come through informal networking, lateral problem-solving communications, and nonhierarchical forms of innovation diffusion. Finally, formal leadership tends to concentrate power high up in the chain of command; empowerment requires a more devolved and decentralized model of leadership. When successfully implemented, empowerment enhances internal accountability, a sense of ownership, professional affiliation, and buy-in with group goals.

Although implied in path-goal theory, Kerr (1977) and Kerr and Jermier (1978) clearly articulated a theory of situations in which less leadership was necessary because it was provided by "substitutes" for leadership. They also identified when leadership was constrained or "neutralized." Howell, Dorfman, and Kerr (1986) further articulated the theory with other moderators of leadership: "enhancers" and "supplements." It continues to generate a lot of support (e.g., Hui et al. 2007).

Two styles of leadership are implied by substitutes theory. First, a delegated style is implied when less leadership is needed. A delegated style allows subordinates relative freedom in decision making and freedom from daily monitoring and short-term review. However, it is important to note that in this theory, leadership delegation is not necessarily an active element, but as frequently it is a passive phenomenon. For instance, as workers become more experienced in their jobs, it is normally expected that the level of supervision should be reduced. Formal or active leadership is withdrawn as unnecessary.

Substitutes for leadership are intervening variables that make nondelegated forms of leadership redundant or even unwarranted. Such variables include task, subordinate, and organizational characteristics. Examples of substitutes provided by the task include innately satisfying work, predictable work flow, and feedback mechanisms built into the task. Examples of the organization's providing substitutes include formalized rules, procedures, and protocols (bureaucratization and centralization), work group cohesiveness and self-management, and a strong organizational culture. Examples of substitutes being provided by subordinate characteristics include a professional orientation and the ability of subordinates to function autonomously because of past experience and education. Cases of substitutes for leadership functioning effectively occur in widely disparate settings: a well-run factory floor using specialized functions, individualized error reports, and highly detailed work protocols; and an effective social services senior management team that has collaborated effectively for years so that the agency head is able to focus on requests for funding and external public relations.

The other variables identified—neutralizers, enhancers, and supplements—function differently than substitutes. Neutralizers constrain a formal leader's ability to influence subordinates' performance. They are moderating variables for formal leadership. They include organizational inflexibility, an antimanagement culture, high need for autonomy by workers, an inability of leaders to influence work incentives such as raises or sanctions, lack of consensus about the best goals to achieve, situations when workers have alternate resources, and when subordinates are distant from the leader. Enhancers have the opposite effect. Enhancers augment the leader's ability to influence subordinate performance. They include the leader's upward and lateral influence, the ability to sanction, the cohesiveness of the work group when there is value alignment with the leader, a strong resource base that the leader controls, a promanagement culture, and a positive image of leadership by subordinates. Supplements also augment the leader's ability by directly strengthening either the tools of leadership, such as analytic aids, or the capacity of leadership, such as training and education. Thus, neutralizers, enhancers, and supplements all moderate the effectiveness of nondelegated forms of leadership.

There are innumerable performance outcomes, depending on the myriad intervening and moderating variables involved. The positive ones from substitutes, enhancers, and supplements include production efficiency, freeing up the leader's time, motivating employees, and enhancing the leader's influence and capacity. The negative ones from neutralizers include reducing the leader's influence and a reduction in group goal achievement. The relationships between the behavior and the different variables are illustrated in Exhibit 5.5.

The theory of substitutes for leadership has made an enormous, highly respected contribution to the literature. First, there is the central insight that more leadership is not always better. Leadership time and resources are commodities to be conserved and used strategically like any others. Second, substitutes theory established an intellectual basis for the empowerment, self-management, and team literatures in which formal or vertical leadership is reduced. Third, substitutes theory provided a clear direction for those redesigning work systems so that leaders' time and energy could be conserved, while workers' effectiveness could be self-managed. Finally, substitutes theory brought together a widely dispersed literature of studies and microlevel insights about when and how leadership functions. The major problem with the theory is that it is really more of a framework than a theory per se. Perhaps it is best viewed as two theories. Although substitutes, neutralizers, enhancers, and supplements are all situational variables, substitutes are intervening variables (as they have been defined in this study) while neutralizers,

Exhibit 5.5

Substitutes Leadership Causal Chain

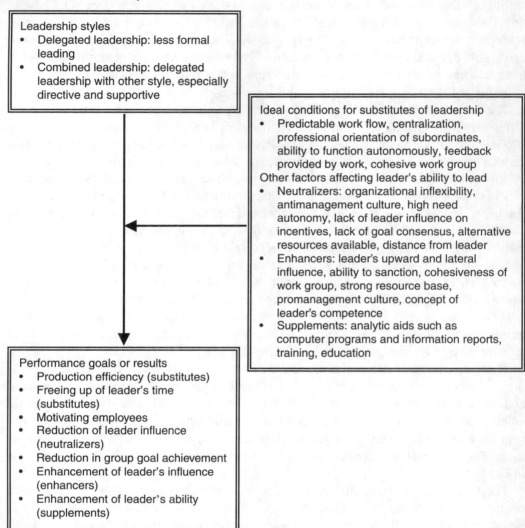

Leadership styles
- Delegated leadership: less formal leading
- Combined leadership: delegated leadership with other style, especially directive and supportive

Ideal conditions for substitutes of leadership
- Predictable work flow, centralization, professional orientation of subordinates, ability to function autonomously, feedback provided by work, cohesive work group

Other factors affecting leader's ability to lead
- Neutralizers: organizational inflexibility, antimanagement culture, high need autonomy, lack of leader influence on incentives, lack of goal consensus, alternative resources available, distance from leader
- Enhancers: leader's upward and lateral influence, ability to sanction, cohesiveness of work group, strong resource base, promanagement culture, concept of leader's competence
- Supplements: analytic aids such as computer programs and information reports, training, education

Performance goals or results
- Production efficiency (substitutes)
- Freeing up of leader's time (substitutes)
- Motivating employees
- Reduction of leader influence (neutralizers)
- Reduction in group goal achievement
- Enhancement of leader's influence (enhancers)
- Enhancement of leader's ability (supplements)

enhancers, and supplements are all moderating variables. Thus, rather than explaining the leadership phenomenon elegantly, it tends to provide a laundry list of situational classes of a disparate nature (Dionne et al. 2005).

Self-Leadership Theory

Accordingly to one of its most common definitions, leadership is the art and practice of effective influence (Bass 1990). Self-leadership is the "process of influencing oneself"

(Manz 1992, 6). The central insight of self-leadership theory is that the attitudes, beliefs, self-designed behavioral patterns, and motivational preferences of individuals make a critical difference in both accomplishment and personal satisfaction in work, whether it involves an executive or a frontline worker. Indeed, self-leadership argues persuasively that those who master effective self-leadership practices are far more likely to be successful in gaining higher leadership positions and in being considered more effective in those positions. (Many of the traits discussed in chapter 11 relate to this discussion. Traits that affect or are affected by self-leadership include self-confidence, decisiveness, resilience, energy, need for achievement, willingness to assume responsibility, flexibility, and emotional maturity. The skill of continual learning is also directly related to self-leadership.)

Although the contemporary notion of self-leadership is relatively new, there are a number of fields that have provided the foundation. In psychology, social learning theory emphasizes the ability of individuals to learn and adapt in complex settings (Bandura 1977, 1986). Intrinsic motivation theory (Deci 1975) emphasizes the ability of individuals to harness the natural enthusiasm that they have for some tasks. Self-motivation was popularized by Norman Vincent Peale in the late 1940s and 1950s (Peale 1956, 1959). In the management literature, self-leadership was preceded by self-regulation (Kanfer 1970), self-control (Mahoney and Arnkoff 1978), and self-management (Luthans and Davis 1979).

In terms of styles recommended, only one style, with numerous subelements, is recommended: self-leadership. This combined style parallels those that have been used to compare other theories. However, the exception to the parallel is that it is self-focused. Thus self-leadership is composed of self-direction, self-support, self-achievement, and self-inspiration. Rather than relying on others for guidance, confidence, goals, or stimulation, the theory asserts that one should rely primarily on oneself, whether one is a manager, office worker, or executive.

Self-leadership is a universal style that does not focus on intervening variables. It does focus extensively on the specific strategies that produce effective self-leadership. Three types of strategies are identified: behavior-focused strategies, natural reward strategies, and constructive thought-pattern strategies. Behavior-focused strategies help us alter how we interact with the world. Global strategies include reminders and attention focusers, removal of negative cues, and the increase of positive cues. Such strategies are particularly useful in helping us to accomplish the necessary but undesirable tasks that confront everyone. Examples of such behavioral strategies include the old-fashioned, but still powerful, "to do" list, organizers, identification and removal of one's distractions and time-wasters, and identification and utilization of those people and artifacts that enhance productivity. There are also specific behavioral strategies. Self-observation requires periodic, disciplined, and honest self-evaluation. It can be thought of as providing oneself with self-correcting feedback. Self-goal-setting is the act of setting one's own goals apart from those set by the organization. Self-reward is the act of "treating oneself" when self-defined goals are achieved and celebrating one's own success. Self-punishment is the act of correcting defective past practice, but not applying self-guilt, which is invariably dysfunctional. Rehearsal is the act of practicing those things that either need improvement or must be conducted with an exceptional level of quality, such as a public speech.

Individuals find different types of work more intrinsically satisfying than others. That is, some types of work have more natural rewards for people. Yet, almost all work can have some degree of intrinsic reward if one has the proper mental attitude. A manager trained as an accountant may not instinctively enjoy "managing by walking around" but may nonetheless cultivate a talent for it through developing an appreciation of the motivation that it enhances and the qualitative data that can be gleaned. By overcoming the negative disinclination and focusing on the positive aspects of work, natural rewards can be greatly enhanced. This literature also points out the liability of "incentivizing" everything that workers do, because the incentives can actually overwhelm the natural reward—and motivation—that is an effective and cost-efficient driver of productivity and quality. Finally, self-management points out that the sequencing, blending, and location of activities make an enormous difference in how the natural rewards of activities are perceived and in the quality of work that is actually produced. Less desirable activities may be scheduled early in the day or week to ensure that they are "gotten out of the way" promptly. Physical activities may be scheduled in the afternoon to break up the monotony of the day. Major management products such as reports, strategic plans, and detailed schedules may need to be done in quiet locations where distractions can be eliminated or kept to a minimum.

"Constructive thought-pattern strategies deal with the creation or alteration of cognitive thought processes. Essentially, this set of strategies includes three primary ways through which thought patterns may be altered: self-analysis and improvement of belief systems, mental imagery of successful performance outcomes, and positive self-talk" (Houghton, Neck, and Manz 2003, 129). Dysfunctional thought patterns are a common hindrance to productivity. Such thought patterns may include self-perceptions of incompetence, difficulty in accomplishing tasks, hostility by others, or futility in making progress. Self-talk is defined as the psychological rehearsal or internal dialogues that we engage in either consciously or subconsciously. It is easy for people to engage in negative or pessimistic self-talk without external feedback to correct it. Negative self-talk about oneself can almost ensure failure, mediocrity, and/or lower effectiveness. Of course, negative self-talk is not the same as self-evaluation, which is done in a timely way prior to performance to allow time for change or after performance to influence future efforts. Negative self-talk largely sabotages high energy levels and ultimately jinxes success. Finally, positive visualization is a powerful tool to encourage effort despite fatigue and setbacks. Although the best empirical evidence comes from athletics, it is a widespread strategy that can help with the preparation of a difficult report, challenging performance goal, or completion of an academic course of study. For example, the student who is unsure whether s/he has the ability to complete a master's program because of competing commitments, and who rarely ever imagines what it will be like to have the degree and the career potential it will bring, is unlikely to enjoy the program, do well, or even finish the program. On the other hand, the student who relishes the intellectual stimulation, enjoys overcoming the logistical and intellectual challenges one by one, and who dreams of the day when s/he will achieve his/her goal, is much more likely to complete the program of study and be more dramatically improved because of it.

Exhibit 5.6

Self-Leadership Causal Chain

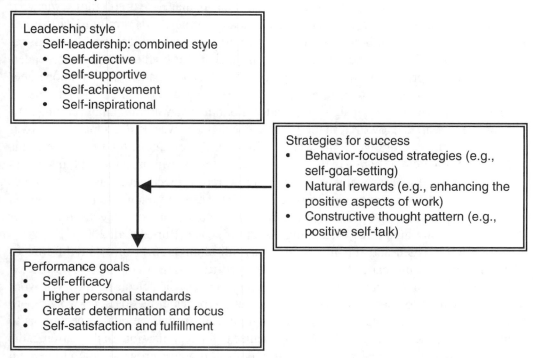

Leadership style
- Self-leadership: combined style
  - Self-directive
  - Self-supportive
  - Self-achievement
  - Self-inspirational

Strategies for success
- Behavior-focused strategies (e.g., self-goal-setting)
- Natural rewards (e.g., enhancing the positive aspects of work)
- Constructive thought pattern (e.g., positive self-talk)

Performance goals
- Self-efficacy
- Higher personal standards
- Greater determination and focus
- Self-satisfaction and fulfillment

Performance variables include enhanced self-efficacy, higher personal standards, greater determination and focus, and greater self-satisfaction and fulfillment. The causal chain implicit in self-leadership is illustrated in Exhibit 5.6.

One strength of the self-leadership literature is that it has a delightful commonsense approach about it. It reminds one of Benjamin Franklin and Aesop who both said that God (or the gods) helps those who help themselves. Self-discipline, self-analysis, self-goal-setting, self-improvement, and so on are fundamental to our success and long-term happiness (Fletcher and Cooke 2008). Optimism, enthusiasm, and a positive attitude do make a difference. Another strength of the self-leadership literature is that it has matured from the somewhat excessive and syrupy nostrums of Peale into a more mature body of thought and research without losing its applied emphasis. Finally, the self-leadership literature is a useful companion to the trait approach to leadership. It points out not only the virtues of a trait such as self-confidence but also the strategies to achieve it. Its major weakness is that self-leadership is not a true form of leadership if leadership is defined as having followers or extending influence to others. Thus, the term self-leadership, like superleadership, is a bit of a stretch and probably not the best choice of terms. A term like self-management would probably have been more apt and less affected.

Leadership functions are delegated not only to self-led individuals but also to teams. That is the topic to which we turn next.

Self-Managed Teams

As with other forms of distributed leadership, the self-managed team literature was very slow to come into its own right. References to teams in the 1950s through 1970s in the mainstream management literature invariably referred to hierarchical teams—teams reporting to a formal leader. The leadership literature did focus on the emergence of leadership in leaderless groups, but the primary purpose was to study leadership formation rather than functioning without a formal leader. Social-exchange and role theory crystallized a number of important social insights for leadership, but they were not analyzed in a self-management context. However, in the 1980s great attention was paid to Japanese innovations in devolution, employee empowerment, quality circles, and similar measures. This initiated a dramatic sea change in the examination of teams. Almost overnight, interest in self-managed quality improvement teams, "empowered" project teams, and various types of self-managing user groups mushroomed. Old theories were reanalyzed in the context of distributing leadership functions in the traditional work group or project setting rather than in controlling the group or ensuring leader influence (Burke et al. 2006).

Formally managed and self-managed teams fall along a spectrum. The differences between formal team leadership and self-managed teams are dramatic only in the extremes. The formally managed team has a "strong" leader who selects members or work assignments, monitors progress, encourages members, provides feedback for work deviations, sets goals, evaluates progress, and communicates organizational expectations to members while communicating team performance to the organization. In the extreme, the self-managed team selects its members, all members monitor progress, encouragement is provided by colleagues, goal setting and evaluation are done in a group setting, work problems (including member expulsion) are handled communally, and external leadership is rotated or assigned by the group on an ad hoc basis.

Self-managed team theory is generally proposed as a universal approach rather than a contingency approach for convenience and clarity. Advocates generally acknowledge that self-managed teams can thrive only under special conditions (which will be identified as the moderating variables), and should be considered *a* type of team leadership, not *the* type of team leadership. The single combined style of team leadership distributes the standard functions of leadership among the group, or allows the group to assign leadership functions based on member talents and availability. Thus, direction, support, participation, achievement, inspiration, and external connectedness are mutually determined and executed. This practice is an appealing form of work democracy, and when functioning ideally, enhances identification with the work, task selection based on talent and interest, flexibility, and innovation. It also reduces the organizational expense of numerous, highly paid leaders. This money can be reinvested in more highly paid professionals who manage themselves individually and in teams. However, when self-managed teams are functioning poorly, they induce frustration, unresolved disputes, "free riders" (members who do not pull their weight), goal confusion, fuzzy accountability, excessive meetings, and other management pathologies.

Katzenbach and Smith (1993) provide a good example of the type of conditions that must exist for self-managed teams to perform well. They point to four moderating variables. The first is a common purpose and approach by the team. Management theory holds that work done by groups must be organized to be efficient, which means a major function of management is to divide and coordinate work (Mintzberg 1973). Under certain conditions, however, such division and coordination can be diffused and organic. Imagine a large, annual family gathering to which many members bring different dishes of food. There is an understanding that the family meal will take place at around five o'clock, so self-selected members busy themselves with what seems necessary. After the meal, another self-appointed group starts to clean up, picking different tasks to work on, with a complete lack of central or formal leadership and direction. This self-organizing example highlights some of the factors contributing to a common purpose and approach: a history of cooperating and working together, a shared project and goal, and common interests. In the organizational world, a common approach is enhanced by a strong culture and philosophy that in turn tend to rely on similar educational background. For example, social work education in a social services agency fosters a common approach. However, because of the multiple disciplinary perspectives represented in many teams and the complexity of technical functions to be executed, many organizations that want to encourage self-managed teams rely on extensive team training (Scholtes 1988). Such training essentially teaches the basic functions of leadership as well as how to distribute leadership functions.

Another great principle of management theory is that without accountability, productivity lags and quality varies beyond permissible levels. The classical management answer has been to provide cascading levels of leadership authority in a hierarchical setting. Katzenbach and Smith are among those who assert that in many settings mutual accountability is as effective or even more effective than vertical accountability. Social exchange theory asserts that most action in work settings is rational and is based on reciprocity. At the tangible level, pay is traded for service and special consideration is exchanged for hard work. Yet, unequal power need not be a factor in exchange. High-performing teams are characterized by an exchange of different types of contributions to team efforts and by an unconditional exchange of "favors." At the intangible level, implicit exchanges include loyalty in return for security, and deference to the leader in return for respect of the worker's expertise. Again, such influence and respect can be equal as well as reciprocal. For mutual accountability to work, then, mutual benefits must be freely and consistently exchanged and power relationships must be relatively equal. A strong and positive sense of shared fate motivates the team. High-performing teams can rely on deep-seated notions of mutuality to rouse team members to exceptional efforts in the face of unusual demands, a deadline, or a crisis.

A third principle of self-managed teams that function well is the need for complementary skills. Role theory provides the basis for this assertion. The best role assignments are based on individual skills and personality. The clarity of roles makes an enormous difference in member comfort, efficiency, and reduced confusion. Further, role differentiation becomes more important with task complexity. Complementary skills, then, are based on the natural talents of team members who are allowed to specialize for efficiency and coordination. However, an important caveat is that the leadership role must also be distributed. Role theory states that those in leadership roles are expected to be competent in basic social skills, have an appropriate demeanor, and be worthy of trust. For the leadership role to be shared, all members must be interpersonally competent, professional, and trustworthy. Thus, while members can and should have different skill sets to contribute to team efforts, they must all have basic leadership competence for a diffused model of management to work well.

The last requirement for highly productive self-managed teams is that they have an appropriate number of team members. Role theory also points out that as the group size increases, the pressure to formalize roles also increases. Role formalization can enhance work uniformity, consistency of expectations, and complex accountability requirements. However, role formalization often decreases flexibility, common ownership of group products, and creativity and innovation. Self-managed teams, by definition, avoid role formalization to take advantage of such potential virtues. Katzenbach and Smith note: "Virtually all the teams we have met, read, heard about, or been members of have ranged from two to twenty-five people. The majority of them . . . have numbered less than ten" (1993, 45). A relatively small number allows team members to interact directly, get to know one another, trust one another, and feel a strong sense of community. A common approach is more likely to be achieved, and the purpose is less likely to become fragmented. And it is very important to note that, for the most part, mutual accountability can still be monitored informally.

The performance variables vary considerably in the self-managed team literature, from an emphasis on individual development through teams to an emphasis on high team productivity. Katzenbach and Smith (1993) emphasize the latter in their "high-performance organization." Like Bass's transformational model, which emphasizes "performance beyond expectations," they stress exceptional production, external alignment, and organizational change, although at a microlevel. They also stress follower satisfaction, mutual development, and decision quality. The causal chain implicit in self-managed terms is illustrated in Exhibit 5.7.

Despite the positive allusions to "team spirit" that have always been commonly associated with athletic teams, there was little concrete theorizing about nonvertical teams until recently. Team theory acknowledges a powerful organizational mode and gives it the central attention that it deserves. Although sometimes overstated as a management revolution that will transform the organizational world (Peters 1992, 1994; Manz and Sims 1993), there can be little doubt that teams with self-led features have had a substantial and growing impact in contemporary organizations. A second strength of this literature is its clear statement that high-quality self-managing groups are neither accidental nor easy to attain, and not for all situations. In fact, self-managed teams take even more sociotechnical design than normal vertical leadership teams do. This was often overlooked in the team organization craze of the 1990s, when many organizations empowered poorly structured and trained teams (which subsequently underperformed or fell apart), or falsely implied that they empowered teams when in reality they only delegated additional responsibilities (leading to burnout and cynicism). With the coalescence of the team literature and the

Exhibit 5.7

Self-Managed Teams Causal Chain

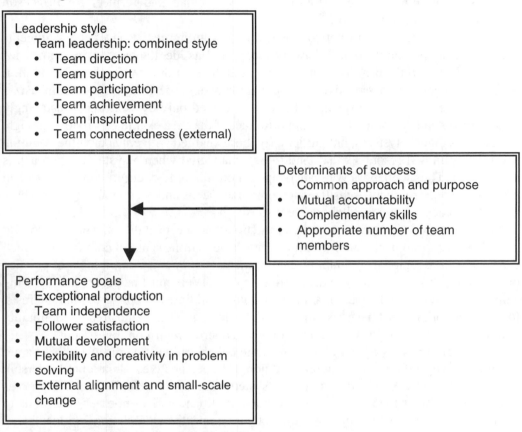

Leadership style
- Team leadership: combined style
  - Team direction
  - Team support
  - Team participation
  - Team achievement
  - Team inspiration
  - Team connectedness (external)

Determinants of success
- Common approach and purpose
- Mutual accountability
- Complementary skills
- Appropriate number of team members

Performance goals
- Exceptional production
- Team independence
- Follower satisfaction
- Mutual development
- Flexibility and creativity in problem solving
- External alignment and small-scale change

Source: Based on Katzenbach and Smith (1993)

increased popularity of team approaches, the connections between the reality and theory of teams has also been somewhat bridged. Nonetheless, team theory is still highly fragmented compared to other aspects of the leadership literature. There is little consistency in nomenclature, concepts, or theoretical models. Until very recently, there has been no coherent attempt to relate self-managed teams to leadership theory (e.g., Day, Gronn, and Salas 2006; Ensley, Hmieleski, and Pearce 2006; Schaubroeck, Lam, and Cha 2007).

Network Leadership Theory

So far the types of distributed leadership have been primarily focused on sharing power within the organization and potentially with clients or client stakeholders. Network leadership focuses on power sharing among organizations. Network leadership deemphasizes the roles of both leaders and followers in order to emphasize the needs of the network, system, environment, or community. It recommends a collaborative style in opposition to a noncollaborative style. It is often part of the discussion about moving from a government to a governance approach, and various types of interorganizational and cross-sectoral forms of cooperation (Klijn, Koopenjan, and Termeer 1995; Jackson and Stainsby 2000; Kettl 2006).

Critical to understanding network leadership is an appreciation of the arguments made about its potential merits. Network theory and its ideological cousins emphasize the need to support the health of communities and the environment for the good of all. It requires a longer-term perspective in achieving many of the desired results. It emphasizes a cooperative, win–win perspective that can be gained only by working painstakingly through problems to frame them as opportunities if they are examined broadly enough. It maintains that all systems, but particularly those charged with enhancing the common good, have limited resources that tend to be squandered when a systemic approach is not utilized. Thus, collaborative leadership is more likely to occur in communities and professional environments sensitized to communal needs and accountability, and where individual leaders share a collaborative disposition.

Network leaders tend to have a particularly strong service mentality, and be very good at consultation and environmental scanning. They have a strong sense of community, which can be a local or regional community, environmental community, community of practice or need (charity), and so forth. Successful network leaders must be perceived as having genuine goodwill and the lack of a hidden agenda, and time to explore mutual interests. Ideally, network leaders have resources available to contribute to the greater community without having to worry about an immediate or concrete return on investment.

The research base is tightly aligned with the collaborative style discussed in chapter 2 and is heavily influenced by public and nonprofit perspectives. Relational leadership theory (Uhl-Bien 2006) is the branch of systems theory that emphasizes the process of leadership rather than the people who populate it (the entity approach that tends to dominate most of the literature and theoretical perspectives). Relationship leadership theory focuses on leadership as a process of social construction with an evolving social order. Network theory tends to have strong normative overtones regarding the need to share power for ethical and pragmatic reasons (e.g., Agranoff 2008a; Cortada et al. 2008; Crosby and Bryson 2010; Newell, Reeher, and Ronayne 2008), and to work together to solve tough problems that might otherwise be unresolvable (e.g., Chrislip and Larson 1994; Heifetz 1994).

Network leaders are judged by their contribution to building community, mutual learning and sharing, cooperative problem solving, and working on "wicked" problems. Rather than trying to get a "bigger piece of the pie," network leaders work to expand the size of the pie for all. Exhibit 5.8 illustrates the causal chain for network leadership.

CONCLUSION

Seven types of leadership were discussed in this chapter. *Informal leadership* occurs to a greater or lesser extent in all organizations, with or without the support of management, because subordinate employees are not without residual power and a few subordinates

Exhibit 5.8

Network Leadership Causal Chain

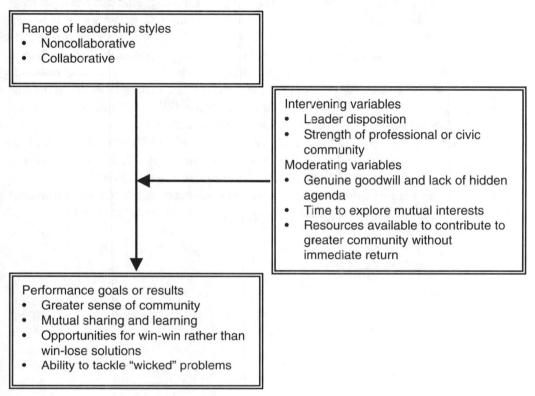

exercise considerable influence with both peers and superiors. *Followership theory* emphasizes the role of subordinates in supporting or resisting their leaders from the ethical and
effectiveness perspective, rather than a personal perspective per se; that is, it emphasizes
followers in the leadership process as a separate evaluative base from leaders. *Superleadership* encompasses the various types of voluntary power sharing (empowerment) that
occur when formal leaders actively develop subordinates, allow participation, and seek
opportunities for appropriate delegation. It has strong echoes in Hersey and Blanchard's
situational leadership theory (1969, 1972), but Manz and Sims's superleadership theory
(1989, 1991) deemphasizes the use of directive leadership and negative incentives. *Substitutes for leadership* theory points out that the answer to leadership issues is not always
more, but less, and sets out propositions for empirical conditions when the absence of
leaders can improve the leadership process (Kerr and Jermier 1978). To whom or what
is leadership distributed? There are three primary answers—individuals, teams, and
networks. *Self-leadership* looks at the characteristics that all workers can practice so as
to be less dependent on formal leaders or superiors, more capable of performing well in
situations with extensive distributed leadership, and ready to accept or expand formal

leadership if and when those roles are assigned. Sometimes leadership occurs through a group of individuals who share leadership functions as a team. The high-performance team theory of Katzenbach and Smith (1993) exemplifies the *self-managed team* perspective as the example used here. Sometimes leadership occurs in an even more dispersed environment, *networks*, in which collaboration with those external to the organization is critical. In sum then, informal leadership, followership, and superleadership emphasize different perspectives on the power-sharing relations in the leadership process. Substitutes theory, self-leadership, and team leadership focus on concrete strategies for reducing formal leaders' roles to enhance better distribution of responsibility to followers. Network leadership takes power sharing outside the organization altogether.

The challenge of integrating these different perspectives with each other as well as integrating them with vertical leadership is addressed in chapter 8. Before we turn to that process, we will look at additional value-based theories of leadership. Values and ethics are a major theme of most of the distributed-leadership perspectives we have just examined but will be the primary content of the approaches we will review next.

Ethics-Based Leadership Theories

Ethics-based approaches are generally in stark contrast to most traditional approaches to leadership studies that either focus on descriptive realities of leader-centric systems and/or the importance of leaders who influence others through their personal charisma, vision, and skill. Such power-based or "heroic" approaches assume that the primary source of wisdom is the leader or that knowledge is for the leader's benefit, that the leader is implicitly the most critical and important decision maker, and that the leader's success is the principal consideration. In contrast, ethics-based approaches assume that the leader is not likely to have all wisdom. Such approaches assert that, frequently, followers either have important contributions to make or may even have all the facts and knowledge necessary for decisions in the leadership process. In this respect, distributed approaches discussed in the preceding chapter and ethics approaches discussed in this chapter are highly compatible. Second, these approaches assume that followers have the same importance as leaders themselves, and sometimes followers are of even greater importance than leaders. Followers accomplish the work and they should be the focus of the leader. Rather than increasing personal influence, good leaders are involved in empowerment. Finally, these approaches stress that ethical leaders must deemphasize their personal interests to be effective, including business settings (e.g., see review by Aronson 2001; Block 1993; Rost 1990; Senge 1990; Dalla Costa 1998; Johnson 2005). While power-based approaches (discussed further in the next chapter) do not endorse the use of power for personal ends, they tend to adopt Machiavelli's cosmopolitan view that influence and power exist, and that one wants as much as possible from a "princely" viewpoint to hopefully do good (Machiavelli 1998).

Ethics-based approaches tend to have three major concerns (Ciulla 2004; Ciulla, Price, and Murphy 2005). The first concern is the *intent* of individuals, whether they are leaders or members of the organization. How does the character and virtue of individuals shape their moral compass to do good? For example, an individual leader may be both ambitious and very careful to comply with all regulations and rules. Such a leader may insist on results and also be sure to do so in authorized and appropriate ways. Nonetheless ambitious leaders tend to be self-centered and thus weak in listening to others and providing developmental opportunities for followers' benefits, and they tend to be blame averse, even when they have indirectly allowed problems to occur. Ambitious leaders' ability to do good, then, is somewhat diminished by limitations in their moral compass.

The second concern involves selecting the *proper means* for doing good. In philosophy, this is often called the deontological or duty approach. Being moral means knowing and following appropriate social customs stemming from laws, rules, and mores. Yet, as situations become more complex, what is the leader's role in dealing with the competing and conflicting values that emerge. Kant (1787/1996) is perhaps the best known for the ethics of duty, via his grand categorical imperatives, in an orderly society.

The third concern is in selecting the *proper ends*. In philosophy, this is often called the teleological or utilitarian approach. An example is when a male manager is approached by an angry female employee who accuses a supervisor of sexual harassment and provides three instances of inappropriate language and behavior. The manager calms down the employee by saying that he will talk to the supervisor. The manager does talk to the supervisor, who admits using poor judgment in speech and behavior. Since the supervisor is hardworking and competent, the manager lets the supervisor off with an oral warning. In this case, the manager's ends are probably distorted by excessive concerns about preventing strife and protecting a good worker, rather than protecting the legal rights of the victim.

Ultimately, all three concerns—good intent, proper means, and appropriate ends—must be functioning for good leadership (as a process) to be robust. Systems with ethical leadership provide a higher quality of life for all individuals involved, higher organizational performance on average, and greater sustainability over time. We now turn to the different perspectives on what is most important in ethical leadership.

PERSPECTIVES ON ETHICS-BASED LEADERSHIP

The range of what ethics theories include or emphasize is extensive. To articulate the emphases more clearly, five "models" that call attention to the differences are provided below. The first is the essential core or foundation for ethical leaders in nearly all theories. The next four models offer contrasting, but not necessarily contradictory, perspectives on ethical leadership that build on basic leader morality.

The Basic Integrity Model of the Virtuous Leader

Nearly all ethical theories focus on, include, or assume basic leader integrity. Thousands of years ago Confucius stated that the strength of the nation is the integrity of its homes. More recently, the military commander and president Dwight Eisenhower noted that the supreme quality of leadership is unquestionable integrity. The basic meaning of integrity is wholeness, and that in turn is based on notions of consistency with one's own words, thoughts, principles, actions, and social setting. The three most common hallmarks of integrity are honesty, trustworthiness, and fairness. When asked about all possible characteristics, the various elements of integrity are often the highest, frequently ranking higher than competence itself.

The first level of honesty involves telling the truth in all oral and written expression. Honest people from this perspective do not tell lies, even by reframing "white" or courtesy lies. Further, they are truthful in both private and public situations. Truth telling occurs in subtle ways such as admitting mistakes or not evading taxes. A higher level of truth telling concerns coming forth with appropriate information when not compelled to do so; this is often called forthrightness. Secrets and "lies of omission" are not associated with honest people.

The second element of integrity relates to trustworthiness, which can involve several elements. Trustworthy people know what their principles are and are able to state them so that others know "where they stand." Of course, trustworthy people are consistent with own their principles (Manz, et al. 2008; Palanski and Yammarino 2009). In the public sector, principles are expected to include dedication to public service, commitment to the common good, dedication to the law of the land, and other civic virtues. Further, in being considered trustworthy, it is very important to follow through on commitments, which is often called credibility. Many people make commitments cavalierly if innocently, damaging their credibility with others. "Trust has been identified as one of the most frequently examined constructs in the organizational literature today" (Burke et al. 2007) and is sometimes used more broadly as a synonym for the concept of integrity as used here (Newell, Reeher, and Ronayne 2008).

A third major element of integrity is fairness. Fairness implies that one knows and follows rules and makes sure that they apply to all. Because those with management and executive responsibilities have a lot of discretion, fairness is important in the equality of treatment as well as in making rational and appropriate exceptions. A management nostrum is that although your enemies may report you, it is your friends who are more likely to get you into trouble. That is, turning a blind eye to the peccadilloes or problems, and/or providing excessive assistance to those close to a leader can be a significant source of vulnerability and can significantly diminish others' sense of fairness. In the above example of the manager handling the sexual harassment incidents of a friend, he needed to take more aggressive action in order to meet the fairness standard. Those who are considered very fair are not involved in "self-dealing" or using their position for personal gain, but rather in sharing gain as equally as possible (Carnevale 1995, 23). Finally, because balancing various responsibilities and concerns is often a complicated matter, fair people take the time to listen well to all sides in disputes.

People of good integrity are perceived as telling the truth, acting consistently, and providing treatment to others that they themselves would like in the same position. Those of exceptional integrity likely exhibit outstanding candor, conscientious follow-through, and unusual astuteness in achieving a balance that meets the competing interests of situations. The factors contributing to the basic integrity model of leadership are shown in Exhibit 6.1.

The Ethical Leader as Moral Manager

Certainly one of the first mandates of ethical leaders and an ethical leadership process is to make sure that the rules, regulations, and expected mores are:

- explicitly stated,
- clearly and fully taught to new organizational members,
- refreshed and updated for veteran members, and
- enforced consistently and fairly for all.

Exhibit 6.1

Ethical Leadership Based on Personal Integrity

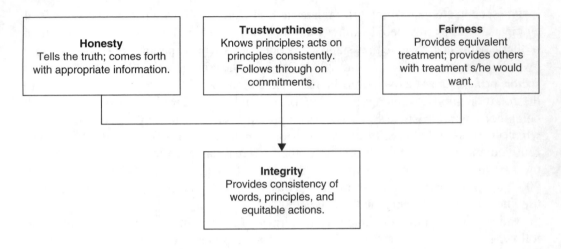

Organizations depend on members to know and follow their "duty" (Trevino, Weaver, and Reynolds 2006). This is particularly true in public sector organizations in which the delegation of authority to work on the public's behalf derives from statute and is articulated through administrative law. Just as the content of what ethical public leaders are supposed to accomplish is stipulated in authorizing statutes, so too are expectations of leaders in avoiding self-serving and inappropriate behaviors stipulated in so-called ethics legislation (legislation clarifying prohibited behavior such as conflict of interest, gift taking, nepotism, etc.). Moral management is a common term used to describe the leadership function ensuring that organizational expectations are understood and enforced (Brown and Trevino 2006). The approach is also sometimes called the duty approach or ethics training. This approach is not only expressed in legislative and regulatory documents but also in codes of conduct, oaths of office, and professional standards documents (Menzel 2007).

The importance of ethical leadership is most obvious when it is absent. Imagine an entrepreneurial public agency, such as an economic development agency, in which the rules and regulations are not clearly stated, so that agency personnel are always guessing just how much initiative they should take into their own hands. Imagine the results of not training police officers or welfare benefits providers extensively. Imagine the resulting chaos of not instructing veteran employees about new legal mandates or providing continuing education in areas of organizational laxness. Imagine the damage to agency reputation when a culture of "anything goes" and lax enforcement pervades it, until finally excesses result in public scandals and judicial or legislative interventions.

There are a number of strengths inherent in this approach. Because the United States and other advanced nations are nations of laws, a duty and compliance approach is consistent (Rohr 1989). A rules approach assists agencies in creating a shared vision and method (Svara 2007). Because the laws, regulations, and organizational rules are often complex or nuanced, an ethics training perspective gives due deference to the time and focus necessary to have sufficient mastery of this aspect of organizational functioning. Not enforcing rules can lead to moral decay and employee disenchantment (Trevino 1992). Finally, knowing the rules and regulations gives employees confidence and enhances the public's trust (Gilman 2005). These are enormously important considerations and are often directly or implicitly included in broader theories of ethical leadership along with the basic integrity model.

The duty or compliance approach also has many potential weaknesses, generally from three sources: an excessive focus on prohibition, poor implementation, or the problem of dealing with executive corruption. When the sole focus of ethical leadership is based on compliance, it is often called the "low road" approach, signifying both a single path to a complex undertaking and the easier route because it is a "technical" solution to the problem of wrongdoing. However, being ethical is not exclusively about prohibiting wrongdoing and reacting to threats against integrity. Being ethical is also about doing the right thing and doing things right, which are active, not passive pursuits. Further, higher stages of morality are not just founded on avoidance behavior, but on principle-centered behavior (Kohlberg 1981), which the compliance approach neglects when not blended with other perspectives.

In terms of implementation, the ethics or code training perspective can fall short when poorly executed because of inadequate materials, superficial or lackluster training, lack of pertinent examples, contradictory role models, and so forth.

Perhaps the trickiest aspect of moral management arises when the authorized source or enforcer of moral management is itself corrupted, or at least perceived to be corrupt. Extreme historical examples make this problem provocative: Hitler orders subordinates to run death camps, a president orders a cover-up of his own overreach of power, or a governor sells government privileges for payoffs. In such instances the wrongdoing is obvious (in retrospect) so it is really a discussion of courage in following social norms rather than improper orders. But the issue is more complex when social rules dictate one thing, but one's own conscience dictates another, as frequently happens with both prolife and abortion advocates. And what about substituting one's own judgment for authorized opinion, given the possibility of individual quirkiness or eccentricity, or downright error? The next perspective focuses on the leader as an important evaluator of ethical norms.

The Ethical Leader as Authentic

If the moral manager perspective emphasizes the external role of authorized values, authentic leadership emphasizes the internal perspective. Predecessors of this general conceptual framework include Argyris (1957, 1993), Covey (1990), Fairholm (1991), and many others. The definition varies significantly across current researchers (Avolio and Gardner 2005). Authentic leaders, according to Avolio and Gardner (ibid.), are self-aware in terms of their values, cognitions, and emotions. Core values of authentic leaders include trustworthiness, credibility, respect for others, fairness, accountability, and other aspects of basic personal integrity that were discussed above. They are adept at self-regulation in terms of their emotional intelligence, self-improvement goals, and balanced congruence between their actual and ideal selves. Authentic leaders control their ego drives and defensiveness, which encourages openness, feedback, and genuine communication. Their self-awareness and self-acceptance increase their transparency in communication of their values, identity, emotions, goals, and motives to others. Because of this, authentic leaders develop positive psychological capital with followers whose self-awareness is also enhanced and whose authentic interaction becomes more likely. However, while the overlap with other ethical theories can be extensive to the degree that proponents of this perspective seek an all-inclusive ethical approach to leadership, it is the emphasis on self-awareness and self-regulatory elements that sets it somewhat apart for our discussion, especially from moral management as discussed above.

The strengths of the authentic leadership approach are numerous. The authentic leadership construct takes into account the individual's role beyond the mere passive acceptance of social norms; authentic leaders are responsible for being self-aware and self-regulating. It pays attention to the mutual and ongoing redefinition of moral norms. It emphasizes the positive aspects of leadership in terms of leaders taking charge of their emotional health and enhancing the moral awareness and emotional health of others. It therefore integrates ethical concerns such as the positive use of influence in a general leadership model.

Critics (e.g., Cooper, Scandura, and Schriesheim 2005) have noted a number of challenges in developing this "very normative approach." First, the definitions of authentic leadership seem somewhat amorphous and all-inclusive, and definitions become circular. Good leaders are authentic and vice versa. There seems to be little consensus as to the exact constructs that make up authentic leadership, authentic leadership development, and authentic followership. Consequently, this leads to significant measurement issues and levels of analysis issues. Finally, as theorists work at setting up more elaborate research protocols, the distance between their research and practitioner accessibility seems ever greater (see George [2003] for a good practitioner application of authentic leadership).

The Ethical Leader as Spiritual Mentor to Followers, Clients, and Constituents

While spiritual leadership as a school of thought only emerged in 2003, it has strong precedents in the servant leadership tradition (Greenleaf 1977) and Kohlbergian ethics (1981).

The spiritual-servant leadership philosophy is an ancient one that is clearly recognizable in the writings of great humanitarians such as Lao-Tzu and Jesus. The basic idea is that the notion that the people are to serve the king, prince, or potentate is backward and fundamentally wrong; it is the leader who is privileged to serve the people. Furthermore, it is the improvement in well-being of the people, their empowerment, and the concomitant humility of the leader that is the measure of leadership greatness. Greenleaf continues to be highly referenced and also the center of significant research (e.g., Graham 1991; Russell and Stone 2002; Sendjaya, Sarros, and Santora 2008). Greenleaf Centers have an extensive following and are found not only in the United States but also in the UK, Europe, and Asia. They promote the servant leadership philosophy, which is particularly popular in the nonprofit community.

Kohlberg established three levels of moral development that have been used by many leadership ethicists. Level 1 is preconventional and includes the obedience and punishment orientation (how can I avoid punishment?), and self-interest orientation (what's in it for me?) of those with immature or undeveloped moral compasses. The second level is the conventional, which includes the conformity stage (instinctively following social norms) and the authority and social-order-maintaining orientation (a law-and-order morality). The highest level is the postconventional, which includes the social-contract orientation (demonstrated in democratic state constitutions and capitalistic legal instruments), and the ultimate universal ethical principles stage (following one's own principled conscience). These levels are relatively easily transferred to the leadership process, as the section on ethical consciousness and conscientiousness below will illustrate. This type of layered intellectual framework undergirds the leader exemplar literature in the public sector (e.g., Cooper 1990; Cooper and Wright 1992; Pfiffner 2003; Callahan 2006; Rugeley and Van Wart 2006).

Although the spiritual leadership movement has a very strong normative thrust, it has taken a more empirical approach than servant leadership, which tends to eschew the atomization of its propositions for concrete testing (see Liden et al. [2008] for a recent exception). Key proponents of spiritual leadership are Louis Fry and his colleagues (e.g., Fry 2003; Fry, Vitucci and Cedillo 2005).

The overall thrust of spiritual leaders is that the authority of action comes from those being assisted, especially those affected outside the organization. It takes a broader view of the stakeholder universe, not limited to direct clients and customers, or even to humans. Even the great scientist Einstein urged "try not to become a man of success, but rather try to become a man of value" and that "only a life lived for others is a life worthwhile."

Four major propositions can be distilled from the researchers in this area. First, it is firmly established on the integrity model above, but a core value not necessarily included in other perspectives is the need for leader humility. This can be argued to be potentially conflicting with the authentic leadership model emphasizing self-confidence, or largely ignored by the moral manager approach. It also advocates altruistic love and "calling" as explicit values. In the public sector literature there is a growing literature on the importance of public service motivation (Perry 1996, 1997; Alonso and Lewis 2001; Moynihan and Pandey 2007). In other leadership perspectives, these concepts tend to be wrapped in less evocative terms such as commitment and dedication. Second, spiritual leaders always put the needs of subordinates and external constituents first. A supervisor might break up his own work pattern to assist a subordinate who was having trouble, or an intake worker may take more time on a particularly desperate client even though pressed for time herself. This also means the developmental role of the leader is primary as it is in superleadership. It also implies a strong empowerment thrust. Third, spiritual leaders engage in emotional labor and emotional healing. Emotional labor is the act of showing sensitivity, empathy, and compassion for others. Emotional labor is most extensive when negative events occur, such as disasters, death, and great suffering. Although emotional labor occurs with subordinates and other organizational members, the perspective recognizes that in some occupations, such as social workers, emergency workers, and teachers, there are far greater expectations that leaders will exhibit emotional labor with clients (Gardner, Fischer, and Hunt 2009; Newman, Guy, and Mastracci 2009). Finally, spiritual leadership emphasizes end results strongly in the community and environment. From this perspective, the Kohlbergian notion of integrating increasingly broad consciousness in terms of both space and time is imperative for the spiritual leader who is deeply aware of and concerned for the needs of humanity and the environment.

One of the strengths of spiritual leadership is that it taps directly into the need to assist and make a difference. Martin Luther King said that an individual has not started living until he can rise above the narrow confines of his individualistic concerns to the broader concerns of all humanity. While social scientists often eschew feelings that have religious overtones, such sentiments are so powerful that they sometimes lead people to risk their lives or change their vocations. Spiritual (or servant) leadership sets up a model that analyzes leaders of compassion and calling, and implicitly encourages all leaders to move closer to a spiritual model. For example, after a long period of corporate greed and scandal, it is easy to see that many business organizations are trying to adopt a more humanitarian and "green" perspective represented in the rise of interest in consciously ethical constructs such as corporate social responsibility and the triple bottom line—people, planet, and profit. However, not only is spiritual leadership in its various forms a universalistic model, it has great potential to be a situational model as well. Some professions are fundamentally more open than others to a servant leadership model, especially in the nonprofit and public sectors. Ironically, another example is the contemporary military. While conventional warfare encourages leadership that is heroic, regimented, and rugged, the nation-building activities that have been increasingly thrust on the military mean that soldiers and their supervisors must attempt to show compassion for the population, assist in community projects, and demonstrate concern for long-term sustainability.

A challenge of servant and spiritual leadership is its abstraction from normal organizational authorization procedures and functions. In more recent iterations, it includes the skill of possessing the knowledge of the organization and tasks at hand so as to be in a position to effectively support others. Another challenge involves deciding whether it is a normative or empirical approach, and whether the ideal methods are prescriptive or descriptive. There is some confusion about whether a more spiritual approach does, or needs to, make a difference to bottom-line efficiency and results, or whether it is a desirable end result in and of itself. Finally, sometimes there is very strong resistance to the normative thrust of servant leadership in the private sector where the market can be seen as the primary source of wisdom, and the concerns of shareholders and owners are paramount to the success of capitalism (à la Milton Friedman 1970). Some managerialist and legalistic leadership approaches in the public sector have a much less aggressive form of resistance to such a religiously based approach.

The Ethical Leader as a Transforming Agent of Change for the Common Good

From the beginnings of the transformational and charismatic leadership renaissance in the late 1970s, major intellectual efforts were made to distinguish change-oriented and bigger-than-life leaders driven primarily by personal ego or "personalized" concerns from those driven by "socialized" concerns. Distinctions between a transformational Mahatma Gandhi and a pseudotransformational Adolf Hitler are important (Bass and Steidlmeier 1999). For example, although Burns (1978) has noted that transformational leaders as a class are concerned about change whether for good or ill, or out of personal ambition or desire to do good, he has also noted that the great ones are "transforming" leaders. Transforming leaders are those who understand the need for change emanating from the people, who clarify those needs, and are able to create wholesome long-term change that benefits society. Such leaders can transcend (or at least balance) their personal needs for fame and success with the good of the community. Ultimately, transforming leaders raise the morality of the people in Burns's perspective. Although his political perspective was heavily weighted toward political processes in which transformational change can be not only transforming but also manipulative for personal aggrandizement and reactionary based on demagoguery, it is easy to see how this can be translated into private and public organizational settings as well. Similarly, in the charismatic literature, Conger (1989) and others have noted the importance of using personal power for good or socialized ends, rather than a personalized power orientation (Kanungo 2001; Parry and Proctor-Thomson 2002). The tools and characteristics of transforming leaders include gathering information from a wide variety of sources including clients and customers, stimulating wholesome discussion about the ideals of the organization relative to its need to survive and grow, molding a shared vision that is not based solely on the beliefs of a single executive, and ensuring that the change focuses on long-term benefits rather than short-term gains.

These themes have been robustly discussed and supported in the leadership literature with a public sector focus. Heifetz's adaptive leadership model (1994) focuses on the need of leaders to focus on the hard work of consensus building in tackling complex contemporary problems. He distinguishes between routine technical problems, which are handled through expertise, and adaptive problems, such as crime, poverty, and educational reform, which require innovative and value-laden approaches. Adaptive problems require diagnosing the situation in light of the values involved and avoiding executive-dominated solutions, finding ways to moderate the inherently stressful change process, staying focused on the relevant issues, and ensuring that the responsibility for problems rests on all primary stakeholders, not just executives. Similarly Bryson and Crosby (1992) have helped public sector leaders focus their strategic planning on community-based needs rather than on more competitively oriented goals, which tend to dominate private sector perspectives. It is only by staying squarely focused on the needs of the community that the public agencies retain trust (Carnevale 1995) and ultimately have a legitimate substantive role at the policy table (Terry 1995) as "conservators" of the public good.

A strength of this perspective is that there is no doubt that change is a major, and frequently critical, function of leaders, especially executives. Transforming leadership theory integrates managerial and normative values into a single model. Change is a heady process that can be negatively affected by ambition, posturing, image management, excessive urges to compete and dominate, egotistic desires to implement one's own vision, thirst for short-term gains, and so forth. Transforming leadership is a model that requires leaders to subordinate their own needs and desires to those of the organization and affected community. Additionally, the whole idea of transforming leadership is particularly suitable to the public sector, given its common good and social focus rather than the profit-oriented and individual focus that is more common to the private sector.

A variety of potential weaknesses can also be posited. First, whenever theories marry descriptive and normative perspectives, the blend is always a bit complex and arbitrary. Good versus bad change and moral motives versus immoral ones are easy to detect only in the extremes. Further, correctness in leadership when measured in historical terms is often as much tempered by success as by morality. The Spanish "liberation" of Mexicans by Cortez from the "dictatorship" of Montezuma and "native" religions would be a different story if Cortez had been killed at his Veracruz landing site, and the emperor had been half as crafty as the conqueror. Second, transforming leadership is still heroic to the degree that it casts change as the primary function of leaders and suggests that other leadership functions are essentially inconsequential management details. Critics can argue that this is like saying that Woodrow Wilson's role in creating the defunct League of Nations was transforming, even though he failed to get his own country, the United States, to join. That is, his idea was grand and uplifting but ultimately the management of the process was a failure. Generals and CEOs are also all too aware that battle plans or product launches require excellent execution—that is, management—for success. A related point is that many who might be considered leaders do not have a mandate or need for transforming change. Nonexecutives and executives in stable environments have little direct use of transforming leadership theory.

In summary, an ethical perspective on leadership is unified in the sense that leaders are supposed to take great stock of their organizational, professional, and societal communities, and integrate the common good in process and product. Both the means and the ends of success are put in a social context that emphasizes equity and sustainability. Undergirding all ethical approaches is the personal integrity of those involved in the leadership process. The honesty, trustworthiness, and fairness of individuals is the foundation of an ethical perspective. However, the variation in the emphasis of different ethical theories is nontrivial. Moral management concentrates on ensuring that legal rules and organizational strictures are carried out. Lax organizational cultures, especially in the fishbowl public sector, can lead to scandals, public resentment, legislative investigations, demoralization of employees, and other bureaupathologies. The "high road" approach to moral management also ensures that the more discretionary elements of decision making are enhanced through professional education. Authentic leaders are those who know themselves so well that their ability to be self-regulating, resilient, optimistic, nondefensive, and other-oriented is enhanced as they manage leadership processes. Stemming from their centeredness, authentic leaders tend to exude both wisdom and an innately positive spirit. Servant or spiritual leaders are extremely other-oriented. They are motivated by heartfelt empathy, concern, and compassion for those who entrust the leadership role to them. Helping others is not a problem to be dealt with for the servant leader, it is the very purpose of leadership. While Mother Teresa was an extreme example of a servant leader, it is easy to find more prosaic examples in leaders and managers in nonprofits and a wide variety of social-work agencies. Transforming leadership focuses on the important business of change, integrating a socialized perspective into the organizational and social evolution process. Unlike servant leadership, transforming leaders tend to focus on processes rather than individual people. Transforming leaders are facilitators of wholesome change, and use their skills to ensure that the need for change does not lead to either authoritarian solutions or chaotic abandonment of wicked social or organizational problems. Exhibit 6.2 summarizes the differences in the major approaches to ethical leadership discussed. Of course the ideal ethical leader could incorporate all these styles all the time. In reality, leaders have ethical preferences and the needs of the ethical landscape will vary significantly, making the distinctions in the various perspectives useful for analytic purposes.

GENERIC LEADERSHIP MODEL BASED ON CONSCIOUSNESS AND CONSCIENTIOUSNESS

Leadership styles are based on the level of social consciousness, self-discipline, and courage of the leader, ranging from unethical to exemplary (Van Wart 1998a).

The most common symptom of leaders with *unethical styles* is that they use their positions for their personal benefit or for a special group at the expense of others. Also, unethical leaders may use their positions and power to promote the interests of friends at the expense of more qualified people or to seek retribution against those who cross them. Less egregious but still unethical are those leaders who simply use their positions as platforms for ego boosting rather than accomplishing good; such leaders tend to hoard all the credit for accomplishments. Moreover, it is generally considered unethical when leaders ignore major responsibilities or decisions that they think may reflect poorly on themselves or because they are simply sloppy or lazy.

Many leaders are *ethically neutral* in their style. They may be unaware of subtle ethical issues, or if they are aware, fail to take the time to reflect on them. A senior manager may not know, because he is not receptive to receiving information about his supervisors, that one of them frequently uses a demeaning style with employees. Or the senior manager may know about the problem but ignore it. Sometimes managers pride themselves on the technical and "neutral" execution of their duties. What are the authoritative guidelines and bureaucratically assigned duties? Managers operating in this mode generally try to emphasize the procedural nature of work, the rules, and technical fairness. Ethics, apart from rule breaking, is not a part of their job. Thus, ethically neutral leaders can range from those who are unresponsive or unaware of moderate ethical issues to those who attempt to structure and conceive of their work as procedural and essentially value free. Ethically neutral leaders are themselves free of improper behavior, but they do not actively encourage an ethical climate.

Exhibit 6.2

Summary of Value-Based Theories (emphasizing distinct focus)

Type of ethical leadership	Alternative names	Major concern	Major emphases	Proponents of particular type
Moral management	Duty approach, ethics training, the low-road approach	• Concern for organizational and social standards	• Ethical compliance with organizational or legal mandates, for example, codes of conduct, professional standards	Legislative bodies; Rohr; Trevino
Authentic leadership	Positive leadership	• Concern for one's own principles and values • Concern for self-regulation ("positive" leadership) leading to confidence, optimism, resilience, and so forth	• Self-awareness • Self-improvement • Open to feedback; non-defensive • "Positive" influences on followers	Avolio and Gardner; Fairholm; Argyris; Covey
Spiritual leadership	Servant leadership, affective leadership, exemplar leadership	• Concern for others (followers or clients): • Concern for the community and environment	• Care and compassion • Hope, faith, and spiritual well-being • Work as a "calling"; emotional labor • Sustainability	Greenleaf; Newman and Guy; Fry; Cooper and Hart
Transforming leadership	Adaptive leadership	• Concern for making wholesome change	• Shared organizational or community vision • Organizational or community adaptation • Intellectual stimulation to improve organization or community	Burns; Bass; Heifetz; Bryson and Crosby; Carnevale

Note: All types assume personal integrity as a requisite foundation for moral action.

The analysis of ethical leadership is nearly as old as philosophy itself. Most of Aristotle's work on ethics is set in a leadership context (Aristotle 1953). His virtue-based perspective of ethics emphasizes the rational process that leaders exercise. People of good character—*ethical leaders*—engage in three primary practices. First, people of good character recognize ethical issues. They understand that many values invariably compete in social settings, and that leaders are often the arbiters of who gets what in terms of allocating values. For example, a seemingly simple decision about extending hours has many ramifications. What will be the effect on the employees, the clients, the quality of work, the manager's own ability to coordinate the hours and get people to staff less desirable times, the cost of operations, and so forth? Second, ethical leaders take the time to reflect on issues that often pit one important value against another. Consider the leader evaluating a problem supervisor: A demeaning supervisor is also extremely hardworking, organized, and informed. He is himself the best worker, and he leads the most productive unit. Nonetheless, the ethical conundrum is that leaders should not put down or degrade their subordinates and clutch all power to themselves in the name of the organization. Third, ethical leaders find ways to integrate the collective good into appropriate decisions. Using the previous example, changing the supervisor's style, without diminishing productivity or the supervisor's substantial contributions, is not an easy task. Integrating appropriate but differing sets of values may mean hard work for the ethical leader. It may also mean finding workable compromises that optimize several important values.

A number of theorists have been interested in identifying not only ethical leaders but also highly ethical, or *exemplary*, leaders (Cooper and Wright 1992; Hart 1992). What characterizes the person of high character? This is an especially important question for public sector leadership because stewardship of the public good is inherently a social process and often very challenging to enact. Two additional elements are generally articulated: contribution and courage.

Making a substantial contribution to a group, organization, community, or system takes sustained hard work, perseverance, and the involvement of many people, which in turn requires trust, empathy, and nurturance. One type of substantial contribution might be the accomplishment of a specific project or good work of some magnitude. A city library director might seek authorization for and implement expanded auxiliary services such as after-school programs in a disadvantaged area, despite its lack of popularity with a policy board dominated by wealthier neighborhoods. A second type of substantial contribution involves raising the moral consciousness of followers or the community. Burns (1978) asserts that it is the responsibility of political leaders to actively guide the transformation of society by stressing justice, liberty, and equality. Leaders themselves should be transformed by the process so that their morality also ascends to a higher, more socialized level. In a similar vein, Heifetz (1994) proposes a facilitative role for leaders in the process of moral consciousness raising. He believes that such leaders articulate the value conflicts of workers, organizations, and communities in rapidly changing environments. Exemplary leaders enable groups to sustain dialogues until coherent decisions can be reached that benefit all in win–win solutions. Leaders do not select the answers or make decisions occur; leaders allow answers and decisions to emerge by mobilizing people to tackle the tough issues. This means that they must bring attention to the critical issues, foster honest and candid discussion, manage competing perspectives, and facilitate the decision-making process in a timely way.

The final or highest level of exemplary leadership is often perceived as the willingness to make sacrifices for the common good and/or to show uncommon courage. David K. Hart (1992) discusses such leaders as they confront moral episodes. Sacrifice involves denying oneself commodities that are generally valued, in order to enhance the welfare of others or the common good. Leaders who sacrifice may give extraordinary time, do without financial emoluments, pass up career advancement, or forsake prestige as a part of their passion to serve others. The best leaders may be those who are able to make sacrifices but nonetheless feel joy about the opportunity to help (DePree 1989; Block 1993). Greenleaf (1977) calls these "servant leaders," who are concerned about empathy, development of others, healing, openness, equality, listening, and unconditional acceptance of others. When they act, they do so with quiet persuasion that places a high threshold on inclusion. They avoid the unequal power paradigm typical in hierarchical organizations and instead use the *primus inter pares* (first among equals) paradigm (Greenleaf 1977, 61–62). Indeed, they assert that the hierarchical model of leadership is often damaging to leaders. Some of the challenges "strong" leaders often face are:

- "To be a lone chief atop a pyramid is abnormal and corrupting."
- "A self-protective image of omniscience often evolves from . . . warped and filtered communication."
- "Those persons who are atop the pyramids often suffer from a very real loneliness."
- " . . . in too many cases the demands of the office destroy these [leaders'] creativity long before they leave office."
- "Being in the top position prevents leadership by persuasion because the single chief holds too much power."
- "In the end the chief becomes a performer, not a natural person, and essential creative powers diminish."
- "[A single chief] nourishes the notion among able people that one must be boss to be effective. And it sanctions, in a conspicuous way, a pernicious and petty status-striving that corrupts everyone." (Greenleaf 1977, 63–64)

However, some leaders are willing to make exceptional and painful sacrifices or decisions that require great courage. Making a tough decision may lead to social stigmatization. Revealing unpleasant truths about powerful people, interests, or groups may result in the loss of a job or even the ruin of a career. In chapter 11 (Exhibit 11.4 on page 282), the case of Marie Ragghianti provides an example of extreme courage. She suffered the loss of her patron, job, and career in her pursuit of the public good. While most leaders do not experience many of these moments, when they do, opportunities for greatness or conspicuous mediocrity and/or failure emerge. Yet, sometimes a decision is not so much

Exhibit 6.3

A Model of Ethical and Exemplary Leadership

The Person of GOOD Character Will . . .

1. Recognize ethical issues

2. Reflect on ethical issues

3. Integrate the collective good into appropriate decisions

The Person of HIGH Character Will Also . . .

4. Make a substantial contribution

   a. Carry out a project or good work, and /or

   b. Increase the moral awareness of the community

OR

5. Exhibit sacrifices or courage for the common moral good

   a. Deny oneself for the common good

   b. Suffer abuse for the common good

dangerous to one's career as so enormous and controversial that it would be far less trouble simply to ignore it. The courage of such decisions can result in ethical greatness if the leader's ethical integrity is mature. For example, Thomas Jefferson despised executive privilege but nonetheless doubled the size of the country with a unilateral executive order when he made the Louisiana Purchase in 1803, an act nearly as defining as the American Revolution itself. For a general model of ethical leadership that differentiates good and exemplary characteristics, see Exhibit 6.3.

Models of ethical leadership are generally proposed as universal theories, although they differ significantly from private sector settings, which have more moral discretion about social responsibilities as opposed to basic corporate/agency responsibilities. An important exception may be the highest level of exemplary leadership, which requires acts of extraordinary courage or sacrifice. Such challenges/opportunities are relatively uncommon and situationally specific.

Exhibit 6.4

Causal-Chain Model Implicit in an Ethics-Based Approach to Leadership Studies

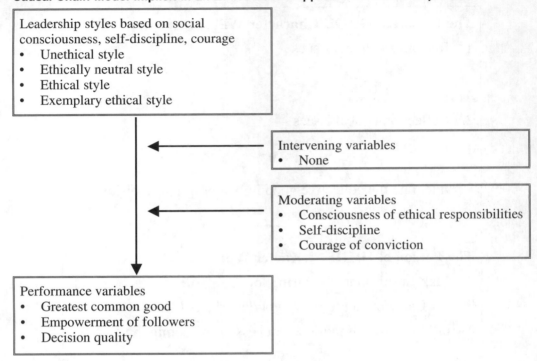

The quality of ethical leadership is moderated by three factors. First, how conscious are leaders of ethical issues and how active are such leaders in reflecting on them? This cognitive element must be joined with a caring ethic that motivates leaders to integrate competing communal values in wholesome ways. Second, ethical leaders are not occasionally ethical; they are constant in practicing ethical reflection. This self-discipline is even more important for people aspiring to be of high character. Great self-discipline is normally required to accomplish important moral projects or increase the moral awareness of the community. Third, the degree of courage that a leader has affects his/her ability and courage to make substantial personal sacrifices and potential administrative martyrdom.

The performance variables for ethical leadership are dissimilar to other approaches that generally emphasize efficiency of production or follower satisfaction. Various theorists in this general approach propose different goals, but increasing the common good and the empowerment of followers are the most frequent. These goals contrast especially with the power-based approach to leadership. Furthermore, ethics-based approaches implicitly emphasize the quality of decision making as demonstrated by the more thoughtful, comprehensive methods they recommend (Cooper 1990). See Exhibit 6.4 for the implicit causal chain for ethics-based approaches.

CONCLUSION

Because it takes such a different path than most other approaches, ethics-based leadership has a number of strengths. For example, it prominently raises the question: For whom is leadership exercised? *In this approach, the context of leadership as a social phenomenon to enhance the common good must be the first consideration.* Other approaches with their more instrumental perspective may emphasize productivity, success, or influence, but this can allow some leaders to exercise excessive narcissism in the name of efficiency or control. Indeed, in many business contexts leaders are taught that social responsibilities are constraints to be avoided or ignored (Friedman 1970; Henry 2003, 54). Often, other approaches add an ethical component, but it generally seems to be a codicil to the theory. Ethics-based leadership is also inspiring because of the examples it cites and the challenges it lays out. Theoretically, ethics-based leadership provides valuable insights and recommendations with respect to the courage needed and the nature of leader character. One major weakness is that it offers little insight into the more pragmatic aspects of leadership. Major ethical conundrums are, hopefully, relatively rare in a manager's routine. Moreover, ethics-based leadership frequently has an abstract, philosophical quality. This is partly a result of its intellectual heritage and partly due to the highly generalized normative base that it advocates. Yet for any of its perceived shortcomings, ethical leadership is certainly foremost in the minds of followers who routinely place trust, integrity, and similar concepts at the top of their preferences with respect to leaders, and is essential in public and nonprofit sector settings in which stewardship is inevitably considered fundamental to the right to serve.

Specialized Approaches to Leadership: Power, Culture, Diversity, and Gender

Leadership is such a complex phenomenon that the transactional and transformational approaches do not fully include many significant perspectives. Four specialized approaches have also added considerably to our understanding of leadership, and they are discussed here. The power approach to leadership studies has emphasized the role and mechanisms of influence and has focused almost exclusively on follower compliance. The world culture approach to leadership research examines the effects of world cultures on perceptions about what constitutes ideal behaviors and how those differing perceptions sometimes complement and sometimes clash. The subculture and diversity leadership research examines the effects of dealing not only with many different world cultures in single organizations but also with the challenges and opportunities of leaders and organizations in harnessing the diversity created in race, age, nationality, religion, and so forth. The gender approach examines the role of a particular group in the diversity universe, women, and asks whether they have a distinctive style, and how women can be better represented in senior leadership positions.

The four approaches to leadership have a particularly focused perspective. All of them limit the types of performance variables on which they focus. The power approach focuses primarily on leader influence, the world culture approach focuses on conformance to social context, the diversity perspective emphasizes broad inclusion of individuals with different life experiences, and the gender studies approach to leadership uses women or feminine stereotypic characteristics as their limiting factor.

THE POWER APPROACH TO LEADERSHIP

Power and leadership are not synonyms, and their research involves different emphases. Nonetheless they invariably intertwine. Power has traditionally been defined as the *potential* to influence others. Much of the power literature examines the major sources of power. One important definition of leadership has been the *ability* to influence followers and others. When that definition is used, leadership is the effective use of various types of power—which implies different leader styles—to influence others.

It should be immediately apparent that the power approach is essentially nonnormative, as opposed to the ethics-based approaches examined in the preceding chapter, which are self-consciously normative. Therefore, the power literature examines how influence is built up and lost, not the social value of how it is used. As a fact of life and a crucial component of applied leadership, the study of influence tactics is important to improve one's technical ability and leadership sway (see chapter 12 for specific influence tactics). On the other hand, as has been noted before, excessive attraction to the acquisition of power can be corrupting, often leading either to personalism (an approach in which all activities are primarily evaluated on their positive or negative effect on the leader) or the imposition of a narrow vision on less-powerful followers. The extraordinary variance in the use and corruption of power can be seen in two World War II leaders, Franklin Delano Roosevelt and Adolf Hitler. Both leaders relished power and brandished it freely. However, Roosevelt was both constrained by a democratic system of governance and motivated by a socialized sense of justice. Hitler, although originally democratically elected, eradicated all democratic constraints to his power, and was motivated by a racist vision for Germany and the world.

Different analyses of power imply different leadership styles. The most prominent analysis of power, by French and Raven (1959), is the one that will be used for the prototype here. They discuss five sources of power: coercive, reward, legitimate, referent, and expert. Coercive power is the ability to punish and use negative sanctions. It can include physical force, resource deprivation, or psychological reprimands. The use of coercive power implies a *forceful or highly directive style.* The power to reward includes praise and recognition, raises, promotions, better assignments, desirable work schedules, sought-after travel and training, and the like. It implies a *remunerative style* based on exchange and bargaining. Legitimate power stems from either holding an authorized position in a formal sense or being part of a tradition in an informal sense. According to Hinkin and Schriesheim (1989), legitimate power is useful in making people aware of their commitments and responsibilities. Those exercising legitimate power use accepted values, agreed-upon norms, or customary symbols to effect member compliance and commitment. The related style of leadership is *symbolic and emotive.* A different but related source of power that is prevalent in public bureaucracies is referent power. Those with expert power have knowledge about subjects (which is content-based), knowledge about processes and past practice, or detailed knowledge about human and physical resources needed to accomplish work. The new boss of an administrative unit may be powerful because of his/her content expertise, but may have to defer to the process and resource knowledge of their direct staff for some time. Those with a *knowledge-based leadership style* tend to analyze, clarify, and inform. Finally, referent power is based on the personal appeal and demeanor of the leader. Those with referent power have the ability to make people feel good, liked, or accepted based on the attractiveness of their character. The related style is *personality based.*

Extreme and excessive use of a source of power or poor use of the implied styles lead to commonly recognized leadership pathologies (Manz and Sims 1989). The leader who relies too much on coercion generally engages in overmanagement or micromanagement and is labeled a bully, dictator, or strongman. The leader who relies too much on reward and exchange can become manipulative or a mere "transactor." An excess of legitimate power may lead to a rigid, tradition-bound, or reactive leader. An excessive reliance on knowledge can lead to either information hoarding or an unproductive disposition toward analysis rather than action. Those who have strong referent power and are perceived as charismatic often fall under their own spell, and, consequently, act as if the organization were an extension of themselves that is largely designed for their benefit. Charismatic leaders are also the most likely to make unwise radical changes.

Many factors intervene regarding the type of power and style used. The leader's personality and natural strengths in using various types of power are key factors. People vary enormously in the degree to which they are analytic, sociable, dominant, persuasive, and so on. In addition to being adept at using a type of power, a leader must also be willing to use it. A leader who has the potential to act firmly under unusual circumstances but fails to do so when actually called upon is not exercising his/her capacity. The followers also affect the type of power and style used. For example, there was a general trend in the second half of the twentieth century for workers to expect less use of a forceful style and more use of a knowledge-based style. However, newly inducted followers or followers in crisis may expect the leader to "take charge." Finally, the system itself has a sizable impact on the selection of power types and style. Some organizations—especially those in the private sector—provide leaders with more expansive position power with regard to reward and coercion. Other organizations—especially those in the public sector—provide leaders with greater legitimate power and select those with expertise to fulfill duly authorized mandates.

The effectiveness of leaders in using these styles is moderated by their ability to use related influence tactics. A forceful style relies on pressure tactics such as monitoring, hints, or warnings, as well as occasional following up with corrective or sanctioning behavior. A remunerative style relies on finding out what rewards are available and attractive and on negotiating agreements or plans about what is to be accomplished. A symbolic style reminds followers of one's own legitimate base and the legitimate needs of the group. It often uses normative or emotional appeals for group achievement. A knowledge-based style uses rational tactics such as the display of facts, careful reasoning, and structured arguments as well as references to one's own expertise. A personal style tends to use ingratiation tactics initially, in which the leader builds up bonds of affiliation, a reservoir of acts of kindness or favors (sometimes called "chits"), or trust in the leader. This style subsequently tends to use personal appeal tactics based on the interest of the follower to satisfy someone they admire, like, feel indebted to, and/or respect. Consultative tactics can be used with all styles, but are particularly critical with remunerative and personal styles of leadership. For more important influence targets, such as increasing productivity by 5 percent, a leader would want to use as many influence tactics as possible.

All tactics can be used appropriately or inappropriately, depending on the context, purpose of the influence attempt, and execution. For example, it is certainly important to build up social bonds with employees and make appropriate accommodations for their unique situations. However, consistently using ingratiation tactics with some employees and not others is fundamentally unfair and creates an out-group. Using ingratiation (such as favors) because of an expectation of personal payback is also inappropriate. In this connection, while leaders make work-related accommodations—favors—for subordinates as a give-and-take part of the process of managing on the organization's behalf, some leaders tacitly demand greater *personal* loyalty rather than *organizational* loyalty.

The performance variable in the power approach is related to the leader's influence with followers. A leader who uses power and influence tactics effectively will succeed in increasing followers' agreement with the decisions or goals of leaders and organizations. Three levels of influence can be discerned between the leader (agent) and follower (target).

> The term *commitment* describes an outcome in which the target person internally agrees with a decision or request from the agent and makes a great effort to carry out the request or implement the decision effectively. . . . The term *compliance* describes an outcome in which the target is willing to do what the agent asks but is apathetic rather than enthusiastic about it and will make only minimal effort. . . . The term *resistance* describes an outcome in which the target person is opposed to the proposal or request, rather than merely indifferent about it, and actively tries to avoid carrying it out. (Yukl 2002, 143)

See Exhibit 7.1 for an illustration of the leadership model implied by the power approach.

The strengths of the power approach stem largely from the utility of looking at the mechanics of influence. Just how do some leaders become so powerful while others fail to be perceived as powerful, although they occupy the same type of position? The "neutral" approach generally adopted in the power literature is akin to the scientific approach of discovering facts and explaining phenomena before judging their merit, utility, or interpretation. On the other hand, there has been a good deal of popular disapproval of the power literature because of its nonnormative approach to leadership. Power becomes corruption so easily and influence becomes manipulation so effortlessly that it is dangerous, critics argue, to study leadership without always including the ethical responsibilities.

WORLD CULTURES AND LEADERSHIP

Culture is the learned and shared customs, beliefs, and values of a people or group (Kluckhohn and Strodtbeck 1961). Customs can include language and laws; beliefs can include religion and underlying assumptions about technology and education; and values can include preferences for the way society is organized and the priorities of the people. Culture ultimately constitutes a way of life. It is a critical component in the study of leadership because of the distinctly different perceptions about what to do, what values to emphasize, and how leaders and followers should interact (Hodgetts, Luthans, and Doh 2006). Consider the difference between Scandinavian ideals of equality and participation stemming from centuries of stability, versus the Middle Eastern perspective that leaders must first survive to lead, given a hundred years of turmoil and a longer history of strife

Exhibit 7.1

Power Approach to Leadership Causal Chain

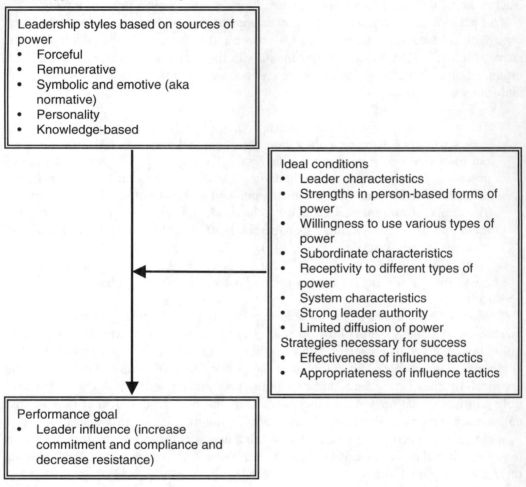

Leadership styles based on sources of power
- Forceful
- Remunerative
- Symbolic and emotive (aka normative)
- Personality
- Knowledge-based

Ideal conditions
- Leader characteristics
- Strengths in person-based forms of power
- Willingness to use various types of power
- Subordinate characteristics
- Receptivity to different types of power
- System characteristics
- Strong leader authority
- Limited diffusion of power

Strategies necessary for success
- Effectiveness of influence tactics
- Appropriateness of influence tactics

Performance goal
- Leader influence (increase commitment and compliance and decrease resistance)

Source: Based on French and Raven's analysis.

and subjugation by colonial and local powers. Culture itself is a conglomerate of ideas in which there is frequent overlap and also disagreement; the discussion here is where the research consensus is strong.

Culture varies because of peoples' and groups' different experiences. The most broadly defined world culture groups are determined by social, political, economic, and historic factors. Powerful social factors include language and religion. Language is a potent factor because of the ability to transmit ideas directly and the easy opportunities for confusion when language is not shared. The example of Canada demonstrates the importance of language to culture. Despite hundreds of years of integration, French Canadians eventually insisted on true bilingualism first in Quebec and then in all of Canada, starting in the 1960s (Pelletier 1966). A second important social factor is religion and one's beliefs about creation and the authoritative sources of right and wrong behavior. Even in the twentieth century, Europe has experienced bitter wars of religion in Ireland and the former Yugoslavia.

Political systems stamp a shared belief system on a people over time, and these can have an important effect on nonpolitical notions of leadership as well. Common classifications (pure types) of political systems are hereditary, authoritarian, ecclesiastic, democratic, and elitist-oligarchic. Hereditary systems are based on familial ties in ruling or leadership; some interesting modern examples of hereditary leadership come from the Kims (Il-sung and Jong-Il) of Korea, the Sauds of Saudi Arabia, and the Duvaliers (informally known as Papa Doc and Baby Doc) in Haiti. Heredity can play a significant factor even in systems that officially are antiaristocratic such as the Kennedys and Bushes in the United States demonstrate. Authoritarian states are those run by a single strong leader who has seized power, with or without the blessing of a majority of the people, as has occurred in Cuba, many African nations, and fascist Germany. Relatively pure examples of ecclesiastic states that assert that religion has primacy in the running of the state are not common but they do exist in Iran and the Vatican, and formerly existed in Tibet. Modern democratic systems were strongly proposed and initiated in enlightened Europe and America in the eighteenth century, expanded in the nineteenth century, and dominated the world belief system after World War II. Nonetheless, many systems are democratic in name only and are in reality elitist-oligarchic systems. Examples of elitist-oligarchic systems include most of the former and current communist countries when particularly strong figures such as Stalin and Mao were not in power, and countries with long, single-party rule as was true in Mexico and Japan for many decades.

Economic systems have an immense effect on a culture over time. Economic systems can vary by their resource base, such as hunting/herding (now rare, of course), agricultural, industrial, service, and financial. Economic systems also vary by the intensity of the role of the state, for example, capitalist, socialist, and command. Although significant shifts in cultures normally take hundreds of years, the changes in the Russian and Chinese cultures by the imposition of different politicoeconomic systems were impressive. Russian (Holzer and Illiash 2009) and Chinese society (Pittinsky and Zhu 2005) formerly embraced extreme power distributions, enormous gender inequality, and were little involved in future and social planning. Today it is expected that power will be more equitably distributed regardless of the reality. Gender equality is far more balanced, and social and family planning is a strong expectation, especially in China.

Although less of an influence in the short term, historical factors can have a tremendous influence over the longer term as cultures have a history of success or failure affecting people's outlook in terms of their assertiveness or fatalism. Examples of dramatic changes include the rapacious Vikings of Scandinavia who metamorphosed into the most equality-minded people in the world in a less than a thousand years, and the rugged individualist culture of colonial and frontier America that evolved into a country that is relatively risk averse as demonstrated by the enormity of private and public insurance, and legal penalties for causing any risk whatsoever to others.

The most sophisticated analysis of culture to date, especially with reference to the effects on leadership, is by House and his colleagues (2004). Based on the work by Hall (1976), Hofstede (1980, 2001), Ronen and Shenkar (1985), and others, House and his associates used nine cultural dimensions to define and describe ten global cultures. Their study surveyed 62 countries, 950 organizations, and approximately 17,300 managers. The ten cultures were represented by:

- Anglo—England, Australia, the United States, Canada, white South Africa, and New Zealand
- Eastern Europe—Russia, Greece, Hungary, Albania, Slovenia, Poland, Georgia, and Kazakhstan
- Germanic Europe—Germany, Austria, the Netherlands, and Switzerland
- Nordic Europe—Sweden, Denmark, Finland, and Norway
- Latin Europe—France, Italy, Spain, Portugal, and Israel
- Latin America—Brazil, Mexico, Ecuador, El Salvador, Colombia, Bolivia, Guatemala, Argentina, Costa Rica, and Venezuela
- Confucian Asia—China, Japan, Taiwan, Singapore, and South Korea
- Southern Asia—India, Iran, the Philippines, Indonesia, Malaysia, and Thailand
- Middle East: Turkey, Egypt, Kuwait, Qatar, and Morocco
- Sub-Saharan Africa—black South Africa, Zimbabwe, Namibia, Nigeria, and Zambia

The nine dimensions of culture used by House and associates are as follows:

- Assertiveness refers to the degree that people in a culture are aggressive, determined, or confrontational in their social relationships. Assertive cultures inculcate tough-mindedness. Germanic and East European cultures typify assertive beliefs, while Nordic culture is very low in assertiveness.
- Future orientation refers to cultures whose individuals delay gratification for future benefits, who plan a lot, and who tend to invest for the future. They are less spontaneous. The northern cultures, Nordic and Germanic European, are extremely future oriented. There is much less emphasis on a planning perspective by those from the Middle East, Eastern Europe, and Latin America.
- Gender egalitarianism refers to the degree to which the sexes are treated equally and have political and economic equity. Roles are more defined by sex, especially related to home care and child rearing versus careers outside the home, when gender egalitarianism is low. Strong gender egalitarianism epitomizes Nordic and East European cultures. The world culture that places the least emphasis on gender egalitarianism is the Middle East.
- Humane orientation refers to societies that emphasize altruism, generosity, caring, and kindness to others. Southern Asia with its Buddhist influences and Sub-Saharan Africa put the greatest weight on a humane orientation. The cultures with the least emphasis on a humane orientation are Germanic Europe and Latin Europe.
- In-group collectivism is the degree to which societies emphasize devotion to family and group cohesiveness. Many cultures emphasize family and close-knit groups such

as Confucian Asia, Eastern Europe, Latin America, Southern Asia, and the Middle East. However, Anglo culture, Germanic Europe, and Nordic Europe put far less emphasis on the family with their individualistic ethics.

- Institutional collectivism refers to loyalty or dedication to social or organizational goals. It is in contrast to cultures that emphasize strong individual goals. Those cultures with strong institutional sentiments, such as affiliation to the state and its goals, include Confucian Asia and Nordic Europe. On the other hand, there is much less natural affiliation with the goals of large institutions in Germanic Europe, Latin America, and Latin Europe.
- Performance orientation is demonstrated by the degree to which those who accomplish a lot are provided greater benefits and rewards. It is also seen by the degree to which excellence and the achievement of difficult goals are promoted. High performance cultures comprise the Anglo countries, Confucian Asia, and Germanic Europe. Low performance cultures are made up of Eastern Europe and Latin America. The work of McClelland (1961) in discussing the "achieving society" provides an excellent insight into this emphasis in American culture.
- Power distance refers to the degree to which different levels of status and power are tolerated and encouraged. In the contemporary world, no culture espouses a high power distance the way it was just a century ago in many cultures such as class-conscious Europe and class-rigid Hindi society with its castes. The Middle East still has the highest tolerance of high power distance (Butler 2009). Only one culture today was found to be exceptionally averse to power distance: Nordic culture.
- Uncertainty avoidance refers to how much a culture uses rules, laws, social norms, and procedures to make things more predictable and to reduce risk. This perspective is again common in the northern Germanic and Nordic European cultures while far less typical in the cultures of Eastern Europe, Latin America, and the Middle East.

Of course these findings represent average beliefs of cultures, which are useful in getting a handle on the differences that we experience when we travel, do business, and try to understand political and social behaviors in other countries. Nonetheless, they also represent stereotypes, since the variation within cultures can often be as great as the variation between cultures. While cultural types can be used to understand predilections, it should not be used to predict or judge the preferences and behaviors of individuals. Pride in one's cultural group is often appropriately expressed today in nationalism that is restrained by simultaneous respect as exhibited in the Olympics. Pride in particular cultural traits, such as Germanic European and Confucian Asian performance orientations or African and Anglo humaneness, is not necessarily inappropriate, as long as such pride does not turn into arrogance and disrespect for other cultural traits. Belief that one's culture (as well as racial group or nationality) is inherently superior, either overall or in a particular feature, is called ethnocentrism. In the extreme, it has led to many wars and genocides.

Even more interesting for the study of leadership was the identification by House and his colleagues of six leadership behaviors relative to their cultural groupings. What leadership behaviors were most identified with which culture cluster?

One leadership trait studied was charismatic/value-based leadership, which includes an emphasis on being trustworthy, self-sacrificing, and decisive as well as being visionary, inspirational, and performance oriented. This is an ideal leader characteristic in the cultures of Anglo, Latin America, Latin Europe, and Nordic Europe. At the other end of the spectrum, the Middle East puts the least emphasis on charismatic-value-oriented leadership.

Team-oriented leadership reflects, as its names indicates, the support of collaborative endeavors of teams and groups and includes integrative and diplomatic behaviors. More team-oriented cultures include Confucian Asia and Latin America, while the least team-oriented culture is the Middle East.

Participative leadership emphasizes the involvement of others in broad decision making and implementation. It encompasses nonautocratic behavior. Nordic Europe and Anglo cultures are very participative, while Eastern Europe, Confucian Asia, Southern Asia, and the Middle East are the least participative.

Humane-oriented leadership reflects generosity, consideration, and compassion, as well as sensitivity and modesty. High in humane-oriented leadership are the Anglo and Sub-Saharan African cultures, while Latin and Nordic Europe are lowest in the study by House.

Autonomous leadership emphasizes individualistic behaviors and the uniqueness and independence of leaders. Those cultures that are high in this leadership dimension are assertive cultures that include the East Europeans and the Germanic cluster. Ideal leaders in Latin America, Latin Europe, and Sub-Saharan Africa are least likely to demonstrate this trait, despite and sometimes because of the presence of dictatorial leaders in these regions.

Self-protective leadership refers to ensuring the security and safety of both the leader and the group. It allows for behaviors that are face saving, status conscious, procedural, and, to some degree, self-centered. Nordic, Anglo, and Germanic cultures did not emphasize this leadership style, while Eastern Europe, Latin America, Confucian Asia, Southern Asia, and the Middle East all did emphasize this in ideal leader profiles.

How does the individual or leader operating in, or in contact with, world cultures behave in order to be competent in this regard? Adler and Bartholomew (1992) recommended five cultural competencies. First, leaders need to have a general understanding of the history of other cultures. Does one understand the broad historical differences between, say, an Anglo culture and a Latin American culture forged from a blending of conquest, colonization, and native cultures? Second, leaders need to be sensitive to the different tastes and preferences of other cultures. Does one appreciate the differences between collectivist and noncollectivist societies? Third, leaders need to work well with people of different cultural backgrounds by showing respect for the different histories, customs, and beliefs. Does one consult with different cultural groups to ensure common understanding and mutual goal sharing? Fourth, high levels of cultural competence require communication adaptation by being either bi- or multilingual as well as by using appropriate vernacular within a common language. Fifth, and perhaps most important, leaders need to be scrupulous in demonstrating cultural equality rather than in allowing cultural superiority. For example, asserting to others that the "American way" of approaching things is always superior is sure to raise the resentment of other cultural groups who perceive many right ways of achieving social or organizational ends. Also a part of this competency is the ability to inspire visions that transcend cultural differences and unify groups in common ways that promote cooperation, effectiveness, and ultimately success.

It should also be noted that there is a growing global culture and increased convergence on an ideal global leadership profile, even though world cultures continue to be vibrant. Increased communication, shared technology, widespread entertainment distribution, convergence on a single economic model, increased support for democratic processes and similar trends have amplified the trend toward a global community. Likewise, as reported by House and associates (2004), there is a greater tendency to expect leaders to behave in a similar manner in terms of performance, integrity, communication, facilitation, and so forth, as well as less tolerance for leaders who behave in ways perceived to be dictatorial, ruthless, noncooperative, and the like. See Exhibit 7.2 for the causal chain from a world cultures perspective.

The strength of the world culture approach is that it recognizes real differences and seeks to explain them in as neutral, unbiased, and nonjudgmental a fashion as possible. The study by House and associates is to be especially commended for its scope, thoroughness, and its conscious effort to link notions of leadership to world cultures. It is an essential resource for those seeking a global understanding of world cultures and working in an international context (e.g., the State Department, Peace Corps, Voluntary Service Overseas, or international trade offices), or for intergovernmental organizations such as the United Nations, World Health Organization, and NATO and nongovernmental organizations in the not-for-profit sector such as CARE, Oxfam America, Refugees International, and the Salvation Army. The approach can be expanded to the next logical level, which is the national level, although the distinctions will tend to be smaller and the comparisons more complex. The weakness of the world culture approach is the ease of overgeneralization and the difficulty in concrete application beyond the very general understanding it provides. The study by House and associates had to make many difficult distinctions that border on being arbitrary, such as in what world culture to include the mixed culture of Israel. Further, many of the terms and concepts are unwieldy conglomerates (charismatic/value-oriented) or vague (autonomous and self-protective) as used in their study. Nonetheless, it is by far the most sophisticated and informative study on world culture to date, and overall, a giant leap forward in the study of this important, but inherently amorphous, area.

SUBCULTURES, DIVERSITY, AND LEADERSHIP

So far, the discussion has been about world cultures, but when examined more closely, no culture is entirely homogeneous, and some have less homogeneity than others. Thus, Confucian Asian cultures tend to be more homogeneous than an Anglo culture such as the United States, which is the case study presented here about subcultures and diversity. To be effective in contemporary organizations, leaders need sensitivity, understanding, and knowledge about subcultures and diversity (Adler, Doktor, and Redding 1986; Cox 1993). Conversely, leaders need to be above prejudice, which is a prejudgment about all

Exhibit 7.2

Leadership Based on World Cultures

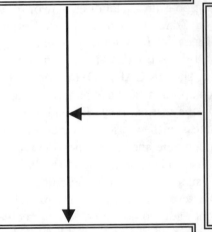

Leadership styles of various world
cultures as a unique blend of six
characteristics and behaviors
- Charismatic/value-based
  characteristics
- Team-oriented characteristics
- Participative characteristics
- Humane-oriented behaviors
- Autonomous leadership behaviors
  (individualistic and independent
  behaviors)
- Self-protective characteristics (for
  both leader and group)
(Nine unique leadership profiles
  identified by House et al. 2004)

World cultures with unique profiles of
shared cultural assumptions. The ten
major ones identified by the Globe Study
project
- Anglo
- Eastern Europe
- Germanic Europe
- Nordic Europe
- Latin Europe
- Latin America
- Confucian Asia
- Southern Asia
- Middle East
- Sub-Saharan Africa

Performance goal
- Conformance to cultural expectations
  of one's group

members of a group based on stereotypes and/or a disregard of facts; it is a suspicion, intolerance, or irrational dislike of other races, creeds, religions, and so forth.

Subcultures are distinct groups that have learned or shared customs, beliefs, or values, and that reside in, but are distinct from, a dominant culture. Subculture groups have similar ways of perceiving the world, identify with similar strengths of their members, or cite similar existential challenges. Consider the enormous differences historically between American Indians and the dominant Anglo culture, in which a collectivist society with very low power distance must interact with an acutely individualistic society in which toleration for power distance is much higher (Warner and Grint 2007). Or consider Confucian and Southern Asian individuals who may demonstrate high levels of deference to authority and guests, which can be construed as insincerity in Western cultures (Slackman 2006). Subcultures can be based on both the differences found in world cultures, as discussed above, and on distinctions found in the human condition, ideological divisions, economic classes within a society, and the like.

In the United States there has been a great deal of legislation to protect the general rights of subgroups and subcultures. In terms of world cultures, extensive protections have been afforded people regardless of race (and color), ethnicity, and national origin. Race is generally based on physical differences, especially with a genetic and acquired characteristic basis. It was formerly based on the major skin color differences combined with the ancient human migrations: Caucasian/white, African/black, Oriental/yellow, and Indian/red. Because the basis for this categorization was based on incomplete science and the tendency to use stereotypes in a demeaning or classist fashion, most of the older categories have been replaced. The U.S. Census provides a good historical metamorphosis. In 1850 the census captured population data for Whites, Coloreds (Free and Slaves), and All Others; in 1880 the census included Whites, Coloreds, Chinese, Japanese, and Civilized Indians; and in 2000 the census included sixteen racial/national/ethnic groups with significant U.S. populations (White, Black, Hispanic, American Indian-Native Alaskan, Chinese, Asian Indian, Filipino, Japanese, Korean, Vietnamese, Native Hawaiian, Guamanian, Samoan, Other Asian, Other Pacific Island, Other Race).

Ethnicity was not formerly a synonym for race, but is often used interchangeably in American contemporary political and popular discourse. Traditionally, ethnicity was used to denote groups with some physical differences—generally minor—from a dominant culture, but emphasizing historical/cultural distinctions. Examples of "ethnic" groups in the late nineteenth century included the Irish and southern Italians whose hair, skin, and linguistic characteristics made them distinct in their first generation or two. By the late twentieth century, the term commonly referred to Hispanic/Latino and non-Hispanic in the United States as captured in census data. However, recent research indicates that Hispanics are well on their way to cultural integration in organizational settings (Romero 2005).

Although the American colonies were founded by Anglo, Nordic, and Germanic sources, by the time of the American Revolution, the Anglo influence was completely dominant and remained so for at least 150 years. Over time most of those with European ancestry became a part of the "melting pot." After World War II the idea of the "salad bowl" metaphor became more prevalent, and although legal integration was enhanced, more emphasis was placed on celebrating differences. Yet over time most groups in the American context tend to blend, and notions of ethnic and even racial differences tend to evolve and lessen, or even disappear altogether.

The introduction of immigrants from different world cultures into the dominant Anglo culture is certainly not the only basis of subcultures. Ideology can create a subculture such as the "counterculture" of the 1950s through the 1970s identified with the early "beat" culture and the later "hippie" culture in which there was a rebellion against perceptions of excessive classism, status consciousness, gender inequality, racism, and other ills in

American society. Subcultures often captured by census and legal protections include age and gender. Consider the differences in generational subcultures (Vanmullem and Honde-ghem 2009) and male-dominated organizations such as law enforcement in which there has frequently been resistance to the promotion of women (Heidensohn 1995). Another important subcultural factor is regionalism in terms of general society (Bass 2008, 983) and organizational culture (Jones 2005).

In organizational settings, the dominant culture represents the dominant customs (e.g., rules, procedures, and practices), values, and beliefs about the mission, and the goals and strategies of the organization. Although the term "organizational culture" sometimes simply refers to the management style of senior management, especially the level of ethical and production-goal rigor, for this discussion we retain the broader meaning that includes the diverse contributions of all employees. Subcultures exist in organizations as they do in social settings, especially in terms of professional groups with slightly different functions to fulfill and perceptions about what goals to achieve. Subcultures sometimes simply have a different emphasis; Hispanic employees as a group may focus more on family–work balance. Other times it is possible for subversive subcultures to emerge when there is a perception either that the organization is hostile to select groups, perhaps due to systematic bias toward a given racial group, or that management as a class is insensitive to the contributions and needs of workers, such as in hostile union environments. The causal chain for the diversity chain is illustrated in Exhibit 7.3.

Leaders in the United States live in a particularly multicultural society (Putnam 2007). A multicultural society is a single society or nation that includes many strong subcultures. Organizational leaders of public and nonprofit organizations have to be especially sensitive to the multiculturalism in terms of their clients, contractors, and hiring practices. In turn, this leads to diverse organizations comprised of individuals from many racial, ethnic, ideological, and social backgrounds and having significantly different life experiences by gender and age, to include only the more prominent categories. An important leadership responsibility is to show respect for all subgroups and sensitivity to the standard range of value differences. However, this provides several challenges to leaders. First, equal treatment may be based on past inequalities, and "righting" those wrongs is a tricky prospect. Minorities in the United States have fewer role models in organizations and therefore fewer mentors. Second, equal treatment may be biased toward the preferred mode of a dominant group. A preference for unbroken career paths is biased toward men. Third, leaders need to be highly supportive and sensitive to cultural/subcultural differences, while promoting a cohesive organizational culture nonetheless. This is a tall order in many organizations but it is has nonetheless emerged as a critical competency for twenty-first century leaders.

GENDER AND LEADERSHIP

An important specialized approach examines the relationship between gender and leadership (Kellerman and Rhode 2007). This subfield begins with the fact that there has always been a disproportionate number of male leaders (Eagly and Carli 2007). Historically, it has often been politically, economically, or socially nearly impossible for women to be leaders.

Exhibit 7.3

Diversity Leadership

Leadership style emphasizing diversity principles
- Knowledge of and openness to learning about different subcultures (whether based on world culture, age, ethnicity, region, gender, etc.)
- Sensitivity to diversity issues (differing value priorities, customs, holidays, communication preferences, nonverbal behavior, etc.)
- Concrete efforts—educative, outreach, and regulatory—to ensure that stereotyping, harassment, passive exclusion, and discrimination do not occur
- Willingness to make concrete efforts to ensure that historical imbalances are rectified (this principle is in the process of legal and social evolution with a general narrowing of the scope and range of action)

Ease or challenges in implementing:
- Degree of integration of diversity representation in the organization, especially in terms of proportional numbers, high-pay career penetration, and hierarchical advancement
- Compatible representation between the organization and its multicultural environment
- Organizational record and practices to listen not only to the external stakeholders as a whole, but to individual communities affected by policies and practices of the organization
- History of cultural tensions or cooperation (such as when there exists a polarized conflict based on racial lines and past legal actions)

Quality of implementation: based on the leader's ability to implement the diversity principles and cultural competence

Performance goals
- Perceived respect and equality within the organization
- Mandated education regarding fair treatment, discrimination, and harassment, aggressive follow-up of reported instances of harassment and discrimination, all leading to relatively few actual grievances and legal disputes (because of a proactive approach)
- Perceived respect and fairness by external constituencies, especially those less privileged
- Acknowledgment and appreciation of diversity but ability to foster cohesive group goals

(See Exhibit 7.4 for a brief discussion of the challenges faced by women political leaders.) In the twentieth century, many barriers in the United States were eliminated by legislation, for example, adding political franchise (e.g., the Nineteenth Amendment), recognizing economic equality (e.g., the 1963 Equal Pay Act, the Pregnancy Discrimination Act of 1978, and the Family and Medical Leave Act of 1993), and providing greater job access (e.g., the Civil Rights Acts of 1964 and 1991, and the Equal Employment Opportunity Act of 1972). Women now make up slightly less than half of the working population (Guy and Newman 1998). Women have been improving in middle-ranked managerial positions, but in top political and organizational positions, they are still enormously underrepresented in most areas (Adler 1996; Ragins, Townsend, and Mattis 1998; Hogue and Lord 2007).

Exhibit 7.4

The Historical Challenges of Being a Woman Leader

Given the many thousands of political leaders (as heads of state) in history, it is remarkable how few have been women before the twentieth century, perhaps as few as three or four dozen. Only a handful have been famous, partially because of the oddity, and partially because of the challenges that they experienced in getting and maintaining power. Some have become women leaders because of a lack of legitimate males to ascend a throne. Eleanor of Acquaintaine (1122–1204) was an independent grand duchess in her own right, nonetheless first married Louis VII of France, found him uninteresting, and annulled the marriage to remarry Henry II of England. She gave Henry many children, and ultimately her lands too. Nonetheless he occasionally imprisoned her because of her passion for politics (portrayed in *The Lion in Winter*). Although 11 years older than her husband, she outlived him long enough to see two of her sons become kings of England. Elizabeth I (the Great; 1533–1603) was aware of the precedent of male consorts assuming power, and staunchly maintained an official public posture as the virgin queen. Historians do not believe that she did, in fact, die a virgin. Cleopatra (III; 69–30 BC) is famous for her use of sexual as well as political prowess. Her claim to power was tenuous at best until Julius Caesar firmly installed her as pharaoh. After his death she induced Mark Anthony to fall—and stay—in love with her for a period of 18 years. Anthony's degree of romantic/political devotion to her is almost unrivaled in history. A number of famous women leaders have assumed or seized power when the opportunity presented itself. Queen Hatshepsut of Egypt actually reigned for 30 years. Upon the death of her husband, "King Tut II," she became regent in 1512 B.C. Rather than give up power to her son when he came of age, she proclaimed herself Pharaoh in 1503 B.C. and continued to rule until her death 21 years later. Militarily and economically, Egypt thrived during her reign, and many great monuments were built in her honor, which included the pharaonic false beard with her image. Angry because he had to wait for more than two decades to ascend the throne, King Tut III had every image of her in the land defaced, in an attempt to obscure the record of history's first great woman political leader. Catherine de Medici ruled France from 1560 to 1574 in a similar vein. She ruled as regent, even after her son was of age, despite the antipathy of the French to the Italian woman. A more interesting case still is that of Catherine II of Russia ("the Great"; 1729–1796). She was a German princess who married a weak and dim-witted tsar. Once his strong-willed mother died, Catherine quickly arrested her husband, had him assassinated, and assumed the throne. In her thirty-four-year reign she built schools, substantially expanded the empire, and promoted religious tolerance. Ironically, the classical and modern democracies have an extremely weak record. There were no "great" political leaders in ancient Greece or Rome. Because women's suffrage was not common until the twentieth century (1920 in the U.S.), women have not had much chance to be political leaders. While the glass ceiling in the organizational world has been penetrated by a small proportion of women, it has remained surprisingly intact in the U.S. in terms of elected political leadership. The U.S. has yet to have a woman as president, vice president, or president pro tempore. There has yet to be a female chief supreme court justice and even the first female supreme court justice was not until Sandra Day O'Connor in 1981. Worldwide the cases of Indira Ghandi, Golda Meir, Margaret Thatcher and Angela Merkel remain rare examples of strong capable women achieving the political pinnacle.

This phenomenon is commonly known as the "glass ceiling." What have remained rich sources of research and debate are: (1) the relative importance of various biological and cultural factors leading to unequal distribution of leadership positions in contemporary society, (2) the value of a distinctly feminine perspective in leadership, and (3) the course of action to correct current biases or to better utilize the feminine perspective. Thus, the subfield itself examines leadership from a number of rather different perspectives. For simplicity, only two will be represented here.

One perspective of gender and leadership assumes that both men and women use similar leadership styles. The question is generally: *Why are there fewer women in leadership positions?* This approach emphasizes moderating variables that affect the degree of success women have with the same styles that men use. Is the lack of a proportionate number of women leaders a function of culture—stereotypes, higher standards for women, lack of proactive advancement on the part of current leader elites, or possibly even active male efforts to retain top positions? Is it a lack of opportunities to learn—fewer opportunities to gain preliminary experiences or the rotational assignments so typical of executive advancement? Is it problems with mentoring—fewer opportunities to participate in the power networks or fewer women executives to mentor others? Do cultural and gender barriers hold women back—disproportionate expectations about family responsibilities and the greater likelihood of taking time off from work for child-bearing or child care.

A second perspective assumes that men and women have different style preferences, and these fundamental differences, whatever their source, are very important. *Research questions usually examine the intervening variables that affect the right style(s) to select.* Generally, it is reported that men are more dominant, assertive, and task-oriented. Women are reported to be more consensual, social, and participative (Grant 1988; Rosener 1990), stemming from their different worldview (Gilligan 1982). The more moderate feminine view is that all of these skills are necessary for organizational success. Indeed, proponents are quick to point out the increasing need for skills in which women are perceived to have an edge such as leading by consensus and utilizing participation. The more radical view is that the feminine approach to leadership is superior because it deemphasizes domination, internal competition, and leader isolation.

When the research question centers around reasons for the low number of women in executive leadership positions, the implicit performance goal is to increase the number of women leaders. That is, how can the imbalance be rectified for the good of women and organizations? Subsidiary performance goals include improving organizational support for women leaders and eliminating the remaining barriers. On the other hand, when the research question centers around the effectiveness of women's preferred leader styles, the performance variables tend to be follower satisfaction and development (e.g., greater satisfaction from greater inclusion) and decision quality (e.g., higher quality based on integrating more points of view). The gender approach causal chain shown in Exhibit 7.5 reviews the two different research perspectives on gender and leadership.

A major contribution of the gender approach to leadership is that it examines the important contemporary problem of gender imbalance at the executive level in almost all fields. Following from this focus, gender research determines which constraints are most important and how the special needs of women can be addressed. Finally, it examines the important debate about whether there is a special feminine approach to leadership and how this affects contemporary organizations. Certainly, as late as the mid-1980s, researchers were still asserting the importance of dominance and masculinity as leadership traits (Lord, DeVader, and Alliger 1986). Are the tables turning?

A weakness of the approach is that the different perspectives seem at odds with one

Exhibit 7.5

Gender Approach Causal Chain

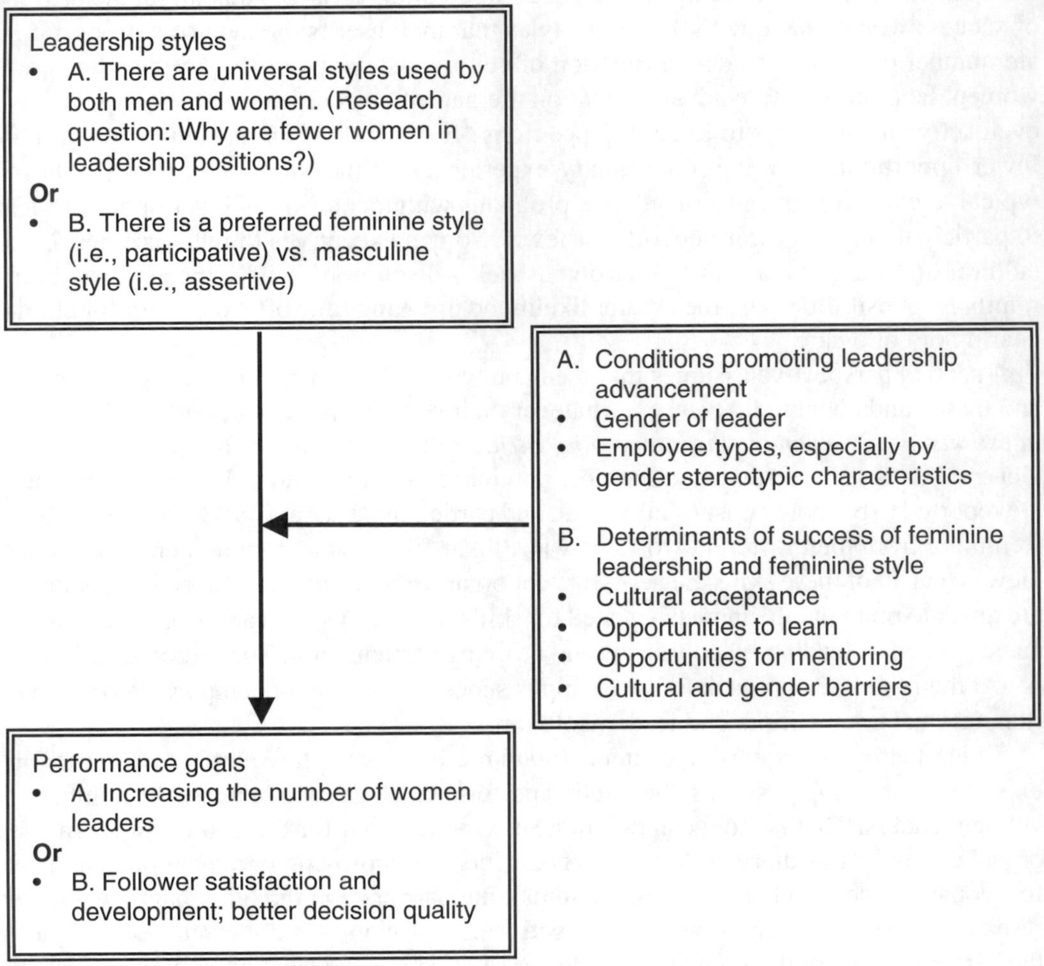

Leadership styles
- A. There are universal styles used by both men and women. (Research question: Why are fewer women in leadership positions?)

Or
- B. There is a preferred feminine style (i.e., participative) vs. masculine style (i.e., assertive)

A. Conditions promoting leadership advancement
- Gender of leader
- Employee types, especially by gender stereotypic characteristics

B. Determinants of success of feminine leadership and feminine style
- Cultural acceptance
- Opportunities to learn
- Opportunities for mentoring
- Cultural and gender barriers

Performance goals
- A. Increasing the number of women leaders

Or
- B. Follower satisfaction and development; better decision quality

another and are not necessarily additive in nature. On the one hand, some researchers assume that male and female leaders are or should be alike in all important aspects, and that enhancing full integration is the ideal (Powell 1990). On the other hand, some researchers point out differences, the value of those differences, and the need to enhance the differences (Grant 1988; Rosener 1990). A technical problem with the field to date is the difficulty of research controls. Because of the sweeping nature of the research questions posed, problems with subtle contamination effects are substantial and rarely overcome in the literature (Lefkowitz 1994). Finally, there is the real issue of how important the differences among women really are. It is possible that the differences between men and women are statistically significant, but nonetheless proportionately smaller than the differences among women themselves (Yukl 2002).

CONCLUSION

This chapter added four more approaches to those that have already been discussed in chapters 3 through 6. In addition to the early management, transactional, and transformational, distributed, and ethics approaches discussed earlier, this chapter covers leadership approaches focusing on power, culture, diversity, and gender.

The classic analysis of power suggests five leadership styles related to the ability of leaders to use (a) force and punishment, (b) remuneration and rewards, (c) norms, legitimacy, and symbols, (d) their personalities, and (e) their knowledge and expertise. In terms of the styles mapped out in chapter 2, these styles are roughly equivalent to directive (forceful), achievement (remunerative), inspirational (personality and symbolic aspects), and strategic (knowledge based). The leader's influence is the focal point of this perspective. It is an approach that is almost antithetical to a focus on ethics and leadership discussed in the last chapter.

The most prominent cultural perspective on leadership focuses on the differences in leadership based on personality, team-orientation, participation, humane-orientation, autonomous behaviors, and self-protective behaviors. House and associates identify nine unique world culture profiles. It is a nonnormative, nonuniversal perspective, asserting that while there are universal ideal characteristics underlying leadership expectations across cultures, there are also substantial differences. A transposed strongman type from either a Middle East or Latin American culture would not be well received in a Nordic European setting, any more than the reverse. Although it repackages leadership styles in unusual ways, we can still see the outlines of most of the leadership styles identified in chapter 2.

The literature emphasizing diversity and leadership focuses on four major elements: knowledge of and openness to learning about different subcultures; sensitivity to diversity issues such as differing value structures and differing customs; concrete efforts—educative, outreach, and regulatory—to ensure that stereotyping, harassment, passive exclusion, and discrimination do not occur; and a willingness to make concrete efforts to ensure that historical imbalances are rectified. This is a normative, universalistic approach that emphasizes supportive, participative, and collaborative styles.

The topic of gender and leadership raises the issue of why more women have not reached the pinnacle of leadership, and whether women bring special—and desirable—attributes to the table such as enhanced collaborative and supportive skills. The literature is bifurcated between a more descriptive analysis that is nonnormative, and a more prescriptive and normative approach that asserts the more collaborative nature of women and the increasing benefits of collaboration in leadership roles.

While the approaches to leadership discussed in this chapter, as well as those focused in previous chapters, provide analytic tools and enormous insights into leadership, an increasing concern has arisen over how, and even whether, macrolevel leadership theory is achievable and can provide useful theoretical guidance and applied utility. It is to integrated theories that we turn next.

8

Integrative Theories

Because of the extreme complexity of the phenomenon, a number of theorists have tried to build overarching frameworks that simultaneously incorporate as many approaches as possible. Integrated frameworks are very useful for the "big picture" perspective that they provide, but they involve overcoming many challenges because the subject is so vast and the perspectives that one can take are so numerous (Avolio 2007; Bennis 2007). Because no single integrated framework has gained wide acceptance, we will review a variety of the better-known frameworks.

After the transformational leadership movement had run its initial course in the 1980s and the early 1990s, some researchers began to focus on how to integrate different research foci. This seemed increasingly urgent as the number of fundamentally different approaches had grown so large and the field had become a bewildering forest of theories and specialized concepts and terms. Rather than simply expanding a single theory to be more inclusive as Bass (1985) had done with transformational leadership (thus with an implicit focus on the organizational-level change role of maintenance), there was an interest in an integrated approach that was more comprehensive in its scope.

An integrated approach provides a broad sweep of the leadership context rather than a set of specific factors, situations, or behaviors, or a perspective. Integrated approaches include multiple types of leadership and often involve different contexts. Those working on integrated models or frameworks have tried to show the complexity of relationships while understanding that this makes it difficult or impossible to validate them as empirically testable theories.

Some integrated approaches focus on consolidating the transactional leadership theories. Shared leadership is an integrated approach bringing together traditional vertical leadership with substitutes, team theory, self-leadership, and superleadership. A leader-member integrative leadership framework by Chemers (1997) incorporates most of the contingency factors of the transactional models. It should be noted that transactional leadership theory and these models or frameworks are largely based on closed systems theory. Closed systems theory lacks a robust, two-way feedback loop involving the organizational environment. It also lacks significant reference to the complexity of stakeholders located outside the organization. Therefore, by definition, frameworks based on closed systems may be useful, but they are ultimately not comprehensive.

In contrast, leadership models based on general system theory tend to include a robust feedback loop and external stakeholder concerns. Several variants can be identified. Open system theory tends to maintain an organizational perspective but to include moderate attention to the environment. Unlike closed system theories, leaders must split their focus between internal and external demands. Change demands evolve from the environment, rather than just leader-member interactions, and can be dealt with in a relatively orderly way through the planning of leaders. This means that leaders not only gather internal data about operations with the related problems that need to be fixed but also gather data about external trends related to the field, market, technological advancements, and so forth. Leaders in an open system perspective tend to emphasize a strategic approach overall.

Another variant of general system theory envisions a dynamic system. The system is viewed as complex and capable of radical and disruptive shifts. Change can be chaotic. Therefore, leaders need to be good at dealing with unplanned change coming from any direction. Little attention is directed to the details of leader-member interactions per se. Instead, many people should be involved in the change process because of the complexity and ubiquity of change. Some theorists utilizing a dynamic approach emphasize that the organization exists *for* the system, rather than that the organization exists *in* a system. That is, they actually focus on the needs of the system as primary, which results in a different normative thrust altogether; the leadership style generally emphasized is facilitative or collaborative rather than strategic. The factors emphasized in different management-leadership theories are highlighted in Exhibit 8.1.

Integrated models are nearly always frameworks that do not attempt to quantify factors, because of the extensive number of relationships and numerous classes of cases that they attempt to identify. Despite less claim on quantitative validation, they do attempt to offer greater utility in other respects. First, there is always a need to coordinate diverse research agendas, and this is particularly important in leadership studies that are so vast. How can the insights of trait, management, transactional, charismatic, transformational, and distributed approaches be brought together? Second, an integrated approach tends to reveal where consensus can be achieved, which can lead to shared nomenclature and concepts. Confusion of terms and concepts in leadership studies is sometimes extreme. Third, an integrated approach can more holistically identify research gaps among the various approaches. What aspects of the phenomenon have yet to be explained adequately? Finally, an integrated approach is highly useful in explaining leadership studies as a research area as well as in training in the field. An integrated approach can help place a specific approach in context without reducing its significance. Integrated approaches should be useful to those setting up training and educational programs in that they clarify connections between fields, and to those learning about leadership in that they combine different perspectives.

One issue that immediately becomes apparent in creating an integrated approach is the decision about how to balance parsimony versus comprehensiveness. Like all research endeavors, theoretical elegance is desirable: explaining the bulk of a phenomenon with as few concepts as possible. A parsimonious approach is easier to understand and to teach. Yet leadership is a highly complex phenomenon, and reducing the number of variables presented simply makes it highly abstract. The applied utility is seriously reduced and the highly parsimonious approach (common in the popular leadership literature) can become a series of generalized assertions that do not have much more weight than wise proverbs or abstract principles.

Exhibit 8.1

Factors Emphasized by Different Management-Leadership Theories

Dimension	Closed system	Open system	Dynamic system
	Internal focus with little attention to the external environment	**Organizational emphasis with moderate attention to external environment**	**System emphasis with primary attention to the external environment**
Type of leadership most emphasized	Managerial leadership	Strategic leadership	Facilitative leadership
Nature of external environment	Not a primary concern; assumed	Orderly if evolving	Chaotic because of complexity and sometimes subject to dramatic systems shifts
Leader's focus	Internal organizational focus; maintenance-control; quality control; production, service, employee-management relations	Equally divided between internal and external concerns; balancing environmental scanning-alignment with internal operations; orderly change	Primarily a systems focus; (a) collaboration; continuous adaptation; (b) openness to environmental and social needs in the organizational setting
Role of change	Technical problem solving, process improvement, replacement of personnel, updating of systems and technology	Planned; ideally "engineered" with extensive leader-expert oversight with an eye to new trends, competition, shifting service demands	Dynamic; frequently unplanned, ad hoc, and experimental; sensitive to the need for radical change
Leader's role in change	Gathers technical facts, monitors production trends, fixes problems, and proactively improves system weaknesses	Gathers data on market trends, and prioritizes change initiatives based on personal, agency or corporate vision	Encourages information to permeate the organization from many sources and allow change to "percolate in" and "bubble up" as much as possible
Traditional examples of theories	• Leader traits • Grid theory • Situational leadership • Path-goal theory • Substitutes theory • Normative decision theory • Leader Member Exchange	• Transformational and charismatic	• Transforming leadership • Servant leadership
Contemporary examples of theories with integrative qualities	• Shared leadership (vertical and distributed) theory • Leader-member integration theory	• Organizational hierarchy theory • Comprehensive leadership competencies theory • Strategic leadership	• Complexity theory • Social change leadership theory

A concrete challenge in creating an integrated approach involves how to graphically represent the relationships identified as important, because so many functions and levels of analysis must be presented in a two-dimensional format. As Chemers candidly admits, "leadership processes are complex enough that not all perspectives can be addressed simultaneously" (Chemers 1997, 163). Some challenges to researchers in this area are variable complexity, levels of leadership, temporal dimensions, organizational purpose (e.g., profit versus common good), and types of outcomes desired. The challenge to present multiple "layers" simultaneously is very difficult. Additionally, how many of the relationships among variables are to be presented? With a highly interconnected phenomenon such as leadership, the number of feedback loops and indirect effects is extensive and important. Showing such relationships is messy for the instructor, but critical for the researcher setting up a rigorous research design.

Because of the vast scope of their integrated frameworks, only thumbnail sketches of eight approaches are provided here. They range from those tending to focus on a closed system, an open system, and on a dynamic system perspective. The examples provided here include shared leadership (Pearce and Conger 2003a), Chemers's "integrative" theory (Chemers 1997), transformational theory (Tichy and Devanna 1986; Conger 1989), strategic leadership (Boal and Hooijberg 2001), social change leadership (Crosby and Bryson 2010), complexity theory (Uhl-Bien, Marion, and McKelvey 2007), comprehensive leadership competencies theory (Van Wart 2004), and multiple-organizational-level leadership (Hunt 1996). Readers are encouraged to consult the original works for full descriptions.

SHARED LEADERSHIP THEORY

Contemporary shared leadership is a loose model or framework showing the relationship of various distributed and vertical styles in a closed system framework, rather than a well-articulated empirical theory at this stage. Nonetheless, it is a theoretical advancement over substitutes theory in which situational variables were essentially a laundry list of contingencies rather than an explanatory theory. Shared leadership is based on the normative assumptions that various types of distributed leadership exist and are useful, and that a major role of traditional or vertical leadership is to enhance the capability and motivation to engage in distributed leadership. Shared leadership has strong parallels in other areas of the management literature. In particular, although there has been little cross-fertilization, the learning organization literature also emphasizes the traditional management overreliance on hierarchy, centralized expertise, status differentials, and in-group competition. Instead, the learning organization literature emphasizes breaking down dysfunctional mental models and creating a sense of shared vision (similar to superleadership), personal mastery (similar to self-leadership), teams, and a systems approach (similar to the integration of vertical functions with distributed functions) (Senge 1990).

The style proposed in shared leadership is a combined style based on both vertical and distributed forms of leadership occurring concurrently (Houghton, Neck, and Manz 2003). It is a multilevel model because different organizational members perform different types of leadership at the same time. Superleadership is necessary on the part of the formal leader to develop followers to accept the responsibilities and challenges of distributed leadership, to provide the participative opportunities to learn and interact, and to prepare to self-lead or self-manage in a group environment. Although self-leadership is practiced, modeled, and encouraged by formal leaders, it is only when subordinates also practice self-leadership that a robust form of shared leadership exists. Another important element of shared leadership is the empowered team, which not only carries out important management functions with relative autonomy but also self-organizes and distributes leadership functions such as accountability and role assignments. In the ideal, shared leadership recognizes the need for some elements of "top-down" leadership, but it emphasizes that the best-run contemporary organizations need to maximize "bottom-up" or distributed leadership as much as possible (Locke 2003).

Overall, three factors moderate the success of shared leadership. The first factor is the capacity of the subordinates or organizational members themselves. If turnover is high, education is poor, training is superficial, pay is unusually low, or recruitment is sloppy, shared leadership has little chance of success. Self-leadership will be weak and inconsistent and team skills will be too shallow to rely on them in substantial ways. In such situations, a strong leader is probably more likely to keep the organization together and keep it producing at modest levels. The second factor is the capability of leaders to develop and to delegate. No matter how capable and committed subordinates may be, some leaders find it very difficult to teach others, much less to share their power. Ironically, units or organizations with more powerful members are ultimately more powerful overall. Therefore, the leader is not really giving up power, per se, but allowing for the possibility of more power to exist in their arena whereby the leader benefits proportionately. The third factor is the general willingness of the organization, through its governing board, chief executive officer, and culture, to allow and encourage the use of distributed-leadership models. This is particularly true in the public sector in which distributed leadership is occasionally attacked with accusations that bureaucracy will run amok or that unelected bureaucrats will make important public decisions. Although these are real concerns, it has not been clearly established that they are more likely to occur because of distributed leadership.

The performance variables of shared leadership are not well-articulated but can be assumed to be similar to those of other leadership models. Production efficiency, follower satisfaction and development, decision quality, and external alignment are all significant outcomes. Management decentralization and leadership devolution are also implied by the model as a preferred outcome. The implicit causal model for shared leadership is shown in Exhibit 8.2.

A major weakness of shared leadership theory as it is currently expressed is the fact that it works at multiple levels of analysis simultaneously. That makes empirical testing extremely difficult. Furthermore, the subcomponents of the theory are not as well articulated as the individual theories themselves. Nonetheless, shared leadership starts to bring

Exhibit 8.2

Shared Leadership Causal Chain

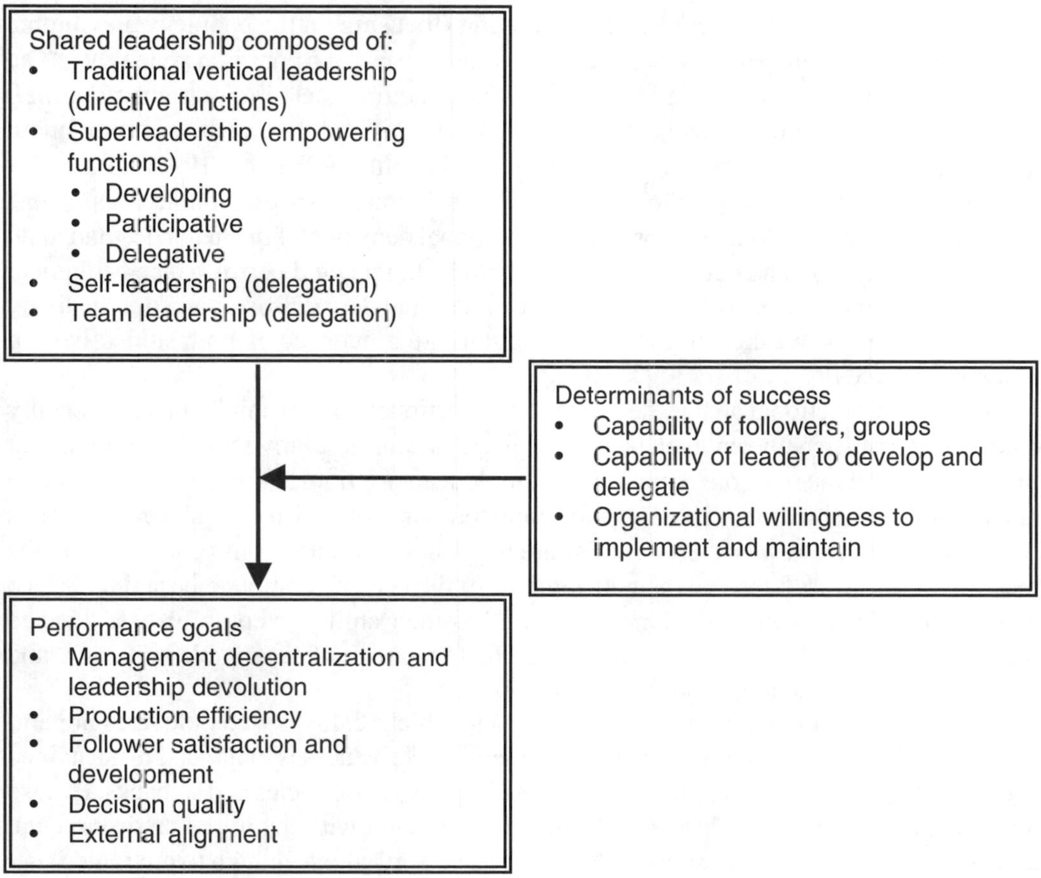

Shared leadership composed of:
- Traditional vertical leadership (directive functions)
- Superleadership (empowering functions)
  - Developing
  - Participative
  - Delegative
- Self-leadership (delegation)
- Team leadership (delegation)

Determinants of success
- Capability of followers, groups
- Capability of leader to develop and delegate
- Organizational willingness to implement and maintain

Performance goals
- Management decentralization and leadership devolution
- Production efficiency
- Follower satisfaction and development
- Decision quality
- External alignment

together the scattered research and thinking that began in the 1980s and then exploded in the 1990s. It provides a more realistic balance of the simplistic forms of "empowered" leadership in the popular literature that are reminiscent of "silver bullet" cures for what ails any organization.

CHEMERS'S INTEGRATIVE THEORY

Chemers's (1997) "integrative" approach emphasizes major facets of leadership based on the type of interaction involved: intrapersonal, interpersonal, or situational. He asserts that the operating principles of leadership shift from one area to the next. That is, the principles in image management, relationship development, and resource utilization are distinct, even though all functions of leadership may overlap in "multidimensional, reverberating, and dynamic" ways. In all areas, the "leader match" concept applies, "which states that the outcomes of leader and follower behavior are determined by the degree of fit between the behavior and demands of the surrounding environment" (Chemers 1997, 163).

He limits styles to three major types: structuring, consideration, and prominence. Structuring (focusing on objectives) and consideration (focusing on the people achieving the objectives) have been extensively covered. Prominence is not a common style type. "The Prominence category acknowledges that leaders sometimes act simply to increase their own ego satisfaction by drawing attention to themselves and their contribution without true regard for goal attainment or other collective benefits" (Chemers 1997, 167).

The first functional area is the "zone of self-deployment" in which individuals must assess their personal characteristics and the situational demands. If the match is good, then comfort, confidence, and persistence are likely to be higher, and performance is likely to improve. If the match between the leader and situational demands is poor, stress is likely and performance is weakened. Leader perceptions are influenced by both subjective and objective sources.

The second functional area is the "zone of transactional relationship" in which socially constructed reality between leaders and followers is central. Many factors are important in this context. One variable is the set of generic leader attitudes that enhances positive outcomes across situations. These include confidence and optimism, which Chemers calls "leadership mettle." Two other variables are the behavioral intentions of leaders and the reaction of followers based on their attributions of the leader's competence and their own perceptions of their abilities and needs, as well as their ability to communicate these to the leader. Cultural ideals and social norms affect the range of acceptable behaviors and attributions of both leaders and followers.

The "zone of team deployment" is the arena in which reality-based outcomes are emphasized. Chemers's model suggests that leaders' effectiveness is enhanced by sustained team efforts, persistence, and member contributions despite obstacles and setbacks. He also notes that a good match of leader skills and temperament with the initial environmental demands does not guarantee success. Nor are team efforts alone enough to guarantee success. Success also requires reality-based assessments based on pragmatic organizational demands and capacities.

Chemers defines performance as productivity, efficiency, and effectiveness. See Exhibit 8.3 for the causal model.

TRANSFORMATIONAL THEORY

Because transformational theory was dealt with expansively in chapter 4, the discussion here will focus solely on the place of transformational and charismatic theories vis-à-vis integrated theories. Historically, the transformational movement reminded the bulk of the leadership researchers of the importance of looking beyond the interpersonal, small group, supervisory, closed system perspective that had tended to dominate from the 1950s to the 1970s. Some aspects of transformational leadership focused on the requirements for leaders to be change masters (Tichy and Devanna 1986). Others focused more on the personality of leaders interacting with followers, whether it was charisma or simply

Exhibit 8.3

Chemers's "Integrative" Framework Causal Chain

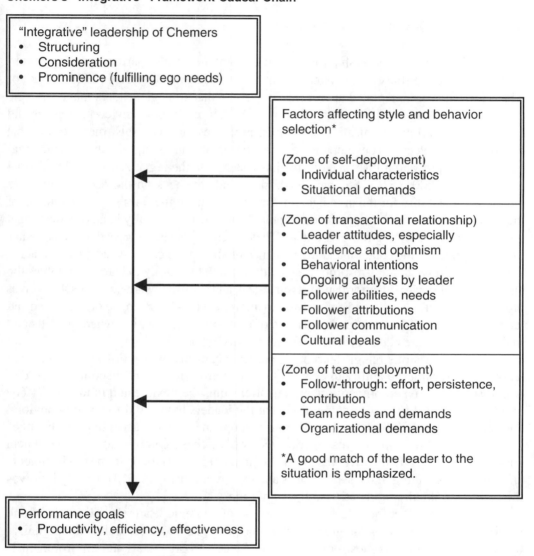

Source: Based on Chemers (1997).

force of character (Conger 1989). Bernard Bass was most successful at providing a quasi-integrated model for both the transactional and the transformational perspectives in his full-range theory (1985). Some focused on change leadership at a more operational or entrepreneurial level (Hammer and Champy 1993). These theories, tending to emanate from business, were inclined to be universalistic, leader-centric, and organization-centered. One could also include Burns's idea of transforming leaders (1978), which is qualitatively very different. Coming from an "enlightened" political science viewpoint, he emphasized the leader's role in elevating the shared interests of constituents, adherents, or followers for the long-term common good.

STRATEGIC LEADERSHIP THEORY

Traditionally, strategic leadership theory had concentrated rather narrowly on upper echelon theory and the study of top management teams. Boal and Hooijberg (2001) called for a broader and more integrated approach. They argue that strategic leaders make strategic decisions, create and communicate a vision of the future, develop key competencies and capabilities, develop organization structures, processes, and controls, manage multiple constituencies, select and develop the next generation of leaders, sustain an effective organizational culture, and infuse an ethical value system into the organization's culture (Boal and Hooijberg 2001, 516). Strategic leadership tends to focus on the people who have overall responsibility for the organization, but the authors argue for a greater inclusion of the environmental conditions in the conceptual framework, especially in an organizational universe that is becoming more turbulent. They assert that a strategic leadership style has three components: the creation and maintenance of absorptive capacity, adaptive capacity, and managerial wisdom. "Absorptive capacity refers to the ability to learn. It involves the capacity to recognize new information, assimilate it, and apply it toward new ends. It involves processes used offensively and defensively to improve its fits between the organization and its environments. It is a continuous genesis of creation and recreation where gestalts and logical structures are added or deleted from memory" (ibid., 517).

A second aspect of strategic learning is adaptive capacity, which utilizes the ability to learn by exercising the ability to change. Given an environment of discontinuities, disequilibrium, and hypercompetition, organizations must be flexible and innovative. "The organization's ability to change requires that the leaders have cognitive and behavioral complexity and flexibility . . . , coupled with an openness to and acceptance of change" (517–518). The final aspect is managerial wisdom, which is a combination of discernment and timing. Discernment "involves the ability to perceive variations in the environment" and "an understanding of the social actors and their relationships" (518). Timing involves the ability to take the right action at the right time.

Many factors affect the selection and success of strategic leadership. First, Boal and Hooijberg point out that strategic leadership becomes far more critical as the organizational environment becomes more dynamic. Since the organizational environment is almost universally becoming exceedingly dynamic, they point to the increased importance of strategic leadership. However, even in a stable environment, organizations need some degree of strategic management for growth and healthy rejuvenation. Second, they point out that leaders can exercise strategic leadership only to the degree that they have discretion. Of course traditionally, public administrators and political bureaucrats tend to have less discretion than their private sector counterparts in order to ensure greater democratic input and higher levels of accountability. Responsible leaders, individually and as teams, are primarily able to exercise strategic leadership to the degree that they have the following traits/skills: cognitive complexity, social intelligence, and behavioral complexity. Cognitive complexity is the ability to assimilate large amounts of information, sift through it, and interpret it as circumstances and purposes change. Social intelligence is the ability to make constructive distinctions among individuals and their moods, temperaments, motivations, and so forth and to simultaneously align and maximize individual and organizational needs. Behavioral complexity is the ability of leaders to perform multiple leadership roles and to have a large behavioral repertoire to select from as circumstances change. (See chapters 11 and 12 on traits and skills for more discussion on these competencies.)

Three other factors moderate success to a somewhat lesser degree. Strategic leaders are able to formulate and project a clear vision of the past and present of the organization, and the concrete needs for future change. The cognitive aspect of a vision involves the outcomes and means of achieving them. The affective aspect is the motivation and commitment necessary to execute the vision. A second element that enhances the likelihood of successful strategic leadership is charisma. The attractiveness of an individual's personality and a trust in their expertise and insight help immensely in the selling and implementation of change. Finally, having change-management experience and skills, as captured in transformational leadership, is a tremendous boost in strategic leadership.

The performance goals of strategic leadership include the traditional goals of efficiency and effectiveness, but emphasize identifying change needs and opportunities and executing them effectively. Performance goals highlight the linchpin role of senior managers and emphasize the role of competition, expanding an organization's market or profit, and ultimately winning in a demanding and often hostile environment. See Exhibit 8.4 for a summary of the underlying causal chain of strategic leadership.

SOCIAL CHANGE LEADERSHIP THEORY

The social change leadership has a disparate literature that tends to focus on the broadest level of systems leadership. It focuses on accomplishing social change by working through collective action in order to contribute to the common good and resolution of public problems by paying attention to the strategies and competencies that contribute to shared policy decision making and implementation. It is strongly antiheroic in tone. Social change leadership shares a lot in common with the ethical-value theories already covered in terms of authenticity of action, a "calling" or passion for service, and a sense of morality rather than competition, success, personal accomplishment or legacy, and so forth. However, leadership theories emphasizing ethics tend to be more universalistic, focus more on the source of ethical action (rather than the results), and be more philosophically oriented.

Social change can occur at many levels, or it can be treated abstractly. Not surprisingly, there are a variety of different foci. For example, at a national/international political level, James McGregor Burns's idea of transforming leadership is pertinent (1978, 2003). He differentiates first-order change, which is largely technical, structural, procedural, mandated, and so on, from a higher level of change that involves attitudes, beliefs, and values. Quantitative change may be good and necessary, but the really hard work of change is

Exhibit 8.4

Strategic Leadership

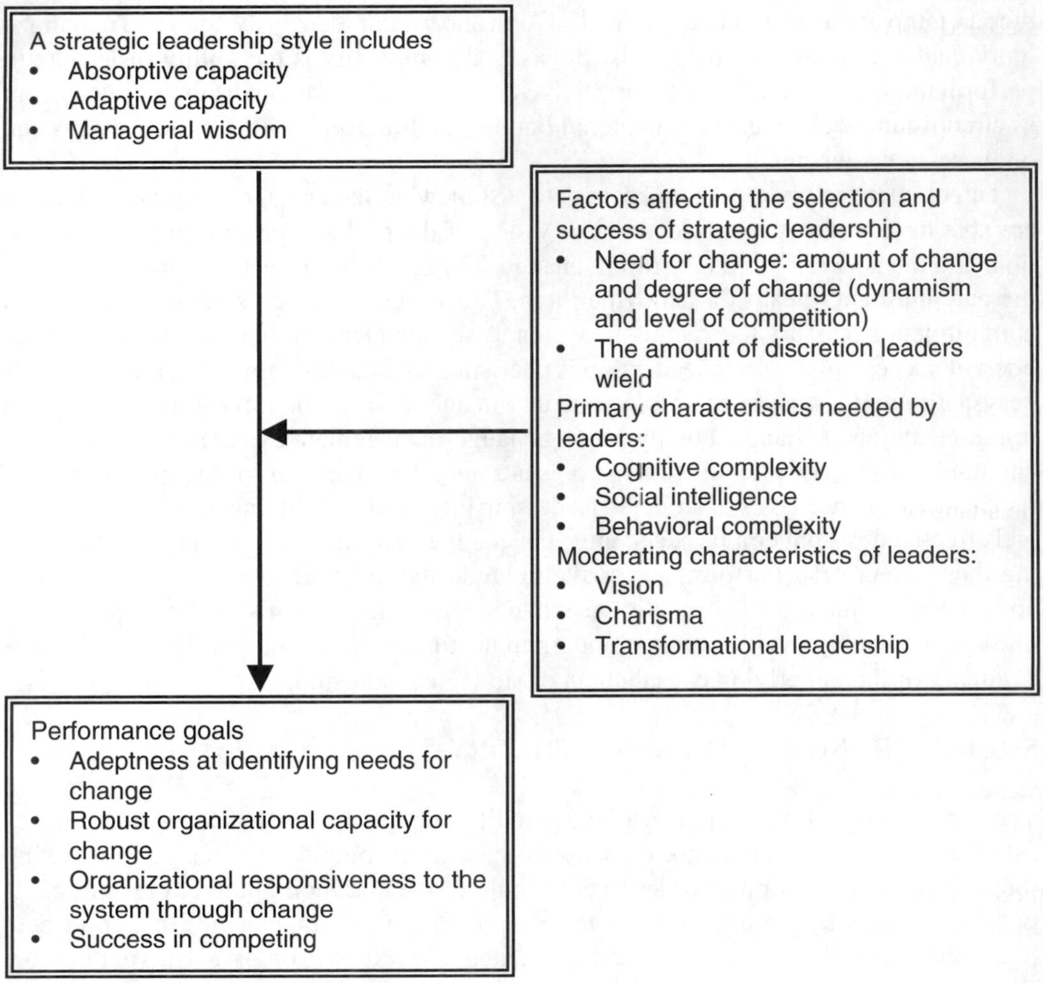

A strategic leadership style includes
- Absorptive capacity
- Adaptive capacity
- Managerial wisdom

Factors affecting the selection and success of strategic leadership
- Need for change: amount of change and degree of change (dynamism and level of competition)
- The amount of discretion leaders wield

Primary characteristics needed by leaders:
- Cognitive complexity
- Social intelligence
- Behavioral complexity

Moderating characteristics of leaders:
- Vision
- Charisma
- Transformational leadership

Performance goals
- Adeptness at identifying needs for change
- Robust organizational capacity for change
- Organizational responsiveness to the system through change
- Success in competing

Source: Boal and Hooijberg (2001).

qualitative and therefore more likely to be more long-lasting. Some leaders may vastly expand national boundaries, as President Polk did, but others are transforming leaders who bring out the best of the political system, as Franklin D. Roosevelt did when he reengineered the economy to protect the vulnerable masses. A related literature about social movements (Tilly 1978, 2004) differentiates such leaders as Mahatma Ghandhi, Mahmoud Ahmadinejad, Cesar Chavez, and Jim Jones.

Many scholars examine social change at subnational, regional, or local levels. John Gardner (1989), a leadership scholar who founded Common Cause, among other accomplishments, strongly urged more focus on public problem solving. The five leadership skills he emphasizes are: agreement building, networking, exercising nonjurisdictional power, institution building, and flexibility. Heifetz (1994) emphasizes the slow and patient process of bringing about adaptation to get answers to the tough problems of society in a way that brings the community together. Similarly, Bryson and Crosby (1992) emphasize the need for collaboration in a shared power world. More recently, Crosby and Bryson discuss what they call integrative leaders "as bringing diverse groups and organizations together in semipermanent ways—and typically across sector boundaries—to remedy complex public problems and achieve the common good" (2010, 211). Svara (1994) emphasizes the facilitative style necessary for mayors and elected chairs of legislative bodies. Luke (1998) has a similar perspective, but promotes the idea that good collaborative leaders are critical catalysts (still a far cry from heroic leaders). Other scholars focus on social activists who make up boards, commissions, chambers of commerce, local organizations, and the like, who fuel positive change (e.g., Chrislip and Larson 1994; Henton, Melville, and Walesh 1997). Agranoff takes a community network perspective (2007). Taking a more entrepreneurial network perspective are Goldsmith and Eggers (2004), who emphasize public private partnerships. A very early example of the social change perspective in administrative (rather than policy) settings was proposed by Cayer and Weschler (1988; updated as Cayer, Baker, and Weschler 2010), who emphasized the adaptive change that managers must make as they wade through the policy swamp. Distinct differences have been demonstrated between traditional hierarchical leaders and social change leadership (Silva and McGuire 2010), as has the importance for leadership success in federal agencies (Fernandez, Cho, and Perry 2010).

Because most social change theories focus on the policy level, they are inclined to deemphasize general management and administrative competence, which tend to be assumed. Understanding of the political and policy process is frequently considered an important factor. Social change theories also tend to emphasize personal integrity because of the trust necessary for successful change, as well as a passion for public service and giving back to the community. Theorists argue that adherents are more interested in creating public value than organizational or personal value per se. Thus, social change theory tends to be somewhat antistrategic, to the degree that a strategic mindset is about competition, market share, winning, personal wealth and reputation, and so on. Most important, the social change leadership theory heavily emphasizes collaborative leadership, sometimes called facilitative, adaptive, integrative, or catalytic leadership. There are at least five major elements of collaborative leadership as expressed by this school of thought. First, there is a tremendous sense of egalitarianism. It is not the size of the contribution to public problem solving that matters as much as the participation in the process. Social change leadership tends to reject hierarchical notions. Second, there is great cultural sensitivity. All public problems must embed a variety of perspectives, whether it is at the level of organizational and client diversity or in terms of cross-cultural differences. Third, there is an openness to the ideas of others. Social change leadership promotes bottom-up communication that embraces as large a number of constituents as possible. Ideally individuals are willing to go without significant personal credit for their contributions for the good of the cause. Fourth, there is enormous stress on consensus building. Making social change with simple majorities means that large groups are frequently either disenfranchised or angry, or both. Such feelings leave open the possibility of bitterness and eventual retaliation. Consensus building requires a great deal of time, patience, and even perseverance in the face of different opinions. It requires all sides to participate in learning about differing perspectives to achieve win–win scenarios, so that the contentious aspects of bargaining and compromising can be reduced. Finally, collaborative leadership requires comfort with ambiguity and complexity. There is no clear sense of the outcomes in social change leadership, other than broad social goals, whether those goals are to reduce poverty or improve a run-down park in which the neighbors, sports enthusiasts, and city start out with very different goals but must ultimately achieve shared agreements if resentment is not to be a major outcome. As public problems are discussed, their complexity and interrelatedness are reviewed, and there is a long period of ambiguity about how to achieve a consensus on how to act.

A social change perspective is dependent on a focus on public problems rather than a focus on (1) administrative efficiency and effectiveness or (2) narrower strategy leading to organizational or personal gain. Thus, supervisors and managers handling caseloads, help calls, and providing a variety of services in day-to-day operations are unlikely to focus on social change. Private sector executives interested in maximizing profits or public sector executives engaged in making painful staffing cuts are more likely to have an internal and self-interested perspective. The success of social change leadership is largely determined by the degree to which adherents not only have integrity, but exhibit strong collaborative leadership qualities.

The success of social leadership is in tackling and then solving society's local, regional, national, and global problems. Those problems can include local economic development, regional environmental problems, national dilemmas about improving education, or global problems having to do with nuclear proliferation. Its success is seen by the integration of goals of various constituents in the consensus-building process, whether that is at the macropolitical level (e.g., the European Union or ASEAN), or in a local nonprofit network working cooperatively and sharing funding. Exhibit 8.5 illustrates the general causal chain inherent in most social change perspectives.

COMPLEXITY LEADERSHIP THEORY

Complexity theory is based on chaos and complex adaptive systems theory. (See the discussion of postmodern theories in chapter 1 for background undergirding this perspective.) Here we will focus on the articulation of complexity theory by Uhl-Bien, Marion, and McKelvey (2007). First, this perspective does not assume a stable environment as is the case in closed system models, or a moderately competitive environment as in traditional open system models, but rather a highly turbulent and complex environment. Organizations must meet complexity with complexity, such as with rapidly evolving structures and quickly customized responses, products, and services. Context "is not an antecedent, mediator, or moderator variable; rather, it is the ambiance that spawns a given system's dynamic persona—in the case of complex system personae, it refers to the nature of interactions and interdependence among agents (people, ideas, etc.), hierarchical divi-

Exhibit 8.5

Social Change Leadership Theory

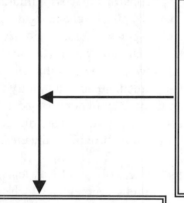

Social change leadership style combines
- Political and administrative competence
- Personal integrity and a passion for public service
- Collaborative/facilitative qualities
  - Sense of egalitarianism
  - Cultural sensitivity
  - Openness to the ideas of others
  - Consensus building
  - Comfort with ambiguity and complexity

Factors affecting style and behavior selection
- Need for collaborative setting: social rather than organizational problem or context
- Success determined by quality of social change leadership exercised (e.g., political and administrative savvy, trustworthiness, and facilitative qualities such as a lack of hierarchical perspective, and lack of competition)

Performance goals
- Solve society's local, national, and global problems
- Integration of goals by those in system or network
  - Individual goals
  - Group goals
  - Organizational goals
  - Society's goals (often expressed as local needs, networks, or public problems)

sions, organizations, and environments" (ibid., 299). Second, leadership is emphasized as a process rather than an activity exercised by individuals.

Complexity leadership theory envisions three primary leadership styles that are executed on a rotating, as-needed basis. All three must be practiced for complexity leadership to be effective, but since it is a process-oriented approach, different members of the organization may emphasize different roles. The first type of leadership is administrative leadership, which is "grounded in traditional bureaucratic notions of hierarchy, alignment and control" (ibid., 299). Although most contemporary organizations exist in different environments requiring optimal flexibility and creativity, this does not mean that traditional functions from human resource management to accountability chains of command cease to exist. Administrative leaders structure goals, engage in planning, build vision, acquire resources, manage crises, and manage organizational strategy. Second, adaptive leadership fosters creativity that fits a knowledge era. Adaptive leadership "is an emergent, interactive dynamic that produces outcomes in a social system. It is a collaborative change movement that emerges nonlinearly from interactive exchanges, or, more specifically, from the 'spaces between' agents" (ibid., 306). The creativity, flexibility, and change that occur from adaptive leaders stems from a complex dynamic process rather an individual's unique actions. Finally, enabling leadership enhances the conditions that catalyze adaptive leadership and allow for creativity and change to occur. Enabling leadership can occur anywhere in the organization, but particularly with middle management. It often overlaps with administrative leadership by simply changing the focus or tone of interactions from control and order to one of responsiveness, flexibility, and creativity. Enabling leadership encompasses the tension created between administrative and adaptive leadership, and between hierarchies and networks, in ways that ensure that adaptive processes are not stifled by the demands for immediate accountability and linearity. In sum, the theory acknowledges that bureaucratic needs will not disappear, but emphasizes that twenty-first-century organizations need not only to tout learning, creativity, and change but also to spend a large portion of their time providing the enabling conditions in constantly evolving situations.

A number of factors affect the need for and success of complexity leadership. To begin with, complexity theory assumes a highly dynamic environment in which constant changes in knowledge, technology, consumer needs, competition, and the like are characteristic and important. Additionally, it assumes that organizations in complex environments must also have requisite complexity rather than rigid bureaucratized processes that are incapable of evolving with sufficient alacrity. Lastly, the success of organizations in these environments depends on exercising and balancing three types of leadership with equal skill: administrative, adaptive, and enabling.

The performance goals, then, include providing suitable organizational structures and processes to support bureaucratic needs, supplying enabling conditions for learning, creativity, and adaptations, producing successful change, and creating an organization that can accommodate radical as well as incremental changes. The major factors involved in complexity leadership are displayed in Exhibit 8.6.

LEADERSHIP COMPETENCIES THEORY

Contemporary competency approaches merge the classical trait approach with the multiple-organizational-level approach discussed below. That is, contemporary compe-

Exhibit 8.6

Complexity Leadership Theory

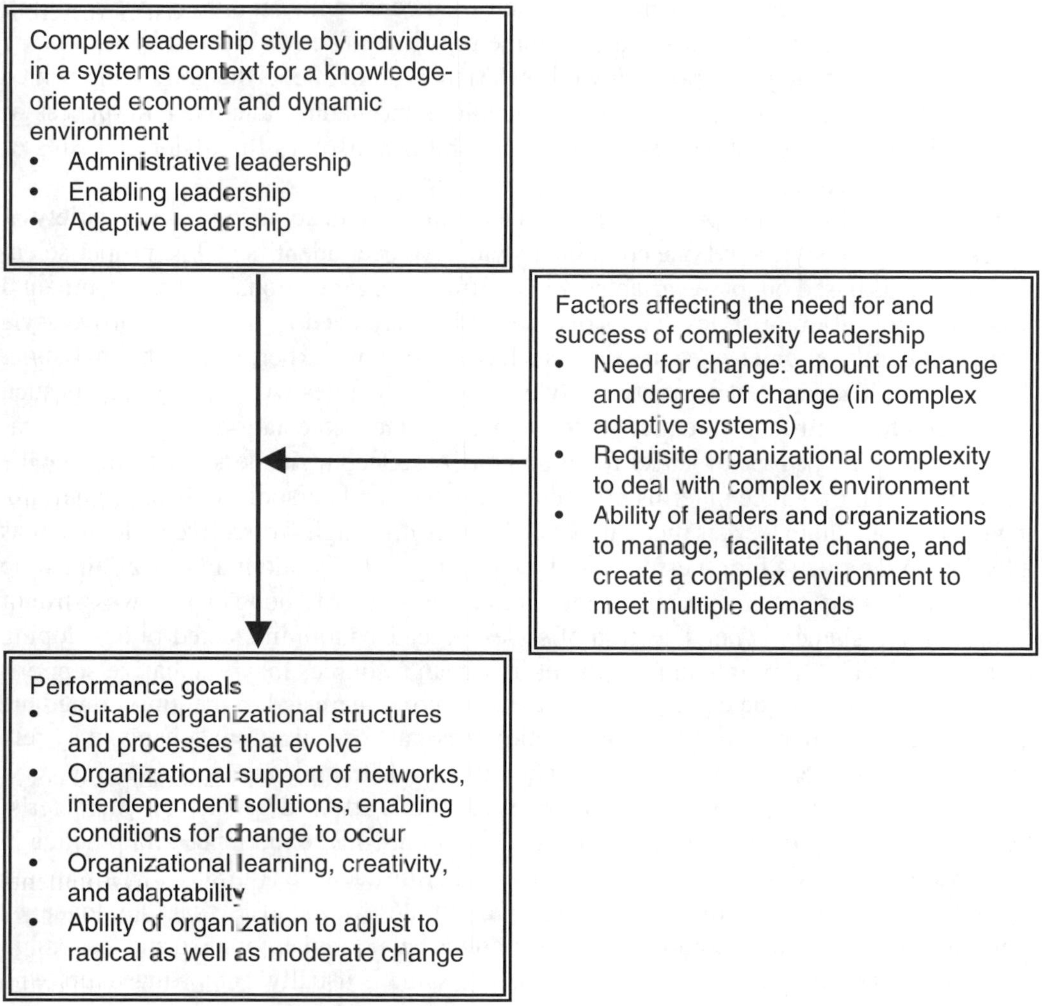

Complex leadership style by individuals in a systems context for a knowledge-oriented economy and dynamic environment
- Administrative leadership
- Enabling leadership
- Adaptive leadership

Factors affecting the need for and success of complexity leadership
- Need for change: amount of change and degree of change (in complex adaptive systems)
- Requisite organizational complexity to deal with complex environment
- Ability of leaders and organizations to manage, facilitate change, and create a complex environment to meet multiple demands

Performance goals
- Suitable organizational structures and processes that evolve
- Organizational support of networks, interdependent solutions, enabling conditions for change to occur
- Organizational learning, creativity, and adaptability
- Ability of organization to adjust to radical as well as moderate change

tency approaches are interested in spelling out exactly which standard competencies are necessary in which sets or classes of situations. By and large, supervisors, managers, and executives work in different situations. For example, supervisors and executives will have some similarities in the skills, traits, and behaviors that they must have to be successful, but they will have some substantial and important differences as well. While both will likely share the need for interpersonal competence, the frontline supervisor must focus more on task-oriented competencies such as operations planning while the executive will be more involved in strategic planning and interorganizational collaboration. Competency approaches try to provide a standardized nomenclature for competencies, as well as more definition and specification about their nature and interaction with each other.

The example used here is Van Wart's leadership action cycle (2004), which is designed to be useful in training and applied settings. Therefore, it breaks leadership down as a competency-based linear process as it would be experienced by hypothetical new leaders. Leaders first assess the organization, their own constraints, and their own abilities. Then leaders begin to set goals and determine priorities. Their actions or behaviors are molded by their strategic purposes as well as the reservoir of talents that they bring, which they have acquired through experience, education, and natural talents. The success of their actions will affect their performance. Exhibit 8.7 displays the major elements of the leadership action.

Reconceptualizing this process as a causal chain, leaders act using a wide variety of styles. Nine pure styles and one combined style have been identified. The proper selection of style is based on three variables. First, different organizational and environmental needs require different styles. The frontline leader may need to use a supportive style more frequently; a chief executive officer has to be more expert at an external style. Although all leaders need a variety of styles, the mix of styles will vary by factors such as the need for control, differential goals and performance expectations, types of motivators utilized, and the type of leader focus emphasized. Second, leaders must examine the constraints that they face in terms of resources, power, and personal skills. A leader taking over a division in a crisis mode may need to rely on a highly directive style, whereas a leader taking over a high-performing division may initially adopt a laissez-faire style as s/he studies the organization for subtle refinements. Third, the leader's own sense of priorities will shape his/her selection of styles. A leader more interested in developing long-term capacity through an investment in human resources may emphasize supportive, participative, and delegative styles. A leader more interested in meeting immediate environmental demands for greater competitiveness and organizational change may rely more on achievement, inspirational, collaborative, and strategic styles.

The degree of success of the various styles chosen is affected by leaders' characteristics and the quality of their behavioral skills. Have they had experience and practice in using various styles? Do they have a natural ability or talent for the styles that they are using? Do they have capabilities and the right attitudes for the tasks that they manage? Thus, managers with high competence in operations but poor interpersonal and leadership skills will generally perform poorly overall. The same is usually true of managers who have good leadership skills but little operational experience because they need to divert much time and attention to basic learning and may need to rely excessively on others for expert judgments in making managerial decisions. As leadership skills and technical competence increase, quality in using various styles is also likely to improve along with overall performance.

Performance itself can be judged from radically different, although not mutually exclusive, perspectives. Technical efficiency requires cost efficiency and program effectiveness. Follower satisfaction is a result of development, competence, and appropriate inclusion in organizational processes and decision making. Decision quality as a performance variable emphasizes a balance of various criteria including leader expertise in the decision arena, follower knowledge, follower impartiality, timeliness

Exhibit 8.7

An Overview of the Leadership Action Cycle

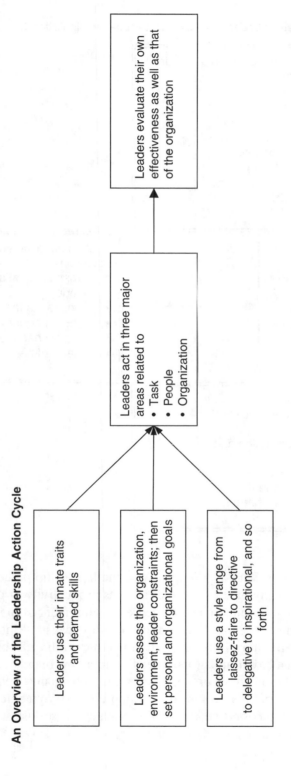

Exhibit 8.8

Competency-Based Leadership (Van Wart's "Leadership Action Cycle")

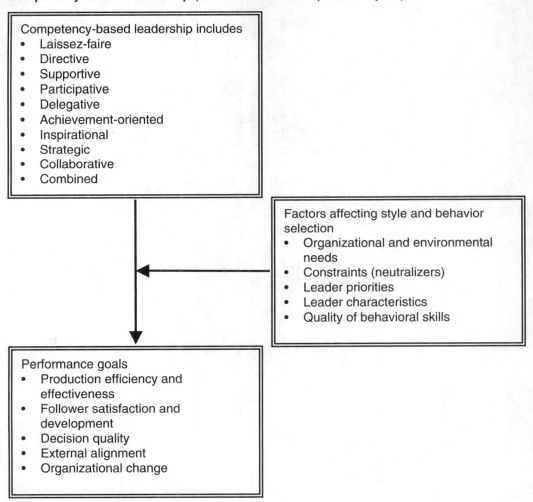

demands, and so on. That is, the quality of the leadership process (quality decisions) is as important as any of the outcomes such as productivity or employee satisfaction. Another performance outcome is the degree of alignment of the organization with the external environment. Poor alignment can occur because of internal dysfunctionality such as organizational rigidity or apathy toward client needs, or it can occur because of a change in the environment itself leading to a new mandate. Finally, performance can be assessed based on the organization's ability to change and be flexible. This type of performance variable becomes more important in a dynamic or turbulent environment. The causal chain for the leadership action cycle is illustrated in Exhibit 8.8. (See Exhibit 17.1 for a fully articulated view.)

MULTIPLE-ORGANIZATIONAL-LEVEL LEADERSHIP THEORY (HUNT'S SYNTHESIS)

Hunt (1996) emphasizes a vertical perspective of leaders at different levels in the organization and the length of time necessary to achieve a broader organizational perspective. Although he proposes only three styles of leadership—direct leadership, organizational leadership, and systems leadership—they are highly articulated. Hunt's formulation follows a popular distinction made by Katz (1955) that management skills are divided by level. Frontline supervisors first need the technical competencies to conduct their jobs; soon thereafter they must master interpersonal skills as well, even as they are expanding their technical scope of knowledge. As senior managers and executives, their need for technical knowledge declines and interpersonal skills level off, but their need for conceptual skills expands as an understanding of changing markets, distant threats, innovations in other fields, and political interventions become more important for the leader to address.

Direct leadership includes the production level. It involves administration or operating procedures and maintenance of individual and collective skills and equipment. Organizational leadership involves the upward integration of subordinate organizational elements with the goals and mission of the organization. It also involves the downward operation, interpretation, and translation of subsystems or programs. Systems leadership involves the development of the mission and the articulation of goals. Additionally, systems management requires the development of strategies, operating principles, and/ or policy development. Executives are responsible for the overall design of the system and subunits as well as the broader operation and control of centralized systems planning over functions such as budget, information, personnel, and so forth.

The appropriate style is largely a function of one's place in the hierarchy. Eligibility for more senior positions is linked to seniority considerations (among others) because of the maturity that organizational and systems leadership normally requires. After selection to leadership positions, a leader's degree of success is moderated by four factors. The capacity of individuals includes their background predispositions and preferences, which are roughly analogous to the traits and skill sets described in this text. Hunt emphasizes cognitive complexity and social cognition as subtle leader skills that strongly distinguish leaders at different levels. He also points to more standard leadership skills of both a transactional and transformational nature. These skills help the leader carefully mediate between external demands, on the one hand, and unit or organizational and follower demands, on the other. An additional moderating factor is the ability of the leader to express and manage the values of the organization or subunit. These values are in turn affected by the social and cultural values of the environment.

Hunt points out that performance can be viewed from many perspectives. He offers four. First, performance can be seen as concrete goal attainment or achievement of specific ends such as profitability. This perspective is especially useful at the operational level. Second, performance can be viewed as strategic goal attainment or the ability to acquire the necessary resources for the organization to survive and thrive. This perspective is useful for executives

Exhibit 8.9

Hunt's "Synthesis" Causal Chain (Extended Multiple-Organizational-Level
Leadership Model)

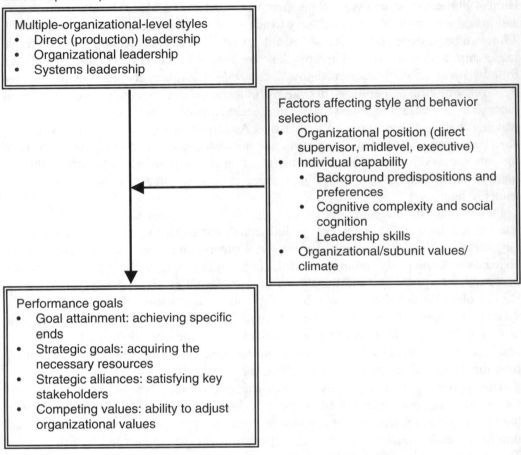

Multiple-organizational-level styles
- Direct (production) leadership
- Organizational leadership
- Systems leadership

Factors affecting style and behavior
selection
- Organizational position (direct
  supervisor, midlevel, executive)
- Individual capability
  - Background predispositions and
    preferences
  - Cognitive complexity and social
    cognition
  - Leadership skills
- Organizational/subunit values/
  climate

Performance goals
- Goal attainment: achieving specific
  ends
- Strategic goals: acquiring the
  necessary resources
- Strategic alliances: satisfying key
  stakeholders
- Competing values: ability to adjust
  organizational values

Source: Hunt (1996)

and senior managers in an environment characterized by competition and independence.
Similarly, the strategic-alliance approach emphasizes the need to satisfy key stakeholders.
This perspective focuses on competition and a collaborative or co-optative approach. Finally,
performance may be analyzed based on competing values. This perspective emphasizes
the ability to adjust organizational values to fit the environment for the varying levels and
types of need for stability, change, production, growth, and human resource development
as they shift over time. (See Exhibit 8.9 for the implicit causal chain.)

In sum, the eight different "integrated" theories must simplify an enormously complex
concept that is used for innumerable purposes. No matter how well-conceived, theoretical
and applied trade-offs are inevitable, ranging from level of abstraction to level of application. Shared leadership and Chemers's integrative leadership models do a good job of
describing leadership interactions with followers in organizational settings, but ultimately

ignore the broader contextual roles of leadership. The narrower transformational theories highlight the need for dynamic leaders, while the full-range theory of Bass fuses transactional and transformational elements. Yet the narrower transformational theories tend to overemphasize change and personality, and Bass's theory is far too abstract to be of much use in applied settings and too universalistic to guide an overarching research agenda. The new strategic leadership theory embraces more than the competitive strategies of executives, but it cannot become too broad or else it loses its powerful thrust in examining the ever-important world of fighting for resources, fame, and fortune. At the other end of the competitive-collaboration spectrum, social change leadership does an excellent job of explaining leadership's role in achieving a better society by merging prescriptive and descriptive factors. Complexity leadership blends both strategic and collaboration foci, and acknowledges traditional leadership functions, all in a highly dynamic environment, but it is extremely abstract and philosophical. Comprehensive leadership competencies provide a useful descriptive listing of the competencies necessary for practitioners, but as it begins to catalog situational specificities, it starts to become encyclopedic and less "user-friendly." Hunt's multiple-organizational-level theory stems from long-held beliefs that leaders at different organizational levels tend to exercise different blends of competencies, but it too is relatively abstract. Exhibit 8.10 compares the integrated theories based on their major leadership style thrusts and groups the styles under Hunt's headings of direct, organizational, and systems types of leadership.

CONCLUSION

It is no easy task to integrate leadership theories into a macrolevel perspective, and corresponding values must be weighed. How many perspectives should be simultaneously captured? If it is a lot, should the theory be very elegant and therefore very abstract? Or should it be comprehensive, and therefore very detailed, multidimensional, and complex? Should it limit itself primarily to a closed system perspective, and perhaps focus on the leader-follower dimension, or should it focus primarily on the organizational perspective or even on the systems perspective? Should it be descriptive and nonnormative, or prescriptive and normative?

Shared leadership focuses on a closed system perspective integrating traditional hierarchical leadership with leadership that empowers, team leadership, and self-leadership. Chemers's integrative approach is another closed system approach that focuses on the traditional structuring and consideration functions (task and people dualities), while blending in prominence or the ego considerations of the leader and led.

The narrower forms of transformational leadership focus on vision or charisma and thus are not particularly integrative; Bass's full-range leadership theory is inclusive of both transactional and transformational leadership. However, the full-range leadership theory is highly abstract and universal. Strategic leadership focuses on the organizational level in terms of learning adeptly and acting boldly in the competitive environment (the absorptive and adaptive functions), while using managerial wisdom to get the timing right and maintain operations sensibly. On the other hand, social change leadership

Exhibit 8.10

Comparison of Different Foci of Various Integrated Theories of Leadership with Representative Scholars

INTEGRATED LEADERSHIP THEORY NAME / TYPE	DIRECT					ORGANIZATIONAL		SYSTEMS	
	Laissez faire	Directive	Supportive	Participative	Delegative	Achievement-oriented	Inspirational	Strategic	Collaborative
Shared leadership (Pearce and Conger)		Traditional	Superleadership		Self Team				
Integrative leadership (Chemers)		Structuring	Consideration		Prominence (fulfilling ego needs)				
Transformational (Tichy and Devanna; Conger)		[Transactional or entrepreneurial*]				Visionary	Charismatic	[Transforming**]	
Strategic leadership (Boal and Hooijberg)		(Managerial competence assumed)						Absorptive; adaptive; managerial wisdom	Collaborative
Social change leadership (Crosby and Bryson)		(Personal integrity; administrative competence)				(Political competence)			Collaborative
Complexity leadership (Uhl-Bien)		Administrative					Enabling	Adaptive	
Comprehensive leadership competencies (House, Van Wart)	Descriptive identification of major styles and the specific competencies necessary in different situations								
Multiple-organizational-levels theory (Hunt)	Direct					Organizational		Systems	

LEADERSHIP STYLE

Notes: Shaded areas indicate an emphasis of the theory.

*The full range theory of Bass would include transactional leadership; some theories of change focus on process and operations systems and are a type of transformational leadership sometimes called "entrepreneurial leadership."

**Burns originally discussed transforming leadership, which entails a collaborative social-good perspective that has been largely taken up by what is called here "social change leadership."

focuses on the collaborative aspects of a systems environment, putting public values front-and-center.

Complexity theory also emphasizes the systems approach, especially the dynamic variety in which radical change is sometimes necessary. It emphasizes that the organization must be as complex as its environment, it must gauge the amount of change necessary, and must function as a cohesive network.

The comprehensive leadership competencies approach is more descriptive and non-normative than most approaches. It tries to be a compendium of the most typical styles and competencies, and to provide a uniform taxonomy to make judgments about classes of situations in which various styles and competencies should be emphasized. It is highly popular in the corporate and agency world because of its applied thrust.

Hunt examines the different skill levels needed based on whether they are expected to provide direct, organizational, or systems leadership. His analysis encapsulates general management wisdom spanning fifty years and overlaps with the leadership competency approach in that it emphasizes situations based on the leader's organizational place in the hierarchy.

This concludes the review of the major theories and leadership approaches. We next turn to an examination of applied leadership theory, emphasizing the elements of leaders' roles and competencies.

PART II

APPLYING THEORY

Leader Assessments

Leaders need information to act effectively, so, logically, leader assessment and evaluation is the first priority. Peter Drucker (cited in Cohen 2010) points out that it is critical for leaders to be adept at looking, listening, and analyzing the organization and the world around it. For example, without good military intelligence a general is unlikely to win a battle; corporate executives without subordinates who are steeped in the details of new initiatives are simply gambling with poor odds; and without an acute sense of technical, political, and/or social trends, leaders of all types will miss opportunities and open their organizations to dramatic downturns (Washington and Hacker 2005). This chapter will focus on the global assessments that a leader needs to make, whether that leader is an agency head or a frontline supervisor. Such assessments help leaders to set long-term agendas, which ultimately dictate how they will balance their time and where they will focus special efforts. Leaders who either skip this step, if they are new to a situation, or allow this function to atrophy if they are ongoing in their position, doom themselves to being, at best, second rate.

At the heart of assessment is asking the right questions. As Oakley and Krug opine, "The single most valuable tool within any renewing organization is skillfully asked effective questions" (1991, 166).

Management theory examines the internal and environmental demands with which all organizations must contend, constraints within which leaders must limit themselves, and the choices leaders make (Stewart 1967, 1976, 1982). This chapter looks at the first two factors: organizational demands and leader constraints. Eight demands will be discussed in the next section. Leaders must be able to effectively assess the capacity of organizations to respond to these demands. Next, constraints will be reviewed. Constraints are those aspects that limit a leader's total discretion, because in reality most leaders are highly constrained. This is especially significant in the public sector. A realistic understanding of these constraints is critical to effective action. Four constraints are examined later in this chapter. Exhibit 9.1 identifies the organizational effectiveness and leader constraint areas in tabular form.

What are some of the general sources that leaders can use to glean information about the organization in its environment? There are at least five major sources of information that leaders can use to assess organizational effectiveness. Absence of any of these sources should be a red flag to proactive leaders and should encourage further investigation. The first source includes the *performance data* that the organization produces. What are the production numbers (cases processed, roads paved, electric customers served, checks or vouchers issued, etc.) in terms of simple output? How does this relate to the number of personnel and amount of the budget (efficiency)? What measures of effectiveness and

---

Exhibit 9.1

Organizational Effectiveness Criteria and the Constraints Leaders Face

Leader Assessment Areas

Organizational and Environmental Demands
1. Task skills
2. Role clarity
3. Innovation and creativity
4. Resources and support services
5. Subordinate effort
6. Cooperation and cohesiveness
7. Organization of work and performance strategies
8. External coordination and adaptability

Constraints
1. Legal/contractual constraints
2. Limitations of position power
3. Availability of resources
4. Limits of leadership abilities

---

quality exist (complaint logs, grievances, lawsuits, external quality control measures)? Simple output data are generally extensive, technical, and highly detailed. Efficiency and effectiveness data are much less common but ultimately more valuable. Leaders who may conceptually understand organizational problems but lack knowledge and a good comprehension of performance data in their organizational area will be hamstrung when trying to fashion implementation plans. A second source of data is any documents that provide *information about the mission, vision, and values of the organization.* This nonquantitative information provides critical information about the organizational purposes, plans, and passions. Public leaders also need to be well versed in authorizing legislation as well as the administrative rules that frame their organizations or areas of responsibility.

Another source of information is the employees themselves. Such information is available through conversations (or interviews), surveys, and focus groups. Employees have critical information about how the organization operates, and, because they form a critical component of several work processes (organizational effectiveness factors), they are uniquely able to discuss perceptions related to their own positions (such as satisfaction). A related but distinct source is the *clients, customers, citizens, or regulated constituents that an agency serves.* An agency can glean information about clients and customers through conversations, surveys, and focus groups. Asking national park patrons, city garbage customers, county road users, or state tax filers what they think of the "service" should be a regular business practice. Regulated constituents—those stopped at police traffic points, undergoing license renewals or site inspections, stopped at borders, required to file paperwork and applications for entitlements, and so forth—should not be exempt from this practice.[1] Regulated constituents (although always harsher in their assessments) not only provide service quality dimensions but also may reveal ethical and legal lapses.

The final source involves using *benchmarks with other units or organizations.* How well does the unit or organization perform compared to others inside and outside the

Exhibit 9.2

A New Agency Director Discovers the Issues for Herself

Having directed a state-level personnel agency in another state, Molly Anderson knew that staff agencies were prone to criticism even when they were doing a good job. Her challenge as a new cabinet-level director in Iowa state government was to get beyond the superficial complaints and to assess the genuine strengths and weaknesses of her new agency. Like almost all large human resource management agencies in government, the agency was coping with issues of decentralization, major recruitment challenges in select fields like technology, broadbanding salary structures, cafeteria-style benefit plans, training upgrades, and salary freezes, despite growth in government and increasing service demands. Yes, surely many of the complaints were legitimate, but many were not fair or were simply out of the agency's control and in the legislature's hands (e.g., salary structure).

Upon taking office, Anderson announced a 100-day assessment period. For nearly three months she read reports, gathered and analyzed data, and talked to people. She talked to the governor and all the legislators on the personnel committees. She talked to all of her 100 employees as individuals and in groups. She talked to other agency directors and to agency directors in other states. She even talked to various customer groups such as line employees and supervisors in other agencies.

On the one hundredth day Anderson presented her report to the governor. Soon afterward, she presented the report to the legislature, her own agency, and the cabinet. Her report clearly stated the strengths *and* weaknesses of the current agency, thus garnering instant credibility. It highlighted an array of problems, some of which needed legislative action, some executive action, and some departmental action. At the end of the first year, less than 50 percent of the agenda she laid out had been addressed, especially in the legislative arena. Nonetheless, the improvement in image, departmental morale, and forward momentum was enormous. Besides, with an extraordinarily thorough assessment under her belt, Molly Anderson had enough to keep her busy for several more years. By that time she would probably need another major assessment!

industry? Does it study best practices and implement them? Is the organization itself a source of best practices?

Several recommendations are commonly provided to leaders about conducting these types of global assessments. First, new leaders should conduct the global assessments early in their tenure, often as their very first major activity. It is not uncommon for new agency leaders to declare a three- to six-month assessment period during which they gather and analyze as much data as possible. Most followers expect a competent new leader to do this and are reassured when it is done comprehensively (see Exhibit 9.2). The second bit of advice is for ongoing leaders: Do global assessments on a routine basis. Such assessments are commonly done as a part of budget and performance appraisal processes. It is just as effective to require new data before a strategic planning session so that new data are linked with new ideas. It is all too easy to let organizational assessment be a pro forma routine when the very dynamism of the organization depends on a vigorous process. Third, leaders need to make sure that they are gathering their information broadly. All organizations need to look at performance, customer, client, *and* document data on a regular basis to be at least average. Benchmark data are more useful to those who aspire to be above average. A similar concern regarding the breadth of the data is quality. The need for higher-quality data is a pressing trend in the organizational universe, as is the need to use knowledge management, which has even brought about the creation of chief knowledge officers in the private sector (Morey, Maybury, and Thuraisingham 2002). Public sector organizations are not exempt (Holzer and Lee 2004). Sometimes the first major initiative of a new leader is a substantial upgrade in the breadth and depth of data collection. Yet, the most important advice of all is simply to be sure that the organization uses the data. Frequently, data are unused; this is generally a waste of resources as well as a source of great frustration for those in the organization.

ASSESSMENT OF THE ORGANIZATION AND ITS ENVIRONMENT

There are many ways to divide the various important functions of the organization. "Total quality" assessments (Walton 1986) and balanced scorecard approaches (Kaplan and Norton 1996) are two of the more popular methods that are discussed in the popular and scholarly literature. This discussion will split important organizational perspectives into eight elements, starting with the basic building blocks of any organization, task competencies, and concluding with the nebulous but critical nexus between the organization and its external coordination and adaptability. Each section will ask three basic questions: How do you know if there is a problem? How do you study the nature of a problem? Finally, what are some of the major strategies that can be used to address a deficiency?

Task Competencies

Task competencies are the finite behaviors, roles, and skills that a worker at any level needs to have to accomplish work successfully. Task competencies may be any combination of knowledge, physical dexterity, interpersonal capacity, or intellectual abilities (Fleishman et al. 1991). For example, a military pilot needs extensive knowledge of aircraft and military tactics, honed flying skills, and the ability to make high-quality decisions under pressure when confronted with large amounts of technical data and extraneous information. Task competencies are critical to the proper functioning of any organization, whether one is talking about the efficient treatment of a customer by an employee working at the counter, an effective treatment by a public sector physician, or the public-speaking skill of an executive. A good organizational reputation, minimization of rework, or maintaining strong funding all ultimately depend on good task competencies.

Identification of task problems can occur in any of three ways; if task competencies are a likely problem, all three identification strategies may be used. One way to understand task skill levels is to study the practices of those whose task skills are best. The best workers normally stand out; studying several workers ensures that different styles will be included in models. This strategy enhances a leader's "depth perception" and assists in identifying model practices. A second strategy is to make individual comparisons. Such comparisons can be based on observation, performance data of the individual (if it exists), and/or work samples or document review. This strategy enhances error detection in general and is very useful in analysis of weak performers. A third strategy is group comparisons, which can be made with the group's past performance, other units in the organization, an industry average, or organizations known for high performance. They are normally based on data review or benchmarking. This strategy is especially useful for units or organizations in which suboptimal performance (e.g., a low performing unit) may lead to redesign and thus new task skills, and for motivating a mediocre organization into refining its task skills to a higher level.

In analyzing the quality of task skills and the range of strategies that may be used to address the problems identified, it is necessary to understand the nature of the work and workers. That is, both task characteristics and subordinate characteristics will identify areas of likely problems and point to more effective strategies. One task characteristic is the degree of structure and routine in the work versus its unstructured, episodic aspects. For example, line work tends to be more routine and management tends to be less structured and more episodic. Another characteristic of work is the feedback provided by the work itself. A road builder will get immediate feedback related to timeliness but may not get good feedback about the durability of concrete roads, a quality that may not be apparent for at least a decade. Another task characteristic is how intrinsically satisfying the work is. Data entry work and paperwork completion are generally not intrinsically satisfying while professional work (usually requiring some advanced study and sense of calling) is more so. There are also the aspects of pressure and hardship. Policing, electric and power line work, and air traffic control are prime examples. Finally, there are the reward structures: standard pay and types of incentive pay (seniority/cost of living, skill-based, merit, gainsharing, etc.), types of recognition, promotion strategies, and so forth.

Because it is people who do the work whatever its actual structure and nature, subordinate characteristics are no less important to observe. What is the level of experience? What is the innate ability of the worker or workers for the specific tasks? What is the level of training and education? To what degree does a professional orientation exist and to what degree is it appropriate? How interested are the workers in the types of incentives that are offered? Some common types of problems that occur from these characteristics include: random errors from new workers and fossilized error patterns from experienced workers; procedural errors from untrained workers; quality errors from insufficiently educated workers; slow production from untalented workers; apathy from unprofessional workers; and plateauing, burnout, and turnover from workers whose incentives are inadequate to the job.

Depending on the nature of the work and the worker characteristics, a number of strategies exist to address deficiencies in task competencies. Leaders need to match the strategy with the type of problem, and be aware that some strategies may be difficult or impossible to implement in a given organizational environment. However, some strategies that seem difficult at first blush can be accomplished through determination and creativity coupled with some patience. Starting with worker characteristics, experience and ability can be improved through improving the recruitment/hiring process. Additional testing can be required (more training-and-education experience, performance examples, ability tests, etc.), and standards can be raised. Another common way to improve task competencies is through improving or expanding training. Perhaps basic training omits an important basic topic. Does continuing education need to cover a specialized or advanced topic? Is the quality of training simply poor (e.g., boring, outdated, irrelevant, inaccurate, etc.) and thus needs to be improved? Or perhaps the training needs to be conducted on a more individualized basis with ongoing workers. Then an appropriate strategy is to improve monitoring and to follow up with technically focused job coaching (normally by the supervisor or a lead worker) or broader training through mentoring with an experienced employee who shares job insights over time. In larger organizations this strategy may need to include the training of supervisors to improve their training and coaching skills. Similarly, although mature workers are generally averse to "retraining" when their competencies are found to be deficient, they are generally more open to "continuing education," which may accomplish the same thing if appropriate training can be identified. A related strategy is the publication of model practices. Such models can be used in training, for job coaching, and as job aids. Still another general strategy that assists with worker motivation is to enhance the sense of professionalism, which increases self-worth, commitment, self-study, and self-training on the job. Leaders pursuing this long-term strategy must be prepared to (1) engage workers in discussions about their work, (2) "empower" workers to make adjustments to improve work quality, (3) allow more opportunities for additional training/education, and (4) recognize those who are "models."

Some strategies to address task competency deficiencies focus more on the nature of the work. The scope of work can be shifted for either greater variety (to reduce boredom or to increase job integration) or greater specificity (if more focus is needed due to excessive job variety). Another strategy is to recognize that workers rarely improve without concrete, ongoing, recent feedback. Feedback systems are powerful teachers but they do take time to implement. (This is often described as the province of performance management.) Examples include requiring workers to keep monthly records of projects or interviews completed, cases processed, and so on, and to regularly provide workers with error rates, work sample reviews, damage reports, and the like. A final strategy is to improve the linkage between work and rewards (e.g., increasing performance-based rewards) or to vary rewards to better fit employee interests and needs (especially because financial reward linkages may be structurally limited by the system).

Role Clarity

Role clarity is the accurate and precise knowledge that workers, groups, and managers have about which activities, functions, and roles they are to master and how their work integrates with others. Mintzberg (1973) summarizes management as the division and coordination of work; when well done, the result is role clarity. Role clarity is also a good example of Max DePree's observation that "the signs of outstanding leadership appear primarily among the followers" (1989, 12). That is, when there are no problems, workers are more efficient and content. Role clarity is easiest when jobs are simple, routines are stable, individual roles do not overlap, and elaborate rules set worker protocols. Yet, the contemporary world of work is moving toward constant work change, job integration and enhancement, teamwork, and more flexible work guidelines due to greater technology changes, customer orientation and customization of service, pressure for constant improvement, and so forth. Therefore, *role clarity is likely to become an increasingly difficult challenge for contemporary leaders.*

How do you know if role clarity is a problem? Unlike task skills, which can often be directly observed and quantitatively measured if necessary, role clarity is difficult to observe or measure directly. Nonetheless, its absence is not difficult to identify. Generally, when role clarity is lacking there is either greater unhappiness or certain types of important work are undone. Qualitative measures (one-on-one discussions, surveys, etc.) will quickly point out problems in this area. Employees will often experience conflict or annoyance when role clarity is weak, expressing this in some form of "Everyone seems to have different priorities" or "They are not doing their job!" Customers will either be shuffled from one employee to another or will not be able to obtain the requisite service at all. Managers (direct supervisors, peers, senior managers) should notice that work production is inefficient or that certain work is ignored because no one takes responsibility for it. Even a single change in the work environment, such as a new worker, a new responsibility, or a changed client, can cause a decrease in role clarity.

Upon what is role clarity based? For role clarity to be high, it assumes that workers know all task competencies. It also assumes the presence of worker cooperation. Generally these conditions precede role clarity and need to be addressed first if lacking. Role ambiguity and role conflict can also occur at a group level. For example, it is not uncommon for workers to disagree about whose job it is to answer customer complaints, respond to special requests, or service a special class of cases that do not fit neatly into anyone's core responsibility. The manager may perceive role clarity problems when s/he wants all employees to attend to certain activities as a part of everyone's job, but the expectation is largely ignored. For example, a manager may expect everyone to help update the unit's Web page, but she finds that it remains hopelessly outdated.

When deficiencies are discovered, what strategies can be used? Fundamentally, problems of role clarity are a manager's responsibility because the division and coordination of work is his/her job. Therefore, serious managerial attention is a prerequisite for adequate solutions when problems exist. One specific strategy is to improve job descriptions by clarifying or updating them. Alternatively, perhaps better role modeling would assist new workers to see how different work connections are accomplished. Ideal or model examples can be pointed out or discussed, either individually or collectively. Another strategy is better job assignments or more thorough goal setting at the individual level. Perhaps the manager is paying insufficient attention to providing a clear mandate or defined instructions. Better goal formation at the group level is another means of refining role clarity. What is the group trying to accomplish and how do individuals contribute to the overall goals? Finally, training may be a solution, especially if new employees are unsure of role responsibilities or there has been a significant work redesign.

Ideally, the overall structure of roles is determined by managerial work design but the details of role integration are worked out by worker self-determination, interactive goal setting (with the supervisor), and mutual accommodation (among workers). However, when role clarity breaks down, leaders must to be ready to step in to be more directive, especially in crises (Kapucu and Van Wart 2006, 2008). For example, the standard protocol for a fire scene is that the first senior commander at a fire becomes the "incident commander" so that s/he can clearly delegate roles and avoid role ambiguity, overlap, and conflict. Even when other more senior commanders arrive on the scene, s/he retains the prime responsibility to preserve this critical work dimension.

Innovation and Creativity

Creativity is the ability to think about ideas or do things in nonroutine ways, while innovation is the adaptation of ideas or ways of doing things (from any source) to a new setting. Managers do not have to be creative themselves to introduce successful and important innovations. They do need to recognize the creative ideas of their subordinates and other organizations and be willing to implement them. (Invention is a term generally reserved for an original innovation that is a significant improvement on a past product or service.) Innovation and creativity require change. As DePree (1989, 33) reminds us, however, "if there is one thing a well-run bureaucracy or institution finds difficult to handle, it is change." That is because efficiency is tied to routines, and quality control is generally tied to consistency. Unfortunately, these virtues can quickly metamorphose into the bureau pathologies of rigidity and deadening negativity. Increasingly, the public sector is being forced to change more rapidly and flexibly, and it would seem that a slow cultural transformation is being achieved. By studying various awards programs, Sanford Borins was able to predict the most common (perceived) causes of change (in order): internal problems, political pressures, a crisis, a new leader, and, lastly, a new opportunity (2000, 502–503).

Like role clarity, problems of a lack of innovation and creativity are primarily perceived in their absence through qualitative means. One signal of such problems is a "firefighting" or reactive management style where problems are constant and solutions are temporary, of poor quality, or after-the-fact. Another is a lack of "ownership" of problems by workers or management—"someone else" is to blame or the system is at fault. These symptoms are accompanied by pessimism about the likelihood of change, which leads to a "why bother?" attitude. Furthermore, the disincentives for change are strong (e.g., failure is punished, those making suggestions must do all the work, suggestions are treated with suspicion or hostility, etc.) and incentives are simply nonexistent.

Sources of creativity can be understood from both individual (Reiter-Palmon and Illies 2004) and organizational (Berson et al. 2006) viewpoints. Individual creativity emphasizes lateral thinking (de Bono 1985) rather than vertical thinking. Vertical thinking is selective, analytical, sequential, negative, and strongly biased toward past practices. However, lateral thinking is generative, provocative, nonsequential, positive, and strongly biased toward new possibilities. Lateral thinkers implicitly allow opportunities for the uncritical generation of alternatives, challenging assumptions, looking at problems from the reverse perspective, only focusing on one problem element at a time, playfulness, and reorganizing standard patterns randomly in order to move past logical inflexibility. Suspending disbelief (i.e., suspending vertical thinking until a new idea has emerged and has been substantially improved) is generally critical to the success of lateral thinking. The best-known method in organizational settings is brainstorming, a family of methods that allows noncritical generation of ideas prior to analysis and selection of the best ideas.

It only stands to reason that organizational culture and attitudes have a major effect on the use of creativity and the amount of innovation that occurs. Common features of organizations that encourage innovation are a positive attitude toward problems, a willingness to make either small or large changes as needed (incremental or radical), a willingness to acknowledge mistakes and failures as major sources of information and teaching, a willingness to question current practice as a standard business tool, and the discipline to occasionally look at how things fit together even when it crosses divisional or internal/external lines (systems thinking). These attitudes tend to create a learning organization, that is, one that readily learns its way through current problems and is proactive in anticipating future problems and opportunities (Senge 1990; Vera and Crossan 2004). Key to creating this environment is an acknowledgment that all ideas cannot come from the top of the hierarchy (Kanter 1983; Hannah and Lester 2009). In a study of innovation in the public sector, Borins (2000) reported that the most likely sources in terms of organizational level were (in order): middle managers, politicians/agency heads/frontline staff (tied), interest groups, and last, others (citizens, clients). For a famous case analysis of creativity in the public sector, see Exhibit 9.3.

When this area is lacking in an organization, there are many ways for leaders to reverse the trend (Yukl 2009). Yet, prior to devising specific strategies, it is important to think about removing disincentives and adding incentives. Because two of the most important disincentives are punishment for failure and extreme skepticism about new ideas, a strong message must be projected that strategic or appropriate failure is acceptable (otherwise experimentation and pilot projects are unwise for managers) and that the generation of new ideas is a mandatory element of doing a good job (Carmeli and Schaubroeck 2007). Incentives can include the resources to implement experiments, pilot projects, and full-scale implementation plans, the public recognition of successful innovation, and even financial rewards when possible. Depending on the organization and circumstances a variety of specific strategies may increase creativity and innovation, for example, such as increasing entrepreneurialism, enhancing competition, benchmarking, experimenting, enhancing team synergy and problem solving, and enhancing training for teams inside the organization and most types of training and education outside the organization (to bring new perspectives back to the organization).

Resources and Support Services

One of Mintzberg's major responsibilities for a manager-leader is as resource allocator. This element of the organizational operation encompasses the degree to which the workers or units have the tools, equipment, personnel, facilities, and funds to accomplish work or to acquire the necessary information or help from other work groups (Yukl 1998, 277). Resource allocation is an issue for most workers because almost all jobs require some degree of planning; it becomes an increasingly larger responsibility as leaders have more

Exhibit 9.3

A Classic Case Study of Innovation: Continuous-Aim Firing at Sea

Perhaps the best known study of innovation is by the naval historian, Elting E. Morison, in which he chronicles the difficulties of transforming the crude art of firing naval guns at the turn of the century into a precision science just a decade later. The case involves not only innovation but also leadership (Morison 1968).

To understand the case, it is necessary to know what the state of the art of naval firing was in the 1890s. The guns on naval ships had to fire in seas that were invariably rolling. Gunners therefore had to estimate the range, adjust the angle of the gun, and then wait for the roll of the ship for the exact moment to fire. Because of the weight of the gun, gear ratios were such that the movement was very slow, so firing was infrequent as well as highly inaccurate.

In 1898, the British captain Sir Percy Scott noticed that one gunner had a superior record of hitting targets. Upon closer inspection, he noticed that the gunner was furiously cranking the gun this way and that. Upon being asked what he was doing and why he was violating operating procedure (after all, did he want to break the gearshift?), he replied that he could aim better if he held the gun stable while the ship rolled. Scott was a bit incredulous. At first he thought it impossible to move the heavy gun fast enough until he realized that the gunner was allowing the gun to remain stable while the ship moved and thus gravity did most of the work if the gunner was in time with the rolls. This spurred Scott to make several other simple improvements such as a better telescopic sight. With these improvements gunners could shoot far more frequently and adjust the stabilized guns to pinpoint accuracy after the first shot or two. One commentator estimated that the efficiency improved nearly 3,000 percent in just six years. While in 1900 naval fire was little better than medieval cannon fire, by World War I battleships could fire several miles with considerable accuracy.

Although Scott faced great challenges introducing these innovations in the British navy, they paled in comparison to the challenges in the American adoption. William S. Sims was an officer in the American navy who met Scott in the South China Sea where he learned all he could of the revolutionary new techniques. Like Scott, he was a determined sort of fellow, and so he ignored the fact that his first half-dozen reports to the Bureau of Ordnance in Washington were ignored. In the second stage, he sent the bureau another half-dozen reports in which he used abusive language and sent copies throughout the Navy to receive attention, which he did. Finally the Bureau of Ordnance responded officially by providing evidence that the new innovations were impossible. In trying out the innovations at the dry-dock testing ground, it was impossible to move the heavy gun quickly enough (ignoring the issue of gravity at sea). The report further stated that poor artillery records were the fault of poor training officers (like Sims), not the guns approved by the Bureau of Ordnance!

Unlike the British case, where the resistance was initially severe but not ultimately stupid, in the final stage Sims had to go outside the Navy itself. Appealing to President Theodore Roosevelt, Sims finally found a receptive audience. The president created a special position for Sims as Inspector of Target Practice in which he was universally acclaimed as the "man who taught us how to shoot."

This archetypal story of innovation has a number of lessons: (1) The changes were not creations of entirely new technology, but innovations and improvements of technology that was in use. (2) The original innovation was actually discovered by an anonymous sailor (a line worker), not an expert or leader. (3) The innovation was uncovered by an observant leader, who then added his own improvements and called for new standardized equipment and procedures. (4) The resistance to change was primarily from the "experts" themselves. (5) Where resistance is particularly severe, appeals to change from outside are occasionally necessary.

senior positions. Frequently, resource allocation is not simply an issue of more; just as critically, the astute leader will consider less (allowing for reallocation) and fungibility (conversion of one type of resource into another or choices among resource needs, such as salary increases versus additional positions, given a constant stream of dollars). In some cases, resources and support services may be the primary focus of a particular leader in terms of expanding resources, constantly fine-tuning allocation, and troubleshooting resource and support problems; for other cases in resource-rich organizations such problems may be relatively insignificant.

At the more concrete and job-specific level, leaders will learn about resource needs through discussions with subordinates, staff, and, to a lesser degree, clients. Do they perceive that they have the necessary equipment, facilities, and support to fulfill their roles efficiently and effectively? Experienced managers can also conduct work observations to detect resource gaps. While weak performance data may not specifically indicate a resource need, they will indicate areas that need to be considered. At a broader level, leaders must observe overall work processes, system performance, and resource opportunities to make sure that the focus is not simply more, but also includes fewer, free, or different resources. Such information can often be gleaned simply by investigating the types of services available. For example, in larger organizations services may be expertly provided at little or no cost but may be unused by a unit, or in a community various types of resources may be available as a volunteer service. Another good source of information is visits to other organizations that conduct similar work for insights into operations and resource usage (benchmarking).

Resource needs should be based on work needs, which are in turn based on the service and product standard levels desired by the law and clients, and by employee needs. The interplay of these factors—legal mandates, client demands, and employee needs—is complex and ever-changing, which is why resource allocation is a critical part of all types of planning. Some managers will find themselves focused primarily on legal demands and have tight resource allocation parameters within which to work. Other leaders will have a relatively wide level of discretion and may be charged with finding many of their own resources (such as through fees, tuition, contributions/donations, and service charges). A frequent but highly important challenge for leaders is the conversion of poorly used resources into better channels. Personnel, clients, and systems strongly resist changes that reduce resource levels (e.g., reductions in personnel, travel, supplies, etc.). Therefore, leaders frequently implicitly negotiate resources as they redesign work patterns or troubleshoot problems.

The strategies used to address resource deficiencies vary greatly depending on circumstances. In some cases resolution of the problem may be as simple as ordering or requisitioning the necessary supplies or filling an authorized position. Or it may be utilizing an untapped resource inside or outside the unit. However, problems may require a strategic linkage with other units in order to better share or partner personnel or expensive equipment. In especially financially tight times, a problem's solution may require a better rationing system along with motivation sessions to make the rationing effort work (Nutt and Hogan 2008). In some instances the leader will spend a great deal of time and political capital in lobbying for additional resources with agency executives or the legislative body itself. Or resolving a problem may require candid discussions with support service providers to ascertain whether changes are necessary. Finally, leaders today must be increasingly aware of and able to reduce or eliminate resources that are no longer being efficiently or effectively used. Such reductions increase leader credibility externally and allow resource reallocation internally. Often, leaders can allocate new resources that are strategically needed only by reducing resources in other areas.

Subordinate Effort

Subordinate effort is the extent to which subordinates strive to achieve work-related objectives and the level of commitment that they exhibit in their jobs. Although seemingly a simple concept on the surface, subordinate effort is actually extremely complex. Different theories address different aspects of human motivation. Process theories tend to focus first, on the work processes and how people learn, and then relate it to workers' perceptions of work accomplishment and especially to reward systems. Classic process theories include operant condition and behavior modification theory (how people learn new behaviors), expectancy theory (how people relate work achievement to rewards), equity theory (how people view comparative reward systems), and social learning theory (how people learn about more complex behaviors and about the culture of a group). Content theories, on the other hand, attempt first to specify the universal internal needs and drives that energize human behavior (as basic human needs are satisfied, they are often supplanted by higher-level needs such as affiliation and achievement) and then to explain how organizational structures and processes can be created to satisfy those needs (e.g., job enlargement or greater self-determination). Classic theories in this area include those of Maslow, McGregor, Herzberg, McClelland, and Argyris.

Classifications of the levels of worker motivation that are useful as a rough gauge are worker resistance, worker compliance, and worker commitment. Worker hostility generally results in covert or overt resistance; worker apathy results in a compliance mentality; and worker enthusiasm may result in genuine commitment. It is not uncommon for these levels of motivation to vary between the job and the organization at large such that workers have a good deal of enthusiasm for their specific job but apathy or even resistance toward the organization in general.

It is also useful to differentiate among three different types of subordinate effort. Constant effort results in the long-range production of basic services or products and tends to be exhibited through sustained effort and work discipline. Peak effort results in short-term project completion, which tends to be exhibited through spurts of effort in times of high demand, crisis, or system change. Problem solving taps the creative component of effort needed to come up with new solutions or to prevent future problems. Different jobs emphasize different types of effort, and yet, workers generally have innate preferences that may or may not suit work demands at a particular time. Exhibit 9.4 defines the different levels of subordinate effort.

As leaders try to assess the level of effort in their organizations, they may first turn to performance data. Such data, when reliable and when comparison is possible, provide fairly good clues about the level of constant effort. While information may be provided by interviews and discussions, it must often be heavily discounted because of various types of bias. However, organizational "climate" surveys are surprisingly accurate in this regard, largely because of the anonymity that they provide. Such instruments survey satisfac-

Exhibit 9.4

Defining the Different Levels of Subordinate Effort

Level of motivation	Types of effort
Worker resistance	• Effort is rarely constant; constant monitoring is necessary; disincentives are important in maintaining work production; workers feel that inadequate pay or poor work conditions do not merit constant effort • Workers refuse to exert peak effort because it is not in the job description, is unfair, or is simply burdensome; instead of increased productivity in high-demand times, work slowdowns may occur • Workers unwilling to assist in problem solving because of the extra energy required or suspicion that management will use innovations "to squeeze more work out of them"
Worker compliance	• Effort is generally consistent but some monitoring is necessary • Some special effort may be put forth in times of high demand, but extra incentives such as additional salary or time off are normally expected • Workers will assist with problem solving when asked, but do not initiate problem solving on their own
Worker commitment	• Constant effort is consistently put forth without supervision • In times of special demand or crisis, peak effort is exerted without prodding • Workers engage in problem solving on their own

tion with training, supervision, senior management, communications, pay, nonmonetary rewards, innate pleasure with the incumbent's job, colleagues' level of effort, and other aspects that strongly affect motivation. Surveys are good at identifying problem areas but not as good at identifying solutions for problems.

The list of factors that may affect motivation is long and heavily influenced by characteristics of both the work and workers. For ideal motivation, workers must have the appropriate ability, training, and resources to effectively accomplish work. Work roles must be clear, as must reward structures. Further, those rewards must relate to worker preferences. The work itself provides more motivation when it is varied, and when workers have manageable involvement, accountability is rigorous, and direct feedback mechanisms are built into the work process. Often, another a significant factor is public service motivation, that is, the sense of serving the common good (Perry and Hondeghem 2008). Of course, the quality of attention (consideration) that workers receive from supervisors and that supervisors receive from managers, and so on, also makes an enormous difference in worker motivation over the long term. Leaders as direct supervisors orchestrate these technical and supportive factors, which are substantial, no matter what level of organizational hierarchy they occupy.

When motivation seems to be lacking, several strategies may be necessary, and, even when successfully implemented, may require some time to take effect. If workers (including managers) are not able to do their jobs well, motivation will be enhanced either by upgrading recruitment (more experience or workers with more native capacity) or training. Enhanced rewards may be one answer, whether those rewards are financial or nonfinancial. Just as important, however, is the customization of rewards. For example, many employees would prefer a job redesign (that better suits their natural abilities and inclinations) to a small salary increase. Disincentives are important, although rarely as effective as positive reinforcements. Nonetheless, without real disincentives for individuals (loss of promotions, salary increases and other perquisites, demotions and separations, etc.), there is ultimately no real accountability for poor or delinquent performance. Yet in the final analysis an enormous aspect of motivation is the quality of supervision, whether it involves directing frontline employees or department heads. Indeed, Buckingham and Coffman (1999) discovered that the single most important factor in the retention of employees (at the transactional level) was the quality of supervision. Therefore, supervisors need to be held accountable for motivation levels of subordinates, and they, in turn, must be supported and trained in management techniques in general and motivation strategies in particular.

Cooperation and Cohesiveness

Cooperation and cohesiveness describe the degree to which individuals effectively and contentedly work in groups or teams in order to share work, information, and resources, as well as to establish strong identifications with the group and the overall organization. Subordinate effort focuses on individual motivation, while cooperation and cohesiveness implicitly focus on motivation at the group and organizational level. Although important to the proper functioning of any organization, they become particularly important when the organization has scarce resources, workers have close proximity or highly interdependent functions, or the organization experiences increasingly rigorous service/ product demands without significant new resources. While such conditions require greater group effort to maintain service levels, organizational stress may lead to infighting and reduced productivity. Given that the organizational universe currently experiences all these trends, cooperation and cohesiveness will only become more important, if more challenging to achieve, in the coming decades (Pittinsky and Simon 2007). Finally, it is important to note that cooperation and cohesiveness affect both microlevel performance and the macrolevel challenges and accomplishments that typify exceptional leadership and great organizations.

Cooperation and cohesiveness are organizational aspects that must be qualitatively identified through interviews, group discussions, and surveys. Leaders need to look for signs of conflict, absence of cooperation and cohesiveness, and lack of group identification. Cooperation and cohesiveness are most conspicuously absent when conflict is present. Such conflict may be among workers, groups, or even parts of the organization and "outside" groups or interests. Conflict is generally quite destructive because it encourages negative sentiments (which usurps individual energy), distrust, dysfunctional behaviors of the organization (such as sabotage and resource hoarding), poor public relations, and inhibition of creativity and innovation. In a more limited and strategic sense, however, organizations should allow and encourage "constructive conflict" in which individuals disagree with one another, have open and robust debates, and yet remain amicable because they value the necessity of examining different perspectives and retain respect for those holding diametrically opposed positions.

It is less noticeable when cooperation and cohesiveness are lacking but open conflict is absent. The negative attitudes accompanying this state are demonstrated by antagonistic or malicious statements about others ("badmouthing"), an "every-man-for-himself" attitude, or simply a lack of trust in others. For example, individual employees may feel that their work is above average while most everyone else is not "pulling their weight," or a line unit may feel the staff divisions such as personnel and accounting are incompetent, unhelpful, and intrusive. The most subtle problem is a lack of identification with the unit or commitment to the organization. This can result in higher turnover, resistance to group or organizational projects, and a distinct loss of organizational dynamism.

The most obvious source of cooperation and cohesiveness is the work structure itself. It is generally encouraged by work unit sizes that are manageable (ideally four to twelve people)[2] so that people can relate to one another on a personal level. It is also encouraged by a balance between centralization and decentralization of responsibilities and authority, the presence of group rewards, and the absence of excessive competition. Other sources include group stability, shared goals and traditions, and pride in the unit/organization's traditions and mission. Leadership also affects motivation by directly enhancing group cohesion, organizational prestige, and organizational vision. The quality of leadership itself—which, when effective, resolves conflict quickly and creatively—encourages group consensus and inspires members to relinquish their self-interests for the benefit of the group from time to time as good professionals and organizational citizens. Leaders who are high in both integrity (e.g., trustworthiness, fairness, and personal consideration) and inspiration (intellectual stimulation, charismatic appeal, and appealing messages) are much more likely to get workers to transcend self-interests. Such motivation is necessary for organizational objectives that require group solidarity and support such as externally induced change initiatives, the weathering of crises, and substantial upgrades in productivity.

Human nature causes cooperation and cohesiveness to constantly deteriorate in the absence of good leaders to rebuild them. Small or imagined slights, ignored viewpoints, lack of appreciation, confusion about what others really do, and so on, can quickly turn around a smoothly operating organization into a balkanized set of factions. Work-structure strategies include adjusting work unit size, even if only into worker-led or self-managed teams, adjusting responsibility-authority relationships to make sure that workers or units do not feel victimized, and decreasing unhealthy competition that pits workers against one another for scarce resources. Although difficult to implement widely in the public sector, work rewards that are aimed at whole units, divisions, and organizations are powerful symbols and motivators in encouraging cooperation. Because excessive turnover diminishes group cohesion, measures to reduce it such as more enhanced personal consideration (primarily through quality supervision), increased pay or salary matches, and work quality enhancement are sometimes necessary. Leaders must also ensure that members of the organization understand and appreciate their shared interests by promoting the use of corporate metaphors or symbols, and using affective language[3] that binds people together in a common mission. Additionally, leaders should ensure that organizational members participate in occasional alignment sessions such as retreats, strategic planning meetings, and even problem-solving caucuses that encourage multiple interests and perspectives. Further, leaders should constantly stress organizational accomplishments, and, where possible, seek local or national recognition for noteworthy achievements.

Finally, because leaders affect cooperation and cohesiveness so substantially, they can be held accountable for it. Motivation to do the big things, take on the big tasks, and confront the big challenges requires the group and organizational motivation that is the special province of leadership. Thus leaders must make sure that they themselves are motivated in order to serve as models of integrity, commitment, and enthusiasm.

Organization of Work and Performance Strategies

Work does not just happen; it must be structured, planned, and accounted for. The organization of work refers to the way it is arranged and structured to maximize efficient and effective use of personnel, equipment, and other resources as well as to the plans and measures used to ensure quantity and quality of production (Holzer and Lee 2004).

There are two important dimensions to the organization of work. The first is degree: Is the work sufficiently structured, planned, and measured, or, perhaps, too structured, planned, and measured? For example, organizations that are growing in size and complexity need a greater degree of specialization, structure, and new performance measures. On the other hand, a very old organization that is moving into a less stable environment and is also shrinking may have too much specialization, structure, and measurement.

A second dimension is the type of structure, plans, or measures that are used. In this dimension it is not a matter of too little or too much, but rather, a fundamentally different type. Perhaps an organization decides to maintain the same number of human resource personnel but to decentralize most of them into various divisions so that they can be closer to their "customers," which is a fundamentally different way of organizing them. Because of the increasing demand for higher performance and the utilization of more complex and sophisticated structures and measures, this area is escalating as a challenge for leaders. Indeed, many public sector leaders may have to wean themselves away from well-mastered and stable forms, such as the hierarchical bureaucracy that was largely perfected in the twentieth century,[4] as they use more decentralized structures and flexible arrangements, but more detailed and accessible accountability systems. Margaret Wheatley notes presciently, "I believe that we have only just begun the process of discovering and inventing the new organizational forms that will inhabit the twenty-first century" (Wheatley 1992, 5). For an example of a public agency that has had to reinvent its structure and performance strategies, see Exhibit 9.5 regarding the U.S. Postal Service.

Knowing whether an organization has the right organization and performance strategies is no easy task. Ultimately, it is difficult to know for sure how much organizational inefficiency and dysfunctionality are in fact caused by the fundamental patterns of the organization and how much are caused by other factors. In many cases very odd and

Exhibit 9.5

**A Continual Quest for Higher Performance Through Changing Strategies:
The United States Postal Service**

Always the largest civilian agency in the federal government, the United States Postal Service has had to assess its methods and organization many times during its history, which dates from the creation of the country. One area of ongoing reassessment is the means of transportation. Starting with horses, it now includes boats, railroads, and airplanes. In fact, the post office began regular airmail in 1918, quickly establishing most of the major U.S. airports, which it eventually turned over to the Department of Commerce and to municipalities. It has used many means over the years including stagecoaches, Alaskan dogsleds, and steamboats, and continues to deliver mail to residents living at the bottom of the Grand Canyon by mule.

A huge landmark for this agency, which currently has a $55 billion budget, 750,000 employees, and 40,000 offices, was the Postal Reorganization Act of 1970. Because of various constraints that had developed over time, just before the 1970 act, the postmaster general had no control over what he could pay employees, the rates charged, the conditions of service, or even the types of transportation used. As the country moved into the technological age, the post office was getting further and further behind. However, the act allowed the post office to become an independent government corporation, thus giving it the the opportunity to be more entrepreneurial.

The Postal Service immediately experimented with overnight delivery in 1971 and made it permanent in 1977. In 1972, the post office finally allowed the purchase of stamps outside of its own facilities. Modern optical scanners were introduced in the 1980s. By 1983, the ZIP + 4 was mandatory for various classes of mail. During this period thousands of uneconomical postal "subzone" or auxiliary post offices were closed. Despite enormous competition from Federal Express and other overnight providers, new electronic distribution methods, such as e-mail, and pressure to keep postal rates extraordinarily low, the new Postal Service continues to pay for itself as it finds new ways of doing business.

cumbersome structures are made to work well by the people who use them, and in other cases organizations that are the models of contemporary practice fail because a suitable culture and resource pattern does not exist. However, strong indications of problems occur from three sources. First, does the organizational structure seem to reflect contemporary practices and needs or does it seem to be primarily an inherited pattern that is maintained due to historical inertia? That is, do people consider the organizational structure to be helpful or do they consider it cumbersome and an impediment to prompt and effective action? For example, many large public sector organizations that are expected to respond more rapidly to changing mandates and technological needs are attempting to de-layer their bureaucracies by eliminating whole sets of midmanagement positions. Or perhaps an agency realizes that its bureaucracy is perceived as hostile and esoteric to clients who resort to elected officials for answers to complaints (through legislative casework) rather than to the agency itself, and thus it establishes an ombudsperson (a client advocate who works for the agency). A second way of perceiving problems is to observe the presence or absence of plans, and then to review their utility. Is the quality of the operations planning high and does the unit do genuine strategic planning? A third way to perceive problems in this area is to determine whether workers and managers know what production goals are, how current production matches those targets, and precisely how individuals are contributing to those goals. Quality data (data that indicate both qualitative and quantitative performance) are an example that will let employees and managers know how they are performing relative not only to past performance but also to the performance of similar organizations.

The sources of good organization are similarly based on appropriate organization designs, various types of planning processes that should routinely occur (even if the plans are for personal use only), and measures to determine the quantity and quality of work. Because of the multiplicity of purposes and environments that occur in the public sector, there is certainly no ideal organizational type. However, trends in this area are clear and worth mentioning. Overall, there is a clear migration away from relatively pure types of hierarchical bureaucracies with many layers, high centralization, rigid rule-maintenance philosophy, nearly exclusive reliance on experts, and stable mass-production strategies. Instead, organizations are leaning toward competition-based hierarchies (typical in the private sector), team-based organizations, adhocracies, and complex hybrids of several types. Features of these organizations include more use of external competition and internal benchmarking, flatter structures, more decentralization, fewer and broader rules that allow more discretion, more consultation with clients and interest groups, and more readily changed structures (such as temporary project teams) that can be dissolved after the project is completed.

Another source of good organization is planning processes whose current trends include (a) operations planning with more input and flexibility, (b) personnel planning that holds employees more accountable for their own personal skill development, and (c) strategic planning that allows for greater learning during implementation and has tougher accountability standards. Finally, measurement systems in the public sector were largely noncomparable in the past, but great strides have been made in comparing states, counties, cities, school systems, and specific types of agencies. Performance measurement has become more sophisticated and requires that better data be available to both decision makers and line workers alike without undue expense or burden, by using more selective criteria (a balance of indicators to capture information in a variety of areas) and more technology (such as automated tracking systems).

Strategies to improve organization of the work generally involve major changes. Devising an alternative structure is certainly a prime example. Perhaps the organization should be restructured so that it is flatter or so that some units have different reporting relations. Perhaps a particular process must be reengineered so that the average process time is substantially reduced or the number of decision rules is decreased, making the work simpler and less confusing. Or perhaps an agency needs to create a new client service location, such as a new fire station, welfare office, or field representative for a large agency such as the Small Business Administration or the Department of Housing and Urban Development. A second strategy is to improve the planning structures and processes in operations, personnel, and strategic thinking. A third way to enhance the organization is to work on the measurement systems: designing a measure where none exists, increasing the comparability of measures, improving utility for the workers who benefit from direct feedback, or providing a better balance of the measures that are used.

External Coordination and Adaptability

External coordination and adaptability describe the degree to which the organization is aligned with its external constituents—legislators, clients, suppliers, comparable agencies, and so forth—and adapts to changing circumstances. As with the competing internal tensions of balancing dependable structures and consistent processes with the need for creativity and innovation, there are competing needs for stable external coordination versus adaptation to a changing environment. The case study on Elmer Staats (Exhibit 9.6) provides a good example of adaptation to the environment (the need for more in-depth policy analysis) with the concomitant need to reorganize internally, shed some responsibilities, and build new task competencies.

Because knowing the quality of the external coordination and adaptability is largely in the eyes of the beholder, it requires a variety of sources and sensitivity to the completely different interests of many parties. As a general method, environmental scanning is one important source of information. Environmental scanning involves paying attention to trends in the area, industry, economy, and technology by reading trade and professional magazines, attending conferences and seminars, and networking in general. Organizations can also create customer surveys that tap into peoples' perceptions of the quality and flexibility of the organization. If the organization is interested in more concrete feedback and suggestions, it can create focus groups.

One source of external coordination is to have full-time positions and units that act as liaisons with external entities such as public information officers, legislative relations officers, complaint units and ombudspersons, satellite units on site in other organizations (e.g., a Nuclear Regulatory Agency inspector stationed full-time at a power plant), and so forth. Another source of coordination occurs when agency employees work jointly with or invite input from external entities through task forces, advisory boards, statutory boards, partnering initiatives, and so forth. Means of increasing communication, include newsletters, press releases, courtesy calls, and informal discussions and written messages such as Listserves, and aids coordination. Adaptation to the environment is largely affected by attitudes but is aided by a strong strategic planning process, an inclination to take advantage of conferences and learning opportunities, and a general openness to doing things differently.

If there seem to be deficiencies in the external coordination and adaptability, then the organization may look at shifting the responsibilities of some people to hold them more directly accountable for better integration in this area. Or it may decide that additional mechanisms are needed for input, for example, an advisory board. When there are deficiencies in external coordination, there is nearly always weak communication that needs to be corrected through increased informal discussion, newsletters, or standing joint meetings. Adaptability is enhanced by creating a learning organization—one that is proactive in handling current issues and anticipating future problems by learning its way beyond them. Learning organizations are education focused, highly collaborative, open to change and innovation, and they lean toward flexibility. Indeed, James Thompson, in discussing important reinvention initiatives that were launched in the 1990s, said, "Leadership may be

Exhibit 9.6

A Leader Assesses His Organization and His Constraints

Great leaders take the time to assess the strengths and weaknesses of their organizations so that they can enhance capabilities and mitigate weaknesses. They also carefully assess their leadership constraints, in the public sector generally to stay within those constraints, but sometimes to shift or reduce them. Our administrative example is Elmer Staats, generally considered the most successful comptroller general of the United States to have headed the General Accounting Office (GAO). The Office of the Comptroller General was set up in the Budget and Accounting Act of 1921, and is fundamentally different from all other executive agencies in several respects. Although the comptroller general is appointed by the president, the term is for fifteen years and removal from office is only by Congress. This creates tremendous independence from the executive branch. Further, the GAO's prime client is Congress, which directs many of the agency's works through specialized requests for reports and is also the receiver of all standard operating audits of agencies. By federal standards it is exceptionally small (now less than 4,000 employees) but exceptionally powerful. It tries to remain thoroughly nonpartisan, but its work auditing agencies and evaluations of policy implementation and possible policy projects always have the potential for controversy. In the main, the GAO has done an exceptional job of avoiding controversy because of its effort to be politically neutral and technically competent.

When Elmer Staats assumed his post in 1966, the GAO had just finished one of those unusual periods of controversy caused by his predecessor's aggressiveness in pursuing defense contractor audits. Comptroller Joseph Campbell had promoted the watchdog side of the GAO; ultimately, Staats promoted the governmental effectiveness side. That is to say, while not discontinuing financial audit and policy compliance functions, he greatly enhanced management audits and largely introduced program evaluation as a major thrust. In assessing the agency, this shift of focus would mean different task skills than had been the norm. Thus, the GAO reduced its hiring of accountants and increased the hiring of systems analysts, computer specialists, economists, social scientists, engineers, and the like. To better respond to congressional needs (external coordination) and to promote role clarity, he changed the structure of the GAO to mirror the congressional committees and subcommittees where possible. To improve subordinate effort and better organization, he "developed a conscious socialization program for new staff that included dress codes, extensive training programs, rotation programs, clear promotion guidelines, rules against fraternization, and a considerable emphasis on esprit de corps" (Cooper 1990, 221). To improve cooperation with audited agencies, he developed stringent requirements for agencies to be able to (1) review draft reports prior to publication, and (2) attach their responses to the report. Audit "creativity" was enhanced by ensuring that audit teams included diversity in disciplinary training as well as in ethnic makeup and gender.

In terms of leadership constraints, the comptroller general during Staats's tenure actually gave up some areas of leadership while substantially enhancing others. After meeting with J. Edgar Hoover, staff of the GAO were generally more inclined to turn over fraud and abuse leads to the FBI. Staats also worked with Congress to create inspectors general in the agencies, so that the GAO could focus more on requests from Congress, which were increasing enormously in number and complexity (congressional requests composed only 10 percent of the agency's business in 1921, and today they constitute approximately 80 percent). This work was endorsed and codified in the 1970 Legislative Reorganization Act.

Thus, through deft organizational analysis, realignment of leadership responsibilities and constraints, and systematic reprioritization of agency goals, Elmer Staats completed the GAO's transformation from an agency of "voucher auditors" and finance investigators into the most sophisticated program evaluation agency in the world.

particularly relevant to what have proven to be the more elusive, higher-order reinvention objectives such as cultural change" (Thompson 2000, 518). Although not as desirable, sometimes leaders must "induce" a crisis (that is to say, highlight the imminent dangers of a situation before it actually occurs) so that the motivation for rapid and significant change is boosted (Kanter, Stein, and Jick 1992).

A list of the practical strategies that can be used when deficiencies exist in any of the eight areas discussed is provided in Exhibit 9.7. Next we turn to leadership constraints, because without a good assessment of this additional set of factors, the strategies used to address problems may fail.

CONSTRAINTS OF LEADERSHIP

As previously stated, all leaders have demands, constraints, and choices (Stewart 1967, 1976, 1982). The preceding section on assessment of the organization and its environment provided in-depth discussion of the types of situational demands that organizational leaders must survey. This section addresses the constraints that leaders must acknowledge and cope with. (The next chapter will deal with the choices leaders make.) Constraints are defined as *relatively* structural or long-term elements that set parameters or limitations on the leader's range of choices. While constraints are never immutable, they are, nonetheless, generally substantial and require considerable time, energy, and luck to change; therefore, even highly effective leaders plan only a few changes in constraints, and even then, over the long term.

Legal/Contractual Constraints

Not uncommonly, legal/contractual constraints are hailed as the greatest set of limitations with which public sector managers must deal. While this assertion is likely overstated, it is certainly true that legal constraints are very important for public servants as custodians of the public good to whom the law is more than a constraint, it is a moral obligation.

Laws authorize the mission of agencies, their general structures, their major, and frequently their specific, processes, and their budgets—often by line item. General laws may also affect agencies because of statutory requirements about the environment, safety, worker protections and standards, health, civil liberties and public entitlements, and so forth, much of which affects the private sector in similar ways. David Rosenbloom points out that the legislative function trumps managerial concerns when he states: "the orthodox managerial values of efficiency, economy, and internal organizational effectiveness retain importance, but they are augmented and sometimes subordinated to representativeness, participation, openness, responsiveness, procedural safeguards, and public accountability" (Rosenbloom 2000, xi). Such laws are, of course, further articulated through various types of rule-making processes that effectively have the force of law. Finally, administrative leaders must generally bow to the general directives of legislative and executive elected officials, which is also known as political responsiveness, and not seek to usurp political authority. "[W]e expect ranking administrative officials wholeheartedly to accept and fulfill their complex responsibilities without exercising broad discretionary power and authority" (Terry 1995, xvii).

Exhibit 9.7

Possible Strategies When Deficiencies Exist in an Organization

When task skills are lacking, weak, or outdated, consider:
- Improving recruitment/hiring processes; for example, increasing testing and/or standards
- Improving training systems
- Publishing model practices
- Enhancing workers' sense of professionalism
- Decreasing (or increasing) task variety
- Improving concrete, ongoing worker feedback systems
- Improving the linkage between work and rewards

When role clarity is ambiguous or lacking, consider:
- Providing better job descriptions
- Improving role modeling
- Clarifying job assignments through interactive goal setting with individuals
- Clarifying group goals through interactive sessions
- Improving the training system
- Devoting more management attention to the area on an ongoing basis

When there is a lack of innovation and creativity, consider:
- Evaluating and reducing the subtle disincentives
- Enhancing rewards for innovation and learning
- Rewarding entrepreneurialism
- Stimulating friendly competition
- Increasing the use of external benchmarking exercises
- Encouraging more experimentation
- Enhancing team synergy in problem solving
- Encouraging outside training and education opportunities

When resources or support services are deficient or lacking, consider:
- Improving utilization of the resource or service
- Ordering new supplies, equipment, and so forth
- Borrowing, sharing, or partnering
- Rationing until a crisis or financial pinch is over
- Devoting time and effort to lobbying for more resources
- Cutting service levels to reduce resource needs

When the effort of subordinates is lackluster or inadequate, consider:
- Improving recruitment if employees are not well suited to positions
- Enhancing training if basic worker skill levels are inadequate
- Improving and customizing rewards
- Establishing better worker accountability for performance and clear disincentives for nonperformance
- Improving supervisors' skills in managing people

When cohesiveness and cooperation are weak or altogether lacking, consider:
- Adjusting group size to create a human scale of work teams
- Improving group rewards
- Decreasing unhealthy competition that leads to resource squabbles
- Finding ways to mitigate excessive turnover
- Encouraging the identification of shared interests and stressing group accomplishments

(continued)

Exhibit 9.7 (*continued*)

- Using more metaphors, symbols, and other emotive elements to encourage the spirit and enhance the visualization of group goals
- Providing structured alignment sessions
- Holding leaders more accountable for handling conflicts and inspiring group cohesion

When the organization of work or performance strategies are suboptimal, consider:
- Devising an alternative structure by flattening, expanding, reengineering, restructuring, etc.
- Enhancing planning structures at operational or strategic levels
- Improving performance measurement systems

When external coordination is poor, or adaptability based on a changing environment is weak, consider:
- Shifting responsibilities of some workers to hold them directly accountable for better integration
- Creating or enhancing the role of an advisory board or similar structures
- Holding leaders accountable for better communications
- Enhancing responsiveness by creating a learning organization
- Inducing a sense of urgency to prevent future challenges and crises

So how can administrative leaders deal with these constraints to minimize their negative effects? First and foremost, an understanding of the law and regulations, often a highly detailed knowledge, is fundamental to minimizing constraint. It is not uncommon for managers and leaders to be paralyzed into inaction because of unspecified fears that they may transgress laws or regulations of which they are unsure. Exactly what are their rights as managers to discipline employees, to expend funds differently than past practice, or to change managerial priorities? Further, sometimes managers are unclear about which issues are, in fact, laws and administrative rules, and which issues are executive directives, and this vastly shifts the likelihood of waivers or change. In a study of innovative managers who had been successful at implementing substantial change, it was found that legal constraints were cited less than 10 percent of the time (Borins 2000, 504). Second, managers can be more optimistic and steadfast at changing rules, and occasionally even laws, if they are outdated, contradictory, vague, or simply ineffective. Administrators must proceed cautiously and patiently when recommending policy changes at any level, but it is a duty to do so when, through their expertise as professionals, they identify areas of potential improvement. The American Society of Public Administration (ASPA) Code of Ethics states: "ASPA members are committed to: . . . work to improve and change laws and policies that are counter-productive or obsolete" (Section II, item 2). Finally, because perhaps the most important function of an administrative leader is the use of discretion in executing policies, and discretion is tremendously enhanced by trust, it is imperative that leaders carefully preserve their reputations through personal integrity (candor, openness, lack of self-dealing, etc.) as well as through competence, courage, optimism, and benevolence (Wang and Van Wart 2007).

Limitations of Position Power

While legal constraints are the primary external constraint, there are a number of significant internal constraints relating to position, resources, and leadership ability.

Quite noticeably, leaders' abilities to act are constrained by organizational structures, job descriptions, and various types of policies having to do with procurement, personnel, budgeting, and so forth. These constraints overlap with legal and rule-based constraints, but extend beyond them to organizational practices not necessarily rooted in law. For example, organizational leaders may be given an additional unit to manage or a job description may be changed due to new needs. Formal means to resist potential leader actions are often used by employees or their representatives such as unions. Under informal constraints, culture figures prominently along with the informal organization. While a leader may have the formal authority to direct subordinates to do something, if angered by the order, they might actively resist by complaining and disputing an order (at a minimum diminishing morale), or covertly they might scuttle the directive through "malicious compliance" (i.e., follow the directive so carefully as to seriously impair production). Generally speaking, of course, the more junior the position is in the organization, the less discretion it possesses or the greater the leadership constraints of position.[5]

Responses to these internal constraints are nearly identical to those imposed by external factors. First and foremost, it is imperative to know exactly what one's position power is—both formally and informally. While all formal powers may not be exercised, it is critical to know what they are and what they are not. By knowing what authority and informal power do exist, one can act more confidently. Just as important, leaders can significantly affect changes in position power over time. That is, by building a record of competence and reliable performance within one's purview (Dull 2008) and also by building good external relations, it is possible to expand one's authority and discretion. Leaders can also request temporary adjustments or waivers to fit specific situations when they are considered knowledgeable and responsible. The greatest informal constraint will generally be a lack of both trust and a sense of shared interests. While developing trust and a sense of shared vision takes time and is always fragile (i.e., it is slow to accrue and fast to dissipate), it is fundamental for keeping informal constraints (which are based on others' self-interest, perceptions, resistance to change, etc.) in proportion.

Availability of Resources

Lack of sufficient resources is a chronic problem at some level for all managers—it is the degree and type that vary. While public sector workers often feel that resources are highly constrained, and indeed they may be, often they may be better off than workers in small companies, struggling companies, or companies in highly competitive industries in which personnel costs are kept at minimum-wage rates.

One key resource for the leader is his/her own time. The typical administrative leader's time is broken into very short chunks as they move from topic to topic as e-mail, telephone calls, employee requests, meetings, correspondence, and memoranda take them from one issue to the next in rapid succession. Many meetings that managers must attend are not their own, and information gathering and environmental scanning are extremely time consuming. Interspersed are a few major projects that the leader typically works on as time and energy allow. Because of the demands of operations management, employee development, and strategic planning, few administrative leaders have the luxury of spending adequate time in all of the areas that they would like. Another chronic resource scarcity is the number or quality of subordinates. Rarely is there an ideal number of employees, including various types of support personnel, or the right types of employees. Even when full staffing is authorized and sufficient, vacations and separations are a challenge. Finally, resource scarcities might include budget (used for operations, travel, etc.), equipment, and facilities. For example, a chronic problem in the public sector is the maintenance of updated computer systems to support massive service programs in human services, law enforcement, and medical insurance. Because of a nonprofit orientation, public sector systems typically eschew state-of-the-art approaches (because of the enormous expense) and "make do" in this area longer than private sector counterparts.

The problem of time for the leader can never be solved, but it certainly can be managed. Leaders need to plan at various levels and monitor their progress in each through goals, objectives, and timelines. Because short-term, close-at-hand issues can easily dominate a leader's schedule, planning becomes critical to carve out time in advance of the interruptions and the routine flurry of activity and daily crises and to ensure long-term goal achievement. As important here as adequate personal planning and time management is the conservation of energy, which can be enhanced by bundling certain types of activities (so that the leader does not become exhausted from "changing gears"), setting adequate time aside in advance for large operational, personnel, or strategic projects, or simply setting aside quality time for contemplation of problems. The problem of scarce human resources may be mitigated by improving delegation, training, and mentoring of employees, or simply prioritizing the work that is to be accomplished so that the most important work is not neglected. In terms of financial and physical resources, the leader may need to make compelling requests, borrow resources that are needed only for peak demand or for a crisis, creatively find new resources, or reengineer processes or needs so that resource demands are lessened. Leaders who are unable to address most resource demands will generally find that they have significantly less leverage with their subordinates.

The Limits of Leadership Abilities

Because of the vast array of traits, skills, and behavioral competencies required of leaders, leadership ability constraints are inevitable, even with leaders who are successful and effective. Mitigating this constraint is a particular theme of this book.

One aspect of the leadership ability constraint is having the right traits, skills, and behavioral competencies for the job. Some jobs may require a great deal of flexibility, decisiveness, operational creativity, delegation, problem solving, and long-term planning. Others may emphasize operations excellence and strong monitoring competency, as well as an ability to clarify specific roles and objectives and manage conflict. Because leaders may not possess the necessary strengths demanded by a particular job, heretofore successful leaders frequently fail when given entirely new assignments; they sometimes simply apply the same skills and abilities to the new situation but with far less effectiveness. A second, but related, aspect of leadership capacity involves having *enough* skill or ability. A leader may have rather good interpersonal skills for one-on-one situations and in settled conditions, but lack sufficient skills to handle intractable, long-term feuding of entrenched factions within a department. Or a supervisor may be able to plan a simple change involving a code revision, but may be completely overwhelmed about how to plan a huge mission and vision transformation due to a philosophical reorientation of policy.

Simply knowing the leadership demands of the job is the preliminary means of dealing with the leadership capacity issue. This is a far murkier, more complex task than a superficial analysis will generally reveal. Indeed, the leader's detailed assessment of the organization, the environment, and constraints s/he faces is critical. This chapter has addressed the issues involved in such a detailed assessment. Furthermore, knowing how one's personal skills and abilities match or do not match the situation is critical. This knowledge can be obtained through serious introspection and self-observation, but is tremendously enhanced by robust feedback from subordinates, peers, and superiors. It can be accomplished through a formal assessment process (such as a 360-degree survey instrument) or through less structured, but nonetheless candid, discussion opportunities. Finally, when leaders know how their skills and abilities match up to the job, they should be able to detect the gaps or weak areas. These can be addressed through additional training or structured experiences, or by using a team approach to leadership in which some functions of leadership are assigned to another person. A list of possible strategies to deal with leadership constraints can be found in Exhibit 9.8.

CONCLUSION

Plutarch commented that to find fault is easy—to do better may be difficult. It is easy to have high aspirations, but without "doing their homework"—that is to say, doing a very thorough job of assessment—leaders will surely do a mediocre job at best. Without thorough assessment, leaders are likely to have incomplete lists of goals and a weak sense of priorities as well as to be very vague about their personal role in achieving greater organizational effectiveness. Has the leader taken the time to study performance data, talk with employees and clients, review important documents that establish the mission and vision of the organization, and seek comparisons with other leading organizations?

Organizational assessment issues start with *task competencies*, which are the microcompetencies that a worker at any level needs to accomplish to work successfully. How good are task competencies of individual employees and of those working as a group? *Role clarity* is the accurate and precise knowledge that workers, groups, and managers have about which activities, functions, and roles they are to accomplish and how their work integrates with that of others. This is increasingly difficult to achieve in an organizational world demanding more teamwork, customization, one-stop shopping, rapid-paced

---

Exhibit 9.8

Possible Strategies to Deal with Leadership Constraints

By definition, leadership constraints tend to be structural and long term. However, effective leaders can mitigate, improve, or even turn around some leadership constraints over time.

When leaders are constrained by substantial or excessive *legal/contractual* constraints, consider:

- Learning about the nature of those constraints in detail so that it is possible to work within them confidently and fully
- Gaining confidence of those setting policy to attain the full latitude of legal discretion
- Requesting policy changes through appropriate channels as a long-term project

When leaders are constrained by substantial or excessive *position* constraints, consider:

- Learning about the details of the position and its power so that it is possible to work within them confidently and fully
- Gaining confidence of those setting policy to attain the full latitude of management discretion
- Requesting (or making) rule changes, or seeking expanded authority

When leaders are constrained by a lack of *resources,* consider:

- Using more delegation, training, mentoring, and planning, depending on the type of resource constraint
- Reconfiguring the organization if resource constraints are chronic
- Enhancing the leader's own time management and planning to conserve the leader's valuable energy and focus

When leaders are constrained by a lack of certain *leadership abilities,* consider:

- Analyzing the leadership demands of the position to determine the critical leadership competencies required
- Analyzing personal strengths and weaknesses through a thorough assessment process
- Addressing some of the leadership gaps by gaining additional training, structured experiences, or a team model of leadership

---

change, and the like. Creativity is the ability to think about ideas or do things in nonroutine ways, while innovation is the adaptation of new ideas or ways of doing things (from any source) to a new setting. *Innovation and creativity* are difficult in bureaucracies because of the value of efficiency and quality control, which are deadening to experimentation, risk taking, and change in general. *Resources and support services* encompass the degree to which the workers or units have the tools, equipment, personnel, facilities, and funds to accomplish work or to acquire necessary information or help from other work groups. Because of increasing scarcity in this area, leaders will need new strategies that will emphasize coordination and sharing.

Subordinate effort is the extent to which subordinates strive to achieve work-related objectives and a level of commitment to their jobs. Chief among the leader's responsibilities is motivating employees to achieve operationally defined goals (transactional level results); excellent leaders inspire subordinates to achieve exceptional results despite ever-present challenges (transformational or charismatic leadership). *Cooperation and cohesiveness* are the degree to which individuals effectively and contentedly work in groups or teams in order to share work, information, and resources, and to which they have strong identifications with the group and overall organization. At a minimum this means containing the various types of conflict and dysfunctional competition that occur; more productively it means instilling camaraderie and pride, which results in enhanced organizational identification and productivity. The *organization of the work* refers to the way that work is arranged and structured to maximize efficient and effective use of personnel, equipment, and other resources as well as to plans and measures used to ensure quantity and quality of production. Because of the dramatic reconstitution of government (often referred to as reinvention), organizational structures and processes are being challenged everywhere to be leaner, flatter, faster, more competitive, and more customer oriented. *External coordination and adaptability* are the degree to which the organization is aligned with its external constituents—legislators, clients, suppliers, comparable agencies, and the like—and adapts to changing circumstances. This means that leaders must be more astute about changing trends and more politically aware, while at the same time being able to communicate and convince the organization of the need to be responsive.

Knowing the exact status of an organization is not enough. Effective leaders must also know their constraints. While constraints are not immutable, they are long-term structural conditions that can be influenced by leaders only over a substantial period of time. Legal-contractual constraints include laws, regulations, organizational rules, and legislative-executive oversight. Limitations of position power include formal sources such as organizational structures and informal sources such as the culture of the organization. The (un)availability of resources includes scarcity of the leader's own time, a lack of sufficient numbers of employees or the right subordinates, and deficient amounts of budget allowance, equipment, and facilities. Finally, the leader's own leadership abilities constitute a constraint inasmuch as the array of traits, skills, and behavioral competencies is so extensive and demanding. Yet, as overwhelming as constraints are at times, the ability to cope with them is in fact the mark of leadership as is the capability of pushing them back to more manageable levels over time. Indeed, leadership could be defined in this perspective as the act of mitigating constraints and enhancing opportunities and capacities to perform strategically and decisively.

With detailed information in hand—about their organizations, environments, and constraints—leaders are prepared to formulate goals and to prioritize them for focused action. That important leadership dynamic is the topic of the next chapter.

NOTES

1. Generally, such information gathering is done on a random basis (a relatively small portion of all clients) in the interest of ease and cost effectiveness.

2. The ideal size of the work group varies tremendously by the nature of the work. Highly routinized functions that are largely independent may have extremely large groups, while more integrated,

customized work may require very small teams. Problem-solving teams are often thought to be ideal when they have four to seven members.

3. Affective language uses evocative symbols and appeals to emotions including pride, camaraderie, patriotism, and so forth.

4. Of course, the twentieth century was not the first to perfect the hierarchical bureaucracy. Ancient Egypt, Rome, and China, as well as the medieval Roman Catholic Church, are historical examples of highly sophisticated forms of hierarchical bureaucracies suited to their cultures and times.

5. There are always exceptions to this general rule. As examples, frontline special project managers may be given wide discretion, and so too are high-level professionals (e.g., lawyers, engineers, or doctors), who are essentially frontline workers or supervisors, that may be required to use extensive discretion and power on a daily basis.

10

Leader Formulation and
Prioritization of Goals

Certainly one of the most important things leaders do is to use their judgment to make decisions—what operational problems to take on and how; which proactive organizational initiatives to purse; how to handle unusual crises; who to hire and who to fire, and the like (Tichy and Bennis 2007). As discussed in the previous chapter, such decisions must be based on the best data and analysis available. Furthermore, decisions are only as good as their articulation, which is generally stated as goals, but can also be guidelines, a "charge," or shared vision. This chapter focuses on generic goal setting in administrative settings (rather than political settings in which it is often very different). Additional discussion in later chapters analyzes decision making in a variety of settings related to problems, creativity, and innovation, enabling followers to adopt change, managing conflict, and providing fundamental organizational change.

This seemingly obvious and straightforward task turns out to be far more difficult and subtle than meets the eye for three reasons. First, leaders have incredible demands on their time. They are bombarded with requests, problems, social obligations, interpersonal responsibilities, and general management functions, none of which directly assist them in this function. Second, organizations have limited resources. There are always more problems to solve and opportunities to explore than there are resources to help. Finally, the process of formulating good decisions with appropriate priorities is simply not as easy as it looks. As it turns out, goal setting is more than a linear process or a creative act—it is both.

THE *SCIENCE* AND *ART* OF GOAL SETTING

There is no better example of how leadership is both a science and an art than the formulation of goals and their prioritization.

Scientific purposes, generally speaking, define and classify concepts, construct useful theories about how things function, and predict the future based on those theories. In practical terms this translates into being knowledgeable about current and future operations, demonstrating relationships between internal and external trends and patterns, and anticipating problems and forecasting opportunities. Even when a leader has good hunches about where organizational problems lurk, these hunches will be very difficult to implement without more specific data about the nature of the problems. Concrete data about the organization must be gathered using methods that can be routinized in function (replicable) and accurate in data collection.

Goal setting as science is only half of the picture, however. Goal setting by leaders is also an *art* (Denhardt and Denhardt 2006) in that action is based on past experience and beliefs, uses customized methods to handle unique circumstances, and encourages passion and commitment to strive for excellence. Further, leaders seek to understand what is significant and what works, use their understanding in practice, and intuit likely outcomes or futures based on different perspectives. The ideal leader has a very different type of challenge in conducting the art (also known as the profession) of leadership. Leaders must have an instinctive understanding based on their eclectic and sometimes inconsistent experience (but informed by as much hard data as possible), be able to use that imperfect understanding in the world of action (but anchored in explicable reasoning), and be able to approximate likely outcomes or futures based on a multitude of different factual data sets (scientific), perceptual realities (quasi-scientific), and normative perspectives (Osborn and Hunt 2007).

A commonplace example will help to illustrate why the science and art of goal setting in relation to management problems is so important. Compare the approaches of two managers, both of whom have a reasonable hunch that subordinate effort is suboptimal. One of the two managers takes a more scientific approach because she gathers more data, analyzes more fully, and prioritizes her strategies more carefully.

Manager A "knows" that his employees are not performing to their full potential. He is eager to work on this problem. Furthermore, he is confident that it is a motivational problem; some of the employees are unmotivated because the pay difference between good and weak performers is extremely modest, and other workers are simply a bit lazy. To correct this problem, the manager gets permission to take all salary increases—annual increases and cost-of-living adjustments—and put them into a bonus pool. All employees will remain at their current rate, and only the top performers will receive a one-time bonus that is not built into their salary base. Over just a few years, the average salary base drops relative to the market, but those who receive bonuses are above the market. Manager A is delighted to discover that the top performers (about one-third of the employees) are doing better and more work than ever, nearly 50 percent of all productivity. Yet, he is disappointed that over half of the workforce is doing even more poorly, that turnover is up, and that filling new positions has become more difficult. However, he has become even more convinced that lazy workers constitute a large and growing portion of the workforce, and that he needs to hang on to his top performers all the more vigorously and simply recruit better workers.

Manager B also knows that her employees are not performing up to their full potential. She has informally assessed worker performance internally and has also visited several high-performing units as a comparison. However, she is unsure of the exact reasons for suboptimal performance and so she sets out to discover the reasons why. Having studied motivation theory, she knows that the major reasons for poor performance are (a) poor innate capability, (b) lack of or poor training, (c) lack of or poor equipment and supplies, (d) rewards that are insufficient—most commonly, insufficient pay, and (e) rewards that are wrong—most commonly, lack of an environment that makes the employees feel highly valued for the work that they perform (essentially poor supervision). This provides her with hunches, but alone does not provide her with a plan, goals, or even reliable data. What does she do?

First she interviews all the supervisors and asks them to evaluate the performance of each employee and to assess the reasons for poor performance, sorting the responses using her five categories. She also conducts a survey of the employees and asks about their perceptions using the five categories. Although the two sets of data do not match perfectly, she feels that she is able to define the problems quite accurately by combining the data. The data collection reveals that the work is not particularly complex, so less than 10 percent of the workers seem to have capacity problems; although better recruitment screening might reduce this problem further, the amount of improvement would be negligible for the effort. The training program is essentially sound, but seems to provide insufficient practice opportunities, and lacks a follow-up mentoring program. This explains approximately 20 percent of the problem and can be remedied without difficulty. Only a few people (less than 10 percent) have significant equipment resource problems, but these problems are also easily remedied. The bulk of the problem is with rewards. Insufficient rewards (money) are a substantial problem for approximately 30 percent of the employees; and wrong rewards (consideration) are problems for another 30 percent. Just as for Manager A, the pool of money for Manager B is limited, so she must be creative about how it is distributed. In order to increase the salaries overall and give slightly larger adjustments to high-performing employees, she sacrifices a position. However, she makes sure that the division understands that average productivity must increase slightly to make up for this lost position. She also implements a supervisory training program because of the obvious problems in this area. It takes her three years to fully analyze the problem, implement targeted solutions, and see results. She finds that productivity has risen significantly, and although the performance of her "star" performers is not quite as high as were Manager A's, the far better performance of the bottom half of her employees more than makes up for this slight differential. Furthermore, turnover has become a negligible problem and the overall reputation of the unit has improved dramatically because of better quality consistency.

In our example, Manager B used a scientific methodology to study her hunch that employee motivation was only one of the productivity problems. She surveyed both supervisors and line workers to get a variety of perspectives, and she studied individual cases as well as the average. She also practiced the art of management because she began with flashes of insight or hunches. Better managers have better hunches; her theory, unlike Manager A's, was that employee motivation was not the only problem. Her data did not all agree, and she had to interpret them in light of her own experience and then act on them as best she could. She did this by prioritizing and customizing a series of strategies. Finally, her zeal and commitment assisted her in working out a long-term solution and motivated others to follow her example.

From this example we can identify some of the skills of good generic goal setting.

GENERIC SKILLS USED IN GOAL SETTING

The skills required for good goal setting, then, include elements of both the scientific and professional ("artful") approaches. First, leaders must have a *deeply informed awareness of organizational needs and the discipline to expand knowledge or experience where it is insufficient.* Heifetz observed that "one may lead with no more than a question in hand" (1994, 276), and Robert Terry noted that "leadership depends on an ability to frame issues correctly" (1993, xvii). Further, good leaders have and use hunches, but test and change them regularly.

Second, goal setting must be based on beliefs as well as facts, leading to a *balance of competing values.* While facts are necessary as a realistic baseline, it is through beliefs that interpretations of the proper short-term versus long-term balance of interests or internal versus external equilibrium are achieved (Van Wart 1998a; Lawrence, Lenk, and Quinn 2009).

Third, leaders cannot set balanced goals—from operational to strategic—unless they have studied both the processes and discrete elements of their businesses and professions, as well as the unruly integration of complex forces. This means that leaders must possess considerable *cognitive complexity* to master detail and order at the same time they master the wholeness and disorder in the organizational universe (Wheatley 1992). As Bennis and Nanus note, leaders assist organizations through "complexities that cannot be solved by unguided evolution" (1985, 18). Just one of the complexities involves deciding on the ideal decision-making framework (see chapter 15 for a discussion of approaches to making decisions).

Fourth, leaders must be able to integrate their individual understanding with group understanding. Leaders, by definition, must be stimulated by their unique vision of organizational needs leading to goal formation, but must nonetheless be informed by group needs and contributions. The German writer/philosopher Goethe opined that the greatest genius will not be worth much if he pretends to draw exclusively from his own resources. This final goal-setting skill is *inclusiveness* (Denhardt 1992). In many instances the leader's role is facilitative and contributing, and thus collaboration is key to success (Kanter 1994; Archer and Cameron 2008).

A MODEL OF LEADER GOAL FORMULATION AND PRIORITIZATION IN ORGANIZATIONAL SETTINGS

The goals leaders select and the priorities they give them are the most important decisions that leaders make. It is well worth our while looking at the process of goal formulation in depth, even though the creative and situational aspects of unique circumstances defy simple explanation.

The Model

Leaders begin the process by gathering information about their organization's effectiveness and their own constraints (chapter 9). That is, they identify the strengths of their organization that they want to maintain, and, just as important, they identify performance gaps they want to improve and opportunities that may require some type of organizational retooling. This is done within the constraints of the doable—those things that are allowed, possible, supportable, and within the capacity of the leader to execute.

This analysis leads to a range of *possible* organizational goals. Such goals are often implicit, especially when they are primarily maintenance-oriented goals and major changes are not envisaged. Preferably, such goals are explicit, written, and discussed prior to acceptance. If leaders are good at forming organizational goals, they will find opportunities to work on aspects of various goals as the year progresses and only deal with the whole on an annual basis during a reporting/planning or budgeting exercise.

From this exercise of thinking and discussion, *actual* goals emerge with specific priorities. Just as important as setting goals is their prioritization. A leader can drown in important but noncritical activities while overlooking a single area that can bring an organization to its knees. For example, it is a very common syndrome that leaders are drawn into numerous "urgent" matters on a daily basis, while they constantly postpone developmental and organizational projects. The general process of goal formulation and prioritization is highlighted in Exhibit 10.1.

The Situational Factors Affecting Goal Selection

A number of factors affect goal selection, both appropriately and inappropriately, from an organizational effectiveness standpoint. Six major factors will be considered here: organizational environment, life cycle of the organization, level of responsibility, type of responsibility, leader personality, and leader tenure. These situational factors affect not only those goals that are considered in the first place but also those that are actually acted upon and their priorities. They range from externally determined factors to factors closely linked to the preferences of leaders themselves. The point is not to avoid certain factors in favor of others, but simply to be aware of them, so that more conscious, and thus conscientious, goal setting can be achieved. A significant finding in our study of leaders and managers was that the factors were not consistently applied across goal areas. That is, a manager might be most influenced by organizational environment in one area, by level of responsibility in another, and leader tenure in still another. Not surprisingly, the most consistent factor, but not necessarily the most dominant in any given goal area, was leader personality.

One factor that affects leaders' goal setting is the *organizational environment*. Is the environment relatively stable or turbulent, or experiencing a transitional period as it moves from one stage to the next? A stable environment will mean that the leader may want to focus more on task operations and maintain smooth relations among employees. There is little incentive for major changes in stable environments and thus almost all change is incremental. In fact, stable periods often induce complacency, making it difficult for leaders to perceive the need for substantial changes or motivate others to endorse major change. Turbulent periods, on the other hand, require that leaders focus more on change issues and less on maintenance activities and employee relations. Leaders may ask fol-

Exhibit 10.1

A General Model of Leader Goal Formulation in an Organizational Context

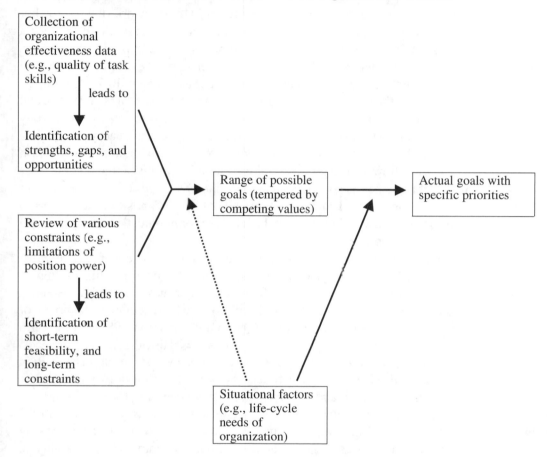

lowers to make sacrifices and may have to make unpopular choices. Of course, leader success will be enhanced by good rapport with employees and with their involvement (Dunbar and Goldberg 1978), but this is more difficult to achieve in times of change. Even transitional periods are difficult for leaders. In transitional periods the organization has not yet fully responded in terms of reduced productivity or legislative support, or the organization has responded to the need for change but the changes have yet to take effect as employees seek to refine and master new ways (moving from turbulent to stable environments).

The areas determining stability or turbulence include revenue sources, organizational mandates, and processes. The periodic shifts in general revenues greatly affect individual agencies' choices. For example, when state budgets are enjoying a surplus, agencies are much more prone to allow new programs, pilot projects, and employee enhancement programs. When state budgets are experiencing a deficit, stringency becomes the rule of the day and the only widely welcomed ideas are those that reduce expenditures. Changes in organizational mandates may include a tighter employee safety policy in the building and energy fields or a looser policy that encourages privatization initiatives. Agencies often receive directives that require more work (a new program) or less work (the removal or cessation of a program), which can upset stability. An example of how dramatic such a shift can be is illustrated by events following September 11, 2001. Immediately after the attack, a few significantly affected public organizations were airports, the Federal Aviation Administration, the Central Intelligence Agency, the Federal Bureau of Investigation, the Department of Defense, the state national guards (called up to assist at most airports), and the Federal Emergency Management Agency. Processes are stable when the technology and client base are constant; however, today new technology and increasingly high client standards are causing significant environmental turbulence. For example, in the past, the public sector was allowed to lag in technology, quite literally years and sometimes decades behind. Public sector use of sophisticated computer systems often came far later than it did in the private sector. Today, however, the public demands Internet access to public organizations, not only for information but also for communication and interactive services that are much closer to the state-of-the-art.

A second situational factor affecting goal formulation is *the life cycle of the organization* (Baliga and Hunt 1988). Life cycle theory asserts that organizations, like biological organisms, tend to respond differently depending on whether they are in a birth stage, a growth stage, a maturity stage, or a post-maturity phase in which decline is occurring or the organization has engaged in revitalization (Quinn and Cameron 1983). In the birth stage, a prospective organization's leaders or champions persuade others of unmet needs, seek resources, and support initial systems design. In a growth stage, an organization works to communicate its vision to its constituencies, promote its services, and establish basic systems to deliver on its mandates. In the maturity stage, the focus becomes increasingly internalized, especially as increased size makes demands for better controls, more consistency, and better internal communication rise to the top of decision-making agendas. Eventually the organization finds that the external environment intervenes again, as external threats and competitors demand a reexamination of basic business practices in light of changed circumstances. While the argument that public sector organizations rarely die has some merit (Kaufman 1976), it begs the question of whether public sector organizations are forced to engage in major changes. Organizations that fail to change with the times may find that their reputations are tarnished (making recruitment difficult), their resources are diminished, and competing programs may be launched in other agencies or such programs may be transferred to other organizations altogether. In this phase, leaders are either successful in introducing major changes that better respond to the environment, or they may face program disbandment or worse. (See Exhibit 10.2 for an example of systems collapse due to ineffective efforts at combating organizational decline.)

Another well-known factor affecting goal formation is the *leader's level of responsibility in the organization* (Katz 1955). Executives and senior managers tend to be most engaged in long-range planning and strategy, allocation of resources, organizational design, external coordination issues, and major change initiatives. Middle managers tend to be more

Exhibit 10.2

The End of a Life Cycle: The Decline and Demise of an Organization

We generally think of the former Soviet Union as a political entity or social system, rarely as a system of public sector organizations. Yet, the demise of the Soviet Union is not well explained in political or sociological terms. It was not invaded; indeed, when it collapsed it was a "superpower" that many thought might eventually dominate the world. The social system was not repudiated by the bulk of its people, who thought that socialist ideals were good in theory, if often poorly practiced by their leaders. For an explanation of the collapse we must look more to the organizational dynamics of the enormous public sector in the country and how it came to die of old age.

Consider the birth of the Union of Soviet Socialist Republics in the teens of the twentieth century. The tsars continued to rule as absolute monarchs over a country that still implicitly encouraged serfdom (peasants were bound to the land through economic rather than legal ties), even though the Revolution of 1905 should have sounded a warning bell.[1] Though probably well meaning, the tsars had rigidly hung onto the past too long and enabled passionate devotees of a racially different system to find popular support.[2] The birth of the new nation included consolidation of political power that was largely completed by 1921.[3] The growth period included the introduction of new social systems such as the nationalization of all property and the collectivization of agriculture in the 1920s through the 1930s. During this period, efforts were made to use mass education or propaganda to promote the new ways. The maturity period from the 1940s through the 1970s included the Soviet Union's ability to fight successfully in World War II, tremendous land expansion of its empire, and the continued refinement of its socialist system of economics, art, and organizations. The decline phase became more apparent to keen observers in the 1980s when the private goods market failed to improve beyond wartime rationing levels despite decades of international prominence. Although President M. Gorbachev tried to reform the ailing system that was little changed since Lenin and Stalin introduced it in the 1920s, the medicine killed the patient and the Soviet Union formally dissolved in 1991.

What happened? How could such a powerful nation implode without external threat? The answers are primarily in the public sector organizations that had long since ceased to operate effectively. Although Stalin's totalitarian tactics seemed to work well in the "state-building" phase—largely through the systematic use of fear and brutality—the country never gave up that rigid, top-down legacy (such as has been seen in some East Asian countries) and had suffered the consequences. Productivity was compromised because all technological improvements had to come from the top, which is rarely where they originate. Moreover, neither labor nor management had true incentives to operate efficiently after Stalin's death in 1954, but rather had incentives to subvert the system for their own benefit. Cronyism, feather-bedding, theft, incompetence, and the like were chronic. The infrastructure was allowed to age and eventually crumble. This was particularly acute in transportation, the hallmark of a prosperous, modern economy. Ultimately the command-and-control economy was unable to reform itself and the life cycle of the organization concluded with decline and death rather than decline and revitalization. The lesson should be clear to all public sector organizations: *Undergo internal revitalization efforts from time to time or prepare for radical reform to be imposed by outside economic forces.*

NOTES

1. Although the 1905 revolt resulted in the formation of a genuine but very weak national legislature, the Duma, its inability to advise Tsar Nicholas II effectively (and occasional dissolutions by him and Tsarina Alexandra) only led to the country's further frustration.

2. There were actually two revolutions in 1917, the February Revolution and the October Revolution, according to the old Russian calendar (or March and November by the Western calendar). The first was a moderate revolution that would have reformed the country by turning it into a constitutional republic; the second, more radical one, turned the country into a highly socialist or communist state.

3. During the period 1918 to 1921, the new Soviet government had to contend with the pro-tsarist White army, a hostile Czech army in Siberia that had earlier been forced into Russian service, British–American invasions in the north, and a Japanese invasion in the West, among other challenges.

interested in lateral coordination, implementation plans, targeted resource allocation, and program monitoring. Lower-level managers and supervisors tend to be more focused on detailed monitoring, staffing issues, frontline production, and process execution. The time frame and complexity of the interests of each group vary accordingly. The executive team should be concerned with the ramifications of their decisions ten or even twenty years in the future; middle managers are most concerned about outcomes in the two-to-five-year range; and lower-level managers are most concerned about decisions affecting the near term (Katz and Kahn 1978; Jacobs and Jaques 1987). While contemporary efforts to devolve some decision-making responsibilities, "flatten" organizations by reducing layers, and delegate more authority for routine problem solving has lessened these traditional tendencies to some degree, they are inherent in the division of labor strategies that hierarchical organizations assume. The extreme compression of goal-setting responsibilities at the lowest levels of the organization, which has occasionally been seen in the private sector where "virtual" organizations (within larger organizations) are intended to be more responsive to a rapidly changing environment, is unlikely to occur in the public sector except in rare instances.

A leader's priorities are shaped not only by the level of responsibility but also by *the type of responsibilities* (Mintzberg 1979). Consider the following senior managers and the different types of perspectives they will likely have: an operations manager, a staff manager, a public relations manager, and a manager responsible for organizational financial soundness. The operations manager will be concerned about production, equipment maintenance and purchases, deadlines, customers and clients, and the proper support of employees (pay, working conditions, etc.). The staff manager (human resources, procurement, facilities, internal services, etc.) will be more concerned with organizational consistency, employees as customers, and internal operations. The public relations manager (e.g., a public information officer) will focus nearly entirely on the media and legislative relations. The financial manager (e.g., a comptroller, auditor, or inspector general) will be most concerned with strict execution of laws and rules, minimization of expenses, and the achievement of work targets. Although these different perspectives are appropriate and (like level of responsibility) built into the bedrock assumptions of hierarchical organizations, they present challenges to the organization as well. Different perspectives can easily lead to intergroup suspicion, strategy suboptimization, and balkanization of resources and organizational efforts if effective executive leadership is lacking. Because of the extreme demands on the chief executive officer (CEO) of larger public organizations, there is often a special layer of assistant executives who are charged with keeping overall organizational interests at heart. For an example of this principle, see Exhibit 10.3, which discusses the role of assistant city managers.

It is only natural that leader likes and dislikes as well as leader perceptions of their own strengths and weaknesses (i.e., the *leader's personality*) should play some role in their goal formulation and prioritization. Common motivational characteristics for effective leaders are the willingness to assume responsibility and the need for achievement. Andrew Carnegie said that you cannot push anyone up the ladder unless he is willing to climb himself. Benjamin Franklin joked that all mankind is divided into three classes:

Exhibit 10.3

The Role of Assistant City Managers

In medium and large cities, department heads are in charge of hundreds, thousands, and occasionally in the case of police and fire chiefs, tens of thousands of employees. Almost all of the departments have distinctly different missions: law enforcement, economic development, electricity, water and sewer, parks and recreation, libraries, fire, and so on. Many of the larger departments have nearly autonomous systems for personnel, equipment, training, and even public relations. So it is not unusual for the identification of employees, managers, and even the department heads to be much more focused on the department than on the city as an entity. Indeed, in more extreme cases, the department may consider the rest of city government a separate organization, perhaps one that is generally indifferent or hostile to its needs. Nowhere is this more obvious than in department-head meetings where department heads as executives view others in the room with suspicion and caution. City revenues are often seen as a zero-sum game; additional resources for one department are at the expense of another. Department heads listen to the announcements of the city manager and promote the positive accomplishments of their departments, but they are cautious about admitting any weaknesses that might be used against their departments as they fight for resources. Cross-departmental activities are often viewed as threats to autonomy and self-sufficient systems.

To combat this natural tendency (which occurs at all levels of government), medium-sized and larger cities create assistant (and deputy) city manager positions. Such positions report directly to the city manager, and even when the department heads still have a direct line to the city manager as well (as is often the case with the fire and police chiefs), it is understood that the assistant city managers speak for the city manager. Their roles are twofold. First, the city manager does not have the time to monitor operations at the department level personally, and cannot afford to have a single source of detailed information (the department head). Second, the city manager needs the department heads to be constantly reminded that they are part of a city-management team, not heads of independent organizations. To make sure that the assistant city managers themselves do not become aligned with specific departments and their parochial interests, it is common to have them rotate departmental portfolios. It is this second role of coordinating departments and encouraging cooperation that can make the difference between a true management team and a loosely connected group of independent executives.

those that are immovable, those that are movable, and those that move. Some leaders who have these characteristics in large measure will seek for great tasks for themselves and their organizations and are willing to assume modest risks in doing so. Others have these characteristics in smaller doses and may prefer to master lesser challenges but do so with exactitude and no significant risk at all. Another set of motivational characteristics is the drive for excellence. Some leaders see excellence in terms of error reduction while others interpret it as exceeding past performance criteria. These conceptions substantially influence the priorities they seek to accomplish.

Because one naturally seeks to play to one's strengths, these very assets subtly shape decisions into the image of their makers. Likewise, avoiding one's weaknesses will shape (or warp) decisions as well. Self-confidence, decisiveness, flexibility, energy, technical ability, communication skills, persuasiveness, and the ability to learn through new experience are all traits and skills that will vary among leaders and affect their priorities. The examples are endless. A new supervisor with little training may lack the self-confidence to initiate a bold new technological approach without extensive information. A highly flexible leader may enjoy allowing several divergent approaches to be employed at the same time. An executive who is exhausted by personal tragedy and recent illness may not have the energy to engage in a restructuring. Yet, the point is the same; leadership cannot be separated from the leader and the unique array of preferences, beliefs, and strengths that a leader possesses. However, this is not to say that the purposes of leadership cannot easily be usurped by the leader. Although leaders ideally attain their positions because of their exceptional abilities, and retain them to serve the law, the public trust, and their followers, it is easy for them to assume that the organization is an extension of them, rather than the reverse. This tendency is known as a personalized power orientation in the academic literature, or narcissism in the popular literature. Although most noticeable in charismatic and authoritarian leaders, it can be an insidious force in almost all leaders at some point. And, as is often noted, the more power a leader has, the more temptation there is to occasionally abuse that power. Exhibit 10.4 looks at both the good and bad effects of leader personality on goal setting.

The final major influence is *a leader's time in office*. Those studying executive behavior over time have observed fairly consistent patterns (Hambrick and Fukutomi 1991). Initially, a new leader is influenced by the mandate of the hiring entity. If the mandate is for change, and/or there is a sense of crisis, some initial changes will occur quickly—primarily in the replacement of some key individuals, the restructuring of the executive functions, or the modification of a technical process that seems to be performing particularly badly. If the mandate is for continuity, initial changes will be minimal and incremental. Those from outside the organization are more likely to make dramatic changes than those selected from within. Initial changes are most likely to be made in the substantive area of the leader's expertise. During the initial period, the executive is likely to gather information intensively and to consider long-term goals and strategies. At the same time, the executive can observe the effect of any changes made and experiment with some tentative strategies. Major or systemwide changes, if they are to occur, are normally made in the second or even third year, when the executive has the experience and wherewithal to implement them. While a slight temporal staggering of a major change plan is customary, the likelihood of major change drops dramatically after that. Even when executives do adopt a major strategy, it is rare for them to adopt another major change initiative in the future. Rather, executives tend to refine their major strategies over time. This often means that they engage in less environmental scanning and may become more complacent. Thus, the most likely way to achieve organizational change is to change the leadership (Tushman, Newman, and Romanelli 1986; Grinyer, Mayes, and McKiernan 1990); however, tenure in office generally provides executives with greater ability to use and wield power to remain in their position despite externally imposed needs.

In the sample of leaders interviewed for this book, the ones who were relatively new to their positions showed a clear preference for information gathering, environmental scanning, and overall assessment as they learned about their new positions. They indicated a clear lack of decisiveness based on a self-awareness of inexperience.

Exhibit 10.4

Personality-Based Decision Making

Certainly one of the most brilliant and adaptive generals of the American military in the twentieth century was Douglas MacArthur. Douglas MacArthur's mentor was his own father, Arthur. Arthur MacArthur was awarded the Medal of Honor in the Civil War, was the commander responsible for taking Manila in the Spanish-American War, and later served as the military governor of the Philippines to set up democratic and judicial systems in keeping with American values. Like his father before him, Douglas was closely allied with the Philippines, at first defending them against the Japanese invasion, and then retaking them in World War II. Similar to his father, he served as military governor for five years, but in his case he served in occupied Japan. His fair-handed treatment won high marks during the reconstruction period over which he presided.

Our case study focuses on his famous role in the Korean War, where he was put in charge of the U.N. forces soon after hostilities began in June 1950. The North Korean forces enjoyed tremendous success, pushing the U.N. forces into a very small, contained area at the southern tip of the peninsula. Rather than accept the conventional strategy of a slow push northward, MacArthur recommended a risky surprise attack at Inchon, high up on the peninsula on the Yellow Sea. The attack would require great resolve as the port has no beaches and is among the ports with the highest tidal variations in the world. Against enormous resistance to the idea from all the U.S. branches, MacArthur was finally able to undertake his plan. On September 15, the U.N. forces invaded Inchon successfully and retook Seoul within a few weeks. More important, over half of the North Korean army was surrounded in the south, eventually leading to the capture of nearly 150,000 prisoners of war. The military route was massive and, in a stunning change of face, the U.N. and South Korean forces had retaken the south and were close to the Manchurian border by November.

Yet MacArthur's very success in overrunning the North may have precipitated the involvement of the Chinese, who entered the war in November with enormous troop numbers to support their defeated communist comrades. The communist counteroffensive was successful, Seoul fell, and the U.N. troops withdrew midway down the peninsula. Determined to push the communist forces back decisively, MacArthur demanded to use a series of offensive tactics including bombing the Chinese mainland bases and blockading the Chinese coast. Unwilling to allow the war to escalate into a direct confrontation with the Chinese on Chinese soil, President Truman called MacArthur's bluff and surprised the world; Douglas MacArthur was relieved of his command in April 1951 in one of the most notorious disagreements in U.S. history.

Where does MacArthur's leadership end and his personality begin? Clearly, his military goals were heavily influenced by his personal preferences (strategic risk taking, winning at almost any cost, and personal persuasion of others to support his military plans) and strengths (self-confidence, decisiveness, and technical brilliance). In defense of his personal style, it should be noted that his "dangerous" invasion plans in Inchon resulted in less than two dozen fatalities and an amazing reversal in a war that was close to being lost. His personal brilliance and the success of the country's endeavor almost completely overlapped. However, his insistence in overrunning North Korea may have brought the Chinese into the war and his bellicose stance might have escalated into a major war with China. When he disagreed with Franklin D. Roosevelt about plans to invade the Philippines, he was able to persuade the president; this same tactic backfired with Truman. This demonstrates how characteristics that made him great also hampered him: Resilience became stubbornness, self-confidence became arrogance, and personal achievement outgrew his policy role. Rather than ending a century-long, father-son tradition on an incredibly high note, his dismissal ended it on a sour note that forever muted his glory.

The trend toward fossilized and rigid behaviors on the part of long-time leaders is not absolute or inevitable, however. Leaders who prize flexibility, stay vigilant to impending crises, remain open to new opportunities, and who enjoy learning from experience are far less prone to become narrow-minded or set in their ways. Indeed, one sign of great leadership is the ability to reformulate strategy even though it requires undoing former successes. This general openness over time is encouraged by leaders with flexible dispositions, powerful internal stakeholders who value change, and an executive team that emphasizes diversity of perspectives and encourages robust discussion (Ancona and Nadler 1989).

The case of an early colonial governor illustrates the effect of a leader's time in office. Peter Stuyvesant became governor of Dutch New York in 1647 after a series of unsuccessful governors had held the post. While the colony had continued to grow, it did so haphazardly, and its safety from attacks by Indians and competing English and Swedes was always a dire consideration. During his tenure, he enforced discipline on the unruly colony, which, from its beginnings, was home to many non-Dutch and various religious sects. He strengthened fortifications and defenses against the Indian attacks that his predecessor had incited, severely limited the sale of guns and alcohol to the natives over the protests of the merchants, and required more orderly settlement of the city itself. He also expanded New Netherlands to the Delaware River, where he annexed the Swedish colony. While his hard work and honesty won him some grudging respect for his management, his intolerance of non-Calvinists such as the Quakers and his heavy, antidemocratic hand kept him at odds with most of the colonists during his rule. Because of this, when the English arrived with a force of only four ships and about 400 troops, the burghers of New Amsterdam refused to support Stuyvesant in military preparations and in 1664 the colony was taken without a fight. Thus, the very style that made the first half of Stuyvesant's career (1647–1655) successful—his discipline, self-confidence, and ability to keep the settlers and the West India Company relatively placated—worked against him later as the colony continued to grow. Despite the great prosperity and security that had been achieved during his rule, the colonists had become tired of his paternalism and preferred to change national allegiance because he had been unresponsive to their growing need for more self-governance.

In sum, effective leaders will be careful to maximize assessment information. In analyzing this information, many situational factors impinge on the range of goals that will be considered as well as on the priority given to them. While these situational factors have a legitimate role in affecting final decisions, they all have the potential to warp the process if used unwisely. For example, many leaders understand the need for change in a turbulent environment or because an organization is in decline but, in their haste to act, they make the wrong changes. Or leaders allow their role or functional specialty to dictate their goals to the detriment of the organization. Or they allow their personal preferences and circumstances to dominate their perspective about how to act. While all these situational factors need to play a role in the process, they must be placed in the context of other factors if high-quality goal setting is to be achieved.

SELECTING MAJOR GOALS

Now we turn from the process of goal setting to its content. In what areas will the leader set goals? What priority will the leader give them? And will goals set in the calm of planning be put into practice in the heat of activity?

Although most of the goal-setting literature addresses leaders assisting subordinates in setting their goals (e.g., Goldstein and Sorcher 1974), the insights apply equally well to leaders themselves. In fact, effective goal setting is an element of a number of leader behaviors that will be discussed in chapters 13 through 15, and include clarifying roles and objectives, developing staff, strategic planning, and articulating the mission and vision. It is certainly one of the most important metaskills for leaders,[1] as evidenced by presidents and CEOs summarizing their accomplishments (goal achievements) as they leave office or seek another one. Another example of the importance of goal setting is how frequently it is asked of senior-level job candidates, even though they may have limited information about a position.

The elements of goal setting were delineated earlier in the chapter. Now we examine some of the more practical guidelines of goal setting.

Set Goals That Are Explicit, Specific, and Have Timelines

Goals are important because they drive people to seek efficiency and effectiveness through higher standards and concrete measures, and perceptions of leadership success are tied to them (Burke et al. 2007). Implicit goals are built into many standardized production functions. Do we meet deadlines, weekly and monthly production schedules, or simply handle operational demands? However, explicit goals are critical for leaders because they set conscious standards and seek accomplishments that would be unlikely to occur without conscious effort. Those goals may be higher standards, resolution of special or nonroutine problems, or progress toward long-range projects.

The single greatest problem in managing is the absence of goals. Without goals, performance and standards are lacking, ambiguous, or unquestioned. Although it is sometimes argued that goals limit flexibility and creativity, they need not do so. Goals should be amenable to change with new information and in an unpredictable environment. Goals should also spur creativity by stimulating action and higher standards, and creating focused challenges. Ideally, goals should measure outcomes or results, rather than the processes used to achieve goals. For example, a decrease in the complaint rate is a better goal than how many training sessions are held to address the problem. Action plans (i.e., strategies) can then detail the processes to be used to achieve the goals. In decreasing the complaint rate, three strategies can be used simultaneously: a series of customer focus groups to improve understanding of the problem, a widely distributed memorandum explaining the need for improvement, and three training sessions reflecting the insights of the focus groups and best practices. Finally, goals should have timelines so that expectations of progress are demanded (even of one-self) and that progress can be monitored. Generally, the more specific timelines are, the better. Without specificity and timelines, goals are in danger of being as useful as New Year's resolutions on New Year's Day. (See Exhibit 10.5 for a discussion of this problem.)

Chief executive officers, because of their long-term perspective, may need to break their goals into manageable chunks. Some large projects, for example, the construction

Exhibit 10.5

Firefighting: A Good Way to Handle Burning Buildings but a Poor Way to Manage Organizations

In the fire service, firefighting has the longest tradition, one that is very honorable and distinguished. It requires fire departments to respond with incredible speed, have highly honed technical skills, rely on predetermined firefighting protocols as extensively as possible to prevent unnecessary risk (despite Hollywood's emphasis on on-the-spot creativity), and focus on mitigating the damage of fires, sometimes by damaging property in the act (through water damage and inner wall inspection). Exciting as it occurs, it has a glamorous image, but leaves firefighters somewhat physically and psychologically drained after the fact. Today, of course, the fire service has other important functions, such as prevention, arson investigation, hazardous materials, emergency medical service, rescue, and so on. In particular, modern professional fire departments emphasize fire prevention as much as firefighting because it is more effective in the long run. Not only fire marshals but all firefighters are charged with prevention activities. Good fire departments systematically collect the building plans of all major public and commercial buildings (a huge undertaking), review the firefighting infrastructure of all neighborhoods, install building and neighborhood plans in computer systems that can be instantly retrieved en route to incidents, and recommend changes to ensure that emergency efforts will not be stymied.

In management, the term firefighting does not have such a glamorous reputation—quite the contrary. It refers to management that is reactive and managers who lurch from crisis to crisis. Managers who are "firefighters" allow minor operational problems that emerge to consume their time day after day. Partially because of the adrenalin rush, and partially because they are exhausted from the daily pressure of quandaries, they rarely have or take the time to analyze problems for systematic patterns or long-term solutions. Long-term planning is neglected because the resources and time are not there. In reality, however, many of the problems being managed are minor and such managers are either micromanaging or allowing slack time to be poorly used. Good goal setting is a strong antidote to the firefighting syndrome. It requires managers to carve out time in advance of the problems, and pushes them to accomplishments despite fatigue, frustration, and distractions. Effective leadership does not ignore the importance of daily technical issues that arise; it simply requires that leaders infuse their goals with long-term and change objectives, achieve specific results in specified timelines, and do so methodically.

of a new facility and the moving of people into it, can and should be fully planned in phases in advance, once the funding is secured. With these types of goals, the two challenges involve the quality of the detailed planning and planning flexibility. That is, are the original plans well researched, detailed, and communicated? Is the planning process able to accommodate changes (be flexible) based on the inevitable challenges that occur in large projects? For more tentative goals, the overall goal must still be explicit, but the action plans may deal with only the first of several phases. For example, a public sector agency head in local government may decide (in cooperation with other elected officials and agency heads) that a highway upgrade from an open-access, four-lane road to a limited-access freeway would be wise for the long-term growth of the city and region. Because the project will require both state and federal transportation funding to match local monies, only the near-term phases will be detailed, although it is critical that the long-term goal be explicit, clear, and convincing. The agency head should make sure in the early phase that engineering plans are drawn up with alternate routes, public input is solicited, robust regional consultation and planning are conducted, and initial (exploratory) groundwork with the state and federal authorities has occurred. Later phases are designed based on the success of the preliminary phases.

Set Goals That Are Related to All Important Aspects of Performance

The coherence of goals is as important as their form. One important aspect of goal setting is the balance of goals across organizational or leadership functions. Today, this idea is often called the "balanced scorecard" approach (Kaplan and Norton 1996). That is, all major areas should receive attention in order to ensure monitoring and improvement. For example, an organization that reviews only the quantitative aspects of operations (amount of production) may be entirely missing the qualitative aspects (customer satisfaction), which are generally harder to capture as data. Yet, the competing principle is that too many goals overwhelm or confuse people, and getting just the right balance of goals and concomitant measures is no easy task. Ideally there are four to ten goals. Of course, a number of these may be maintenance goals (which are generally easier to monitor) rather than improvement/change goals that usually require more energy and focus.

A particular challenge to consider in goal setting is the need to make sure that the goals are truly significant to the people in the organization who must carry them out. Goal selection (cognitive appeal and balance) and articulation (clarity and inspirational appeal) are highly important if people are not to consider goals annoyances or irrelevant. Unless people believe in the importance of the goals that are chosen, they are unlikely to be motivated to pursue them in the daily fray of pressures and problems.

Set Goals That Are Challenging but Realistic

One of the most concrete results of social science research on goal setting is that people respond best to goals that are challenging but realistic (Earley, Wojnaroski, and Prest 1987; Locke and Latham 1990). If goals are all easy, people frequently become complacent. Thomas Edison stated: "Show me a thoroughly satisfied man and I will show you a failure." Indeed, folk wisdom[2] and historical achievements[3] point to the value of challenge as a necessary ingredient for great achievements. Yet, if goals are too difficult, followers will become frustrated, annoyed, or simply fail. Thus, while easy and moderately challenging goals are equally likely to succeed, the latter are more likely to increase results, without increasing in failure rates. Extremely challenging goals are more likely to produce great results, but the likelihood of failure, sometimes spectacular failure, increases exponentially. Achieving the right balance is no easy task, but it is critical so that goals are motivating and achievable.

To balance goals, one must consider the degree of difficulty; some more difficult goals may need to be balanced against some easier goals. In addition, good goal development is based on good data about organizational functions and past performance. The leader needs to know what areas are already strong, which areas have performance gaps, and which present new opportunities.

Consult with Subordinates, Superiors, and Others and Communicate with Them Afterward

Although leaders make the final determination of the goals that they will personally seek to accomplish, they are unwise to do so without abundant input. Consultative practices allow the leader to test goal appropriateness, glean new data to refine the goals, communicate prospective goals to others, and rehearse the strategies for self and others. When dealing with the goals of subordinates, management by objectives in which specific operational objectives and timelines are interactively negotiated between the employee and superior has been found to be very effective in most settings.

Much of the time, goals are related to a system or network of which the leader is only a part, even though the leader is in a specific organizational setting (Friedrich et al. 2009). Sometimes leaders have the task of encouraging intergroup leadership. Pittinsky and Simon (2007) recommend four strategies to enhance intergroup cooperation: encourage contact to build mutual trust, proactively manage shared resources and interdependencies to enhance positive experiences, promote superordinate identities that include all entities under a single conceptual framework, and promote dual identities of an organization that are less restrictive on a monolithic viewpoint.

It is generally not enough merely to have goals; they must be communicated as well. Writing them down is useful for personal clarification and record keeping. Periodic review of goals demonstrates whether or not progress has been made. Further, leader goals should generally be public. Leaders should be talking to their employees about their goals (which are inevitably highly intertwined with organizational goals) as well as discussing goals in memoranda, newsletters, and reports. Leaders who fail to do so are often poorly understood and have less assistance from organizational members in achieving their goals.

BALANCING GOALS

This section expands on the concept of goal coherence, referenced in broad terms in the previous section. In keeping with the theme of this book regarding the technical, follower, organizational, and ethical aspects of leadership, goal formulation and prioritization can be categorized along these lines, too. How many of the major goals of leaders fall into each of these four metacategories? This is a useful tool because it helps to ensure that no areas are deprived of attention, even though leaders inevitably weight their goal clusters very differently to match the variety of circumstances that they face. In order to describe the differences, extensive examples from our study of senior managers are provided to demonstrate the natural goal variations that occur.

Technical Performance Goals

Even though the degree of emphasis varies greatly, a few generalizations can be made from the leadership literature. Generally, the more junior the leader, the more functionally specialized the area of responsibility, the more stable the environment, the more organizational production and performance are judged on purely technical grounds, then the more leaders will tend to emphasize technical goals.

No leaders are exempt from some technical performance requirements. For example, despite their preeminent roles as superpower leaders, American presidents are often strongly faulted for underachieving in technical areas. Ronald Reagan was faulted for improperly monitoring the Department of Housing and Urban Development (HUD), which experienced atrocious mismanagement under Secretary Samuel Pierce Jr. John F. Kennedy was faulted for botching the Bay of Pigs military operation that was intended to topple the Castro regime in 1961. George H.W. Bush was faulted for improperly managing the technical aspects of the economy—even though a president's ability to have a major effect in this area is muted at best—and this cost him a second term in office. Jimmy Carter was faulted for not delegating enough, which caused him to micromanage and to lose sight of broader objectives. Therefore, although technical performance is often dismissed as a nonleadership responsibility (Zaleznik 1977), it is not possible to escape it if one is an organizational leader.

In the study that accompanied this book, technical performance was perceived as the most important aspect for 43 percent of the managers. In contradiction to the literature, this was not particularly affected by the leader's level. As stewards of public service, members of this group (even those monitoring many services, such as city managers) felt strongly that a high-quality product was a baseline responsibility.[4] Leaders in technical areas with critical outcomes, such as firefighting or public health, or with functional specialties such as human resource management, were slightly more likely than other types of leaders to place technical issues as their highest priority. However, close to one-third placed technical performance issues last in their priorities.

Our example of a technically oriented leader is Texas County Judge Harold Keeter. Swisher County is small; it has less than 9,000 in population, and county personnel amount to just forty-eight people including all elected officials. In Texas, county judges not only administer the county judicial system but also preside over county commissioners' meetings and act as CEO unless that has been delegated to a county manager (only in large urban counties). Because the county is small, Keeter hears all probate, juvenile, and criminal cases personally, generally around a dozen cases a week. He also sets the commissioners' agenda, communicates and coordinates with the other elected officials in the county (e.g., the sheriff, attorney, treasurer, and recorder), and drafts and maintains the county budget. Fiscal stress in this rural county has meant that careful financial management is an ongoing concern. While he would like to delegate some of this detailed work, this judge knows that the county simply cannot afford such a luxury. Therefore, despite his elected status, he often functions as a line worker (he estimates nearly 50 percent of his time). Attention to personnel largely takes the form of solving problems and monitoring performance. The judge tries to maintain about 30 percent of his time on long-range projects such as economic development initiatives. However, his goals and time in this area are always being squeezed by the technical nature of most of his work, and he knows that without vigilance he would never quite get to future-oriented goals because of the press of daily technical demands.

By examining his job, we can see why Judge Keeter's primary focus is on the technical cluster. Although he is an elected official with wide executive responsibilities as county judge, the organization itself is very small and he is called upon to act as the direct supervisor for production activities in many cases. Furthermore, he is not only called upon to manage a very narrow functional area—the county judicial system—he also acts as the primary implementer in this area. Although the county may need some economic stimulus and rejuvenation, popular expectations of county government rely on it for technical stability and consistency in basic county functions: law enforcement, county roads, judicial issues, and so forth. Thus, while we would be surprised if Keeter's goals and activities were not primarily focused on technical issues, he is concerned that they dominate his time excessively to the detriment of his goals for strategic improvement in county government.

Follower-Development Goals

The importance of followers is much heralded in both the popular and academic leadership literature (e.g., Max DePree [1989], Tom Peters [1992], and leader-member exchange theory). Thus, important aspects of leadership, and some would say the most important, are leading and developing followers.

Goals that are oriented toward follower development (broadly viewed as working with and managing people) can hardly be absent from any leader's agenda. However, focus on follower development goals, according to the leadership literature, tends to be more pronounced at the junior and middle levels of organizational management (except when the leader is attempting to make cultural changes), in broad supervisory positions as opposed to narrower staff position areas, in noncrisis situations, and when personnel shortages exist or management is called upon to do difficult things.

In the study of local government managers carried out for this book, follower development was perceived as the most important aspect for 31 percent of the managers (second place). It was considered the second most important factor by a large number of those surveyed, so that, overall, state and local managers in this study viewed follower development and technical goals as almost equal in importance. Although the factors cited in the literature were apparent, the ability to follow through on conscious goals and leader personality seemed to be the most important factors driving follower development focus. Although considered important by most leaders relative to the three goals, there was a very strong self-awareness that technical demands (including technical personnel problems) often diminished follower development goal achievement greatly. In other words, very few leaders actually spent as much time as they felt was important on follower development (in contrast to technical goals). There also was a distinct trend for those who indicated achievement as a very high priority to have poor follower development follow-through, even if they rated it as very important. This trend was among those leaders who had task-oriented personalities.

An example of a leader who gives a primary focus to follower development is Steve Ross, fire chief in Amarillo, Texas, whose department has 450 employees. Like many other midsized fire departments in the United States, the Amarillo fire department is a highly technically oriented organization concerned with fire prevention and suppression, emergency medical service, hazardous materials mitigation, and crisis management. Intensive and constant technical training is intended to keep skills high at all levels of the organization, and fire commanders in the department spend much time scheduling, conducting, and sometimes even participating in technical training. Even the most senior commanders monitor operations minutely, and delegation has become a fine science. Despite the intense technical orientation of an emergency business, Chief Ross knows he must make sure that the people providing the service are supported and cultivated. Because of the technical competence of the senior commanders, he can focus more on consulting, motivating, team building, and managing conflict. Several of his personal goals have to do with his followers. One goal is to have senior managers, who tend to be promoted on technical skills, improve their management skills. Another of his goals is to have a more inspirationally led department that will achieve higher levels of motivation, camaraderie, and performance. As in many fire departments, the generally high levels of bonding within the department do not always prevent petty and parochial attitudes nor do they keep performance levels optimal. Therefore, the chief's technical concerns are minimal because of the organization's basic competence, and he hopes to achieve realignment through the reorientation of the followers themselves.

Chief Ross fits our profile fairly well as a leader who emphasizes follower development goals. He refers to himself as a division director more than as a chief, thus identifying himself as a senior manager. In addition, he is attempting to transform the culture of the organization into a more professional one. He has broad organizational responsibilities, and, except in rare cases, can leave technical matters to his senior commanders.

Organizational Alignment Goals

Leaders have a special role in ensuring that their organizations are in alignment with the external environment—clients, customers, the legislative body and advisory boards, interest groups, community groups, and other organizations, to mention only the most prominent. Leaders in this regard are the key nexus between the external and internal worlds of the organization. Just as organizational leaders by definition have followers, they should also be ahead of others in spotting external trends, seeing opportunities, and avoiding threats. This means that leaders have a special responsibility for organizational change.

As already illustrated, not all leaders will have organizational alignment goals as their main emphasis. Some have a great deal of technical work to supervise, or, in some cases, do themselves. Others are in well-organized and situated organizations where they can focus primarily on the employees who actually perform the work. Yet, it is the unusual case where a leader does not have some organizational alignment responsibilities. This focus expands as leaders are more senior in the organization, as the external environment changes or destabilizes, and when the organization needs to look at adding or deleting activities or changing its structure and processes.

In the study accompanying this book, organizational alignment was perceived as the most important aspect for only 21 percent of the leaders. This was reflected in a question about whether they spent the bulk of their time on "refining and maintaining" or on "innovating and transforming." By four to one, the managers in the study indicated that they actually spent the bulk of their time in refinement and maintenance activities. Thus, despite the bias of the group toward education and continual learning, the more powerful factors in goal preference and follow-through seemed to be the very stable environment and strong service orientation of the local and state managers surveyed.

Our example of organizational alignment is Jim Jeffers, the city manager of Plainview, Texas ("the home of Jimmy Dean"). Plainview is a small city of under 25,000 people; approximately 200 people work for the city. In stark contrast to most of the cities in West Texas and rural areas in general, in the past twenty years the city has experienced significant growth and has become more prosperous. All the larger, old companies in town, such as Archer-Daniels Midland, Wayland Baptist University, and Excel-Cargill (beef packing), have expanded. In the past score of years, Azteca Corn Milling has located in Plainview and is now the largest company of its kind in the world, and the new Wal-Mart Distribution Center has become the largest in the region. When asked why this exceptional growth has occurred, Jeffers is quick to respond: location and a fine city council. Yet, the larger cities in the region, Lubbock and Amarillo, have the same location and stable councils as well, and, one could argue, better labor pools. As the city manager of Plainview for the past seventeen years, humility has become an instinctive characteristic. Yet when Jeffers discusses his goals—economic development, street redesign, improved staff development, change in the recruiting system, increased pay for city employees, design of a more sophisticated budget management system—technical performance issues take a back seat to realigning the organization. The technical competence of his employees is very good, he adds; they simply need assistance with the big picture, interdepartmental cooperation, and innovation. Recently, he has found that his time and energy are being sapped by more mundane technical and personnel issues. Having the resources, he has just hired an assistant city manager to share the executive load, to handle some of the more technical responsibilities, and to provide additional fresh insights. Although he maintains that he has had little to do with the consistent growth of the city (despite a large number of important city–community partnerships), he wants to be sure that his attention is focused on keeping Plainview first in regional development.

Jeffers is an excellent example of the leader who focuses on long-term organizational alignment but eschews the credit by giving it to others. He has the senior position in an organization that can afford to allow him to focus much of his time on strategic and change issues, if he so chooses. Because this focus is becoming more difficult to maintain, he has brought in an assistant city manager. Because Plainview is in an enviable position for a small rural city, many of his goals are modest in terms of change and realignment, and they include improved recruitment, staff training, and street design. Yet, he is constantly scanning the environment for new major initiatives and for ways to enhance the reputation and infrastructure so critical to hearty economic development.

Nowhere is the science and art of goal setting in evidence more than in balancing.

When is one too technically oriented? When is one not paying enough attention to those who produce success? When is one too focused on organizational alignment issues? The leadership literature from the 1950s through the 1970s focused on technical and follower development aspects of leadership (popularly known as task and people orientations, or, in the academic literature, "initiating structure" and "consideration"). The transformational literature (starting in the late 1970s) emphasized the important and unique roles leaders have in aligning organizations. Studies of local and state managers revealed a distinct bias toward technical and follower goals in both prioritization and follow-through. Nevertheless, almost none of the leaders/managers viewed organizational alignment as unimportant; they just did not give it equal attention in most cases. However, the leaders in the local government manager study identified many of their skills in organizational alignment and change management as their weakest.

Service and Ethical Focus

Ralph Waldo Emerson asserted, "It is one of the most beautiful compensations of this life that no man can sincerely try to help another without helping himself." Those working in public service understand and deeply feel this sentiment. By giving a portion of ourselves, we become whole and fulfilled. Even motivational psychologists such as Maslow have asserted the fundamental importance of higher-level needs, for example, self-actualization and the role of helping others in that process (1954).

It is generally unquestioned that helping others is a structural part of the public sector and should be an ingrained quality of the exemplary public servant in general. Nonetheless, helping others both competes with other priorities and has bounds. The legendary case of Robin Hood illustrates the issues well. The bandit robbed from the rich (who after all, have the most from which to steal) and was wise enough to provide a small portion to the needy in the region. The local magistrate and constable, the Sheriff of Nottingham, was exceedingly unpopular because of his oppressive taxes and harsh methods, which transformed the outlaw into a folk hero. Thus, Robin Hood acted outside the law to promote the common good, a tricky proposition in all but the most extreme circumstances. A more recent, but less idealized, case occurred in the Department of Housing and Urban Development in 1989 when a consultant working for the agency stole $5.5 million and claimed to have given it to charitable organizations. Marilyn Harrell was forever after given the epithet "Robin HUD." Indeed, highly sophisticated moral arguments have been advanced and acted upon in the past century to justify aggressive wars, ethnic cleansing, political oppression, and extreme administrative intrusiveness. The issue of when to go outside the political/legal framework—although fascinating and important—will not be covered here because it is an enormously complex and large subject, covering topics as diverse as whistleblowing to administrative leaks to civil disobedience. (However, for a relevant case, see chapter 17, which discusses the British public servant, George Washington, who eventually repudiated his former government and helped set up a new and more legitimate one, at least from the American perspective.) What is important is to consider the weight given to ethical issues.

No exact weight is possible because circumstances vary so widely. In routine administrative decisions such as equipment purchases, ethical issues may be so minor as to be nonexistent. But it is rare that ethical issues do not lurk in the background of major decisions, and they may build the platform for appropriate decision making. At its heart, being ethical is considering others before oneself or one's interests. It has a bewildering number of perspectives, including: concern for the public at large (e.g., taxpayers), concern for clients, concern for the disenfranchised (especially those unable to defend their own interests), concern for the organization as a public good, concern for employees as instruments of the public good, and concern for the law as the authoritative will of the people. To what degree should these ethical norms be considered differently, for example, in a regulatory agency versus a social service agency, or in an entrepreneurial agency, such as a state lottery, versus a county hospital serving the indigent?

The example of ethical leadership here is not from the research on local managers conducted for this book, but from the former secretary of U.S. Health, Education, and Welfare (HEW), Donna Shalala. In a 2004 speech, Shalala identified twelve points in her leadership practice as a member of the cabinet that not only kept her out of trouble when many of her colleagues were challenged and even her boss was impeached, but also kept her personally focused and more effective.[5] Although some of her points refer specifically to political executives, her underlying principles are pertinent to all public servants.

1. "Always adopt the attitude, 'The buck stops here.'" If the ethics of responsibility for challenges and accountability for mistakes do not start at the top, they will only haphazardly exist below.
2. "Choose people based as much on the content of their character as their expertise." Moral character does count—a lot—and should be a major part of any selection process. Expertise is simply not enough.
3. "The game is often won in the huddle." Planning requires teamwork, which requires a genuine openness to the ideas of others.
4. "Bureaucrat is NOT a four letter word." In order to send this message as a presidential appointee, Shalala's first appointees were from careers in public service.
5. "You must accept bad news and learn from it." Although the good news is fun, it is the bad news that tests leaders' characters. Can they hear bad news without losing equanimity, and even profit by it?
6. "Stop shoveling." When you make a mistake, admit it. Those who do not admit mistakes are like those in holes who only keep digging—deeper and deeper. Cover-ups are often more damaging than initial mistakes or infractions, and can be dangerous from a legal point of view.
7. "You can't cultivate honesty and integrity in the dark." Transparency is always the best long-term policy. As secretary of HEW, Shalala always had a notetaker in the room during meetings.
8. "You can't subordinate policy to politics." As a political appointee, it is best to carefully protect the facts and the science, even when it is unpopular to do so—it will increase one's trustworthiness and long-term effectiveness.

9. "You have to look at issues through a prism." Leaders have a responsibility to look at issues from many perspectives before making important decisions that affect the public good. This is because the public good is itself a collection of interests and perspectives.

10. "It is your friends, not your enemies, who get you into trouble." First, working too closely with friends will provide a perception of favoritism. Second, friends will often want you to bend the rules or make exceptions that in the light of day look bad or are simply wrong.

11. "Ethical employers care about their employees." In the worst cases, business executives require employees to buy stock while selling their own, or provide themselves with substantial bonuses while downsizing and freezing salaries. More common to the public sector is benign neglect, in which the leader functions only as taskmaster and evaluator. To inspire great deeds, ethical leaders must instill a sense of trust.

12. "If you don't tell people where you are going, you might end up somewhere else." Leadership is a group process, even though the leader may have special responsibilities and prerogatives. People must be consulted and informed constantly, despite the leader's busy schedule. Effective two-way communication is antecedent to success.

Shalala summed up by saying, "It was never simple but always satisfying to lead ethically." Further, her practical advice is to build ethical considerations into the decision-making process itself, rather than to consider ethical dimensions as a final test or afterthought. Wise though her advice may be, however, it is up to individual decision makers to integrate this perspective into production, interpersonal, and organizational goals.

CONCLUSION

Goal setting is an art in that it requires numerous personal judgments, customized responses, and intuitively based actions without full knowledge. Yet, the effective leader also knows that good goal setting is anchored in the discipline of data collection and analysis, implicit hypothesis and theory testing, and prediction based on this scientifically conceived approach. Implicit theories about complex organizational phenomena that have not been tested by data gathering and analysis are often simply wrong, or so simplistic or partial as to be largely useless.

As leaders go about setting goals, they are affected by many factors related to the situation. What is the organizational environment like? At what stage is the organizational life cycle? What is the leader's level of responsibility and type and functional responsibilities? What is the leader's personality? Finally, at what stage is the leader in his/her career? There are four ideals to strive for in goal setting. Goals should be explicit, specific, and have concrete timelines; they should be related to all important aspects of the organization's performance; they should be challenging but realistic; and leaders should be sure to consult widely in setting goals and to communicate them afterward.

Particular attention should focus on goal balance. The primary tool in this regard is an examination of technical, follower, and organizational goals, as well as ethical dimensions. Because of varying situational factors, no ideal goal proportion is asserted. Leaders in stable environments, in smaller organizations and in junior positions, for example, may place disproportionate emphasis on technical and/or follower development goals. Those in dynamic environments and very senior positions may emphasize organizational alignment issues including organizational change. All leaders need to be able to integrate the ethical framework of goal setting and decision making that will create buy-in and trust. These descriptive generalizations should not detract from the prescriptive recommendation about balancing them consciously, whatever the exact weight. Although the most common tendency is for managers to neglect organizational goals in favor of the technical and follower-development issues that seem to demand a leader's time as soon as they enter the office door, it is not unheard of for some leaders to advocate more organizational realignment than their organizations are prepared to handle.

Oversimplifying for clarity, then, effective leaders *must set goals* and do so *consciously*. Without goals, leaders and their organizations tend to wander. John F. Kennedy stated that even effort and courage are not enough without purpose and direction. Leaders must make sure that their goals are informed and balanced. Without data, leaders are just guessing; without balance, the leader may ultimately be warping the organization. And, obvious though it may sound, leaders *must act on their goals* or *revise them*. Just as the road to hell is paved with good intentions, so, too, is the road to organizational decline. Indeed, it is questionable whether a person can even be considered a leader if s/he does not conscientiously set, balance, and achieve goals.

As with other major dynamics of leadership, effective goal setting and prioritization— along with the self-discipline to fulfill one's aspirations—seem to be simple common sense, and they are. However, in practice it is all too often "more honored in the breach than in the observance." In the next chapter we begin a catalogue of those traits that most frequently enhance leadership effectiveness. Not surprisingly, at least half of these ten traits—decisiveness, resilience, energy, need for achievement, and flexibility—are leader characteristics that enhance the likelihood of goal accomplishment.

NOTES

1. Although goal setting is not on the list of skills in chapter 12, it could easily be considered a contender as an additional skill.

2. The pithy aphorisms of many Americans from Robert Kennedy (only those who dare to fail greatly can ever achieve greatly) to Arnold Palmer (the most rewarding things in life are often the ones that look like they cannot be done) attest to this long-held, popular belief.

3. A few of the many remarkable achievements identified in this book include the remaking of New York, the carving of Mount Rushmore, and the very establishment of the United States itself.

4. I am relatively confident that a larger and more diversified sample would find a distinct trend linking higher levels of responsibility with lower levels of technical goal focus. However, my hypothesis is that the linkage is more muted than in the private sector, where the organizational environment shifts more rapidly and radically.

5. Donna Shalala presented these comments at the national conference of the American Society for Public Administration on March 28, 2004, in Portland, Oregon.

Traits That Contribute to Leader Effectiveness

We have known for over a half-century that a purely trait-oriented approach to leadership is woefully insufficient to do more than give a very general indication of leadership capacity. First, the leader's situation or contingencies simply have too great a bearing to predict more than a portion of leader effectiveness (Stogdill 1948, 1974). In other words, to say that a "decisive" leader will always be more effective (which may be true in crises and situations demanding change) disregards the more numerous leadership situations in which leaders need to be cautious, contemplative, and inclusive. Leaders with "high energy" can do damage in situations where they lack basic technical competence because they are disposed to push ahead with action while lacking sufficient understanding of the situation at hand. Second, and already implied in the previous examples, traits do not always follow simple more-is-better linear progressions. For example, a moderate "achievement orientation" is generally better than a high achievement orientation because of the excesses of ambition (Yukl 2002). "Willingness to assume power" is highly qualified by the nature of the leader's use of power (Burns 1978). Yet, even with these qualifications, it is also important to note that both traits and skills are generally rated as more important than most behavior competencies by practicing managers and leaders. The U.S. Office of Personnel Management (OPM) conducted a major study in 1991, consisting of 10,000 managers and lead workers, which is extensively cited in the following chapters. Traits and skills crowded out work behaviors as most important by dominating more than 80 percent of the top competencies investigated (U.S. OPM 1997). So even though their utility is highly contextually determined and the actual nature of traits is often subtle and nonlinear, their overall importance should not be doubted.

We have also known for a long time that it is important to distinguish among different types of leadership competencies. There are relatively innate or long-term dispositions (traits), broadly applied learned characteristics (skills), and actual behaviors (concrete actions). Possession of certain traits and skills is an indicator of likely or future effectiveness; behaviors are the (present or past) indicators of the effective use of traits and skills in organizational contexts. The generic term "competency" generally refers to discrete abilities to accomplish a job, regardless of traits, skills, or behaviors. So far, so good.

However, agreement tends to break down quickly in the attempt to patch together specific lists of traits, skills, and behavioral competencies. Numerous studies done over the years in many contexts have led to innumerable lists. There are several challenges here. The concepts used to define leadership—whether they are traits, skills, or actual behaviors—are analytic inventions used to categorize the amazingly vast terrain of leadership. Therefore, people use different terms to define slightly different concepts; for example, persistence versus resilience. This is a terminological problem. Another is the operational definition problem. No matter how the concepts are divided and labeled, it is nearly impossible to define exactly when one concept such as energy ends and another such as the drive for achievement begins. These are challenges not only to leadership researchers but also to serious practitioners studying leadership. Although this book does not adopt a single list from one of the common comprehensive sources (e.g., Kotter 1982; Howard and Bray 1988; Bass 1990; U.S. OPM 1992, 1999; Yukl 2002), because of its unique purpose and perspective, it strives to be as consistent as possible with them. This chapter will discuss ten traits; chapter 12 will discuss six metaskills; and chapters 13–15 will discuss twenty-one behavioral competencies; it is a total of thirty-seven competencies. One should also add as single competencies leader assessment of the organization (chapter 9), leader constraints (chapter 9), leader prioritization (chapter 10), and leader development and evaluation (chapters 16 and 17, respectively). One could also add each of the different leader styles as competencies. That brings the total to fifty competencies.

The ten traits that will be discussed in this chapter include six personality characteristics: self-confidence, decisiveness, resilience, energy, flexibility, and emotional maturity; two classic motivational drives, the willingness to assume responsibility and the need for achievement; and two value orientations, personal integrity and a service mentality (although emotional maturity has both value and personality attributes). As general traits these are all relatively stable dispositions by adulthood. They are all amenable to significant improvement, and a few, to substantial improvement by training and education in specific situational environments. For example, with good education and training and years of experience, self-confidence on the job is enhanced greatly, one feels more confident about being decisive in critical situations and appreciates opportunities for achievement. Yet, while modest and incremental improvements can be made, it is wise to remember that traits are deeply anchored in the personality and radical changes are unlikely.

SELF-CONFIDENCE

Self-confidence is *a general (positive) sense about one's ability to accomplish what needs to be accomplished.* It is composed of several subelements. Self-esteem is a positive regard for oneself and one's abilities in a general sense. Good self-esteem helps during the awkward learning phase prior to mastery of a new skill set. Self-efficacy is the belief that one has either the specific abilities necessary or the ability to work with others who have those abilities. This is the aspect of self-confidence that is most influenced by training and experience. Yet another aspect of self-efficacy is innate. It has to do with feeling that one's actions make a difference, rather than having a more fatalistic attitude (Rotter 1966; Miller, Kets de Vries, and Toulouse 1982; Hannah et al. 2008). This means that people with high self-efficacy tend to be more optimistic about influencing their own fate. As Virgil aptly noted, "They can conquer who believe they can." Finally, self-confidence is related to courage (which will be included in the concept here even though it could be considered a separate factor). Without self-confidence, courage is almost impossible.

Self-confidence is important because it provides self, subordinates, and others with a sense that things are under control and a proper direction is being set. It assists leaders to encourage self and others to assume more challenging tasks, set higher expectations, make decisions in crises more confidently, and plan changes with more assurance (Sy, Cote, and Saavedra 2005; Luthans 2007). Charismatic leaders are especially adept at infectiously enhancing others' self-confidence, too (House 1977; Shamir, House, and Arthur 1993). Further, some degree of self-confidence and at least a passable façade are necessary for many other traits—particularly decisiveness, resilience, energy, and the willingness to assume responsibility. On the other hand, an extreme lack of self-confidence may lead to a lack of activity, vacillation, defensiveness, paranoia, and overcautiousness.

In a U.S. Office of Personal Management study, self-confidence was included in a slightly larger category called self-direction. Out of twenty-two factors, it ranked eighth in importance for executives; however, it ranked third for new supervisors (U.S. OPM 1997). This is strongly consistent with other studies (see Bass 1990 for a general review; Kotter 1982; Boyatzis 1982; Howard and Bray 1988). In a recent study by Thach and Thompson (2007) self-confidence ranked seventh for public sector managers but fourth for those in the private sector out of twenty-three items. In our small study of local government managers, many identified self-confidence as a weakness. Although there was a slight correlation of self-confidence with tenure in a job, many veteran administrators expressed doubts about their self-confidence, too. Howard and Bray's (1988) research indicated that self-confidence in midcareer is a particularly strong indicator of long-term success. Intuitively, one would expect many leaders to lack strong self-confidence early in their careers but to develop it later with increased experience. Nonetheless, some of the respondents in the study for this book said that the lack of self-confidence was not entirely negative; it aided them to be more inclusive and thoughtful before acting, and ultimately encouraged them to be more flexible.

Indeed, the negative aspects of excessive self-confidence are substantial. Some problems with overconfidence include lack of caution, micromanagement, and arrogance. Excessive confidence can lead to foolish risk taking and mistakes resulting from lack of checking with others. It can lead to micromanagement when leaders think that their skills are superior and thus they must do or supervise all important tasks personally. Even when leaders' skills are clearly superior, this stifles subordinate initiative and learning. Finally, too much self-confidence can be perceived as arrogance when others' ideas, perceptions, and concerns are not considered.

Guidelines

1. *Assess personal strengths and weaknesses in order to address them.* Because lack of self-confidence is partially due to actual skill deficiencies, it is important to know what these deficiencies are. Conversely, it is important to know one's realistic strengths.

2. *Seek training or experience to remedy skill or knowledge liabilities.* Training, experience, and practice significantly improve effectiveness and self-confidence.

3. *Practice positive self-talk and positive visualization.* Much as we would all like to have a positive coach behind us all the time, it is rarely the case. Therefore, we must coach ourselves and encourage ourselves. People with low self-confidence often mentally rehearse pessimistic outcomes and practice self-doubt. Positive self-talk can be a healthy conscious antidote to negative attitudes. It is even better to visualize positive outcomes. (For very good and readable discussions of this concept and self-management in general, see the work of Manz and Sims on "self-leadership" 1980, 1987, 1989, 1991.)

DECISIVENESS

Decisiveness is *the ability to act relatively quickly depending on circumstances without excessively damaging decision quality.* For leaders, decisiveness is really just one aspect of a larger concept: degree of follower participation in decision making (Vroom and Yetton 1973; Vroom and Jago 1988). Generally speaking, follower inclusion in decision making should include a range of options, from no input (directive leadership), to minimal input, to substantial input but with the leader making the decision, and finally to subordinate decision making individually or in groups (delegation; discussed in chapter 13). This can be arrayed as a spectrum of leader options:

DIRECTIVE DECISION MAKING

Directive: No consultation in decision making
$\updownarrow$
Minimal Participation: Leader decision after minimal follower consultation
$\updownarrow$
Moderate Participation: Leader decision after substantial input
$\updownarrow$
Delegation: Decision by follower or as a group

DELEGATIVE DECISION MAKING

Decisiveness, as generally used, emphasizes action at the directive end of the degree-of-participation spectrum. However, decisiveness is not identical to directive decision making because frequently decisiveness occurs after consultation.

Ultimately, it is the situation that should dictate how much inclusion (of both subordinates and external sources) to utilize. Situations demanding decisiveness generally require minimal levels of subordinate participation or checking with outside authority. The most notable reason for decisiveness is crisis; another important reason is efficiency and time management. Subelements of decisiveness include a willingness to make unilateral decisions when appropriate, an ability to act quickly in crisis (and to correctly diagnosis when a crisis is occurring), and the ability to remain calm under stress.

Decisiveness is important in crises (a critical time for leaders) because it gives followers a sense of confidence that matters are being taken care of and it tends to lend substantial credibility to the leader (Mulder and Stemerding 1963; Mulder et al. 1986). In noncrisis situations decisiveness can be useful for decisions for which the leader is uniquely responsible and qualified, such as employment levels or work distribution issues, where levels of agreement are low and discord would likely result, or where it is simply inefficient to consult with others because a decision is not important or others are uninformed. To the degree that decisiveness represents a preference for action and initiative, it relates to the drive for achievement (Spencer and Spencer 1993). The opposite trait, indecisiveness (also known as vacillation or hesitation and attributed to uncertainty), is often identified as one of the most damning traits a leader can have (Yukl 1998, 259).

In the OPM study, decisiveness ranks ninth among the twenty-two traits studied in the federal government for new supervisors. Apparently, new supervisors simply have to check with too many people and gather too much information for it to be higher. Yet, it was rated as important or very important by over 80 percent of the respondents for executives, ranking it fifth out of twenty-two traits, skills, and behaviors. Studies of personality types of public sector executives, using a Myers-Briggs Type Indicator, show that the predominance of those occupying leadership positions have judgment-oriented rather than a perception-oriented personalities, indicating a clear bias toward decisiveness (Barber 1990; McCauley and Lombardo 1990). In a public–private comparison study of twenty-three items, time management—a cousin of decisiveness—was ranked only tenth in the public sector but sixth in the private sector (Thach and Thompson 2007). In our study, a number of participants indicated decisiveness as a weakness. One pattern identified was an inability to bring data gathering to a close. People wanted to get more technical information and consult with more people on contentious issues. Here, the cause seemed to be a personality disposition toward caution or mild procrastination. Another pattern that the study group self-identified was decisiveness involving murky personnel issues in which employees were in conflict or a marginal employee who would sporadically engage in unacceptable behavior or substandard performance. Here, the problem was analytic: deciding what the problem was and handling it with compassion and firmness.

The excesses of decisiveness are very serious for leaders. One problem is that leaders who value decisiveness highly and employ it too often or too quickly are likely to be rash. What appears to be a crisis at first blush may be no more than a momentary problem, or the crisis may leave more time for deliberation and response than one supposes, and a hasty reaction may actually make the situation far worse. This is a particular problem when a policy or order is issued, but then quickly has to be amended or countermanded. The other problem with excessive decisiveness is its addictive quality. Being decisive is efficient (at least in the short run), and it also gives the leader a great sense of power. However, excessive decisiveness quickly leads to reduced information availability and authoritarianism resulting in worker alienation. For an example of the tricky balance that must be achieved by effective leaders, see Exhibit 11.1 on decisiveness and law enforcement.

Exhibit 11.1

Decisiveness and Law Enforcement

While going through an extensive leadership development program, Sheriff Wayne Lambright was enthusiastic about trying out new managerial tactics. He wanted to make a number of changes, and given the strong authority of his position, he could easily mandate those changes. However, he was also burdened with a low wage rate so he needed to make sure that his deputies felt as if they were "part of the team." "From what I have been exposed to in the class," he noted, "I have made an effort to adjust the way I go about change within the organization. I have gone—for the most part—from the 'me' to the 'we' style of management." Yet, he was also careful to point out that the transformation of styles would never—could never—be complete in his position. "There are times when the 'we' must make way for the 'me' style because of the mandates of the law. Of course, it is not really me, but I must be careful to be the forceful spokesperson for the law." And almost as an afterthought he added, "and, of course, when we are in the midst of a major public safety issue and I am present, I am very decisive because that is expected of the senior commander on the scene."

Guidelines

1. *Study decision making.* The study of decision making not only assists leaders in refining their analytic skills in making decisions (especially case methods in formal education) but just as important, it helps in deciding when to be decisive and when not to be. Discussions and analysis of the role of subordinates in decision making are reviewed in detail in Vroom's normative decision model (Vroom and Yetton 1973; Vroom and Jago 1988). (For more discussion on delegation and problem solving see chapter 13 and chapter 14 on consultation, and see chapter 15 for more discussion on decision making.)

2. *Do not procrastinate in gathering information for or making important decisions.* Because of the hurly-burly of management, it is easy to put off tedious data-gathering schemes, and because of possible negative ramifications, it is easy to delay important decisions until another day. Yet, important decisions are a key function of the leader's role and should not be relegated to when-time-allows status. Leaders need to decide the time parameters of decisions, gather the information with appropriate speed, and then act decisively in a crisis or other leader-centered situations.

3. *Prepare for possible emergencies and crises.* By definition, emergencies and crises have an unexpected or sudden element. However, preparation for possible or likely emergencies or crises is an important element of a leader's job and makes decisiveness much more authoritative and accurate when done properly (Tichy and Bennis 2007). In fact, most emergencies are known in advance but are simply less likely possibilities than more optimistic scenarios (Boin and Otten 1996; Weick, Sutcliffe, and Obstfeld 1999). Examples include sudden or severe budget cutbacks, loss of key personnel, service demand spikes, and sustained underfunding leading to unauthorized service gaps. Yet, good managers should have implicit, or sometimes explicit, alternative plans for such plausible future events, which may even be discussed with staff as

advance emergency planning. Even in the case of sustained long-term underfunding, the leader may need to prepare a white paper on the brewing crisis and alternative courses of action for policymakers and agency executives.

4. *Stay calm.* When asked how he became a hero, John F. Kennedy replied that it was involuntary; they sank his boat. It was not the courage to undertake a dangerous task but the courage to remain calm during one that was his pride. In a crisis, which is the primary reason for decisiveness, pressure to make important but unpleasant decisions with limited information is acute. If one does not stay calm, the likelihood of jumping to the most obvious or immediate solution is far more likely. Yet, in most complex management crises, such hasty decisions are generally suboptimal, and may appear rash once the ramifications of the actions are understood. While some people are predisposed to staying calm under duress, most people must cultivate this ability. Of course, among the best means are the advance planning discussed above or prior experience. Other more physical tactics (useful during the crisis itself) include breathing and relaxation exercises. Finally, leaders need to learn the self-discipline of remaining calm by reviewing their performance after the fact, in order to gain insight from past experience and improve future performance under stressful conditions.

RESILIENCE

Resilience is generally defined *as the ability to spring back into shape, position, or direction after being pressed or stretched.* With people, this means that after the weariness of long hours, distractions, or misfortune, a person is able to recover his/her direction, strength, and good humor relatively quickly. Synonyms are "hardiness" (Bartone et al. 2009) and the old-fashioned term "stoutness."

One subelement is persistence. This is the ability to stay the course despite hard work or setbacks. It assumes that one is seeking to accomplish long-term goals (see achievement below). The ditty attributed to Calvin Coolidge is apropos here:

> *Nothing in the world can take the place of persistence.*
> *Talent will not; nothing is more common than unsuccessful men with great talent.*
> *Genius will not; unrewarded genius is almost a proverb.*
> *Education will not; the world is full of educated derelicts.*
> *Persistence, determination alone are omnipotent.*

Woody Allen said something similar, if more humorous: "Eighty percent of success is just showing up." People who are good at persistence generally have stamina to endure, patience to wait for unfolding opportunities, and flexibility (discussed below) to find new ways to achieve long-term goals. The architect of Mount Rushmore, Gutzon Borglum, the leader of a band of courageous stonecutters who had to invent new methods as they carved a mountainside into four great presidents, persisted for fourteen years to complete his project against great adversity. The other subelement is the ability to rebound, which is generally called stress tolerance in the management literature. People who have high stress tolerance can stand high levels of psychological and/or physical discomfort related to their jobs in the short term, and are able to quickly regain their energy (see discussion below), good spirits, and optimism. People who have determination but no stress tolerance often accomplish great things but at a terrible personal sacrifice, sometimes dying early before their dream is accomplished. Such people are admirable but ultimately sad. People who have high stress tolerance but lack determination are pleasant companions and hold up well, but tend to drift and to be low achievers.

The importance of resilience is threefold. First, resilience improves energy, long-term goal achievement, and ultimately the interest and ability to assume responsibility as a leader. Second, resilience contributes to leaders' good psychological and physical health. In a similar vein, Margaret Wheatley points out that healthy, self-renewing organizations tend to be resilient rather than stable (1992, 88). Third, resilient leaders are considered more dependable. There is more likelihood that they will have the resoluteness to achieve goals, and that they (and others) will not be worn down by fatigue, disillusionment, or ill health (Luthans, Vogelgesang, and Lester 2006).

The trait of resilience is not significantly touched upon in the 1992 OPM framework, except for an allusion to coping with pressure (U.S. OPM 1997), despite being prominent in other lists (Stogdill 1974; Howard and Bray 1988; Yukl 1998). However, this was remedied in the 1999 OPM study, which added resilience as an "emerging leadership competency." In the study by Thach and Thompson (2007), an element of resiliency, stress management, ranked fourteen out of twenty-three. In our study of local managers, a self-perceived lack of resilience was not a major concern, but tended to indicate a sense of diminished achievement. One particularly astute observer, who complained of both personal problems and flashes of temper, noted: "It seems my lack of resilience lessens my energy, which in turn lessens my achievement. I am not sure what to buck up first." In a study done by Borins (2000), persistence was among the highest factors related to success in award-seeking projects.

In terms of excesses, it is hard to have too much resilience, unless it is the presence of persistence without the countervailing effect of stress tolerance. Nonetheless, excessive determination without flexibility can lead to a dysfunctional narrowness or unattractive doggedness that will accept only a predetermined outcome regardless of the situation or new information. Such people are considered too rigid. Sometimes persistent people who lack flexibility and/or creativity are also considered obstinate or low achievers (Morrow and Stern 1990). Lack of stress tolerance is a common problem among leaders as well as in high-stress occupations such as police work, air traffic control, dispatch, and so on. It becomes particularly severe when personal and professional periods of stress incidents overlap, such as when a death in the family and an office relocation occur simultaneously.

Guidelines

1. *Know what your long-term goals are*. Without long-term goals, resilience is nothing more than buoyancy without achievement. By determining what the

long-term goals are, they become articulated values, and hence, are more likely to be staunchly fulfilled.

2. *Be patient and flexible in achieving goals.* Those who are impatient in achieving goals are often considered selfish, self-centered, or even bullies, even though their goals are for the common good. As the proverb goes, "Good things happen to those who wait." Further, when there is resilience without flexibility, opportunities are lost and leaders will be accused of rigidity.

3. *Learn to tolerate stress but then let it go.* Everyone must find his or her own strategies for accepting stress for periods of time, just as everyone should also find ways to release that stress. Strategies for accepting stress include being highly organized, being well prepared, rehearsing the overall importance of the task or job, reminding oneself of the trivial nature of many stressors (e.g., the behavior of a competent but annoying colleague), taking breaks during work to become refreshed, eating and sleeping well, being supported by colleagues or superiors, and knowing when to take a complete break (time off, vacation, or work rotation). Strategies for releasing stress include humor, camaraderie, regular exercise, and "leaving the job at the office." After especially high group stress has developed, group debriefings or celebrations are very powerful methods of reenergizing and rededicating for long-term goal achievement.

ENERGY

Ralph Waldo Emerson's observation that "The world belongs to the energetic" is borne out by behavioral science. To have energy is *to have the physical and psychological ability to perform.* It is a better indicator of long-term leadership success (at least in terms of advancement to leadership positions) than many traits (Howard and Bray 1988). The first element of energy is physical vitality and stamina. Those with good health and physical endurance are more likely to excel in this aspect. However, physical vitality and stamina are as much a state of mind as a state of health. Franklin D. Roosevelt was famous for his energy even when he was eventually confined to a wheelchair because of polio. A second element of energy is mental interest. Those with mental interest can have a work focus and concentration at a technical level, and enthusiasm, commitment, or passion at an emotional level. Third, those with energy have a high activity level; that is, they do a lot so they accomplish a lot. An example of someone with both mental interest and a high activity level is Thomas Edison. He is a man normally associated more with invention than leadership, yet, he managed the business of invention so brilliantly that he became the model of the modern scientist, systematically trying hundreds, and sometimes thousands, of combinations on his way to a predetermined invention. His mental interest was so keen that he would announce his next invention prior to doing the research. He and his research team in Menlo Park, New Jersey, would work at least two shifts a day most of the year, and twenty-four hours a day when close to a breakthrough. Because of his passion, focus, and extraordinarily high energy level, he created over 1,000 U.S. patents, including the phonograph, lightbulb, alkaline battery, motion pictures, the forerunner of the electron tube, and the carbon telephone transmitter. He also produced the first electric power plant and nearly single-handedly created the American electric industry.

The importance of energy for leaders is that it contributes so heavily to task accomplishment, and indirectly to a drive for achievement and a willingness to assume responsibility. Those with low energy are less likely to set high goals for themselves and others or to be interested in the stresses and strains of leadership. The importance of energy is probably best seen in its absence. Lethargic people are the antithesis of what most people think of when they envision leaders. Similarly, those who are ill generally have a substantially reduced ability to lead effectively. Leaders without mental interest in their work are mechanistic in their orientation at best, and may even be demotivating. Leaders with a low activity level are seen as complacent and especially poorly qualified to take on large projects and change initiatives.

Almost all of the major comprehensive trait studies highlight the importance of energy, however defined. For example, in a general study by Morrow and Stern (1990), low activity level was by far the most important factor identified in low-performing leaders (although high activity level was rarely mentioned for those designated as high-performing leaders because the trait was assumed). Howard and Bray (1988) found that energy level was particularly useful in predicting success in midlevel managers, suggesting that those who are able to maintain a high energy level and avoid complacency in a private sector environment do significantly better. In the study related to this book, those indicating energy level as a positive factor pointed out its importance in overcoming obstacles that arise in work on projects. Those with energy-level problems indicated that they had personal issues distracting them (such as an ill daughter in one case), their work situation was contentious, or work goals were in dispute or ambiguous.

Although most problems with energy level are related to its absence, some problems from excess energy are possible. Energy without reflection, planning, or thoughtful purpose can lead to action without understanding. Empty activities can distract leaders not only from the more important activities that need to be done but also from contemplation time that is always in demand. Busyness does not necessarily equate with high activity level as it is used in a positive sense here. Also, high energy coupled with a high achievement orientation and strong self-confidence can lead to dysfunctional leadership behaviors if it is not softened by traits such as a service mentality and emotional maturity.

Guidelines

1. *Maintain good health and psychological well-being*. All things related to good health invariably enhance energy. Thus, good diet, sleep, and exercise are the foundations of long-term productivity. Further, avoidance of negative psychological syndromes—for example, anger, jealousy, self-pity, nervousness, and resentment—is indispensable for maintaining one's energy level because they sap energy and creativity. Building on resilience, energetic people are able to cope with stress well.

2. *Cultivate dedication to the profession and interest in the work at hand.* As the proverb states, the secret of life is not to do whatever you like, but to like whatever you do. Tom Peters's famous passion for excellence is largely based on a passion for the work itself, which he insisted could be cultivated (Peters 1992, 1994). Some of the best examples of this passion for work are seen in those who practice charity. Mother Teresa gained worldwide renown for energetic dedication to the poor and sick of Calcutta as well as for her ability to place unwanted orphans, which led to the creation of an international humanitarian organization.

3. *Seek to eliminate "energy distracters."* Energy distracters are almost limitless, and everyone seems to have his or her own weaknesses. As has already been mentioned, poor health and lack of enthusiasm diminish energy as types of distracters. But just as debilitating are interpersonal conflicts, goal confusion, task ambiguity, and excess socializing. Although interpersonal conflict cannot always be avoided, it should be recognized that the sacrifice of energy it can cause is enormous. Goal confusion depletes energy because one is unsure of purpose and direction. Task ambiguity diminishes both the speed and quality of accomplishment. A common distracter is excess socializing with employees, colleagues, or clients. While personal interaction is critical for managers and leaders, there is a fine line between accomplishing mission goals and wasting time, and the latter is something that effective leaders avoid.

NEED FOR ACHIEVEMENT

Those with a need for achievement are *those who have a strong drive to accomplish things and generally to be recognized for doing so.* The need for achievement has three elements. First, achievement is about task accomplishment. Task accomplishment for a line worker might be successfully closing cases or completing a workload on time. For a manager, it might be winding up a special project or finishing work within budget, without personnel conflicts or major problems. Or for a change-oriented leader, it might be clarifying the vision of the organization in the minds of the employees. Timely and effective task completion is often referred to colloquially as "hard work." The author Stephen King (1981) notes that what separates the talented individual from the successful one is a lot of hard work; the sentiment is as true for leadership as for writing. A second element of achievement is competition. What is the relative status of the achiever's level of accomplishment compared to others? This is the element most commonly associated with record breaking, a need for acknowledgment, and ambition. A third element is excellence. How well is the task accomplished or more skillfully done than most others? This dimension may be seen as excellence in quality, lack of errors, or consistency, or as customized, innovative, or new-and-improved.

Because of the natural inclination of organizations to add rules that either impede productivity or flexibility, employees tend to displace organizational goals (Merton 1940), and the environment tends to shift (Kanter 1983), achievement-oriented leaders and managers are critical to long-term productivity and success. Task orientation ensures that distractions and challenges do not obstruct accomplishment, even if hard work, sacrifice, or tough-mindedness are called for. As a wit noted, a diamond is only a lump of coal that stuck to its job. Competition helps people rise to their best level, whether it is in softer comparative forms of diagnosis or broad ratings (e.g., poor, average, very good), or for harder, completely exact ratings (e.g., nineteenth place). The drive for excellence ensures that standards either continue to rise, or if already high, that they do not drift too low.

The best-known research in this area is David McClelland's (1965, 1985). He studied the interaction of three variables: the need for achievement, power, and affiliation. He defined an achievement orientation in a similar manner to that above and found a curvilinear relationship with leadership. That is, a moderate drive for achievement is more likely to result in leadership advancement because high achievers often have difficulty suppressing the competitive spirit when working in a team setting and excellence is often defined in personal terms. Further, high achievers are sometimes loath to delegate. Miner had a similar, long-term research agenda, which indicated the importance of an achievement orientation in successful management (1978). Research surveys that study a large numbers of factors generally place achievement orientation toward the top (McCauley and Lombardo 1990; Rankin 2001). The 1992 OPM competency study placed achievement under the general rubric of self-direction, but the 1999 OPM study placed it under the parameter of entrepreneurship.

As discussed in McClelland's research, the need for achievement can easily become excessive if not tempered with other traits such as a service mentality, personal integrity, and emotional maturity. Task orientation can become so intense that the people doing the task are ignored or bullied. The competitive element can lead to managerial self-centeredness and a loss of subordinate loyalty. The drive for excellence can lead to micromanagement or rigid perfectionism.

The example cited in chapter 1 (see Exhibit 1.3) about Robert Moses is instructive here. His accomplishments on behalf of New York were magnificent: the development of Jones Beach, the beautification of most of the parks, and the creation of most of the major bridges, tunnels, and highways in and around New York City. Nonetheless, he accomplished these ends through the ruthless exercise of power. He did not seek wealth; he died a poor man. He did not seek power for its own sake after he learned early in his career that he lacked the ability to connect with people in popular and electoral terms. Yet, he did seek power so that he could implement his interpretation of what New York needed, which was clearly biased toward the middle and upper classes. Thus, his affinity for monumentalism (large projects that would last), stately beauty (projects that would require substantial space and resources to build), and cohesive artistic conceptualization (projects masterminded by a single individual) did bequeath the city a great legacy. Nevertheless, his leadership legacy was generally considered highly flawed because of his ruthless tactics, his penchant to personally micromanage all elements of projects (which he designed himself), and his inability to consider the needs of others (especially the poor).

Guidelines

1. *Delineate and prioritize goals*. A surprising number of managers believe that their goals are widely understood and accepted, when in fact their goals are

poorly understood and only partially accepted because they have not been clearly delineated in discussion and writing. Annual discussions about macrogoals are important, and should include ample opportunities for individuals to personally relate to those goals. A number of goal-setting principles apply as discussed in chapter 10. Goals must be relevant to workers; while overarching organizational goals are important at that level, they may not be particularly relevant to line workers in a specific unit. Goals must be clear and specific; good goals generally identify what is to be accomplished and how (the concomitant strategies). Goals should have deadlines when possible; even if they are estimations, deadlines help people ensure that work toward goal achievement is orderly and timely. Goals should be differentiated enough for clarity but not overwhelming in number; while too few goals means that they may not be articulated enough, too many goals means that some will likely be ignored. Finally, it is important to prioritize goals; this process helps with timelines and allocation of scarce resources.

2. *Strive for challenging but realistic goals.* The literature on goal setting, as well as the anecdotes of leaders, identifies this as a particularly important human dynamic. In relatively well-managed situations, people will tend to achieve the goals that are set, especially their own, even if they are difficult. To be well managed, the goals must generally be recorded, used as frequent benchmarks during the year, and have some type of accountability mechanism in place to reward individuals for goal achievement at regular intervals (such as in annual evaluations). This process is all the more powerful if those doing the work have had a say in the goal setting; indeed, most social science research has indicated that employees will set higher standards than their superiors when put in charge of goal setting (Latham and Yukl 1975). The only caveat is the distinction between challenging goals and unrealistic ones. Challenging goals encourage individuals to strive and work harder; they should be "beyond one's grasp but within one's reach." Unrealistic goals, on the other hand, cause frustration and confusion. The line can be fine, and sometimes in the heat of optimistic goal-setting sessions excessive goals may be suggested. The careful leader does not discourage striving, yet is careful to steer subordinates away from almost sure failure. Of course, goal setting does not always result in success; the possibility of failure (and the lessons it has to teach) are also an important part of the goal-setting process.

3. *Harness opportunities for positive coordination, competition, and higher standards.* Goal setting, done properly, is very powerful in helping to coordinate people and activities by ensuring articulation of the important elements of work. It can also be very useful in encouraging discussion to ensure that people understand and are motivated in the work they are doing (Earley, Wojnaroski, and Prest 1987). Group discussion and individual consultation are very important in this regard. They can also ensure that comparisons and competition that are fostered lead to higher standards rather than dysfunctional or cutthroat behaviors.

4. *Balance task completion goals with other types of goals.* Invariably conventional goal setting encourages task completion, higher standards, and some form

of competition (even if only self-competition). Yet, there are other important organizational goals that should not be left out of the goal-setting mix. Even a tough-minded businessman like Donald Trump (2009) acknowledges that while the bottom line may be central, other explicit goals should be reserved for team building, employee development, long-term vision, and integrity issues. Because goals lead to performance measures, and it is well known that what gets measured gets done (and other aspects tend to be ignored), it is important not to omit people, values, and overall mission from operational listings of these powerful midlevel work mechanisms (see Kaplan and Norton 1996).

WILLINGNESS TO ASSUME RESPONSIBILITY

The drive for achievement and a willingness to assume responsibility are often confused, but, although often related, they are different drives. A willingness to assume responsibility means that *individuals will take positions requiring broader decision-making duties and greater authority*. Thus, while the drive for achievement is the drive for accomplishment and competition, the drive for "higher" positions involves greater responsibility and the use of power. Frontline employees may have a great desire to accomplish their work and to do so as perfectly as possible, but not want the greater responsibility required in supervisory positions. Or employees might be competitive about getting the best merit increases and preferred assignments, but not be eager to exercise power in the complicated interpersonal issues that arise in managing a division. However, like the drive for achievement, there are extremely important caveats that will be discussed with the research in this area.

One element of willingness to assume responsibility is willingness to take on different responsibilities. This often means learning new tasks, developing skills, and realigning one's competencies for the new position. For example, the frontline worker who excels at work in case management and is then promoted to unit supervisor must stop doing case work one day and focus on administrative planning and interpersonal relations the next. That worker must stop trying to process six cases every day and start organizing twenty-five work schedules, reading a barrage of memoranda from the central office, dealing with a steady flow of client complaints, handling occasional employee grievances, managing her own time among endless meeting, monitoring, and reporting activities, and so on. Those with an inclination toward assuming responsibility like the opportunity for personal change, the excitement of expanded responsibilities, and the recognition that greater authority brings. Additionally, those seeking advancement receive greater status, money, and/or perquisites (such as a better office); however, this is far less evident in the public sector than in the private sector. See Exhibit 11.2 for a case in point. Those with a strong need for these emoluments are said to be ambitious, which, in and of itself, is not necessarily bad, unless the need is unchecked (e.g., leading to unscrupulous tactics to "get ahead") or the recipient accepts the benefits without rising to the demands of greater responsibilities. The negative aspects of taking on different responsibilities for the individual can include increased stress, demand for training, and the prospect of greater accountability with the possibility of failure.

Exhibit 11.2

The Willingness to Serve and Sacrifice in Order to Be a Leader

We often think of leadership as something to which everyone aspires and that will generally lead to greater perquisites, including financial gain. Yet, if this is not uniformly the case in private sector organizations, it is frequently untrue in public service leadership. Consider the case of Sam Medina, a Hispanic judge in West Texas (Rugeley and Van Wart 2006).

Sam Medina began life as a member of a family of migrant workers in the United States. He was constantly made to feel the social stigma of his socioeconomic class and downright discrimination as a migrant worker child. The inequities of life were seared into his psyche and he vowed to do well and to do good. Equity to young Sam could best be achieved through the fairness of the law. So even though no one from his family had ever gone to college, and few had even completed high school, Sam graduated with honors from law school. As a lawyer, he had a backlog of cases and quickly secured financial independence. Thus, Sam Medina did well, as he swore he would. However, even though he helped many in his law practice, he did not feel that was sufficient. He wanted to make a social contribution. He wanted to be a role model as a Hispanic judge in a judicial system that was conspicuously lacking minority representation.

This public service leadership could not be attained without a substantial sacrifice. First, Sam would have to stand for election and take the chance that he would be publicly defeated or denigrated in the electoral process. Second, and more important, he would have to accept a salary less than the tax payments in his lucrative, private sector practice. After consulting with his family, he decided it was worth giving up income for the opportunity to serve.

He won the election in 1998 and currently serves as a judge in the 237th District Court in Lubbock, Texas. Since then he has had the opportunity to help streamline the state's court system and to become a member of the Board of Regents for Baylor University. His desire to do good and his willingness to assume responsibility despite sacrifice have ensured that he is in constant demand as a Hispanic speaker and social advocate throughout West Texas. He has become a role model for children, professionals, and public servants.

The other element is a willingness to use power. Power is necessary to direct, negotiate, lobby, advocate, impose discipline, and the like. Part of this attribute is liking power itself, which is often called dominance. Dominant people (a neutral term as used here) like the influence that power brings and therefore tend to study the use of power. The other attribute is the ability to use power in more forceful ways, which is often called assertiveness. Leaders sometimes have to be tough and able to do unpleasant tasks such as dismissing likable but incompetent employees. Not all people enjoy the use of power, and therefore they eschew leadership positions. (When dominance and assertiveness are considered excessive or inappropriate, they are generally described as being domineering or aggressive.)

The importance of willingness to assume responsibility is seen most prominently when there is a leadership vacuum. Despite the various perquisites of leadership, it is common to have a deficit of people with the right skills, experience, and motivation to accept responsibility. Although there are always candidates to assume leadership positions, situations can develop in which they all seem unsuitable, and the right people are unwilling to assume responsibility or are altogether lacking. Such problems are surprisingly common: finding a city manager for a jurisdiction with a contentious council, finding a good generalist manager for a technical unit in state, federal, or academic administration, or finding a good leader for an elective administrative position in county government (e.g., county sheriff, attorney, recorder, treasurer, etc.). Another symptom of a problem in this area is passivity: Because assumption of genuine responsibility is neglected or simply overlooked (e.g., the responsibility to motivate, plan strategy, articulate an inspiring vision, etc.), the organization lacks the necessary dynamism to prosper. The lack of drive in this area is especially acute when the organization is plagued with problems, is experiencing high stress, or needs to undergo substantial change.

The major studies in this area are those by McClelland (1965, 1985) and Miner (1978). Both researchers found that willingness to assume responsibility was positively correlated to advancement and effectiveness. McClelland, however, takes great pains to point out that the way power is exercised is as important as the drive itself. He distinguishes two ideal types of power usage. The negative use of power (which he calls personalized power orientation) frequently involves using power egoistically—for self-aggrandizement, for personal rather than group goals, impulsively, and/or to create dependencies (and further enhance one's power). The positive use of power (which is called socialized power orientation) involves using power unselfishly, to advance group goals occasionally even at the expense of personal needs, conscientiously, and for the development of others. McClelland's research (1985) also indicates that both the need to achieve and willingness to assume responsibility may not be as strongly correlated with advancement for technical managers as for nontechnical or generalist managers. Howard and Bray's (1988) research suggests that advancement is strongly linked to willingness to assume responsibility early in a career, but is less indicative of advancement later in one's career when energy, self-confidence, and achievement orientation are more highly correlated. Van Wart and Kapucu (forthcoming) note that the willingness to assume authority spikes in importance during crises. While listed on most of the other major comprehensive trait lists, this attribute is omitted from the 1999 OPM study except obliquely in terms of entrepreneurship, political savvy, and accountability.

Guidelines

1. *Understand the different responsibilities of different positions.* Management and leadership are fundamentally different from line work, and many people are better suited and happier in the latter than in the former. The decision about whether "advancement" is appropriate for an individual is easier in the better-paid, more prestigious professions—medicine, law, and academe being good examples. That is, line workers have enough prestige and income to eschew advancement unless genuinely drawn to it. However, many other professions implicitly push employees toward advancement either because of the system (e.g., the military's implicit up-or-out promotional system) or because it is the only way to get adequate income and status (especially in disciplines where frontline pay is very low, such as social services, transportation, and corrections, but management levels pay relatively well). Such industries do well to set up a parallel track for nonmanager advancement to divert those who seek advancement solely to attain

lifestyle improvements. Leadership and management require training and skill development, hard work, and self-discipline in order to be effective. Leaders must be willing to understand the range of needs of the job and to undertake the requisite personal changes and sacrifices, rather than just assume the position and accept the perquisites. Leadership also requires greater accountability. A mentor of Lee Iacocca said, "Always remember that everybody makes mistakes. The trouble is that most people won't own up to them" (Iacocca 1984, 35).

2. *Develop a socialized power perspective.* Because one's relationship to power goes deeply to one's core nature, this is not easy to change. Nor is it easy to self-assess because, as Henry Kissinger pointed out, power is a great aphrodisiac. However, a socialized power orientation leads to greater long-term success (both in terms of advancement and organizational effectiveness) and psychological well-being. Because one's use of power is a social phenomenon, it is nearly impossible to study it without learning from the reflection of others (their perceptions). Leadership survey data can be very valuable here. Lower scores in integrity, fairness, participation, and delegation may actually be a reflection of the use of power in ways that are considered too personalistic.

3. *Learn to use a variety of influence strategies and to use them appropriately.* Many have defined leadership primarily in terms of the exercise of influence. For example, Katz and Kahn define leadership as "the influential increment over and above mechanical compliance with routine directives of the organization" (1978, 528), and Rauch and Behling define it as "the process of influencing the activities of an organized group toward great achievement" (1984, 46). Therefore, one must learn to use a variety of strategies in various combinations to suit a variety of situations. Various strategies are identified in the next chapter. Just as important is the appropriate and ethical use of influence strategies. Those with a service mentality, personal integrity, and emotional maturity—the last three traits discussed in this chapter—are far less likely to use power inappropriately.

FLEXIBILITY

Flexibility is *the ability to bend without breaking and to be adjustable to change or capable of modification.* In terms of management, it has two main elements. Adaptability is certainly a key component of flexibility as a positive leadership trait. Those who are adaptable are willing to use alternatives, substitutes, and surrogates. This is the attitudinal aspect; one who is flexible in this sense is not stubborn. A second aspect of flexibility is the cognitive element: alertness to the existence of alternatives and the ability to see that substitutions can sometimes be improvements. Synonyms for this aspect are watchfulness and preparedness. Flexible leaders do not see most decisions as single yes/no choices, but as a series of options with different benefits and costs. It is one thing to be willing to use an alternative that is pointed out or obvious, but it is quite another to see such opportunities in the stream of activities that engulfs leaders. "A wise man will make more opportunities than he finds" (Sir Francis Bacon). Flexibility relates strongly to resilience (bouncing back to challenges often requires finding a new way), achievement (accomplishments are too slow without some flexibility), and the skill of continual learning (to be really good at flexibility requires constant learning).

Flexibility has always been an important leadership trait (Stogdill 1974) because it is so critical to all the change functions. Such behaviors include problem solving, managing technical innovation and creativity, managing conflict, managing personnel changes, and managing organizational change. Flexibility is becoming even more important in the contemporary organizational environment. The public sector environment is more complex and ambiguous, and resources have to be rechanneled or shared more often. In high-performing organizations in particular there is a trend toward less control and more flexibility to give lower-level managers and frontline employees more discretion and autonomy. Today workers are particularly intolerant of leaders whom they perceive to be inflexible or rigid.

Most comprehensive trait lists identify flexibility prominently; for example, the quantitative OPM study in 1997 found it rated as the sixth most highly rated trait/skill. Howard and Bray (1988) distinguish between goal flexibility (which is the ability to adapt overarching objectives to a changing environment) and behavioral flexibility (which is the ability to adjust one's behaviors and to use more concrete problem-solving approaches). A study by McCauley and Lombardo (1990) identifies elements largely based on flexibility (resourcefulness and "doing whatever it takes") as two powerful indicators of leadership effectiveness from multiple perspectives. Thach and Thompson (2007) found it ranked fourth in their comparative study. In the local government study for this book a number of managers noted that they were strong either in decisiveness or flexibility, but not both. This is not surprising, because a knack for coming to a decision quickly and moving on to other work goals often forestalls the ability to see other options. Additionally, a few managers discussed the problem of "excessive" flexibility in terms of a perception of vacillation. This is a problem typical of those who are highly flexible—a sense by others that any method will do and there is a lack of, or weakness in, rules or structured protocol. The antidote to this concern is a restatement of overall objectives and a reiteration of any important rules or laws that cannot be ignored or bent. Yet, whether managers were inflexible or too flexible, this was by far the greatest trait critique of managers by subordinates and others in this study.

Guidelines

1. *Distinguish critical objectives from noncritical means.* Psychologically it is hard for us not to lock into "packages"; that is, objectives and the means of obtaining them become fused in our minds as a single concept. For example, in our drive for teaching effectiveness, we may identify class size as an important variable and insist on its reduction no matter what. All things being equal, smaller classes do produce higher effectiveness because of greater concentration of attention and resources. However, effectiveness is affected by many other elements as important as class size, such as class homogeneity, number of special learning needs, and level of auxiliary resources. Thus, both class size and teaching effectiveness can be increased if other factors are

better managed so that the range of student abilities is narrowed, students with special needs are attended to elsewhere, and additional resources such as classroom aides, high-quality self-study materials, and equipment are increased.

2. *Appreciate the creativity of decision making.* Decision making is not just about efficiency and speed (decisiveness) or asserting one's will as a leader (dominance). It is also about maximizing information and alternatives in order to sift through numerous permutations for the most effective resolution. Not only does this increase the likelihood of a high-quality solution, but it increases constituents' contribution at the same time. An appreciation of creativity in decision making also encourages willingness to learn from failures and more skill in handling the surprises and enigmas that constantly crop up in management.

3. *Appreciate the power of innovation and change.* Much problem solving and decision making involves reacting to past problems. Flexibility helps people accept the changes that must be made to improve long-term processes or change the objectives to suit new realities. Conversely, a positive attitude toward innovation and change will invariably result in increased levels of flexibility.

A SERVICE MENTALITY

A service mentality is defined as *an ethic of considering others' interests, perspectives, and concerns.* It has two major elements. The first element is a concern for others: the public at large (e.g., taxpayers), customers and clients, and employees. This is the attitudinal aspect. For example, when a decision about expanding hours of operation comes up, the leader with a service mentality will tend to downplay his/her own needs (because such a move may increase responsibilities and resistance from employees), and instead focus on balancing the needs of taxpayers, clients, and employees. The second element is more behavioral: a preference for including others in decision making to the degree that it is possible and appropriate. One can have a concern for others and act on their behalf, but not directly involve them in decision making. This is often important in time-sensitive situations and crises (see decisiveness), and in relatively insignificant or highly technical issues. However, consistently acting on others' behalf without consulting them, even assuming genuine goodwill, is a type of paternalism antithetical to a robust service motivation. A preference for decision-making inclusiveness can consist of a whole range of options from minimal consultation prior to the decision to full delegation of authority.

Putting aside the obvious and important ethical dimension related to this trait for the moment, a service motivation has clear, practical benefits. Many of the most celebrated rulers in history have had a service "mentality." Alexander the Great regularly consulted with his troops to keep morale high; Caesar Augustus included the public prominently in his decision making despite his imperial title; Germanic and Nordic leaders from Attila the Hun to Leif Erikson were highly dependent on follower goodwill to maintain power; and even the absolute monarchs of modern world history, such as Elizabeth I and Catherine the Great, wielded power largely because of their deft use of the royal "we" rather than the kingly "I." Perhaps more telling is the number of rulers in history such

---

Exhibit 11.3

The Arrogance of Contemporary Leadership Scholars

For thousands of years great philosophers have yielded great insights about human nature, society, and most certainly about leadership, too. In fact, great philosophers would often spend nearly as much time giving public advice to leaders as to the people at large. Lao Tzu in 604 BC advised that "He who loves the world as his body may be entrusted with the empire." Confucius noted that "Good government obtains when those who are near are made happy, and those who are far off are attracted." The famous Greek triumvirate of philosophers—Socrates, Plato, and Aristotle—were frequent commentators on good government and leadership. Plato's famous plea for philosopher kings—where "Political greatness and wisdom meet in one"—still rings true in our leadership yearnings today. A common theme was the importance of the people's good in ruling. The great Chinese philosopher, Mencius, stated that "The people are the most important element in a nation; the spirits of the land and grain are next; the sovereign should be the least important." The medieval philosopher Alcuin, who was a personal adviser to Charlemagne, reminded him on the eve of his famous coronation in 800 AD that "The voice of the people is the voice of God."

Certainly one of the greatest of all premodern scholars of leadership is little known in the Western world. Abu Mohammed Al-Farabi lived from 872 to 950, and because of his access to the greatest library in the world of his day in Damascus, he studied and built on the work of the ancient Greeks, Romans, and Chinese philosophers. Similar to modern-day scholars, he divided leadership abilities into twelve acquired traits and six learned skills. Key among the acquired traits were those related to a service motivation and personal integrity: (1) lack of greediness, (2) honesty and sincerity, (3) generosity and high-mindedness, (4) high interest in society's affairs, and (5) a commitment to justice and equity. In addition to these ethical traits, however, was a series of technical abilities: (6) competence, (7) imagination, (8) memory, (9) intelligence, (10) eloquence, (11) an interest in continual learning, and (12) energy. Learned skills included wisdom, knowledge, analytical skills, vision, physical and mental stamina (resilience), and awareness of other civilizations. His highly detailed observations hold up extraordinarily well when compared with modern leadership research, as examination of the lists of Stogdill (1948, 1974) attests. In fact, his lists largely anticipate those used in this study over 1,100 years later!

---

as Charles I in England and Louis XVI in France, who lost power because of insulation from the people and their concerns, especially after the Age of Enlightenment began. Although in the classical age of "modern" management (the 1920s through the 1970s), technocratic and/or strategic elements of leadership were emphasized at the expense of a service-oriented ethic, since the late 1980s this trait has come back into vogue in an era of increased competition, employee mobility, and customer militancy.

A service ethic did not play a significant role in the specification of leadership traits in the modern mainstream literature until strong ethical themes were introduced into the field in the late 1970s with Burns (1978) and Greenleaf (1977). Of course, many classical philosophers from around the world who have studied leadership qualitatively have given service mentality a prominent place among the traits. (See Exhibit 11.3 for an example of an Arabic scholar who was far ahead of his time.) Burns stressed the importance of elevating followers' motivations in times of change such that more selfish and short-term interests could be transcended for the greater corporate good. Similarly, Greenleaf emphasized the critical moral responsibilities that leaders have to their followers and maintained that such responsibilities exceeded those to the corporation. Even then, this aspect of leadership was generally not included in most trait and competency studies, with the notable exception of public sector studies. Nonetheless, it did figure prominently in the work of many management and organization theorists such as Tom Peters and Peter Block. In its 1992 study, the OPM included client orientation, and in the 1999 study split this trait-competency into service motivation and customer service. More recently, in his study of British executives from both the public and private sectors, Rankin (2001) found that a service ethic was tied for second place among important leadership competencies. Yet, whether a service ethic is better classified as a trait, skill, or managerial behavior, it has become very important in practical terms in most organizations in the past twenty years, and it was certainly already ethically important before that.

Having a moderate degree of some traits can be optimal for leadership effectiveness, but it is difficult to have too much service mentality. Paying close attention to the interests of the public at large, clients, and employees can really be only a liability if their interests are taken out of context and thus become overweening. The public may not be aware of technical demands, clients generally do not care about expense to the state, and employees tend to focus on their personal needs. While expanding decision-making processes to include as broad a group as possible, leaders occasionally not only have to go into executive mode for technical reasons, such as emergencies, but most experts believe that leaders must also promote their own integrated vision, however they ultimately include others in the molding and refinement of that vision over time. The exact role of the administrative leader's vision continues to be a matter of debate in the public sector.

Guidelines

1. *Remember the oath of office to serve the public good.* Few public administrators are formally required to take an oath of office today, but it is still implicit in the nature of the work. This notion is captured in the first principle of the American Society of Public Administration (ASPA) Code of Ethics: "Serve the Public Interest (Serve the public, beyond serving oneself)." Guidelines 3 to 6 state "(3) Recognize and support the public's right to know the public's business. (4) Involve citizens in policy decision making. (5) Exercise compassion, benevolence, fairness, and optimism. (6) Respond to the public in ways that are complete, clear, and easy to understand. (7) Assist all citizens in their dealings with government . . ." (ASPA Code, I.7).

2. *Demonstrate respect and concern for subordinates.* Respect for subordinates is both a managerial and ethical responsibility. Beyond a general respect (ASPA Code, III.4), however, leaders are expected to help others by providing support and encouragement to upgrade competence (ASPA Code, V.1), encouraging professional engagement for professional growth (ASPA Code, V.3), and ensuring that others receive full credit for their work and contributions (ASPA Code, III.2).

3. *Expand decision making to include as many people as feasible.* Significant organizational decisions are generally improved with broader input and sometimes even joint decision making. Both leaders and followers become better educated about the issues and technical challenges involved, and there tends to be more

commitment to implement decisions as agreed upon. Leader discretion about when to expand decision making, and how, is critical. Expanding the decision-making process is less efficient and takes resources. Therefore, as with any other resource, it must be used thoughtfully. Sometimes leaders may decide to have a full and extended discussion with all members of the community (such as when a new value or vision statement is being considered). Sometimes leaders limit a discussion to select parameters such as identification of the best of two alternatives for efficiency. And sometimes leaders only consult with individuals or groups, and make an informed executive decision, such as when a controversial issue must be decided (e.g., various perspectives remain opposed) or some groups have clear vested interests (e.g., employee pay). Nonetheless, good leaders will minimize the constraints of efficiency and group disagreements over time, to expand decision-making inclusiveness to its broadest appropriate level.

PERSONAL INTEGRITY

Dwight D. Eisenhower once commented that the "supreme quality for a leader is unquestionable integrity. Without it, no real success is possible, no matter whether it is a section gang, on a football field, in an army, or in an office." Another great military leader, the victorious Desert Storm Commander Norman Schwarzkopf, noted that leadership is a potent combination of strategy and character. But if you must be without one, he added, be without strategy. Personal integrity is *the state of being whole and/or connected with oneself, one's profession, and the society of which one is a member, as well as being incorruptible*. The term "ethical" is often used as a rough synonym; so are "honest" and "fair," but they are essentially subelements of integrity, albeit particularly important ones, which are addressed below. The most overarching elements of personal integrity are consistency and coherence in practicing personal values, whatever those values may be. A person who is consistent will act in the same way each time s/he is confronted with roughly equivalent situations. Thus, when a leader's preferred subordinate asks for a favor that was just denied to another subordinate, the leader will *not* try to find an excuse to grant the favor in one case but not the other. A person who is coherent in their values has values that fit together well and can therefore be more easily explained to others. The leader who expresses a belief in empowerment, but who in reality reviews all work and makes sure that each step is personally approved, is not being coherent. High levels of coherence require a thorough self-examination of values and an ability to express them to others succinctly. This is less common than is proclaimed. For example, when people say they have "strong values" they are implying certain values such as high standards for truthfulness and fairness, but we do not really know exactly what they are referring to. It could also mean that they are strongly against abortion or strongly in favor of capital punishment.

The second element is honesty, the state of being honorable, which, at a minimum, refers to restraint from lying, cheating, and stealing. The principle opposite to lying is truthfulness. Those who are very truthful not only avoid telling falsehoods or misleading information, but also are forthcoming with relevant information. A special case involves keeping promises. Highly honest people will take care to follow up on promises, even when some sacrifice is required in order to do so, for example, working overtime. The larger principle involved in cheating and stealing is self-dealing. Not taking things or taking advantage of situations (for selfish purposes) are minimum thresholds of honor. The higher standard here is placing others' interests as high (or higher) than your own. A special case particularly pertinent to the public sector involves vigorously safeguarding the trust that has been bestowed on one: stewardship. (In extreme cases this takes special moral courage; see Exhibit 11.4 for the famous case of Marie Ragghianti.)

Another commonly incorporated special element is fairness; it involves impartiality and a lack of prejudice or discrimination. A minimum level is required to ensure that people are treated with equality according to the rules. However, fairness also means taking all circumstances into consideration—the rules may be only part—which may mean an overriding or bending of the rules after review. That is, special or mitigating circumstances may justify a different conclusion. The employee who does not call in to report his absence at the beginning of the day will not normally receive a demerit when it is learned that he was taking his wife to the hospital. Because employees often have different responsibilities, make different types of contributions, have different needs, and like to be rewarded and recognized in different ways, fairness is more difficult in execution than merely following the rules or being consistent in mechanical ways.

Although the moral dimension of this leader characteristic is clear, the practical implication is not so obvious. In study after study, followers report that integrity and its related elements are the most important aspects of leadership—even before expertise and competence! This makes sense when one considers the ramifications. If your leader is not honest, what good is competence? Or if your leader does not have integrity, how good will organizational success be, even if it is achieved? For example, in the OPM study (1997) of 10,000 managers with 151 behavioral categories, the first two items in all three levels of management (executive, management, and supervision) were ethics related. Honesty and integrity were also first in the leadership competency study by Thach and Thompson (2007). The first item was "models high standards of honesty and integrity," and the second was "create a work environment where individuals are treated fairly." Nonetheless, it is important to realize that personal integrity is not the *sole* criterion by which followers evaluate leaders, even if it is first among many. The classic example is illustrated by the case of Bill Clinton during and after the Monica Lewinsky scandal. Democrats and Republicans alike disapproved of his handling of the situation from an ethical perspective, and even a majority of Democrats thought it substantially diminished his capacity to lead effectively. However, his overall handling of the government and public policy as well as his representation of the United States in foreign affairs were enough to keep his overall job effectiveness ratings relatively high. Yet, like Ronald Reagan, whose presidency was tarnished by the Iran-Contra affair, Clinton's personal scandals destroyed the prospects for the distinguished legacy he had hoped to achieve.

Despite overwhelming evidence about the importance of leader integrity, many early leadership experts specifically studying characteristics did not include it on their lists of top

Exhibit 11.4

Extreme Moral Courage

It is one thing to be honest and to maintain one's integrity in the daily routines of life; it is quite another when one's job is in jeopardy, and possibly one's life. This is the story of Marie Ragghianti, whose profile in courage demonstrates how severe the test can be on rare occasions (see Hejka-Ekins 1992).

In 1974, Ragghianti was offered a position as extradition officer in Tennessee governor Blanton's administration. During this time she learned about the Board of Pardons and Paroles. She excelled at the job, and, within two years, she was offered a seat on the board itself. In fact, when she was installed by the governor, she was also appointed chair of the three-person board. Yet, even as she was taking over her new position, she began to have concerns. First, she was concerned about rumors of the selling of gubernatorial pardons. Second, she was concerned about how energetically advisers to Governor Blanton insisted that loyalty and cooperation were important to the job, and that service in the position itself was at the governor's pleasure.

Within a few months in the position, she was sure that the accusations were true because she was constantly being pressured to approve pardons that were highly inappropriate. However, she did not know exactly who was involved. Upon meeting privately with the governor and discussing the rumors of the sale of clemency decisions, she was fairly sure that he, too, was involved. This was all made more obvious to her because he refused to allow the extradition of one of his chief financial benefactors, Bill Thompson, to another state. Thompson was highly involved in recommending pardons, although he had no information from the Corrections Department, and he seemed to speak with the authority of the governor.

At this time, Ragghianti realized that she was at a critical juncture. She had been selected as a "front" because she was thought to be loyal, uninformed, and malleable. Indeed, she felt a loyalty to the administration that had provided such opportunities to her, but she was not uninformed and she had to decide how malleable she would be. Being loyal and malleable about management or policy issues within the purview of the governor's authority was one thing. Selling pardons to hardened criminals such as murderers was quite another, especially when she had to acquiesce to breaking the law each time it occurred because the board had to approve it.

Ragghianti had three progressively more difficult choices. She could go along with the governor's recommendations and ignore the improprieties; she could resign and remove herself from the scandals; or she could seek to expose the scandal as an insider. She knew that life would never be the same if she blew the whistle. It was not.

She secretly went to the FBI, which soon raided the governor's files and convened a grand jury. Soon she was urged to resign by the governor himself, but she refused, requiring him to officially fire her. He was unwilling to do so immediately, but Ragghianti knew that a case was being built against her. Within fourteen months, the governor felt he had enough "evidence" and fired her for improper billing of the state among other things. However, she fought the dismissal in court on grounds that the governor lacked good cause for doing so. Mysteriously, the chief witness in her case, her former assistant, was murdered. Nonetheless, approximately a year later she won the amazing court case, was reinstated in her job as chair of the board, and was reimbursed for a year's back pay. While she was able to complete her term, those around the governor were soon indicted, although only a few went to prison. The governor's conviction did not come until several years later for a related scandal with better evidence, but he eventually served three years in prison also.

With the change of administration, Ragghianti was out of a job and also out of a career. As a highly publicized whistle-blower, she was too controversial. Rather dispirited, she moved from the state. After a while she took up journalism and again had jobs related to rehabilitation in correctional systems. Eventually she found her professional stride and fully regained her peace of mind. However, like others who have called a halt to systemic corruption, she paid a very high price in terms of career and emotional torment. Although she was pleased with her boldness years later, she was uncertain she would have had the necessary courage had she fully realized the danger and distress that her convictions would cause.

traits. (Among important leadership generalists Burns in 1978 and Greenleaf in 1977 were unusual in the prominence they gave normative considerations.) In fact, even the OPM's initial study of leadership in 1992 made personal integrity only a subelement of one of the twenty-two competencies. That was rectified in the 1999 study in which integrity and honesty were listed among twenty-seven key competencies. Other private sector leadership experts who have emphasized this element are Kotter (1990), who named integrity as one of his big four, Kouzes and Posner (1987, 1993), Covey (1989, 2010), and, to a lesser degree, Yukl (2002). In the public sector literature, where the connection has been made more consistently, David Carnevale is an example of a management expert who places integrity central to practical leadership in *Trustworthy Government: Leadership and Management Strategies for Building Trust and High Performance* (1995), although many others have emphasized trust, integrity, and similar ethical concepts (Gardner 1989; Rost 1990; Fairholm 1991; Phillips and Loy 2003; Ciulla 2004; Newell, Reeher, and Ronayne 2008; and Fairholm and Fairholm 2009).

Guidelines

1. *Examine and explain principles behind actions.* As Mintzberg points out, leaders are inevitably in environments that are dense with interruptions, short decision time frames, and conflicting values (1973). Thus, it is extremely common *to try to be* rational and fair as one moves from situation to situation, and yet fall prey to important inconsistencies in practice over time and be largely misunderstood in any case. Only by disciplined examination of one's practices and the competing practices framing decisions (Van Wart 1998a) can one really hope to attain the high level of consistency that is expected of leaders. Furthermore, without this ongoing examination, it is unlikely that a leader will be able to explain the coherence of actions effectively, a prime leadership responsibility.

2. *Keep decision making as transparent as possible.* Of course, there are many cases in which decision making must have some level of limited access related to national security, privacy issues, sensitive commercial transactions, and so forth. Yet, in the larger scope of public management, these cases are still few in number and partial. Even when decisions are made in secret, today people expect the principles to be laid bare. Economic development directors may have great latitude in offering incentives on a confidential basis, but the public expects the use of consistent principles that are widely accepted. Disciplinary actions may be executed in private (with full disclosure to the offender), but the principles of those actions must be made clear. And as an act of good management, budget data, adverse trends affecting the organization, downsizing, and the like should be disclosed to subordinates as soon as possible. Even though individuals may not be part of the decision process itself and may not agree with the decision that is made, this does not mean they do not have the right to know the factors that go into making the decision. Indeed, most employees will respect adverse decisions far more if they see that the process was an open one.

3. *Provide opportunities for candid feedback.* This guideline supports the previous two. How can leaders examine their actions and principles if they do not
get feedback? How can leaders be sure that decision making is perceived as
transparent if they do not receive feedback? Once this guideline is accepted, the
issue is implementation. First, multiple sources of feedback are needed: forth-
right advisers, confidential feedback from subordinates, systematic feedback
from citizens and clients, and potentially direct feedback from interest groups
or legislators. Second, in addition to balanced feedback, good leaders integrate
the feedback constantly, as both a source of problem resolution and a long-term
guide to principled action.

EMOTIONAL MATURITY

All the traits listed thus far do not ensure that an individual will have the good relationships,
interpersonal trust, and long-term staying power of good leaders. Those with emotional
maturity are far more likely to have these qualities. Emotional maturity is *a conglomerate
of characteristics that indicate a person is well balanced in a number of psychological
and behavioral dimensions.* Although all adults like to think of themselves as emotionally
mature, in reality, few people are without significant personality foibles, thinly masked
(if mild) manias or phobias, substantial quirks, and other personality coping mechanisms
that inhibit ideal personal interaction and organizational leadership patterns. In fact, the
experts on leadership derailment have identified the top culprit as being a problem in this
area (McCall, Lombardo, and Morrison 1988). A related (and somewhat overlapping)
concept that has become popular recently is emotional intelligence (Goleman 1998). Four
elements are commonly identified with emotional maturity: self-awareness, self-control,
responsibility for actions, and a socialized power orientation.

Self-awareness makes it possible to be objective about one's strengths and weaknesses. Ideally one is both proud of and humble about strengths, and cognizant of and
open about weaknesses (Zaleznik 2008). This enables a person to be oriented to constant
self-improvement. Similar to resilience, this element of emotional maturity also helps
one to accept setbacks as inevitable and to learn from failures and adversity in general,
rather than becoming excessively frustrated, bitter or protective. Those who lack self-
awareness tend to exaggerate their strengths, overlook their weaknesses, be self-satisfied
(closer to smugness than self-confidence), and whine or feel victimized when things do
not always go well. At a broader level, self-awareness includes an understanding of and
ability to articulate your underlying values (Collins 2009).

Emotional self-control leads to both evenness of emotions and emotional balance
between oneself and others. Those with good emotional self-control lack mood swings,
angry outbursts, and tendencies toward narcissism or paranoia. It is often called self-
regulation in the academic literature (Moss, Dowling, and Callanan 2009). As Bennis and
Nanus note, "The management of self is critical. Without it, leaders may do more harm
than good. Like incompetent physicians, incompetent managers can make people sicker
and less vital" (1985, 56). Similarly, one of the study participants for this book said, "The

greatest challenge in managing conflict is controlling human emotions. Don't feel the right decision based on emotion; make the right decision for the organization and your personnel." Of course, all humans have moods and experience anger, but mature people are able to curb their moods and anger in appropriate ways, especially those who are in positions of responsibility. For example, mature leaders do not immediately express anger at subordinates accused of significant misdeeds; rather they verify the infraction, decide on the alternative courses of action, and choose the best means of achieving a positive outcome. While the expression of anger is occasionally useful as a *conscious* strategy to get the attention of an individual or group that has severely misbehaved or underperformed, much more often a calm and fair demeanor is useful in getting the violator to own up to the problem and either take corrective action or accept a punishment. Reactive anger (the type to which we are most prone when untrained or unrestrained emotionally) nearly always leads to inappropriate statements by the leader and resentment on the part of the recipient. Emotionally mature leaders are remarkably good at avoiding cycles of interpersonal hostility or the making of enemies, even while they are expressing sentiments perceived as unpleasant or taking unpopular actions required by their responsibilities.

The third element commonly associated with emotional maturity involves taking responsibility for actions, patterns of actions, and the consequences of actions. The premier example of this trait may be President Harry Truman's famous phrase on responsibility: "the buck stops here." Those weak in this area tend to blame others for problems (scapegoating) while personally taking credit for successes, are insensitive about the needs of others and see the worst in people, and invariably take a short-term perspective. On the other hand, those strong in this area tend to share responsibility for mistakes in their capacity as leaders of the group, even when they are not directly at fault, and to give as much credit as possible to others to encourage and reward them. Sensitivity to others is at least partially derived from the fact that building up the morale and confidence of followers is a leader's major responsibility, and that finding the best in others and amplifying it is a fundamental leadership mandate. Finally, leaders who take full responsibility for their actions pay a lot of attention to the long-term ramifications of their actions (and inaction). That is, discipline is balanced with development; goal achievement is balanced with goal setting; and meeting production quotas is balanced with understanding long-term productivity trends.

The final element is called a socialized power orientation. Because of the potentially distorting effect of power, it is critical that leaders use it wisely. Yet even great leaders are sucked into dysfunctional behaviors because, as Lord Acton noted, all too often "power corrupts, and absolute power corrupts absolutely." First and foremost, a socialized power orientation means using one's formal power (especially to punish or order) as infrequently or lightly as possible given the context. Good leaders tend to be followed because directives make sense and their expertise is respected, not simply because they command. Projects and work plans are considered based on their practicality and general merit. The leader surrounds him/herself with the best and brightest people, and those people are able to be critical of the leader's ideas. Finally, leaders with a socialized power orientation are able to relinquish power when it is time, rather than holding on to it at all costs. On the other hand, a personalized power orientation results when power has insinuated itself into a leader's psyche. One manifestation is that the leader uses formal authority frequently and blatantly. "As the boss I have decided that our new goals will be the following . . ." or (to a new employee) "You will be terminated if you do not meet the following standards." Another example involves grandiose or self-serving projects that are more for the leader's aggrandizement or career than for the organization. Although this is more common in private sector chief executive officers and political leaders, it is not unheard of in administrative leaders. Those with a personalized power orientation draw advice from those whose loyalty is unquestioned but who are likely to be sycophants. Such leaders not only hold on to power, they constantly try to acquire more—by new authority, added resources to direct, or additional information to use as leverage against others. A classic example of the distorting influence of a personalized power orientation is seen in the case of J. Edgar Hoover, whose legacy of great contributions to the American justice system was ultimately overshadowed by his personalized power orientation. (See Exhibit 11.5 for a brief description of his life.)

The public sector leadership literature emphasizes a service mentality and personal integrity as robust concepts but gives short shrift to emotional maturity. On the other hand, the private sector leadership literature gives expansive treatment to emotional maturity, while stinting on service mentality and personal integrity. Although these are natural tendencies of entrepreneurial versus public service sectors, it is also generally true that these conceptualizations are often "repackaged" under other value traits. Thus, emotional maturity is not a specific category in either of the two major OPM studies (1992, 1999) or Bhatta's cross-country meta-analysis (2001), but it is twelfth in Thach and Thompson's survey (2007) as a slightly narrower concept, emotional control. It is a component of the major private sector experts—although variously named. Yukl discusses emotional maturity (2002, 186–187), Kotter mentions emotional evenness (1982) and emotional health (1990), Stogdill's descriptions (1974) of cooperative and dependable behaviors fit this category, as do Howard and Bray's (1988) classifications of self-objectivity and realism of expectations, and Bennis and Nanus's (1985) conceptualizations of self-regard and positive outlook.

Guidelines

1. *Assess personal strengths and weaknesses.* This can be done in many ways, for example, periodic self-assessments of accomplishments and failures, the encouragement of informal feedback from others, and systematic feedback through standardized leadership forms.
2. *Exercise self-control and self-discipline.* This is an injunction for proper channeling of emotions into productive avenues, not for repressing feelings. Although difficult to mitigate in the short term, mood swings, outbursts, and other emotional disorders such as narcissism and paranoia can be decreased over time with counseling, exercise, and self-awareness initiatives (e.g., Covey leadership training).

Exhibit 11.5

Technical Brilliance and Emotional Immaturity: The Complex Legacy of J. Edgar Hoover

There is no other major American administrative agency more connected with a single figure than is the Federal Bureau of Investigation (FBI) with J. Edgar Hoover. His contributions to the agency were immense, but so too were his failings. An "all-purpose," national police force to handle federal crime was not fully created until 1908 when Theodore Roosevelt commissioned the Justice Department to staff its own investigative bureau. Before that it had relied on the Treasury's Secret Service or private services from Pinkerton. In the 1920s the small agency got into political trouble for overzealous investigation of "radicals" and Hoover was installed as its director in 1924, having worked there for five years. His mandate was to reform and professionalize the agency.

His contributions emanated from both his length of tenure and his brilliance. He was director of the FBI for forty-eight years—through the presidencies of Coolidge, Hoover, Roosevelt, Truman, Eisenhower, Kennedy, Johnson, and Nixon. During that time the agency grew from fewer than 100 employees to more than 20,000. He introduced civil service exams, emphasized the hiring of college graduates, brought in professionals from fields other than law enforcement, demanded exceedingly high standards of training, introduced countless technical improvements—such as comprehensive fingerprint filing systems, started the first national crime laboratory, and expanded the scope of professionalism in the field by creating the National Law Enforcement Academy for local law enforcement. He also brought tremendous confidence to the American public, who believed that "G-men" were highly effective in fighting gangsters, kidnapping, espionage, interstate crime, and other federal felonies. Unfortunately, this confidence was not always well deserved. The agency's weaknesses mirrored Hoover's own, and these largely stemmed from his lack of emotional maturity.

Certainly Hoover was intolerant of criticism and was largely incapable of personal self-assessment as well. He surrounded himself with sycophants who were careful never to offer a view that would not be consistent with his own. Hoover punished those who displeased him, even obliquely, with abrupt changes of assignment to the least desirable locations and work details. It was an open secret that civil service protections did not extend to FBI agents during his tenure.

Because of his lack of self-awareness and his ability to create an extraordinary power base, he exercised remarkably little self-control in some areas. His political power translated into a personal authority in the agency that demanded total loyalty and consistency with his views. Thus, his biases against minorities, especially blacks, and communists were always exaggerated in bureau actions. Furthermore, he would occasionally pander to political requests from the White House, exchanging gossip about political figures for enhanced security and agency resources.

Early in his career Hoover learned to take personal credit for the apprehension of major mobsters, even though he was rarely involved as time went on. He also made sure that any failures or mistakes were attributed to subordinates, and they were summarily dismissed. Even more unsavory was his use of secret files for political extortion, an obsequious use of the media, and a dysfunctional insistence on total agency autonomy—even from Congress and the president.

Ultimately he considered the public interest to be synonymous with his own well-being and stature. Although his flagrant tendencies toward self-aggrandizement, power-mongering, bullying, and prejudice were well known to Washington insiders at his death, he was something of a folk hero in the nation at the time. A series of exposés by both popular and academic writers soon revealed the details of his unethical practices (e.g., keeping secret files of political figures in his personal office) and his long-time resistance to dealing with important problems such as organized crime and civil rights atrocities. Despite his exceptional care in cultivating a beneficent reputation during his lifetime, his legacy is now associated with maniacal brilliance and administrative despotism.

3. *Take responsibility for your actions*. A natural human reaction to problems is to "pass the buck," but mature leaders avoid that tendency. Harry Truman's long-term stature as president was much augmented by his strength of character in this regard.

4. *Develop a socialized power orientation*. The lure of power, like the lure of money or fame, can be insidious and can usurp both one's effectiveness and humanity. A socialized power mentality means that one always remembers from whence the power was derived, whom the power is to help, and the ultimate stewardship role that public sector leaders have.

CONCLUSION

Traits were defined in this chapter as relatively stable characteristics or dispositions that are either comparatively innate or learned early. However, they are amenable to modest adjustment over time (either for better or worse), especially with conscious effort, although radical adjustment in adulthood is unlikely. The traits identified as important in this chapter were self-confidence, decisiveness, resilience, energy, need for achievement, willingness to assume responsibility, flexibility, service mentality, personal integrity, and emotional maturity.[1] The first five are personality traits, two are motivations (need for achievement, willingness to assume responsibility), two are value orientations (service mentality, personal integrity) and one is a blend of personality trait and value orientation (emotional maturity). See Exhibit 11.6 for a summary of the traits, their definitions, and their guidelines.

Several broad assertions can be made with some confidence about traits. First, despite the demise of pure trait-based leadership theories because they are insufficient to directly predict behavior or success without reference to context, they are enormously important nonetheless. When followers judge leaders, they tend to do so in terms of traits more than behaviors. Even discounting part of this tendency because of ease of understanding and conceptualization, traits are clearly powerful predictors of success or failure in *very general* terms.

Second, there is inevitably a good deal of synergy among certain traits. More self-confidence tends to increase and improve decisiveness. Greater resilience enhances energy, which in turn leads to greater ability to achieve, and ultimately to greater willingness to assume responsibility.

Third, certain traits and trait sets balance one another. This is important in preventing leaders from either being denied opportunities or derailing their careers. Most notably, the value traits (service mentality, personal integrity, and emotional maturity) that have an other-oriented perspective balance all of the other self-oriented traits. Yet, even among the self-oriented traits, flexibility balances decisiveness and resilience balances need for achievement.

Fourth, the traits do not have an identical pattern. For some, more is generally better (a straight-line pattern), and these include self-confidence, resilience, energy, flexibility, service mentality, personal integrity, and emotional maturity. However, a moderate degree

Exhibit 11.6

Summary of Chapter 11

Leadership trait	Subelements of trait	Major recommendations
Self-confidence *The general (positive) sense that one has about one's ability to accomplish what needs to be accomplished*	• Self-esteem • Self-efficacy • Courage • Optimism	1. Assess personal strengths and weaknesses in order to address them. 2. Seek training or experience to remedy skill or knowledge liabilities. 3. Practice positive self-talk and positive visualization.
Decisiveness *The ability to act relatively quickly depending on circumstances without excessively damaging decision quality*	• Willingness to make unilateral decisions • Ability to act quickly in a crisis • Ability to remain calm under crisis	1. Study decision making. 2. Do not procrastinate in gathering information for or making important decisions. 3. Prepare for emergencies and crises. 4. Stay calm.
Resilience *The ability to spring back into shape, position, or direction after being pressed or stretched*	• Persistence • Stress tolerance	1. Know long-term goals. 2. Be patient and flexible in achieving goals. 3. Learn to tolerate stress and then let go of it.
Energy *The physical and psychological ability to perform*	• Physical vitality • Mental interest • High activity level	1. Maintain good health and psychological well-being. 2. Cultivate dedication to the profession and interest in the work at hand. 3. Seek to eliminate "energy distracters."
Need for achievement *A strong drive to accomplish things and generally to be recognized for it*	• Task accomplishment • Competition • Striving for excellence	1. Set and prioritize goals. 2. Strive for hard but realistic goals. 3. Harness opportunities for positive coordination, competition, and higher standards. 4. Balance task completion goals with other types of goals.
Willingness to assume responsibility *The taking of positions requiring broader decision-making duties and greater authority*	• Acceptance of different responsibilities. • Willingness to use power (in acceptable ways)	1. Understand different types of responsibility and be accountable. 2. Develop socialized power orientation. 3. Learn to use influence strategies appropriately.
Flexibility *The ability to bend without breaking and to adjust to change or be capable of modification*	• Adaptability • Alertness to alternatives	1. Distinguish critical objectives. 2. Appreciate creativity of decision making. 3. Appreciate the power of innovation and change.

(continued)

Exhibit 11.6 (*continued*)

Leadership trait	Subelements of trait	Major recommendations
Service mentality An ethic of considering others' interests, perspectives, and concerns	• Service to public at large • Service to clients and customer • Service to employees	1. Remember the oath to serve the public. 2. Exhibit and promote professionalism. 3. Demonstrate concern for subordinates.
Personal integrity The state of being whole and/or connected with oneself, one's profession, and the society of which one is a member, as well as being incorruptible	• Consistency/coherence of values • Honesty • Fairness • Inclusiveness in decision making	1. Examine and explain principles behind actions. 2. Keep decision making as transparent as possible. 3. Provide opportunities for candid feedback.
Emotional maturity A conglomerate of characteristics indicating that a person is well balanced in a number of psychological and behavioral dimensions	• Self-awareness • Self-control • Responsibility for actions • Socialized power orientation	1. Assess personal strengths and weaknesses. 2. Exercise self-control and self-discipline. 3. Take responsibility for actions. 4. Develop a socialized power orientation

is often best for the value traits: need for achievement and willingness to assume responsibility. More than any other trait, decisiveness is highly specific to the situation, so that good leaders can be both highly decisive at times (e.g., crises) and highly nondecisive at others (e.g., when either group participation or delegation are appropriate).

Fifth and finally, an authoritative trait list is not possible because different people define the concepts differently for different purposes. Is resilience a trait or simply an element of energy? Some popular authors list as few as four traits, and social scientists identify dozens. This is not to say that there is not a great deal of empirical evidence regarding which broad trait concepts are important. There is. However, defining and operationalizing them will vary in significant ways from study to study. For this study, ten traits were identified that were consistent with the literature. Due to the public sector emphasis, the value traits were articulated more fully than in most lists of this length.

Next we turn to leader skills, the complementary leader characteristics that tend to be more refined by education and experience.

NOTE

1. A number of important traits and skills were omitted from this "top" list for a variety of reasons. One of the most commonly listed traits is intelligence. Intelligence has been shown to have a strong correlation with leadership, but some research has shown that too great an intelligence gap can be

dysfunctional. Thus, as with many other traits, a moderate amount may generally be better than an excess. However, while lack of intelligence is a distinct liability, raw intelligence is probably generally overrated in leadership because of the different types of intelligence that humans possess. In reality, indirect proxies of intelligence are in evidence in several of the skills, especially analytic ability. Thus, while intelligence is the base of this competency, it is the training and disciplined use of the intelligence in analytic patterns that is emphasized here. A second common skill/trait is demeanor, which can also categorized as deportment. This is certainly an important competency for executives who function in the public eye and who must instill confidence by their presence and bearing as much as by their ideas. It is not as critical for lower-level leaders, however, and so it was not included. Finally, assertiveness, dominance, or masculinity were formerly popular on many trait/skill lists. However, the world has finally become a bit more gender neutral, and feminists can seriously argue that masculinity and dominance are no longer necessarily assets in a team-based environment. Indeed, they may often be liabilities in the matrixed, networked, and group environments that have become so common.

Skills That Contribute to
Leader Effectiveness

George Eliot pointed out that God gave Antonio Stradivari the talent he needed to be the world's greatest violin maker, but that nonetheless it was Antonio and not God who refined that skill and brought it to fruition. This chapter focuses on leader characteristics that are particularly susceptible to refinement.

Many of the points in the introduction to the previous chapter on traits bear reiteration and amplification for this related topic about the broad skills that contribute substantially to leader effectiveness. One important set of distinctions is among traits, skills, behaviors, and competencies. The difference among traits, skills, and behaviors is largely one of degree. Traits were defined as relatively innate or long-term dispositions. For example, some people are born with more resilience (i.e., persistence, tolerance of stress) than others. However, one can nonetheless improve persistence by having clear goals and practicing patience and self-discipline, and one can learn and practice techniques to reduce stress.

Skills—the focus of this chapter—were defined as broadly applied, learned characteristics of leader performance. They are heavily affected by later training, education, and practice, as is evidenced by written communication skills. On the other hand, some skills, such as oral communication, do have a substantial innate or "hard-wired" component. Nonetheless, many famous leaders began life as relatively introverted and unexpressive, and later learned to use spoken language powerfully (if through practice rather than as a "gift"). Skills are similar to traits in that they are broad; they are similar to behaviors in that they are generally more directly observable than traits.

Behaviors—the focus of the next three chapters—were defined as the concrete actions that are taken in performing work. They can be thought of as types of skills, but they are more narrow in concept and specific in usage. For example, delegation is a management behavior that assists in the distribution of work, in the development of employees, and in allowing leaders to focus on more strategic operational concerns. For ease, traits, skills, and behaviors can all be called competencies. Job competencies are the traits, skills, and behaviors most important for a *specific* position or class of positions. For example, decisiveness may be a key competency for an executive charged with making life-and-death decisions related to public safety, but may not be particularly important for a financial executive whose analytic and technical competencies need to be sharper. While sharp demarcations among traits, skills, and behaviors are hard to make, the distinctions can be useful in analyzing one's own performance, in appraising performance, in writing job applications, and in other specific uses.

It is also worth repeating that although the skills in this chapter sometimes seem so broad at times as to be vague, they are incredibly important. Who can imagine a powerful leader who does not have some exceptional abilities in communication, social interaction, and influence skills, for example? While almost all leaders have weaknesses, some weaknesses in the skills identified in this chapter are generally easily noticed and can result in organizational malfunctions or problems if not balanced by the talents of others on the leadership team. The U.S. Office of Personnel Management, for example, includes all but one of these skills in their twenty-eight competencies (2006).

Six leadership skills are discussed. They are communication skills, social skills, influence skills, analytic skills, technical skills, and a proclivity for continual learning.

COMMUNICATION SKILLS

Whether one is talking about leading others, directing operations, or effecting major organizational change, communication is a fundamental part of the process and therefore a key skill in the leader repertoire. Lee Iacocca commented that "the ability to communicate is everything" (1984, 18), and in a similar vein but in regard to administrative leadership, Paul Van Riper commented, "effective organization men are masters of language" (cited in Cooper and Wright 1992, 37). Communication is defined broadly here, not simply as the act of giving information, but as *the ability to effectively exchange information through active and passive means.* This means that communication is conveyed both directly through language and indirectly through gestures, posture, and so forth. It also means that it is a two-way process that ensures accurate receipt of the message but also includes receipt of information by the leader as well. For example, giving a clear order is certainly an element of communication, but it may not be an effective communication in context if the leader has not listened to subordinates' advice beforehand, explained the rationale if a quizzical look ensues, or "softened" the message if the recipient becomes withdrawn.

There are four main elements of communication skills in regard to leadership. Oral communication is often considered the most prominent, and this would certainly seem to be the case for leadership in politics, social movements, and very large, private sector organizations. Even though it may not seem quite as crucial in many governmental settings, nonetheless it is generally at the top of the list in surveys of government managers. Oral communication itself takes different forms, such as speaking with individuals, small groups and large groups, and communicating via electronic media. Some individuals are quite good at everyday "one-on-one" interactions but atrocious at group and large group settings. Other individuals are actually better in group settings because they are stimulated by being on stage. Still others perform well in front of groups but, because of lack of training, come off badly in the media. Another important distinction is the ability to relay technical versus emotive messages orally. The ability to give a clear order and the ability to inspire troops going into battle are both important but entirely different. While some leaders are blessed with both skills, most tend to be better at one type of message than the other, and some are good at neither.

Written communication skills include using e-mails, memoranda (both information/ discussion pieces and directives), reports, and special-purpose documents such as performance appraisals, letters, public relations materials, and written public statements. Both underreliance and overreliance on written communication skills are common, depending on the biases of leaders. Generally, it is the written record that lasts most effectively over time for all of those *not* prominently in the public eye. Even then, an interesting example can be drawn from Abraham Lincoln's Gettysburg Address. In writing the speech on the way to Gettysburg, Lincoln felt pleased with the product. However, afterward he noted that it did not seem to be particularly well received because it was too short for the event. In fact, some people thought that his entire speech was simply the preamble. Yet, history appreciated the density and clarity of the written language and it has become one of the defining moments of American political expression. Less, of higher quality, is often the best answer, as the following quip attributed to Franklin Delano Roosevelt suggests. In responding to a thorough bureaucrat who had inundated Roosevelt with too much information, he responded, "Are you laboring under the impression that I read these memoranda of yours? I can't even lift them." In contrast, preliminary research on leadership in an electronic environment indicates that quality of communication is largely determined by quantity, i.e., more is better and much electronic communication is too succinct (Kelly et al. 2008).

Listening performs several functions (Hoppe 2006). Most obviously, it is a source of information about facts, trends, problems, and performance. Embedded in this source is information about people's attitudes, moods, and motivation levels. Just as important, quality listening is an act of respect; therefore, it often provides a stronger bond than do speaking and writing.[1] The great value of listening in communication has long been appreciated in classic Chinese philosophy. A famous example is Lao Tzu's epigram: "He who knows, does not speak. He who speaks, does not know."

Perhaps even more unappreciated than listening is nonverbal communication (Sinclair 2005). Immense stores of information are conveyed nonverbally, but the information relayed is far more subtle and embedded than information that is spoken and written. It includes eye movement, facial expression, body posture, gestures, and body movement. When someone is asked to explain a technical discrepancy and s/he looks up (which research on brain functions has suggested indicates a creative cognitive search), we generally become suspicious. Or if a leader is trying to inspire people about the prospects of a great change, and s/he constantly glances down (generally indicating a cognitive search for specific pieces of data), we generally are uninspired because we sense s/he does not truly grasp the big picture. Also, as with other aspects, nonverbal communication can be done well or poorly. The leader about to announce changes who strides into the room with confidence and grace instills confidence; the leader who shuffles into the room and looks nervous does not.

In the U.S. Office of Personnel Management (OPM) study (1997) looking at the importance of twenty-two competencies for new and experienced executives, managers, and supervisors, oral communication was uniformly ranked first and written communication was second or third. The spread among the levels of leadership (executives versus managers and supervisors) was small to moderate. New leaders are expected to have very strong communication skill at entry, but not some other competencies, such as articulating vision, which can be strengthened later. Indeed, every major public sector competency study has given communication skills consistent emphasis (Bhatta 2001). Rankin's British, mixed-sector study ties communication for second place in importance (2001). Stogdill (1974) places fluency in speaking on his short skills list, and Howard and Bray (1988) list oral and written communication separately on theirs. Although some leadership experts do not explicitly indicate communication as a key competency (e.g., Yukl 2002; Kotter 1982, 1990), it is implicit in almost all the competencies or elements that they do emphasize. Although it is rarely listed as a major competency in its own right, listening is often noted in broader studies. The top behavioral competencies for executives in the 150-item OPM study (Van Wart 2002) listed three with pronounced listening elements in the top ten. Empirical studies have also demonstrated the importance of quality listening to promote trustworthiness and credibility (Klauss and Bass 1982; St. John 1983). Numerous studies have indicated that nonverbal behaviors are not only important (e.g., Stein 1975; Friedman and Riggio 1981), but also often provide more trusted cues to the listener than verbal behaviors (Gitter, Black, and Fishman 1975; Remland 1981). Typical of many self-assessments of leaders in the field, in a recent study of local managers they noted that the ability to communicate well orally and in writing were their weakest skill areas (Van Wart 2001).

Guidelines

1. *Assess communication skills to identify strengths and weaknesses.* Because there are so many types and methods of communication, assessment is not a simple proposition. The skills for good e-mail communication are not necessarily those needed for writing a good analytic report. Therefore, any assessment of communication skills has to be discrete enough to identify the specific subcompetencies. For example, if a general perception exists that a leader's writing skills are deficient, follow-up assessment should be conducted to see if that really means (a) too little written communication, (b) the wrong type of communication (using e-mail when a more formal document is appropriate), or (c) poor quality in specific methods (e.g., rambling and ungrammatical reports). The means of assessing communication skill include personal self-assessment, assessment by others in the workplace, and assessment by experts or coaches.

2. *Develop a plan to address weaknesses.* All communication skills are simply too important to have significant weaknesses. Therefore, any perceived weakness should be addressed. Means to do so may be as simple as increasing the quantity of communication, paying more attention to the weakness, self-study (e.g., reading a manual), or formal and informal instruction, which might include writing classes, joining Toastmasters,[2] or communication coaches. Some basic communication tips are included in Exhibit 12.1.

Exhibit 12.1

Basic Communication Skills Tips for Leaders

Communication in General

1. In general, it is difficult to communicate too much to people in the organization. Ample communication tends to include people, teach them, and make them feel better in crises.
2. For important messages such as standards setting or evaluations, however, clarity is more important than quantity.
3. Less-is-more is also true for vision, mission, and inspiring statements where pithiness and symbolism are important.

Oral Messages

Informal

1. Do not talk just to friends, supporters, and those close at hand. Often more important information and contacts are critics, competitors, and end users!
2. It is especially important for leaders in large organizations to find opportunities to talk to people in regional and field offices on a regular basis.

Formal

1. In one-on-one communication, learn to "pace" your communication partner. That is, try to appreciate his/her style in the communication process. If the other person is "open," you are more likely to be heard and to be able to persuade.
2. In talking to groups, use:

   • either a memorable idea, physical prop, story, or symbol for all major points,
   • expressions of interest or passion for the topic,
   • a simple but clear structure such as a five-part frame (introduction, three major points, and a conclusion), and
   • one or more practice sessions to rehearse the material.

Written Messages

1. In informal writing such as e-mails, be sure never to say confidential things that could possibly be passed on—they will be!
2. In formal writing, remember that people generally have very high standards. All formal writing should have a clear purpose statement, appropriate style and structure, and flawless grammar.
3. When possible, give drafts of important documents to others to proof and critique, and reread the draft yourself after several hours have gone by. If it is very important, read it the next day. It is also useful to read once slowly for grammar, and once for meaning.

Listening

1. There is no substitute for taking a genuine interest in what others have to say.
2. When possible, paraphrase others' ideas to ensure accurate understanding and demonstrate attention. Use expressions such as, "So what you are saying is . . . ," or "Let me see if I properly understand your meaning. You are saying that . . ."
3. Try to build off of others' ideas. For example, good salespeople know that it is easier to listen to what you want, and then to sell it to you, regardless of the product that they represent.

Nonverbal Messages

1. Remember that physical alertness and attention to tasks often say more than words. Attitudes such as boredom, apathy, and lack of confidence all have unmistakable physical manifestations, even though we may try to hide them.
2. Watch a videotape of yourself if possible to study your nonverbal patterns. Be sure to watch the tape at least once without the sound.

SOCIAL SKILLS

Because leadership is about dealing with people, social skills are a major pillar of a leader's skill set. Theodore Roosevelt noted that: "the most important ingredient in the formula of success is knowing how to get along with people." In support of this assertion, researchers who study derailment find that weak social skills are among the most common sources of executive career failure (Lombardo and McCauley 1988). As it turns out, people are generally rather unforgiving of social ineptness, lapses, or even innocuous oversights of courtesy by leaders. Despite their obvious ramifications, social skills are subtle and difficult to pinpoint. Social skills overlap extensively with communication and influence skills and are occasionally subsumed under them, but here we will deal with them separately because of the magnitude and range of elements that each concept covers. It should also be noted that, like communication and influence, social skills have significant innate components. For example, extroverts are "hard-wired" to deal with social settings in different ways than those who are introverts. Yet, even though extroverts are disposed to be the talkers and introverts the listeners in social interactions, it is not uncommon to see extroverts become masters of eliciting conversation from others and introverts become captivating speakers. It is because of the enormous effect that a person can have on his/her social skills (over a lifetime) that they are located with skills rather than traits.

Social skills are *the ability to interact effectively in social settings and to understand and productively harness one's own and others' personality structures*. There are three major elements in social skills. One element is personal likability, which, for leaders, focuses on aspects such as optimism, kindness, tact, and respect for others. Optimism is a positive frame of mind, even when people are tired and work is not going well (Jennings 1943; Zullow et al. 1988). Kindness helps people trust a leader (Fleishman 1953). Tact allows people to retain their dignity. Respect for others allows leaders to cultivate people's diversity and to see others as assets rather than costs in professional settings (Fiedler 1967; Priem 1990). In the psychological literature, likability is also known as agreeableness (Judge, Piccolo, and Kosalka 2009).

A second element of social skills is expressiveness. One aspect of expressiveness is simply being sure that the right thing is said or done at the ideal time. Encouragement occurs when people need it most because "man lives more by affirmation than bread," in the words of Victor Hugo. Social scientists have consistently found that positive reinforcement and encouragement are more effective in general than are disincentives. Nonetheless, critique is sometimes necessary, too. Good criticism is delivered in ways that will be understood by the receiver. In some cases this may involve tact, but in many it may also require well-thought-out directness. Leaders who are strong at expressiveness are also particularly capable of putting emotions or professional passions into words. This is important in order to make people feel personally valued, infuse meaning into work, and "rally the troops" for joint efforts (Stohl 1986).

Social perceptiveness is the third element of social skills (Newcomb 1961). A baseline of social perceptiveness is an honest understanding of one's own motives, values, drives, and preferences. This leads to an understanding of the motives and actions of others, which is of inestimable value in leadership. Thach and Thompson (2007) found that this single dimension ranked eleventh among public sector executives, and even higher for private sector leaders. Another more sophisticated dimension of social perceptiveness is a deep understanding of interpersonal dynamics. Interpersonal dynamics is alternately the glue of the organization and the source of bureaucratic politics. Good or bad, insight into—and effective use of—interpersonal dynamics are critical in demanding leadership positions (Stogdill 1948).

A special case of social skills is charisma. Charisma is the natural ability to inspire devotion or allegiance, literally meaning "gift of God's grace." True charismatics, who are extremely rare, have such intense social skills that they can charm almost anyone, at least in the short term. Although some of the world's great leaders have been charismatics, many have not been, and this is borne out in contemporary studies of leaders (Bennis and Nanus 1985). Further, many charismatics do not become leaders. Charisma certainly can help leaders achieve things, but like any other trait or skill, charisma can lead to mistakes and evil as well. Famous charismatics of the twentieth century included Rasputin (adviser to the last tsarina of Russia), Hitler, the Reverend Jim Jones, who encouraged nearly a thousand of his followers to commit suicide in South America, and the Ayatollah Khomeini. The example of Rasputin is highlighted in Exhibit 12.2.

The importance of social skills is easy to understand. They lead directly to a form of power (personal power discussed below). They enhance communication, which also allows for better information gathering. They increase the ability to engage in effective team building. And they reduce unnecessary problems due to bad personality traits (e.g., rudeness or diffidence) while increasing the ability to finesse awkward social situations (e.g., the social peccadilloes of others).

Different researchers have emphasized slightly different aspects of social skills. To review the literature, Stogdill discusses social skills as diplomacy, tact, and being socially skilled (1974). Kotter stresses optimism (1990). Rankin discusses tact and being "socially skilled" (2001). Howard and Bray break down social skills into more components by listing personal impact, perception of social cues, and social objectivity (1988). The OPM studies characterize them as interpersonal skills (1992, 1999, 2006). Although all the major public sector competency studies of other nations studied by Bhatta (2001) reference social skills, they are especially highlighted by New Zealand ("building and sustaining relationships") and Australia ("cultivating productive relationships"). Of course, social and personality preferences (which do not necessarily equate with social skills) are a whole field of psychology and can be determined by personality assessments such as the Myers-Briggs Type Indicator (MBTI).

Guidelines

1. *Take a critical look at your social skills and identify those that are weak.* While most of us enjoy our distinctive personality and are often proud of our quirks, and while some distinctive personality traits may be an asset, our unexamined or

Exhibit 12.2

Charisma for Good or Evil

Charisma means the gift of god's grace. Charismatics emanate a sense of power, as if from a divine source, that very few can resist. True or natural charismatics are exceedingly rare, but people with great communication skills and/or great power often take on significant charismatic elements. Not all who become leaders are charismatic; one need only look at most politicians to observe that few have any charismatic quality at all. Indeed, the pervasive nature of television and the invasive nature of modern reporters may make charismatic behavior more difficult to sustain because charisma can be diminished by overexposure.

Charisma, like other personality characteristics, is itself neither noble nor bad; however, it can be used for good or evil. Almost without exception, all the great founders of religions—as well as great prophets—have been charismatic: Jesus, Moses, Mohammed, Confucius, Buddha, and others. Great generals and great heads of state often acquire charismatic qualities, even if they were not innate; for example, Alexander the Great, Charlemagne, Joan of Arc, Elizabeth I, Napoleon, George Washington, Churchill, Ghandi, and Douglas MacArthur (see Exhibit 10.4 in chapter 10).

Charisma becomes bad or even evil when it is used to manipulate individuals to do what is not really in their best interests, or primarily as a tool for the self-aggrandizement of the holder of charisma. A famous example is (Grigory) Rasputin, who was born a peasant in Siberia in 1871, and became a monk. He was entirely self-trained in religious teaching, and, like the peasantry at the time, was exceedingly superstitious. Early on, his religious exaltation gave way to a belief that he had a direct connection to God, and that as an instrument of God, his beliefs were immutable and his presence was purifying. While publicly he focused on absolute devotion to God, privately he taught redemption through sin, which led to carnal rituals of orgies followed by ecstatic confessions. Despite this odd dualism, his popularity among the peasants grew.

His celebrity enabled him to meet Nicholas and Alexandra Romanov, the tsar and tsarina of Russia, in 1907. Tsarina Alexandra, herself a religious zealot, was also mother to an heir of Russia who, as a hemophiliac, was constantly in grave danger. Rasputin immediately enthralled Alexandra with his "power," and she came to depend on him completely. Because the tsarina had great sway with her husband, Rasputin was able to affect ministerial appointments. Because of his power with the royal couple, he also wielded almost complete dominance over appointments in the Russian Orthodox Church. Unfortunately, his recommendations for appointments were entirely based on their loyalty to Rasputin, and thus a whole class of incompetent sycophants was installed just after Russia had suffered defeat at the hands of the Japanese and had experienced a popular revolution. When Nicholas II went to the front in World War I to personally direct the troops, he left Alexandra as acting head of state. She quickly replaced all ministers not of Rasputin's liking. Her blind devotion to Rasputin, and Nicholas's blind devotion to his wife, had disastrous consequences.

In December 1916, members of the royal family finally assassinated Rasputin, although too late. He was given a great deal of poisoned wine during a huge meal, but, unaffected, he only asked for more. Running out of poison, the executioners finally shot him seven times and hid his body under the ice in a lake. When an autopsy was later performed, it was discovered that he had drowned to death.

Yet, the fate of the autocracy was already sealed. Within a few months of Rasputin's death the country was seized by revolution, and, in March 1917, the tsar abdicated while still at the front. Fearful of their capture by royal sympathizers, the communists executed the entire royal family in July 1918, bringing to an ignominious end the 300 years of rule by the Romanovs, enormously aided by a charismatic peasant.

untrained social skills may preclude effective leadership. Sources of feedback can include reviewing patterns of responses from other people, anonymous feedback instruments, and personality assessment seminars. What many people blame on bad luck (such as being passed over for promotions or distinctive assignments) is often traceable to a subtle personality or social skill defect that could be mitigated or even turned into a virtue.

2. *Develop a plan to address social weaknesses.* The "hard-wired" aspects of our personality and social training make this difficult to do, especially in the short term. Yet, diligence and practice can turn liabilities around. Tactless people can learn discretion if they come to understand the ramifications of not being tactful (such as loss of friends and lack of professional advancement). Verbally awkward people can refine their speaking at Toastmasters. Negative people can learn to stop negative "self-talk" and to practice positive, can-do mental routines that translate into greater optimism (Manz 1986; Manz et al. 1988).

INFLUENCE SKILLS

All leaders have various types and amounts of power, and this gives them the potential to affect people, resources, and outcomes. Bennis and Nanus stated that "power is the basic energy needed to initiate and sustain action or, to put it another way, the *capacity* to translate intention into reality and sustain it" (1985, 17; emphasis added). Influence skills are defined as *the actual use of sources of power through concrete behavioral strategies* (see Bass 1990 for a discussion of the distinctions, 226–227). For example, while criminal judges have extensive powers derived from their legal positions and expertise, they may or may not use these powers as a form of influence. They may give the jury detailed instructions about the points of law to consider (legitimizing certain options and rational persuasion) or may choose not to; indeed, in extreme cases judges who feel the points of law have been ignored by the jury may use their judicial power to influence the final decision by nullifying the jury's verdict.

The simplest analysis of power is based on the position, the person, or a combination of both.[3] Power based largely on position includes traditional authority (sometimes called legitimate power), control over the environment, and the power to reward and punish (coerce). The power of authority stems from established law or rules, elections, or custom. Control over the environment includes the ability to change the technology, physical environment, or patterns of work. Coercive power is the ability to punish, and reward power is the ability to provide financial, psychological, career, or other benefits.

At the other extreme is personal power that is technically called "referent power." Referent power is the ability to influence outcomes based on various types of personal persuasion. A clear case of referent power is exemplified by a leader of a social movement who exerts great influence but lacks a formal position of power. Dominance and assertion are also forms of referent power (Anderson and Kilduff 2009). Some types of power are combinations of both position and personal power. Expert power stems from professional and technical knowledge; remember Sir Francis Bacon's adage that knowledge is power. Expert power partially resides in the user (personal), but it is exerted in the name of the group (position). A related type of power involves control over information in an organization setting. It is largely based on the authority of position, but the use of such power becomes a form of expertise and personal leverage.

Leaders (or agents) exercise power over others (targets), and ultimately increase or diminish their power through the wise and effective use of concrete influence strategies. Eight influence strategies are discussed below.

Legitimating tactics and pressure tactics are two influence strategies that stem largely from authority. *Legitimating tactics* either emphasize the consistency of an influence attempt with established policies, procedures, or past practices, or they directly assert the right of the agent as an appropriate decision maker to make the request/order. Of course, such tactics are useful in directly asserting one's own authority, but they are also useful for informing/reminding others of the nature of the administrative grant of authority and its bounds, as well as the responsibilities that flow from such authority. Reward and coercive power are often—but not always—used with legitimating tactics to assert authority, although generally after the target has already acted and thus as an incentive to influence future actions. Using legitimate authority excessively or awkwardly is annoying at best and brutal at worst. Those who do so may be referred to as authoritarians, rule-mongers, or nitpickers (by lower-level workers referring to senior managers).

Pressure tactics involve the use of demands, threats, or pestering to influence. More than any other influence strategy, pressure tactics emphasize punishment, including prospect of dismissal, poor evaluation, no raise, fewer resources, shunning, and so on. Subordinates use pressure tactics by threatening to quit, grievances, legal actions, work slowdowns, or nagging. In a perfect world, pressure tactics would not be necessary; everyone would do what they are supposed to do, on time, and in the proper fashion. Since it is not a perfect world, pressure tactics supply a range of influence strategies from the subtle hint and gentle reminder to the overt warning of potential dire consequences. Effective leaders use the full range of pressure tactics, carefully matching the need and the strategy, and compliance with later rewards and punishment. However, administrators who overuse pressure tactics or use them too bluntly are quickly labeled as bullying, bothersome, or intimidating.

Exchange tactics involve mutual exchange of favors, either in explicit agreements or implicit and loose understandings. They emphasize reward power. At the macro level, mutually agreed exchange is not only the basis of the capitalistic economic system, but also ultimately the basis of free-floating employment systems. That is, applicants agree to certain work obligations and conditions while organizations agree to certain compensation, benefits, and support. At the micro level where most leaders operate most of the time (outside the hiring process), exchange tactics are often used to influence extra or unusual work or effort, or to get special working accommodations. Leaders may promise compensatory time later for overtime now, or line workers may promise to increase productivity if they are allowed to go to a special training program. Although exchange tactics emphasize rewards, it is understood that punishment may be meted out to those who renege on agreements. In proper bounds, exchange tactics are appropriate ways of managing work and accommodating the ebb and flow of circumstances and needs of the organization and the workers. However, excessive reliance on exchange tactics can lead to dysfunctional bargaining regarding relatively routine work assignments (a tactic that used to be common in many labor union environments) or feelings of unfair favoritism by others if not carefully managed.

Position-based power and the influence tactics that derive from it have generally been the foundation of power for leaders in most organizations. Nonetheless, effective leaders have rarely relied exclusively on position power tactics, and in the past century movement has been toward using the least amount of position power possible. The reasons are many: higher levels of education, greater access to information, more localized decision making, and so forth. Thus, leaders must not be afraid to use their position power but must do so far more strategically than was true in a culture that allowed more authoritarian patterns.

Rational persuasion and consultation are two influence strategies that are based largely on expertise and control over information. *Rational persuasion* is the use of facts and logic to convince the target that a request or proposal is likely to successfully achieve an objective. This is both the most common and the most endorsed type of influence strategy used in bureaucracies. However, often other types of strategies are embedded within a "rational" proposal. Important and appropriate as rational persuasion may be, it is often overrelied upon as a strategy, and its limitations are often underestimated. Some problems of rational persuasion are: fundamental assumptions are often unstated and unchallenged, facts are easily selectively manipulated (consciously or unconsciously), and convictions, commitment, and passion may be more important than rational logic for success.

Consultation is the act of involving the target in the process of planning, in providing substantive feedback, or in making changes. The agent gains information and "buy-in," and the target may affect decision making while also getting information. Consultation, which is much vaunted today, is clearly a powerful influence tactic in the hands of leaders who cannot have too much information or buy-in. The problems of consultation include the inordinate amount of time and energy that it requires, and the possibility of accusations of manipulation by those who use it superficially or selfishly.

Emotional appeals, personal appeals, and friendliness stem largely from referent (personal) power. In *emotional appeals* (also known as inspirational appeals), the agent stimulates enthusiasm and commitment by arousing certain values, preferences, or shared beliefs of the target or by rousing self-confidence. For example, emotional appeals are effective means of increasing enlistment in the armed forces during times of war even though the pay is low and the danger is high. During peacetime (in volunteer enlistment systems), armed forces tend to rely more heavily on rational persuasion and exchange tactics in order to influence citizens to sign up. Effectively made emotional appeals enable people to make sacrifices for the organization or unit and feel good about it during times of hardship or crisis, unite people with shared beliefs, and can enhance the sense of self-worth and satisfaction of those targeted. Ineffectively or inappropriately done, emotional appeals are cloying or manipulative, or they set up emotional expectations that are unmet.

Personal appeals are based on feelings of loyalty, friendship, or human compassion. Personal appeals are often prefaced by expressions such as "Could I ask you, as a friend, to . . . ," or "I would not ask this if I were not in a bind, but. . . ." People generally like to help others, especially if the request is modest and reasonable. When this is done on a reciprocal, ongoing, and appropriate basis, the sharing of such "favors" introduces a culture of mutual assistance and support. Even powerful leaders will make personal appeals to enhance shared bonds. Unfortunately, some people become addicted to personal appeals in order to make up for their own poor planning or deficient discipline, and are unable or unwilling to reciprocate.

Friendliness (or ingratiation) is the use of affable behavior or praise, or the provision of unrequested assistance directed at the target in order to increase the responsiveness to future requests and orders. On one hand, basic friendliness is an expectation of social intercourse, even in work settings in which the parties hold unequal positions; enthusiastic and widely distributed friendliness is normally considered a virtue. On the other hand, friendliness becomes smarmy ingratiation when the agent's motives are solely instrumental, self-serving, or manipulative. This is particularly obvious when praise becomes flattery that is either exaggerated or untrue, or acts of "unrequested assistance" essentially become bribes to win favors. See Exhibit 12.3 for a listing of sources of power and their relationship to influence tactics.

A few additional comments are necessary to frame the discussion about this vast and complex area of power and influence. First, all people have both power and influence; they are simply not equal in type or amount. Organizational leaders structurally have greater (but not exclusive) position power, but personal power is more likely to be evenly distributed. Second, the corollary is that influence works both ways. While the implicit understanding is that effective leaders have greater influence on balance, such leaders are acutely aware of and harness the process of influence exchange. As Max DePree notes, "Leaders must be genuinely open to the influence of others" (1989, 37). For example, organizational leaders who use their formal power too aggressively find themselves successfully defied in the long run by procedural challenges or sabotage, or may find that such tactics ultimately result in passivity, turnover, or smoldering conflict. Third, all sources of power and their related influence tactics are themselves neutral in an ethical sense. It is the way power is enhanced and the context of the use of influence tactics that should be judged. For example, firing an employee who refuses to get treatment for alcoholism is quite different from firing an employee because of personal dislike. Effective leaders increase their power over time and use all influence strategies. Ethical leaders use this power and different influence tactics with great care to appropriately balance organizational needs, professional standards, legal requirements, and the public good, as well as their own needs (Van Wart 1998a). Leaders who use power and influence *primarily* for personal gain—whether for personal privilege or career enhancement—are likely to be judged harshly by others, even if they are "brilliant" and/or successful (Kets de Vries and Miller 1984; Kets de Vries 1985; Raskin, Novacek, and Hogan 1991).

It should also be pointed out that this survey discusses only individual sources of power and influence; it does not discuss group or political aspects. Common political tactics include forming coalitions, co-optation (inducing a major opponent to join your side by offering favors or employment, in order to weaken the opposition), and gaining/maintaining control over decision processes. Despite claims of putative political neutrality, these tactics are frequently used at the executive levels of public agencies, and their use (and abuse) needs to be understood by savvy senior executives, but will not be discussed here.

In the leadership literature, the significance of influence and negotiation is estimated

Exhibit 12.3

Sources of Power and Related Types of Influence (for individuals)

Potential sources of power		
Position/personal power dichotomy	**Expanded French and Raven subtypes**	**Methods of influence**
Largely position power	• Authority • Control over work environment • Reward • Punishment	• Legitimating tactics • Pressure tactics • Exchange tactics
Mixed position and personal power	• Expertise • Control over information	• Rational persuasion • Consultation
Largely personal power	• Referent	• Emotional appeals • Personal appeals • Friendliness

to be very important. Influence and negotiation skills are mentioned by many leadership experts as at or near the top of their lists; for example, Stogdill (1974) discusses persuasiveness, Howard and Bray (1988) include it in their leadership skill cluster, and Rankin (2001) uses it in a similar capacity. Yukl gives it the most comprehensive treatment in his study of leadership (see especially his two-chapter treatment in his fourth edition, 1998; his 2002 fifth edition cuts the treatment to a single chapter). The 1997 OPM study placed it fifth in importance, and the 1999 OPM study added political savvy and partnering as major competencies in addition to influencing and negotiating. In contrast, while Thach and Thompson (2007) do place influencing on their list of key competencies, it is closer to the bottom, at sixteenth, for both private and public organizational leaders.

Guidelines

1. *Leaders must be prepared to assess—candidly and thoroughly—their sources of power and their ability to use influence tactics.* The amount of power and the effectiveness of influence will vary widely among different individuals with whom the leader interacts. The more one is aware of one's strengths and weaknesses, the less likely power will be squandered or influence attempts will be ineffective.
2. Generally speaking, power is not amassed quickly. It is acquired over time. Even when someone steps into a new executive position, it is generally because of the power that the individual has built up over a career. Highly effective leaders understand power and its importance, *and develop the discipline to augment it over time. This is especially true of personal power.*
3. *The understanding and cultivation of influence tactics over time is also essential to high effectiveness.* Effective leaders are able to: use the least power necessary, especially formal power; use the right influence strategies for different situations rather than always using the same few; and use multiple influence strategies simultaneously for more important or difficult objectives.

4. Effective leaders are very careful *to guard against the corrosive effects of power and influence*. While power and influence are standard requirements of the leadership stock-in-trade, they can easily lead to self-centeredness, selfishness, blind spots, manipulation, insensitivity, rudeness, arrogance, and other personal pathologies. See Exhibit 12.4 for examples of the corrosive effects of power on various leaders.

ANALYTIC SKILLS

Analytic skills are defined as *the ability to remember, make distinctions, and deal with complexity and ambiguity*. Much of what people think of as intelligence is covered under analytic skills. Many elements of this skill cluster are more aptly described as traits because of a large innate element. Nonetheless, analytic skills can be much affected by environment, education, training, and self-study, which are all emphasized here. It is also important to remember that people may have good analytic skills in one domain, such as work processes (which can also be divided into concrete/physical or conceptual aspects), while having weak analytic skills in other domains, such as social or political aspects (Streufert and Swezey 1986).

There are at least four major elements that comprise analytic skills. The most obvious is memory. When people have good memories, they have a clear advantage in making distinctions because the data are immediately accessible. Because memory is based on exposure to information, those we typically think of as having a "good memory" can either remember information from a single exposure or can recall detail after a long period of time with few exposures. (Of course, because memory is based on exposure to information and because some people will have been exposed to great amounts of information over time, they may be able to remember a great deal of information by dint of experience.) Good memory in concrete work might involve knowing the specific language of seldom-used statutes in code enforcement, or it might involve remembering the process used to solve a problem from several months before. Good memory in social settings might involve remembering the names of people one met only once before or remembering people's spouses, children, or other personal details. Political memory might include knowing the key decision makers and the decision protocols that they are expected to use, or perhaps a complex grievance process (see Willner 1968 for a discussion related to great leaders).

The second element of analytic skills is discrimination. Discrimination is the ability to distinguish and use different conceptual dimensions. For example, good carpenters must be able to distinguish the characteristics of different types of wood, and fire marshals must be able to distinguish among fundamentally different sources of fire such as electrical causes versus combustible liquids and gases. Good discrimination also takes an ability to see more than "black-and-white" distinctions; it involves using subtlety and nuance to make better decisions. For example, a subordinate's proposal to address a new organizational arrangement may be good overall, but it can be improved in cost, timing, and communication dimensions. While leaders keep up their technical discrimination skills, they must also refine an entirely new set of discrimination abilities. A common example of

Exhibit 12.4

The Corrosive Effects of Power

Lord Acton's famous 1887 dictum that power tends to corrupt and absolute power corrupts absolutely should be a somber admonition for those privileged with extraordinary influence. Philosophers and wits have noted the corrosive effects of power on personality for hundreds of years. A smattering of examples includes the following:

- Aesop (550 BC): Any excuse will serve a tyrant.
- Francis Bacon (1624): The desire of power in excess caused the angels to fall.
- William Pitt (1770): Unlimited power is apt to corrupt the minds of those who possess it.
- Percy Shelley (1813): Power, like a desolating pestilence, pollutes whatever it touches.

Yet, despite how common this wisdom is, examples of the corrosive effects of power on people, groups, companies, and nations are practically a weekly occurrence. Needless to say, authoritarian leaders cannot help but fall prey to excess, whether we are talking about Josef Stalin of Russia; Idi Amin of Uganda; other African dictators such as Emperor Bukassa of the Central African Republic, Mengistu of Ethiopia, and the Nguemas of Equatorial Guinea; or Caribbean dictators such as the Duvaliers. Pol Pot of Cambodia serves as a disturbing example. This radical idealist caused 1.5 million of his countrymen (one-seventh of the population) to perish while he was in power (1975–1979), in order to "purify" the country. Democratically elected presidents are no strangers to the tantalizing corruption of power; witness Richard Nixon's abuse of the law and Bill Clinton's sexual license. Entertainers and sports figures, such as Mike Tyson, Robert Downey Jr., and Robert Blake occasionally learn that their celebrity and wealth cannot keep them out of jail. Administrators are famous for secret abuses of bureaucratic power; well-known examples include J. Edgar Hoover and Robert Moses (highlighted in Exhibits 11.5 and 1.2, respectively). Whole countries are seduced by power, whether they are led by dictators like Adolf Hitler (who was initially elected), or by superpowers like the United States, which expected to use its superior force in tiny Vietnam to achieve its military goals.

An interesting example is seen in the corrosive effect of administrative power on legislators. Members of the U.S. House of Representatives normally draw their power from the mandate of their constituents and their ability to sway their colleagues through persuasion, ideology, and bargaining. However, Speakers of the House have substantial administrative power to shape the process. By the late nineteenth century, Speakers had acquired the power to appoint the standing committees and name their chairs, as well as personally chair the all-powerful Rules Committee. The dominance of Speakers reached its extreme under Joseph Cannon (Republican from Illinois), who came to power in 1903 and greatly reduced the influence of individual members. As if his power to appoint committee members and chairs and to determine what legislation would be allowed to come to the floor were not enough, he went one step further—too far as it turned out. To complete his domination of any wayward colleagues, during debate he simply refused to call on anyone who was not supportive of his position. Progressive Republicans banded together with Democrats not only to get rid of this bullying Speaker but also to change the power structure of the House altogether. No longer could the Speaker participate on the Rules Committee, chair positions were based on seniority, and appointment to standing committees was no longer his or her sole domain. And never again would Speakers be allowed to abuse their power to recognize members in floor debate in such a flagrant manner. Yet, later Speakers were certainly not immune to the siren call of power, especially when additional power was restored to Speakers in 1974. Speaker Jim Wright (who served roughly currently with President Reagan), despite his gracious public manner, wielded power mercilessly and sometimes selfishly, as ethics peccadilloes finally caught up with him. Speaker Newt Gingrich used his power as Speaker to dominate the national political agenda to such a degree in the 1994–96 period that the public at large revolted, returned Clinton to the White House, and seemed to cause greater-than-expected House losses for Republicans in 1998. Gingrich ended up stepping out of office completely because of his precipitous drop in standing, after a period of being the most influential Speaker since "Uncle Joe" Cannon.

leadership discrimination is the ability to resist contamination of personal and professional arenas. A line worker may avoid a colleague who is delightfully gregarious but who is also sneaky; a manager must simultaneously acknowledge both elements but keep them conceptually separated. Or a line worker may judge a well-liked colleague's work more favorably but a manager must keep social and technical performance elements distinct, which is not to say the social/interpersonal contributions are dismissed or discounted.

Cognitive complexity is the ability to consider and use different dimensions simultaneously or use different levels of complexity in different domains (Streufert and Swezey 1986; Hunt 1996). For a manager to do a good job in performance appraisals, some degree of cognitive complexity is an asset because of the complex nature of workers' contributions and liabilities in the work environment. Not only must the manager consider the individual dimensions of accuracy, speed and work volume, communication, record keeping, problem solving and creativity, collegiality, responsiveness, and flexibility, but the cognitively complex manager will understand and address these factors as they interact with each other and the requirements of the work environment (Boal and Hooijberg 2000). Cognitive complexity increasingly becomes a way of life as managers move up the hierarchy, and they have to make many discriminations in different domains as well as subtle judgment calls about what to emphasize for the organization's good (Jaques 1989). For example, a manager may achieve success in a low-performing division by focusing on the interactive effects of recruitment, training, clear work protocols, process improvement, and tougher accountability and discipline. When transferred to another division that is already high performing, the manager may have to focus on the subtle dimensions involved in advanced team building, improved reward and bonus systems, and external benchmarking.

The final element of analytic skills is ambiguity tolerance (Wilkinson 2006). Ambiguity tolerance is the ability to suspend judgment while new data are being gathered. On one hand, many analytic skills involve the ability to set up and remember patterns or mental models (also known as mental schemas). These models generally provide a means of sorting vast amounts of information quickly and simplifying decision making by categorizing data and issues into known "pigeonholes." That is, mental models help us to cope with information overload and act quickly on information. However, mental models are based on past information and past analysis. They become a liability when either the past trend is no longer accurate or past analysis was inadequate or faulty. Managers who tolerate ambiguity well are more willing to pay attention to anomalies in order to determine whether a new or contradictory pattern emerges, or more willing to appreciate that new environmental trends may mean the configuration of new, and yet-to-be-elaborated, mental models.

Analytic skills are universally acknowledged as important to leadership, but they are discussed in very different ways. Some researchers talk about analytical skills primarily in the service of applied aspects such as problem solving (U.S. OPM 1992, 1999; Rankin 2001). Others refer to this aspect of leadership in more abstract terms such as intelligence (Kotter 1982). However, most researchers have a variety of concepts to capture analytic skills such as general mental ability and decision making (Howard and

Bray 1988), conceptual skills (Yukl 1998),[4] and being intelligent (clever) and conceptually skilled (Stogdill 1974). A study by the American Management Association (Bhatta 2001) identifies intellectual abilities as a metacategory composed of logical thought, conceptualization, and diagnostic use of concepts. New Zealand also identifies intellectual capability a metacategory for its public managers; the metacategory is composed of intellectual processes, problem solving, and strategic assessment (Bhatta 2001). The 1997 OPM study identifies problem solving as the second-most important executive skill behind oral communication, and the third-most important supervisory skill behind oral and written communication.

Guidelines

1. *Assess your various cognitive abilities*. What are your strengths and weaknesses? What is most critical to improve? What aspects can be improved through self-discipline?
2. *Enhance analytic skills through targeted experience as well as extensive training and education*. Experience is a useful teacher in providing basic information and data; that is, it provides the content of knowledge for analysis. Training and education become superior teachers in enhancing the actual tools of discrimination and pointing out nuance. Therefore, because of the enormous complexity of the contemporary management world, it is nearly impossible to be an exceptional, or even an above-average, leader without extensive training and education in management.
3. *Enhance reflectiveness*. Even training and education can go only so far. Leaders must deal with unique combinations of issues and new problems. Furthermore, there simply is not time to learn *all* the solutions expounded in high-quality training and education curricula. Training and education enrich one's repertoire, but a certain amount of analytic work is the customization of knowledge, discrimination, cognitive complexity, and ambiguity tolerance through reflection. Unfortunately, some leaders have the skills but lack the discipline or patience to reflect. Reflection can involve sitting in a quiet room, or doodling with a series of problems in order to see if there is a higher pattern and solution. But in a more physical mode, reflection can also be conducting a series of personal site visits with an open mind about the issues that will be heard, the strengths and weaknesses that will be observed, and the work that will emerge from the experience.

TECHNICAL SKILLS

Although leaders rarely do the technical work themselves, especially at more senior ranks, their mastery of technical skills generally remains important. Even an executive, Stone noted, "must know enough of the general field not to get lost in the labyrinth. If he does not know the program at the onset, he must master quietly its major elements. Otherwise he will be unable to command the loyalty and respect of his specialists and weld them together as a team" (Stone 1945, 215). Long ago, Katz (1955) stated that technical skills were most important for supervisors and least important for executives. More recently this was borne out by a large OPM study (1997) in which technical skill was the only one in which supervisors were perceived to need more competence than executives. However, it is generally understood that executives in narrow functional areas such as accounting or safety compliance need significantly more technical competence than their generalist brethren such as city managers, agency directors, or executive corps members who are considered troubleshooters (the original concept behind the U.S. Senior Executive Service). See Exhibit 12.5 for an insight into leadership in a functional area and its relationship to technical creativity.

It is also understood that leaders—especially those with an entrepreneurial bent— who want to have a more significant impact on the operations frequently have stronger technical skills and involvement. This last facet, however, is very much a two-edged sword in practice. On one hand, such executives are occasionally the pioneers needed to make important changes in products or processes that would fail without major executive involvement. On the other hand, excessive executive focus on technical issues and personal expertise is just as often a major source of career derailment because of a tendency toward arrogance, micromanagement, and underachievement in other core executive competencies (Lombardo and McCauley 1988).

Technical skill for leaders *entails the professional and organizational knowledge and practice associated with an area of work*. It involves three major elements. The most conspicuous element consists of the technical information and skills of the discipline. For example, managers in transportation generally have and need engineering degrees, primarily in civil or aeronautics engineering; in hospitals, nursing or medical degrees; and in forest and park management, biology or natural sciences degrees (Carnevale, Gainer, and Schulz 1990). In many areas a degree may not be necessary per se, but extensive knowledge is necessary nonetheless. Training managers may not have a degree in education but they should have extensive knowledge about learning theory and training techniques. Leaders, especially at the supervisory level, are often hired or promoted based on technical skills. Yet, over time, many complain that they lose touch with these skills, and this is a frequent complaint from subordinates as well. In a study of local managers, 22 percent stated that this aspect of technical competence was their weakest skill area (although an equal number identified it as the strongest) (Van Wart 2001).

Part of this basic competence repertoire has always included information about the organization—processes, rules, employees, facilities, clients, interest groups, elected overseers, culture, and so on. This is often not much of an issue for those promoted internally in an organization, especially if they have had the luxury of several rotational assignments or cross-functional team opportunities. It is often a major issue for external hires who may have to focus considerably on understanding the organization for the first six months or so. However, sometimes this is an asset in the long run because such leaders have broader experience and can use comparative practices as a source of personal benchmarking.

Since the quality management revolution that occurred in the late 1980s and 1990s, many basic management skills are now expected of frontline workers and can be thought

Exhibit 12.5

Technical Creativity Versus Leadership Ability

In an interesting set of studies about technical abilities, leadership abilities, and age, H.C. Lehman (1937, 1942) studied chemists. In the first study, he found that chemists, on average, make their greatest technical contributions between the ages of twenty-eight and thirty-two. At this point the chemists were completely trained and had some experience in the field, but still had lots of fresh ideas. That is, excessive socialization had not diminished their ability to "think outside the box." In the second study, Lehman found that the optimal age for eminent leadership was forty-five to forty-nine. That is, it took time for others to appreciate their technical contributions, for them to rise in organizational roles, and for them to polish their social skills, which tend to increase rather than diminish over time. Additionally, in a later study, Lehman found that great leaders in a variety of professional fields tend to be those who have gifts of ability that are recognized at an early age, and thus receive special attention and/or training (Lehman 1953). Of course, in all of his studies Lehman was studying those who had achieved eminent leadership status. Therefore, great technical ability early in a career certainly does not guarantee eminent leadership status later; rather, it serves as a powerful advantage that may or may not be exploited.

of as an extension of organizational knowledge and skills. Such knowledge and skills might include managing and leading teams, leading meetings, basic operational problem solving, and rudimentary operations planning. Unfortunately, these basic skills are often assumed of leaders at all levels, resulting in insufficient training or feedback in this area. Military and quasi-military organizations are the exception in that the planning of meetings, teams, operations, and the like is considered a critical craft of the trade.

Technical skills and credibility are not on all the major competency lists for leaders. Kotter (1982, 1990) omits it altogether and Howard and Bray (1988) identify only the basic management element. Indeed, there are certainly many examples in the management world of executives who, with little technical and organizational information, have accomplished a great deal in spite of, and sometimes because of, this absence of knowledge and experience. Yet, this class of cases is not the general rule, and weaknesses in technical skills often prove to be enormous liabilities. The meta-analysis by Stogdill (1974) identified both the technical knowledge and basic management components separately. Rankin's study featured technical skills relatively prominently (2001). As mentioned, the OPM studies identify technical competence, which OPM relabels as technical credibility in the latter studies (1992, 1999, 2006). It is more implied than stated on the competency lists of other advanced democracies (Bhatta 2001).

Guidelines

1. *Assess your technical skills and the need for technical competence.* The level of technical competence can sometimes be assessed using a self-inventory, but it is much enhanced by asking candid subordinates how they would evaluate such skills or by using an anonymous survey instrument. If subordinates are queried,

then it is often wise to get the opinions of superiors or colleagues as well, because they often have different perceptions about the level of and need for such competence. Those technical competencies that can easily be acquired should be mastered as a routine aspect of ongoing personal development. Yet, because professional technical expertise is not a critical issue for many leaders who are managing programs, clusters of programs, and whole agencies, those technical skills that take considerable time to enhance must be carefully weighed against the other areas that demand attention and improvement. As management becomes more of the core job, so too must those skills become the core focus. This means that increasingly, senior managers keep up technical skills on their own time or altogether delegate specialized expertise to others.

2. *Develop a plan to improve selected technical skills.* No matter how modest or ambitious such plans may be, technical skills generally improve only through self-discipline. If knowledge of the state-of-the-art in the discipline is slipping, then it may be necessary to incorporate a thorough reading of a major journal once a month and to attend technical sessions at conferences several times a year. If meeting skills are weak, then it may be necessary to purchase meeting software and/or ask for a critique of each meeting at its conclusion.

CONTINUAL LEARNING

Although continual learning has always been a significant competence, its importance has been rising in the past few decades because of increased change and uncertainty in all organizations (Vera and Crossan 2004; Berson et al. 2006). Broadly defined, continual learning means *taking responsibility for acquiring new information, looking at old information in new ways, and finding ways to use new and old information creatively.* It relates closely to and builds on several other competencies. "Cognitive complexity is required to develop better mental models, but emotional maturity is also required to learn from mistakes, and flexibility is required to change assumptions and ways of thinking and behaving in response to a changing world" (Yukl 1998, 257). In addition to cognitive complexity, we can assume other analytic skills such as memory, discrimination, and ambiguity tolerance are also critically linked to continual learning. For a detailed example of this complex skill, see Exhibit 12.6 about the father of consumer advocacy in America.

Because some aspects of continual learning are emphasized through other competencies, only two elements are identified here. Essentially, they equate to an ability to learn proficiently in basic and advanced modes. The first element is the ability to glean and use new information and data. The basic learning mode requires people to review and monitor data and trends. The data and trends are both internal and external to the organization. Examples include operations, client demand, technology, and the economy. Basic learning requires using new information in standard ways. Although basic learning sounds routine, and should be, the challenge lies in the vast amount of information to monitor and review as well as in the number of standard processes and problem-solving protocols one must learn and use in the contemporary management world. To keep one's workload

Exhibit 12.6

The Father of Consumer Advocacy in America: Harvey W. Wiley

No better example of the importance of skills can be found than that of Harvey W. Wiley (1844–1930), chief chemist of the U.S. Department of Agriculture for twenty-nine years, who was the primary force behind the passage of one of the most important pieces of legislation in American history, the Food and Drug Act of 1906. Despite enormous obstacles, he was able to get this strong act passed, an act that he had personally drafted. The manufacturers of both food and drugs were wholly against it and brought fierce pressure on Congress to stall action. Further, many states' rights advocates felt that this was not a proper federal issue and infringed on the states' ability to enforce their own welfare. Certainly, it was not the power of Wiley's position that aided significantly in the legislative fight, because he had only the rank of bureau chief. Nonetheless, he prevailed over all odds by a combination of technical and analytic brilliance, well-honed influence skills, superb communication abilities, and the capacity to continually learn as he waited for the opportune "policy window."

Technical and analytic skills: Despite his meager upbringing in Indiana and the interruption of the Civil War, through self-discipline Wiley obtained a bachelor's degree in 1867. After being an instructor at various institutions, in 1871 he also received an M.D. (which was not a rigorous course of study at the time). Still feeling the need for higher-quality training, he acquired another bachelor's degree in science from Harvard, and later toured Europe to investigate the state of scientific inquiry. For his day, he had the best scientific training possible. Of his many technical contributions, two are especially prominent. First, his work (as chief chemist) resulted in important modifications in sorghum and beet sugar manufacture, vastly expanding the American market in this area. Second, he wrote the three-volume *Principles and Practices of Agricultural Analysis,* which remained the mainstay textbook for nearly forty years.

Influence and social skills: Although Wiley did not have enormous legitimate power (formal authority), he did use his position as chief chemist to testify before Congress year after year in his never-ending battle to provide the public with greater information about food and drug ingredients and about harmful additives. As a coalition builder, Wiley spent thirteen years adding groups to the list of those who actively supported legislation. He started with his fellow state chemists and a few in agriculture who were concerned about those using unethical and dangerous methods to sell products. By the turn of the century, he got the attention of the progressives and muckraking media such as *Collier's Magazine,* which did frequent pieces stemming from his work. By 1905, he had won over the American Medical Association, the Women's Christian Temperance Union, the public at large, and the president as active advocates. His powers of rational persuasion were so great that in the months before passage of the legislation he spoke at a national canner's association—at which he had been warned not to appear with threats to physical safety because of their vehement opposition—and yet received an ovation for his work in promoting the integrity and well-being of their industry! And he was also a master of inspirational appeals of all kinds. Some of his appeals were high-minded calls for the safety of the public from unscrupulous business people with their invisible poisons. Other appeals took the form of roiling accusations of the mass deaths of children caused by unsavory medicines and adulterated foods.

Communication skills: Wiley was a natural writer; he produced 9 books, 60 government bulletins, and 225 scientific papers during his lifetime. His speaking ability was entirely learned, however, insofar as he had to overcome stage fright. Yet he learned the craft of public speaking so well—successfully including humor, customizing his talks to particular audiences, and mastering voice control—that he came to be in tremendous demand on the speaking circuit. This ultimately provided him with the public fame to match his academic renown.

Continual learning: His quest for more information and state-of-the-art practices has already been amply illustrated: His return to school after earning an M.D., his ability to learn new skills such

(continued)

Exhibit 12.6 *(continued)*

as public speaking rather than relying on his writing prowess alone, and his ability to continually monitor and learn about the congressional policy process as he waited for his opportunity to promote national standards. Indeed, after retiring from the Department of Agriculture in 1912, he assumed a job as a section editor at *Good Housekeeping,* where he promoted good nutrition, and helped the Good Housekeeping Seal of Approval become an extraordinarily sought-after symbol of product integrity.

Wiley's leadership is interesting, then, on two scores. First, his followers were not really the hundreds of employees who reported to him at the Bureau of Chemistry but were really the public at large over whom he had no formal authority, as well as Congress and the president who clearly followed his lead. Second, given his exceptionally modest formal power as a civil servant, in opposing huge commercial and political forces his technical, persuasive, and communication skills had to be extraordinary. His ability to continually adapt these skills enabled him to work toward his lifetime ambition: a safe food and drug supply for the American people.

Source: Cooper and Wright (1992).

reasonable, it is tempting to review data superficially, ignore it altogether, or resort to the same old methods for solving problems, even though they may be poorly suited to the issue at hand. Those who are good at basic learning are disciplined about staying abreast of operational and environmental data, and finding the best standard methods for accomplishing the work.

The second element is the ability to expand knowledge. Advanced learning involves creating new knowledge that leads to innovation (using known products/processes in new ways) or invention (discovering altogether new products/processes). It also requires disseminating that knowledge. An example may be helpful to distinguish between basic and advanced learning. A manager in a social service agency discovers that a variety of clients seem to be getting poor information in several areas and error rates for some routine benefits calculations are increasing. She decides that the cost/benefit is not worth determining exactly who is causing the problem, and that it is better to invest resources in several short, in-service refresher training sessions at staff meetings (i.e., she is operating at a basic learning level). To her surprise, despite a brief period of improvement, the problem seems to be getting worse after a year. Now she believes the problem is more extensive than she thought at first, so she commissions a study to determine who is making the mistakes and why. The study reveals that most of the experienced workers have left for better pay and working conditions, new worker training is less comprehensive, the quality of new recruits has fallen, and the caseload has increased by over 10 percent. In response to her study, she recommends to the agency director a comprehensive reform package that includes modest salary adjustments, numerous process changes (streamlining), a significant technology infusion to substantially increase worker productivity, an expanded training curriculum, and a better system to track case manager performance levels. This latter example demonstrates advanced learning.

It is important to note that although advanced learning is often founded on basic learning, the utility and viability of basic and advanced learning modes are generally situationally determined, and advanced learning is not always the better of the two modes. However, it is generally the case that advanced learning takes more resources and is less practiced, or practiced more poorly than basic learning. In addition, all high-performing organizations have cultures that promote advanced learning. Therefore, wise leaders enthusiastically engage in and encourage advanced learning practices.

Aspects of continual learning have been reflected on leadership competency lists for some time, if obliquely. Stogdill refers to leaders as being creative (1974). Kotter describes leaders as being intelligent and having diverse interests (1990). Howard and Bray also refer to diverse interests as well as creativity (1988). Rankin (2001) refers to it only very indirectly as problem solving. The 1997 OPM study found that problem solving and creative thinking were rated second and eleventh in competency rankings for long-time executives and that the spread in creative thinking skills between supervisors and executives was very large. In the 1999 study, the competencies related to continual learning were expanded to four areas: problem solving, creativity and innovation, strategic thinking, *and* continual learning.

Guidelines

1. *Focus on the benefits of learning.* Learning is hard work and can feel like a nuisance or nice-to-do-when-I-get-time activity. Therefore, it is critical to keep the benefits of (continual) learning in mind at all times. First, it provides entrepreneurial opportunities for organizational and personal advancement. As Bennis and Nanus note, continual learning means responding to the future in the present (1985). The unpleasant opposite reality is that a lack of continual learning may lead to organizational malaise career blockage. Second, it keeps people up to date with their business and the world, which in turn makes life more interesting.

2. *Learn from surprises and problems.* Dealing with surprises, problems, mistakes, and failures is not a distraction from work; it is the work of leaders. Leaders have a responsibility to take a proactive mental attitude toward challenges. Indeed, many times problems and failures, properly confronted, give way to unforeseen and substantial opportunities. As many have noted, the only people who never fail are those who never try.

3. *Find ways to challenge assumptions and mental models.* Because leaders have the ability to change assumptions and mental models, it is their responsibility to find ways to be vigilant about questioning them. Such challenges might be about work processes and standards, or about notions of what certain people can accomplish or ways that clients should be treated. Indeed, without challenging assumptions, innovation is hardly possible. One especially important set of assumptions to challenge concerns organizational performance (see chapter 9 on organizational assessment). Ultimately, challenging assumptions should be a form of self-discipline that complements external competition; can things be done better and are people achieving their best?

4. *Invest in learning despite turbulent or difficult times.* There is rarely a really good time to devote to learning; it must simply be a way of life for most leaders. The methods of learning vary widely. Leaders can engage in the usual activities such as

seminars, conferences, reading, site visits, rotational assignments, mentoring, and the like, but they can also commission experiments and special studies, examine best practices, benchmark, and maintain good information networks. Because learning takes time, it is useful to have a longer time horizon. Furthermore, learning should be thought of not only as an individual activity, but also as one that is done by groups, teams, and even an entire organization.

CONCLUSION

Theodore Roosevelt noted that some gain success simply by their extraordinary gifts of talent, but that is rare indeed. Most gain success, he noted, by their ability to cultivate natural talents. Success, he asserted, generally comes to people who have "developed those ordinary qualities to a more than ordinary degree." His insight applies to the skills cited in this chapter. Some people have innate genius in a given area, but most people must develop their talents to be effective.

The six broad-based skills discussed here are important and multifaceted. Exhibit 12.7 provides a summary of the skills, subelements, and major recommendations covered in this chapter. However, our review of traits and skills would not be complete without a discussion of some of the other characteristics that are frequently mentioned in the leadership literature but do not appear among the six presented here. Although significant, the three leadership characteristics below are more structural than the traits and skills emphasized above.

As mentioned before, intelligence is not listed as a *trait* that emphasizes the innate elements of mental brilliance. Instead, cognitive *skills* have been discussed that focus more on the learned aspects of mental ability. The argument can be made that a cognitively well-trained, well-disciplined person of mediocre mental acuity will generally outperform an untrained genius. Research has overwhelmingly confirmed this (Stogdill 1948, 1974). Of course, it should be added that the concept of intelligence is multifaceted, and that somewhat different types of intelligence are useful at lower managerial levels ("crystallized understanding") as opposed to the more fluid types that are useful at higher levels (similar to basic discrimination versus cognitive complexity, as discussed under analytic skills). One interesting counterintuitive finding relates to the optimal degree of difference between the leader and the led. Early on, Hollingworth (1926) found that a moderate discrepancy in intelligence was optimal. He found that exceptionally intelligent individuals were less likely to be leading those of average ability because of communication problems and were more likely to be conceptually and socially isolated. Many studies have revealed similar findings, including one by Ghiselli (1963), who speculated that those of exceptional intelligence often make better concept pioneers than they do leaders who must be sure to relate to the goals and values of followers. In order to get around the problems associated with intelligence as a primary trait, the concept is sometimes melded with knowledge and relabeled as wisdom, although the sense of intelligence is applied or practical rather than abstract (e.g., Sternberg 2003).

A second important area relates to physical aspects such as appearance and age. Individuals with a better appearance based on grooming, comportment, health, height, or

Exhibit 12.7

Summary of Chapter 12

Leadership skill	Subelements of skill	Major recommendations
Communication skills *The ability to effectively exchange information through active and passive means*	• Oral skills • Writing skills • Listening skills • Nonverbal skills	1. Assess communication skills to identify strengths and weaknesses. 2. Develop a plan to address weaknesses (see Exhibit 12.1).
Social skills *The ability to interact effectively in social settings and to understand and productively harness one's own and others' personality structures*	• Personal likability (extreme form: charisma) • Expressiveness • Social perceptiveness	1. Take a critical look at your social skills and identify those that are weak. 2. Develop a plan to address social weaknesses that are critical.
Influence skills *The actual use of sources of power through concrete behavior strategies*	• The effectiveness with which one uses influence strategies (see Exhibit 12.3) • The range of influence strategies that one has to use (see Exhibit 12.3)	1. Assess sources of power and ability to use influence tactics. 2. Develop the discipline to augment power. 3. Understand and cultivate influence strategies. 4. Guard against the corrosive effects of power.
Analytic skills *The ability to remember, make distinctions, and deal with complexity*	• Memory • Discrimination • Cognitive complexity • Ambiguity tolerance	1. Assess cognitive abilities. 2. Enhance analytic skills through targeted experience, training, and education. 3. Enhance reflectiveness.
Technical skills *The basic professional and organizational knowledge and practice associated with an area of work*	• Technical information and skills of the profession • Information about the organization • Basic management knowledge/skills	1. Assess your level of technical skills and the skills actually necessary for the position. 2. Develop a plan to improve selected technical skills.
Continual learning *The taking of responsibility for acquiring new information, looking at old information in new ways, and finding ways to use new and old information creatively*	• The ability to glean and use new information and data • The ability to expand knowledge (knowledge creation)	1. Focus on benefits of learning. 2. Learn from surprises and problems. 3. Find ways to challenge assumptions and mental models. 4. Invest in learning despite turbulent or difficult times.

attractiveness, have been found to have a distinct edge in many studies. However, many other studies have failed to find differences based on these characteristics. It seems that the nature of the appearance that makes a difference is situationally specific. Those serving in leadership positions in military or quasi-military organizations are more likely to be selected and perceived as leaders if they are well groomed, possess a proud carriage, and are physically robust. Political leaders have a distinct advantage when they are attractive and tall. Leaders in many services and information agencies may find that appearance is not particularly significant. However, in one recent study it was found that comportment (the professional manner in which people carried themselves) was considered one of the more important characteristics for leadership across all agency categories (Van Wart 2001). Furthermore, although the 1990s represented a high-water mark for casual attire, the popular media are reporting a return to more conservative dress trends as the marketplace becomes more competitive.

Age is another interesting factor that is enormously important. A study by Standard and Poor's (1967) provides a fairly reliable baseline. Seventy-four percent of American executives were over age fifty. Forty-eight times more executives were in the seventy-one to eighty age-range category than in the under-thirty category. While an updated study might shift these data slightly toward a younger profile today, it is unlikely that the senior executive profile will vary tremendously. Of course, there are variations by industries, because many are more age-rank lockstep than others. In general, the public sector tends to exhibit this age-rank lockstep fairly consistently. Some organizations, such as the military, seem to prefer that senior executive leaders be in the age range of fifty-five to sixty to reflect maximum experience; many others prefer ages fifty to fifty-five to maximize physical energy; and a few prefer executives younger than age fifty; for example, information agencies in which industry changes require extreme mental nimbleness and technical expertise. The number of executives appointed older than age sixty seems to drop precipitously; however, many older public sector executives successfully retain their positions for long periods, thus keeping the number of executives at age sixty-five or older quite substantial.

A final aspect that has received considerable attention is the connection between social background and leadership. Most studies find a significant but modest effect from social and economic background on the likelihood of being in a senior leadership position (e.g., Porter 1965). While this relationship was very pronounced before the twentieth century when society was more clearly class-based (Matthews 1954) and class membership was more rigid, the connections still seem to have a bearing. An important mediating factor is that greater wealth tends to mean more education and better universities in general. Economic and social connections also play a role, albeit not as prominent a role as they once did.

As important as these last three characteristics may seem, they pale in comparison to the importance of communication skills, social skills, influence skills, analytic skills, technical skills, and the ability to continually learn. One may be highly intelligent, physically robust and attractive, and come from a prestigious family, yet never come close to being a leader, much less a highly effective one. Leaders must be masters of language, interaction, influence, ideas, credibility, and change. Although part of the leader's hand is dealt at birth and in early childhood, these are areas that can be enormously affected by self-disciplined study and practice.

Of course, leader characteristics are only half of the competency mix. To understand the dynamics of leadership one must also look at how leaders act in work settings. It is to this behavioral aspect of leadership that we turn next.

NOTES

1. Lee Iacocca said: "You have to be able to listen well if you're going to motivate people who work for you" (1984, 54).

2. Toastmasters is an organization dedicated to improving oral communication skills by providing people opportunities to speak to groups in a supportive atmosphere.

3. The most famous taxonomy is from French and Raven (1959) who describe five types of power: legitimate, reward, coercive, expert, and referent. The power and influence literature is enormous and complex. Good starting points for understanding this literature are Bass (1990) and Yukl (2002).

4. Yukl describes this category as "good judgment, foresight, intuition, creativity, and the ability to find meaning and order in ambiguous, uncertain events" (1998, 253).

13

Task-Oriented Behaviors

Although it is useful to understand the traits and skills that leaders use in a variety of contexts, the study of leadership is woefully incomplete without an examination of the discrete types of actions that leaders practice—well or badly. Like traits and skills, *behaviors* can be very broadly defined so that there are few categories, or they can be very discretely defined with hundreds of items. For example, the large, early behavioral studies of the 1950s focused on condensing hundreds, even thousands, of items down into a few major categories—focusing, for example, on the task at hand (also known as initiating structure) or focusing on the people doing the work (also known as consideration or relations-oriented behavior). A third "mega" category has always lurked in the background. Katz discussed conceptual skills in 1955 in addition to technical and interpersonal ones; the transformationalists have emphasized the ability to create large change; and biographers have emphasized the effect of great leaders on the course of events. In other words, leaders must have skills in successful interaction and act as an interface for the organization and environment at large. It is these three categories—task-, people-, and organization-oriented behaviors—that will form the basis of the next three chapters.

Task-oriented behaviors can vary in three fundamental ways. First, they can vary by level. The conventional wisdom was that ideally those with good technical skills were promoted to supervisors. Supervisors with good interpersonal skills were promoted to managers. And managers with good conceptual skills were promoted to executive roles. In reality, this useful but oversimplified conceptualization is much violated in practice, and it obscures a host of important distinctions that will be explored in this chapter.

How do managers at various levels actually spend their time, and what do they think is most important? Although different studies will come to slightly different conclusions, a reanalysis of data generated by the U.S. Office of Personnel Management (U.S. OPM 1997) using the behavior categories defined by this study is typical. In a content analysis of 150 narrowly defined competencies that supervisors, managers, and executives in the federal government identified as being crucial or very important, we can obtain a concrete sense of the priorities of public managers. High priorities are captured by looking at the top 20 discrete competency preferences; medium priorities are captured by looking at the top 100. Low priorities are those ranked 101 and above. For contrast and simplicity, here we identify only executives and supervisors in the text because managers fall between these two classes in over 90 percent of all cases, and the exceptions are relatively minor.[1] See Exhibit 13.1 for the results of the task competency study comparing supervisory to executive priorities.

Exhibit 13.1

Overall Priority Given to Task, People, or Organization Behavioral Competencies by Federal Supervisors and Executives Based on Ranking of 150 Discrete Competencies (as percent)

	Top 20 Competencies		Top 100 Competencies	
	Supervisors	Executives	Supervisors	Executives
Task-Oriented Competencies	44	35	34	31
People-Oriented Competencies	39	26	26	22
Organization-Oriented Competencies	17	39	40	47

Note: Based on an analysis of OPM data on 1,763 executives and 3,516 supervisors. Domain rankings (i.e., task, people, or organization) were based on percentages of those rating specific competencies related to that domain as very important or crucial and whose position involved that competency. Percentages add down. Two competencies were excluded from the original study because they were traits, and several dozen competencies were dually counted. With dual counting, the top-20 list of executives and supervisors actually include 23 "hits" each, the top-100 supervisor list includes 112, and the top-100 executive list includes 121. Proportions in Exhibit 13.1 reflect these adjustments.

Supervisors divide the bulk of their high-priority attention relatively equally between people (39 percent) and tasks (44 percent); organization-oriented activities get a scant 17 percent. This focus shifts significantly when the top 100 competencies are analyzed. Supervisors' attention becomes quite balanced, with task-oriented behaviors (34 percent) now following slightly behind organization-oriented behaviors (40 percent), and slightly ahead of people-oriented ones (26 percent).

The profile is quite different for executives. Their top priority attention goes to organization-oriented behaviors (39 percent), followed closely by task-oriented behaviors (35 percent); relatively speaking they give scant attention to people-oriented behaviors. Unlike supervisors, whose priorities even out as the competency listing becomes more expansive, executives' focus on organization-oriented behaviors actually increases (47 percent), task-oriented behaviors decline to 31 percent, and people-oriented behaviors decrease to 22 percent.

Shifts in emphasis will occur across industries, organizations, and situations as well. For example, it is well known that a task-oriented focus tends to increase when there are technical problems, when there is a crisis needing immediate attention, when employees are new or training is deficient, and when clients' or customers' interests are relatively stable and well known (i.e., organization change is not necessary). The reverse is generally true as well. A leader's task-oriented focus tends to decrease when operations are running smoothly, employees are well trained and self-managed, when client and customer demands are shrill and/or changing, or when a long-term crisis requires a fundamentally different approach.

THE UNDERLYING LOGIC OF EACH OF THE BEHAVIOR DOMAINS

There is a fundamental logic to each behavior domain, and this is well established in the action research literature. Before leading, people should have information and knowledge that form an ongoing set of activities or behaviors. This is called the assessment phase. In the task domain, it is referred to as monitoring and assessing tasks. In the people-oriented domain, it is consulting. In the organizational domain, it is called environmental scanning.[2]

Leaders have to decide what to do. They must process information and knowledge and draw up explicit or implicit plans of what they will do or what should be done by others. In the task domain this is generally called operations planning. In the people-oriented domain we will call it planning and organizing personnel. At the organizational level it is generally referred to as strategic planning.

The implementation function involves several behaviors in each domain. In the task domain, leaders must clarify roles and objectives for followers, inform, and delegate. In the people domain, leaders develop staff, motivate them, and build and manage teams. In the organization domain, leaders articulate the mission and vision, network and partner, and perform general management functions related to human resource management, finance and budget, and so forth. While similarities in the activities across domains are not as consistent in implementation, they are nonetheless apparent. Clarifying roles, developing staff, and articulating the mission and vision have common elements. So do informing, motivating, and networking and partnering. Delegating and team building are highly connected as well. Performing general management functions tends not to have a parallel activity at other levels in this taxonomy.

Since the early 1980s, many have added "change" as a mega-category similar to task and people domains (see Yukl 1998, 61). Although elevating change behaviors is important, this conceptualization has resulted in a blurring of distinctions among the different types of change (e.g., technical change versus reorganizations) and the different discrete skills that flow from these distinctions. Therefore, it is more useful to think of change as a function of each behavioral domain. Essentially, change behaviors are special types of implementation skills that, for many, are the very essence of leadership. The task domain includes technical problem solving and managing technical innovation and creativity. The people level involves managing conflict and managing the change process of personnel (which time and again is hailed as the Achilles' heel of major change). At the organization level, change is performed through decision making (choices that affect the organization in significant ways) and managing overall organizational change processes.

Dividing each domain into seven behaviors results in twenty-one midlevel behaviors that allow for a relatively detailed analysis of the needs, abilities, and performance of leaders. Exhibit 13.2 summarizes the logical organizers for the three behavior behaviors. The remainder of this chapter discusses each of the task-oriented behaviors in more detail.

MONITORING AND ASSESSING WORK

Monitoring and assessing work involves *gathering and critically evaluating data related to subordinate performance, service or project qualities, and overall unit or organizational performance.* It involves using both quantitative and qualitative indicators, and therefore

Exhibit 13.2

Summary of the Three Behavior Domains

	Leader actions: behavior domains		
	Task	People	Organizational
Assessment/evaluation functions	1. Monitoring and assessing work	1. Consulting	1. Scanning the environment
Formulation and planning functions	2. Operations planning	2. Planning and organizing personnel	2. Strategic planning
Implementation functions	3. Clarifying roles and objectives	3. Developing staff	3. Articulating the mission and vision
	4. Informing	4. Motivating	4. Networking and partnering
	5. Delegating	5. Building and managing teams	5. Performing general management functions
"Change" functions	6. Problem solving	6. Managing conflict	6. Decision making
	7. Managing innovation and creativity	7. Managing personnel change	7. Managing organizational change

it is exhibited in a wide range of discrete behaviors. Supervisors tend to focus most on the work of individual employees, work standards and procedures, and problem identification (individual cases); executives focus on overall program effectiveness and efficiency, fund balances and resource levels. However, midlevel managers often have special responsibility for monitoring and assessing the details of organizational performance.[3]

Monitoring can be disaggregated into three important aspects. The first aspect involves defining what is important to monitor and observe. The world is too full of data to monitor everything in detail; therefore, indicators must generally be strategically selected and defined. Furthermore, because routine data gathering is expensive, one wants as few indicators as possible, but nonetheless enough to provide an accurate picture of operations and organizational health. The definition of indicators might include process/progress indicators as well as output indicators. Different indicators are often needed to track different qualities: timeliness, accuracy, presentation, cost, effectiveness, and so forth. Some indicators are needed for different levels of analysis: individuals versus groups versus the entire organization. Some indicators are needed for areas that only indirectly affect service or production, such as absenteeism, employee satisfaction, and turnover. The relatively recent emphasis on the appropriate selection of critical indicators has led to the popularity of the "balanced scorecard" approach (Kaplan and Norton 1996).[4] The public sector lagged in this area for many years, but the performance measurement movement has blossomed since 1990 (see the work of Epstein 1992; Hatry 1999; Ammons 2001; Holzer and Lee 2004; and others).

A second aspect of gathering data is the consistent and disciplined review of the information. It is not uncommon for data reports to go unanalyzed, for studies and technical analyses to go unread, and for individual and unit performance statements to be hastily glossed over. The problem is that managers, especially as they become more senior, are bombarded with so much information that it can be a full-time job to review and analyze it. Understandably, managers learn to be selective and skim because they generally track trends and have redundant sources of information. Yet, the liabilities of not maintaining a rigorous review of data can be enormous. Emerging crises may be missed, which can result in financial overruns or media exposés. Weak review of data may result in poor understanding of problems, which in turn can lead to misdiagnosis and loss of technical credibility.

The third aspect of data gathering is the integration of qualitative sources. Problems cannot be detected and understood solely through data and performance reports. The popular acronym MBWA means "managing by walking around" and is a reminder to managers that valuable information can be gleaned from direct observation and casual conversations. Inspections of various types—for example, work samples and site visits—are helpful in paying attention to the details of production and facilities. Various types of review meetings can be used to monitor project progress or evaluate results after the fact.

While monitoring the work implies a relatively passive set of activities in order to gather information neutrally, the second subelement, assessing the work, refers to the more active decision making that occurs once the information has been collected. Simplifying for clarity, managers decide that the data are either within an acceptable range or not. If the data indicate that performance standards or organizational health factors are within an acceptable range, they will generally integrate any minor adjustments and follow up on a low-priority basis as opportunities arise. However, monitoring occasionally results in surprising data, information about problems, and revelations about potential crises. This causes issues to receive high priority and to be put at the top of the action queue for interventions. In terms of the behavioral taxonomy presented here, acceptable data generally flow most naturally into operations planning, clarifying roles and objectives, informing, and planning personnel activities. However, unacceptable data flow more frequently into technical problem solving and conflict resolution, and sometimes into organizational decision making. Various leader change skills are often necessary.

Careful monitoring and assessing of unit or organizational work are important as the basis of planning, clarifying, delegating, problem solving, developing, and, indirectly, most other behavioral competencies. The task can be tedious and time-consuming, but it serves as the basis for leadership accountability. Are the rules being followed, the plans being implemented, and standards being maintained as expected? Although it is possible for managers to spend too much time performing this competency, more often than not managers do too much of a single type of monitoring and assessing such as analyzing quantitative data in the confines of their offices at the expense of MBWA. Occasionally managers have "analysis paralysis," which means that they spend so much time analyzing and are so loath to making decisions without extensive data that they act too late or fail to act at all (Loveday 2008).

Studies have generally shown that more monitoring and assessing correlates to greater effectiveness (Komaki 1986). Thach and Thompson (2007) ranked employee performance management as fourteenth of twenty. In addition, monitoring and assessing have, to some extent, a positive "Hawthorne effect"; that is, the mere act of explicit attention by superiors tends to produce more and better work (Larson and Callahan 1990). In terms of public managers, an OPM study of twenty-two midlevel competencies (including some traits and skills) indicated that the related but narrower concept of "internal controls" was ranked dead last in importance by executives and close to last by supervisors and managers (for whom it was the most important of the three groups). In a more comprehensive discrete analysis, supervisors gave this competency both focus and range of attention. Executives did not give it a high focus but had a moderate range of discrete behaviors (see Exhibit 13.3).

Guidelines

1. *Define and measure key indicators of progress and performance.* Leaders need accurate and timely data, which can only come from a variety of measures that are carefully selected and scrupulously maintained. Process indicators allow leaders to detect problems early and correct them. Performance indicators assist leaders to plan, make decisions, and make changes in the organization. It is a leader's responsibility to make sure that there are good indicators and to add to or change them over time.

2. *Compare progress with plans.* The data from monitoring can provide an "early warning system" only if they are used and analyzed. One of the primary tools for problem recognition is the comparison of data with plan specifications. Such plans can be budgetary, work quotas, project schedules, contractual, and so on. The detailed comparison of data and plans becomes particularly important with large complex projects, when services or production are being changed, or when there has been a lot of organizational upheaval or change.

3. *Maintain a variety of sources of information.* Data should be both quantitative and qualitative. Quantitative data should include a variety of quality measures, measures for progress and final performance, financial and customer data, as well as data about employee conditions and development. Qualitative data add greatly to a leader's insight into the data. Qualitative data are gleaned by "walking around," providing an open-door policy, making site visits (especially unannounced), and conducting occasional surveys of employee or customer opinions (a combination of a quantitative and qualitative technique).

4. *Ask clarifying questions.* Walking around is not enough. Leaders talk to a variety of people. They must engage people by asking discerning questions and probing for information. Sometimes these questions are intended to confirm what leaders believe to be true, to find out different perspectives of an issue, or to learn about new problems. Quality questioning demonstrates not only insight but also interest in both the work and worker.

5. *Encourage open and honest reporting.* Quality data are likely only in an organizational climate that encourages accuracy and honesty. The Enron corporate

Exhibit 13.3

Number of Federal Executives and Supervisors Rating Task-Oriented Competencies among the Top 20 or Top 100 Competencies

	Executives		Supervisors	
	Top 20 competencies	Top 100 competencies	Top 20 competencies	Top 100 competencies
Monitoring/assessing	0	7	1	8
Operations planning	1	10	0	5
Clarifying roles	0	7	3	8
Informing	1	4	2	7
Delegating	2	2	2	2
Problem solving	3	5	1*	5
Managing innovation	1	3	1	3
Total	8	38	10	38

Note: Based on a study of 150 competencies. Competencies selected based on a rating of very important or crucial by those who reported that competency applied to their position.

*The discrete problem-solving competency measured here was the highest for supervisors for all behavioral domains and the highest for executives in the task domain.

scandal of 2002 was precipitated by executives who led the way in manipulating and distorting data. Public sector equivalents occur when law enforcement departments do not rigorously investigate recalcitrant members, or when whistle-blowing mechanisms are not in place and whistle-blowers are not protected. On a more personal scale, leaders must be careful not to "punish the messenger," as well as to respect those who criticize, and to reward those who are willing to step forward regarding undetected problems.

6. *Conduct review meetings.* There should be a constant exchange of data about progress and performance among leaders and workers, as well as among partners. Such meetings provide an opportunity to compare data with plans, to identify problems, to brainstorm solutions, and to adjust plans. Additionally, review meetings should be conducted after large projects ("postmortems") to see what lessons can be learned for the next time.

OPERATIONS PLANNING

All types of rigorous planning assess current conditions, decide on what should be done, and detail how it should be done. Operations planning in particular *focuses on coordinating tactical issues into a detailed blueprint.* Therefore, in operations planning organizational directions have already been set, policies established, and overarching strategies selected. Similar (but not identical terms) for this concept are tactical planning, action planning, program planning, implementation, and project management.[5] Contingency planning is a special type of operations planning that takes into account either the problems most likely to disrupt operations (e.g., employee absences or resignations) or unexpected crises that would jeopardize the central mission or basic safety (e.g., crisis planning).

Generally speaking, operations planning involves deciding on a planning model, determining what logistical elements are necessary to include, coordinating the plan with others,
and implementing the plan. Formal elements of operations planning result in schedules,
memoranda, and work orders, as well as coordination with budgets and strategic, comprehensive, emergency, or other official plans. The informal elements include individual
consultations, group meetings, and leader reflection. Sometimes operations planning is so
decentralized that it is almost invisible. For example, in many case management systems
where workers are relatively well cross-trained, the only immediately apparent operational
planning decisions are the hiring of staff, scheduling of vacations, and direction of special
projects in which workers manage their own workflow. At the other extreme, operations
planning may be centrally planned in great detail and involve shifting workers among
locations, changing work schedules (say from the day to the swing shift), making small
changes in the services offered, adjusting the presentation of services, and deciding the
exact allocation of allowable costs. This more detailed scheduling is common in military
and quasi-military operations (e.g., corrections and law enforcement), high-quantity
production operations (e.g., in agencies like public hospitals, the U.S. Immigration and
Naturalization Service, U.S. Customs Service, Internal Revenue Service, motor vehicles,
audit agencies, and other inspections functions), and research/scientific operations (e.g.,
the National Aeronautics and Space Administration and the Centers for Disease Control
and Prevention). Operations planning functions vary enormously not only by agency but
also by position. Some management and expert positions are defined largely by their operations responsibilities (e.g., operations commanders for fire departments, or the senior
central staff charged with writing policy manuals based on legislative language), while
others (at all levels) have few operations functions because of the nature of the work or
because operations functions have been specialized in other positions.

Some organizations become victims of overplanning, especially centralized planning
that leads to rigidity and lack of regionalization. Planning rigidity has been endemic to
all advanced civilizations; Publius reminded his Roman brethren: "It is a bad plan that
admits no modification" (maxim 469). Likewise, some leaders spend nearly all their
time in an operations mode without paying enough attention to the people side of the
job. However, generally far more dangerous for an organization or leader is a lack of
operations planning. (See Exhibit 13.4 about winning wars through tactics rather than
strategy.) The major glitches that occur because of poor operational planning infuriate
employees, clients/customers, and organizational partners. Although good operations planning is little noticed, poor operations planning can be glaring, and leads to accusations of
unprofessionalism, incompetence, or nonfeasance. Taken together, both monitoring and
assessing and operations planning are often taken for granted; nonetheless, they provide
the basics for most other competencies and the basis for most of the work that leaders do.
Even though substantial portions of these competencies may be delegated, leaders who
are sloppy—or allow sloppiness—in these areas often come short in their careers as some
"unforeseen" problems dog them or a crisis occurs due to an inability to forecast.

Many tools are used in operations planning. Some focus on scheduling elements.
Most common are deployment charts (e.g., ranging from Gantt charts to planning

Exhibit 13.4

Winning Wars Through Tactics Rather than Strategy

Winning wars through superior strategy has long been highly esteemed, and, in fact, almost revered by many historians and moviemakers. Yet, good military men know that good strategies rely as much on solid operations deployment as on fresh or clever ideas. George Herbert pointed out the importance of small operational differences in winning battles. "For want of a nail the shoe is lost; for want of the shoe the horse is lost; for want of the horse the rider is lost." That rider was the deciding element in the apocryphal battle, of course, as was that battle in the war.

Sometimes operations planning—or tactical planning in military campaigns—may be *more* important than strategies. This is true when brilliant strategies become well known; the enemies of Rome came to know the Latin strategies all too well but seldom were able to match their brilliant deployment. Frequently, good strategies become irrelevant or overextended and the victory goes to those with tactical endurance. The Germans began World War II with far superior strategies but ended up losing badly in the end. In World War II, they simply went around the impregnable French Maginot Line of military defense that separated Germany and France. Rather than going up against the line of forts that separated the borders, they invaded France though neutral Belgium. The blitzkrieg ("lightning campaign"), professional military, and superior equipment were initially crushing. Yet, in the end, it was overextension that defeated Germany, when it squandered its air superiority in the Battle of Britain and its army in the unnecessary campaign against the Soviets. Ultimately, the Allies reconquered Europe one city and province at a time through well-managed tactical operations.

In some wars, the strategies are so incoherent that tactics reign supreme. This was generally true throughout wars in the Middle Ages. The Hundred Years' War between France and England (1337–1453) is an excellent case in point. Because of the marriage of Eleanor of Acquitaine (i.e., the French Bordeaux region) to Henry II, England could claim it as well as Normandy very distantly through the lineage of William the Conqueror. English armies roamed through France time and again, and the English controlled large portions of the country for extended periods. Yet, the English strategies were generally most dependent on the inability of the French military factions (Orleans and Burgundy) to trust one another, the military incompetence of the French kings, and the lack of a modern French identity. Had British strategies been more coherent, all of western France might today speak English as the city of Bordeaux once did. In addition to their ability to exploit the even greater strategic disarray of the French, the English were consistently more brilliant in operations planning, despite being on enemy soil and being generally outnumbered in the great battles. In two of the great battles of the period, Crecy (1346) and Agincourt (1415), the English showed their tactical brilliance using similar basic strategies. The outnumbered English quickly found better terrain on which to fight—atop slight inclines with flanks that offered cover for lethal archers (forests or towns). The English archers, by far the best in Europe, used the newer longbow technology to great effect, while the French continued to rely on the crossbow and armor. Because these tactics worked poorly against well-fortified cities and castles, the French relied upon them, staying walled in when the English were in the area, and the English avoided them, leaving much of the country a patchwork of hostile domains. It was only with the inspiration of Joan of Arc that the French finally became determined to rid the country of the English, which they did as much by encouraging local revolts as by winning conventional battles and campaigns.

grids), which show the flow of the steps, the people involved, and sometimes time schedules or other critical aspects. Critical path analyses (e.g., PERT charts: program evaluation review technique) examine the shortest time frames for complex projects to ensure that bottlenecks are anticipated. Other tools focus on making the work more efficient before the scheduling occurs. Workflow plans show the physical progress of work through the organization, and flowcharts detail process steps allowing for better analysis and improvements. Other efficiency and effectiveness tools can include mapping techniques, task analysis, unit-cost analysis, performance measurement, and time-and-motion studies.

The research on planning has consistently correlated it with effective leadership (Shipper and Wilson 1992; Kim and Yukl 1995). It also reminds us that much planning is done informally and that planning takes many forms (Kotter 1982). The original midlevel competencies of OPM identified planning and evaluation as sixteenth of twenty-two categories. However, despite the overall importance of various types of planning (especially strategic), operations planning itself is often ranked relatively low compared to other major competencies. The planning category was eliminated in the updated OPM listing (strategic *thinking* was included), and operations planning was only indirectly covered by technical credibility. Somewhat surprisingly, the discrete OPM listing of competencies reveals that federal executives and managers actually spend more time and energy in operations planning activities than do supervisors.[6] For example, executives ranked "establish organization objectives to provide direction for assignment of resources" thirteenth while supervisors ranked it thirty-seventh (still the highest in this category for them). As expected, executives tended to focus on budget alignment and resource allocation issues, while supervisors paid more attention to deadlines and work design. Managers tended to focus most on the coordination between strategic and operational plans as well as the proper selection of projects and program parameters.

Guidelines

1. *Identify the type of action planning necessary.* "Operations planning" is generally the term used for ongoing prioritization and scheduling activities while "program planning" is the term for setting up a new ongoing operation. Special or unusual programs are generally subsumed under the term "project management." These are all tactical-level operations in which policy issues have largely been settled and the detailed logistics need to be worked out.

2. *Determine the logistics that need to be planned.* What is the scope of planning functions to be coordinated? The most common elements include how, when, who, how much, and how well. Of course, the first issue is what needs to be done: the action steps in their logical order. Time scheduling is almost universal: when do the steps need to be accomplished? Who is responsible for each step? Are there cost issues to coordinate and to monitor in the planning process? How will the project be monitored for quality assurance as it proceeds, or how will it be evaluated at the end of the batch or project? The more complex the planning (of whatever type), the more critical it is to document such requirements in condensed planning grids and to remind people of responsibilities, deadlines, problems, and standards. This is especially true in a work world in which increased job enrichment (jobs with numerous types of tasks) has led not only to more interesting work but also to increased fragmentation.

3. *Consult and coordinate to ensure planning accuracy and buy-in.* Consultation and coordination should occur before, during, and after operational planning as necessary. Major planning issues should be resolved before scheduling-type activities occur. Leaders engaged in operations planning will often need to consult with people about specific issues or to customize planning to individual needs to the greatest degree feasible. After plans are drafted, it is often useful to give people a chance to review them in order to detect errors before implementation. While routine operations planning may need little consultation and coordination, entirely new or different operations plans may require extensive review or even public relations–type promotion to "sell" them to those implementing them.

4. *Implement the plan.* Implementation includes transmitting or posting the plan, explaining the details of the plan as they arise, and evaluating its effectiveness. Deviations from normal operations—problems—are a major aspect of leaders' work. Problem solving is dealt with as an entirely separate competency. Even though problem solving gets *much* more attention as a critical leader competency, it is important to remember that the number, severity, and tenacity of problems is highly correlated with the quality of the operations planning done in the first place. That is, good operations planning anticipates or prevents most problems before they arise. Some managers are good problem solvers because they are weak at operations planning, and thus as numerous problems arise downstream in the work process, they become proficient at solving them. This is generally a less efficient, less effective, and less professional way of managing work.

CLARIFYING ROLES AND OBJECTIVES

Clarifying roles and objectives refers to *working with subordinates to guide and direct behavior by communicating about plans, policies, and specific expectations.* It is dissimilar to informing in that it is primarily directed at subordinates, whereas informing focuses equally on supervisors, colleagues, clients, and outsiders. Clarifying roles and objectives involves more active feedback and performance loops than does informing. It is also related to developing staff, but it is more short term and position specific in focus.

There are three subelements of clarifying roles and objectives. (1) Defining job responsibilities ensures that job occupants know the major functions of what they are expected to accomplish. (2) Setting performance goals ensures that job occupants know what standards they are expected to obtain. (3) Providing instruction ensures that they fully understand the tasks, processes, and knowledge to execute each major function and perform at the required standard.

Clarifying roles and expectations is most important with subordinates who are new, when roles and expectations are changing, when roles and expectations are not clearly articulated in policies, procedures, and formal training programs, and with those who have little professional experience. Thus, a supervisor of an area requiring extensive technical training, but whose agency's formal training programs are minimal and infrequent, may spend an inordinate amount of time performing this function (Mahoney, Jerdee, and Carroll 1965). On the other hand, a supervisor who has an excellent agency training program or is able to hire well-trained professionals with experience may find that this function is very modest in time demands.

Role clarity is most likely to be clearest in positions in which the range of functions is relatively narrow and consistent. In medium and large companies, it is common to divide production, sales, and administrative support functions. There are many times when functions overlap for efficiency, such as when a salesclerk also assists with returns. However, there are a number of instances in which functional overlap leads to high risk factors. In the fiduciary area for example, it is standard practice to ensure that those collecting and handling money and financial transactions are not the same as those recording receipts and disbursements, in order to reduce the likelihood of embezzlement. In the private sector, a well-known problem occurs when an organization is responsible for assisting customers to save and invest money while simultaneously being allowed to manage and invest organizational funds, which sets up potential conflicts of interest. The removal of the Glass-Steagall Act separating depository and investment banks contributed to the great recession starting in 2008 (Wallenstein 2009). Government agencies frequently have combined regulatory and "service" functions that need to be carefully managed to protect against "cozy" relationships or a lopsided mission balance. A recent example of this issue arose with the Minerals Management Service, which is an Interior Department bureau responsible for regulatory compliance of safety standards as well as for (maximizing) revenue collection, with $10.68 billion being disbursed to the federal, state, tribal treasuries and conservation funds (Minerals Management Service 2010). The agency was rocked by a bribery scandal in 2008 (Savage 2008) and was subsequently shown to have been extremely lax in the enforcement of environmental safety issues, having issued excessive waivers and disregarded environmental risks (Dlouhy 2010).

This function varies across organizational levels more than many other competencies. Clarifying roles and expectations tends to be a primary activity for supervisors and a background activity for executives. In a study of 150 discrete competencies (Van Wart 2002), supervisors ranked helping employees with job performance as 11, advising employees about standards as 12, conducting formal performance appraisals as 17, providing regular guidance as 28, and assisting with job-related problems as 31. Executives ranked these same activities 63, 71, 84, 52, and 106, respectively. However, when it came to directing *broad* policies and guidelines for program planning and development, executives ranked it 26 while supervisors ranked it 81. Managers ranked explaining *significant* goals, activities, and policies to subordinates as 17; executives and supervisors ranked it similarly as 34 and 33, respectively.

Problems resulting from too little or poor clarification of roles and objectives are a major cause of employee frustration, confusion, and turnover (Buckingham and Coffman 1999). Common examples include the following: the employee finds out what the performance standards are only when s/he receives the annual evaluation; employees neglect an important job area because they are unaware of it; employees focus on an area of minor importance; employees rehearse ineffective methods of performing work because they are not corrected. Because people need time to learn and may not understand the language or concepts the first time they are told, this function commonly requires repetition, rephrasing, and confirmation of understanding. Managers who are unclear, not expressive, or impatient may be unaware of how difficult they make it for their subordinates to perform well. Although much less common and generally less problematic, it is possible to focus too much on role and objectives clarification, which can lead to role rigidity, lack of creativity, and micromanagement.

In the research literature categorizing major leadership competencies, clarifying roles and objectives is generally subsumed under larger categories such as initiation of structure (Stogdill 1959), work facilitation (Bowers and Seashore 1966), directive leadership (House and Mitchell 1974), or supervision (Page 1987). Although the major OPM studies do not refer to it directly, it is assumed in their oral and written communication competencies. Only Yukl makes it a separate category (1998). In a study of local (senior) managers, it was self-reported as one of the most pronounced weaknesses by a factor of 8 to 1 (Van Wart 2001).

GUIDELINES

1. *Mutually define job responsibilities.* When job incumbents are new or changing positions, it is critical for the superior to meet with them in order to define their major job responsibilities and the results they are expected to attain. The review should cover a position description, if there is one, or should generate some sort of mission statement for the job. Occasionally, this guideline is useful for ongoing employees when the supervisor is new or when the agreement about work priorities seems unclear. As with all clarifying behavior, it is important to listen to subordinates' ideas carefully and to consider them genuinely, even though the superior is ultimately responsible for the final selection of responsibilities.

2. *Establish priorities among job responsibilities and establish a scope of authority.* Not all of the major responsibilities will have equal priority. What priority will be given to each responsibility? That priority may be partially decided by the season or a logical sequence. Or some priorities may always be higher in terms of total focus and time. A clear understanding of the different weights assigned to each area is critical. Ideally, these priorities are reflected in the performance appraisal process as well. At the same time, it is important that the subordinate's scope of authority be clearly delineated. Common areas of authority are lines of reporting, finance, decision-making autonomy, and external contacts. Common levels of authority in each of these areas are *no* authority (e.g., the subordinate has no employees reporting to him or no independent budget), *moderate* authority (e.g., the subordinate may make significant unilateral decisions but must seek approval before executing), or *full* authority within normal bureaucratic oversight (e.g., the subordinate has numerous subordinates, full signature authority, and the ability to meet independently with important elites outside the organization).

3. *Mutually set goals for each priority area.* Priorities and goals are different. A priority involves how much attention to direct and where. A goal is a specific performance objective to be met. For example, a manager may work with a supervisor in a case management system (in which line workers have a series of

clients or cases to handle) on priorities and goals. Because of a series of retirements and unusual turnover, priorities for the supervisor for the upcoming year
may be mutually determined to be (in order): staffing (recruitment and hiring),
training and integration of new workers, monitoring the quality of work, general
supervision (e.g., problem solving), and general administration (e.g., scheduling). Each of these priorities should have one to three goals; most jobs have at
least a handful of concrete goals (which in turn may have multiple indicators)
but should not have more than about a dozen (or there will generally be a loss
of focus). Staffing may be reflected as an average percentage of authorized lines
that are filled. Training and integration may be determined by the percentage of
new employees fully trained, an average case review score (number of errors
found in files by an independent reviewer) three months after training, and a
new-employee turnover rate. Monitoring the quality of work may be reflected
by an average case review score for the entire unit. General supervision may
be determined by a productivity level (average number of cases per employee
per year), and overall turnover. General administration may be reflected by the
absence of major problems and the accomplishment of special projects.

4. *Pay attention to the basics of goal-setting theory*. Research on goal setting
(performance standards) highlights that those leaders who do it well improve
quantity and quality significantly, and sometimes dramatically (Earley, Wojnaroski, and Prest 1987; Locke and Latham 1990). There are four elements to
good goal setting. Good goals tend to be clear and specific. For example, a goal
of being "efficient and effective" is vague and nonspecific. An efficiency goal
can be effectively translated into quantifiable completion rates, process rates,
and output measures. Effectiveness can be translated into accuracy rates, standards on important quality dimensions such as timeliness, or outcome measures
(such as number of people employed three months after the completion of a job
training program). Good goals are challenging but realistic (often called "stretch
goals"). When allowed to determine their own goals in an energized environment, most people will set hard but realistic goals for themselves and try hard
to achieve them. Of course, what constitutes challenging but realistic goals is
contextual. An extremely high-performing unit that has lost several of its best
workers may find maintaining current standards a challenging goal. On the other
hand, relatively new employees can substantially improve their productivity
by simply dedicating themselves to reaching the next performance level. Good
goals include deadlines or time frames. For projects, deadlines demarcate step
completion as well as overall project completion. Time frames for continuous
types of work allow comparability of one period with the next, or one person/
unit with another. Good goals involve feedback loops. They should be mutually
set whenever possible (as suggested in management by objectives, or MBO).
Further, they provide an opportunity for people to monitor their own progress
(self-feedback), as well as frame discussions of problems with others (not only
one's superior, but subordinates and colleagues as well).

5. *When providing instruction, be sure to pay attention to the basics of informa-tion and learning theory.* It is worthwhile to keep four elements in mind. First, people work better when they understand the rationale behind an instruction or direction. Of course, there are exceptions to this principle, for example, time constraints, but generally this is an important part of the socialization process. Second, use clear language. This means that the communicator avoids making offhand comments or numerous assumptions about what the recipient knows. Instead the communicator defines terms and concepts, is careful to indicate the order of events, presents material in "bite-sized" steps or chunks that are num-bered or labeled, and reinforces oral instructions with written notes or materials. Third, good instruction provides examples or demonstrations whenever possible. A sample of an ideal work product is an invaluable teaching device, as is the demonstration of how a piece of equipment works. Finally, good instructors check for comprehension. In formal training, this may be measures on a test, exercise, or participant simulation. In informal settings, it may involve asking the learner to rephrase the discussion or demonstrate the behavior. Sometimes it simply means asking questions to probe for understanding or monitoring actual performance.

INFORMING

Informing *provides business-related information to subordinates, superiors, peers, or people outside the organization.* Three important functions are accomplished by inform-ing activities. First, informing facilitates coordination of work. Second, informing shapes the mood about work and strategies that will be most effective. Third, informing serves a public relations or image function. For example, in a single afternoon a supervisor may call several outside vendors to move deliveries up, talk to another supervisor about some client complaints, respond to a subordinate with a request for technical information, tell another employee about a special request for the central office to which they will need to respond, write a memorandum to the manager about the unit's accomplishments for the year, and end the afternoon with a briefing about a budgetary shortfall.

Informing occurs through oral communications (i.e., one-on-one discussions, telephone calls, group meetings, and briefings) as well as written communication (i.e., e-mail, memo-randa and letters, news and promotional articles, postings, reports). The more technical aspects of informing simply provide the information that people need to do their jobs and to coordinate tasks. Informing also provides an opportunity for managers to shape mood and strategy by selecting information to relay and the manner of delivering it. Bad news may be provided as an opportunity for improvement or a reason to work harder; good news as a cause for celebration and encouragement. Finally, informing is an opportunity to promote individuals, the unit, or the organization.

Occasionally, there are reasons to constrain information in both the private and public sectors. In the private sector, information about trade secrets and competitive advantage is often tightly held. In the public sector, privacy concerns occur in cases related to confidential information, employment issues, and the like (e.g., the Privacy Act of 1974). However, much more information is guarded than is generally wise (Bass 2008, 745–756). Freely communicated information tends to foster goodwill and realism. Withholding information (or simply failing to make it available) often leads to accusations of secrecy and concerns about mismanagement or corruption.

In Mintzberg's classic study of managerial work (1973), three of ten roles are heavily affected by informing behaviors: liaison, disseminator, and spokesman. The OPM midlevel competencies of oral and written communication (which are first and third most important for executives and supervisors, respectively) are key aspects of informing. The more discrete aspects related to informing were ranked as moderately important by federal managers with "informing subordinates about developments and their impact on organizational activities" being in the top twenty for all levels of managers (Van Wart 2002).

Guidelines

1. *Determine what information others need and want.* People need information from leaders whose jobs make them linking pins in the organization (Likert 1967). Talk to people about the types of technical or routine needs they have related to production, coordination, and job assistance. Of course, people need information about changes and problems so that they can respond effectively in their various roles. People not only *need* information, but they *want* it in order to be involved and to have their concerns allayed. This is particularly important when there is a crisis or emergency. If people are not well informed during a difficult period, rumors tend to circulate and subordinates tend to feel alienated, neglected, and/or powerless. Today's employees are particularly critical of information lapses, and managers who do not inform their superiors of potential problems are generally held in low regard.

2. *Determine the best way to relay information.* Sometimes the best form may be a confidential face-to-face session, and at other times it may be a general meeting. Good leaders are very careful about the means, quality, and number of sources that they provide. As the old adage points out, knowledge is power, and thus, informing is the use and demonstration of that power. Revealing confidential information too broadly, concealing general information from public dissemination, and relaying sloppy messages that are misinterpreted are examples of serious problems that a manager may be blamed for if s/he is slipshod about informing. The more important the information, the more sources of information the leader may want to use. Frequently, leaders want to ensure that subordinates and others have direct access to technical information (i.e., reports, user groups, training sessions, etc.) so that they can focus on more strategic information.

3. *Manage information flow strategically.* First, it is important to guard against information overload. Communication overload causes several problems. It may result in diminished productivity due to trivial information acquisition, the ignor-

ing of all information, inappropriate interpretation of information, or failure to distinguish critical data. Therefore, good communicators restrict information to relevant issues, but provide expanded access on a special or as-needed basis. For example, a three-sentence memorandum might identify the significant aspect of a policy change, but the entire policy document might be included as an electronic attachment. The practice of highlighting information is critical for busy people who are bombarded with data but who want to know the core information. Second, information can shape the mood of the recipients. Information can stir people to action, caution them to be more careful, or enthuse them about a difficult project. Good communicators and effective leaders also manage information flow for propitious opportunities. On the other hand, information manipulation, excessive secretiveness, or distortion will eventually result in an unfavorable impression of a leader.

4. *Inform people about accomplishments and promote successes.* Potentially, one of the best aspects of a leader's job is the dissemination of information about what the unit or group has achieved. This encourages subordinates, raises the reputation of the unit or organization, and often results in preferred access to resources in the future. Leaders who do not share accomplishments miss opportunities for goodwill; leaders who take too much credit engender distrust.

DELEGATING

Delegating is *a type of power sharing in which subordinates are given substantial responsibilities and/or authority.* While it is related to other forms of participative leadership such as consultation and joint decision making and is often arrayed with them as the most robust form, it is actually a distinct category. Whereas the initiation and locus of action is with the leader in consultation and joint decision making, that shifts to the recipient in delegation. The discussion about delegation should be balanced with the discussion on decisiveness in chapter 11. The issue is not whether decisiveness (e.g., unilateral directions) or delegation is best; *both* are critical for good leadership. The issue is *when* and *how* to use them and the intermediate forms of leadership between them (e.g., consultation and joint decision making).

Delegation has two major elements: the designation of responsibility and the allocation of authority. Responsibilities involve the assignment of duties, whereas authority is the level of decision making allowed. Thus, a manager may be given a second program area to manage (additional responsibility) but not the additional authority to make nonroutine decisions. Or a manager may be given additional authority to make hiring decisions as funds are available in an area that s/he already manages. Common areas in which the level of authority varies include budget and financial decisions, hiring and discipline decisions, problem-solving solutions, and program changes. It is possible for leaders to be delegated many responsibilities and little authority (common with frontline supervisors), or for them to have just a few responsibilities and substantial authority (common for managers of special areas such as budget, audit, or highly targeted operational areas).

Most common, however, is an increasing level of both responsibility and authority as a leader ascends in the organization.

While responsibilities are largely quantitative, authority is largely qualitative. That is, levels of authority range from minimal to nearly complete authority. Authority is completely circumscribed when all nonoperational and nonroutine decisions must be turned over to the next level of management. This is common for supervisors in large production-type organizations. Authority is minimal when nonroutine decisions must be determined jointly with the next layer of management, or all decisions must receive prior approval and the approval process is not necessarily automatic. This is common with midlevel managers seeking to make program changes (an area in which authority is usually carefully guarded). Authority is substantial when the approval process is largely perfunctory, or when notification and action are simultaneous. This is common for senior managers as they expend, hire, and make program adjustments within broad decision parameters already delegated to them. Authority is full when decisions are not subject to immediate review except under extraordinary conditions.[7] Even frontline supervisors often have full authority for routine decisions relating to operations (e.g., scheduling, appraisals, work rejection, etc); however, the more robust forms of authority that affect organizational well-being (major program changes, shifts in organizational philosophy, major legal actions, etc.) are primarily reserved for executives.

The virtues of delegation are many. It can improve decisions when subordinates are competent in or closer to the issues to be handled. It generally leads to greater job satisfaction and is a form of job enrichment. Delegation helps busy leaders free up their time for other responsibilities. Finally, it is a powerful form of personnel development. Subordinates learn about how to handle responsibility and authority wisely only by getting gradually larger increments of it over time. Thus, delegation is an essential training opportunity that superiors should bestow upon subordinates as circumstances merit.

The reasons for not delegating can be both legitimate and illegitimate. If subordinates are not competent because of lack of training, experience, or temperament, then it is unwise and unfair to delegate to them, at least in the short term. However, providing this training and experience is part of the long-term responsibility of leaders, even when the employee skills pool is shallow. Many responsibilities are core to a leader's function of providing direction and should not be delegated because of a loss of necessary power. Finally, some responsibilities and authority cannot be delegated because of issues of confidentiality. Yet, all too often, leaders fail to delegate for the wrong reasons. Some simply fail to consider others' judgment as good as their own, which, even if true at the moment, may be because the leader "hoards" information and experience. Some fail to overcome the anxiety that they will diminish their own power. Some are too concerned that a mistake will be made "during their watch" and believe that they can prevent it only by closely guarding their decision-making authority. In rational terms these leaders are emphasizing accuracy and the short term over the benefits of personnel development, succession planning, and long-term organizational vitality. Ultimately, they are putting their personal comfort level and perceptions of safety before the organization's need for fully engaged employees and a long-term talent pool.

Delegating is rarely its own major category in leadership taxonomies. Stogdill (1959) and Yukl (1998) are the exceptions. Generally delegation is subsumed under the broader category called supervision or discussed separately as empowerment. In an analysis of 150 competencies, delegation was very highly ranked, although only in two items (Van Wart 2002).[8] In terms of giving "subordinates authority and discretion to carry out work activity and make decisions," executives ranked it eighth and supervisors fourteenth. Both supervisors and executives ranked "empower employees nearest the data with authority and responsibility to make decisions" in the top twenty competencies. In a study of local managers, it was ranked the single most serious behavioral weakness, with almost no one identifying it as a strength (Van Wart 2001).

Guidelines

1. *Assess opportunities for delegation.* Delegation should be done with forethought. In fact, delegation may mean an analysis of the leader's responsibilities and work-load as well as the subordinate's. Therefore, a work analysis should be done from time to time, even if that analysis is an informal listing of job duties. Furthermore, increasing levels of authority in terms of decision making or independence is a good way to reward and develop subordinates.

2. *Emphasize personnel development and empowerment when possible.* Certain types of tasks or situations are more appropriate for delegation. Certainly when the subordinate is as qualified or more qualified to handle a responsibility because of time, experience, or closeness to the work, delegation should be strongly considered. Tasks that are not critical but are time sensitive are also good candidates. That is, while the superior may do a better job, competing demands that make it difficult or impossible to accomplish all tasks may make delegation a suitable alternative. This is common when meeting times conflict. It is also important to delegate not only tasks that are easily within the subordinate's range but also some tasks that might require a moderate stretch in the subordinate's capabilities. The pain of small failures should not necessarily be regarded as negative: "Those things that hurt, instruct" (Benjamin Franklin). Of course, excessive delegation causes burnout and is a major reason for turnover of high-quality employees.

3. *Balance responsibilities and authority.* Most managers feel far more comfortable delegating responsibilities than delegating the complementary authority. To employees, this feels like additional workload without the tools (i.e., the authority) to accomplish it and can make them frustrated and angry. However, empowerment means that employees are given the requisite authority. Of course, grants of empowerment should be accompanied by assignment of accountability, too. Misuse of authority (malfeasance or misfeasance), and nonuse of authority (nonfeasance) should result in lower evaluations, or, if severe, punishment.

4. *Specify conditions of delegation carefully.* To the degree possible, it is very helpful to specify the new responsibilities, the scope of authority that accompanies them, and the rewards and punishments for not meeting standards or using authority

well. Ideally this is preceded by a discussion and verbal contract and is followed up with a written statement. This is best done before delegation occurs. Sometimes it is done after delegation has occurred because conditions or the implicit contract have changed, or aspects were not fully understood initially. When the conditions of delegation are poorly articulated and work is not accomplished or problems occur, employees complain (sometimes correctly) that it is not their fault, that they did not have the authority, or that the work was someone else's. These types of problems can largely be forestalled with clear reporting responsibilities so that the superior can monitor progress until the responsibility is being well handled on a uniform basis.

PROBLEM SOLVING

Problem solving involves *the identification, analysis, and handling of work-related problems*. It is related to, but different from, other important competencies discussed in this book, including operations planning (discussed earlier in this chapter), conflict management (chapter 14), and decision making (chapter 15). Operations-planning schedules work in order to prevent problems to the greatest degree possible (and contingency planning devises alternative strategies for routine or critical problems); operations planning has a proactive and long-term focus whereas problem solving is reactive and short term. Conflict management is a special type of problem involving people and therefore often requiring different skills and solutions. Problem solving and decision making use similar logic because they are part of a single continuum. They also have an extremely important distinction: problem solving tends to be more case by case and production focused, whereas decision making is oriented toward direction setting and policy with an eye to the organization at large. Although it is a slight exaggeration, supervisors tend to focus more on problem solving and executives focus more on decision making.

Just as the flow of work tends to be the responsibility of line workers, fixing problems, breakdowns, and interruptions are major responsibilities of management. Many managers go from problem to problem at a frenetic pace (Mintzberg 1973). Managers who are good at solving problems are more likely to be successful, and thus to be promoted. However, problem solving can be addictive to some managers because of its adrenaline rush and hands-on nature, which can choke out more forward-thinking management behaviors. On the other hand, some managers find problems annoying, distracting, and/or overwhelming so they procrastinate in dealing with them, pass them off to others ("buck passing"), or ignore problems altogether. Thus, managing problem solving is as important as the skills that go into problem solving itself.

It is useful to mention some of the common tools that are associated with problem solving. Depending on the type of problem to be solved, different types of tools are more likely to be used (Scholtes 1988). If it is an obvious breakdown in operations planning, then the tools discussed in that section such as flowcharts and work mapping might be used. If the nature of the problem is unclear, then identification tools such as check sheets (which are simple means of collecting data), Pareto charts (which rank problem elements), cause-and-effect diagrams (which link related types of problems by families), and "is/is-not" analysis (which identifies when, where, and how the problem occurs) might be most useful. If it is a control problem or a deviation from standards, then more common tools are control charts, time plots, and scatter diagrams (all of which are methods of graphing trends in order to detect variations and problems). If new solutions are necessary, brainstorming and nominal group technique (a variant of brainstorming that enhances input from all group members) may be the best tools if time is available.

Many of the major competency taxonomies refer to problem solving, although sometimes under other names such as disturbance handling and demand reconciliation. The OPM identifies problem solving as an important midlevel category in both its 1992 and 1999 studies of federal managers; it ranked second for both executives and supervisors and third for managers (U.S. OPM 1997). In a discrete analysis of 150 competencies (Van Wart 2002), problem solving was identified as the very highest behavioral competency for supervisors, and sixth most important for executives and managers ("take corrective action when problems arise").[9] Of course, when the problems involve assisting individual workers with problems, supervisors are far more likely to focus on them (thirty-first) than executives (106th); when the problems are broader, executives are somewhat more likely to focus on them. In a study of local managers (Van Wart 2001), more respondents identified this as a strength than any other competency and none identified it as a weakness. Although the importance of a competency and perceptions of the strength of a competency are entirely separate, it does suggest that many managers are biased toward action-oriented management strategies and that organizations tend to reward them for this behavior.[10]

Guidelines

1. *Identify and classify problems.* From their many sources of information and contacts and because of the nature of their jobs, managers at all levels are bombarded with real and potential problems. Because problem solving is time consuming and energy depleting, often there are many more problems than a manager can reasonably handle. This results in the need for problem management. First, the leader must briefly assess the type of problem, its severity and criticality, and identify the most responsible party to solve it. This is a kind of triage effort. (1) Which problems need to be handled *immediately* because they can be solved quickly, are critical, or are severe and are likely to be solved successfully? Quick and easy problems should be handled at once whenever possible for responsiveness and to avoid neglect of simple issues. Critical problems (e.g., safety concerns or legal infractions) need to be handled immediately even if no certain solution exists, to promote learning from initial efforts. Severe problems that are not critical (e.g., chronic turnover) that are solvable should be handled quickly so they do not fester. However, severe problems with unclear solutions should be further analyzed. (2) Which problems need to be deferred? Generally, there are two times when problems are deferred. First, during a crisis, all but the most

critical problems are deferred. Second, problems that need more analysis are generally deferred in order to bring in others, gather more data, use more robust problem-solving techniques, or implement more complex solutions. This class of problems is very important for the effective manager, so deferral is more a matter of managing the problem than giving it a lower priority (see the next guideline). (3) Some problems are referred to others or ignored altogether. Some problems can be appropriately delegated, or passed on to colleagues or a superior. Some problems can be ignored because they are trivial or not relevant to the work (e.g., unfounded gossip). Some small or unclear problems are temporarily "shelved" as the manager monitors operations and the environment to see if additional episodes occur or if s/he detects a significant trend line that would merit action.

2. *Analyze difficult problems*. Good leaders heed Charles Kettering's advice: "Do not bring me your successes; they weaken me. Bring me your problems; they strengthen me." While some problems can be handled instinctively, or because of a crisis need to be handled decisively, a leader's true skill in fixing problems lies in handling the difficult ones, handling multiple problems with a single solution, finding innovative solutions for problems, or best of all, turning problems into opportunities. This type of problem solving invariably requires some genuine reflection or empirical analysis. Good problem solvers do not jump to solve every problem. They savor many of them as they cull reasons for the problem, look for connections, and allow their minds to mix and match problems together for broader solutions. For example, a good but troublesome employee might be matched with a challenging special project that will give him the attention s/he craves. Many problems are poorly understood and additional information is required in order to resolve them. Yes, the revenues at the city-owned civic center may have been going down, but to what degree is that the result of the popularity of the venues presented, the fees charged, the ticket prices, the advertising, the parking, the perceptions of safety, the general ambiance of the building itself, or other types of competition that have developed? The manager should not simply rely on gut impressions, because several problems may be occurring simultaneously, and fixing only one (such as constructing a new building) may solve only a small part of the overall problem. Some of the many strategies that can be used to approach problem solving are illustrated in Exhibit 13.5.

3. *Generate alternatives*. Ambiguous and difficult problems also invariably can be approached multiple ways. Rarely is there a single way to attack the problem, and rarely is the first "good" solution the best solution that can be devised after further reflection and comparison. Generating alternatives hones thinking and provides opportunities to graft portions of one solution onto another. Generating alternatives is often required by policymakers or executives in order to include important constituencies in or outside the organization.

4. *Choose an alternative*. The choice of an alternative is the decision that is the most visible part of problem solving. Other than the time frame for the choice, which is largely implicit in the analysis step, the major issue is the degree of participation

Exhibit 13.5

Five Improvement Strategies

All problems share a similar decision-making protocol: identify and clarify the problem, identify the alternatives, choose an alternative, implement the decision, and evaluate the results. Because of the different types of problems, however, different strategies are employed to emphasize different aspects of the decision-making process. Some of the more common strategies for problem solving in organizations are the following:

1. *Collect data or collect better data.* One of the most common situations when a problem arises is that the existing data do not provide the basis for an informed decision about a problem. When this happens, good problem solvers must clarify data collection goals, develop procedures and operational procedures, work with people to collect quality data, and check for data reliability. This strategy sometimes leads to obvious solutions, and sometimes it simply provides the substance for a more rigorous analysis of the problem. Some of the activities on which one might focus are:

   • Study the needs and concerns of customers.
   • Conduct time-and-motion-type analysis.
   • Analyze exactly where problems are occurring.
   • Experiment with a process.

2. *Define the process more accurately.* Sometimes processes are not well defined, or have been adjusted over time so that confusion exists. Just a clear map of the process may help substantially with obvious improvements as well as with training. Common elements of this strategy are flowcharts of the process and diagrams of the physical work flow.

3. *Standardize a practice.* When variants of practices exist, and the variants are not related to substantial and useful customization, then standardization may be important. Standardization helps with quality control, consistency (fairness), and quality improvement. The most important element of standardization is the identification of best practices. It is also important to test these practices to ensure that they work well in all cases. Standardized processes are easier to measure, monitor, and fix. Important mass-production processes should be under statistical control; that is, they should be monitored continuously and the data should be charted regularly for process consistency.

4. *Error-proof the process.* What are the common mistakes that are made in a process? How can those mistakes be reduced or eliminated? Some of the common methods for simple problems are: changing and improving forms, providing better written directions, providing overlapping methods of information (such as both a written and graphical presentation of information), and providing a checklist for the user.

5. *Reengineer a process to streamline it.* Sometimes a process is too long and unwieldy. This occurs over time with the ad hoc addition of steps and with changes in technology and locations. Reengineering allows for rationalization of the process; that is, reengineering allows people to examine the entire process at a single time to reintroduce simplicity and efficiency. Noncritical steps are eliminated. Because many of these noncritical steps may be approvals, workers may need to be made aware of new accountability that may fall to them for process accuracy and timeliness.

in the decision. Managers must be prepared to make some decisions unilaterally, some with consultation or jointly, and to delegate other decisions entirely, even when they have identified the problem, conducted the analysis, and generated alternatives themselves. Good problem solvers understand that both narrow and broad participation have their strengths, and vary their inclusiveness according to the characteristics of the problem situation. Narrow participation is faster, especially in times of crisis, more efficient, especially for trivial or easy problems, more suitable when the decision maker is well informed about all aspects of the problem, more fitting when the goals of employees diverge substantially from those of the organization (e.g., salary issues), and more appropriate when confidentiality is an issue. On the other hand, broader participation enhances buy-in of multiple constituencies, encourages involvement and a sense of ownership, is more likely to provide a systems perspective because of multiple perspectives, tends to be very important when others have critical information, is more apt to arrive at an innovative solution, and is much better at providing development opportunities for others to learn about management or the issues affecting the organization (Vroom and Jago 1988).

5. *Take responsibility for fixing problems.* Just because a solution is decided upon does not ensure that action will occur, that is, that there will be effective implementation. There must be a commitment to follow-through. Many challenges can diminish problem implementation. For example, perhaps an executive enjoys the creative aspects of problem solving but is weak at handing off problems to others because of vague communication and weak rewards (or even attention) for those who do follow up. Perhaps a manager decides on one solution but becomes distracted by a series of other pressing problems and loses interest in the issue. Perhaps a supervisor makes a serious effort to implement a solution, but it was so poorly conceived that s/he becomes overwhelmed with the mess created rather than rising to the occasion. Problem implementation, then, requires many of the leader characteristics discussed in earlier chapters: willingness to assume responsibility, energy, resilience, flexibility, continual learning, technical and analytic skills, communication skills, and sometimes even courage.

MANAGING TECHNICAL INNOVATION AND CREATIVITY

Managing technical innovation and creativity involves *establishing an environment that encourages and provides the tools for learning, flexibility, and change, and that also provides implementation support for new or cutting-edge programs/processes.* It is useful, but not critical, for leaders themselves to have new insights into situations and be able to make organizational improvements from their own insights. It is more important today for leaders to be able to recognize and support the ideas of others than to be the source of those ideas themselves (Makri and Scandura 2010).[11]

This competency—managing the technical aspects of innovation and creativity—is highly related to two others that will be discussed in later chapters: managing personnel change and managing organizational change. Frequently, these ideas are combined into one or two behaviors or concepts; indeed, they certainly are highly intertwined. However, they are separated here and elsewhere (see Yukl 1998) because (1) the concrete microbehaviors constituting each are quite often different and (2) the change behavior domain is so large and important but also very difficult for contemporary managers. While managing technical innovation involves the encouragement and implementation of learning and ideas on an individual or incremental basis, managing organizational change focuses on wholesale shifts in the policies, directions, major processes, or culture of the organization (see chapter 15).[12] Although a part of the difference is the sheer scope of change, often there is a qualitative difference as well. Whereas an innovation might be the integration of a new geographic information system (GIS) for program analysts, an organizational change might be the *systematic* redistribution of resources based on the findings of that new GIS analysis. Yet, just because new technology is available, or a new policy is promulgated, it does not mean that people will like, accept, or implement it. Thus, managing personnel change—mental attitudes, physical readjustments, and the ability to cope—is quite separate from the other technical and structural aspects of change (see chapter 14). Examples of brilliant technological breakthroughs that go unutilized for years because of resistance by personnel are common in public sector organizations, as are examples of line workers and supervisors who ignore or even sabotage organizational change policies with which they do not agree.

Because *managing* innovation and creativity is really mostly about *increasing* it throughout the organization at a grassroots level, it is highly related to the concept of the learning organization. Senge's overall definition of the learning organization is "where people continually expand their capacity to create the results they truly desire, where new and expansive patterns of thinking are nurtured, where collective aspiration is set free, and where people are continually learning how to learn together" (Senge 1990, 3). A much more popular overall definition is Garvin's: "an organization skilled in creating, acquiring, and transferring knowledge, and at modifying its behavior to reflect new knowledge and insights" (Garvin 1993, 79).

Although all the major writers on the learning organization speculate about the reasons for its ascendance as an idea (even if the reality has been less than common), it is useful to look to a prominent public sector theorist for the specifics within that particular environment. In the first major essay in the public administration field that discusses learning organizations in light of the attention that Senge brought to the concept, Kettl (1994) provided four major reasons in support of the learning organization in the public sector. First, he speculated about the end of bureaucracy as we know it (which he more aptly called the "twilight of bureaucracy") because of the need for faster and more responsive organizations with less expensive overhead (flatter). Second, he pointed out the increased government reliance on external expertise, causing organizations to become more like networks and also causing a whole new set of learning dilemmas surrounding contracting and partnerships. Third, he highlighted a decline of confidence in centralized science solutions, which meant a loss of confidence in expert staff teams managing all organizational change. Finally, knowledge about problems has become highly decentralized, because of the speed of change and the degree of customization more commonly required; therefore, problem solving also needs to stay more localized when possible. In summary, learning organizations should (theoretically) thrive in environments that are very dynamic and in which knowledge is highly dispersed but necessary for successful adaptation. This can be compared to the environments in which traditional bureaucracies exist—whether they are hierarchical bureaucracies more typical of the public sector or rational bureaucracies such as those found in the private sector—where the ideal conditions are stable and knowledge is highly centralized. For a concrete example of the reasons that people innovate in the public sector at the program level, see Exhibit 13.6.

Despite widespread agreement about the enabling conditions for learning organizations (Kanter, Stein, and Jick 1992), they have not flourished as they might because of the exceptional challenges confronting them. First, by definition, the structure is less clear. Typically, learning organizations are flatter, have looser formal links, and look more like networks. While the links are looser in terms of rules and regulations, tight informal links are required in terms of cooperative synergies. Because of the need for constant reorganization to adapt to new problems, they tend to be self-organizing and "messy" (Wheatley 1992). Individuals have larger, but far less defined, roles. When these features are properly functioning they give rise to learning organizations, but, improperly implemented, they lead to confusion, lower productivity, infighting, and lack of organizational focus, among other dysfunctionalities. Second, this type of amorphous structure gives rise to a high degree of stress for many individuals who prefer more "organized" environments, stable conditions and standards, sharper role clarity, and high job security. Those who do work in less structured environments expect higher incentives (e.g., pay, working conditions, and perquisites such as training) for staying in the organization. Further, because of the loose management structures, the more creative types of people bred by the organization are easily alienated and more likely to move to other organizations if conditions are less than ideal. Third, learning organizations require highly trained individuals. This requires background education in the discipline, organizational knowledge about systems, processes, culture, and the like, and training in the specific skills necessary for the job. But it also requires advanced skills to make greater use of learning by sharing, comparing, systems thinking, competing, and suspending disbelief. That is, advanced learners not only learn about basic knowledge and skills, but also become adept at learning how to learn in order to solve entirely new problems that confront the organization. However, the cost of hiring and training employees rises dramatically as better-educated individuals demand better salaries and the cost of constant training, including self-training, increases exponentially. Thus, recruiting and retention problems for learning organizations are particularly challenging.

Often, managing innovation and creativity, as well as change in general, are not integrated into the regular managerial competency taxonomies of leadership theorists. This is not to say that it is not acknowledged as being very important (indeed, some define change skills as being the core of leadership), but just to say that it is often handled separately. The OPM's mid-level competency lists give central importance to either creative thinking (the 1992 listing) or creativity and innovation (1999). Executives ranked creative

Exhibit 13.6

Reasons for Innovation

Jonathan Walters (2001) studied what inspires innovation at the program level. He discovered six "drivers" of innovation.

1. *Feeling frustration with the status quo.* For example, Walters pointed out the frustration that Stephen Goldsmith felt with the status quo when he was elected mayor of Indianapolis. The hierarchical approach to all business was insufficient for some of the big problems he confronted. Therefore, he opened up many public services to competition by the private sector (such as road repair) in order to stimulate new thinking and new motivation.
2. *Responding to crisis.* Crisis is often a powerful driver. Some of the examples Walters identifies are a program in Arizona to find and close abandoned mines after an accidental death, and a recycling program in Seattle, which was in part inspired by the landfill crisis the city was experiencing. Sometimes it is to prevent likely disasters and catastrophes in the future. Past natural and man-made disasters such as tornadoes, floods, and terrorist incidents are strong motivators of innovations for the future.
3. *Focusing on prevention.* Sometimes there has been no crisis or disaster, but a problem is seen emerging and innovation prevents its development. Prevention strategies are most common in health care, safety, and child development.
4. *Emphasizing results.* Some government programs assume results, whether or not they exist. Yet, some programs may actually exacerbate problems more than help them. Welfare programs around the country, which had developed out of the nightmare of the Great Depression and a sincere interest in helping the poor, were widely perceived by the 1990s to be a major cause (not mitigation) of poverty. Welfare innovations in the 1990s were directed at emphasizing results (poverty reduction, training, self-sufficiency) in a changed world. The innovation represented by the Oregon benchmarks program is one example of an emphasis on results. That innovation provided a wide array of measures on community health and tried to provide a tight connection with the question: How are public policies influencing these indicators?
5. *Adapting technology.* This driver is really rather obvious but not always so easy to implement. Some of the major contemporary opportunities in this area include the Internet and geographic information systems. The Internet provides numerous opportunities for enhanced information, responsiveness, co-production of services (ideally lowering government costs), and cost-containment (especially in materials production and dissemination). Geographic information systems allow for better data analysis, tracking and monitoring, and systems planning (especially overlapping systems such as in land-use planning).
6. *Doing the right thing.* Sometimes programs are more about helping people than about results and efficiency per se. For example, the city of Tulsa began a national trend in the early 1990s with a new style of debriefing for rape and abuse victims. Rather than have police debrief the incident in the same law enforcement setting that would be used to interrogate violent offenders, specially trained counselors debriefed victims in more private and comfortable settings. The program was an innovation based on doing the right thing for victims; however, the side benefits also became evident quickly: Victims were far more likely to testify against their assailants.

thinking 11 in importance and supervisors ranked it 16, out of 22 competencies. It was slightly higher in rankings for incoming leaders. In the discrete (1997) analysis of 150 competencies, "establish an environment that encourages innovation" was ranked 12 and 15 for executives and supervisors, respectively (Van Wart 2002). An organizational perspective was, understandably, more pronounced for executives. "Seek opportunities to move the organization toward future goals" and "stress innovation as a means to move the organization forward" were ranked 40 and 50, compared to 103 and 88 for supervisors.

Interestingly, for federal managers innovation issues related to technical improvements ("explore new work methods, systems, or decision-making automation or other technology") hovered only around 100 in rankings for all groups. In a study of local government managers, this competency was frequently mentioned as a major strength by some and as a weakness by others.

Guidelines

1. *Create an environment that fosters learning, flexibility, and change.* In a fast-moving environment, learning and change are constant, which requires an attitude conducive to flexibility. Leaders need to be able to convey the importance not only of innovation and creativity through words but also through actions. Are people supported in training with time off? Are new ideas listened to with enthusiasm? Is there an attitude that no practices are unchangeable? Are there rewards for learning new skills and for innovations? Are innovations disseminated systematically? Although it is individuals who actually learn, they often do so in teams: Is team learning—such as in improvement projects or user groups—encouraged and rewarded?

2. *Encourage a mindset that will encourage high-quality change and innovative learning.* An organization can support lower levels of learning—what Senge would call personal mastery (technical training) and team learning—without really engaging in the types of learning that characterize learning organizations with their absorption of innovation and thirst for useful change. This requires several special qualities. First, significant problems must be seen in the context of broader organizational patterns rather than as discrete events. That is because most problems have ramifications for many people, and the problem solvers are generally only a small subset. Therefore, it is quite possible for them to solve a problem by making matters more difficult for someone else. Second, organizational members must systematically challenge assumptions and mental models (patterned ways of interpreting information based on past experience). Mental models are useful in assisting people to deal with large amounts of information, but they can frequently be based on beliefs or information that is outdated, situationally specific, or simply incorrect.

3. *Provide the tools and opportunities for learning and innovation.* Leaders as managers can provide a number of tools for fostering a learning and change-friendly environment. One is simply to ensure that organizational members have the resources necessary such as time off or the money for training/conference registrations or materials. Leaders can encourage others to see the opportunity to learn from failures and surprises. Not only is this generally a more productive attitude, but it enhances a positive work environment as well. Leaders can sponsor and support experimentation. Ideally, organizations try out new practices on a small scale, with good experimental practices (such as a control group, equivalent time frames, random selection) to the degree possible. Another practice, which

became very popular in the 1990s, is benchmarking. The best-known version of this is when an organization looks at the practices of a high-performing organization in an area of their strength. Through discussions, site visits, and creative discourse, a team adapts practices to its own organization. Ideally, this practice leads to inspiration rather than slavish mimicking. Benchmarking can be interpreted more broadly to mean any rigorous use of comparison. Therefore, it is also possible and quite useful to benchmark against other similar units (e.g., the average), other units in the organization, and even one's own past performance. This aspect of benchmarking is closer to trend analysis. Yet another tool that can be used is competition. Often the public sector discourages a competitive mindset and promotes equal access and conformity to authorized standards. Yet, competition can also be a useful approach at times. It is particularly appropriate at the group level when products and services do in fact compete with others in or outside the public sector and when there is a sense of apathy. Friendly professional competition can even be useful within a unit if it does not lead to information hoarding or alienation, but rather leads to stimulation and striving. However, intercolleague competition must be carefully balanced with team goals, because, as David Sarnoff quipped, "Competition brings out the best in products and the worst in people."

CONCLUSION

Task-oriented competencies include monitoring and assessing work, operations planning, clarifying roles and objectives, informing, delegating, problem solving, and managing innovation and creativity. See Exhibit 13.7 for a review of the major points of the chapter. For many people, task-oriented competencies lack the glamour of other leadership competencies. Some leadership experts prefer to think of them as management—a more technical aspect that is easier to teach and in greater supply (Zaleznik 1977). Yet, detailed studies over the past fifty years have indicated that task-oriented competencies are a cornerstone of leadership (Trottier, Van Wart, and Wang 2008). Several general observations will summarize this chapter.

First, task-oriented behavioral competencies form a basic dynamic for leaders at all levels and in all positions. Leaders need to get things done, done right, and especially, to fix problems and stay up to date. However, as one would logically expect, the task-focus is not consistent across levels and types of positions. Just as line workers tend to focus almost all of their attention on concrete tasks, executives at the other end of the spectrum focus on broad organizational tasks that can seem far removed from the operational business of the organization. Thus, it makes sense that while executives cannot neglect task-oriented management competencies, they can attend to them more efficiently and delegate them more effectively (which is itself a competency). Indeed, leaders must be careful not to let the daily operational aspects of business crowd out the other major leadership foci.

Second, the most prominent task-oriented behavior—problem solving technically

Exhibit 13.7

Summary of Chapter 13

Task-oriented behavior	Subelements of behavior	Major recommendations
Monitoring and assessing *Gathering and critically evaluating data related to subordinate performance, service or project qualities, and overall unit or organizational performance*	• Defining what is important to monitor and observe • Consistent and disciplined reviewing of the information sources • Integrating qualitative sources	1. Define and measure key indicators of progress and performance. 2. Compare progress with plans. 3. Maintain a variety of sources of information. 4. Ask clarifying questions. 5. Encourage open and honest reporting. 6. Conduct review meetings.
Operations planning *Coordinating all tactical issues into a detailed blueprint*	• Deciding on a planning model • Determining what logistical elements are necessary to include • Coordinating the plan with others • Implementing the plan	1. Identify the type of action planning necessary. 2. Determine the logistics that need to be planned. 3. Consult and coordinate to ensure planning accuracy and buy-in. 4. Implement plans and follow-through.
Clarifying roles and objectives *Working with subordinates to guide and direct behavior by communicating about plans, policies, and specific expectations*	• Defining job responsibilities • Setting performance goals • Providing instruction	1. Mutually define job responsibilities. 2. Establish priorities among job responsibilities and establish a scope of authority. 3. Mutually set goals for each priority area. 4. Pay attention to the basics of goal-setting theory. 5. When providing instruction, be sure to pay attention to the basics of information and learning theory.
Informing *Providing business-related information to subordinates, superiors, peers, or people outside the organization*	• Facilitating coordination of work • Shaping the mood about work and strategies that will function best • Serving a public relations or image function	1. Determine what information others need and want. 2. Determine the best way to relay information. 3. Manage information flow strategically. 4. Inform people about accomplishments and promote successes.

(continued)

Exhibit 13.7 *(continued)*

Task-oriented behavior	Subelements of behavior	Major recommendations
Delegating *Power sharing in which subordinates are given substantial responsibilities and/or authority*	• Designating responsibility • Allocating authority	1. Assess opportunities for delegation. 2. Emphasize personnel development and empowerment when possible. 3. Balance responsibilities and authority. 4. Specify conditions of delegation carefully.
Problem solving *Identifying, analyzing, and handling work-related problems*	• Recognizing problems • Investigating problems • Resolving problems	1. Identify and classify problems. 2. Analyze difficult problems. 3. Generate alternatives. 4. Choose an alternative. 5. Take responsibility for fixing problems.
Managing innovation and creativity *Establishing an environment that encourages and provides the tools for learning, flexibility, and change, and that also provides implementation support for new or cutting-edge programs/processes*	• Creating, acquiring, and transferring knowledge in an organizational context • Modifying organizational behavior to reflect new knowledge and insights	1. Create an environment that fosters learning, flexibility, and change. 2. Encourage a mindset that will encourage high-quality change and innovative learning. 3. Provide the tools and opportunities for learning and innovation.

defined—is one of the hardest to learn and one of the easiest to get lured into overutilizing. Problem solving comes out at the top of nearly everyone's list in terms of importance. It often requires technical understanding, the ability to work with people, and good comprehension of the overall system within which problems occur. It takes time to build up the experience base to handle the variety of problems that occur, and really good problem solvers have an indefinable creative spark. Problem solving has a dark side, too. It is especially easy to devote nearly all one's time to problems because they are rarely in short supply. Yet, this means that problem prevention may not be adequate, that people in the organization may be receiving less attention than they need and would like, and the more robust elements of organizational direction setting are being overlooked.

Finally, some task-oriented competencies—monitoring and assessing, operations planning, clarifying roles and objectives, and informing—are critical but frequently underappreciated. When these competencies are performed well, they tend to prevent many problems from occurring downstream in the management process and to allow for more effective delegation. Some leaders learn to practice some of these competencies outside the office by reading reports and writing memoranda at home. Some leaders carefully discipline themselves to review roles and objectives annually, quarterly, or even more frequently to ensure clarity of operational focus. Some leaders effectively share these responsibilities with others, especially those from operations planning, ensuring that there is buy-in and quality assurance. Leaders who fail to keep up with these basic competencies are the very leaders who may be unlucky and find their careers derailed or their organizations lurching into crises because of "unforeseen" problems that better basic management might have identified and fixed.

Thus, while some people prefer to think of task-oriented behaviors more as management than leadership, such behaviors are nonetheless critical to effective leadership no matter how they are classified. Next, we turn to the other classical cornerstone of leadership dynamics, people-oriented behaviors.

NOTES

1. Managers had a *higher than expected emphasis* in the following areas: inform subordinates about developments and their impact on organizational activities; gain support of key individuals to ensure goal accomplishment; explain significant goals, activities, and policies to subordinates; keep abreast of the organization's performance and effectiveness; maintain internal control systems to ensure protection against fraud, waste, and mismanagement; monitor status of funds, ceilings, and travel; authorize expenditure of funds. Managers had a *lower than expected emphasis* in the following areas: provide career growth opportunities for self; match subordinate interests and abilities with the job; provide regular guidance to subordinates; coordinate activities with other organizations within the agency to accomplish work. Yet, even though these minicompetencies are not consistent with linear supervisor-to-executive trendlines, they are generally logically consistent with what midlevel managers do: focus on programs, control, and manage organizational functions.

2. Although evaluation is sometimes considered a separate phase, such as in the literature on decision making, this is generally not the case in the leadership literature, which folds evaluation into the assessment phase. Evaluations are in one sense the end of action sequences, but just as logically they are also the beginning of them.

3. When federal managers were asked about the importance of keeping abreast of the organization's performance and effectiveness, they ranked it 38th as opposed to executives who ranked it 49th or supervisors who ranked it 82nd.

4. Kaplan and Norton (1996) identify four overarching areas in which a variety of indicators should be selected that are organization specific: customers, finance, internal business process, and learning and growth.

5. Typically, tactical planning focuses on adjustments or implementation of strategic plans; action planning is related to problem solving; program planning is related to new program implementation; implementation is a very broad term for all these types of activities; and project management is the scheduling of large-scale projects.

6. Executives had one operational planning item in the top 20 and 10 in the top 100; supervisors had none in the top 20 and only 5 in the top 100.

7. The nature and frequency of review, which relates closely to authority, can almost be considered another dimension of delegation. For example, a middle manager may not be given additional authority beyond his/her normal ability to spend, hire, and solve problems. However, over time because of reliability, reputation, and/or connections, a middle manager's decisions may be reviewed less frequently or rigorously. Indeed, it is not uncommon for longtime supervisors and managers to demand high levels of authority, despite the desire of superiors to curb that authority. Junior managers are often successful in such struggles because of their competence and focus; occasionally, managers asserting such authority in the face of opposition find that they are reassigned or subject to intensive micromanagement in order to "bring them back in line."

8. The original study included only two items directly related to delegation.

9. The highest competency was related to honesty and integrity.

10. It also certainly reflects the nature of the convenience sample that formed the basis for this study—self-selected participants in a management training program.

11. Those leaders who can implement only their own good (or not so good) ideas generally hold their organizations back today. The exception is probably the entrepreneurial leader whose technical ideas and vision blend in bold ways to create an opportunity to reengineer a process or program. However, even in this case, it requires the entrepreneurial leader to be accurate, brilliant, and realize that future refinements (the critical improvement process following a significant process change) invariably need to come from others.

12. Of course, implementing a major "culture change" is invariably long term and therefore has an incremental quality; nonetheless, and more important, it is comprehensive and planned, unlike technical innovation, which is more piecemeal and opportunistic.

People-Oriented Behaviors

John D. Rockefeller, an oil tycoon at the turn of the twentieth century, was famous for his brilliant insight into the U.S. oil business. He had a well-earned reputation as a ruthless competitor and sometimes shady oil baron who wrested oil-rich land from less-than-eager sellers. Yet, when asked what quality he most valued in his chief aides, he said, "I will pay more for the ability to deal with other people than any other ability under the sun." Indeed, despite his brutal dealings with those outside his organization, the loyalty of his senior managers and their ability to work with others were the key to his successful organization. If people skills are important for a business empire despite the allure of wealth, then they are doubly important for the leaders interested in the personnel-intensive public sector.

We now turn to the other behavioral competency cluster that evolved in the 1950s: people-oriented behaviors. The Ohio State studies define "people-oriented" behavior or "consideration" as supportiveness, friendliness, concern, and inclusiveness (Hemphill and Coons 1957). The University of Michigan study also emphasizes "relations-oriented" behavior, which includes helpfulness, trust, thoughtfulness, delegation, and recognition. Along with task-oriented and relations-oriented leadership, the Michigan study also includes a third category, participative leadership (Likert 1961, 1967). This element of leadership emphasizes managing group processes constructively, especially information flow, meetings, and decision making. It relates both to task and relations behaviors in that leaders must organize and work through groups as well as treat them with consideration.

Sometimes the term "leadership" is used as the super-category of all major behavior clusters (as well as the organizational cluster, which we will address in the next chapter). This is how the term "leadership" is used in this book. However, sometimes leadership is defined as a midlevel competency similar to the other broad categories that have been discussed so far, such as decisiveness, communication, and problem solving. When leadership and management researchers use the term in this more limited fashion, then leadership generally refers to elements of the people-oriented behavior domain (essentially what we will discuss in this chapter).[1] For example, Mintzberg notes that leadership, only one of ten roles he identifies, "involves interpersonal relationships between the leader and the led" (1973, 60). Similarly, the U.S. Office of Personnel Management (OPM) definition of leadership as one of twenty-two competencies is: "inspires, motivates and guides others toward goal accomplishment; coaches, mentors, and challenges subordinates; adapts leadership styles to a variety of situations; models high standards of honesty, integrity, trust, openness, and respect for the individual by applying these values to daily behaviors" (U.S. OPM 1997, 3). However, that competency list also included interpersonal skills: "considers and responds appropriately to the needs, feelings, and capabilities of others; adjusts approaches to suit people and situations." More recently, the OPM added "developing others" to its top executive competency list (2006).

Seven people-oriented competencies are discussed in this chapter: consulting, planning and organizing personnel, developing staff, motivating, building and managing teams, managing conflicts, and managing personnel change. These "soft" competencies have been somewhat more difficult to delineate quantitatively in the research than task-oriented competencies in terms of performance. They have been much easier to correlate to satisfaction, but the correlation of satisfaction with performance is frequently nebulous and complicated. Although they are both important and are related, satisfaction and performance issues should be differentiated in the discussions that follow. Nonetheless, a relatively concrete sense of the comparative emphasis that executives and supervisors place on the people-oriented skills in this chapter is provided in Exhibit 14.1. Overall, supervisors are somewhat more focused on people-oriented skills. In particular, supervisors have a slightly stronger focus in consulting, planning and organizing, personnel, motivating, and managing conflict.

CONSULTING

Consulting involves *checking with people on work-related matters and involving people in decision-making processes*. It can be done in one-on-one meetings ranging from a minute in the hallway to an hour in a formal session, through telephone calls, e-mail, or other written communications. To a lesser degree it can be done in group settings as well. Consulting can occur in small-group gatherings, staff meetings, all-organization meetings, or various types of group- and mass-written communications. Both the postmodern (e.g., Uhl-Bien 2006) and community change theories (Crosby and Bryson 2005) of leadership have emphasized the importance of this competency, as well as broadening it from a leader-centric perspective to a network or systems perspective.

As a competency, consulting has two distinct elements. First, it refers to soliciting information from people: suggestions, ideas, and advice. The information may be solicited in a closed-ended manner, such as by asking, "What do you think is the problem causing the client's lack of response to our request for more information so that we can process their claim?" Solicitation of information can also be open-ended, such as, "So, how do you think things are going?" or "Do you think it is possible to reduce our process cycle time and, if so, how?" The second element is an invitation to be involved in decision making to some degree. That degree may be highly indirect and informal, or it may be highly direct and structured. Finally, for purposes of definition, consultation refers to checking with and involving all organizational members, not just subordinates, but bosses, peers, and other employees as well. Indeed, although consultation with one's subordinates is a critical dimension, consultation with one's boss may be no less important for planning and career purposes.

Exhibit 14.1

People-Oriented Competencies Rated in the Top 100 by Federal Executives and Supervisors

	Executives		Supervisors	
	Top 20 competencies	Top 100 competencies	Top 20 competencies	Top 100 competencies
Consulting	3	6	4	7
Planning and organizing personnel	0	4	1	4
Developing staff	1	4	0	6
Motivating	1	3	2	5
Building and managing teams	1	5	1	4
Managing conflict	0	2	1	2
Managing personnel change	0	2	0	1
Total	6	26	9	29

Note: Based on a study of 150 competencies. Competencies selected based on a rating of "very important" or "crucial" by those who reported that competency applied to their position.

Consulting is related to but distinct from many other competencies. Unlike informing, consulting requires an active feedback mechanism. Consulting emphasizes questions and data collection whereas informing emphasizes data dissemination. Consulting is related to other assessment/evaluation competencies: task monitoring and assessing, which focus on internal technical data collection and analysis, and environmental scanning, which focuses on external technical data collection and analysis. Whereas the other assessment/ evaluation competencies emphasize "hard" data, consulting emphasizes "soft" data (although this exaggerates distinctions for purposes of clarity). Consulting is also related to decisiveness (one of the leader trait competencies), delegating, and decision-making competencies. As a decision-making model (one of the two fundamental elements of this competency), consulting falls between decisiveness (authoritarian decisions) and delegation, as will be discussed further below. (Readers interested in the full context of decision making should refer to those sections.) Finally, consulting undergirds decision making inasmuch as broad-based and important decisions generally have extremely heavy data demands that can rarely be met without consultation, as well as using other data sources. In addition to ensuring decision quality, consultation assists decision making by enhancing buy-in, decision education, and legitimacy. Despite its relationship and overlap with other competencies, it is distinct enough so that when managers are asked about the quality of consultation, they have no problem whatsoever understanding and responding to the question.

Nowhere are the distinctions among subtypes and other competencies more important than with consulting, decisiveness, and delegation. In the simplest sense, they can be arrayed on a spectrum with authoritarian decision making at one extreme, consultation as a decision-making model in the middle, and delegation at the other extreme where authority is given over to subordinates. Yet, analysts and managers quickly realize that these scenarios, while useful for clarity, tremendously understate the subtlety of decision processes, especially in the consultation range. A well-known and lucid analysis of this type is that of Vroom and Yetton (1973), who distinguish two types of consultation in addition to two types of unilateral decision making and delegation. Essentially the decision participation range for this leader-subordinate model is:

- Autocratic decision model 1: You make the decision yourself with the information that you have available to you.
- Autocratic decision model 2: You make the decision yourself but after getting information from others. You may or may not tell others why you need the information; however, the emphasis is on collecting data, not getting advice or input.
- Consultation decision model 1: You share the problem or decision issue with *individuals* and ask for input; however, you make the decision unilaterally, and your decision may or may not reflect others' preferences.
- Consultation decision model 2: You share the problem or decision issue with a *group* and ask for input; however, you make the decision unilaterally, and your decision may or may not reflect others' preferences.
- Delegation decision model: In this model the leader structures the decision making and facilitates the final decision by the individual or group. The leader does not try to influence the group except to ensure a process that facilitates decision quality and consensus. The leader implements the decision by the group or individual.

The main factors Vroom and Yetton point to in determining the correct approach in any given situation are the importance or nature of: decision quality, subordinate information, problem structure, subordinate decision acceptance, subordinate alignment with organizational goals, and subordinate consensus. They also point out that many decisions can be skewed toward efficiency (such as in times of crisis) or toward employee development, depending on the context and leaders' disposition.

For our purposes we will distinguish only two types of consultative decision making, although a more fine-grained rubric is possible. *Participative decision making* is when subordinates and others are actively involved in providing ideas and suggestions in the decision-making process. Although the leader ultimately makes the decision, it is clear that the others have substantial opportunities to influence the decision because of data or opinions that they offer. In quality participative decision-making environments, others know that while their ideas may not determine every given decision, they do have influence over a significant proportion of decisions over the course of multiple decisions. *Joint decision making* is similar to Vroom and Yetton's delegation model above. That is, the leader manages the decision-making process—especially the decisional parameters—but does not make the actual decision. Leaders still have significant influence because of the narrowness of the decision parameters and the opportunity to control the process (including policing any process violations).

The literature on decision making is extensive, and thus this element of consulting is vast. In terms of specific leadership taxonomies, consulting is often subsumed under supervision, participative leadership, leadership (as a people-oriented competency), consideration, interpersonal skills, and supportiveness. The OPM subsumes this skill at the midlevel as a combination of leadership and interpersonal skills (1992). Yukl delineates it as a separate competency (1998). Still, the definitive analyses of this and related competencies have been done by Vroom and Yetton (1973) and Vroom and Jago (1988). In our analysis of the discrete competencies of federal managers, consulting is striking in the importance it is accorded. Questions related to getting information rank 7, 9, 32, and 71 for executives. Questions related to encouraging participation in decision making rank 3 and 73. In fact, because the first two executive competencies in the overall list are leader characteristics, consulting is the highest of all executive behavioral competencies ("Involve relevant people in decision making"). Supervisors also rank the discrete competencies very highly but focus much more strongly on consultation as it relates to employees themselves (e.g., "encourage open communication and input from employees") and issues related to performance. This emphasis on consulting is also reflected in the study of local government managers, who mention it as among the top four strengths identified but many of whom also refer to it as a weakness (Van Wart 2001).

Guidelines

(See also guidelines for decisiveness in chapter 11 and delegation in chapter 13.)

1. *Evaluate the decision environment surrounding substantive decisions.* Although all decision environments have a unique blend of conditions, the parameters of those environments are relatively standard (Vroom and Yetton 1973). The following are the standard parameters that a decision maker should consider. What information is needed and who has it or can best get it? Generally, the more information that is already in the leader's domain, the more likely s/he is to take a primary role. However, even when leaders have all the technical information, certain types of interpersonal and judgmental information may not be immediately available to them without consultation. How critical is time in making the decision? Classically, the greater the time pressures, the more the decision is made in an "executive mode." On the other hand, some leaders always seem to be in a crisis mode because they are overwhelmed by decisions that should have been delegated and shared. How important might the development and inclusiveness of others be? Some (potential) loss of decision quality may be well worth the inclusion it brings and the learning that comes with it. How likely are others to cooperate with the leader and/or group in making the decision? Some issues are so divisive or so inherently personal that leaders are loathe to bring them into a group discussion.

2. *Seek as much input as possible for substantive decisions.* Even if decisions are determined unilaterally, others like to know that they have been consulted for relevant information. Not only does it make subordinates and others feel respected and useful, good information is critical for good discussions. For example, it is not uncommon for decision makers to ask why critical information was not forwarded

to them before a critical decision was made that subsequently resulted in failure due to the oversight. Invariably, the answer given is, "Because you never asked me." The response is not glib and needs to be taken as a serious warning to decision makers; it is ultimately their responsibility to solicit information actively, and not to assume that notification of a decision process will be sufficient to get all the relevant data, especially from taciturn subordinates who may nonetheless be the closest at hand. Therefore, leaders must encourage others to provide information, develop listening skills, (demonstrably) record ideas, and show that they are building on the ideas of others (see Exhibit 14.2 for an example). Leaders who do not show good receptiveness get far less information over time because others lose interest in relaying it to a less-than-fully interested party. This is one of the most common areas for a large gap in perceptions to exist, as demonstrated in leadership feedback exercises. It is a particular problem for leaders who are highly experienced and have less experienced people in the decision environment, or who are by nature highly decisive, loquacious, or quick-witted.

3. *Utilize the ideas, suggestions, and input of others for substantive decisions to the maximum degree feasible.* The general rule of thumb is that one should seek to maximize decision inclusiveness to the degree that time, decision quality, cooperation, and so forth, will allow. Completely autocratic decisions should be as limited in number as possible. Good leaders let others know what the implicit guidelines for decision inclusion are, so that decisive decisions do not seem arbitrary or peremptory. In particular, maximum inclusion tends to ensure maximum information, buy-in, and development. Depending on the nature of the decision, maximizing decision inclusiveness means pushing it down the participation/delegation spectrum as far as feasible. Even when a decision maker retains a great deal of authority in a participative process in which only information was requested (not decision alternatives), public or private acknowledgment and appreciation of the contribution are much valued by others.

PLANNING AND ORGANIZING PERSONNEL

As was mentioned when discussing operations planning, the planning function can really be separated into several distinctly different competencies. For example, those good at tactical planning are not necessarily good at strategic planning. Similarly, those good at the tactical and strategic aspects are not necessarily strong at the personnel aspects of planning. Planning and organizing personnel involves *coordinating people and operations, and ensuring that the competencies necessary to do the work are, or will be, available. It also involves self-planning.*

One obvious element of planning and organizing personnel is simply fitting people to schedules and making the appropriate changes as work and personnel needs change. In our discrete analysis of federal managers, executives ranked "schedule work assignments, set priorities, and direct work of staff" 56th of 150 competencies surveyed. However, this competency moved up to 30th for managers and 13th for supervisors. Other items

Exhibit 14.2

Dick and Jane: The Management Version

Dick and Jane grew up in the same neighborhood at the same time, both went to the same state university, and both got master's degrees in public management. In fact, Dick got his graduate degree before Jane by several years. Yet, Jane was now the division head and Dick was only a frontline supervisor. It seemed to Dick that Jane was better liked and trusted than he, even though he was more outgoing and worked very hard to be completely fair. But their respective career progressions were not the issue today.

Today he was going to Jane because he was angry about the fact that he had not received an exemption from the statewide hiring freeze for the Information Technology Specialist 2 that he wanted to hire. The freeze came just as the job was posted and was effective for all those to whom an offer had not been made. While he had not yet offered the position at the time, he felt sure that he would be granted an exemption—until his immediate supervisor declined to make an exemption request. He was appealing to Jane.

For her part, Jane knew that Dick had an appointment and she knew the broad facts of the case. She often thought that her undergraduate degree in counseling psychology was extremely useful for this part of the job. She still remembers the lectures on "Rogerian" psychology when active listening skills were taught: *maintaining attention, expressing empathy for the person while listening neutrally to the facts, restating others' points for accuracy and clarity, suspending preconceptions, and avoiding premature judgments.* Indeed, to this day she keeps some aphorisms framed on her wall: "He listens well who takes notes" (Dante), and "Give every man thine ear but few thy voice" (Shakespeare).

When Dick came in, Jane greeted him at the door with a warm smile and asked about his family, whom she knew. After the pleasantries, she asked Dick to tell her the problem, allowing him to start at the beginning. Occasionally she interjected summaries of his points and once she asked a follow-up question. After he had fully expressed his case, and in fact was beginning to repeat himself, Jane asked for potential solutions. She explained that under the current fiscal constraints she was unlikely to get an exemption unless she offered up another position. Did he have suggestions of a slack area? If she were able to receive permission for a "term" employee (for a two-year term with full benefits), rather than a regular classified position, did he think the applicant would be agreeable? At the conclusion, she said that she would talk to Dick's supervisor, who, she stated, was supportive of the request but simply realistic about the challenges involved in the exemption. If the supervisor had another unfilled position, she would suggest that it be traded for the Information Technology Specialist until the hiring freeze was lifted. If not, she would make a strong request for a term appointment. If that failed, he would have to wait until the freeze was lifted.

Dick left the office knowing that the probability of filling the position immediately was still only fifty-fifty. Despite the lack of guarantees, he knew that Jane had listened to his needs carefully and would do all that she could within her scope of authority. Dick was no longer angry, because Jane respected and appreciated him. Yes, he had always liked her. Jane listened.

in this vein showed a similar pattern. "Adjust work schedules to changing priorities" was ranked 100th by executives but 39th by supervisors, and "prepare staffing plans with projected number and type of staff" was 129th for executives and 98th for supervisors. Another aspect of finding people to fit into schedules is to ensure that the critical competencies of jobs are understood and available. This aspect overlaps with the human resource management competency discussed in the next chapter under performing general management functions such as authorizing personnel lines, recruiting, and hiring. In large systems, personnel planning includes personnel needs analysis and employment forecasting tools.

Another element is matching the talents, interests, and preferences of people to the work. In our study of federal managers, executives ranked "match subordinate interests and abilities with the job" as 44th and supervisors ranked it 53rd. People are not cogs in a machine; reflecting their interests and natural abilities in assembling jobs, projects, and teams makes an enormous difference. In identifying the core competencies of managers in working with people, Buckingham and Coffman (1999) identify talent and job fit as the two most critical elements of selection and development.

A third element is personal time-management skills. A leader's ability to manage others is largely determined in the long term by his or her ability to self-manage. Good time management means that you have a clear sense of what you want to accomplish and that you have a plan to do so. It further means that you have analyzed the use of your time and that you plan the daily and weekly activities that will contribute to goal achievement. It also means that wasteful activities are avoided and that many "reactive" activities are productively harnessed as strategic opportunities to further long-term plans. Finally, it means that time for reflection and the planning process itself is allotted and guaranteed, because without it, the subtleties of good planning will not occur.

The importance of planning as a broad skill with technical aspects has long been recognized (Fayol 1949; Drucker 1974). Indeed, the old management acronym POSDCoRB, which was heavily weighted toward supervisory and middle management concerns, is a good example. The acronym stands for planning, organizing, staffing, directing, coordinating, reporting, and budgeting. But planning and organizing in this sense are directly related, and the directing and coordinating functions are indirectly related. Emphasizing the personnel aspect of planning is not common in studies of this type except for Page (1987), who separates strategic planning from planning and organizing. It is more common to describe planning as a more comprehensive category in leadership taxonomies (e.g., Morse and Wagner 1978; Luthans, Rosenkrantz, and Hennessey 1985). This is the case in the 1992 OPM study, which includes planning and evaluation (16th out of 22 for executives). This category was dropped from the 1999 study, which emphasized the strategic elements of leadership, such as strategic thinking, although generic human resource management was cited in both. In a study of local government managers, personnel planning was occasionally mentioned as a strength, but never mentioned as a weakness (Van Wart 2001).

Guidelines

1. *Ensure that specific staff assignments are understood and accepted.* Scheduling can be a routine, unquestioned process or it can be the cause of much frustration and griping. Three aspects of good scheduling are sufficient data, fairness of policies, and clarity and feedback. Getting sufficient data about organizational needs and potential personnel demands is critical for a schedule to be coherent. The more that organizational needs can be mapped, and the more that specific demands of employees can be anticipated, the less chance that scheduling will be subject to excessive changes. Such data can be collected by analysis of organizational

needs, group meetings, and group communications, and augmented by individual communications. When scheduling is complex and a good deal of negotiation is involved, it is better to circulate draft schedules rather than to continually publish updated schedules that erode confidence. Another aspect of scheduling is the set of policies that is used and perceptions of fairness. Employees are conscious of others' assignments and will tend to be highly critical of those assignments if they do not agree with or understand them. Therefore, while leaders do want to retain flexibility, it is best to do so using broad principles. For example, departments that have three shifts to cover must decide how to prioritize requests (e.g., excused for seniority), and what types of exceptions can be considered (e.g., authorized training for the time of the course). Finally, the clarity of the group assignments is critical. This is less likely in ongoing operations, but is crucial in new or changing operations in which roles are unclear and whole functions may be neglected if individual and group responsibilities are not identified. Where new assignments are being made, it is ideal to build in a feedback loop to ensure that the information has been received and understood.

2. *Match staff preferences and competencies to the work as much as possible.* It is a truism that people are different. Therefore, even though units and departments may have relatively consistent work products, the more the individual preferences, personalities, and experiences of employees can be accommodated, the better. Some people may prefer the "inside" jobs so that their work centers around a desk, while others may prefer the jobs that take them outside the office on a regular basis. Because of different personality structures, some people may be better interacting with others, some in producing detailed analysis, and still others at getting new projects done quickly. Different experiences may mean that some employees are better at financial analysis while others have experience with negotiating contracts. The challenges of integrating fairness and flexibility were mentioned above. Thus, a major aspect of customization or specialization of scheduling involves building an appreciation of the different roles people play and the importance of "playing to people's strengths."

3. *Stay on top of scheduling changes.* Changes create major opportunities for operational glitches and even systems malfunctions. The oft-heard refrain is: "I thought that so-and-so was going to do that." Feedback loops and confirmation of changes are the best ways to prevent problems.

4. *Review long-term organizational competency needs to ensure organizational capacity.* Good leaders are constantly assessing the overall competency needs of their organization or unit. Gaps are common because of retirements or staff shortages; long-term weaknesses are inevitable as competency needs evolve faster than members of the organization adapt on their own. Those planning and organizing personnel have a responsibility to document such gaps and weaknesses so that they can be addressed through formal training, staff rotation, one-on-one coaching, inspirational exhortation, selection criteria changes, and so on.

5. *Manage your personal schedule effectively.* Some leadership analysts place this among the chief qualities for effectiveness. It is hard to respect leaders who do not have the discipline to manage their own time well or to address all their major responsibilities. This includes the daily and weekly scheduling of activities and the ability to reorganize priorities constantly, without losing sight of long-term goals. It includes the ability to use the natural energy cycle to maximum effectiveness; creativity does not occur when you are tired, and passive activities do not need high energy levels. It certainly includes an ability to make sure that one gets things accomplished, which is reflected in the new emphasis on results that pervades the organizational environment (Bhatta 2001). The need for achievement (chapter 11) is not enough. This means understanding how one uses time, avoids procrastination and unnecessary activities, and uses serendipity (unplanned events) to further planned goals.

DEVELOPING STAFF

Developing staff involves *improving subordinates' effectiveness in their current positions and preparing them for their next position or step.*[2] It is highly related to clarifying roles and responsibilities, which focuses on initial instruction and specific definition of job responsibilities and performance goals; that is, clarifying establishes a baseline of information and direction. Developing staff focuses more on assisting employees to be comfortable in their positions, reach higher levels of productivity over time, and prepare for future prospects. Therefore, it builds on the baseline that clarifying should have established. In most respects clarifying and developing can be seen as two elements establishing a continuum from a short-term, technical focus to a long-term, career focus. Developing also relates to continual learning in that employees and the leader him/herself must improve and prepare for the future. It relates to problem solving and innovation/ creativity in that these skills are rarely learned easily or quickly. Finally, it relates to motivating through showing concern and giving individualized assistance.

There are three major elements in developing staff: supporting, coaching, and mentoring. Supporting is the emotional component of development. People generally do better over time when they have socioemotional encouragement. Support helps a person identify with his/her job, focus energies on productive issues, and accept criticism or hardships. Employees who feel that they have friends at work are shown to be more productive and more likely to remain (Buckingham and Coffman 1999). Supportiveness from a superior (with direct authority) reduces unnecessary anxiety and paranoia when mistakes are made or organizational changes are occurring. Because a primary responsibility of a supervisor is to point out errors, weak performance, or areas for improvement, a supportive relationship will generally facilitate the acceptance of criticism and even disciplinary actions. Supportiveness is especially important in times of special hardship, because without it organization members are very likely to give up or abandon the organization.

Coaching helps employees do a task more effectively. After employees have received their initial instructions and training, and have been made aware of the standards that they are expected to meet, they are still not at peak performance. While the primary responsibility lies with the employee to improve performance—speed, accuracy, presentation, and the like—this responsibility is shared with the superior whose job it is to provide intermittent on-the-job training and suggestions. While initial training may or may not take place on the job, coaching nearly always involves observing actual performance in the job setting. An analogy with sports works well. Youth who are taught sports are frequently drilled (trained) on the component parts of a sport so that they can perform each element proficiently (e.g., lay-up shots in basketball, kicking in swimming, and passing in football). Later they receive individualized coaching as they perform these and other discrete elements together in realistic conditions on the court, in the pool, or on the field. It is also important to note that the training provided in the clarifying phase and the coaching during the developing phase are *both* critical, and weakness or omission of one lessens the value of the other. It is not uncommon for the performance of relatively well-trained new employees to be subsequently ignored by superiors (lack of coaching), so that higher levels of proficiency are ultimately modest and completely self-directed. Even worse, it is not uncommon for organizational members to be thrown into job settings with scant training and clarification, with the expectation that they will learn complex functions entirely through coaching (thus the poor reputation of "on-the-job training"). This generally places unrealistic expectations on the coach in terms of time and oversight responsibilities, and deprives the learner of the more systematic approach that is utilized in training.

Mentoring refers to supporting a person's career and is sometimes referred to as career counseling. (Sometimes on-the-job training/assistance is called mentoring, but this is really a misnomer.) Mentoring involves providing advice on the culture of the organization and profession, the right job-related decisions to make, and the best way to interpret significant issues or concerns. Mentors also act as models of successful or ideal performance or behavior. Not infrequently mentors assist in identifying or providing special opportunities for the individual whom they are assisting.

The research on developing staff is abundant, especially on supportive behavior, and is often labeled "consideration" in the leadership literature (e.g., Bowers and Seashore 1966; House and Mitchell 1974; Stogdill 1974). The literature on coaching and mentoring as leadership behaviors placed in a major taxonomy is less prominent (yet, for examples, see Morse and Wagner 1978; Luthans, Rosenkrantz, and Hennessey 1985; Mumford et al. 1988). The OPM studies referred to development responsibilities under a number of headings in earlier studies; developing staff was identified as the term of choice (and the only additional category) in the OPM 2006 revision of executive competencies. Thach and Thompson (2007) rank it third in their study. In a study of local government managers, this behavior was identified as a problem three times as much as a strength (Van Wart 2001). A specialized study of people-oriented leadership was conducted by Buckingham and Coffman (1999). See Exhibit 14.3 regarding their recommendations coming from the "world's greatest managers."

Guidelines

1. *Show courtesy to and interest in everyone, and demonstrate positive regard for others to the greatest degree possible.* Courtesy and good manners are part of

Exhibit 14.3

How the World's Greatest Managers Develop Staff

In a fun-to-read management best seller, Buckingham and Coffman (1999) compiled information from 80,000 managers regarding the elements of great management. While some of the conventional management wisdom applied, in some cases they found that it did not and was fundamentally at variance with managing for excellence.

The most iconoclastic finding of their study was that "great" managers select strictly for talent (innate ability and interest), not skills, knowledge, or experience. ("The secret to great performance is all in the casting.") Following through on this belief leads to a number of significant conclusions. They do not believe, for example, that with enough training people can do anything they set their mind to. Nor do they think that great managers spend much time trying to fix people's weaknesses. And finally, they think it is okay to play favorites, that is, spend the most time with the best workers because they are the most productive, creative, and talented. Because these recommendations are so contrary to conventional management wisdom, they entitled their book: *First, Break All the Rules* (1999). Their message, then, is that great managers select the right people (those with the right talents) and then focus on those people's strengths. Too many managers get caught up in production-line recruitment, selection, and work structuring, and ignore the human contribution to success. Too many managers, they contend, focus on fixing problems reactively rather than building strengths proactively.

Ultimately, they were able to distinguish the best organizations from those that were mediocre or poorly managed with just a dozen questions. While none of the dozen questions refers to money, eight relate to developing staff. For example, excellent companies have high numbers of employees who can respond affirmatively to these three questions:

- "In the last seven days, have I received recognition or praise for doing good work?"
- "Does my supervisor, or someone at work, seem to care about me as a person?"
- "Do I have a best friend at work?"

Two of their questions relate to coaching employees:

- "Do I know what is expected of me at work?" (This is the very first question in their list).
- "Is there someone at work who encourages my development?"

Finally, three of the questions relate to mentoring and career development:

- "At work, do my opinions seem to count?"
- "In the last six months, has someone at work talked to me about my progress?"
- "This last year, have I had opportunities at work to learn and grow?"

Their overall findings, then, are not really so iconoclastic. The very best organizations develop their employees as much as they recruit them. Others investigating organizational excellence, such as Peters and Waterman in *In Search of Excellence* (1982), have emphasized the same point. In great organizations, although not ignored, minimal time is spent in focusing on "fixing" personal weaknesses and creating detailed rules beyond the important basics. Rather, the focus of such organizations is always on finding the right employees, paying attention to their professional and personal needs, providing them with career flexibility, and focusing on their strengths.

the fabric of modern democratic society. A role of authority does not exempt one from these basic social responsibilities; indeed, it makes them that much more noticeable, and lapses or weaknesses are amplified. Even under difficult conditions, such as when disciplining employees, courtesy should generally be carefully maintained. Although it may be appropriate for leaders to show anger on *rare* occasions for the *conscious* effect that it will cause, leaders cannot afford to lose their tempers spontaneously in modern organizations. Yet courtesy and good manners are only the formal structure of consideration. Showing interest in others demonstrates a higher level of support. Good active listening skills assist greatly in showing interest (see Exhibit 14.2 as an example of active listening). Paying attention to people means that you think they are worthy of your time and that their ideas and contributions count. The deepest level of support involves positive regard for people. This can be a positive acceptance of the totality of a person—strengths and weaknesses—with or without affection or trust, or it can be a more active emotional bond of friendship that includes trust and liking. Positive regard does not mean that the weaknesses, errors, or "sins" of others are overlooked; it simply means that no matter what a person may do, their basic humanity is appreciated and their value as a human being is always remembered. Positive regard in this sense is the emotional equivalent of the more legalistic notion of fairness. Of course, displaying courtesy, interest, and positive regard is relatively easy with those whom one naturally likes. The challenge for leaders is to extend these behaviors as broadly as possible. When leaders do not, they can easily create "in" and "out" groups that have negative effects in the work environment. Indeed, such groups can easily demonize one another, which leads to extreme organizational dysfunction (Graen and Cashman 1975; Graen and Uhl-Bien 1995).

2. *Promote a person's self-esteem and reputation.* A leader can support a subordinate's self-esteem by praising consistent work, accomplishments, and positive qualities. This can be enhanced by promoting a person's expertise and reputation to superiors and peers. Subordinates can be introduced to other significant or important people inside or outside the organization, and can be given assignments with visibility.

3. *Listen to personal problems that affect work performance and take the time to counsel subordinates.* Balancing and separating one's personal and professional lives often present a challenge even under normal conditions. Therefore, when subordinates have problems and issues in their personal lives, it often adversely affects their professional performance. Supervisors must take the time and show the compassion to understand the basic problem so that they can determine how to help most appropriately. If it is a severe personal or psychological problem that is not work related, then the supervisor may need to indicate their understanding, suggest community resources (e.g., a marriage counselor), and be ready to determine what work-related accommodations may be appropriate on a temporary basis (e.g., some time off with or without pay). If it is a severe problem that causes performance issues (e.g., drug and alcohol related), then the organization may furnish professional counseling through an employee assistance program. While such cases require a good degree of firmness and reiteration of rules and policies, empathy is being underscored here and can sometimes be the deciding factor in whether or not the person makes it through the difficult period success-

fully. However, for most routine or temporary issues a friendly ear is enough, with some detached advice and appropriate encouragement. Although managers should not normally allow themselves to assume the role of therapist, "light" counseling, from listening to advice, is often part of the job.

4. *Analyze subordinates' overall performance and identify deficiencies.* For a person to develop, one must have a realistic assessment of overall strengths and weaknesses. Leaders must take the time to analyze how well subordinates are doing through observation, review of work products, and conversations with the subordinate. Not only does the leader need to analyze performance strengths and deficiencies, but it is important for the manager to help the subordinate to participate in the analysis or self-diagnosis. Often, the subordinate has a relatively good grasp of weaknesses and problems so that the manager is simply providing additional encouragement, structure, and resources for improvement. Sometimes the subordinate may be unaware of the problem, or be emphasizing the wrong areas for attention, about which the leader may need to be more proactive in guiding the employee.

5. *Monitor and correct errors.* At a more detailed level, in order to develop people it is necessary to pinpoint specific errors, mistakes, and problems as they arise on a daily, weekly, or monthly basis. Timely and precise error correction is a foundation for performance improvement and prevents many problem trends from occurring, such as unsatisfactory practices that become routine or fossilized behavior. This is most obvious and critical for frontline supervisors who are coaching new employees. New employees are most open to correction and suggestions, and generally appreciate close monitoring and directions for improvement. Although more subtle and requiring finesse, monitoring and correcting are needed even at senior levels in order for people to develop. The department director who turns in sloppy reports, the division director who neglects to perform performance appraisals on his own employees, and the section chief who treats her subordinates in an arbitrary manner are all examples of when monitoring is necessary and correction is useful.

6. *Provide career advice and encouragement.* Leaders let subordinates know how to do well in their current position, but also can help employees discern and prepare for future careers. What training is required? What standard of performance is expected? What auxiliary requirements such as length of time or proof of worthiness are crucial? What are the intricacies of applying for a different or better position? What are the realistic expectations of achieving other options? Of course, the leader as model is an important form of career advice; successful bosses are more likely to have successful employees (Graen et al. 1977). Part of the modeling that is useful to employees is to observe the superior's development activities. Just as important as providing information and modeling behavior is to be active in encouraging subordinates to think of either enrichment or advancement opportunities. Overall, good bosses early in one's career can make a tremendous difference between a lackluster career and a very good one.

7. *Provide special opportunities for subordinates to prepare for a future position.* Because leaders have superior resources and authority, they can often provide special opportunities for individuals or whole groups. Advancement is often contingent on a range of assignments, certain types of assignments, special training, advanced education, and access to people or networks outside the subordinate's sphere. Leaders can allow people to take additional training, authorize reimbursement for educational classes, allow subordinates to represent the division in meetings, provide opportunities for them to attend conferences, and so on.

MOTIVATING

Motivating is a very general term that refers (for the purpose of defining the competency here) to *enhancing the inner drives and positive intentions of subordinates (or others) to perform well through incentives, disincentives, and inspiration.* The research on motivation is vast and old, and extensively overlaps and intertwines with the leadership literature. For example, the famous 1924 "Hawthorne studies" at Western Electric by Elton Mayo and his Harvard colleagues demonstrated not only the power of motivating behaviors of leaders but also the complexity of motivation (Roethlisberger 1941). (See Exhibit 14.4 for a review of this much celebrated case.) In a sense, most of what leaders do has a positive or negative effect on the attitudes, drives, intentions, and efforts of followers, so nearly everything could ultimately be subsumed under the topic if broadly defined.

One large aspect of motivating that will not be included here because it has been included under other management competencies has to do with the whole area of structuring the work. Workers are tremendously affected, for good or ill, by the way work is structured. Management sets the basic conditions including pay (always a powerful motivator but generally in short supply) and working conditions (hours, work space, equipment, travel, etc.). The quality of training and instruction affects employees' ability to do the work and their acculturation (see clarifying roles and objectives). Organizing the work so that it is coherent and efficient has been covered in operations planning, personnel planning, and developing staff. Providing assistance as technical issues arise is also a part of clarifying roles and objectives. Finally, involvement adds considerably to morale, and indirectly to performance, and is covered in informing, delegating, consulting, and teamwork. It is important to note that lower-level leaders often have little say in the conditions of employment, an area that is generally reserved for senior managers and executives, and that even they are often severely constrained by external mandates (e.g., legislatively authorized pay scales) and fiscal pressures. (See Exhibit 14.5 for a discussion of the relationship of rewards and compensation philosophies.) Indeed, good leaders must often motivate despite poor/mediocre pay and unsatisfactory working conditions, as well as poor organizational training systems, convoluted and unfairly mandated organizational designs, and time pressures reducing the ability to assist and be involved. While effective leaders will work to improve the structure of work over time, many of these issues can be only partially ameliorated and a few will prove intractable, so that good leadership is defined as much by motivating in spite of structural challenges as it

Exhibit 14.4

The Study of Worker Motivation and the Hawthorne Studies

Certainly one of the most celebrated management studies ever done was the research conducted at the Hawthorne plant of Western Electric in Hawthorne, Illinois, under the general direction of Elton Mayo of Harvard starting in the 1920s. In one of the studies, the efficiency experts at the plant decided to test for the optimum level of illumination. Two groups were identified, with one being an experimental control. As the level of illumination increased, so did productivity. Yet, it was hard not to notice that the productivity of the control group also rose at nearly the same level. Not surprisingly, as the researchers provided additional adjustments to the environment such as more rest breaks and snacks, productivity rose even more. What was shocking was that when the light was dimmed and the new work enhancements were eliminated, productivity did not decline significantly. When interviewed, the workers discussed how important and good they felt on the basis of being studied, even when perquisites were eliminated. These studies led to a number of conclusions.

First, it was established that mere attention to human beings will affect their behavior, in this case positively. Researchers must be sure the effects that they find are not the result of the attention the subjects receive instead of the effect they think they are studying such as levels of illumination. The bias introduced into research by the observers became known in social science as the Hawthorne effect.

Second, it was established that workers are not cogs in machines. The fundamental elements of motivation, what Maslow would call physiological needs and what Herzberg would call hygiene factors, do not generally account for high-performance situations in which worker satisfaction must include a sense of achievement and significance. This study later became a major cornerstone of the human relations school of the 1950s and 1960s.

However, later the case was reopened and the data were reanalyzed by a number of researchers. Two of these research teams tempered the original findings and pointed out the importance of diligence in field experiments. Franke and Kaul (1978) pointed out that two workers were fired during the experimental period, thus substantially enhancing the sense of worker discipline. Parson (1978) pointed out that the plant had also moved to a modified differential monetary reward system (a type of piecework system). The harder workers worked, the more money they got. They were also provided better feedback about their productivity. A third researcher (Jones 1990) reasserted the significance of the higher motivation factors—achievement and significance. Given that the levels of productivity were so dramatically improved, it seems likely that there were a variety of contributing factors, even if researchers argue about the exact degree of variance explained by each factor in this particular situation.

This leads to several more conclusions. Third, work structure does make a difference. For example, good feedback enhances worker information and motivation. Fourth, basic motivations to avoid pain, such as firing, also make a difference. Fifth, basic motivations for optimum exchange, such as increased income, make a substantial difference. All this points out that motivation is complex and operates on multiple levels. Leaders need to understand that maintaining high levels of motivation is extremely challenging, given structural constraints they must work within and limits on their own time and ability. Nonetheless, enhancing worker motivation is certainly one of the most central conceptions of leadership in organizational settings.

is by removing them. These are aspects of motivation that will define the term here and on which we will focus now.

Elements of motivating include positive incentives (e.g., recognition and rewards), disincentives (e.g., disciplining), and inspiring. Recognition involves intangible incentives such as showing appreciation and providing praise. It includes actions such as informal positive verbal comments, informal tributes or awards in public settings like staff or division meetings, written praise in notes or annual evaluations, and formal commendations

Exhibit 14.5

Rewards and Compensation Philosophies

Pay systems use fundamentally different philosophies in establishing pay criteria. In *social exchange theory,* the ideal situation is where the greater the effort and performance by employees, the greater the reward they receive. This is emphasized in merit-based pay systems for individuals and gainsharing plans for individuals or groups. Extreme forms pay solely on commission (e.g., real estate), product (e.g., the entertainment industry), or piecework (e.g., doctors in traditional practices seeing and billing patients). Social exchange theory also takes into account the context of the employment market. Employees with skills and experience that are in greater demand get more rewards. Thus, managers and professionals with their experience or nurses and information technology workers with their coveted skills can demand greater rewards upon entering employment. Some of the newer skill-based pay systems (emphasizing potential) are a variant of this school of thought. On the other hand, *equity theory* stresses fairness and valuation of different types of contribution. Fairness means that similar jobs and similar results are rewarded in similar ways.* The valuation of different types of contributions ensures that short-term results do not overwhelm long-term organizational needs for stability, experience, loyalty, and potential. This second aspect of equity theory allows for the greater acknowledgment of seniority (accrued experience and loyalty) as well as potential (skills and capabilities that may be used in the future). Despite ubiquitous griping, lockstep seniority pay systems with their numerous grades and steps are remarkably popular with workers because of the security and the predictability that they offer. For a period, unions became so cynical of management that they wanted all pay increases strictly defined by seniority; today many public sector organizations are still organized in this fashion. The more "enlightened" systems often use a mix of rewards: a cost-of-living increase (essentially seniority raises) and a merit increase based on the annual evaluation. However, because the cost-of-living increase has traditionally eaten up most of the money available for raises, and because most employees cluster heavily in the 3.5 to 4.5 range on a five-point scale (minimizing merit increase differences), the actual differences are often trivial in such systems. A much more powerful factor has been the original pay base, insofar as raises are often based on percentages rather than flat amounts for all employees; thus, employees with higher base rates get significantly larger pay increases. In the past decade the system of differentiating raises by strengthening merit evaluations, emphasizing qualitative differences in performance, and reducing or eliminating cost-of-living increases has become more common, in an effort to reward better employees and stimulate better performance. That is, the trend has been toward emphasizing social exchange theory rather than equity theory.

*This is the most common meaning of equity theory narrowly construed. It often refers to pay similarity for groups or classes, especially for women and minorities. Although the Equal Pay Act of 1963 did much to rectify discrimination in pay by grade or classification, it has not removed pay inequity by organizational level in that white men continue to dominate—on average—the upper ranks of most political, bureaucratic, and entrepreneurial organizations. Examples include Congress, the presidency, the judiciary, the Senior Executive Service, the chief executive officers and boards of Fortune 500 companies, and so forth.

ranging from letters of positive acknowledgment to plaques and trophies. Recognition generally costs nothing and is an immensely powerful form of motivating. Nonetheless, recognition is utilized less than it should be according to most respected researchers. "Recognizing is one of the most neglected managerial practices, even though it can be one of the most effective for building commitment, increasing job satisfaction, and improving working relationships. Everyone, from the clerk in the shipping department to the vice president for operations, wants to be a winner or a hero" (Yukl 1998, 105).

Rewarding involves tangible incentives such as promotions, increases in pay (e.g., base pay increases or one-time bonuses), increased discretion, superior work assignments, perquisites (called "perks") such as a better office or special supplies, additional responsibilities/authority,[3] and so forth. As already discussed, pay and promotion rewards are generally more highly constrained in the public sector than in the private. Nonetheless, rewards do exist and are important to execute carefully. Performance standards, fairness, and clarity of reward determination are key to good implementation. Stated differently, rewards need to be based on performance goals that are important to the organization (e.g., not based on personal loyalty), and represent different types of contribution (e.g., high productivity vs. a "social" goal such as mentoring), using clearly explained guidelines. In utilizing recognition and rewards to their maximum, it is important to find out what individuals or groups find attractive, so that the incentives will be as motivating as possible. While one employee may find a public commendation of performance success sufficient, an employee who has been "underfilling" a position (performing higher-level responsibilities while maintaining a lower-level classification and salary) for several years may be difficult to appease with anything other than a reclassification and pay increase.

Sometimes employees do not work very hard despite positive incentives such as pay, recognition, and supplemental rewards; sometimes negative disincentives are necessary to set the acceptable bounds of behavior and to punish poor work and rule infractions. Of course, it has been well established that positive rewards are generally more motivating in terms of higher performance because they require less supervision and better suit the positive mindset of high quality. Thus, negative disincentives should be used more strategically and less often in most management situations. Negative disincentives include any sanctions that reduce perquisites, pay, work flexibility, status, honor, and pride, or even terminate employment and impose fines or imprisonment for actions that violate or defy administrative rules or laws. Disincentives can be very mild, for example, a verbal rebuke for carelessness, or extremely harsh, for example, a charge of criminal misconduct. If positive incentives are too uncommon, disincentives are too common and too relied upon. Disincentives are necessary in organizational settings, but they are very difficult to use effectively. The unpleasant aspects of disincentives can easily lead to resentment, scheming, work sabotage, and litigious court battles. Further, negative disincentives can lead to even poorer performance, rather than the improved performance that is the ultimate goal, because of discouragement and loss of self-esteem. Yet, without the bounds that they set, someone is likely to go too far or not far enough, and not only under- or misperform in their own capacity, but disturb or anger other workers as well, if only by their obstreperous behavior. Some of the more important dos and don'ts of negative sanctions are discussed in the guidelines section below. Taken together, positive and negative disincentives work at the lower end of Maslow's (1954) hierarchy of needs such as meeting basic living needs (via income), security, and basic human interactions (e.g., positive work relations).

In stark contrast to providing disincentives is the motivational technique of inspiring, which works at the higher end of Maslow's hierarchy—achievement, self-actualization, and spiritual connectedness. Inspiring involves providing encouragement to work for group and organizational goals regardless of personal benefit (Maxwell 2008). Unlike positive and negative incentives, which tend to rely heavily on the effect on the individual and the near term, inspiring relies on the effect on the group and the long term. The classic example of inspiring is illustrated by soldiers at war who risk their lives for very low pay and in terrible conditions, but do so with pride and satisfaction. More mundane examples include getting people to volunteer for organizational betterment teams, agree to work extra long hours without positive incentives, accept mentoring assignments despite the drain on time, or strive to work harder—not for personal benefit but for the good of the organization. Of course, positive benefits are more likely to accrue to the individual if the organization is successful as a whole, and inspiring behavior does not mean that both the individual and the organization cannot prosper simultaneously. Indeed, inspiring tends to emphasize that all fail if the organization fails (the rational appeal). It also uses emotional appeal ("do it for the team") and personal appeal ("do it as a favor for me"). When the motivational appeal of inspiring is effective, short-term sacrifice is seen as a justified and virtuous contribution or badge of honor. Although inspiring is merely useful in helping with daily work such as tackling an unpleasant task, it becomes crucial in dealing with crises and striving for long-term successes.

While the original work on motivation is based on behavioral conditioning, initially the work of Thorndike, Pavlov, and others, and later popularized through Skinner (1953, 1971, 1974), it was converted into management terms by Vroom (1964). Expectancy theory sets out the stimulus-response chain that must work effectively for high performance to occur through positive incentives. First, workers have to know that their efforts can in fact lead to good performance (this linkage is called expectancy by Vroom). There are many reasons why they might doubt this linkage: lack of innate ability, poor training, unclear assignment, lack of ambition, or even interest. The second linkage is between good performance and the delivery of work-related rewards (what Vroom calls instrumentality). Just because good performance is achieved, will rewards occur? This linkage breaks down when rewards are not awarded based on performance (but perhaps based on seniority or personal connections), are awarded inequitably (e.g., when the employee making an improvement gets the praise and the employee's superior gets the raise), or are altogether lacking. The final linkage, valence, is between the reward and the desirability of the reward to the recipient. Additional compensation may be a weak motivator if the recipient is more desirous of time off, more support (less stress), or better working conditions. Vroom speculates that these stages function in a roughly multiplicative fashion so that a "weak link" in any stage tremendously reduces motivation. Good managers monitor all the stages, not only identifying problems for the group as a whole but also examining the barriers to positive motivation for each individual. See Exhibit 14.6 for a figure identifying the basic elements of expectancy theory.

Perhaps the best-known leadership theory related to leadership style and motivation is path-goal (House 1971; House and Mitchell 1974). It holds that different leadership styles are more effective in different conditions, largely using the logic of expectancy theory. Supportive leadership emphasizes consideration for the needs of subordinates

Exhibit 14.6

Vroom's Expectancy Theory

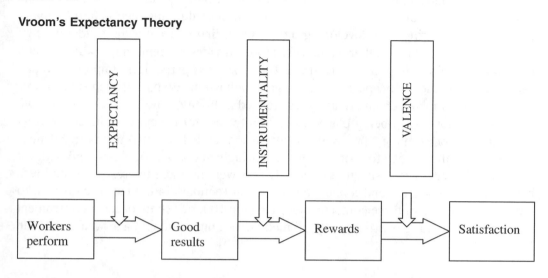

and establishing a friendly work climate. It is especially important when the work is intrinsically less interesting because it is repetitious or boring. It is also useful when the work is dangerous or stressful. Directive leadership provides specific instructions, orders, and structuring for subordinates. It is useful when there is a lack of training and experience, and when work is unstructured or complex, and subordinates need direction to work coherently or organize quickly. Participative leadership provides opportunities for subordinates to share their opinions and ideas, and sometimes to share in decision making. It is useful when knowledgeable workers can help with work-related problems, or when highly trained workers are better than the leader at structuring new or unclear work. Achievement-oriented leadership emphasizes challenging goals, excellence, and high standards. As transformational theories implicitly acknowledged later in the field's development, an achievement focus actually functions on a different basis and is, therefore, not as mutually exclusive as the other three categories are. It is particularly important when morale is weak, goals are low, or long-term strategies are unclear. As with other contingency models of leadership, path-goal theory emphasizes that leaders pay a great deal of attention to the characteristics of situations and their followers, and then pick the right style to suit. Weak leaders, according to most contingency theories, rely too heavily on one or two styles, and use them in inappropriate situations. The extroverted, "nice-guy" leader may fail to give commands in a crisis and inspire the group to set challenging goals. The linear, "tough-guy" leader may fail to support people when they are discouraged or fail to take advice and include people when he is less capable than his followers of tackling the problems at hand. The consensus-builder leader may fail to distinguish situations in which he needs to act with authority or not overburden inexperienced followers with decisions that they are unequipped to handle. (See chapter 3 for an extended discussion of path-goal theory.)

The research on motivation in leadership is extensive, but it is placed in very different conceptual packages that are rarely identical in what they include and exclude. Many researchers include all the aspects of motivating discussed in this section *in addition to* consulting, delegating, and developing others into a single "leadership" category (e.g., Mintzberg 1973). On the other hand, Yukl (1998) divides recognizing, rewarding, and motivating/inspiring into three categories. Therefore, it is particularly important to discern how motivation concepts are operationally defined in comparing such studies. In a study of federal managers, motivating was ranked as highly important, with one or two of the subcompetencies being placed in the top twenty for executives and supervisors respectively. For example, "provide recognition and rewards for effective performance" was ranked fifth (of 150) for both groups. Inspiring behaviors ranked 31st and 54th for executives/supervisors, respectively.[4] Supervisors were far more interested in employee behavior problems (21st) and conducting disciplinary actions (74th) than executives, who did not place either of these competencies in the top 100. In a study of local government managers, motivating was frequently pointed out as both a strength and weakness (Van Wart 2001).

Guidelines

1. *Recognize as many people as is possible and appropriate.* Because recognition is effective in motivating people and costs nothing except the effort, it should be an important practice for leaders. Leaders can recognize improvements in performance, maintenance of high standards and reliability, out-of-the-ordinary work accomplished for the group, displays of good organizational citizenship, commendable efforts that failed, solutions to problems, and so on. It is important not just to reward a few good performers or those with high-visibility jobs. Leaders who never recognize a subordinate may be sending a message that either they find the person's work unsatisfactory or that s/he is part of the "out" group, even if this is not true. Frequent and timely recognition is more motivating than recognition long after the fact, such as in an annual evaluation. For management purposes, specificity in recognition is particularly important for a number of reasons. First, recognizing specific behaviors illustrates an understanding that makes the praise more believable. Second, it reinforces ideal practices whereas general recognition does not necessarily do so. Third, specificity reduces the risk that recognition is perceived primarily as a popularity contest.

2. *Use an appropriate form of recognition.* There are many forms and levels of recognition, and it is important to use as many as possible for appropriateness and variety. While managing by walking around, the manager should be able to intersperse verbal praise as well as occasional suggestions for improvements. Most staff meetings should have a recognition component in which the leader quickly reviews current or special accomplishments. Written notes recognizing praiseworthy activities are very motivating. This requires that notes stipulating improvement areas also be written to balance personal records; however, negative notes and evaluations are better accepted when both the positive and negative

aspects of performance are in writing. Informal appreciation lunches can be as motivating as formal awards programs. "Nice try" discussions should quickly follow failures; such discussions can then easily segue into analyses of what went wrong and how things might be done differently next time.

3. *Explain how rewards and significant commendations are distributed.* People must know the rules of the game in order to follow the rules, and be motivated to seek high levels of performance. If a desirable internal position will be opening in the next year or so, it is useful to tell those eligible what you will be looking for so that they can groom themselves for the position if they are interested. If priorities have shifted, it is important to let people know this as soon as possible so that they are not surprised later. The act of explaining how rewards and commendations are distributed will ensure that managers are clear about the elements and standards of performance that they will later be identifying and tracking.

4. *Find out what rewards are attractive.* More money is always nice, but money may not be available, and it may not be the prime motivator in every case. A sense of what people value in rewards, as well as what type of recognition is meaningful, is a critical task in using recognition and rewards most effectively.

5. *Explain rules and procedures to ensure that subordinates understand the consequences of deviations.* When rules and procedures are not explained and documented, the liability generally flows up to the manager! For example, when an employee has not been provided training on sexual harassment and reported incidents are not followed up by the supervisor with documented coaching, then the employee may be absolved of legal culpability while the supervisor and the organization may become the legal target. It is important for managers to respond to infractions promptly and fairly, without showing favoritism to any individual or group. Additionally, it is important to note that not administering punitive action for noncompliance may result in lost credibility, encourage wayward behavior, and ultimately redound upon the leader.

6. *In order to avoid hasty and wrong conclusions, always investigate the facts before using reprimands and punishment.* Any savvy leader (or lawyer) knows that there are two or more sides to every story and that it is imprudent not to have the data from alternate perspectives before acting. When infractions are reported, leaders need to be trained to withhold judgmental or accusatory comments until additional information is gathered. Comments such as "I will not stand for that" or "That is unacceptable on the part of Matt" before an issue has been discussed with the accused can be construed as a prejudgment or bias. Further, if the original data are wrong, skip over significant facts, or omit substantial mitigating factors, then the leader is put in the position of contradicting her/himself. Comments that show concern but neutrality are much wiser: "I will look into that as soon as I can," "I will talk to Matt immediately to see what the problem was," or "We will need to investigate to see exactly what transpired." Some additional suggestions are: to remain calm and collected during the process, to express a sincere desire to help the subordinate, and to try to engage the target person in the problem resolution process.

7. *Use punishments that are fair and commensurate with the seriousness of the violation.* The general management practice of progressive discipline covers much of this guideline. This practice recommends that disciplinary actions be administered sequentially such that the target has the opportunity to understand problems/concerns and to take self-corrective actions. Assuming minor or low-grade problems, a target should first get coaching—recommendations on how to improve without a reprimand being involved. Next the target receives an oral warning—a clear statement that improvement will be necessary. Such warnings should be documented as notes in an activity record or desk personnel file. After one or more oral warnings the manager moves to a written reprimand that is maintained as an official document, whether or not it is sent to a central personnel file. An especially important opportunity in this regard is the annual evaluation in which written reprimands should be cited. Next, punitive action can be taken to include: suspension with or without pay, no pay raise, a fine, demotion of responsibilities (informal) or classification (formal), increased or special supervision, and ultimately termination of employment. In a fully articulated progressive discipline sequence a lesser formal punishment or two would precede termination. It is important to note that discipline is fact and situation specific: No set regimen can be determined in advance without knowing the specific facts and context. For example, some low-performing employees may gradually move up to written reprimands, improve for extended periods, and later have deteriorating performance requiring starting over at the oral reprimand level. Or occasionally an employee's violation is egregious or serious, requiring skipping steps in the chain. To use the example from above, the first case of sexual harassment may be egregious and documented, requiring a stern written warning and a corrective course of action (e.g., mandatory training and a distance restraint). Or, if an employee commits a serious enough violation, such as theft of government property, the organization may elect to move immediately to termination. Of course, due process must be carefully followed, such as a pretermination hearing (generally known as Loudermill rights[5]) and appropriate post-termination grievance procedures.

8. *When attempting to inspire, use energetic or emotional language with symbols, metaphors, and inclusive terms such as "we," "us," and "our."* Inspiring is both a technical and emotional undertaking. In technical terms, inspiring is assisted by language that captures the imagination or strikes clear mental images. "Fred, imagine what it would be like if we could announce that we had solved this problem at the annual retreat." Or, "This first phase of data gathering and logistics will be like setting the pylons for a bridge: hard work that is largely unappreciated. But once we have accomplished that, the program edifice that we can achieve will be a means of transport for thousands of needy clients from poverty to self-reliance." Appeals are not only to rational logic (especially self-interest), but also come in the form of emotional appeals (e.g., emphasizing group membership and pride) and personal appeals (based on the request of the leader). Effective appeals en-

able people to appreciate the long-term benefits of hard work and sacrifice. The emotional element is the sincerity and energy that it takes to make inspiration work. Lethargy and lack of trust are sure killers of inspiration.

BUILDING AND MANAGING TEAMS

The array of groups that organizations use is extensive (Hackman 1990). Unfortunately, the nomenclature for this complex area varies extensively. "Intact" or "functional" work groups (i.e., all the members of a unit) are generally distinguished from "true" teams, which have various distinguishing features such as selective membership (discussed below). Teams are indispensable in most organizations today and require a special set of skills to manage. Yet all groups—work groups and teams—share some common needs in terms of the values, identification, and group bonding that enhance the likelihood of optimal performance. This aspect is generally referred to as team building. Therefore, managing teams *involves creating and supporting "true" teams in addition to traditional work units, and team building involves enhancing identification with the work, intramember cooperation, and esprit de corps of both work groups and teams.*

There are three important parameters that capture most of the differentiation of groups in organizations. One parameter is group membership. Is group membership inclusive of all the members of a unit more or less automatically, or are members selectively recruited or assigned? Additionally, are all the members selected from within a work unit or are they chosen from a variety of units? Second, what is the work function and scope of the group? Is it to produce a service or product on an ongoing basis (a basic operational function), or is it to make a specialized, part-time, or one-time contribution to the process? Third, what is the degree of authority for independent decision making of the group? Are most ideas proposed, monitored, and approved by a leader with formal authority in the area (as is common in traditional work groups), or does the team have some degree of independence in how their work is handled, especially problem/process selection, problem identification, and solution implementation? The most independent teams, "self-managed teams," are capable of substituting team structure for most conventional leadership by an individual (Cohen and Bailey 1997; Kirkman and Rosen 1999). Needless to say, even these three parameters give rise to a large number of group permutations.

Traditional groups are those composed of all members of the unit who take care of ongoing operations and have a formal leader who makes most of the important decisions. Frequently called work groups in the team literature, they continue to be an indispensable element of organizational effectiveness, despite the rise in use and importance of team structures. When these intact operational work units are given a high degree of internal decision-making authority in which members are charged with work structuring or even the hiring of new members, they are generally called self-managed teams. When the group has selective membership, a specialized objective, and some independence, but is still from the same unit or work area, it is called a project team. When the membership is from a variety of areas, it is called a cross-functional team. Both cross-functional work teams (e.g., executive teams or standing interdepartmental committees) and cross-functional project teams (e.g., task forces or ad hoc interdepartmental committees) are common.

Both traditional work groups and different types of teams have their benefits and liabilities. These benefits are important for leaders to understand in order to choose the best mechanism for the work at hand. The liabilities are equally important because they point out the implementation challenges that can be overcome but are very common. Some of the strengths of work groups are clear membership, clear lines of authority, efficiency of operations, and stability. Thus for the large flows of daily work, work groups are well suited, with the work group leader (i.e., line manager) acting as the "traffic cop" for coordination and the queuing up and resolution of problems. The liabilities of work groups are also significant: lack of creativity, stifling of individual initiative, excess of rule maintenance (as much by the members for protection as the leader for control), and aversion to change. Because business operations can change so much more quickly in an era of rapidly evolving telecommunications, policy shifts, responsiveness to client tastes and preferences, and so forth, work groups are not well suited to handle the volume of problems, customized operations, and organizational modifications that typically occur—teams are.

The benefits of teams include: the ability to select appropriate skills for a particular project, the creativity and synergy they engender (especially in handling nonroutine work), their flexibility of structure (hence the difficulty of naming them clearly), and the fact that most of them can be easily disbanded. When they have a high degree of self-management, they generally report a higher degree of satisfaction as well. Thus, a regional care facility for the deaf and blind might have, in addition to a dozen work groups, a variety of standing cross-functional committees to monitor operations and quality control, a cross-functional project team to oversee the implementation of a new computer system, and a variety of project teams in various units to reduce costs in laundry, to monitor patient counseling treatments, to review all security precautions for the campus, and so on. Teams also have many potential liabilities as well. Liabilities include: lopsided representation, coordination problems, divided loyalty and role stress/confusion, time consumption, lack of commitment, and challenges in implementation. For example, because team responsibilities are generally in addition to regular duties, first loyalty often goes to regular responsibilities in busy times, both in terms of meeting attendance and task completion. Team members may agree to responsibilities in good faith but have no strong incentive to carry through. Team meetings can consume a great deal of time and energy, sometimes seemingly disproportionate to their value if they are not well managed. Often, teams are poorly established, so that both their mandate and authority is unclear. Even the scheduling of meetings and routine maintenance of the team such as note taking and responsibility tracking can easily deteriorate, as the team leader struggles with multiple responsibilities. See Exhibit 14.7 for a discussion of common problems.

It should also be noted that efforts to increase the positive effects of diversity are normally considered a part of building and managing teams, just as handling the negative aspects of diversity are grouped with managing conflict (the next competency to be discussed). Diversity has the potential to increase the creative power of teams, one of

Exhibit 14.7

Ten Common Problems That Teams Encounter

An excellent, common-sense review of teams is provided by Peter Scholtes (1988). Chapter 6 of his book reviews the types of problems that are commonly encountered by teams.

- *Floundering:* Teams commonly have problems starting, moving from one stage to the next, and even finishing up the project. They may be overwhelmed by the task in the beginning, lack the expertise to tackle the problem, have problems with consensus, or have problems letting go of the project.
- *Overbearing participants:* Often when members of the group have higher rank or status based on credentials or expertise, they insist on a disproportionate role in team decision processes. Although such members can contribute a great deal, they also discourage discussion of topics on which they do not agree and thus can diminish both creativity and the legitimate role of other participants. Overbearing participants generally do not talk much; they simply insist on holding sway when they do.
- *Dominating participants:* When members of the group insist on airing their opinions and views at length, regardless of their level of expertise, they dominate by force of personality. This diminishes the role of some and is simply frustrating or boring for others.
- *Reluctant participants:* The opposites of dominating participants are reluctant participants. While quiet participants are not necessarily a problem, it is a special challenge to elicit their ideas, and excessive introversion saps the energy of the group.
- *Unquestioned acceptance of opinions as facts:* Teams often have to elicit a variety of types of information and data from participants. Often, opinions are expressed authoritatively as facts, and other members of the group are reticent to express their skepticism when support is not supplied.
- *Rush to accomplishment:* When a member or members do not take the time to assess problems thoroughly, or take the time to analyze their decision and action processes, they risk accomplishing the wrong thing or making important mistakes.
- *Attribution:* Attribution is the normal process of assigning motives to actions that we observe. However, attribution can be problematic when it is not based on solid data and insight. When team members disagree as a part of the creative process, negative or largely unfair attributions become a likelihood. These negative attributions make all further interactions of the group very difficult.
- *Discounts and plops:* These are times when a team member makes a comment or suggestion, and the idea is either discounted (contradicted or potentially even ridiculed) or "plops" (completely ignored). In the creative process many ideas must be vetted that are not ultimately acted upon, so the trick is to make sure that the feelings of participants are treated with respect even though all their ideas may not be used.
- *Wanderlust:* This phenomenon happens when team members lose track of the meeting's purpose, either because of a lack of team discipline or they want to avoid a sensitive topic. Discussions wander off in many directions at once, or stray off the purpose of the team for an extended period.
- *Feuding team members:* While creative differences are helpful and healthy for teams, feuding team members are not. These feuds often predate the team and very well may outlast it too. The challenge for the team is to keep these feuds from dominating the discussion or tenor of the meetings.

their most valuable features, as well as ensure adequate representation and fairness.

Leaders can substantially enhance the conditions for facilitating team effectiveness. Of course, making sure that the task structure and team structure fit well requires thinking through design issues in advance. Providing clearly defined objectives and scope of authority is critical. What is the team tasked with, in what time frame, and with what authority? Leaders need to make sure that the team membership mix is appropriate in technical skills, interpersonal skills, number, and representation. Teams in which volunteers generally self-select does not mean that some members cannot be specifically invited for better balance or to fill skill gaps. A team should be given some authority, and generally substantial authority, which needs to be clarified upon its establishment. Just because teams have good members and well-defined missions does not mean that an external leader's responsibilities are over—generally far from it. Teams need strong outside champions to assist with resources and implementation issues; they also need adequate information and occasional guidance during the project to make sure that they are "on track."

In the research on leadership, managing "true" teams is rarely mentioned as a major competency, except by specialists in that area. However, more generically, team building is commonly designated as a major competency or competency cluster. The OPM placed team building in their top competencies in both the 1992 and 1999 versions (along with diversity or cultural awareness). Likewise, New Zealand and Australia place it in their top half-dozen competency clusters (Bhatta 2001). Yukl places team building with conflict management (1998). Federal managers ranked promoting teamwork within the organization as fourth (executives) or seventh (supervisors) out of 150 competencies; in addition at least four other elements of team building were identified by executives in the top 100 competencies. Local managers mentioned team building as a problem far more often than as a strength (Van Wart 2001).

Guidelines

1. *Analyze the work in order to assess the best group structure to use.* A natural tendency is to use one or two group structures for all work design. Today leaders must be far more sophisticated in using a variety of structures well. Sometimes a traditional work group structure is best, for example when the work is running smoothly, worker satisfaction is high, and efficiency is the foremost value. However, as worker characteristics include substantial experience, specialized expertise, or forms of work alienation, and/or work context demands frequent customization, rapid change, solution of numerous problems, or implementation of entirely new challenges, then traditional work group structures are likely to be suboptimal. Various forms of delegation can include either individuals or groups; delegation to individuals was discussed under both delegating and consulting. An example of group delegation is in the area of quality control. A single, rather narrow area of quality-control problems might be handled by an ad hoc project team tasked with "fixing the problem." The project team is tasked not only with analyzing and clarifying the problem, but proposing and potentially implementing a solution. A somewhat larger problem that spans several divisions might be handled by an ad hoc cross-functional project team. If quality control were being delegated to that group on an ongoing basis, then a cross-functional work team (e.g., a standing committee on quality control) might be used.

2. *When setting up new or special teams, be careful to think through the design elements carefully.* Typical issues include membership, mandate, authority, linkage, and group incentives. Membership varies by the type of work necessary. If it is a problem-solving team, then three to seven is generally considered optimal. If it is a standing committee to review or institute policies, then it may need a membership of six to fifteen, with subcommittees for detailed work. A mandate is important even for small groups so that unnecessary confusion is not induced. Preferably such a mandate is in writing. At the same time, the grant of authority should be addressed. Does the group need to get approval prior to action? Does it need to check in with management about its progress from time to time? While advisory groups are sometimes useful, members are generally less committed because of their limited role. Another important question to resolve is just how the team links to the management structure. Will there be an internal liaison? Is there an official executive champion outside the team? How will the team leader be selected—appointed in advance, nominated by the group, or possibly rotated? Finally, what types of incentives motivate the team as a whole and the members individually? Will team members need some relief from their regular duties? Will acknowledgment for success be adequate for the extra work incurred? Does the annual evaluation adequately include team contributions? Will the team members be eligible for an additional perquisite if the team is successful? If the team project is important to the organization, will the team be held accountable for sloppiness, slowness, or poor quality?

3. *Provide teams with special training.* When team structures became more popular in the 1980s, there was a widespread acknowledgment that the basics of running teams were extensive enough to warrant wholesale training. After all, if team structures are designed to expand or substitute for management, then background on team process and analytic tools only makes sense. A great deal of the quality-management training that was popular in the 1990s was in response to these needs. An excellent example of the types of team manuals that were created is *The Team Handbook* by Peter Scholtes (1988). Training for teams can include tips on getting started, analytic tools (e.g., the use of Pareto charts and nomination group technique), monitoring group progress (e.g., end-of-meeting reviews, alignment sessions), troubleshooting problems that teams commonly incur, and tips for disbanding, among others.

4. *When team building, use and emphasize common interests and shared values.* Whether it is traditional work groups or teams, groups work better when they have similar values, common goals, and shared interests. Although heterogeneity and diversity add to creativity and comprehensiveness, it is the sharing of common interests that coheres groups and enables high performance (Katzenback and Smith 1993). Team leaders or team-building facilitators should help the group establish those common interests and thus strengthen the sense of collective fate. Sessions that examine the values of members, the importance of the mission, and the various perspectives of the participants—when well facilitated—add

tremendously to the sense of group community and dedication. A well-known model of team development involves four phases: forming, storming, norming, and performing. Teams that have substantial missions but have not worked together in the past sometimes pay insufficient attention to forming, only to find the storming phase of group development that much more difficult to overcome, and the specter of distrust to be that much greater (Scholtes 1988, sections 6-1-6-9). Although competition among teams spurs creativity and goal stretching, as a rule of thumb, competition among team members of a single team is mildly counterproductive at best, and disastrous at worst.

5. *When team building, enhance group identity and morale.* Groups that have a strong identity are more likely to perform well. Therefore, the "trappings" of group identity can make a significant difference. A good group name, a logo, a slogan, a special meeting place, or even a drawer for group materials can all assist in creating an identity. Social interactions also make a big difference. Including food helps people bond—snacks, lunches, or even beverages. Sometimes it helps and is appropriate to convene a group at a nonstandard time if the work is important (e.g., a retreat setting on a Saturday). Of course, recognizing group importance, progress, and successes are extremely important. If the work at hand is not important, even if it is the solution to a specific problem, then it should not take the team's time. Those engaged in team building need to point out this importance, and even inspire the group on occasion if the group has or will have significant challenges. Success for groups may be a long way off and thus recognition of progress can provide the encouragement to work hard and renew efforts. Further, the success of resolving a problem, initiating a new program, or meeting new standards of excellence should be recognized in meetings, newsletters, and ceremonies as necessary.

MANAGING CONFLICT

Conflict management is used to *handle various types of interpersonal disagreements, to build cooperative interpersonal relationships, and to harness the positive effects of conflict.* It is most highly connected with the competency of team building because managing conflict is often a prerequisite to team building. It is also related to clarifying roles and objectives, because much conflict arises out of unclear responsibilities and work linkages. It is also related to problem solving in two ways. Interpersonal conflict is a special type of problem that managers must manage; additionally, successfully managed and integrated, conflicting perspectives breed a creative ferment that can contribute to problem solving. Although the following discussion refers to conflict as if it always involves others, in reality it may involve the manager as well. Nonetheless, the same principles apply; the manager who is personally involved in conflict must be particularly vigilant to be fair and follow good conflict management precepts diligently.[6]

The three main elements of conflict management are identified in the definition above (Fisher and Ury 1981; Rahim 1992; Thomas 1992). Essentially, conflict management involves reactive, proactive, and creative aspects (Runde and Flanagan 2010). The reactive portion of conflict management applies when the conflict has already occurred—either escalating out of past disagreements or arising suddenly out of a clash of opinions or personalities. In these cases, the manager's job is to resolve conflict (the most common conception of conflict management). Generally the types of conflicts that occur are divided into two major categories, although in reality most problems are a blend of the two types. Some conflicts arise out of differences of opinion about how things should be done. In the extreme case, good friends strongly disagree about the course of action to pursue, the method to adopt, and so forth. The second class of conflicts has personality as its basis. In the extreme case, colleagues fight over inconsequential issues (which may not even be work related) because of a lack of trust or personal animosity. In personality-based conflict, facilitators often:

- share concerns about the conflict and the well-being of the protagonists,
- try to retain neutrality,
- strongly discourage personalistic and unprofessional behaviors such as insults or refusal to interact at work,
- build on positive perceptions while carefully exploring negative perceptions, and
- insist that protagonists try to find ways to change dysfunctional behaviors.

In problem-based conflict, facilitators often:

- first seek to identify shared values and objectives (normally wider in scope than the conflict),
- then seek disclosure of perceptions of critical needs from each party,
- next look at a variety of ways to address those critical needs, and
- ultimately persist until the protagonists agree on a solution/course of action.

When a series of related issues is present, conflict managers generally seek to resolve the issues jointly rather than allowing them to be handled separately, so that there is maximum ability to exchange and negotiate across issues. When issues have both a problem and personality basis, ideally facilitators work on personality problems first (to build trust and cooperation). However, managers may have to simultaneously inhibit protagonist personalism and unprofessionalism, while primarily pursuing problem resolution because of time or other constraints.

Good managers do not just resolve the conflicts that arise, they are proactive in creating environments in which the likelihood of dysfunctional conflicts is minimized. Such managers are skillful at highlighting the different types of contributions of various individuals and are aware that good teams need a variety of people with different talents and personalities. They are also skillful at highlighting the importance of professionalism and what it means. Professionals understand that personal conflicts are out of place in the work setting, and that cooperative interpersonal relationships are key to retaining a work focus. This is not to say that professionals have no preferences about whom they work with or disagreements about approaches; however, professionals do not let personal preferences get in the way of the work, and they find ways to work through disagreements on their own.

Yet, conflict management can be more than reactive or proactive—it can be creative. Conflict has positive aspects that, when properly cultivated, bring significant value to work groups and teams. For example, the complete absence of conflict may indicate an unhealthy level of "groupthink." Groupthink describes a process in which everyone thinks in a nearly identical fashion and relies excessively on traditions, which results in their being blind to emerging problems and uncreative in handling new challenges. This insight is not new. The great eighteenth-century legislator Edmund Burke said, "He that wrestles with us strengthens our nerves, and sharpens our skill. Our antagonist is our helper." Managers good at conflict management do not try to eradicate conflict but rather try to channel it in productive ways to enhance friendly rivalry and group originality. Modest levels of competition among group members spur more demanding individual goals, while simultaneously improving group goals.

Although many researchers subsume conflict management under the general categories of leadership and interpersonal management skills, Luthans, Rosenkrantz, and Hennessey (1985) and Yukl (1998) both identify it as a special competency category. The OPM has done the same in its competency typologies. Among the 22 competencies identified in the earlier version, it ranked 15th among federal executives and 11th among supervisors. The increased focus is even more pronounced when looking at discrete aspects. For example, when rating the minicompetency of resolving problems among parties, the executive ranking was 22nd (of 150) and the supervisor ranking was 10th. Even more striking was the question regarding resolving complaints from employees (which might or might not involve a conflict). The executive ranking was a paltry 95th while the supervisor ranking was 25th (Van Wart 2002). Thach and Thompson's (2007) study notes that it is 5th among public sector leaders, but only 9th among their private sector counterparts. As we would expect, managing the more detailed aspects of people problems tends to be more important at lower levels. This competency was commented on the most by local government managers who identified it as a strength by two to one (Van Wart 2001). This correlates with employee responses on manager feedback forms stating that when conflict management is a problem in a unit or division, employees hold leaders highly accountable, even when problems involve intractable personality issues. Thus, good leaders do not ignore this area, even when it is not their forte.

Guidelines

1. *In conflict resolution, set the stage for positive interactions and analysis.* Negotiators know that they must establish credibility as facilitators of the peace process as well as get people to come to the bargaining table and stay there long enough to enact a settlement. The same general principles apply in conflict management. Facilitators establish credibility and rapport by expressing both concern for each of the parties separately and the need for improvement in the situation. Maintaining

impartiality is critical so that participants trust that the process and both sides of the story can be told without prejudice. As a fundamental ground rule, the person managing conflict must establish that personal attacks and other unprofessional behavior will not be accepted, and must be willing to enforce this standard if the parties are acrimonious. Instead of allowing negative feelings to be expressed, the facilitator should elicit recognition of mutual contributions and the benefits of joint cooperation. Only when the participants feel that they are involved in a fair process that will respect their rights and interests are they likely to engage in discussing the reasons for the conflict without excessive shrillness, while simultaneously disclosing the needs that they want met. It is important for the facilitator not to let these needs be defined too narrowly, so that the mix of solutions can be as broad as possible. For example, if two case managers are arguing over travel and load equity, because one travels to fewer but more complex cases and the other handles more cases but easier ones, the needs are not necessarily equalization of travel and load (although that is certainly a possibility), but more mutually acceptable and efficient redistribution of the work. Because the types of specialized roles currently being played might be suitable to the participants and good in terms of work production, the final solution may have more to do with increasing their appreciation of their respective roles than with changing their roles.

2. *In conflict resolution, seek common ground for genuine consensus.* When participants in a dispute trust the process, they are more likely to consider a range of acceptable solutions. Brainstorming a variety of ideas provides a range of acceptable solutions that allows for a creative and mutually agreeable one to be hammered out. Frequently, side benefits can be identified at the same time, so that the solution is not just the cessation of a negative situation, but potentially a positive enhancement of the process. Because the different parties may each have one or more different issues to resolve, it is important not to allow them to be handled separately, because generally some of the hardest issues are left to the end and can be handled only in the quid pro quo atmosphere that allows everyone to get something of value, while minimizing what each party must give up. Finally, good conflict managers are able to keep the parties discussing the issues until a win–win proposition is found that is satisfactory to all.

3. *Create an environment that reduces the likelihood of dysfunctional conflict.* Good managers are effective in preventing most conflict from arising in the first place. For example, they take a proactive approach to emerging situations so that they do not escalate into personal feuds. This may mean exploring and eliminating dysfunctional mental models (Argyris 1993). Such models are based on assumptions that are faulty because they are old, partial, or simply untrue. Good managers create an environment in which the diversity of contributions and talents of different players are appreciated. Nonetheless, managers who work with low performers need to make sure that their performance does not

continue to be substandard, since co-workers are highly frustrated by incompetence, shirking, or excessive inefficiency. Additionally, good managers can instill a professional atmosphere that discourages unprofessional behavior such as distorting important work patterns because of personality issues. That is, the professional work at hand takes precedence over personalities. Finally, in a well-managed environment the manager can often place the responsibility back on the parties in conflict to work it out for themselves if the issue is problem based rather than personality based. Allowing participants to manage and discover their own mutual accommodation can lead to a greater sense of professionalism and shared mission.

4. *Utilize the positive aspects of conflict.* Some conflict is actually healthy. In a high-performing environment, openness to different ideas and approaches is embraced. Debates are understood as necessary for idea refinement and the analysis of weaknesses. In fact, heated discussions are often understood as a prelude to bursts of creativity. Members of such groups may argue vociferously in a committee meeting but go to lunch together immediately afterward without a hint of ill will just as golfers or handball players may aggressively fight over a point, only to laugh about it later. In many situations, then, friendly competition (a type of contained conflict) is considered not only appropriate but also necessary to keeping analytic and creative skills well honed.

MANAGING PERSONNEL CHANGE

When organizations are in trouble, some of them rally by making the major changes necessary to survive and prosper. However, some organizations do not, and, consequently, either founder financially or simply eke out an existence as a sick organization (despite good products or important services they may offer). Necessary change may not occur for various reasons: because management and labor are locked in labor disputes, leaders lay blame for problems elsewhere, everyone is concerned about his/her job and future, everyone wants others to change, and yet no one wants to personally engage in change. The old management quip applies: "I don't mind change as long as I am not personally affected." In these instances leadership is weak and often brought down by an inability to manage personnel change. Managing personnel change involves *establishing an environment that provides the emotional support and motivation to change*. It focuses on the people side of change. It is highly related to—and indeed is the other half of—either microlevel or macrolevel change: managing technical innovation and creativity, and managing organizational change. This competency is born of the reality that good ideas or a good plan are simply not enough. People must want to change and be assisted through what is often an uncomfortable or even painful process (Washington and Hacker 2005).

It is instructive to think about personal and emotional aspects of dramatic change in order to gain insights into the organizational setting. Examples from one's personal life might involve a divorce, the loss of a loved one, or an unexpected and large loss of income (such as a sudden drop in the stock market). Organization-wide or radical process change in a unit can cause similar reactions in people (Woodward and Bucholz 1987). The first stage in this well-known pattern is denial. In this phase there is disbelief. Perhaps the information is incorrect or the situation will revert on its own accord to what is known. "But he lives such a healthy life." "But the market has been doing so well." Or "I am sure that this situation is only temporary." The second stage is anger. Who is responsible for the mishap? Such anger is as often self-directed as it is other-directed. "If only I had . . ." "She should have known better!" The third stage is mourning. "I will miss him so much." "I am so lonely living alone." The final stage is adaptation where one picks up one's life and moves on. "I will miss her but I need to form new relationships." "Because of the financial setback, I will have to change my plans, work a bit harder, and move my retirement back a year." For major change, the trick is generally not to skip these phases, but to move through them, to let go of the past, so that one is prepared to embrace the future. Of course, the phases of the cycle are rarely so clear or linear in reality, and people often get stuck in one phase.

There are many reasons people may resist change—often fiercely. Some reasons are more rational and some are more emotional, but they must all be overcome if change is to be embraced. On the rational side, change may have some relatively high costs in financial terms, for example, the purchase of new equipment, and in personal terms, for example, the replacement of familiar routines with the inconvenience of new ones. Change may serve as an economic threat to those who could suffer a loss of income, and even potentially of their jobs. Similarly, change may cause a loss of power as new strategies shift status from people familiar with a process to others. On the more emotional end of the spectrum, one of the main reasons for resistance to change is a lack of trust in those proposing it. When this is the case, people are suspicious of hidden agendas and menacing repercussions that may be kept from them "until it is too late." People also resent the intrusion and interference that accompany change programs. Often, people deny that change is even necessary. The absence of clear signals and the ability to blame external trends may lead people to assert that the status quo is the best option. If the organization has downplayed the need for change too long, it may be difficult to change as much as would be helpful for the organization. Even when the need for change is acknowledged, it is common for people to deny the feasibility of change. Perhaps past change efforts have been unsuccessful, or perhaps there is a sense that the quality of leadership is insufficient to technically implement change effectively. Because many change efforts are unsuccessful, and because many people experience a series of minifailures even during successful change processes, foreboding about personal failure can be great. Finally, many change efforts represent not only a shift in resources, processes, and strategies, but, at heart, a change in values that people may resent and resist. Perhaps the agency is decreasing its role in direct care provision, reducing service levels, or shifting its expectations of clients in ways contrary to what employees have long been accustomed to think and believe in.

Those who lead change efforts cannot afford to brush aside these reasons for resistance. While it may be impossible to address all of these types of concerns fully, successful change efforts must address most of them or else apathy, lack of cooperation, and even defiance will doom change efforts. The guidelines discuss the types of strategies that are generally necessary to minimize resistance to change.

In recent years, the competencies related to change have received more focus in the leadership literature. In the 1960s and 1970s, the literature was dominated by routine task- and people-focused competencies with little real attention to change. By the 1980s, a number of leadership theorists pointed out the shortcomings of such a limited conceptualization (Zaleznik 1977; Bass 1985; Schein 1985). Now, most theorists propose it as the third leg of the management trilogy in some fashion (Hunt 1996; Chemers 1997; Yukl 1999, 2002). The emphasis on change as a mega-factor in leadership has, in turn, meant the articulation of specific change competencies. Thus, for example, when the OPM restructured its conceptualization of competencies in 1997, it added a mega-category (one of five) called "leading change." In a study of federal managers, supervisors focused much more on acting as a liaison between workers and management to facilitate organizational change (22nd out of 150), while executives focused far more on seeking opportunities to change the organization to meet new goals (40th out of 150).[7] Local managers reported a good deal of attention paid to this issue, with about half feeling that it was a strength and about half reporting it as a major weakness.

Guidelines

1. *Generate a sense of importance or urgency about the need for change.* Whenever possible, change efforts should be initiated with data, examples, and anecdotal evidence of the need for change. Such evidence might be performance reports, discussions of legislative mandates, customer complaints, or economic trend data. People are naturally attached to the past and need assistance in the form of documentation or proof to separate from it. If the change is substantial, it is important to create a sense of urgency. For example, it may be necessary to outline the costs that will be incurred or the liabilities that will arise by not taking action.

2. *Involve and empower people in change processes.* By doing so, people's sense of self-determination and their ability to monitor their self-interests increases the likelihood of buy-in. In some cases subordinates may be put in charge of designing the overall change effort. Yet, even when the overall effort is to be designed by the executive or executives in charge, there should still be ample opportunity to involve people in the details, in monitoring the progress, and in making suggestions for corrective actions.

3. *Be honest about the challenges of change.* Major change initiatives always entail setbacks, process failures, and course corrections. Even champions of change may have moments of frustration, fatigue, and discouragement. If there has not been a realistic preview of the challenges, many people may balk at the first sign of difficulty and prematurely label the change a failure. Thus, identifying the need for perseverance and flexibility is important at an early stage. When the changes are traumatic, such as downsizing, it is generally a mistake to downplay the consequences and to minimize the degree of change necessary in the hope that things will miraculously improve. Rather, it is better to identify the realistic

threats to job security boldly, make the necessary cuts as soon as they are clearly identified and practical, and emphasize fairness and continued support to those who will be adversely affected.

4. *Ensure that people are well informed about the progress of change.* Lack of information breeds rumors, suspicion, and distrust. Further, lack of information may falsely signal a loss of support for change. Reports on the progress of change, even when there have been setbacks or a lack of forward movement, indicate interest and support for change initiatives.

5. *Exhibit ongoing support for the challenges of change.* This can be done in a number of ways. One of the most powerful is to participate in change activities personally, either continuously or from time to time as appropriate. Another form of support rejects easy solutions that do not fix underlying problems. This indicates that support is neither superficial nor uninformed. Another type of support praises efforts toward progress, rather than waiting for completion. Sometimes this is most important when the progress is slowest and most halting. Yet another form of support is to explain the "vision" behind the change in different ways as the process continues, so that people have different insights into what they are trying to accomplish. Fresh explanations also motivate in that they remind people that the work is all the more important for its challenges.

CONCLUSION

The people-oriented competencies reviewed in this chapter include consulting, planning and organizing personnel, developing staff, motivating, building and managing teams, managing conflict, and managing personnel change. (A review of the elements for these competencies is provided in Exhibit 14.8.) As a competency cluster, people-oriented behaviors are important for both supervisors and executives, but, true to the conventional wisdom, lower-level managers have a slightly stronger emphasis in this area in terms of where they focus their attention. Both executives and supervisors (in the federal study) give substantial attention to this area. Supervisors give slightly more attention to consulting, planning personnel, motivating, and managing conflict overall. The competency that had the lowest level of attention was managing personnel change.

To the degree that we define leadership primarily as leading others, these competencies are core to the leadership endeavor. Indeed, one school of theorists largely defines leadership as the people- or relations-oriented competencies. But even if the leadership definition that one prefers does not identify people-oriented competencies as the very highest priority, it is hard to conceive of them as not being vital and substantial because they are so instrumental in the dynamics of leading. These competencies may be no easier or harder to learn than other competency clusters; however, they are certainly more subtle.

Next we turn to the last competency cluster, organizational-oriented behavior. Leaders must not only ensure high-quality technical results and that people are involved, coordinated, cultivated, and energized, they must also see the "big picture," interact with external people and issues, develop corporate skills, and make decisions and changes based on macrolevel needs.

Exhibit 14.8

Summary of Chapter 14

People-oriented behavior	Subelements of behavior	Major recommendations
Consulting		
Checking with people on work-related matters and involving people in decision-making processes	• Soliciting information from people • Inviting people to be involved in decision making to some degree	1. Evaluate the decision surrounding substantive decisions. 2. Seek as much input for substantive decisions as possible. 3. Utilize the ideas, suggestions, and input of others for substantive decisions to the maximum feasible degree.
Planning and organizing personnel		
Coordinating people and operations, and ensuring that the competencies necessary to do the work are, or will be, available; it also involves self-planning	• Fitting people to schedules and making the appropriate changes as work and personnel needs change • Matching the talents, interests, and preferences of people to the work • Using personal time-management skills	1. Ensure that specific staff assignments are understood and accepted. 2. Match staff preferences and competencies to the work as much as possible. 3. Stay on top of scheduling changes. 4. Review long-term organizational competency needs to ensure organizational capacity. 5. Manage personal schedule effectively.
Developing staff		
Improving subordinates' effectiveness in their current positions and preparing them for their next position or step	• Supporting: the emotional component of development • Coaching: helps employees do a task more effectively • Mentoring: refers to aiding a person's career development and is sometimes referred to as career counseling.	1. Show courtesy to and interest in all, and demonstrate positive regard for others to the greatest degree possible. 2. Promote a person's self-esteem and reputation. 3. Listen to personal problems that affect work performance and take the time to counsel subordinates. 4. Analyze subordinates' overall performance and identify deficiencies. 5. Monitor and correct errors. 6. Provide career advice and encouragement. 7. Provide special opportunities for subordinates to prepare for a future position.

(continued)

Exhibit 14.8 (*continued*)

People-oriented behavior	Subelements of behavior	Major recommendations
Motivating		
Enhancing the inner drives and positive intentions of subordinates (or others) to perform well through incentives, disincentives, and inspiration	• Providing positive incentives (e.g., recognition and rewards) • Providing the negative disincentives that are sometime necessary to set the acceptable bounds of behavior and to punish poor work and rule infractions • Providing inspiration that encourages work for group and organizational goals regardless of personal gain	1. Recognize as many people as possible and appropriate. 2. Use an appropriate form of recognition. 3. Explain how rewards and significant commendations are distributed. 4. Find out what rewards are attractive. 5. Explain rules and procedures to ensure that subordinates understand the consequences of deviations. 6. In order to avoid hasty and wrong conclusions, always investigate the facts before using reprimands and punishment. 7. Use punishments that are fair and commensurate with the seriousness of the violation. 8. When attempting to inspire, use energetic or emotional language with symbols, metaphors, and inclusive terms such as "we," "us," and "our."
Building and managing teams		
Managing teams involves creating and supporting "true" teams in addition to traditional work units, and team building involves enhancing identification with the work, intramember cooperation, and esprit de corps of both work groups and teams	• Creating and supporting "true" teams in addition to traditional work units • Enhancing identification with the work, intramember cooperation, and esprit decorps of both work groups and teams	1. Analyze the work in order to assess the best group structure to use. 2. When setting up new or special teams, be careful to think through the design elements carefully. 3. Provide teams with special training. 4. When team building, use and emphasize common interests and shared values. 5. When team building, enhance group identity and morale.

(continued)

Exhibit 14.8 (*continued*)

People-oriented behavior	Subelements of behavior	Major recommendations
Managing conflict		
Handling various types of interpersonal disagreements, building cooperative interpersonal relationships, and harnessing the positive effects of conflict	• Managing conflict that has already occurred—either escalating out of past disagreements or arising suddenly out of a clash of opinions or personalities • Proactively creating environments in which the likelihood of dysfunctional conflicts is minimized by enhancing a sense of professionalism in which employees work through their differences openly and maturely. • Using the positive aspects of conflict for creativity, dynamism, and to avoid "groupthink"	1. In conflict resolution, set the stage for positive interactions and analysis. 2. In conflict resolution, seek common ground for genuine consensus. 3. Create an environment that reduces the likelihood of dysfunctional conflict. 4. Utilize the positive aspects of conflict.
Managing personnel change		
Establishing an environment that provides the emotional support and motivation to change	• Reducing the reasons to resist change, such as fear, mistrust, and personal risk • Increasing the reasons to support change such as the prospect of a better future, involvement • Providing personal involvement and support for the challenges and pain of change	1. Generate a sense of importance or urgency about the need for change. 2. Involve and empower people in change processes. 3. Be honest about the challenges of change. 4. Ensure that people are well informed about the progress of change. 5. Exhibit ongoing support for the challenges of change.

NOTES

1. Of course, this returns to the debate about the proper definition of leadership discussed in chapter 1. The other major definition of leadership emphasizes change or transformation.

2. While leaders generally focus on developing staff and subordinates because of proximity and responsibility, they also often develop others—colleagues, clients, and even superiors. Although not discussed here, this aspect is consistent with the competency as defined.

3. While additional responsibilities and authority can sometimes be construed as rewards, they are not always considered as such by recipients. A common organizational dysfunction involves "rewarding" high-performing employees with so many responsibilities and so much authority (without significant changes in pay and classification) that they become overburdened, burn out, and eventually seek employment elsewhere. Another common problem is to "reward" with additional responsibilities but without the concomitant authority, which often feels like work is simply being piled on, and that one is really being penalized for competence!

4. However, this item captured only a portion of inspiring behaviors: "motivate subordinates and peers toward future goals."

5. In *Cleveland Board of Education v. Loudermill* (470 U.S. 532, 1985), the Supreme Court firmly established that procedural due process will apply where a public-sector employee is dismissed, including a pretermination opportunity to respond. In practice, many jurisdictions request a response in writing, within a limited time frame, prior to dismissal. Grievance procedures supplement this process after the termination order.

6. Of course, not only are managers themselves involved in conflicts from time to time, but they also can engage in dysfunctional behaviors. When the manager is engaged in a conflict with a subordinate, it is easy to use power to try to force compliance (the "I'm-in-charge" syndrome). When the manager is engaged in a conflict with a colleague, such as another department head, the frequent response is simply not to interact with the person (the "separate-kingdoms" syndrome). When the manager is engaged in a conflict with a superior, it is common to take a legalistic response (the "that's-not-in-the-rules" syndrome).

7. On the other hand, executives ranked acting as a liaison 74th, and supervisors ranked seeking opportunities to move the organization toward the future 103rd.

Organizational-Oriented Behaviors

There are many similes used for organizational leadership. One of the best is to think of an organizational leader as the captain of a ship. The captain must make sure that the ship is provisioned, schedules are kept, and tasks delegated (chapter 13). The captain must also be sure that the crew is trained, motivated, and works in teams (chapter 14). The captain also has to navigate the ship. The Roman philosopher Publius observed that anyone can hold the helm when the sea is calm. It is when storms approach and strike that the wisdom and skills of the captain are truly tested. So it is with administrative leadership in which anticipating and even harnessing the dramatic external events that occasionally occur are singularly defining events.

The third category of behavior in the dynamics of leadership, then, are those that are organization oriented. They include scanning the environment, strategic planning, articulating the mission and vision of the organization, networking and partnering, performing general management functions such as human resource management and budgeting, decision making, and managing organizational change. The emphasis of these competencies shifts to an external perspective and a systems approach (e.g., "big picture") and more attention is paid to organizational culture and organizational change (and crisis).

Historically, there has been a substantial difference between supervisors and executives in their emphasis on organization-oriented competencies. Managers and executives were given more system responsibilities and expected to be more global in their perspective. Supervisors were expected to pay close attention to microlevel production and personnel issues; they were not expected to be particularly aware of the system or external affairs. However, today the flattening of the organization, the decentralization of responsibilities in many areas, the increased level and speed of change, and so forth, has pushed the importance of many of the organization competencies down to levels lower than those of the past.

The study of federal managers conducted for this book tends to support the traditional emphasis more than the contemporary emphasis. Most dramatically, only 17 percent of supervisors' top competency concerns were in the organization category, while 39 percent of executives' concerns were. This emphasis is moderated but substantial when looking at all concerns (the top 100 of 150 competencies). Organization-oriented competencies move up to 40 percent of the total for supervisors and 47 percent of the total for executives. Refer back to Exhibit 13.1 for a comparison of the different domains; proportions reflect some exclusions and dual counting established in the study. However, these data may be disproportionately affected by two factors. First, the data were collected in the early 1990s before the federal government made a concerted effort to adopt more contemporary practices. Second, the federal government, because of its size and the requisite specialization that this generally causes, will always tend to emphasize more differentiated leadership models.

The study further found that differences between the supervisory and executive levels varied among the different competencies (Van Wart 2002). In terms of quantity of attention, scanning the environment was relatively similar at both levels and only modest differences appeared in networking and partnering, decision making, and performing general management functions. Yet, while the *level* of attention was similar, the *nature* of the attention often varied substantially. In environmental scanning, executives focused on budget and policies issues whereas supervisors were more sensitive to specific client needs. In decision making, the scope of decision varied enormously. The greatest differences in attention were found in strategic planning, articulating mission and vision, and managing organizational change. The largest differences are mainly the result of structural factors; supervisors and executives tend to have different roles and functions. The most important function in terms of criticality was decision making, although it was not as extensively elaborated by numerous microcompetencies as others. This confirms Bass's comment that "the intensity of leadership acts may be much more influential than the frequency with which the acts occur" (1985, 8). On the other hand, activities that were not quite as intense, but were represented by many competencies included networking, scanning the environment, performing general management functions, and, for executives only, strategic planning. The least-emphasized competencies were articulating the mission/vision and managing organizational change. (See Exhibit 15.1 for a detailed comparison of the different competencies.)

SCANNING THE ENVIRONMENT

Scanning the environment, also known as environmental scanning and external monitoring, involves *gathering and critically evaluating data related to external trends, opportunities, and threats on an ongoing and relatively informal basis*. It is similar to both monitoring/assessing and consulting in that it is informal, ongoing, and generally not systematic, except that the focus is on external rather than internal affairs. It is related to strategic planning in its external perspective, but the data-gathering phase in strategic planning is generally conducted on a more formal, short-term, and systematic basis. It provides the base for most organization-oriented competencies, especially networking/partnering and decision making.

Even in the most stable times, environmental scanning is important. It provides leaders at all levels with fresh ideas, enhances credibility, and ensures vigilance with regard to unexpected events. For example, a manager in the Department of Veterans Affairs may learn about a new medical practice that saves money, a county flood-control manager will inspire confidence in the flood-control board when able to speak of comparative practices, and an agency director may be better prepared for a "copycat" scandal by monitoring events in other states. The importance of environmental scanning increases substantially

Exhibit 15.1

Number of Federal Executives and Supervisors Rating Organizational-Oriented Competencies among the Top 20 or Top 100 Competencies

	Executives		Supervisors	
	Top 20 competencies	Top 100 competencies	Top 20 competencies	Top 100 competencies
Scanning the environment	1	8	1	8
Strategic planning	1	8	0	4
Articulating the mission and vision	1	4	0	4
Networking and partnering	2	15	0	12
Performing general management functions	0*	11	1	8
Decision making	3	6	2	5
Managing organizational change	1	5	0	3
Total	9	57	4	44

Note: Based on a study of 150 competencies. Competencies selected based on a rating of "very important" or "crucial" by those who reported that competency applied to their positions. Two competencies were excluded from the original study because they were traits and several dozen competencies were dually counted. With dual counting, the top 20 list actually includes 23 "hits," the top 100 supervisor list includes 112, and the top 100 executive list includes 121. Proportions in Exhibit 13.1 reflect these adjustments.

*The item "Make decisions on significant personnel actions" was ranked 20th for supervisors (and thus included in the top 20) and 21st for executives.

in times of rapid change, tightening resource constraints, or prospective paradigm shifts. The most common examples here are related to sudden or long-term budget reductions. The great recession that began in the general economy in 2008, but hit the public sector one to two years later is a case in point. Leaders and managers who do not see major budget reductions coming, and are therefore slow to act, generally exacerbate the crisis substantially. The prudent manager who sees a midyear rescission coming will start pruning expenses and postpone all noncritical financial commitments. The manager who does not know that a budget shortfall is likely may have to return 10 percent of the budget in the second half of the year.

Three elements of this competency can be identified. First, environmental scanning involves broad and informal monitoring and consulting outside the organization. The various "environments" include political, demographic, technological, economic, local market, and industry arenas. Data are gathered by talking with people (clients, citizens at large, legislators and their staffs, competitors, suppliers, other stakeholders), attending conferences, reading, and doing research in targeted areas. This element emphasizes breadth.

The second element involves identifying external trends, opportunities, and threats. In the enormous flow of information that is provided by the environment, what are the critical issues to monitor and potentially to act upon? Among many other less important issues, a public power director may be simultaneously monitoring dropping oil prices, increased private sector competition, and a greater demand for subsidization of the general fund.

The third element involves investigating external trends of significance in greater detail. When critical trends are observed, the savvy leader puts out more "feelers," and may even spend a considerable amount of time and energy to gather strategic data to move directly to a decision mode. The election of several new council members who have been openly critical of city governance may spur some department heads to request ideas for improvement from the public and to assess operations in light of that commentary. For some historical examples of the importance of good environmental scanning in the public sector, see Exhibit 15.2.

The research has long shown the importance of environmental scanning for executives (Pavett and Lau 1983; Kraut et al. 1989; Ginter and Duncan 1990). It has been acknowledged and emphasized at nonexecutive levels only more recently as a result of the quality management revolution of the 1990s and decentralized strategic management initiatives in select public sector industries such as education. Nonetheless, it is not always highlighted as a metacompetency or even midlevel competency in leadership taxonomies. For example, in Howard and Bray's famous competency study at AT&T, there is no explicit category for either environmental scanning or strategic planning among the twenty-six identified (Howard and Bray 1988). The emphasis on organization-level competencies was largely ushered in during the 1990s, after the economic upheavals and infusion of transformational theories in the 1980s. Typical of this emphasis was the Office of Personnel Management (OPM) inclusion of external awareness on its 1992 competency list (22 items), which it retained in its 1998/2006 models. It was ranked 19th for executives and 20th for supervisors, but this masks the largest absolute difference among the 22 competencies between the two levels. A discrete analysis shows that the scanning done by lower-level managers is extensive but very much focused on specific clients, whereas middle and senior managers pay far more attention to trends, policy ramifications, and organizational issues, as one would expect (Van Wart 2002). A comparison of the competency profiles of major corporations in 1996 shows that strategic elements had grown considerably in importance (U.S. OPM 1999). Further, it is identified among the executive competencies for the countries that have experienced the most radical public sector transformation in the 1990s—Australia and New Zealand (Bhatta 2001). In a study of senior U.S. local managers who were very aware of their communities, it was twice as frequently assessed as a strength than as a weakness (Van Wart 2001).

Guidelines

1. *Identify multiple relevant sources of external information.* All sources of information are incomplete and biased to some degree; therefore, multiple sources provide a balanced perspective. For example, client complaints are a very valuable but highly skewed source of information. Complaints identify critical weaknesses or system breakdowns that leaders need to understand and address. Client data supplied by random surveys provide a much broader, more balanced picture of the scope of client problems, but do not provide the level of insight that complaint data do. It is common for most client complaints to be isolated incidents; surveys

---

Exhibit 15.2

The Importance of Environmental Scanning

The quality of environmental scanning is related not only to the breadth and quality of information gathering but also to good data analysis and follow-up. For example, following the September 11, 2001, terrorist attacks on the World Trade Center and the Pentagon, analysts noted insufficient information, insufficient analysis of the information that was available, and an absence of follow-up despite previous terrorist attacks (e.g., on the Trade Center itself and the bombing of the Alfred P. Murrah Federal Building in Oklahoma City). Environmental scanning is important for all organizations; however, the importance of good environmental scanning is more obvious in military and public safety functions where lives are at stake. Three short examples from American public sector history dramatize the importance of failures in this function.

In 1876, General George Custer, a seasoned military man, took a force of 675 soldiers to the Little Bighorn River in Montana to engage the Indians there who had been ordered to disperse. He had decided to ignore orders to wait for three other generals to arrive with an additional 1,400 troops. Although he knew his men would be somewhat outnumbered, he also knew that his men had superior weapons, training, and leadership. He had become famous in the Civil War for leading daring and successful cavalry charges against great odds. He divided the group into three units so that they could attack from both sides of the river; his own unit had 267 soldiers. What he had failed to learn, however, was that the Indian force was three times the size they had guessed and that the Indians had many of the new repeating rifles that his own men did not. The rest is history.

In 1941, the U.S. military knew that war with Japan was likely if not inevitable. Warnings had gone out to military commanders on November 27, 1941, but without a specific location. The attack was expected to occur in the Philippines. Shortly after 7:00 A.M., a military message from a radar station (a new technology) was sent to headquarters at Pearl Harbor that there appeared to be a large airplane squadron coming in from the north. It was ignored as being impossible and a likely malfunction. Despite these warnings, the Japanese surprise was complete, leaving 2,403 killed and destroying 17 ships. It was the most stunning battle defeat in U.S. history.

In January 1986, children across America watched as the first "teacher in space," Christa McAuliffe, took off from Cape Canaveral. Seventy-three seconds after takeoff the space shuttle Challenger blew up. The problem was a failure of the O-rings, gaskets that join together the segments of the shuttle. The O-ring problem was well known to technical experts and National Aeronautics and Space Administration (NASA) administrators, and the specifications for launch stipulated a temperature of at least 53 degrees. However, because of below-normal temperatures, the launch schedule was slightly delayed, but under building political pressure, NASA officials ordered the launch despite the low temperature and over the objections of contractor Morton Thiokol. The children learned a lesson different from the one that had been planned.

---

help to identify which are aberrations and which are patterns. Together, complaint and survey data can provide a leader with a client profile that is both broad and deep, and the weaknesses of one are offset by the strengths of the other.

2. *Reflect on the significance of external trends.* Today senior managers are bombarded with enormous amounts of information. Lurking in those data may be clear signs of an economic downturn, a tight job market, the obsolescence of a service due to new competition, growing client dissatisfaction, or a deteriorating public relations image. However, it is a leader's responsibility to review and reflect on data to distill these trends, which may not be immediately apparent.

3. *Follow up on the significant external trends.* External monitoring should lead to internal adjustments. Sometimes those adjustments are relatively rapid and ad hoc. For example, many public sector organizations found themselves woefully behind the technology curve in the 1990s. Their organizations needed large infusions of technology and personnel to support that technology. However, because technology was also a growth area in the private sector, trained personnel were in extraordinary demand and public organizations often were unable to compete, largely because of inadequate salaries. Environmental scanning indicated that the problem was not simply poor recruitment, bad timing, or other technical problems, but rather systemic issues that were structural. Therefore, special compensation schedules were often instituted for information technology (IT) staff, which were elevated several pay grades from where they would normally be classified.

4. *Link scanning and strategic planning.* Good environmental scanning by leaders is a prelude to the data gathering that occurs in strategic planning. It should inform and guide the strategic planning exercise and provide an intuitive check on the more systematic and formalized data gathered. To extend the previous example, the IT industry "bubble" burst after the new millennium upgrades. Technology costs dropped and IT workers became relatively abundant at all levels as the IT industry laid off tens of thousands of workers. The new strategic planning issue for leaders in public sector human resources and IT is whether or not to restore the former salaries for incoming IT workers.

STRATEGIC PLANNING

A short definition for strategic planning is a blueprint for action. A more substantial definition is *a disciplined effort to produce fundamental decisions and actions that shape and guide an organization* (Bryson and Crosby 1992). It emphasizes the future, astute analysis, wise option selection, and coherence among decisions. It is often considered one of the major hallmarks of great leadership, because without it, major and lasting organizational change is unlikely. It is also extremely important in providing a common frame of reference for the organization and because it defines the feedback loops so critical for contemporary high-performing organizations (Halachmi 2003).

It is related to but can be distinguished from operations planning, personnel planning, environmental scanning, and decision making. Whereas operations planning is largely internal and tactical, strategic planning is more externally focused, broader in focus, and longer in time frame. While personnel planning emphasizes the development of people, strategic planning emphasizes the "fit" with the environment. As discussed in the previous section, the data-collection phase in strategic planning is more disciplined and structured than the ongoing external monitoring in environmental scanning. The process used in decision making and strategic planning is similar; however, here, strategic planning refers to the comprehensiveness of the decisions and the systematic alignment of current and future decisions in a broad organizational context. These distinctions are not insignificant. For example, good supervisors may engage in operations and personnel planning without ever being involved in strategic planning at all. Many executives are very well connected and well informed about what is going on in the environment and their organizations but are incapable of translating this into effective strategic planning. Likewise, many executives are almost constantly involved in decision making and quite good at it, but then fail to systematically review and coordinate these decisions in a comprehensive organizational process. Such a failure substantially weakens communication, broad input, empowerment, and institutionalization of change.

Strategic planning is part of the strategic management complex in contemporary organizations: strategic planning, performance measurement, program evaluation, and performance budgeting (Haas 2003, 899). Performance indicators provide the indicators of success. Program evaluation provides the in-depth analysis of efficiency, effectiveness, appropriateness, impact, etc. Performance/strategic budgeting provides the linkage of strategy and indicators with funding (Khan 1998). Because of the more entrepreneurial and market-based environment in which public organizations are situated, strategic management issues and competencies are increasing in importance for leaders.

The elements will be discussed in terms of the four building blocks of strategic planning, and the typical strategic planning process will be covered in the guidelines. The first element of strategic planning involves defining the mission of overall organizational purposes and the overall vision of the preferred future of the organization. What is the organization fundamentally about and where does it want to position itself in the future? Good strategic planning clarifies this "big picture perspective," as well as adjusting it or even occasionally changing it. Formerly, many public sector organizations merely assumed their missions and visions, but in the 1990s, explicit exercises to articulate these concepts were introduced and public statements became commonplace. Unfortunately, many of these statements really function just as public relations hyperbole that have little to do with real strategy (e.g., market niche, core competence, realistic goal setting, etc.). Compare the raft of mission statements "to be the best in the world," and those that implicitly exhort employees to try harder, for example, Federal Express's mission statement to deliver a package anywhere in the United States by 10:30 A.M. or Southwest Airline's guaranteed lowest price. A state police agency might define itself as the leading police agency in the state emphasizing standard setting for local government agencies, or it might define itself as a coordinating and support agency emphasizing cooperation and specialized services, such as computer and securities fraud, high-quality laboratory work, and freeway traffic control.

The second element of strategic planning involves defining objectives of organizational purposes at the departmental or unit level. Different operational units contribute different aspects to the overall purpose. State police agencies will have different objectives for routine investigation, detective work, traffic control, drugs, special operations, white-collar crime, police laboratory, public relations, and so forth, depending on how they are organized, what the agency is authorized to do, and how it envisions its own mission. Strategic issues at this level involve the selection of areas, the amount of resources allocated, and their coordination.

The third element involves defining alternatives and selecting the best ones to accomplish objectives. In strategic planning, the selected alternatives are generally called strategies. Because of the variety and number of white-collar crimes committed, police agencies have to be highly strategic about which of those crimes to actively pursue and what specialized skills will be required. That is, a major part of the strategy involves what types of cases to turn over to other jurisdictions depending on their nature, severity, and scope.

The fourth element or level is related to the goals and their concrete measures. What are the specific targets for accomplishment and what are the indicators of success? Goals and measures generally should have an array of outputs and outcomes. The goals of a traffic control division may include a decrease in speeding and a reduction in traffic deaths. These might translate into an output measure of 100,000 stops (not necessarily tickets) and an outcome measure of highway deaths that are reduced to a level below the national average.

Although long acknowledged as an important executive function, strategic planning (except in specialized military settings) has not been placed on most leadership competency lists until recently (see the discussion of this under environmental scanning). More often than not it has been lumped with planning. In its 1992 study, the OPM included aspects of strategic planning in three of its top 22 competencies: planning and evaluation, vision, and external awareness. For executives, these competencies were ranked 14th, 16th, and 18th; for supervisors they were ranked 21st, 15th (higher due to tactical aspects), and 20th (U.S. OPM 1997). Clearly, this competency is far more important at the executive level than at the supervisory level. The category of strategic thinker was ranked 8th in the Thach and Thompson competency survey (2007). In the in-depth analysis this emphasis shows up: executives placed one of the microcompetencies in the top 20 whereas supervisors place none there, and executives identified 8 in the top 100 whereas supervisors only identified 4 (Van Wart 2002).

Guidelines

Note that the process is not as linear as depicted; in particular, the second through fourth steps are largely concurrent, as are the fifth and sixth steps. Furthermore, each organization customizes strategic planning to suit its needs and will define its nomenclature differently.

1. *Define the strategic planning process itself.* Because organizational strategic planning must be broad and comprehensive, it needs to be planned. Decisions need to be made about the time and resources to commit to the project. In addition, important decisions need to be made about the type of process to use. The traditional corporate-style strategic plan tries to design carefully cascading objectives, strategies, and goals with substantial centralized input and approval. In another model, only the broadest mission and objectives are set centrally, and divisions or units are encouraged to behave as relatively independent strategic business units. Consequently, more decisions are made as required by evolv-

ing situations. This second approach is known as logical incrementalism in the strategic planning literature (Lindblom 1959; Mintzberg and Quinn 1991). This step also designs the level of inclusiveness and role of stakeholders in the process (Freeman 1984). This aspect is particularly critical and complex in the public sector (Nutt and Backoff 1993).

2. *Collect systematic and comprehensive data.* There are at least three types of data that need to be collected. First, the organization should have a great deal of performance data that can be summarized for comparison over time and with similar organizations. Second, it is likely that a number of special program evaluations (Newcomer 1996) or specialized organizational assessments (Van Wart 1995) have occurred in the intervening period between the current and previous strategic planning process, which also provide data. Third, environmental data can be included from generalized environmental scanning as well as from more formalized scanning of the process itself. Examples of this more proactive approach include forecasting using experts or leading indicators, trend extrapolation, and impact assessments.

3. *Review the mission and capabilities of the organization.* During the process of strategic planning is a good time to review the basics and to make sure that the organization is well aligned with its environment and its own competencies. At the macro level, the organization reviews its mission and overarching vision. Most of the time this level of analysis is largely pro forma; however, major changes in the environment (such as major legislation or dramatic shifts in the service environment) or new leaders may cause a more robust review. Another perspective for large agencies with a variety of missions competing for resources is portfolio analysis (Wind and Mahajan 1981), which, in the public sector, must substitute a broader value base than the strictly economic one generally used in the private sector. Good strategic planning processes always engage a rigorous analysis of objectives and their related strategies. Well-known techniques are the analysis of strengths, weaknesses, opportunities, and threats (known as SWOT) developed at Harvard in the 1920s, and the review of core competencies (Prahalad and Hamel 1990).

4. *Identify major issues and alternatives.* First, the scope of change that the organization will attempt must be defined. Rarely do organizations make a radical shift in their mission and overarching vision nor should they. When they do, however, it is important to be highly conscious of the major shift in purpose and direction. Second, good strategic planning processes generate numerous possible alternative strategies. Such strategic analysis encourages creativity and insight and is the heart of the entire process. When this aspect of strategic planning is superficial or deemphasized, the entire process tends to be a formalistic exercise with little strategic utility or broad buy-in (Mintzberg 1994).

5. *Select alternatives (strategies).* Listing alternatives is not enough; choices must be made. When choices are not made, resources tend to be squandered, or the strategic process tends to break down. This is particularly clear in military strategy.

In Korea in 1950, Douglas MacArthur was presented with a variety of military strategies that included strengthening the southern foothold and trying to retake the country from there, or launching a surprise attack in the northern part of the country. He selected the more risky but high-payoff strategy of attacking at Inchon Bay in the north within striking distance of Seoul where he had to deploy all available resources (see Exhibit 10.4 for additional information about MacArthur). Agencies must constantly decide the best strategies to deliver services given scarce resources. Sometimes those service delivery strategies represent a radical departure from past practice. (See Exhibit 15.3 for comparative historical examples of the need for strategy.) One rigorous example of strategy selection is competitive analysis in which the characteristics of customers, suppliers, rivals, potential substitute products, and potential new service entrants are investigated (Porter 1980, 1994).

6. *Develop a step-by-step plan.* Planning mechanisms include traditional strategic planning documents (e.g., "strategic plans," annual reports, or comprehensive plans) as well as budgeting documents. Plans may include a definition of the work products and the components of the process; that is, the mission, objectives, strategies, and goals and measures. Plans may include a system of feedback and evaluation for the organization. They may also function as a system of accountability and control in terms of setting up expectations and performance targets. This perspective is emphasized in the strategic planning analysis approach that emphasizes the formal aspects of the system (Lorange 1980).

7. *Implement the plan.* One of the greatest of all complaints about strategic plans is that they "sit on the shelf" unused. Therefore, plan implementation should not be assumed. Typical reasons for nonuse include: insufficient or nongenuine stakeholder involvement; insufficient or superficial strategic analysis; lack of integration of strategic planning with budget and appraisal systems; and a lack of commitment to keep the plan up to date and use it between formal planning periods. Good plan implementation includes attention to data collection, use of strategic targets for rewards and "fire bells" (organizational indicators that performance is inadequate and needs immediate action), and a commitment to updating. Further, sometimes an intermediate strategic process substitutes for a more comprehensive approach called "strategic issues management." Such an approach emphasizes immediate identification of critical or timely issues (Ansoff 1980).

ARTICULATING THE MISSION AND VISION

Articulating the mission means *defining and expressing an organization's purpose, aspirations, and values.* The term is defined broadly here and includes aspects of vision and values as well. It has been empirically asserted that although great leaders do not have to possess charisma (Bennis and Nanus 1985), they do need the ability to express a coherent and compelling vision.

Exhibit 15.3

Ancient and Modern Examples of Strategy

Strategy is a plan to put one's strengths to greatest advantage while minimizing one's weaknesses. Strategic planning involves weaving together many strategies to achieve overall success in a field of endeavor. Two points are important to remember. First, the success of a single strategy does not guarantee the success of a strategic plan. As the saying goes, it is possible "to win the battle, but lose the war." Second, both stratagems and strategic plans must evolve over time. An ancient and a modern case illustrate these points.

The ancient example of these two concepts comes from the great Carthaginian general, Hannibal. His overall strategy was to take an armed force to Italy, through the Alps, to make the Romans leave the Carthaginians in peace. His specific strategy was to outmaneuver on the battlefield. Having been badly beaten by Hannibal in two previous battles, the Romans decided to put together the largest force they had ever mounted, 70,000 infantry and 6,000 cavalry. When he went to the Battle of Cannae in 216 B.C., Hannibal had 50,000 infantry and 10,000 cavalry. On the open plain Hannibal placed his weakest troops in the center and held back his best on either side. Flanking each side of them were cavalry. When this great battle began, Hannibal's center eventually yielded to the Roman troops. Although the line held, the Romans pushed it further and further to the center. Meanwhile the strong Carthaginian troops swung around both sides and began attacking the Romans on both flanks. The Carthaginian cavalry, the only place where they had superiority, had easily driven their counterparts from the field. After that, they attacked the Roman rear. The Carthaginians lost approximately 6,000, the Romans nearly 70,000. Having learned their lesson, the Romans never again faced Hannibal in the open field; unfortunately, Hannibal did not have the means and skills to overcome the major towns. After fourteen years in southern Italy, Hannibal had to return to Carthage to defend her from a Roman invasion (his own tactic), unbeaten in the field, but soundly beaten in the war.

A modern, nonmilitary example of strategy and strategic planning comes from the U.S. Forest Service. Its overall strategy for seventy-five years was to fight fires aggressively in national forests by using well-trained firefighters, excellent equipment, and special techniques such as fire breaks. Over time, the Forest Service became better and better able to fight fires with the use of airplanes to parachute firefighters in before major conflagrations occurred. However, by the 1990s, the Forest Service realized that the fires were becoming more intense, more difficult to contain, and more dangerous. Their overall strategy had, as they say, "backfired." Because of the absence of undergrowth fires—fires that flash through forest floors but fail to burn the old growth—the fuel on the forest floors had accumulated dangerously. The overall strategy would need to be changed. In 2000, the National Fire Implementation Plan called for "controlled burns" to try to better simulate the natural cycle of fire in forest evolution. Today the U.S. Forest Service no longer uses a single strategy for extinguishing fires. Rather, in some cases it fights fires vigorously, in others it allows fires to burn themselves out, and in still others the Forest Service actually sets the fires themselves.

Articulating the mission is related to strategic planning, organizational change, informing, and motivating. It is often a highly visible part of strategic planning. However, mission articulation also occurs outside the strategic planning process and serves nonstrategic purposes as well. It also relates strongly to managing organizational change, for which it is particularly critical. To the degree that it relays basic information, mission articulation is related to the skill of informing; in terms of inspiring greater productivity and sacrifice, it is related to motivating.

Articulating the mission has both explicit and implicit aspects (Johnston 1998). The explicit elements are the various types of mission statements that are used as a part of strategic planning, public relations, budget documents, and internal communications. The creation of these documents became more prevalent in the 1990s when major economic and technological changes caused large shifts in the organizational universe. A legislative mandate (e.g., authorizing legislation, charter, articles of incorporation, bylaws, statutes, or executive orders) is a type of mission statement in that it sets the legal parameters in highly detailed and legal terms. However, in common parlance, mission statements refer to "a brief written statement" that "can be used as a contract of accountability for citizens, clients, and other external constituencies" (Kearns 1998, 1412). That is, as important though mandates may be for legal and technical purposes, they are not easily understood by the public and employees and they are not particularly useful either for motivation or for the evolving strategy formulation and articulation that all organizations must engage in.

The implicit aspects of mission articulation are as important as the explicit elements. That is, it is a special charge for leaders to have a deep understanding of the mission of the organization, to convey its meaning both inside and outside the organization, and, most important, to facilitate its evolution. Edgar Schein (1985) asserts that managing the culture of an organization is by far the most important responsibility of a leader. For those holding this view, articulating the mission along with strategic planning and organizational change are the most important competencies for executives. This is more difficult than it sounds, however, because missions (1) tend to be much "messier" and more complex than is commonly supposed, (2) tend to be somewhat contentious because of the very different views of stakeholders, and (3) are not easy to make dynamic, much less exciting, after many compromises have been made to achieve a reasonable consensus. See Exhibit 15.4 regarding political and administrative leaders who have done an exceptional job of articulating a compelling vision.

The three most common elements of mission articulation can be divided into the mission proper, vision, and values. The mission is the commonly understood interpretation of the organization's legal mandate or what Gulick called the "central dominant theme" (1937, 37). The organization's purpose includes the services or products that it is to provide, the clients or customers who are targeted, the geographical context of the organization, and the general public needs that are to be filled by the agency. Generally speaking, the legal mandate is the most stable (putting aside the vicissitudes of the budgeting process), the mission (implicit and explicit) is slightly less so but is still highly stable, and the vision is the most variable by design.

The vision includes the aspirations of the organization, the overarching goals that it wants to achieve, the broad strategies that it intends to use to achieve its purpose, and the special niche or competencies that it expects to excel in. If the mission emphasizes the past coming into the present emanating from legal mandates, legal authority, historical tradition, and the fundamental good that is accomplished, vision emphasizes the present going into the future in terms of evolving purpose/objectives/goals, optimism about improvement, new priorities, and the dynamic aspects of organizational life that are highly affected by the quality of leadership and management. Thus, while mission statements are often more somber and formal, vision statements tend to be more inspirational and lively.

Exhibit 15.4

A Compelling Vision

Many people think that articulating the mission and vision is the competency that best separates great leaders from good leaders. This is particularly clear in the political case. Consider the presidents who are most commonly considered "great" in the twentieth century: Theodore Roosevelt, Franklin Delano Roosevelt, John F. Kennedy, and Ronald Reagan. The first Roosevelt was fond of using his "bully pulpit" to advance a country blessed with the greatest national park system in the world. The second Roosevelt had a vision of the U.S. government, and played the role of active social architect as the country struggled first with the Great Depression and then World War II. John F. Kennedy's vision of a robust scientific and cultural America propelled the country to put a man on the moon by the end of his decade and to establish public support for the arts. Ronald Reagan came to the presidency when the country was trying to come to grips with a new world economy (propelled by both nationalization of oil in the Middle East and growing world competition with American products) and a stinging military loss in Vietnam. His vision of a vibrant, "can-do" America inspired the country while it began the difficult task of realigning its economic institutions. Examples of other inspirational leaders from around the world might include Mahatma Gandhi in India, Charles de Gaulle in France, Margaret Thatcher in England, and Nelson Mandela in South Africa.

Although administrative examples are generally not as well known, they are just as important for those who lead in organizations. Consider the ability of some of the early American administrators to articulate a clear mission and vision for their agencies. Alexander Hamilton envisioned a strong central government for the United States, even when the colonies had initially chosen a loose form under the Articles of Confederation. As the first secretary of the Treasury, Hamilton fought tirelessly for an activist government. In particular, he established the first national banks, an early precursor to the Federal Reserve System, and established a national currency. He also nationalized all colonial debt stemming from the American Revolution, thus establishing a tradition of integrity and trustworthiness in U.S. debt policies. The first postmaster general was Benjamin Franklin, who espoused during the Revolution that "we all hang together, or surely we will all hang separately." Reliable and modestly priced interstate mail delivery is essential for hanging together. Finally, there is John Marshall, who served as Chief Justice of the Supreme Court from 1801 to 1836. Taking over the court when it was held in very low regard as a minor department, he refashioned it to become a co-equal branch of government. He successfully asserted the Supreme Court's unique right to uphold the Constitution, even when it meant declaring an act of Congress unconstitutional or an action of the executive branch in violation of the law (*Marbury v. Madison*). A similar right was asserted to declare state laws unconstitutional (*Fletcher v. Peck*). The Marshall Court also prevailed in asserting the supremacy of federal law over state law, but only where the Constitution gave the national government direct or implied powers (*McCulloch v. Maryland*).

Thus, great administrative leaders such as Hamilton, Franklin, and Marshall are also distinguished by their ability to clearly articulate their agency's mission and vision.

While mission statements focus on the "what," vision statements focus on "how." The vision aspect of mission articulation is highly related to strategic planning, but whereas concrete performance targets are the end result of the latter, the former emphasizes overall direction and philosophy.

The values aspect of mission articulation is an enormous and complex area that is frequently difficult for leaders to address well (Van Wart and Denhardt 2001). Values are expressed through the various operating philosophies of the organization having to do with governance systems, organizational structures, and systems of accountability. Consider the difference in values: between an equity-oriented public agency providing services and an entrepreneurially oriented, privately owned contractor; between a steeply organized county jail bureaucracy and a "flat" county attorney's office; and between a state lottery department focused on innovation and profit and a state department of transportation focused on permanence and value. Examples of contemporary value debates include the degree to which the organization will emphasize monopoly versus competition, regulation over market incentives, adding programs versus changing programs, centralized systems over decentralized systems, individual work versus work in teams, simple jobs versus multidimensional jobs, generic services versus customized services, tradition versus innovation, seniority versus performance-based systems, and emphasis on system needs versus employee needs. Value statements can highlight all major types of values affecting the organization (public good, legal, organizational, professional, and individual). Alternatively, value statements can emphasize only those values that are often neglected in the organizational context (e.g., an agency in a highly regulated environment might want to emphasize humane values such as employee development and involvement, as well as client needs and rights, to offset its natural tendency toward rule rigidity).

In practice, statements of mission, vision, and values are presented in innumerable formats. Sometimes such statements are integrated and sometimes they are separate. The format seems to matter less than that they are broadly conceived, widely understood, and have a real presence in the organization.

Research on mission articulation comes mainly from the strategic planning, change, and transformational leadership literatures. Not surprisingly, it was rarely indicated as a major competency before the 1980s. Kouzes and Posner's (1987) ten-element leadership taxonomy focuses exclusively on people- and change-oriented practices, and devotes two categories to mission articulation (Inspiring a Shared Vision: [1] envision the future, [2] enlist others). The OPM (1997) placed it among its top 22 competencies; it was ranked 14th among executives and 21st among supervisors, the largest difference between these two groups for any competency. In the Thach and Thompson (2007) public sector competency study, two elements of mission and vision articulation (being inspirational and being visionary) ranked 9th and 15th, respectively. Ironically, their study indicated that being inspirational is even more important in the public sector (perhaps because of less monetary leverage over employees), while vision was less important (perhaps indicating the need for greater levels of change and innovation). In a study of local managers, mission articulation was (self-) assessed as the weakest among the organizational competencies, with few listing it as a strength.

Guidelines

1. *Clarify the mission/vision, what is working, and key competencies.* Leaders must have deep insight into what the organization is about in order to express its purpose with conviction and even passion. They must be able to positively assert the accomplishments of the organization, as well as those things that are working well. Further, leaders must know the inherent strengths of the organization so

that they can capitalize on those strengths and avoid unwise diversification. An example of a successful mission change involves the firefighting profession. In the 1960s and 1970s many professional fire departments realized that their key competencies—rapid response to public safety needs—fit well with emergency medical dispatch. By looking at their key competencies they were able to include a related service, broaden their mission/vision, and retain what they were already good at.

2. *Identify areas of opportunity and growth through key stakeholders.* Key stakeholders include employees, clients, taxpayers at large, legislators, partner organizations, and interest groups. In the previous example, it was only in those fire departments in which a critical mass of enthusiasm was generated from stakeholders that successful integration of the disparate activities of firefighting and emergency medical services occurred. Where the firefighters themselves were largely opposed to service diversification or when special interest opposition (from hospitals or other extant providers) was particularly intense, service acquisition was either forestalled or unsuccessful.

3. *Arouse commitment to the mission and instill optimism for the future.* Yukl (1998, 342) summarizes the transformational literature, which has extensively studied arousing commitment and instilling optimism:

   • Articulate a clear and compelling vision.
   • Explain how the vision can be attained.
   • Act confident and optimistic.
   • Express confidence in followers.
   • Provide opportunities for early successes.
   • Celebrate successes.
   • Use dramatic, symbolic actions to emphasize key values.
   • Lead by example.
   • Empower people to achieve the vision.

4. *Continually assess and refine the mission and vision.* Mission articulation is an evolving process that involves many people learning from both successes and failures and finding new ways to improve. Good leaders constantly ask questions such as: What type of progress is being made toward achieving the vision? How successfully is the organization living up to its values? How valuable is the purpose of the organization? When mission articulation is stagnant, goals tend to be too easy, failures too readily accepted, and organizational dynamism too low.

NETWORKING AND PARTNERING

These two concepts are commonly used as synonyms (e.g., Grayson and Baldwin 2007; Gerencser et al. 2008) but are treated here as distinct. Networking means *developing useful contacts outside the leader's direct subordinate-superiors chain of command.*

Networking occurs through scheduled and unscheduled meetings (e.g., a "courtesy call" to a counterpart, or the numerous informal contacts that occur at conferences or regional meetings), telephone calls, observational tours, and written messages. Partnering means *developing working relationships that are voluntary but substantive outside the organization or within the organization but outside the normal chain of command.* These competencies become more important at senior levels in organizations, in which more external adjustment is necessary, more environmental scanning is expected, and more discretion is allowed. They are also more important in organizations or divisions in which lateral dependence is high. Lateral dependence is higher when processes/products change rapidly and a constant flow of information about the environment is necessary, processes or responsibilities are structurally shared with other divisions or agencies, or resource constraints require closer cooperation with the other agencies or groups. For example, an audit division might represent a relatively rare case in which networking and partnering would be low because of the confidential nature of the work, while a social service case management division might engage in an enormous amount of networking and partnering through and with personal contacts, professional organizations, nonprofit providers, private service vendors, related agencies at other levels of government, and so forth. Strong networking and partnering competence contributes to one's referent and expert power.

Networking and partnering are related to many other competencies, in particular environmental scanning, delegating, consulting, and motivating. Networking is related to environmental scanning because both seek external information; however, networking is more focused on building relationships over time and the public relations function of the contacts. Consulting and networking also have commonality in that they involve "checking with people"; however, the former is an internal function and the latter is an external function. Similarly, while both consulting and networking-partnering seek to heighten productivity through encouraging people at both the mutual exchange and the achievement levels, the focus is internal to the unit or organization in one case, and external to it in the other. Partnering and delegating are related because they both concern the legitimate and effective sharing of responsibility; however, whereas delegating does this with subordinates, partnering does this outside the unit or agency.

Three elements comprise this competency. The first is information sharing, which correlates most strongly with networking. Through networking, both routine and strategic information is shared. Routine information might be related to general levels of productivity or normal personnel changes. Strategic information might be related to special opportunities due to new types of technology, a new funding program, or an economic shift. Information sharing is often common and extremely valuable when it is time to solve problems. A human resource manager may call a colleague in another city when s/he is having problems with a benefits program or rewriting disciplinary procedures. A procurement manager may pick up valuable tips while at the monthly professional lunch for procurement personnel.

The second element is providing mutual support or professional "favors." This level of interaction is similar to moving from acquaintance to friendship. Friends are people that one can generally turn to when some modest level of assistance is needed. The primary type of favor is simply the contribution of time that is a valuable resource for all leaders. Taking the time to talk through an extensive problem, supporting an event that is time consuming, sitting on an advisory board, or critiquing a plan prior to public distribution are examples of favors. Favors may also include the temporary donation of appropriate resources—loaning equipment/personnel or contributing discretionary funds to a legitimate project. In times of emergency, those with a reservoir of favors that they have done other people are less likely to feel stranded.

The third element is responsibility and benefits sharing. This strongly correlates with partnering. The sharing can be a joint program, major resources, or a team approach to a task that would normally be performed on a strictly contractual basis. For example, fire departments often have joint assistance programs to enable personnel to cross jurisdictional lines for exceptional conditions such as the outbreak of large or multiple fires. Resource sharing commonly occurs at the local government level in police and other public safety areas such as dispatch and specially trained personnel, and in economic development projects such as public-private stadiums. An example of incentive partnering is when a transportation agency (the principal) and the engineering firm that has contracted to build a major structure (the agent), agree to incentives for early completion or quality upgrades and to mutually work toward achieving those higher standards. Several things happen to the relationship. The principal is more engaged in the process and in suggesting alternatives when problems arise. Regular review and progress meetings have a more robust brainstorming and creative element to them. And finally, both parties try to keep the relationship more cooperative and mutually beneficial, rather than legalistic and at arm's length. Higher levels of partnering generally require a substantial degree of reciprocal influence, an important type of which is called co-optation. Co-optation engages potential opposition by bringing them into the planning process. See Exhibit 15.5 for a discussion of this concept involving the Tennessee Valley Authority.

Not surprisingly, the most attention to networking and partnering comes largely from the literature on executives and strategic planning. A number of Mintzberg's (1979) ten roles relate partially to them: figurehead, liaison, monitor, disseminator, and spokesman. However, until recently, networking was often not found on general leader competency lists. Yukl (1998) was an exception in identifying networking. The OPM did not include it in its 1992 competency guide but did include partnering in its 1998 guide, where it was identified as an "emerging competency." The definition provided by the OPM is instructive: "Develops networks and builds alliances, engages in cross-functional activities; collaborates across boundaries, and finds common ground with a widening range of stakeholders. Utilizes contacts to build and strengthen internal support bases" (U.S. OPM 1999, 49). An examination of discrete networking-partnering competencies finds that they are more focused on programs and broad networks for executives, and focused on specific clients or small client groups at the supervisor level. Executives, in particular, engage in a large number of networking-partnering activities. However, it does not appear that they are generally critical in the short term insofar as the top ones are ranked only 18th and 19th. This correlates with qualitative studies indicating that executives seek to

---

Exhibit 15.5

Partnering: Is It Cooperation or Co-optation?

The best known example of partnering in public administration is probably the case of the Tennessee Valley Authority (TVA), both because it involved long-term political controversy and because of a famous administrative study by Phillip Selznick, *TVA and the Grass Roots* (1949). During World War I the federal government built two nitrate plants and a dam in Tennessee. For years there was debate about what to do with these resources, with bids going out to sell them to the private sector at one point. However, in 1933 Congress created (at Franklin D. Roosevelt's request) the TVA as a model regional planning authority (despite its success, the model was not duplicated). It was set up as a federal government corporation. (Today less than 20 are fully owned by the government.)

The authority's functions are electricity generation, flood control, agricultural and industrial development, and improved river navigation. From a small operation in 1933, it has grown to an organization with nearly 50,000 employees and a $6 billion budget. Today it serves 7 states, has 160 power distribution centers, 29 dams, 3 nuclear plants, and 11 coal-fired plants (Schultz 1998).

Successful though it may have become in later decades, it initially faced strong opposition from local interests even after it was created. Despite its mandate to help the region, there were many concerns about unfair competition (especially in electricity generation in which its consti-tutionality to do so was challenged), outside meddling, and economic disruption. Conscious of their need to get the support of local interests, a strategy of "co-optation" was developed.

> Co-optation referred to the strategy employed by the TVA Board of Directors in gaining the ac-ceptance, and ultimately the strong support, of initially hostile local interests by granting their representatives membership on the board. TVA, as a result, influenced and cajoled the local interests far more profoundly than the local interests influenced TVA; in short, TVA co-opted the local interests but was required to modify slightly its own purposes in so doing. (Henry 2003, 68–69)

Interestingly, later studies have shown that the long-term consequences of co-optation are more reciprocal (Couto 1988) than Selznick had originally thought. However, what remains clear is that without the aggressive community partnering that the TVA engaged in, it could never have expanded into the highly successful, mega-government corporation that it became.

---

participate in as much networking-partnering as they can, but allow it to be "bumped" when more pressing internal activities arise. Respondents in the local manager study were evenly divided in terms of it being the strongest and weakest of the organizational competencies. That is, some managers enjoyed the external focus and were good at it; those who were more focused on internal operations found networking and partnering to be their greatest weakness.

Guidelines

1. *Look for occasions to make linkages and to stay in touch with outside contacts.* There are innumerable opportunities to make and build contacts: professional meetings, community functions, ceremonial occasions, voluntary associations, working lunches, and others. Those leaders who cut themselves off from these types of networking opportunities, even though they may have more time to

work on operational concerns, may find that they are perceived as distant or professionally narrow in scope (Kaplan 1984). Of course, there are a few rare individuals who spend so much time networking that they neglect operational functions; this is especially true when people are looking for a new position or playing a major role in a national professional organization.

2. *Provide assistance (favors) for others.* Bonds are often built up through the exchange of favors. In the public sector this involves primarily the contribution of scarce time. Taking the time to help others with their problems or offering slack resources to others builds up tremendous goodwill and a team spirit. Of course, the offering of favors must be within the bounds of proper discretionary authority and must not involve misuse of public resources for personal gain.

3. *Choose strategic alliances for joint collaboration.* It is rare that a unit, division, or agency does not have to collaborate extensively with other constituencies. Perhaps the collaboration involves a jointly sponsored conference, shared facilities or personnel, or a cooperatively run project. An academic department at a state university, for example, might have joint degrees and jointly appointed faculty with other departments, a loaned executive program with the city, branch campus programs that it coordinates with continuing education, and internship programs that it cooperatively runs with a series of local employment agencies. These relationships are created and maintained by leaders with good networking-partnering skills. Of course, not all alliances are strategic, and those leaders who do not effectively discern the nonstrategic alliances may either squander resources or even engender ill will. Among the questions that need to be asked are: Does the partnership really add to the capacity of the organization? Is the partner really reliable and willing to follow through on the understanding?

PERFORMING GENERAL MANAGEMENT FUNCTIONS

Bureaucracies have complex subsystems that must be understood by managers and leaders in order to function effectively. Performing general management functions means *carrying out structural responsibilities related to the organization—human resource management, budgetary and financial management, and technology management are key among them.* In particular, some of the major aspects of human resource management include personnel policy (e.g., administrative law and discipline policy), staffing (recruiting and selection), classification, compensation, performance appraisal, and labor relations. Financial management includes the elements related to budgets (e.g., preparation of operations and capital requests, justifications, revisions) and financial control such as monitoring (e.g., authorizing, reporting, analyzing, and forecasting) and resource allocation (especially for projects and reallocations). Technology management (which today is almost synonymous with information management or information technology) includes office system communications (e.g., telephony, e-mail, and Internet), data processing systems, management information systems (e.g., reports that display and analyze performance data), and geographic information systems (e.g., data mapping by geographical markers). Managers often have a variety of other organizational responsibilities such as procurement, facility management, safety issues, and figurehead functions for executives. This competency, then, is essentially the ability to build and maintain the management infrastructure and to coordinate the various subsystems of the organization.

Although such functions are commonly ignored in discussions about leadership, and instead are considered elements of management, they are included as a leadership competency here because of their critical necessity in bureaucracies that are designed to be highly regulated. Sloppy selection practices can easily lead to a negligent-hiring lawsuit; outmoded classification systems become sources of unfairness and frustration; weak budget requests leave divisions or units starved for resources; poor financial monitoring guarantees occasional overspending; and ineffective IT does not allow organizations to attain productivity increases demanded by the current environment. In the public sector, leaders are not only held to a higher legal standard for the proper functioning of the management systems, but the expectations of employees (who are not focused on the bottom line but rather on organizational effectiveness) for competence in these areas is generally higher too.

Performing general management functions is most closely related to operations and strategic planning. Both of these competencies have a coordinating function related to the work of the organization. However, general management functions tend to focus on the technical expertise needed to administer human resources, finance, and information technology. Indeed, some leaders become specialized in these areas, some leaders (although generalists) focus on creating major changes in these areas (such as a new compensation and classification system), and still other leaders are only indirectly responsible for these areas.

Typically, performing general management functions is a part of management competency lists (often disaggregated into two to five categories), but omitted in leadership taxonomies. Some leadership experts do include competence in these functions indirectly (Mumford et al. 1988; Neider and Schriesheim 1988), but invariably the people in the process are emphasized more than the mastery of the process itself. The management literature has always reflected a greater appreciation of the complexity and importance of these functions, starting with bureaucratic theory stemming from the late nineteenth century. The ultimate expression of this was in the acronym POSDCoRB, which identified seven principles of management (planning, organizing, staffing, directing, coordinating, reporting and budgeting) by Gulick and Urwick (1937). Two of the seven refer to staffing and budgeting. A more modern and comprehensive version of this management paradigm is given by MacKenzie (1969) who identifies approximately six of twenty-five competencies as general management functions.

Consistent with OPM's public sector focus on management skills for leaders, it has long included human resource management and budget expertise among its competencies. In the 1990s it included technology management. Early in the 1990s human resource management was in the middle of the 22 metacompetencies (9th for executives and 10th for supervisors), while financial and technology management were nearly at the bottom of the major competencies (20th and 21st for executives, and 22nd and 18th for supervisors). A discrete examination shows that leaders rarely place these functions in the most critical category, but they perform a lot of them. Personnel functions were emphasized over financial and technology management. However, both the nature of the audience (federal managers) and the time the study was conducted (the early 1990s) probably affected these data more than other competencies. The larger the bureaucracy, the less all but the most senior executives have to do with budget and finance. In addition, technology management has exploded as an issue in the past decade, with new systems and enormous expenditures requiring far higher levels of leadership competence. Not surprisingly, a study of local managers (who are invariably more in the generalist mold) considered this an area of strength, rather than an area of weakness by eight to one (Van Wart 2001).

Guidelines

1. *Acquire a basic management education.* Basic management curricula are included in business programs, public administration programs, and comprehensive training programs (e.g., the Certified Public Manager program). Classes or modules generally include human resource management, finance, budgeting, and information technology, as well as courses that supply knowledge and skills useful for performing these functions such as statistics, research methods, and systems analysis. (Nonpolitical) senior executive leaders generally need these skills as they come through the ranks, even if they are later able to delegate many of the tasks requiring them. Of course, budget skills actually become more important at the most senior levels because of the resource allocation discretion bestowed at the highest levels.
2. *Learn the specifics of organizational management functions.* Although the commonality among public sector personnel, financial, and technology systems is enormous, the differences are critical in both functional and legal terms. Technical and legal oversights are most common for those shifting from the private sector where the norms may not be as detailed and the penalties for errors not so high. Managers and executives who personally "do not know the rules" are less respected generally, and more prone to employee and legal challenges.
3. *Integrate general management functions into an annual cycle and regular routines.* Good managers know the annual due dates for budget submission, budget approval, financial closeout analysis, employee appraisals, data reports, and so forth. They also have regular management routines to scan financial, personnel, and performance data in order to prepare for major management events and to identify trends that need attention. Leaders who lose track of these regular routines fail to give sufficient notice to employees for data that must be supplied, and fail to identify the early warning signs when things are not performing as they should.

DECISION MAKING

All actions engender some form of decision making in the broadest sense, even common-sense and repetitive actions that require little contemplation. However, as it is used in the academic literature (and in the most common lay usage as well), decision making denotes a substantial thought process with the generation of alternatives and the selection of the most favorable one, generally affecting policy or substantial numbers of people. Here, we reserve decision making for *making major organizational choices by understanding the fundamental values and factors involved and by structuring an appropriate decision framework.*

Decision making is distinguished from its "close cousin," problem solving (see chapter 13), which is limited in scale and rarely considers more than a single decision framework. The manager of a city trash collection division uses problem solving to resolve a safety and health problem triggered by an unacceptably high incidence of employee injuries. On the other hand, the city manager engages in decision making with the council when considering whether to privatize part or all of the trash collection service. Just as problem solving supports operations planning and enhances technical innovation and creativity, decision making supports strategic planning and enhances organizational change. Conflict management is another specialized type of decision making, which is treated as a separate competency (chapter 14) because it is essentially problem solving that involves people; that is, it is limited in scale and uses a specialized decision framework. Decision making is also related to decisiveness (chapter 11) and delegation (chapter 13). Decisiveness is the specialized characteristic of leaders to act relatively quickly depending on circumstances without excessively damaging decision quality. However, important though decisiveness may be at times, most leaders need to exercise it only occasionally. Delegation also affects decision making in terms of the level of participation of subordinates. In decision making, however, delegation is only one option, which also includes sole determination by the leader, the inclusion of constituents other than employees, and the ceding of responsibility to another authority altogether.

Decision making is an important but complex competency because effective leaders do not constrain themselves to the use of a single decision framework. Some situations require radical systems changes such as occurred with the change in the welfare paradigm in 1996, the security problems evoked by September 11, 2001, or the shift in the forest fire suppression model in the late 1990s (see Exhibit 15.3). Others require a legal framework in which rule adjudication is the proper focus, such as the use of eminent domain or the dismissal of a recalcitrant employee. Some situations invite "democratic" modes of choice selection, whether that entails empowered employees, a union election regarding a strike, or a request for a referendum. Other decisions may be better structured around, and with the cooperation of, the special interests of those directly involved—be they clients, landowners, or perhaps other levels of government. Some decisions should pay homage to the implicit traditional values of the community such as dealing with historical landmarks and cultural icons, while others need to allow or encourage decisions to be made in a hurly-burly political process, for example a controversial annexation issue.

David Rosenbloom (1998, 354–355) identifies a number of common problems that occur in decision making. They include:

- lack of clear goals;
- getting the interests of a special group or client confused with the public good;

- excessively rigid adherence to rules or past practice;
- oversimplifying problems because of the specialization of the experts handling them;
- excessive use of "quantification" and under-appreciation of qualitative factors;
- under-utilization of program and policy evaluation.

The elements of decision making include: (1) understanding the factors in the decision environment, (2) understanding the values involved, and (3) understanding and being able to utilize the appropriate decision framework. These three elements are discussed next.

Numerous factors affect the way that decision makers handle problems. Sorenson (1963) called these factors the upper limits of decision making. Simplifying for clarity, these factors or upper limits help us determine whether decisions (or problems) are relatively obvious and easy, or complex and wicked (i.e., issues that are largely unresolvable and in which the goal is merely mitigation and the means unclear). One factor is the clarity of the issue, which can include issues that are (a) instinctive, (b) simple, (c) well defined but without a clear solution, or (d) poorly defined. Some decisions can be handled instinctively because both the means and ends are clear, such as in following a procedure. Some decisions are simple after some contemplation, such as a standard problem eliciting a standard solution. Real problem solving occurs most frequently when the solution is unclear, but the problem can be relatively well structured and defined in "rational" terms. Bureaucracies excel at problem solving of this type because of their expertise and rules. Decision making is more likely to occur when problems are poorly defined and nonrational elements are involved, such as when the public seems to demand a service increase in times of financial austerity. A second factor is the restraint on information or time needed to resolve a problem. Problems of any complexity can require an unlimited amount of information gathering and an unrealistic amount of time to fully comprehend. Herbert Simon (1947) concluded that the best we can hope for is bounded rationality: a finite and practical amount of information in a reasonable amount of time to handle the numerous problems that confront an administrator at any one time. A third aspect is the type of issue to be resolved. Some problems are generic, predictable, or recurring. On the other hand, other problems are novel or unique. Managers need to be able to distinguish, with their limited time and information, which problems are recurring and can be handled efficiently with a standard problem protocol, and which ones are new or unique and merit a substantial amount of the manager's time and energy. Managers who are unable to distinguish types of problems well end up solving the same problem again and again, or worse, miss a new problem that leads to a major liability such as a lawsuit or financial shortfall. The final decision factor is what number of decision makers should be included. Some problems and decisions can and should be settled unilaterally by the decision maker. More complex ones require the involvement of a variety of constituents that may include employees, clients, political players, or others. Involvement may merely be consultation, or limited participation, or even full delegation or transfer of decision authority.

The second element of decision making is understanding the values involved (Van Wart 1998a). The most common and easiest values for administrators in bureaucracies to handle are the values of efficiency, effectiveness, and legality. What is the cheapest option? Which option will have the best effect on clients over time? Is the suggested procedure legal or consistent with policy? Because many of these types of decisions are largely operational and routine, they tend to be handled as problems. However, administrators have other values to consider in many cases such as fundamental change, political consensus, special group consensus, traditional values, and altruistic values. For example, when administrators are only considering efficiency, effectiveness, and legality, they generally assume that the solutions found will be within the confines of a system. But sometimes it is the system itself that needs to be changed. Being willing to suggest or make a radical change is a highly important value in the minds of most contemporary leadership experts. Or perhaps the discovery of an insect that causes great havoc to farmers' crops might cause an agriculture department administrator to elevate the issue to the political level for a supplemental appropriation. Or perhaps an unusual client case needs to be reviewed by senior administrators for an exemption from the standard rules because of special circumstances. Although there is no definitive way to determine the values in any decision, effective leaders develop an instinct to know which values should be most highly considered in which cases.

The third element in decision making is understanding and being able to utilize the appropriate decision framework. Going from largely bureaucratic to largely political decision frameworks, the most common include the reasoned-choice model, the incremental model, the mixed-scanning model, and the garbage can model. The reasoned-choice model is the most amenable to bureaucratic solutions and was discussed under problem solving (i.e., problem identification, analysis, alternatives generation, choice, implementation, and evaluation). It is a combination of an ideal or economic approach ("rational man") and a pragmatic approach ("administrative man"). Its major strength is its wide utility for administrative problems and its efficiency. Its weaknesses are the common biases of the bureaucrats who use it: oversimplification, expert bias, procedural rigidity, and inability to fix major systems problems.

The incremental model (Lindblom 1959) acknowledges that there are many decisions to make and that they require too much information to explore fully. Further, given the limited information available, it is unwise to make radical adjustments to problems or policies whenever it can be avoided. Rather, the wise course of action is to make an adjustment that will require the fewest resources to make an improvement and then see what happens. These small adjustments are possible when the best information is on hand and they take the least time to investigate. Depending on the results, another small incremental change can be made when the time is ripe. With these "successive limited comparisons" come the benefits of building on past experience, reducing the risk of a major failure, and building in the opportunity to learn from small successes and failures. The weaknesses are that some of the best adjustments might be those requiring substantial amounts of new information and time, and, more important, that sometimes radical changes are needed because the approach has become fundamentally flawed for handling the situation that has evolved. This depiction of decision making is still considered the most common for complex problems and policy changes.

The weaknesses of the incremental model led to the mixed-scanning approach (Etzioni 1967). Mixed scanning recommends that decision makers first scan the external environment for radical economic, technological, or competitive shifts. Simultaneously, the decision maker examines the organization for major systems malfunctions such as production drops, public relations fiascoes, or human resource troubles. If any of these are in evidence, then the decision maker deploys major time and energy to investigate the major problem, and is prepared to make/recommend a major change in the organization. However, generally the internal and external scanning will not reveal a major problem, at which time the decision maker reverts to an incremental mode across the innumerable areas of responsibility. It is intuitively appealing and often hailed as the ideal executive model for leaders in that it requires decision makers to be attuned to the "big picture" but simultaneously to make the small adjustments that constitute healthy organizational evolution or continual improvement. One weakness is that most leaders tend to be good at either the transformational mode or the incremental mode, but rarely both. Further, the advice as to when to make major or incremental changes is entirely in the eyes of the beholder.

The most descriptive of the political process is glibly called the "garbage can model" (Cohen, March, and Olsen 1972), which is similar to Kingdon's (1984) organized anarchy model or Allison and Zelikow's (1999) government process model. It is most common in the legislative forum for there to be multiple problems, players, and solutions floating in the policy environment. It is important to note that problems and solutions are not connected, and it is as possible that an important solution will find an appropriate problem as vice versa. Opportunities occur (or are created) in the environment, generally for limited periods of time, for players to promote certain types of problems and solutions that fit their needs and disposition. Ultimately, the selection of problems to handle, solutions to use, and players who will decide are determined as much by luck, timing, and ideological appeal as by "rational" (i.e., efficiency and effectiveness) considerations. The garbage can metaphor simply alludes to the messiness of the process (e.g., the legislative process is like sausage making) and the fact that although almost all of the elements are present, only certain problems and solutions are plucked out for serious deliberation. Even those considered may fail to be chosen and thrown back into the garbage can for possible consideration in another permutation at another time. The strength of the model is its descriptive appeal in legislative settings, but much less so for administrative settings. The weaknesses of the model are its atheoretical penchant and its lack of prescriptive advice.

Many models and discussions about decision making are found in a literature distinct from leadership research. The leadership literature has tended to focus on problem solving, decisiveness, and employee participation. A more recent focus has been on good judgment or wisdom (Sternberg 2007; McKenna, Rooney, and Boal 2009). In terms of leadership competency taxonomies, the trait literature typically includes decisiveness in fuller lists (Stogdill 1974), and the behavioral competency lists tend to include either problem solving (Yukl 1998) or decision making (Howard and Bray 1988), but not both. Some use related substitute terms such as judgment or analytic/integrative ability. Researchers before the 1980s tended to focus on the problem-solving aspects; the newer research, especially that of the transformationalists, tends to focus on using decision making to make major changes. The OPM's 1992 taxonomy included problem solving and decisiveness, which both ranked very high for executives and supervisors (2nd and 5th of 22 competencies for executives and 2nd and 6th for supervisors). A discrete analysis of decision competencies finds that decision making is not the most extensive (like networking and performing general management functions), but it is far more critical. For example, of 150 micro-competencies, decision-making activities ranked 3, 7, 14, 23, 46, and 54 for executives. In 1998, the OPM added five emerging competencies, two of which have some overlap with decision making: political savvy and entrepreneurship. These competencies focused on the complex political environment and sensible risk taking that modern administrative leaders must be able to engage in. This was considered a strength by local managers 4 to 1, with their can-do attitude and their proximity to policymakers (Van Wart 2001).

Guidelines

1. *Analyze factors in the decision environment.* Leaders need to be able to efficiently decide the nature of the decision environment. How clear is a potential solution? What is the critical information that is needed to make a decision with an acceptable risk or error? What type of problem is it? Does the problem have novel or unstructured characteristics? How important is the problem, or should it be postponed or ignored? Who should be included in the decision mix and at what level? Leaders need to be careful not to handle all problems in the same way. For example, leaders who always insist on the widest inclusion of others in the decision process may find that very little gets accomplished, while leaders who rarely use inclusive practices may get much more done but have very little buy-in from the affected groups. Good factor analysis allows for parsimonious use of precious time, resources, energy, and focus.

2. *Determine the values implicit in the decision environment and different decision-making approaches.* Because values are subtle, they may not be immediately apparent. The problem of a high error rate in a social service agency may seem to be a simple efficiency-effectiveness issue related to defective training. However, many other values may be involved. Very low pay may lead to a lack of satisfaction. An excessive rules orientation may deaden the workers' altruistic motivations. A strict management culture may maximize alienation. Workers then feel unappreciated, unable to "make a difference," and micromanaged. Values become only that much more complex, and often ideologically conflicted, in the policy environment.

3. *Select or design the appropriate decision framework.* In a routine operational mode, leaders need to be able to use either an incremental approach to fine-tune procedures (which is nonrisky and efficient) or a reasoned-choice approach for select problems that deserve more substantial analysis. In the longer term, the ideal is a mixed-scanning approach. In this approach, the leader scans for big shifts in the environment or big problems in the organization requiring rare but major changes

and a detailed analysis, and an incremental model for most commonplace changes. Finally, an eclectic and messy garbage can framework is primarily a legislative model of decision making, but it certainly has applications in the organizational world. Senior administrative leaders are frequently called upon to become involved in policy matters and must feel comfortable and even be proficient in the organized anarchy of legislation with its reliance on luck, timing, and appearance. Agency leaders who are unable to see the temporary opening of policy windows will invariably lose substantial funding opportunities. For example, when economic development tops a community's list of priorities, a school system is foolish not to frame and promote quality of schools as a critical recruitment issue for both prospective parents and employers moving to the area.

4. *Implement the decision framework.* Because different frameworks require different skills to execute well (e.g., analytic precision versus opportunistic flexibility), leaders need to be careful in working within those frameworks that are not natural to them. In addition to needing to ensure that the decision process is accomplished, decision implementation should include an evaluative element. See Exhibit 15.6 for an example that shows the negative consequences of not following these guidelines.

MANAGING ORGANIZATIONAL CHANGE

Because change is so important for leaders and involves such an extensive set of activities, it has been divided into three competencies in this taxonomy. Already reviewed in the task domain was managing innovation and creativity. This aspect drew heavily from the learning organization literature. It focused on frontline or microlevel changes. Another separately reviewed area of change was managing personnel change. Although the people aspects of change are critical for both innovation diffusion and organizational change, it was handled as its own topic for clarity and to avoid duplication. Organizational change is the broadest level of change. It involves *large-scale change in the direction, structure, major processes, or culture of the organization.*

The organizational direction may refer either to the philosophy of the organization or its policy. For example, the Food Security Act of 1985 (also known as the 1985 Food Bill) totally changed the culture of the Soil Conservation Service (SCS). It "linked farmers' eligibility for U.S. Department of Agriculture (USDA) programs to conservation performance. The highly erodible lands provision, sometimes known as conservation compliance, required farmers to use conservation measures on erodible land in order to remain eligible for USDA programs such as price supports and crop insurance. These requirements placed a considerable burden on SCS field staff and altered the relationship of the SCS to its clientele" (Helms 1998, 438). Organizational change may occur through a change to structure as reflected in an organization chart. Examples include the inclusion or exclusion of federal agencies in the cabinet, or the creation of the Executive Office of the President in 1939. Another type of organizational change occurs with the change of major processes. The radical changes in the U.S. Postal Service since the

Exhibit 15.6

Critique of a Decision-Making Fiasco: The Orange County Bankruptcy

Some of the best examples to use are negative ones in order to illustrate why the "rules" are important. One well-known example of a decision-making fiasco occurred in Orange County, California, in the 1990s (Simonsen 1998).

Robert Citron had been the elected treasurer for nearly twenty-five years. Although an elected official, as a county "row officer" he had frontline administrative duties—the investment of the $7.4 billion in funds for the county and other government jurisdictions in the county. His success in getting substantially better return-on-investment averages for the government funds he managed had made him something of a celebrity in his profession by the early 1990s. Approximately 37 percent of the county's revenues came from investments, compared to the national average of less than 10 percent. There could be little doubt that government cash management and investment strategies had been woefully sloppy or excessively cautious through the 1990s. Cash flows were sometimes not invested at all, and investments were generally limited to only the safest but lowest-yield securities. But Citron was beginning to change that. He argued that wise investment included a diversity of strategies including higher-risk securities. However, he did not fully follow his own advice, and on December 6, 1994, Orange County declared the largest government bankruptcy in U.S. history. How was the decision making flawed? (See the guidelines for decision making.)

Citron did a poor job of analyzing the decision environment. The instrument that he invested heavily in was a special type of derivative called an "inverse floater." Derivatives were not well understood even by experienced investors and many new types had emerged in the 1980s. The factors affecting the use of derivatives were highly complex, and as later inquiry found, Citron had a very weak grasp of their nuances and pitfalls.

Citron ignored the extreme divergence between private and public sector values about investment. In a capitalist system, private investors can use highly risky strategies in hopes of higher returns if they are so disposed. However, it is expected that governments will play the very conservative, long-term odds in investment, because they are essentially investing forever, and risky strategies will eventually lead to disaster. The values, then, are generally long-term effectiveness and high security over short-term efficiency and high risk. Citron reversed these values.

Citron did not select an appropriate decision-making framework. First, he made radical adjustments in investment, rather than the more cautious incremental model common to government. Second, those he genuinely included in the decision making were those who stood to profit from the strategy—his investment advisers. He did not educate other constituents in the system, such as the County Board of Supervisors or noncounty investors, about the real risk.

Finally, he failed to implement his own decision framework well. Rather than diversify the risks, he placed almost all of the fund (approximately 90 percent) in a single, high-risk strategy. Further, he did not divulge the problem until it had swelled to enormous proportions.

The fallout from this example of poor decision making was tremendous. Citron was sentenced to a year in jail and a $100,000 fine (strictly based on mismanagement). The county did pay off the bulk of the creditors' claims, but it did so very late, with some "rollover losses" of up to 20 percent, and by incurring substantial long-term debt to pay off investment debts. In order to make up the difference, 3,000 jobs were cut, nearly eliminating social services in the county. Finally, because of the extraordinary precedent set by the successful declaration of bankruptcy by a large and wealthy county, the bond market reduced ratings across the country, forcing thousands of other governments to pay a higher premium on borrowed monies.

1970s (see Exhibit 9.5) with ZIP codes, express mail, and electronic address sorting are a testament to how large processes can fundamentally alter the organization. A similar example would be the enormous retooling required of the Internal Revenue Service in order to accommodate electronic tax filing. Finally there are wholesale attitudinal changes, better known as culture changes, that may not be as sharply demarcated as reorganiza-tion, but, when successfully implemented, lead to change as dramatic. The major shift in many government organizations in the 1990s to move away from being formalistic, inward-focused, and excessively change-averse organizations resulted in substantial performance improvements. Common culture shifts included a move toward a stronger focus on customers, quality, improved efficiency, and employee development.

As already noted, organizational change is highly related to managing innovation and creativity and personnel change. It is also related to, and essentially builds on, other organization-level activities. Environmental scanning and networking are important for most changes in order to achieve good alignment, which is almost always a factor in change at this level. Strategic planning is necessary to institute the change over time. Many comprehensive organizational changes take three to five years to fully implement. Decision-making skills are integral to organizational change. Perhaps most noted in the leadership literature, however, is the necessity of articulating the (reformulated) mission and vision. Managing organizational change involves utilizing all these competencies in ways that keep the organization adapting and evolving in the most effective manner possible.

Many consider organizational change to be the supreme leadership competency, not only because of its fundamental importance for the long-term health and survival of the organization (Schein 1985), but also because of its difficulty (Kanter, Stein, and Jick 1992). Kanter, Stein, and Jick (1992, 5–9) point out five challenges for those trying to institute organizational change:

- It is hard to make changes stick. The originators of innovations are generally not the same as those who need to take advantage of them.
- There are clear limitations to the use of managerial authority in making change.
- Attempts to carry out programmatic change through a single effort are likely to fail because of the resistance of systems to change.
- The need for change may make it harder. The inclination to change is generally greatest when the ability to do so is least because of diminished resources.
- Some of those best at new practices in one realm may show severe limitations in another, which undermines the overall effort.

The elements of managing organizational change include providing a rationale for change and a plan for change, and then implementing the change. Providing a rationale for change simply means getting information and making sense of it. Apart from the analytic function, people are going to be highly resistant to change unless they feel that the change is built upon reliable data and that there is a compelling case for change. The information should come from a variety of sources including environmental scanning, the executive team, organizational surveys, performance data, program evaluations, legislative mandates, financial analyses, networking, benchmarking, and visioning.

The plan provided for change must be practical, challenging but realistic, and widely understood. It must consider not only the technical aspects, but the social aspects of the change process as well. Planning processes can occur in three ways, depending on the circumstances and skills of those involved. Sometimes the plan is created primarily by the chief executive officer. The leader is often called upon to personally provide the plan when the circumstances are dire and high visibility is needed for morale boosting. In quite a contrasting scenario, when the leader feels strongly that change is necessary but the organization is not yet ready to be proactive, the leader is essentially staking her/ his credibility on the success of change. The virtue of this approach is that it fulfills a leader's more heroic role; the weakness is that the leader must commit nearly all of his/ her time and spare resources to the initiative for an extended time frame. Organizational change is sometimes planned through a strategic planning process. As a part of the regular cycle of planning, the organization (or some major part of it) decides that significant steps must be made to realign and renovate the way business occurs. The virtue of this approach is that it is already structured to identify goals and performance measures; the weakness is that the cycle may not coincide with external events and opportunities for change. Finally, sometimes a special structure is created to initiate and later monitor change. This is known in the organizational development literature as a parallel learning structure. It might be a quality council or a special task force. It commonly uses one or more special organizational planning conferences that can range from one to three days and include either the executive team only, a sample of people from throughout the organization, or sometimes everyone in the organization if it is small. Teams or standing committees then take charge of various aspects of the change. It has the virtue of being more organic and integrated; it has the weakness of being difficult to get started and being resource intensive to carry out. This is a common approach for smaller-scale organizational changes, such as the setting up or closing down of a major site in which there are numerous aspects of work restructuring and physical plant considerations to divide among groups and individuals.

Implementing the change involves the who, what, when, and where. Laying out the responsibilities provides the capability for technical monitoring. Executives need to know if the plan is meeting its objectives in a timely way. Units, teams, and individuals also need direct feedback on their conformance with goals. Because large-scale organizational change efforts cannot be fully preplanned the way an engineering project can, the implementation must allow for learning and adaptation. Generally, whoever promotes the plan is responsible for the adaptation process as well. In recent years, however, there has been much more receptivity to the use of various types of cross-functional improvement teams that are empowered to identify problems and recommend solutions to keep major change efforts on track.

The literature on organizational change is rather scattered. Historically, the most detailed research was done in organization development (e.g., Lewin 1951; Beckhard 1969; Bennis 1969; Schein 1988; French and Bell 1999). The "quality" and total quality management literature is a rough successor to that tradition. The "excellence" literature championed by Tom Peters touches upon organization change as well. Closer to home, the charismatic and transformational leadership literatures highlight organizational change as a major leadership function. Weber's sense of charismatics as those with the force of personality to create a new entity is intuitively appealing. Transformationalists generally play down the force or cult of personality aspects and substitute the more cognitive or visionary aspects of change. (See Exhibit 15.7 for a well-researched example of charisma and transformation in the public sector.) As a specific leadership competency, organizational change did not fare well in the major taxonomies until the 1990s. The 1992 OPM taxonomy included several competencies that were modestly related: creative thinking and vision. The 1998 taxonomy included a metacategory—leading change—and most of the eight elements (reduced to six elements in 2006) were related to organization change. In a discrete analysis of federal managers' organizational change competencies, executives ranked the competency (somewhat surprisingly) as only modestly important and frequent (1 in the top 20 and 5 in the top 100), and supervisors placed it even lower, as would be expected (0 in the top 20 and 3 in the top 100). Interestingly, local managers reported that this was often their major weakness and rarely reported this as a strength.

Guidelines

1. *Analyze the organization and its need for change.* Leaders should use their strategic position to gather data and be prepared to make a compelling case for change.
2. *Create a shared vision and common direction for change.* It does little good for everyone to agree that there needs to be change if they disagree about the causes and the direction that the change should take. Creating a shared vision is often enhanced by making some dramatic, symbolic changes, using vibrant and evocative language, and involving many people in the process.
3. *Leaders must also realistically determine the politics of change.* Who is going to oppose the change? Who can be co-opted? Who is likely to hold out? What is the best way to line up political support? How can some key positions be filled with supporters? Who can act as competent change agents?
4. *Design an implementation plan for major changes.* Decide who will construct the plan. It may be the leader her/himself, enabling structures, or task forces. Make sure the plan includes the who, what, where, and when elements.
5. *Institutionalize and evaluate major changes.* Change the relevant aspects of the organizational structure. Monitor the change for lack of progress as well as for the need to make adjustments. Be sure to support people in the change process.

CONCLUSION

This chapter reviewed organization-level competencies—scanning the environment, strategic planning, articulating the mission/vision, networking and partnering, general management functions, decision making, and managing organizational change. See Exhibit 15.8 for a review of the competency definitions, elements, and guidelines. As has been widely demonstrated in the literature, leaders who are executives give this category much more attention and assign it more importance. The reverse is true for supervisors,

Exhibit 15.7

Comparative Examples of Organizational Change

Identifying rigorous comparative examples of organizational change is extremely difficult because both the participants and situations tend to vary so much in complex settings. A rare exception is a set of studies done by Nancy C. Roberts (Roberts 1985; Roberts and Bradley 1988). She studied an effective educational leader in two different settings. In the first setting, the leader achieved major organizational change, and, in the second setting, the same leader did not. The relatively limited differences in the two cases allow for more powerful analysis than usual.

In the first study, the leader was the superintendent of a public school system that was experiencing large mandated cuts that were perceived as a crisis. She followed most of the classic steps in organizational change. She met with people in a variety of venues and exhibited commitment, passion, flexibility, persistence, and, above all, energy. She formulated a useful mission statement and compelling vision statement from the early meetings. She also delegated much of the work to task forces and principals but was careful to monitor progress and encourage productivity through concrete performance plans. She reassigned some of the key "lieutenants" in the system to act as dynamic change champions. High involvement of employees and parents at all levels meant high levels of buy-in for the implementation plan. Her competence, commitment, and honesty elevated attributions of her to "charismatic" after approximately two years. The school district was not only successful in accommodating the mandated cuts, but simultaneously improved programming and services because of the coherent change process that occurred under her leadership.

Largely because of this highly visible success, she was appointed shortly afterward to be the state commissioner of education. As with all public education systems in the past thirty years, many ideological issues were being discussed in the state (from vouchers to teacher standards to class size to curriculum reform). However, there was neither a perceived crisis nor did any new radical change idea have strong support in the system. She followed a similar pattern to shape her administrative direction—multiple public meetings, evolution of a new mission and vision, installation of a few key change champions, and delegation of specific objectives. In this setting the commissioner was considered a competent administrator but failed to be perceived as introducing either cultural or systemwide organization change. Indeed, she was not really advocating a system overhaul as much as a series of administrative changes to improve efficiency and effectiveness. Nonetheless, in total, the changes were extensive. However, many failed to win acceptance or to be implemented. Overall, in her new position she was considered effective, but neither charismatic nor exceptional. Some of the impediments she faced and did not overcome were the lack of a perceived crisis, the presence of powerful players in the system (the teachers' union, the governor, the legislature, etc.) whom she failed to convince of all her ideas, and her inability to project her energy and commitment as effectively in her vastly expanded scope of responsibilities. Her ability to craft a cohesive change plan as superintendent, then, was not matched at the commissioner level where many of her ideas were victim to the ideological crossfire of different interest groups and points of view.

although lower-level managers have probably been significantly affected by the flattening of organizational structures and the empowerment that was emphasized in the 1990s. Yet, given the more extensive legal framework and administrative rule articulation in the public sector, supervisors may never reach the highest levels of involvement in the organizational competencies that are found in the most progressive private sector organizations.

This chapter and the preceding two have described two conceptual categories—behavioral domains (three of them) and discrete competencies (twenty-one of them). We now focus on a topic of particular interest to those seeking to improve themselves as well as their subordinates—leadership development.

Exhibit 15.8

Summary of Chapter 15

Organizational-oriented behavior	Subelements of behavior	Major recommendations
Scanning the environment		
Gathering and critically evaluating data related to external trends, opportunities, and threats on an ongoing and relatively informal basis	• Carrying out broad and informal monitoring and consulting outside the organization • Identifying external trends, opportunities, and threats • Investigating external trends of significance in greater detail	1. Identify multiple relevant sources of external information. 2. Reflect on the significance of external trends. 3. Follow up on significant external trends. 4. Linking scanning and strategic planning
Strategic planning		
Making disciplined efforts to produce fundamental decisions and actions that shape and guide an organization	• Defining the mission of the overall organizational purposes and the overall vision of preferred future for the organization • Defining objectives of organizational purposes at the departmental or unit level • Defining alternatives and selecting the best ones to accomplish objectives • Selecting detailed goals and their concrete measures	1. Define the strategic planning process itself. 2. Collect systematic and comprehensive data. 3. Review the mission and capabilities of the organization. 4. Identify major issues and alternatives. 5. Select alternatives (strategies). 6. Develop a step-by-step plan. 7. Implement the plan.
Articulating the mission and vision		
Defining and expressing an organization's purpose, aspirations, and values	• Interpreting of the organization's legal mandate or central dominant theme • Defining and expressing the aspirations, overarching goals, broad strategies, and special niche or competencies in which the organization expects to excel	1. Clarify the mission/vision, what is working, and key competencies. 2. Identify areas of opportunity and growth through key stakeholders. 3. Arouse commitment to the mission and optimism about the future.

(continued)

Exhibit 15.8 *(continued)*

Organizational-oriented behavior	Subelements of behavior	Major recommendations
	• Expressing values through the various operating philosophies of the organization having to do with governance systems, organizational structures, and systems of accountability	4. Continually assess and refine the mission and vision.
Networking and partnering *Developing useful contacts outside the leader's direct subordinate-superiors chain of command. Developing working relationships that are voluntary but substantive outside the normal chain of command*	• Sharing information • Proving mutual support or "favors" • Sharing responsibility and benefits (partnering)	1. Look for occasions to make linkages and to stay in touch with outside contacts. 2. Provide assistance ("favors") to others. 3. Choose strategic alliances for joint collaboration.
Performing general management functions *Carrying out general structural responsibilities related to the organization*	• Using human resource management knowledge and skills • Using budgetary and financial management knowledge and skills • Using technology management knowledge and skills	1. Acquire a basic management education. 2. Learn the specifics of organizational management functions. 3. Integrate general management functions into an annual cycle and regular routines.
Decision making *Making major organizational choices by understanding the fundamental values and factors involved, and by structuring an appropriate decision framework*	• Understanding the factors in the decision environment—complexity, information availability, type of decision, involvement of others • Understanding the values involved—efficiency, effectiveness, legality, and the values implicit in the types of change or consensus supported	1. Analyze factors in the decision environment. 2. Determine the values implicit in the decision environment and different decision-making approaches.

(continued)

Exhibit 15.8 *(continued)*

Organizational-oriented behavior	Subelements of behavior	Major recommendations
	• Understanding and being able to utilize the appropriate decision framework, including the reasoned-choice, incremental, mixed-scanning, and garbage can models	3. Select or design the appropriate decision framework. 4. Implement the decision framework.
Managing organizational change *Managing large-scale change in the direction, structure, major processes, or culture of the organization*	• Providing a rationale for change—getting information and making sense of it • Providing a plan for change that is practical, challenging but realistic, and widely understood • Implementing the change, which involves the who, what, when, and where issues	1. Analyze the organization and its need for change. 2. Create a shared vision and common direction for change. 3. Realistically determine the politics of change. 4. Design an implementation plan for major changes. 5. Institutionalize and evaluate major changes.

PART III

DEVELOPING AND EVALUATING LEADERSHIP

16

Leadership Development

Leadership in organizations has become more difficult in the past few decades for a variety of reasons (Barzelay 1992; Hannah et al. 2008). First, the rate of change in organizations has increased substantially almost universally. Public and nonprofit organizations are still adjusting to the movement from a traditional bureaucratic paradigm to a post-bureaucratic paradigm that integrates much higher levels of customer service, devolution, co-production, competition, and so forth. This makes the job of leadership more interesting, but also more confusing and risky (Kanter, Stein, and Jick 1992; Gauthier 2008). Second, the range of leadership activities required of leaders is simply greater. In addition to the greater change-management skills implied by the first point—technical, organizational, and personnel change skills—contemporary managers must be better at the organizational skills identified in this study—environmental scanning, strategic planning, articulating mission and vision, networking and partnering, performing general management functions (Van Wart and Berman 1999; Holzer 2008, 21). A dynamic environment in which resources are scarce and frequently shrinking requires leaders to accurately assess what is happening and mobilize internal and external stakeholders to adopt practical plans. This is hard work. Third, in a more cynical age it is more difficult to be a leader. Followers are not only more cynical about institutions (Henry 2003, 11–12), but also more likely to be cynical about the individuals who lead them. While public administrators are generally considered trustworthy in comparison to politicians, they are still not exempt from tough scrutiny.

THE NATURE OF LEADERSHIP DEVELOPMENT

Today's dynamic, challenging environment translates into a need for more leadership development throughout leaders' careers. Three fundamental types of leadership development are possible: self-study, structured experience, and formal training and education.

Types of Leadership Development

The first type of leadership development is *self-study*. Self-study is the raising of one's consciousness before, during, and after either developmental experiences or formal training (Lord and Hall 2005). It can certainly be argued that without self-study—which is to say, self-recognition of the issues and skills of leadership—no leadership development can occur. However, self-study here refers primarily to the learning that occurs outside formal training and structured developmental experiences provided by the organization. Individuals often begin preparing for leadership long before they assume such roles by engaging in both technical and broad education. Leaders frequently pursue advanced degrees in order to ensure a deeper understanding of their field and management practices. Individuals should also cultivate work-specific personal development plans based on their self-observations about what knowledge and competencies they need to enhance. Numerous attitudinal traits and skills described earlier in this study correlate directly with self-study. Important traits include resilience, energy, need for achievement, and emotional maturity (see chapter 11). The skill that directly relates to this aspect, which is enormously important, is continual learning (see chapter 12). Because this aspect of development was covered under self-leadership in chapter 5, it will not receive additional coverage in this chapter.

The second type of leadership development is provided by *structured experience* (Day 2000). Experience is a powerful teacher (McCall, Lombardo, and Morrison 1988; Revell 2008; Amit et al. 2009). Three elements have been identified as particularly important in enhancing the developmental opportunities embedded in experience. First, experience is valuable when work offers challenging but realistic assignments. People report learning more and appreciating the experience when work offers some real challenges. Indeed, failures also offer valuable lessons. However, the realism of challenges must be kept in mind. Unrealistic goals are discouraging and produce frustration and anger (Locke and Latham 1990). Second, the variety of experiences is critical for optimal executive development. Those trained in a "silo" of experience and who have never worked in different areas of the organization will have difficulty understanding the language, norms, and mindset of many parts of the organization. The leader who has never been anything other than a financial analyst or accountant will find it exceedingly difficult to appreciate and communicate with the operational divisions. Similarly, the leader who has always been involved in line operations may make very poor use of staff divisions. Third, the quality of feedback received makes an enormous difference as well (Kim and Hammer 1976). Suggestions about how things work, why success or failure is achieved, and how to do better are critical for optimal learning. This means that as leaders are developing, their supervisors must take the time to understand the quality of their work as well as to discuss it in detail. Top organizational leaders also continue to need quality feedback, but they must usually design and analyze it themselves.

A third type of leadership development, *formal training and education*, is a major focus of this chapter. This type should vary as leaders progress through the organizational hierarchy and take on progressively broader and more externally sensitive responsibilities (Van Wart, Cayer, and Cook 1993). Training in supervisory skills focuses on supervisors' direct interaction with subordinates and on getting work done by, with, or through other people. Specific interpersonal skills and clearly identifiable personnel practices are important targets. Many of the topics focus on organizational procedures and policies that supervisors must master in procurement, ethics, equipment and facilities, hiring, training of employees, information management, privacy and security issues, and so forth. Common topics for supervisory programs involve methods of evaluating employees, conducting selection-hiring processes, handling and preventing sexual harassment, disciplining employees, developing communication and active listening skills, motivating people, delegating, team building, coaching employees, becoming proficient in meeting management, grievance prevention, basic conflict management, basic counseling for employees with problems, employee goal setting, and confidence building. To the degree that leadership is an explicit topic, transactional and the simpler contingency approaches are often used, such as Hersey and Blanchard's highly popular situational leadership (1969, 1972) and Blake and Mouton's managerial grid (1964, 1965, 1982, 1985).

Just as supervisory skills training focuses on specific interpersonal skills and specific group processes and procedures, management development focuses on more complex interpersonal skills like labor relations and interrelated group processes like organizational climate in an attempt to find organizational solutions within a changing and complicated environment (Ernst, Hannum, and Ruderman 2010). The focus shifts from individuals to groups and from the problems of a unit to the management of programs. There is often a focus on the improvement of general analytical skills (as opposed to the specific analytical skills of technical professionals) and the ability to make balanced judgments based on a variety of data sources. Standard topics for such programs include workforce planning, labor relations, budgetary and financial planning (including contracting, capital planning, auditing, negotiation), risk management, problem analysis, and information management. More advanced topics in interpersonal skills are often included, such as team building (Morgeson, Lindoerfer, and Loring 2010) and participative management (Morse 2008). To the degree that leadership is an explicit topic, it is more likely to use more sophisticated contingency models such as Vroom's normative-decision model (commercially marketed as Kepner-Trego training), management theory (e.g., Mintzberg 1979), and team and self-leadership theory (e.g., Manz and Sims 1987, 1989, 1991, 1993).

Executive development is the most conceptual, as well as the broadest and most externally oriented type of training. Programs for executives tend to focus on the role of the organization in the public sector environment and to facilitate the executives' skills in coping with external opportunities and threats, and recently, the need for strategic alliances, collaboration, and the search for better shared governance (Kee, Newcomer, and Davis 2008; Quinn and Van Velsor 2010). Typical courses for executives focus on media and public relations, public speaking and contact skills, multisource leader feedback, strategic planning, intergovernmental relations, policy analysis, political and social trends, legislative and lobbying processes, and advanced general management topics. Leadership is itself often a formal topic. More common approaches include transformational and visionary leadership, collaborative leadership, as well as integrated approaches (U.S. OPM 1992, 1997, 1999). Executives are most likely to participate in programs outside the organization because of the specialized and high-quality resources required, confidentiality, and the small pool of participants from which to draw in all but the largest organizations. A good example of this is the Federal Executive Institute, an executive training program for the entire federal government (see Exhibit 16.1).

Exhibit 16.1

An Example of Executive Training: The Federal Executive Institute

The largest, oldest and most respected executive seminar center for the Federal government is the Federal Executive Institute (FEI) in Charlottesville, VA. Their major program is called Leadership for a Democratic Society. This four-week program brings together managers and executives (generally GS-15 and SES I and II) from twenty-five to thirty domestic and defense agencies for a unique, residential learning experience. The objective is to help agencies in the development of their career executive corps, linking individual development to improved agency performance. The themes of FEI's Leadership for a Democratic Society program reflect and enhance the common culture of senior federal executives. Personal leadership, organizational transformation, policy, and global perspective components support an overarching emphasis on our government's constitutional framework.

Enhancing Leadership Development

Finally, it is essential to note that organizations are also very important in enhancing leadership development. Ideally, organizations create multiple avenues for leadership development so that formal training, structured developmental opportunities, and incentives for self-study all exist. Further, such diversity can provide a highly favorable environment and synergy among the types of training. Some of the concrete methods by which organizations can enhance leadership development include that they:

- provide financial support for continuing education;
- provide an array of supervisory, management, and executive leadership programs;
- provide rewards and awards for those who are innovative and create improvements;
- provide rotational assignments;
- assign pay increases partially based on skill development;
- allow time for learning experiences and experimentation;
- place development as an explicit category in the annual evaluation for all employees;
- evaluate supervisors at all levels on their ability and success in providing management and leadership development (leadership succession);
- bring in outside speakers and guests to stimulate new ideas;
- encourage outside field trips to benchmark best practices;
- integrate "live" projects into formal training programs (action learning);
- provide multisource feedback on a standard schedule and with institutional support (see Appendixes A, B, and C);
- are proactive in establishing a "learning organization" that embraces new ideas and openness (Senge 1990; Garvin 1993).

The aggregate effect of these supportive activities is enormous, as research has repeatedly shown. An example of such a study is provided in Exhibit 16.2.

Exhibit 16.2

The Positive Effects of a Supportive Environment

Huczynski and Lewis (1980) conducted a study specifically to see which variables were most important in effecting transfer in a management training situation. They used a single training program and divided the participants into those who demonstrated substantial transfer and those who did not demonstrate much transfer. Certain factors in the situation they investigated became apparent. First, trainees who chose to take the class (rather than being sent without much choice) were significantly more motivated than other employees to try to transfer the new learning to the job. Second, trainees who had the opportunity to talk about the goals and objectives of the course with a superior were far more motivated to transfer learning. Third, superiors could substantially effect transfer by making sure that when the trainees were most amenable to transfer—immediately upon their return to work—they were not overwhelmed with a backlog of work. Superiors also encouraged implementation of new learning by maintaining a supportive attitude. Thus, in this study of transfer, learning principles were held constant, trainee characteristics played a small role, and work environment played a substantial role in determining the amount of transfer that occurred.

STRUCTURED EXPERIENCE AND ASSOCIATED DEVELOPMENTAL METHODS

Because the best development relies on providing challenge, variety, and feedback, multiple types of activities may be needed to foster a strong leadership learning environment. Of course, the types of developmental activities will vary substantially based on the level in the organization. Although the following activities will be described as if the learner is always the recipient of development, this is not to say that providers of leadership development do not also gain from the experience as they structure it and provide feedback. Teaching requires people to take implicit or "gut" knowledge and make it explicit. It also requires people to refine their ideas and increase their overall sophistication about the relationships inherent in leadership. Five specific methods of structuring experience follow, as well as a discussion of the superior's role in creating a supportive environment.

Individual Learning Plans

Leaders at all levels of the organization should encourage those reporting to them to submit individual development plans that map out future learning goals, as well as employee accomplishment reports that emphasize past training and development. A development plan requires a person to specify a strategy to improve skills, abilities, and knowledge—whatever her or his current level. The assumption behind development plans is that everybody can and should try to improve current capabilities. Employee accomplishment reports should include both production achievements and personal growth achievements. Such accomplishment reports ideally are connected to performance ratings, pay increases, and promotions over time. The most comprehensive strategy is an individual annual report that includes the annual accomplishment report (the past year's) and an individual development plan (next year's). It is a powerful tool for supervisors who wish to hold those reporting to them responsible for their own development while maintaining a say in the authorization and reward of training and developmental activities.

Consciously designed, fully articulated annual plans for development do not spring full-blown to paper once a year unless a less formal, ongoing assessment of development needs has occurred during the year. Leaders and their supervisors need to be on the lookout for special learning opportunities and new competency deficits created by new respon-sibilities. While many microlevel skills do not rise to the level of inclusion in an annual development plan, they can nonetheless be critical in optimizing job success. For example, leaders must often take time from busy schedules and learn about technical systems for approvals, information relaying, budgeting and finance, and so forth. Understanding the details of such systems may not be critical because subordinates can provide the needed information; however, a basic understanding of the more technical aspects can facilitate direct access and help leaders shape their requests for information more astutely.

Job Rotation

In a true job rotation, a trainee is given a series of different job assignments in various parts of the organization for specific periods of time and is exposed to a variety of tasks or decision-making situations. There are several types of modified job rotation as well, for example, rotating jobs in a unit among employees who work together. Another ex-ample involves placing a senior manager or executive as an intern in another division or agency for an extended period of time. Sometimes governmental organizations will allow two high-level managers to "swap" jobs for up to a year. The federal sector refers to this technique as developmental career assignments.

Job rotation enriches both the organization and the employees involved. When the rotation takes place at the lower levels of an organization, especially within a unit, it spreads skills more evenly throughout the work group. Trainees can fill in for absentees or wherever else they are needed. Employees appreciate each other's work more, and group problem solving is tremendously enhanced. The benefits of job rotation for senior employees are slightly different. These employees gain an overall perspective of the organization through job rotation and can make better decisions. It is especially useful for leaders-in-training to experience both line and staff positions. Job rotation can also be an excellent means of assisting employees in exploring alternatives.

Traditionally, job rotation serves as a form of executive development for employees chosen early in their careers for promotion. Bright and motivated young employees engage in a number of assignments throughout the organization to ensure that they have an excellent firsthand grasp of a wide range of essential organizational components. Af-ter working at a series of jobs, the employees acquire a permanent job and are allowed to rise rapidly through the ranks. Public safety and armed forces organizations have traditionally been the biggest advocates of job rotation at all levels. For example, well-articulated development systems in the military require a variety of assignments prior to advancement; completing such assignments is informally referred to as "punching your card." The federal government attempted to increase job rotation assignments at higher organizational levels when the Senior Executive Service (SES) was created in 1978. Traditionally the United States has been the advanced democracy with a bureaucracy dominated mostly by specialists. However, most analysts consider the rotational aspect of the SES to be only a modified success, at best (Ungar 1989).

Job rotation is not without its problems. If the work area or organization is struggling with large workloads, rotational assignments can initially decrease productivity and efficiency. When the workload is too pressing, the trainee may feel great stress and may not receive support in the training. A lot of one-on-one training is required to assist the trainee to learn the basic work requirements and to monitor progress. An unmotivated trainee can view rotational assignments as transitional and thus have a shallow learning experience. These and other potential problems only emphasize that job rotation cannot be conducted in a random, unstructured, or casual way if it is to be consistently successful.

Specialized Developmental Assignments

In order to gain the advantages of a broader perspective and an enhanced range of skills, it is not always necessary to leave one's job on a rotational basis. One can gain these benefits from additional special assignments concurrently with one's regular job. Managers can be asked to chair a problem-solving committee or task force, assume a new general management function such as budget preparation, start up a new operation, substitute at an important meeting, or manage and write an important study. Sometimes such assignments do not require being in charge, but just observing. Attending meetings and conferences, conducting site visits, and shadowing an executive are examples of useful observation experiences.

Special assignments have particular relevance in an organizational universe moving toward flattening, decentralization, and multitasking, insofar as they mimic the nature of most work today. The proverbial final item at the end of everyone's job description—"and other work as assigned"—is an everyday reality for most managers and supervisors. Leaders need to be prepared to take on a variety of special tasks in addition to their normal line or staff work, and discussions about these challenging assignments should focus on the opportunities for development. Of course, the downfall of special assignments is typical of many developmental problems—poor planning, excessive challenges in carrying out the assignment, and poor feedback and support from one's supervisor.

Coaching

Coaching, the most commonly used developmental technique at all levels, is the backbone of on-the-job-training. In (basic) coaching, employees learn from an immediate supervisor or a co-worker. More than anyone else on the job, the coach is in closest contact with the employee and therefore best knows the employee's skills and actual performance. Coaching occurs on a one-to-one basis, uses the trainee's actual job experience as a source of learning, and is done on-site. Coaching is used to train new employees and to maintain and upgrade the skills of current employees. In other words, coaching should really never stop. It offers the opportunity for employees to learn from their own mistakes and successes instead of learning only from generalized examples. The technique is often casual, which helps the learner to relax, but the informality may lead to sloppy implementation.

While coaching frontline employees is often a major function for supervisors, it is much less an expectation at all levels of management. The management group that generally receives the most coaching is the new supervisor because of the shift from a technical to a management position. The assumption at other levels, even when managers are moving into new positions and to higher levels, is that the managers have the experience and background to figure out the job with the limited structured training that is provided. Coaching on technical processes and background information is normally conducted by subordinates at the manager's request. In general, managers and executives who need coaching because they are new, inexperienced, or encountering a new or special problem must seek out their own coaching. This means that they must recognize the need, identify a competent source, and follow through on their own. Because most managers have frenetic jobs with dozens of issues swirling about them at any given time (Mintzberg 1979), it is easy to see why managers often fail to seek out coaching even when they clearly recognize the need to do so. Occasionally managers can sidestep the immediate need for coaching by assigning the task or issue to a competent subordinate. This can save the manager's time, allow the manager to learn by example, and provide a professional experience for the subordinate. However, it is not always appropriate or possible to delegate all tasks that the manager does not understand. Typical coaches for managers are subordinates, the boss, a colleague at the same level, human resource personnel, executive staff, and other specialists in the organization.

Because of the chronic weakness of individualized on-the-job training and developmental feedback at all levels of management, there has been an increase in the popularity of executive coaching. Executive coaches can be hired consultants from outside the organization or high-prestige trainers with special training from within the organization. Some of the advantages of executive coaching are flexibility, confidentiality, and convenience. Because of the expense of an outside consultant, or the consumption of time of an internal consultant, such training is normally reserved for very senior managers. It is particularly useful when provided in conjunction with other programs in which the executive is getting a wide array of management-style performance data (such as through leadership survey feedback) or when the executive is implementing a special project (a form of action learning). Although there are some very positive examples of executive coaching in the public sector (Olivero, Bane, and Kopelman 1997), it has not gained the same popularity as in the private sector.

Mentoring

Mentoring, unlike executive coaching, is quite popular as a concept in the public sector. Mentoring refers to a protégé relationship in which a more senior and experienced individual shares information about the organizational culture, career opportunities, and networking aspects of a job. Unlike coaching that focuses on specific learning goals such as fixing a technical problem or learning about a specific process, mentoring focuses on the "big picture." Mentors are often from other areas in the organization.

Mentoring for those new to the profession, but who have high potential, such as those from master of public administration or master of business administration programs, is often more generic and discipline related. Public-management students may be matched up with a city manager, a county department head, or a state government executive during the latter stages of the program of study. High-quality internships like the Presidential Management Internship program usually build mentoring into the overall structured experience. There is no consensus about whether formal or informal mentoring is more effective. However, there is little doubt that in order to be effective the mentor has to be a true role model who is sincerely interested enough in the relationship to devote the time. Given that time is often a senior manager's most precious commodity, good intentions are often not equivalent to good follow-through.

Mentoring senior managers has received special attention in relation to enhancing diversity. Because of the long-term, historical dominance of white males in senior positions in almost all sectors of organizational and political life, special efforts at providing support through mentoring programs are popular. Unfortunately, mentoring to enhance diversity has frequently run into problems with finding suitable diversity role models, stereotyping, resentment by peers, and sometimes exclusion from the true power networks. Although mentoring programs are generally informal or developmental, staff support and the provision of structured formats often helps ensure quality.

The Superior's Role in Creating the Supportive Environment

Earlier in this chapter the importance of a positive organizational climate was discussed. This section addresses the particular importance of the supervisor in this process. To begin with, the supervisor can identify and inform subordinates about training opportunities. Opportunities can be discussed with individual employees, and the particular benefits of certain programs can be highlighted related to their management development needs. Providing time off for training is often important and occasionally means rescheduling an individual's work for a period of time. Often, a supervisor can request a specific learning objective and identify a special task to work on after training. This acts as a powerful motivator to the individual receiving the training.

When a subordinate comes back from training, a report on what was learned and its utility for the unit or organization is helpful to the individual and other employees. This can be done in a staff meeting or in a memorandum. A one-on-one meeting with the subordinate is particularly useful to review the material and identify applications or work improvements based on what was learned. Placing developmental accomplishments and goals in the annual work review is especially important in demonstrating to subordinates that these tie directly to important job evaluation functions. Indeed, it has been repeatedly demonstrated that even the confidence that the supervisor exhibits in a subordinate has

Exhibit 16.3

The Pygmalion Effect

Most people are not aware that trainees' abilities can be enhanced simply by using the right approach. Enhancing ability through psychological means is called the Pygmalion effect. In the play and movie *My Fair Lady* (based on George Bernard Shaw's play *Pygmalion*), Eliza Doolittle is a cockney flower vendor with low expectations of herself. To win a wager, Professor Henry Higgins agrees to teach her Oxford English so that she can pass as an aristocrat. When he announces his purpose, she says, "Go on," in nasal cockney tones. In six months, however, his high expectations win out, and she indeed passes as an aristocrat. Eden and Ravid (1982) tested this thesis in a training study. Two identical groups of trainees were given the same training program. However, one group was told by a highly credible source—a psychologist—of their tremendous ability. Even though the trainer was not informed about this experiment, the trainees in the experimental group performed dramatically better. Thus, high expectations affected the trainees' perceptions of their ability and increased their motivation.

a tremendous effect on subordinate behavior, better known as the Pygmalion effect (see Exhibit 16.3 for an example of such a study). Overall, the attentiveness of the supervisor can have a disproportionate effect on the perceived value and ability to utilize training; however, busy supervisors frequently overlook such opportunities, thus sending an unintended message that training is not as critical as other functions are.

FORMAL TRAINING DESIGN

Although the implementation of training programs is important, the design of programs is generally even more important. Good design takes into account learning theory, costs and benefits, training objectives, and special constraints. Learning theory looks at the way trainee characteristics, the work environment, and principles of learning interact to influence the quality of learning and retention, as well as concrete transfer of learning to the workplace and long-term maintenance (Baldwin and Ford 1988). Good programs are generally designed with a clear idea of who the participants are in advance so that learning needs can be pinpointed. Preliminary surveys or assessments help to identify their special needs. It is also important to have a realistic idea of the work environment from which the trainee comes and to which they will return. The learning theory literature has provided solid evidence that a select number of principles operate in nearly all substantial training programs. Seven fundamental training principles will be discussed below.

Setting Goals

Setting goals is an important way to focus and enhance motivation (Kim and Hammer 1976). Ironically, motivation is rarely addressed directly in training programs despite its obvious importance in job or training settings. Because goal setting has been found to be so effective in stimulating motivation, two levels of goal setting are discussed.

The first level of goals includes those that bring the employees into training. These goals may stem from employee characteristics such as belief in training and the motivation to succeed, or from work-environment factors such as promotion and salary potential and encouragement by supervisors (Burke, Weitzel, and Weir 1978). Or the goals may be more specific, for example, a need to master minimum competencies, raise performance to higher standards, gain cross-training for organizational flexibility, or learn about a new technology. The goals also may be developmental, such as the desire to cross-train for career breadth, explore new career opportunities, take a break in the job routine, or explore current state-of-the-art theories and practices (Latham and Baldes 1975).

A second level of goals is employed in the training itself. The training program usually will be composed of many learning tasks that should each fit in with specific learning goals. Instructors call those goals the desired learning objectives. A major challenge to the trainer is to relate participant and instructional goals. When trainees complain that training is not relevant to them or not sufficiently practical, the connection between the trainees' goals and the instructor's goals is weak or nonexistent.

The instructor needs to clarify as many of the participant and instructional goals as possible (Wexley and Latham 1981). Participant goals can be assessed through a variety of means. A needs assessment usually provides valuable data on participant goals prior to the beginning of the program. Instructors can also get information about the goals of participants during the program. A questionnaire administered during the first session or a diagnostic test can help the instructor clarify the specific goals of trainees. Participants' goals can usually be highlighted without deviating from instructional goals by good instructors familiar with teaching the material.

Goal-setting theory has generally indicated that easy goals are not the most effective in terms of motivation, satisfaction, or accomplishment, which all track together relatively consistently (Latham and Yukl 1975; Reber and Wallin 1984). Rather, the most motivating goals are those that are hard but realistic. The realism of hard goals is often in the clarity with which they are laid out, the organizational support they receive in implementation, and the accuracy of the expectations on which they are based. Therefore, providing hard but realistic goals takes both insight and finesse. Furthermore, most employees do not balk at hard but realistic goals when they are confident that they will receive the requisite support and will ultimately be successful with moderate persistence. Thus, confidence building, listening, and flexibility are all necessary to attain hard but realistic goals.

Increasing the Similarity of Training to the Work Environment

One of the primary ways to increase the effectiveness of training and have it transfer to the job is to increase the similarity of the training to the work environment (Baldwin and Ford 1988). Early researchers have stressed that if the same stimulus and response elements are in both the training and the job, transfer to the job is more likely and retention of verbal behaviors and motor skills increases. This notion is called "identical elements" (Crafts 1934; Wexley and Latham 1981). Identical elements can include the conditions of the training program, such as the surroundings, tasks, equipment, and other physical elements. Just as important, psychological identical elements refer to the degree to which trainees attach similar meanings to the training and job context. Increasing similarity between training and work can occur with discrete skills, intermediate skills, and complex skills. Three progressive steps increase the similarity of training to the work environment: use of examples, modeling, and simulation.

The *use of examples* is a cognitive technique that describes the relationship between what is being taught and the specific job or range of jobs. Often training discussions are general and analytical, with the only detail being the generic labeling of elements. Examples make the labeling concrete and help students visualize what is being taught. Examples can be used in several ways. An instructor who is lecturing about negotiation might discuss a recent labor-management clash. By taking the time to illustrate general points with details of a specific example, the instructor gives the trainees the time to digest points and to weigh the ramifications of what is being discussed. Another way to use examples is through case studies; students are given scenarios related to the topic and job and asked to devise, either in groups or individually, possible courses of action. For example, students can be given a scenario of an imminent labor-management conflict and be asked to propose solutions. A third way is to bring student examples into the discussion. This method becomes increasingly effective as the participants' level of experience rises and the trainees are likely to have relevant examples to share. For example, most midlevel managers and all senior managers would have a range of examples germane to labor-management negotiations. A particularly robust form of example, the case study, will be presented as a discussion method later in this chapter.

A second way to increase the similarity of training to the job is through *modeling* (Moses and Ritchie 1976; Kinslaw 1990). The use of descriptive examples is a cognitive technique, but modeling is a visual or graphic technique—that is, the desired behavior is shown to the students or trainees. Modeling can occur in a class as well as in the field (Decker 1982). When instructors demonstrate situations for students, they are modeling the correct behavior. Or an instructor may use a training film in which the situation is illustrated. The instructor may take the trainees out of the training environment and into the job environment for field experience. Using the prior example of teaching negotiation skills, the instructor might script a discrete learning lesson and role-play a situation with one of the trainees. A training film on negotiation might follow several disputes through to the conclusion. Because of the confidentiality involved, students might not be able to observe negotiations, but they could talk to representatives from labor and management in their work environment.

A third means of increasing similarity between training and the job is with *simulation*. In simulation activities, the trainees do more than observe correct behavior, they perform it (Bligh 1972; Beard 1970). Class simulations can be nonautomated (e.g., role-plays and management simulations) or automated (e.g., machine and computer simulations). A management training program can involve a management training exercise that lasts for several days during which all the students take on different roles as they proceed through a series of events. For example, an instructor might assign all the class members to one of two sides in a negotiation and have them move through a contract negotiation process. The instructor teaches the students to get them ready, coaches them during the exercise, and critiques them afterward.

If trainees are placed into a job situation as a part of the instruction, the distance between training and job is closed entirely. It is best if this placement occurs at the end of a training sequence. Ideally, the trainee would learn general principles by hearing examples first, seeing the correctly modeled behavior next, and then practicing the behavior with guidance and immediate feedback (Goldstein and Sorcher 1974). Throwing trainees into a live situation too quickly can cause them to panic and not learn much. Guided practice in actual work situations, internships, and apprenticeships are excellent ways to conclude training. When careful coaching is provided in these situations, the number of errors is quickly reduced and the learners master skills swiftly and well.

Teaching Underlying Principles

The teaching of underlying principles is another well-established learning concept (Bourne 1970). While increasing similarity between the training and the job is training focused, teaching underlying principles is education focused. Some training is so skill and task specific that general principles are omitted. Regulation updates, frequent as they are, often sacrifice discussions of background principles to quick communication because it is expected that the recipients are already versed in the principles. Although this approach might be realistic in a limited number of cases, normally this is a poor practice in training situations. The trainees' understanding can always be enhanced by the teaching of general principles, which, in turn, contribute to transfer (Latham, Wexley, and Pursell 1975).

Training in personal computer applications presents a good example of the danger of not teaching general principles. It is possible to introduce people to computer applications without teaching them any of the underlying principles. However, the individuals may have such a limited understanding that they forget a step in the procedure and are unable to rediscover the solution on their own. Someone with broader training will be more likely to figure out problems because of a deeper understanding of general principles.

Several notes of caution are necessary in reference to the teaching of general principles. First, the integration of general principles into applied learning in a balanced and smooth way that does not confuse the trainee is a constant challenge for instructors. Second, general principles are often overemphasized in educational settings and underemphasized in training settings, due to their distinctive roles in providing generic versus specific understanding and skill development. Although university education stresses generic learning, it places a great burden on the students to relate the learning to their own limited experiences. A training program that overstresses general principles is likely to neglect examples, models, and simulations. A training program that understresses general principles is likely to lack intellectual stimulation and long-term transfer and maintenance because of the evanescent skills being taught.

Increasing the Organization of the Material

Increasing the organization of the material is a simple learning concept but is not easily translated into instruction (Gagné 1962). A content specialist may give a brilliant lecture that is tightly organized, but the learners may retain little of the material if the structure and sequence are not readily apparent to them. The structure of the material should usually be outlined for trainees, verbally and/or visually. Occasional references to the outline will help make the points fit into place and be retained by trainees.

Auxiliary readings are excellent for adding variety to courses but can be difficult for learners to comprehend and retain if the learning points are discussed only after the reading. Although many instructors believe that learners should learn through discovery in auxiliary readings, this may be a poor organizational strategy. Helping learners to organize the reading prior to and during the activity may lead to far more effective results. Adjunct questions are a good way of focusing attention on the more important points in the reading. Questions given to learners before they begin reading will help them integrate the readings with the lecture and discussion.

Definitions and labels are also important in the organization of material. Learners need consistent terminology and definition of terms, even though there may be active debate in the field about the best definitions. Instructors must make heuristic decisions about the best definitions for the class, noting diversity of opinion if necessary. Although the labeling and definition of behaviors and concepts is more difficult than the labeling and definition of tangible things, they are just as important. For example, when discussing discipline problems with new managers, the trainees may need to learn what authority they have to deal with insubordination. However, first it is important to know what the concept of insubordinate behavior means. How is it specifically defined? Because major personnel and legal issues are involved, the term insubordinate behavior must be conceptually and specifically defined to ensure clarity and consistency of trainees' understanding.

Instructional organization usually poses a problem only when it is lacking. One way for the trainer to check instructional organization from the participants' point of view is to look at tests or exams as tests of the instructor instead of the participants. If more than a few students miss a point or question, the instructor is well advised to assume that he or she has failed to make the point as clearly as it should have been made. The army puts it more bluntly: If students fail to learn, the instructor failed to teach—so always examine the material from the learner's perspective.

Actively Involving the Learner

Active involvement of learners in the learning process has been reemphasized in recent research, but it is actually an ancient learning principle. The Socratic method teaches by using questions to discover basic truths. It requires learners to constantly question and probe their experiences and understanding. Whether active involvement is stressed as a part of the initial instruction or separately after instruction, it is basically practice. Three aspects of active involvement will be reviewed here: manipulation of material, frequency of practice, and timing of practice.

Manipulation of the material is now considered to be one of the most important ingredients for learning retention. Any manipulation of the material will tend to lead to vastly superior recall as compare with no manipulation at all. For example, the recall of individuals who take notes is significantly better than the recall of those who do not. Exercises and small-group activities require learner manipulation after the instructional input. Even occasional use of the Socratic method in the classroom, such as using questions rather than statements to introduce material, can significantly enhance the learning process.

Frequency of practice is also important. A single opportunity to practice may not accomplish much. However, if recognition is all that is required, then minimal practice may suffice. For example, law enforcement personnel may need only to recognize a situation in order to refer a citizen to the appropriate agency for service. If comprehension is necessary, the law enforcement officer may need to understand a process that is used only occasionally or in which process aids (e.g., the instructional materials themselves) will be available for reference. If mastery is necessary, complete recall may be needed because time and legal constraints may not allow for instructional aids or delays. For example, a law enforcement officer must know exactly what procedures to follow in actual enforcement situations in order to meet due process constraints and safety standards. Clearly, moderate comprehension requires more practice than mere recognition, and full mastery requires more practice than comprehension. Although much of the practice may be allotted to noninstructional time, instructors need to build in several opportunities for practice under their supervision.

Generalizing about when practice should occur is difficult because the timing of practice varies with the situation. In the ideal, some sort of modified practice should occur during the initial instructional phase in the form of note taking, questions, and exercises. Following this phase, but still in the context of the training setting, practice should continue under guided conditions. The final phase of involvement is an unguided practice phase, in which the participants can self-correct with activities provided by the instructor. However, this ideal scenario may not be practical or possible in many situations.

Giving Feedback

The term feedback refers to the knowledge of results of practice (Locke 1980). If there is no instructor-monitored practice, there can be no external feedback. Practice includes exercises, tests, discussions, papers, and in-training observation of behavior in apprenticeships or simulations.

Feedback can take many forms. It can be verbal praise and/or suggestions for improvement. It can be test scores, productivity reports, and performance measures. Feedback can be a subtle physical behavior by the instructor: a nod or shake of the head, a smile or a frown, or a pat on the arm. Good trainers tend to look for ways to increase the amount and immediacy of feedback (Yukl and Latham 1975). Although task performance has an implicit feedback function apart from the instructor, the trainee who receives instructor feedback is likely to outstrip those who are not assisted by personal attention. For example, mentoring is a particularly powerful technique because participants constantly receive customized feedback on performance.

Three major uses of feedback have been identified (Wexley and Latham 1981). First, it is used to reduce errors. Through feedback, trainees learn quickly about wrong behaviors and receive instruction about right behaviors. Therefore, trainees do not spend much time practicing wrong behaviors. Second, feedback makes training more interesting and significantly enhances trainees' motivation. Third, feedback should lead to high standards and goal setting.

The usefulness and effectiveness of feedback can be enhanced by following certain guidelines. First, the interval between the practice and the feedback should always be kept as short as possible. Second, positive feedback is as important as negative feedback because of its motivating quality and the encouragement of correct behaviors. Negative feedback is useful in error reduction. Thus, it is important to establish a good balance between positive and negative feedback. Third, ideally in training systems feedback is extensive and detailed, and then tapers off over time as trainees become more proficient. Selective feedback with more skilled or mature workers is generally preferred and is more efficient; abundant instructor or supervisor feedback often annoys competent employees.

Providing executives with feedback is more difficult than doing so for other learners. In training settings, executives often enjoy feedback in discussions as they bring up particular issues. Customized leadership survey feedback with individual conferences is another way to provide high-quality feedback. Mentoring and executive coaching techniques excel at providing high-quality feedback. In work settings, senior managers and executives often suffer from a lack of diverse and honest feedback. Lack of quality feedback is a primary source of leader derailment, according to McCall, Lombardo, and Morrison (1988).

Using a Variety of Techniques and Stimuli

The use of a variety of techniques and stimuli is a powerful way to enhance both learning and retention to the fullest. By varying techniques, a trainer can engage several of the learners' senses. If a trainee merely hears something in a lecture, the chances of his or her remembering it (effective encoding), even after only a few days, are minimal. If a trainee hears and sees something, perhaps in a lecture and on a blackboard, the chances increase that he or she will remember the material. If something is heard, seen, and written down (the tactile sense), the chances of retention increase still more. And if the learner also has the opportunity to verbalize the new material, perhaps through questions or role-plays, it results in the greatest chance that he or she will remember it. For an example of a study that investigated this principle, see Exhibit 16.4.

Different sensory and cognitive channels used in the learning process provide all learners with a greater opportunity for encoding. Because everyone has different learning-style preferences in terms of aural, visual, and tactile inputs, using different sensory channels ensures that all learning styles are covered. The use of different sensory channels also seems to increase both interest and motivation. Variety enhances interest by reducing boredom. It enhances motivation by providing a challenge to integrate differently displayed material (Blum 1968).

Learning can be varied through stimulus variety and technique variety. Stimulus va-

---

Exhibit 16.4

Using a Variety of Techniques to Enhance Recall

In a classically designed study, Duncan (1958) demonstrated the importance of variation in training to teach general skills. He set up experimental and control groups of college students to test two variables: the degree of variation in training and the amount of training. In other words, he wanted to see if learning transfer would be greater with one highly practiced task or a number of less practiced tasks (with an equivalent amount of total training time). He also wanted to see if the amount of training time allocated would favor one method or the other. The results showed that subjects learned the general skill better with a variety of tasks than a single task—whether the total amount of time was short or long. Duncan (1958, 72) hypothesized that "training with a variety of stimuli forces [subjects] to concentrate carefully on every stimulus, making use of all the cues that stimulus provides." In fact, in this experiment the groups with the highest number of tasks (ten) learned best, indicating that the value of task variety plateaus only at very high levels. The ramification for trainers is that they should maximize the number of tasks for a learning objective. The challenge is to make sure that the variety of tasks and stimuli are of high quality.

---

riety can take the form of examples; that is, several different examples can be used for the same point. Stimulus variability in modeling situations can occur by changing the sex, age, and organizational levels of the participants in the modeling. In simulations, the participants can change roles. Stimulus variety keeps the technique constant while changing the participants' perspectives through different examples, models, or roles.

Variety in techniques can involve mixing an aural technique (e.g., lectures) and an application technique (e.g., exercises), or through a visual technique (e.g., reading) and an oral technique (e.g., debate). Or it might involve a sequence of techniques, beginning with reading, moving to lecture, model demonstration, and discussion, and concluding with an exercise, simulation, or test. Note that the test in this sequence is an extension of the learning process, not simply a means of assessing the amount of learning.

In sum, leadership and training are related in many ways. The quality of training affects all employees in an organization in the broadest sense. Prospective leaders should get different types of training as they move from one level to the next. And leaders have a special responsibility for training those reporting to them. Developing staff is an important competency covered in chapter 14. Whether leaders are participating in or managing training programs, it is important to remember the basics of good program design. It is fundamental to know the background of participants and the work environment from which they come. But it is just as fundamental to know that humans learn better following general principles of learning. Programs should maximize these principles to the degree possible. Good programs tend to use participant goal setting, ensure ample similarity to the work environment, teach underlying principles of the content area, provide clear objectives and a well-thought-out instructional plan, involve the learner, provide abundant feedback, and use a variety of stimuli throughout the program. With the basic principles of effective training in mind, we can now turn to specific methods.

COMMONLY USED METHODS IN FORMAL TRAINING PROGRAMS

No decision is more important in the design of a training program than the selection of the methods of instruction. The selection of methods begins immediately after decisions are made about who the audience is to be and what topics are to be covered. As important as audience and content issues are, they only determine the general need for and function of the training. The methods used will give the training or development program its distinctive shape. The methods and strategies chosen affect most of the other elements of program design, in particular, the number of participants, training times, location, cost, and instructors.

Instructional methods have been divided into four families in this book: (1) lecture methods, (2) discussion methods, (3) printed and electronic materials, and (4) practice and feedback techniques. The methods in each family are similar in terms of presentation and the learning principles that they emphasize. Because the learning principles of each method (and family) have both strengths and weaknesses, mixing methods from the different families tends to enhance learning outcomes.

Lecture Methods

Five lecture methods will be discussed in this section: standard lectures, team teaching, guest speakers, panels, and participant presentations. All of these oral methods of presenting information have similar strengths and weaknesses. Learners with an aural preference like lecture methods, but these methods are less suitable for learners with visual or kinesthetic preferences. Lecture methods are an excellent choice for presenting a great deal of information efficiently, stressing underlying principles, and highlighting the internal organization of the material presented. However, they tend to lack opportunities for participant involvement as well as feedback and a direct connection to the work environment.

In the *standard lecture* format, the trainer talks while the audience listens and absorbs information. In a more active lecture situation, trainees take notes. Main ideas can easily be stressed and summarized. The verbal aspect of the format is strengthened by the use of quotes, examples, statistics, and comparisons. It can also be strengthened by using visual displays such as PowerPoint presentations or opaque/overhead projection, flip charts, white boards, teaching props, slides, videos, or handouts. Ideally, trainees hearing a lecture should have good listening skills and a fairly consistent range of abilities or experiences. The trainer must have strong basic lecturing skills and the power to hold trainees' attention. This means that the trainer must have credentials in the content area and a good mastery of presentation skills to ensure interesting delivery. While it is the single most popular method for both trainers and trainees, it is often the most abused. Learners' attention span is generally much shorter than the lecturer's interest in talking, which results in wasted participant time. Interspersing short, tight lectures among other methods is often the ideal from the learners' perspective.

Team teaching is a variation of the standard lecture method. Several formats for team teaching are possible. In one common format, different instructors present different topics. Alternatively, two instructors may teach different aspects of the same subject. When the topic is highly technical, different experts can add complementary expertise to the presentation. Teams are also useful when the presentation time is extensive, especially if the training is a half-day in length or more. Team teaching adds significantly to the dynamic quality of the presentation because of the change of presenter and the interaction between presenters. Good teams not only frequently rotate the lead but also present information collaboratively through simulated dialogues. Of course, team teaching is more expensive in terms of instructional resources and requires more coordination for good execution.

In terms of training principles, the use of one or more *guest speakers* is nearly identical to standard lecture and team teaching. Guest speakers can be the primary means of conveying the desired learning objectives, but more often they are used to augment a standard lecture format and other teaching methods. A program structured around guest speakers can be a particular challenge for a training coordinator; without tremendous coordination of the speakers' material, thematic links between the presentations are likely to be weak and repetition is unavoidable. These problems are especially common when the guest speakers are not present for one another's presentations, a situation that prevails when using high-prestige speakers.

Panels add texture to a training program but do take a lot of time to arrange. They are common in management and executive development programs as well as professional conferences. There are two main types of panels: sequential and moderated. Sequential panels use two or more speakers who speak in succession. Speakers prepare the outline of their remarks in advance and may or may not modify their remarks based on what the other speakers say. When a panel is used in training programs, it is often to introduce a variety of expert opinions after the group has discussed the basic issues. For example, an all-day seminar on current budgeting practices might conclude in the afternoon with budgeting directors from local, state, and federal agencies making presentations based on their particular experiences. Question-and-answer opportunities for participants are often planned with sequential panels, although they are frequently truncated because of time. The moderated panel format is common on television news shows that discuss, rather than report, the news. A less common technique because it is difficult to employ, it is nevertheless powerful when successful. It relies on a strong moderator who understands the topic, prepares questions in advance, and insists on panelists' brevity in responding.

Participant presentations are probably underused in many programs because of the problems they present. They can take a great deal of time; other participants can find them dull and rambling; and the participant presenters may lack experience, be nervous, or fail to devote the necessary time. However, the method can be a powerful one in motivating trainees to take an active part in their own learning. A few guidelines can increase the success of participant presentations. Participants must know of the requirement before, or at the beginning of, the program. Written instructions should provide information about the topic, presentation guidelines, presentation tips, resources available, and importance of the assignment. Strictly limiting the presentation time improves presentation quality and audience attention substantially. The old saying, "less is more," invariably applies to student presentations.

Discussion Methods

Discussion methods, especially case studies, occasionally are used as the dominant training method, but more often they are auxiliary to lecture and other methods. Most training programs, especially those depending primarily on lectures, use some form of discussion method. In general, discussion enhances participants' active role in the learning process. Although inefficient in terms of time, discussion methods more than make up for this weakness in terms of dynamic human interaction. In this family of methods, we will address question-and-answer techniques, large group methods, small group methods, case studies, and individual conferences.

The standard open-question format follows almost every live lecture. Unfortunately, the *question-and-answer technique* is rarely used effectively because the lecturer's concern for the logic and comprehensiveness of the lecture usually takes precedence over concern for the listener's curiosity and enthusiasm. A classic example is the lecturer who ends his or her peroration one or two minutes before the prescribed ending time and asks if there are any questions. For the standard question-and-answer technique to become robust, several things must happen. First, the instructor's attitude must change from viewing questions as distractions from lectures to viewing them as an effective way to enhance learning through increased participation and interaction. Second, question-and-answer opportunities must not be relegated to the last few minutes of the allotted time. Third, rather than asking participants if there are any questions in a fashion that implicitly suggests that they do not understand the lecturer's presentation, the lecturer must encourage the participants to ask questions that add to the presentation—questions that share perspectives, discuss ambiguities, relate their own examples, and even insert some of their own subject-oriented humor. Achieving high-quality question-and-answer discussions is indispensable in management development and leadership programs.

True *large-group methods* involve participants in such a way that they are in charge of their learning objectives for a substantial block of time. Although there are a number of alternative methods, we will discuss group brainstorming (with some nominal group elements). For example, an instructor for a train-the-trainer seminar series should discuss the importance of training before beginning to talk about training principles and methods. Collectively, the participants in the room already know why training is important, but they do not have all the information on an individual basis, nor is their understanding organized. The instructor poses the question to the class: "Why is training important?" The instructor acts as the group's secretary, writing down the responses in a list. When all responses have been recorded, the instructor asks the participants to cluster the responses. Students cluster related entries and throw out overlapping entries. Before generating a new list, the participants are asked what the best order for the responses might be in terms of importance. Responses can be put in order informally or through voting. The new list is sequential, ordered, and entirely generated by students with only moderate input from the instructor.

Like large-group methods, *small-group methods* (also known as work groups or buzz groups) have many variations. The task-solution format will be highlighted in our discussion of this important technique. For example, in a seminar on ethics, public sector managers discuss the ethical uses of discretion. To identify the actual range of discretion, the managers are asked to list all of the areas in which they have some degree of discretion. They do this in small groups in which the members share their perceptions with one another while one person acts as the recorder. In fifteen minutes the group members have identified a dozen or more concrete examples from their own experiences. The facilitator then brings the participants back together and records a master list. The first small group shares all of its list. Later groups add only new items.

The *case study method* has long been a favorite teaching method of law schools, business schools, public sector executive training, and other disciplines for their advanced curricula. There are many variations of this old and powerful technique. We will describe the oldest format, which is a large-group method involving considerable participant preparation time. (Short case studies for small-group settings are popular and effective.) In the traditional case study, a problem situation is presented in writing, although it can also be presented with video material as well. The trainee is given time in advance to consider the case and sort out the issues. Written cases commonly vary from 500 to 5,000 words. The full case study utilizes ample detail and complex descriptions of situations and personalities. The case brings the reader up to the point where an action is necessary to deal with a problem or series of problems. Because of the complexity of the case, there is rarely a right answer, but there are many wrong answers if participants do not consider this complexity and do not come up with a sufficiently sophisticated solution.

Learning does not always occur in a group setting. In fact, it is desirable to try to build *individual conferences* into many types of training programs. This is especially true with long courses of instruction, when participants are highly motivated, when skill development is complex and interrelated, and when participants are being prepared for higher assignments. Individual conferences can also be useful for troubleshooting problems and coaching. Examples of individual conferences can be found at all levels of training. At the end of a one-day orientation program, each participant can be assigned to a seasoned employee who answers a few structured questions and who encourages the new employee to ask questions. New supervisors may be given personal feedback on the behavior modeling they are practicing. This feedback is especially valuable in difficult and high-stress situations such as counseling and administering discipline. Managers often profit greatly from individual conferences after receiving anonymous feedback from employees and supervisors about their leadership style. Executives benefit from opportunities to rehearse how course material might be relevant to changing policies in their respective organizations. As with any training and development activity, it is important that the participant knows in advance what the purpose of the individual conference is and what the desired outcomes are.

Printed and Electronic Materials

The importance of printed and electronic materials in training varies tremendously. Some forms of training might not include any printed and electronic materials at all, but most training programs have substantial print and electronic materials as an important teaching tool. Other training programs rely exclusively on printed and electronic materials. Three major roles can be distinguished. When printed materials are supplementary, not written specifically for the training program, or used outside the formal training session, they are used as *auxiliary reading materials*. When the materials are integral to the training program, written specifically for the training program, or used as the major reference and orientation for the program, they are general *training manuals or textbooks*. When the training manual is written as the primary teaching method for a program that relies on self-instruction, the method is called *programmed instruction*. Programmed instruction is different from the other members of its instructional family in that questions and answers are provided for participants to self-process. Assuming that participants take advantage of this interactive feature, it is less passive than pure lecture or print formats. Other types of print and electronic materials include handouts, written exercises, various types of visuals such as overheads, and other types of in-class materials that are largely teaching tools rather than methods per se.

Print and electronic materials have strengths similar to those of lecture methods. They are good at teaching underlying principles and providing clear organizational techniques. Print and lecture methods can reinforce one another but do not compensate for the weaknesses generally characteristic of both. Printed material can be used prior to class meetings, during and after classes, or with no classroom format at all. Except for programmed instruction, printed materials do not address learner involvement nor do they provide feedback. The capability of programmed instruction to involve learners and give feedback is a major advance in printed material, but programmed instruction is more expensive to design than other printed and electronic material and may not suit many situations.

Practice and Feedback Techniques

Practice and feedback techniques are most effective in two training principles: actively involving learners and giving them feedback. Although more cognitive techniques, such as standard lectures, are efficient in relaying general principles, there is no certainty that trainees will retain and store the information in a lasting and accurate fashion. To be involved, learners must pay attention, and feedback helps motivate learners to pay attention. It is rare for practice and feedback techniques to be used alone, but they are extremely effective in enhancing learning when combined with lecture, print and electronic, discussion, and other developmental techniques.

One common flaw of many instructional programs is that the design calls for input to be completed before any output (practice or discussion) and feedback begin. This design allows for little integration of the learning and may mean that learners will be overwhelmed with information that they cannot encode. Learners may resort to memorization in the

Exhibit 16.5

Weak and Strong Instructional Designs

Weak Instructional Design

Input ⟶ Output and Feedback ⟶ Output ⟶ Feedback
Such as lecture   Discussion   Test   Grade
and readings

Strong Instructional Design

Input ⟶ Output and Feedback ⟶ Input ⟶ Output ⟶ Feedback ⟶ Output ⟶ Feedback
Such as   Discussion   Lecture   Individual   Comments on   Test   Grade
readings   conference   exercise

short term, but it is likely that the information will rapidly fade from their memories. A more effective model of learning is formatted in a series of cycles and uses short input sessions followed by output and feedback. This model gives learners a chance to build experience and cognitive understanding as the learning proceeds. Overconcentration on input ignores learner needs. The real test of good instructional design is a variety of integrated output (practice and feedback) opportunities. A comparison of weak and good instructional designs is provided in Exhibit 16.5.

Some practice and feedback methods that will be discussed here are role-plays, survey and self-assessment techniques, and site visits. Many other techniques will not be discussed; these include note taking, adjunct questions, individual exercises, demonstrations, simulations, and tests.

Role-Plays

Through role-playing, trainees build self-confidence, get specific guidance, and receive constructive feedback as they interact with fellow employees. In the ideal situation, the tell-show-do-review model is used. First, the participants are told about the correct behavioral sequence and discussion is encouraged (tell). Next, the participants see the correct behavior demonstrated, either in person or through a videotape (show). The demonstration is briefly analyzed. The participants then have the opportunity to play the role themselves (do). In the final step, the participants get constructive feedback from the instructor or peer learners (review). Often role-playing is thought to involve only the do-step of the model, but true role-playing involves all the steps. Role-playing is one of the most effective strategies for modeling and changing behaviors. Done properly, it has been shown to have dramatic results in the workplace after extended periods of time (Latham and Saari 1979). In addition to the teaching of physical skills, role-playing has been broadly and successfully used in the development of interpersonal skills that are critical to leadership: coaching employees, interviewing, disciplining, handling difficult clients, listening and giving constructive feedback, and being assertive. Exhibit 16.6 provides an example of a successful supervisory leadership program that uses role-playing.

Exhibit 16.6

The Effectiveness of Role-Plays

Latham and Saari (1979) conducted a study to test the importance of similarity of training to the work environment, especially the effectiveness of role-plays. Forty-one firstline supervisors were randomly assigned to a training program or control group. Nine teaching units included such topics as orienting a new employee, giving recognition, motivating a poor performer, reducing absenteeism, reducing turnover, and so on. The trainees were first given an orientation on the topic and some examples. Then they were shown a model: a training film showing correct and incorrect behaviors. Finally, the trainees were required to role-play the correct behaviors and to be critiqued by classmates. The training program produced highly favorable reactions from trainees, and, more importantly, improved participants' performance significantly over that of the control group more than a year later. What makes this an extraordinary accomplishment is that the entire training program was only eighteen hours long.

Survey and Self-Assessment Techniques

Although there are a number of useful survey and assessment techniques available, only the 360-degree feedback or multirater type will be discussed here. Typically, participants will be asked to send out four to ten questionnaires to subordinates, colleagues, and their primary supervisor for feedback on the participants' leadership style. This information is sent to a central source (other than the participant) for tabulation. Some large training departments perform this service internally, but it is often subcontracted to outside experts. The internal or external expert then debriefs the participants about the results. Customarily, the source of individual responses is kept strictly confidential, and the participants are allowed to keep their personal assessments of themselves private as well. One-on-one debriefing is important in this method, but a single instructor may be unable to use individual conferences, so participant dyads (two participants per group) can be an effective substitute. The self-selected dyads have relative confidentiality and ample debriefing time, and the instructor can circulate to answer specific questions. Whether the self-assessment or survey format is used, assessment techniques are powerful tools in explaining leadership concepts and making them personally relevant to participants.

Appendix A provides a multisource leadership assessment form called the Assessment of Organizational Conditions and Leader Performance, which is based on the material presented in this book. The form can be given to supervisors, colleagues, and subordinates. It provides sixty questions related to organizational resources and constraints, leader priorities, leader characteristics, leader behaviors, and overall leader evaluation, and may be reproduced without publisher permission. Because the questions are sequenced with the text, it allows easy reference for those using the instrument for development. If one scores poorly on delegation, it is not difficult to refer to the appropriate section in chapter 13 on delegation. Appendix B provides general instructions for the use of the assessment form. Appendixes B.1 and B.2 provide additional tabulation and debriefing forms. Even without the benefit of feedback from others, the leadership action cycle can be used as a self-assessment only, thus becoming the basis of a personal individual learning plan for leadership skills improvement.

Site Visits

Site visits, also called field trips, facility or study tours, and fact-finding missions, are powerful ways to enhance various of types of training and development programs. Taking program participants to a site allows them to see the facilities and equipment, talk with the personnel, analyze programs up close, and see physical dimensions of organizations. A site visit focuses specifically on seeing how a new piece of equipment works, where different departments are located, who key personnel are, or how a program operates in its physical surroundings. In advanced programs, it is a particularly powerful way to display either model practices, on the one hand, or the tough working reality of a system, on the other. For example, in a program to train new assistant district attorneys in Queens County, New York, a series of site visits is used. Although the new law recruits know the principles and precedents of the legal system, they do not have a sense of what police personnel face on a daily basis; what assistant district attorneys really do; and how the district attorney's office, with 250 lawyers and 40,000 cases a year, functions as a part of the system. The following description provides an example of the prominence of the site visits in that program:

> Much of the training dealt with nuts and bolts—intake procedures, mock suppression hearings—but a lot of it had the feel of day camp for future prosecutors: a school bus filled with eager young people, heading from the Queens Criminal Courthouse to a variety of destinations—the N.Y.P.D. shooting range where they fired .38 revolvers and 9-mm plastic Glocks; the police ballistics-and-drug laboratory, where they learned how evidence is analyzed; the Queens House of Detention, where they saw what it means to be behind bars; the Medical Examiner's Office, where they came face to face with death; the 103rd Precinct House in Jamaica . . . , where each rode in a patrol car on the night shift, to see how cops spend their working hours. (Pooley 1991, 40)

CONCLUSION

Whereas previous chapters have discussed the mechanics of leadership, this chapter discusses how to consciously develop it. We have learned that the demands on leaders are greater because the rate of change in organizations has substantially increased the skills necessary, while we have simultaneously entered an age more cynical about leaders. Allowing leadership to develop haphazardly is likely to leave individuals with critical skill gaps and blind spots, and to leave organizations with succession deficits.

There are three fundamental types of leadership development. Self-study is the raising of one's consciousness before, during, or after either actual work experiences or formal training. Self-study is the attitude in which the learner takes responsibility for the learning process wherever it occurs, but especially when it is outside structured experiences or formal training. While self-study has been only briefly discussed in this chapter, it is extensively referenced in the traits and skills chapters under the topics of resilience, energy, need for achievement, emotional maturity, and continual learning. It is also explicitly discussed in chapter 5 in the section on distributed leadership (see especially self-leadership).

The second leadership development involves providing structured experiences in the work setting. Learning through experience is particularly valuable when work is challenging yet the goals are realistic. Leaders' development is enhanced by a variety of experiences, especially when quality feedback is included so that they can improve and self-reflect.

There are five specific methods of structuring work experience. Individual learning plans are a means by which a person analyzes his or her skills and abilities in order to draft a specific strategy for improvement. Job rotation enriches both the individual and the organization by spreading skills and improving problem solving. It is particularly important for senior employees to have had a variety of assignments during their tenure to gain a better overall perspective of the organization. Specialized developmental assignments such as committee or task-force assignments, new job tasks, or substituting for one's boss are all ways in which the learner gains a broader perspective and skill range. Coaching is the most common technique at all levels. It occurs on a one-to-one basis on site and uses actual experience as the "classroom" from which to teach. Mentoring is a protégé relationship where those who are more experienced share the "big picture" information about culture, opportunities, and networking. Finally, a supportive environment encouraged by the superior goes far in maximizing the training effect of these or other experience-based leadership development methods.

Examined in the greatest detail, formal training and education is the third type of leadership development. The developmental needs of leaders vary extensively as they advance through ascending levels of the organization. Supervisory-skills training focuses on organizational procedures and the basic interaction skills that supervisors use with subordinates, while management development focuses on managing programs and more complex interpersonal skills like labor relations. Executive development tends to focus on the strategic, networking, and public relations skills needed to lead the organization in a dynamic, political environment.

Formal programs require good training design, which is implemented through the effective selection and combination of methods. Good training design does more than take associated costs and benefits, objectives, and constraints into account; it also takes into account learning theory. Seven fundamental principles of learning theory have been discussed. Setting goals both focuses and enhances motivation. Training effectiveness is improved by increasing the similarity of the training to the work environment via the use of examples, modeling, and simulation. Trainees' understanding of underlying general principles can significantly contribute to transfer, especially over the long term. A clear and structured organization of the materials can be achieved through the use of definitions, auxiliary readings, adjunct questions, and the like. Another tried-and-true learning principle is the active involvement of the learner through manipulation of the material and practice—doing. Feedback is knowledge of the results of practice, which is used to reduce errors, make training more interesting, enhance motivation, and encourage high standards and goal setting. By using a variety of techniques and stimuli, a trainer engages more of the learner's senses, which in turn, creates a greater opportunity for encoding and more enjoyment for the learner.

Selecting the methods of instruction is the means by which training principles are operationalized. Four families of methods have been reviewed. The lecture family includes standard lectures, team teaching, guest speakers, panels, and participant presentations, which are all excellent choices for passing along information and principles to learners efficiently. This family of methods is most suited to learners with an aural preference but less so to those with visual or kinesthetic preferences. Discussion methods are often auxiliary to lecture methods, but are important because they tend to counterbalance the weaknesses of lecture methods. Examples of discussion methods include question-and-answer, large-group, small-group, and case study techniques. Additionally, long courses of instruction can benefit from individual conferences, especially where the trainee is highly motivated and the skills are complex.

The third family, printed and electronic materials, can be used as auxiliary reading materials, training manuals or textbooks, or programmed instruction in which the training manual is the primary teaching method for a program of self-instruction. Finally, practice and feedback techniques are very effective in enhancing learning when used in conjunction with lecture, print or electronic, discussion, and other developmental techniques. Role-playing builds confidence and gives the trainee an opportunity to receive guidance and feedback. Survey and self-assessment techniques open a confidential "window" through which the personal relevance of leadership concepts can be examined. Finally, site visits are a powerful way to display model practices or the gritty reality of a system.

Improving leadership development in an organization is most likely when there are multiple avenues for it to occur and the organization takes the issue of leadership succession seriously. Ideally, organizations either offer or sponsor numerous training programs for their leaders. Work itself is shaped into learning opportunities through job rotation, coaching, mentoring, and so on. And in the organizations best at supporting leadership development, supervisors at all levels engage in confidence building and work hard to provide the necessary resources such as access to formal and informal opportunities, time to participate, and the monies they often require.

In sum, because leadership in organizations has grown more difficult over time, the dynamics of leadership development are that much more important to master, practice, and foster.

Evaluating Leadership

We conclude this book with a discussion about how to evaluate the dynamics of leadership—a job not much easier than leading itself. This begins with a review of the current literature and how it assists us to conceptualize and evaluate the basic fundamentals of leadership. Where have the advances in the literature occurred, and what are the research gaps? Next, we explore an individually oriented evaluation strategy by reviewing the components of the leadership process as expressed in the action research model that undergirded this text: the leadership action cycle. To bring the discussion full circle, we return to the definition of leadership as it affects one's goals and the evaluation of one's accomplishments. The very different ways that leadership can be defined are not just academic distinctions; they are profoundly important for operationalizing leadership in all applied settings. Yet, it quickly becomes apparent that context matters as well. It is important to review some of the major contextual factors as they may, or may not, change the preferred or operational definition. This brings up the question of the need for style range, and along with it, a debate about the degree to which leaders can vary and personalize their style. Finally, once a definition is determined, at least in terms of the context, one must look at who does the evaluating and for what purpose.

We close the chapter with an example of perhaps the greatest administrative leader in U.S. history: George Washington. The argument will be made that his successes in performance, follower loyalty, and alignment of his duties with national needs was based more on his administrative skills than his military or political skills. As a military man, he certainly had more failures than successes, and possibly only one brilliant success during the American Revolution. As a politician, he disliked factions and frequently was nearly derailed by the politics of his own army staff or his divisive cabinet. In the end, it was the mix of traits, skills, and behaviors that we identify with an administrator that enabled Washington to succeed, and, ultimately, inspired the epithet Father of the Republic.

EVALUATING THE PUBLIC LEADERSHIP
RESEARCH LITERATURE

This discussion provides an overview of recent trends in public sector leadership research, highlighting where leadership theory has been of late, and briefly defines the boundaries and context of public leadership. It then outlines the fundamental shifts that were discussed in chapter 1. Coverage is given to six specific areas in which either the mainstream or public leadership fields have made advances. The section concludes with a review of the opportunities and challenges for a public leadership research agenda.

Defining the Boundaries and the Evolving Context of Public Leadership

In defining the broad boundaries of public leadership Morse, Buss, and Kinghorn (2007) note at least three types of public sectors. First, there is political leadership involving legislators; elected executives such as presidents, governors, and mayors; and other various stakeholders in the political process. Second, there is organizational leadership, also known as bureaucratic or administrative leadership, primarily aimed at those leading and managing employees, programs, and organizations for the public good. Third, there is collaborative leadership, which focuses on leading in a shared power world where citizens must have broad access and engagement, where more organizations must be included in policies and solutions, and where accountability is more broadly distributed. Each of these types is important and each will be referenced. The primary focus of this chapter, however, is the administrative leadership affecting more than 23 million employees in the United States alone.[1] As Morse (2008) notes, it is very difficult to disentangle the types because of the enormous overlap; at the same time, it is important to provide a narrower focus of this sweeping topic for heuristic purposes.

While there are many fundamental "eternal verities" related to leadership that seem to defy culture and time, much of what is interesting about leadership is affected by context. When environmental shifts occur, social values tend to evolve, organizational structures adjust, preferred leader styles alter, and competency needs are affected (Bass 2008). To the degree that it is possible, research needs to identify the more long-term stable elements of leadership and those that are more topically affected. What are the recent shifts in the organizational environment? Focusing on the American context, the demographics have shifted to a more multicultural and educated society. Communication is much more computer and technology mediated. Organizations are more team based, networked, globally connected, flatter, and purport to be more empowered and participative. The public at large as citizens, consumers, and organizational members is much more cynical and distrusting.

Abramson, Breul, and Kamensky (2006) point out that in a world in which public sector expectations and mandates, technology, structures, resources, workforce demographics, and norms are evolving, the challenges of management must also evolve in tandem. They identify six major trends that have direct or indirect effects on management: (1) change in the formal rules of government in order to allow more flexibility and customization of services, (2) the expanded use of performance measurement, (3) the increased emphasis on competition, choice, and incentives, (4) the expectation of performance on demand, (5) the requirement for greater citizen engagement, and (6) the greater use of networks and partnerships. Ultimately, all these trends make leadership challenging and make the business of providing scholarly and applied materials available that much more critical.

These trends and others have had a real impact on leadership. For example, the massive reductions in middle management in the 1980s for the private sector, and in the 1990s for the public sector, may have been instigated by economic pressures but were made possible by improvements in communication and data processing. This encouraged more use of teams, networks, and the concomitant empowerment strategies, all of which had an enormous effect. Leaders at all levels found it necessary to broaden the range of their styles and to shift their emphasis from directive styles toward more participatory, delegated, and collaborative modes. Because these latter styles are no less difficult to implement successfully—indeed, they may be more difficult to implement—managers-as-leaders have had their work cut out for them in making this transition.

The recent leadership literature adds to and/or changes ongoing approaches developed over the past century or more. The literature started with a great-man approach in the nineteenth century. A "traits" approach dominated the first half of the twentieth century but was very one-dimensional and failed to adequately address the various contexts of leadership. Useful, if simplistic, situational and contingency models were put forward in the 1960s, such as the managerial grid and situational leadership. In the 1970s, somewhat more sophisticated models such as path-goal theory and normative decision theory were advanced. The field expanded greatly in the 1980s and 1990s with the surging interest in transformational and charismatic leadership. Executive and external perspectives became central to the literature. Normative discussions about the personal morality and appropriate role for the various types of public leaders have been ongoing in the academic literature since the 1940s. Although elements of distributed approaches have roots that can be traced to the 1970s and earlier (e.g., substitutes theory), the distributive approach did not fully evolve until the team, self, and superleadership models appeared in the 1980s, and matured when Pearce and Conger's work appeared in 2003. In recent years, postmodern, collaboration, and networks are some of the powerful trends that have had an enormous impact. Yet more traditional approaches have also made significant progress. No brief synopsis can do justice to a vast and complex field. (See Bass [2008] for a more inclusive review of mainstream literature.)

Reviewing Some of the Recent Fundamental Shifts in Leadership Studies

The shift in focus of much of the contemporary leadership literature was discussed in chapter 1, and reflected in other chapters (especially 5 through 8). Those shifts include the following:

- A move toward postmodern thinking
  - Science is not neutral; there is no universal ideal for leadership and all theories, even "descriptive" studies, have biases, which are normally unstated
  - The whole is more than the sum of its parts, so empirical analysis of leaders often distorts our understanding
  - Leadership is a process not a person (past leadership studies have tended to be too leader-centric)
  - Radical shifts are poorly understood by traditional "normal" science, which cannot anticipate tipping points and butterfly effects

- An emphasis on horizontal and distributed types of leadership such as teams, employee empowerment, self-management, and employee development
- An articulation of community change leadership as a domain (in addition to the individual-organizational perspective, on one hand, and the strategic-political models, on the other) and the collaborative leadership paradigm in general
- Efforts to advance integrated and comprehensive approaches

These shifts are all maturing with robust theories, research, and examples to support them for the most part.

Reviewing Some of the Advances in Traditional Research Approaches

More traditional approaches have been somewhat overshadowed, but never fully eclipsed. Some of the areas of advances include transformational leadership, ethics and leadership, research methods, leadership in crisis management, biographical case studies, and trait and competency approaches.

Transformational Leadership

Although some studies still usefully point out the utility of transactional approaches (e.g., Vecchio, Justin, and Pearce 2008), the debate over the effectiveness of transformational leadership versus transactional leadership (e.g., Schriesheim et al. 2006) has subsided. A more reasonable acknowledgment is that both styles are needed in different situations to differing degrees (O'Shea et al. 2009). One of the key elements, change, has received a significant amount of research on the public sector side. For example, Fernandez and Pitts (2007) investigated the array of factors enhancing or diminishing change in an educational setting. Wright and Pandey (2010) found more transformational leadership at the municipal level than has been assumed by scholars. Dull (2008) examined the prime importance of credibility for public leaders, and Washington and Hacker (2005) studied the critical need for public managers to fully understand policy changes for better implementation.

Although charismatic leadership is typically considered a subtype of transformational leadership, it continues to receive a great deal of interest. Sosik (2005) found that approximately 11 percent of the positive performance variance was due to the presence of charisma in the case of five organizations. Work by de Hoogh et al. (2005) spotlighted the subtle but significant differences in the operation of charisma in the private versus public sectors, finding that leader responsibility makes a difference in charismatic appeal. Javidian and Waldman (2003) also found that charismatic leadership is a potent force in the public sector. Innumerable studies and books have examined negative charisma, such as Cha and Edmondson (2006) looking at the long-term disenchantment effect. Related to negative charisma is an increase in research on the nature of other types of negative leadership by various writers (Rosenthal and Pittinsky 2006; Schilling 2009).

Among the other aspects of transformational leadership that have received considerable attention are the effects of vision (e.g., Strange and Mumford 2005) and the role of positive emotions and mood contagion (e.g., Bono and Ilies 2006). Strategic leadership is closely aligned with transformational leadership, but it focuses more on how ideas are selected and decisions made, and their subsequent implementation (e.g., Boal and Hooijberg 2001; Pajunen 2006). Discussions of strategic leadership at the administrative level have generally been more muted in the public sector because of issues related to democratic accountability.

Ethics and Leadership

The mainstream leadership literature has finally started to come of age and look at ethics in more than an ad hoc framework. Three different perspectives have emerged (Trevino, Weaver, and Reynolds 2006) that are distinctive enough to describe. Still, the ideal-type models sketched here inevitably have a good deal of overlap as articulated by various theorists, all of which assume a basic integrity or trust foundation.

The ethical leadership model (e.g., Brown and Trevino 2006) focuses on moral management at a more transactional level and ethical standards at the organizational level (Waldman and Siegel 2008). What do leaders do to support ethical and moral behavior, and what do they need to do in order to make sure that organizations themselves are ethical?

A second model is the servant leadership model (e.g., Greenleaf 1977; Liden et al. 2008), which focuses on supporting followers via participation, empowerment, and development. How can leaders make sure that the organization is about the employees and end users? A more recent version of servant leadership is spiritual leadership, which emphasizes membership and calling (Fry, Vitucci, and Cedillo 2005) to balance transformational needs that focus primarily on the organization (Parolini, Patterson, and Winston 2009).

A third model is authentic leadership, which tends to focus on self-awareness, honesty, and transparency (Avolio and Gardner 2005). How can leaders have integrity in a multi-faceted world? These themes have been extensively discussed in public sector literature for some time, appearing in journals such as *Public Integrity* and indirectly in both ethics and management writing (Menzel 2007). A current example of a relatively new theme is "affective" leadership, which stresses the need to take into consideration the emotional labor so common in the public sector (Newman, Guy, and Mastracci 2009).

Trust has continued to be an important topic in the prevailing current of thought (regardless of the research paradigm). Trust is invariably highlighted by popular writers such as Covey (2010), and the mainstream literature has shown the power of positive organizational behaviors as emerging from select traits such as hope, optimism, resiliency, and other variables (Luthans 2007), and has provided careful analyses of the subelements of trust (Burke et al. 2007). Extensive research has been done about trust in government. This includes Newell, Reeher, and Ronayne's edited volume (2008) on building trust through values-based leadership, self-awareness, coaching, using teams, networking skills, and collaboration effectively, and providing high performance (good value). Empirical research has shown that although citizen participation and involvement can positively affect trust, agency or government performance is ultimately the stronger factor (Wang and Van Wart 2007).

Research Methods

Because of the complexity of approaches, factors, and interactions, the strength of research methods is a major concern relative to the perceived credibility of the field. Although popular and quasi-academic products are not expected to provide the same level of rigor, the scholarly literature should provide clearly enunciated constructs, carefully conceived hypotheses, and well-crafted empirical arguments (Yammarino and Dansereau 2008). In a 2005 meta-analysis, Yammarino et al. explored the conceptual accuracy of seventeen approaches to leadership: Ohio State, contingency, participative, charismatic, transformational, leader-member exchange, information processing/implicit, substitutes, romance, self-leadership, multiple linkage, multilevel/leaderplex, individualized, path-goal, vertical dyad linkage, situational, and influence tactics. Their concern was that the four major levels of analysis, "individuals or persons (independent human beings), dyads (two person groups and interpersonal relationships), groups (work groups and teams), and organizations (collectives larger than groups and groups of groups)," are commonly but inappropriately blended, thereby confounding good theoretical modeling practices (Yammarino et al. 2005, 880). They found that "while the literature is vast and growing, relatively few studies in any of the areas of leadership research have addressed levels-of-analysis, and inference drawing. Nevertheless, the findings reported are encouraging, as levels issues are still relatively new to the leadership field and some progress has clearly been made in the last decade" (879). Simultaneously, the postmodern approaches have emphasized qualitative techniques such as biography and narrative inquiry.

Leadership in Crisis Management

All organizations can and do have crises from time to time. Their frequency and severity are much affected by the quality of leadership (Tichy and Bennis, 2007). Good leaders have contingency plans (mitigation) to prevent many crises altogether, prepare for a variety of plausible events, respond quickly and effectively when crises occur, and are able to move the affected community and responding organization(s) back to normalcy after the event in a reasonable time frame. For example, NASA was in a crisis mode during and after both the Challenger disaster in 1986 and the Columbia disaster in 2003 (Garrett 2004; Donahue 2006). Boin and 't Hart (2003) examined the difficulty involved in making major changes in crises as well as transformational changes after the fact.

Emergency response agencies have a special challenge in dealing with catastrophic events that are very large and unusual or that simply catch agencies off guard (Farazmand 2001). The Katrina/Rita crisis has both entered the national psyche and received tremendous scholarly attention. An entire special issue of *Public Administration Review* in 2007 looked at the roots of administrative failure in the wake of Katrina. The failures of leadership in this event got wide coverage in all the major public administration journals. For example, Kapucu and Van Wart (2006, 2008) compared the administrative successes of the "horde of hurricanes" that inundated Florida in 2004 to the leadership failures experienced in New Orleans with Katrina.

Biographical Case Studies

It was not many years ago that case studies of administrators were scarce and nearly always atheoretical. The biographies of outstanding leaders not only commemorate the qualities of professionalism and perseverance but also serve as valuable teaching tools. This deficit has been remedied by numerous biographical case studies as well as books devoted to significant administrative leaders. In the journal *Public Integrity*, cases include those of George C. Marshall, known for the Marshall Plan (Pops 2006/07), Dag Hammarskjold, the strong-willed leader of the United Nations from 1953 to 1961 (Lyon 2006/07), and Sam Medina, an everyday moral exemplar (Rugeley and Van Wart 2006). "Administrative profiles" have also been highlighted in the *Public Administration Review* such as a profile of Sean O'Keefe at NASA (Lambright 2008). The IBM Center for the Business of Government provided a volume including short profiles in leadership, specifically seeking out administrative leaders who were not cabinet secretaries (Morales 2007). Of course, many biographies about political and business leaders are published in the popular press, but the biography of Colin Powell (Harari 2002) stands out for its focus on administrative leadership.

Trait and Competency Approaches

Trait and competency research is alive and well in the organizational world, despite ongoing debates (Hollenbeck, McCall, and Silzer 2006: 399). These debates pit applied and pure researchers against one another. Critics argue that competency models are based on unrealistic assumptions: a single set of characteristics that adequately describes effective leaders, independence of context and trait interaction, and senior management bias for simplistic presentations. Essentially, they argue, competency models are a "descendant of the long-discredited 'great man' theory." Zaccaro (2007), while acknowledging the potential of a trait-competency approach, notes that the value will also be limited unless researchers combine traits and attributes in conceptually meaningful ways that predict leadership. Contemporary critics argue that competency models are excessively individually oriented and leader-centric from discursive and constructionist perspectives (Carroll, Levy, and Richmond 2008). Proponents argue that competency models have utility because they summarize the experience and insight of seasoned leaders, specify a range of useful behavior, provide a powerful tool for self-development, and outline a framework useful for leadership effectiveness. Yukl, Gordon, and Taber (2002) utilize confirmatory factor analysis to provide empirical support to competency approaches. Their hierarchy taxonomy uses task, relations, and change behavior metacategories. Mau (2009) notes the prevalence of competency models in both the private and public sectors, and compares the approaches used by the United States, Canada, and Australia, while Beinecke and Spencer (2009) compare health leadership competencies in eight countries.

Although there are more than 88,000 units of government in the United States when states, counties, municipalities of various types, school districts, and special districts are counted, the civilian federal government is in a class of its own because of its size, constituting about 11 percent of the employees in American government (U.S. OMB 2010). Because of its resources and prestige, it has unique opportunities to lead when it chooses to do so. One area where it has been generally strong is in leadership research.

One reason for the quality of federal data is because it has been very strong at setting up the systems to critique itself through the General Accountability Office (GAO), Merit Systems Protection Board (MSPB), and inspectors general of the various agencies. The reports of these agencies and offices are, in general, exceptionally well-researched and cogently written. The quality of data provided means that academic research has much to work with, and analyses of the degree of success as well as the analysis of its leadership are forthcoming (e.g., Light 2008). The Office of Personnel Management (OPM) has long tried to provide leadership in applied leadership models (U.S. OPM 2006), which has encouraged the use of rigorous competency models by academics as well (Van Wart 2003, 2004). Using their own data set, Thach and Thompson (2007) provided a detailed competency comparison of private and public (and nonprofit) organizations. While there was a great deal of similarity, significant differences emerged whereby business emphasized time management, self-knowledge, and marketing. In contrast, the public and nonprofit sectors emphasized conflict management and being inspirational.[2]

Research Gaps, Weaknesses, and Concerns

A number of the major gaps identified in recent reviews have been at least partially addressed. In terms of importance, leadership studies in the public sector have blossomed from being marginalized when Terry (1995) did his review, to being a recognized area of research interest. In addition to public leadership scholarship, enough materials have been generated with a public sector focus that classes in the area are no longer entirely derivative of materials from business, psychology, and education scholars (Denhardt and Denhardt 2006; Van Wart 2008; Fairholm and Fairholm 2009).

Public leadership theory has followed into more formal aspects of postmodern theory (e.g., complexity and chaos theory), but has integrated collaborative, collective, and network issues with gusto. For example, the affective leadership research of Newman, Guy, and Mastracci (2009) is clearly postmodern in approach. As organizations have flattened in the corporate and agency worlds, distributed theories looking at self-leadership, team leadership, and shared leadership have matured, yet there is room for growth in the administrative leadership arena. Transformational leadership studies have taken greater care in their use of constructs and have narrowed their specifications to be more useful and to help build nonuniversalistic theory. Much work needs to be done in this regard. The mainstream has finally caught up with the public sector ethics literature in terms of articulation of conceptual framework. Traditional positivist methods have improved in the field as a whole in terms of levels of analysis and careful model building. However, both the mainstream and administrative leadership fields are still rife with impressionistic models utilizing convenience data sets. Some areas of special interest and need have developed with urgency. Crisis management in the aftermath of 9/11 is one case. The development of teaching materials, case studies, and more sophisticated trait and competency models are other examples where materials that were formerly scant or out-of-date with current leadership emphases have blossomed. Finally, the field as a whole has settled into a better understanding of integrated theory building when compared with the simplistic trait models of the first half of the twentieth century, the two-factor matrices of the 1960s–1980s, and the interesting but exaggerated debates about leadership versus management and transactional methods versus transformational methods from the late 1970s through the 1990s. Today, with the addition of more theoretically grounded distributed-leadership literature, and the enriching nature of postmodern approaches warning us of the excesses of positivism (and its attendant methodologies) and the reification of power, there are finally a variety of comprehensive approaches with a better appreciation of the virtues (and limits) of those approaches.

Nonetheless, there are still a few concerns that are apparent from reviewing the field as well as reviewing manuscripts for publication. One concern is that the strong convictions of many scholars interested in the field tends to lead to implicit, if not explicit, statements of certitude that they have "the answer" to the leadership question. Such assertions are useful for popular books sold in airports with their breezy lists of favorite tips and personalized models. This leads to an unhelpful assertion or inference that one type of leadership study is more important than another. An example of this occurred in the mainstream during the 1980s when transformational leadership roared onto the scene, with the dismissal of management as routine and plentiful, if not downright trivial and potentially insidious. Second, there is still a substantial problem with studies being able to locate the context of their "problem" in the bigger picture (e.g., a proper clarification of the level of analysis), which consequently reduces their generalizability and usefulness as normal science. Nevertheless, the recent advances in both the mainstream in terms of better balance and the public leadership literature in terms of self-consciousness and depth have been impressive.

Summary About the Status of Public Sector Leadership Studies

While the importance of public sector leadership is profound, historically it has lagged behind the mainstream. However, public sector leadership is slowly becoming its own specialized area of study. Political, organizational, and collaborative leadership are distinctive subareas within public sector leadership. An important development in all fields of leadership study is postmodernism. In leadership studies, postmodernism is a broad critique of the literature as being too status-quo oriented with an emphasis on positivism, empiricism, static power structures, and leadership from the top down. This perspective aligns with studies emphasizing gender issues, contextual/ethnographic research strategies, complexity/chaos theories, and integral or community approaches, among others. Focusing on organizational leadership, the aspects that have developed most in recent years include distributed or horizontal leadership, biographical case studies, crisis management leadership, analysis of federal leadership and applied competency models useful for government, network/collaborative leadership, and integrated frameworks or holistic perspectives of leadership. The field of public sector leadership is generally more nuanced in terms of specifying types of leadership, the factors involved, and the use of different perspectives. As important, it has achieved a critical mass and can be considered a recognizable and maturing field of interest. This has meant that teaching academic public sector leadership classes has become much easier (Van Wart and O'Farrell 2007).

USING AN ACTION RESEARCH MODEL OF LEADERSHIP TO EVALUATE INDIVIDUAL LEADERS

A pragmatic use of leadership theory and modeling is to provide concrete tools for the evaluation of individual leaders. There are too many approaches to review them all. Therefore, the leadership action cycle discussed in this book will serve as the applied example and as a final review of chapters 9 through 15. While the cycle is presented in a linear form for simplicity, it is actually both cyclical and overlapping. The full view of the leadership action cycle presented throughout the book is shown in Exhibit 17.1.

Leader Assessment

Because leaders need information to act effectively, leader assessment is logically the first priority. Leaders need to make both global assessments that steer their overall decisions about goals and priorities and more detailed assessments that improve quality, follower development, and strategic alignment. Leaders who skip this step when they are new to a situation or allow this function to atrophy if they are ongoing in their position doom themselves to being, at best, second-rate. At the heart of assessment is simply asking the right questions and having the discipline to ensure that one has genuine answers.

What types of broad questions do administrative leaders need to ask? Eight areas were identified in the organization and its environment. What is the level of task skills of those in the organization? How clear are the role duties? How well does the organization or unit foster innovation and creativity? How does the level of support and resources match the demands on the organization? Just how much effort do subordinates put forth and how motivated are they? What is the level of intra-unit cooperation and cohesiveness? How well is work organized, and what is the quality of the performance metrics to assess actual productivity? Finally, what is the level of external coordination and adaptability of the organization with outside clients, funders, and legislators?

During the assessment phase the leader must also examine a series of constraints within which s/he must work, at least in the short term. Prime among them are the legal and contractual constraints that figure so heavily in the public sector. Leaders must realistically examine their position power as well as the limitations on it. The availability of resources always restricts options. And finally, leaders must be realistic about their own leadership abilities so that they can avoid excessive commitments, impetuous decisions, and failing to utilize alternatives that can complement their weaknesses with others' strengths.

Exhibit 17.1

The General Management and Leadership Competencies Associated with Administrative Activities (Leadership Action Cycle)

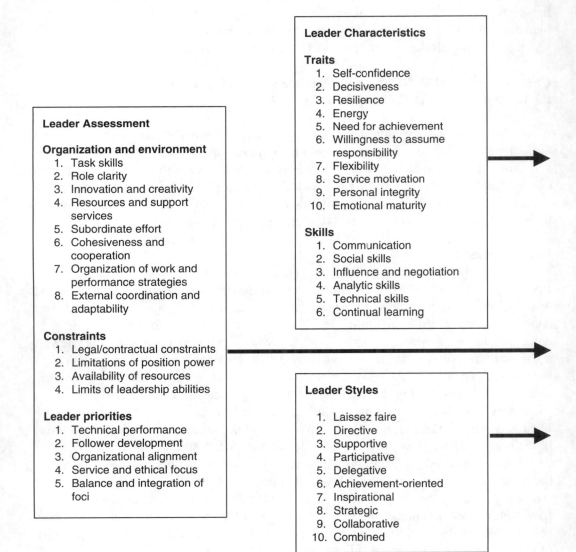

Leader Characteristics

Traits
1. Self-confidence
2. Decisiveness
3. Resilience
4. Energy
5. Need for achievement
6. Willingness to assume responsibility
7. Flexibility
8. Service motivation
9. Personal integrity
10. Emotional maturity

Skills
1. Communication
2. Social skills
3. Influence and negotiation
4. Analytic skills
5. Technical skills
6. Continual learning

Leader Assessment

Organization and environment
1. Task skills
2. Role clarity
3. Innovation and creativity
4. Resources and support services
5. Subordinate effort
6. Cohesiveness and cooperation
7. Organization of work and performance strategies
8. External coordination and adaptability

Constraints
1. Legal/contractual constraints
2. Limitations of position power
3. Availability of resources
4. Limits of leadership abilities

Leader priorities
1. Technical performance
2. Follower development
3. Organizational alignment
4. Service and ethical focus
5. Balance and integration of foci

Leader Styles

1. Laissez faire
2. Directive
3. Supportive
4. Participative
5. Delegative
6. Achievement-oriented
7. Inspirational
8. Strategic
9. Collaborative
10. Combined

Leader Behaviors

Task-oriented behaviors
1. Monitor and assess work
2. Plan operations
3. Clarify roles
4. Inform
5. Delegate
6. Solve problems
7. Manage innovation and creativity

People-oriented behaviors
1. Consult
2. Plan and organize personnel
3. Develop staff
4. Motivate
5. Manage teams and team building
6. Manage personnel conflict
7. Manage personnel change

Organizational behaviors
1. Scan the environment
2. Strategic planning
3. Articulate the mission and vision
4. Network and partner
5. Perform general management functions
6. Decision making
7. Manage organizational change

Leader Evaluation and Development

Development
1. Self-study
2. Experience
3. Education

Evaluation
1. Technical performance
2. Follower performance
3. Organizational alignment
4. Service mentality and ethical focus

There is no better example of how leadership is both a science and an art than in the formulation of goals and their prioritization. Goal setting by leaders is a science, in that concrete data about the organization must be collected using methods that can be routinized, and such that data collection is dispassionate. The need for scientific collection of data in assessing the areas discussed above, such as the level of task skills, role clarity, innovation and creativity, and so forth, is critical to good decisions. Even if a leader has good hunches about where organizational problems lurk, those problems will be very difficult to fix without specific data about the nature of the problem. In practical terms, this translates into leaders who are articulate and knowledgeable about current and future operations, able to demonstrate the relationship between internal and external trends and patterns, and able to anticipate problems and to forecast opportunities.

Goal setting as science is only half the picture, however. Goat setting by leaders is also an art in that action is based on experience and beliefs, uses customized methods to handle unique circumstances, and encourages passion and commitment to strive for excellence. Further, leaders seek to understand what is significant and what works, use their understanding in practice, and intuit likely outcomes or futures based on various perspectives. The ideal leader has a very different type of challenge in conducting the art of leadership. Leaders must have an instinctive understanding based on their eclectic experience, be able to use that limited understanding, and be able to predict likely outcomes.

Both the science and the art of leadership are shaped by one's definition of leadership and the context. Those aspects are discussed later in this chapter.

Leader Characteristics

Leaders come to various leadership situations with more or less potential. Traits are the most innate elements of the leader's capacity repertoire. Although refined later in life, traits are characteristics that, for the most part, are shaped very early on. Ten of the most important were reviewed. Self-confidence is the general (positive) sense one has about one's ability to accomplish what needs to be accomplished. Decisiveness is the ability to act relatively quickly depending on circumstances without excessively damaging decision quality. Resilience is the ability to spring back into shape, position, or direction after being pressed or stretched. Energy is the physical and psychological ability to perform. The need for achievement is a strong drive to accomplish things and be recognized for those accomplishments. Willingness to assume responsibility means that individuals will take positions requiring broader decision-making duties and greater authority. Flexibility is the ability to bend without breaking, adjust to change, and be capable of modification. A service mentality is an ethic of considering others' interests, perspectives, and concerns. Personal integrity is the state of being whole and/or connected, with oneself, one's profession, and one's society, as well as being incorruptible. Emotional maturity is a conglomerate of characteristics that indicate a person is well balanced in a number of psychological and behavioral dimensions.

Leader skills also have innate aspects, but are more fully shaped by later education and training. Six were identified. Communication skills involve the ability to effectively exchange information through active and passive means. Social skills involve the ability to interact effectively in social settings and to understand and productively harness one's own and others' personality structures. Influence skills involve the actual use of power through concrete behavior strategies or tactics. Analytic skills require the ability to remember, make distinctions, and deal with complexity. Technical skills include the basic professional and organizational knowledge associated with an area of work. Continual learning means taking responsibility for acquiring new information, looking at old information in new ways, and finding ways to use new and old information creatively.

Leader Behaviors

Leaders have to get work (tasks) done, work with and through people, and ensure that their organization or unit is well aligned with the environment. Seven behaviors were identified with each category of leadership behavior. Task behaviors begin with monitoring, which is gathering and critically evaluating data related to subordinate performance, service or project qualities, and overall unit or organizational performance. Operations planning involves coordinating tactical issues into detailed blueprints. Clarifying roles and objectives refers to working with subordinates to guide and direct behavior by communicating about plans, policies, and specific expectations. Informing provides business-related information to subordinates, superiors, peers, or people outside the organization. Delegating refers to a type of power sharing in which subordinates are given substantial responsibilities and/or authority. Problem solving involves the identification, analysis, and handling of work-related problems. Managing technical innovation and creativity involves establishing an environment that encourages learning, flexibility, and change, and that also provides support for new cutting-edge programs/processes.

The first of the people-oriented leadership behaviors is consulting, which means checking with people on work-related matters and involving people in decision-making processes. Planning and organizing personnel involves coordinating people and operations and ensuring that the follower competencies necessary to do the work are, or will be, available. It also involves self-planning. Developing staff refers to improving subordinates' effectiveness in their current positions and preparing them for their next position or step. Motivating means enhancing the inner drives and positive intentions of subordinates (or others) to perform well through incentives, disincentives, and inspiration. Managing teams involves creating and supporting "true" teams in addition to traditional work units. The related competency of team building involves enhancing identification with the team, intramember cooperation, and esprit de corps of both work groups and teams. Managing conflict is a behavior used to handle various types of interpersonal disagreements, build cooperative interpersonal relationships, and harness the positive effects of conflict. Managing personnel change means establishing an environment that provides the emotional support and motivation to change.

Organizational behaviors begin with scanning the environment, which is the gathering and critical evaluation of data related to external trends, opportunities, and threats on an ongoing and relatively informal basis. Strategic planning is the disciplined effort to produce fundamental decisions and actions that shape and guide an organization. Articulating the mission refers to defining and expressing an organization's purpose, aspirations, and values. Networking is the development of useful contacts outside the leader's direct subordinate–superior chain of command. Performing general management functions means carrying out general structural responsibilities related to the organization, such as those connected with information technology, human resource management, or financial management. Decision making refers to making major organizational choices by understanding the fundamental values and factors involved, and by structuring an appropriate decision framework. Managing organizational change involves large-scale change to the direction, structure, major processes, or culture of the organization.

Leader Styles

Leader styles are the consistent clusters of behavior that tend to be implicitly understood by both followers and leaders. Leaders may use many or few styles, and they may be good at many, one, or even none of the styles. Better leaders generally have a range of styles that they can use, and consciously adapt a style to the situation or conversely adapt a situation to a style at which they are adept. Ten archetypal styles were identified.

A laissez-faire style, characterized by passive indifference about the task and subordinates, is essentially a nonstyle. A directive style is one that lets subordinates know what they are expected to do, gives specific guidance, asks subordinates to follow rules and procedures, and does scheduling and coordinating. A supportive style involves showing consideration of followers, displaying concern for their needs, and creating a friendly work environment for each worker. A participative style refers to consulting with subordinates and taking their opinions into account, providing advice rather than direction, and creating a friendly work environment for the team. A delegative style allows subordinates relative freedom for decision making and from daily monitoring and short-term review. An achievement-oriented style involves setting challenging task goals, seeking task improvements, emphasizing excellence in follower performance, and showing confidence that followers will perform well. An inspirational style uses intellectual stimulation for new ideas or processes and inspirational motivation for group goals, as well as using charisma. A strategic style focuses on the organizational context, the ability to gain and retain resources, and the opportunity to gain comparative advantage in public settings and competitive advantage in private settings. A collaborative style focuses on representation, external networking/partnering, goodwill, and "expanding the pie" (an external win–win perspective). A combined style uses two or more of these styles simultaneously in a single fused style such as a combined directive and supportive style with an underperforming employee.

Leader Evaluation and Development

When leaders evaluate what they have accomplished, they have begun the leadership action cycle over again as they reassess what they need to do next or do differently. Our evaluation focus was on the act of improving leadership skills. Three primary means are discussed: self-study, experience, and formal training. Self-study involves raising one's cognitive awareness before, during, or after experiences and/or training. Structured developmental activities occur in conjunction with work, and include individual learning plans, job rotation, specialized developmental assignments, coaching, and mentoring. Formal training was discussed in terms of seven fundamental learning principles that should be incorporated in quality programs, as well as four major families of methods that harness the learning principles to accomplish specific learning goals.

REVISITING THE MANY POSSIBLE DEFINITIONS OF LEADERSHIP

It is time for us to review the major definitions of leadership covered in chapter 1. Five possible definitions were discussed. Leadership can focus strictly on the ends or actual performance. An example of such a definition could be: Administrative leadership is the process of providing the results required by authorized systems in an efficient, effective, and legal manner.

Leadership can focus on the means by which things get done, which is to say the development and motivation of followers. Here the definition might be: Administrative leadership is the process of developing/supporting followers who provide the results.

Leadership can emphasize the alignment with the external needs and opportunities that results in substantive changes. A definition along these lines is: Administrative leadership is the process of aligning the organization with its environment, especially the necessary macrolevel changes, and realigning the organizational culture as appropriate.

Leadership can also emphasize the spirit in which it is conducted. In the public sector this inevitably means a "public service" commitment. The definition here might be: The key element to administrative leadership is its service or stewardship focus in which leaders are dedicated to responsiveness, openness, awareness of competing interests, dedication to the common good, and so forth to enhance the public trust.

Finally, a definition may include all of these major elements. Administrative leadership is a composite of providing technical performance, internal direction and support to followers, and external organizational direction—all with a public service orientation. This definition recognizes that leaders perform many different functions, and thus, implicitly, that being a great leader is difficult. However, leaders may not always focus on all roles either because the situation does not demand it or they must be more selective with their time, talents, and energy.

One's definition of leadership will ultimately vary with one's situation and normative preferences.

THE ROLE OF CONTEXT

The context of leaders affects not only their definition but also their style and performance. Of course, leaders are themselves a part of their context. Five major sets of contingencies were reviewed. These have enabled researchers to examine the context or various elements of leadership. One set of contingencies is leader characteristics, which include the leader's general traits and skills, concrete behaviors, and attributions of followers. Another set of contingencies is task characteristics. What is involved in role, task, and organizational clarity in the leader's area of responsibility? How much task ambiguity and complexity exists? How much task interdependence is required? Here a leader's level of authority in the organization is important. A third set of characteristics has to do with subordinates. The level of subordinate traits and skills will generally affect leader style substantially. The level of task commitment is another crucial factor. And just as leader attributions of the followers are important, so, too, are the follower attributions of the leader. A fourth area is organizational characteristics. What are the power relationships and what is the organizational design? The type of and need for external "connectedness" is another variable. The level of environmental uncertainty is also an important factor. The fifth category is a perceptual one that includes factors such as the leader's ethics and gender.

WHO EVALUATES AND HOW?

After all is said and done, who evaluates leaders? Evaluation may occur at many levels and for many purposes.

Evaluation of leadership may be by and for oneself. Self-evaluation may be primarily for short-term improvement in the job or for long-term improvement in one's leadership capability. It may occur through formal mechanisms such as productivity reports or benchmarking, or it may occur primarily through self-reflection.

Leadership evaluation can be done by or for followers. At some level this is both inevitable and constant because followers are exposed to, and very affected by, leader competence and commitment. How much the evaluation of followers matters to individual leaders, as well as the organization as a whole, varies. Some leaders focus their energies primarily on the positive regard of followers, while others are concerned mainly with the positive regard of superiors or legislative overseers. Feedback can be provided through a formal mechanism such as a leadership survey form, or informally in casual conversations and open discussions.

Leadership evaluation is done by superiors or the authorized body to whom the leader reports, which in some cases is simply the voting public. Most administrative leaders have formal processes of evaluation that they experience. Smart leaders usually seek intermittent feedback as well so that they are able to adjust their performance to the formal demands of those who have a major role in shaping their jobs.

Leadership evaluation also occurs outside the organization. Clients, indirect consumers of services, partner agencies, and vendors are some of the others who may evaluate a leader's competence and performance. For a welfare agency, some of those who have a stake in how the agency is led include welfare recipients, prospective employers, other social service and public safety agencies, and nonprofits with contracts for services.

Perhaps the toughest and subtlest evaluator of all is time. What effect will a leader have in the long term? Will one's contribution be so significant as to be associated with a level of development or an era of the organization? Standing the test of time may not necessarily be memorialized in the annals of the agency, but can simply be the testament that people will offer in recognition of, and appreciation for, a job well done. Generally only the most dedicated and passionate are concerned with excelling at this level of evaluation.

A FINAL EXAMPLE OF A GREAT ADMINISTRATIVE LEADER

It can be argued that George Washington's greatness, and the reason that we think of him as the Father of the United States, is not so much his military prowess or political acumen, but rather his "extraordinary administrative abilities" (Twohig 2001). Especially important were his public servant traits: a service motivation, personal integrity, and emotional maturity. In the three major public service periods of Washington's life, one can see his administrative abilities maturing and expanding.

When he was twenty-one to twenty-three years old, Washington served in senior positions under the British/American forces as the French began encroaching on the Western frontier of Virginia. The commanders under whom Washington served were ineffective and outwitted by the enemy French and their Indian allies in major battles. At twenty-three, he assumed the command of the Virginia Regiment and spent four years building forts, establishing effective military networks, negotiating with friendly Indian tribes, and generally defending the Western frontier. Under his able leadership, western Virginia was secured and the brunt of the hostilities occurred elsewhere. Although somewhat brash in this period, the young Washington's contributions were not military exploits and tactical genius, but self-confidence, energy, willingness to assume responsibility, communication skills, as well as excellent technical skills (his training as a surveyor was invaluable). Further, he learned to do operations planning, delegation, problem solving, consulting, developing and motivating his troops, managing conflict, strategic planning, partnering, and decision making. These qualities would serve him well later when his scope of command increased dramatically.

After an extended period of managing a large thriving southern plantation and extensive business holdings, Washington was called upon to be the commander in chief of the American army in 1775. Although he was responsible for a few personal military successes in the war, such as the Boston siege and the battles of Trenton and Princeton, it was not his military victories that won the war. Indeed, he suffered more losses than victories. His more impressive accomplishments were keeping a ragtag army whole even when it was despondent, out of supplies, and unpaid (people skills); retaining excellent relations with the legislative body authorizing and financing the war, despite the confusion that frequently typified its internal workings (organizational skills); and keeping his eye on both short- and long-term administrative and military functions (task skills). Despite the arguably superior military skill of the British professional forces, they were unable to break the organizational integrity of the American army, whose resilience, pragmatism, and resolve proved pivotal. Despite bleak moments after the fall of New York and the winter at Valley Forge, the American forces eventually cornered the British at Yorktown. This was not a brilliant military victory; the British had only 8,000 troops, which both the American and French forces outnumbered. In addition, 15,000 French sailors prevented the British navy from providing a means of retreat to New York. Rather, the victory was a tribute to Washington's ability to have mounted such a vast force after such a long campaign and to organize his disparate forces and allies against a deft military foe.

Finally, there is Washington the statesman and president. In 1789, six years after giving up his commission as commander in chief of the American army, Washington was elected president of the United States, and then again in 1792. During this time he organized the original cabinet, formally composed of the Departments of Treasury (which functioned as a multifaceted, domestic executive agency initially), State, and War. In addition, he appointed major administrative officers such as the attorney general (which began as a half-time position) and the postmaster general (who headed the department with the most employees for most of the nineteenth century). Under his aegis the First National Bank of the United States was created, establishing the new country's financial integrity by repaying the debt in full and creating a reliable and consistent system of money and finance. Even more important, he established the tenor of the civil service: integrity, honor, and service before fame or fortune.

Several factors make George Washington a great, rather than merely a good, leader. Foremost, he ensured that the overarching goal was achieved. He did this by accomplishing the myriad technical details required and staying the course doggedly. Securing the Western front required building forts and negotiations. Winning the war with the British meant avoiding a decisive battle until the British had been worn down and distracted at home. Being the first president meant establishing the infrastructure of government. As a leader, he was exceptional at integrating broad organizational needs with task-level demands. When he accomplished each job, he stepped down and returned to his estate.

Although his military skills may have been average, his people and political skills were enormous. Whether it was his soldiers or his fellow statesmen, Washington was everywhere admired for his integrity, balance, and civic determination. He was invited to take on different tasks because he could be depended on to analyze the job, do what it took to accomplish it, and then retire. He was also able to bring out the best in those who reported to him. During the American Revolution, he shifted the focus of command to different theaters of war and different generals depending on the necessities of war, not on his personal preferences or ego. Prior to Yorktown, he had not personally managed a military command for many years. His ability to harness two of the most remarkable (but personally antagonistic) geniuses in the nation, Alexander Hamilton and Thomas Jefferson, in a single cabinet was an extraordinary feat. His political skills were exceptional in that he was able to stay out of policy and political squabbles so that he could get his (administrative) job done.

A final testament to his greatness was his ability to adapt to remarkably different jobs. Being a general, military commander in chief, and a president require different skills, especially given the vastly different contextual situations. Washington assessed what needed to be done and set his priorities and goals. While he utilized his own traits, skills, and expertise, he supplemented his abilities with the help of many others. Further, he was able to shift roles and leadership styles in an instant. As commander in chief of the American armies, he had to become a subordinate and supplicant to the Continental Congress, which he did in an able and gracious fashion. While he was generally a facilitative and consensus-building president, he personally led 11,000 soldiers to western Pennsylvania in 1794 to put down the Whiskey Rebellion when a liquor excise tax was resisted. Federal authority was not again questioned in this way until the succession of the South sixty-five years later. Thus he commanded both with *direction* and *support*. He expected ample *participation* from both his generals and his cabinet. He fully *delegated* campaigns and administrative operations. He always *achieved* his goals but did so in a way that incorporated the goals of his country and *inspired* others. He was never caught unaware of *external* issues and devoted the time necessary to work with Congress and other constituencies.

George Washington was a great leader not because he achieved a single set of skills and abilities, but rather because he mastered and practiced an evolving array of leadership competencies.

CONCLUSION

We began the book with three related points. First, leadership is a complex phenomenon. Second, leadership varies significantly from one situation to the next. And third, those wishing to study the dynamics of leadership must be willing to consider more sophisticated models if they want more than platitudes.

The review of theories provides a kaleidoscope of perspectives, from closed-ended approaches that focus on leader member exchanges, to internal participatory-team approaches, to open systems strategic and competitive approaches, and to collaborative community-change approaches.

This book presents an action research model of moderate sophistication in order to capture the complexity of leadership itself. The model is based on current research in the field, but is intended to be applicable and relevant to practitioners and students. Including all assessment and priority factors, leader characteristics, styles, and behaviors, and leader evaluation and development considerations, seventy variables were reviewed in detail and incorporated into the action model. A leadership survey form is provided as an appendix (see Appendix A) for those wishing to utilize the model in an applied setting to obtain feedback. Models of complex phenomena are useful not only for general understanding and one's own long-term developmental purpose but also for instruction, as a checklist in specific operational situations, and as an analytic tool in new situations.

It is hoped that the review of the large literature in the first half of the book and a breakdown of leadership functions in the second half have offered the reader both theoretical and applied approaches for better understanding the dynamics of leadership.

NOTES

1. OMB historical tables, 2009, reflecting the data from 2007.

2. It should be noted that the first item is similar to other competency priority listings: honesty and integrity. The other matched top competencies are somewhat more highly ranked than similar lists in the past, but these data reflect holistic assessments discussed above: collaboration (team player) and developing others. Adaptability was fourth for the private sector and fifth for the public and nonprofit sector.

Assessment of Organizational Conditions and Leader Performance

---

Name of the person being assessed:

_____

You are:

The person being rated	_____	(self)
A subordinate	_____	
The superior	_____	
A peer or colleague	_____	

Background information: You are being asked to contribute to an organizational and leader assessment. The instrument should take between twenty and twenty-five minutes to complete. A cover letter will stipulate the terms of confidentiality, the return address, and whether to use this form for responses or a separate form that can be scanned. The survey has two parts. The questions regarding organizational effectiveness may or may not reflect a particular leader's effect on the organization. For example, leaders who are new or have a relatively small range of discretion may not have a major impact. Because leadership is ultimately about improving organizational effectiveness, however, these questions are vitally important no matter how great or small the leader's past role. The second part of the assessment focuses on the leader's traits, skills, and management behaviors. Leader traits are generally predispositions toward effectiveness, rather than guarantees of success. The leader skills selected here are those generalized capabilities that are used in many management behaviors. The leader behaviors are divided into those that are task-oriented, people-oriented, and change-oriented.

Important guidelines for respondents:

- In nearly all cases, the organization, area, or unit being referred to is *the area under the jurisdiction of the person being assessed*, not the organization at large. The exception is when the person being evaluated is the chief executive officer.

- Reserve 5's for truly exceptional behavior. Most people are exceptional in a few things; almost no one is exceptional in all leadership areas.
- Reserve DK/NA (do not know/not applicable) for cases when you have no idea or the question seems completely inapplicable.
- Even though a number of the questions are broad or composite in scope, provide an average score for the range that you feel applies.

PART 1

Organizational Conditions

Unless a special scale is called for by a question, rate the following statements about organizational conditions using the following scale:

> 5 = strongly agree
> 4 = agree
> 3 = neither agree nor disagree
> 2 = disagree
> 1 = strongly disagree
> DK/NA = do not know or not applicable

OVERALL ORGANIZATIONAL EFFECTIVENESS (ORGANIZATION-WIDE)

1. The technical management of routine performance and problem solving of the organizational area is optimal.
   Disagree   Agree
       1   2   3   4   5   DK/NA

2. The management of employees' needs—enhancing satisfaction and creativity—is optimal.
   Disagree   Agree
       1   2   3   4   5   DK/NA

3. The management of change—either to improve current systems significantly, replace processes altogether, or make changes in organizational culture—is optimal.
   Disagree   Agree
       1   2   3   4   5   DK/NA

4. Which of the three areas is most in need of attention in your opinion (technical management, employer's needs, management of change)?

ORGANIZATIONAL FACTORS AFFECTING SUCCESS

5. Task skills (as a result of recruitment, experience and/or training) are generally excellent in the organizational area.

Disagree   Agree

   1   2   3   4   5   DK/NA

6. Role clarity—for individuals, teams, and entire units—is generally excellent in the organizational area.

Disagree   Agree

   1   2   3   4   5   DK/NA

7. The unit/organization is characterized by high levels of creativity and innovation.

Disagree   Agree

   1   2   3   4   5   DK/NA

8. Resources for the organizational area are generally optimal for employee pay, technology, facilities, support staff, training and development, travel, and so forth.

Disagree   Agree

   1   2   3   4   5   DK/NA

9. The level of subordinate effort (in terms of both well-managed time and subordinate enthusiasm) is generally excellent in the organizational area.

Disagree   Agree

   1   2   3   4   5   DK/NA

10. Formal groups/units and other teams are characterized by high levels of cooperation and mutual support in the organizational area.

Disagree   Agree

   1   2   3   4   5   DK/NA

11. The organization of work groups and the performance strategies they use to ensure high levels of productivity and quality are generally excellent in the organizational area.

Disagree   Agree

   1   2   3   4   5   DK/NA

12. The coordination of the organizational area with other external constituencies—other areas or agencies, legislative overseers, and public interest groups—is generally optimal.

Disagree   Agree
   1   2   3   4   5   DK/NA

13. Overall, how would you rate the level of organizational effectiveness, with 5 being high?

Low   High
   1   2   3   4   5   DK/NA

CONSTRAINTS ON LEADERSHIP

14. Rate the degree of constraints placed on the leader by legal/contractual restrictions (such as legal limitations on rewarding and punishing employees, mandatory purchasing/travel/process requirements, union contracts, etc.). Many legal/contractual restrictions would be a 5; few legal/contractual restrictions would be a 1.

Few constraints   Many constraints
   1   2   3   4   5   DK/NA

15. Rate the degree of constraints placed on the leader by the level of their position in the organization. A chief executive position would be a 1; a frontline employee's position might be a 5 (but might also be lower depending on delegation and empowerment).

Few constraints   Many constraints
   1   2   3   4   5   DK/NA

16. Rate the constraints on leadership based on the level of resources. Few resources would be a 1; extremely lush resources would be a 5.

Few resources   Many resources
   1   2   3   4   5   DK/NA

PART 2

Leader Traits, Skills, and Management Behaviors

LEADER TRAITS

17. The leader exhibits a high degree of appropriate self-confidence.
Disagree   Agree
    1   2   3   4   5   DK/NA

18. The leader exhibits decisiveness in situations calling for decisive action.
Disagree   Agree
    1   2   3   4   5   DK/NA

19. The leader is resilient in handling setbacks and disappointments. S/he is also persistent in promoting long-term organizational goals and new projects that require time to provide results.
Disagree   Agree
    1   2   3   4   5   DK/NA

20. The leader generally exhibits high levels of energy.
Disagree   Agree
    1   2   3   4   5   DK/NA

21. The leader demonstrates a high regard for excellence and motivates others to achieve excellence forcefully.
Disagree   Agree
    1   2   3   4   5   DK/NA

22. The leader exhibits flexibility in responding to situations and also adapts her/his leadership style to the situation.
Disagree   Agree
    1   2   3   4   5   DK/NA

23. The leader generally demonstrates a public service mentality and a customer service orientation specifically.

Disagree				Agree	
1	2	3	4	5	DK/NA

24. The leader has very high standards of fairness, integrity, and honesty.

Disagree				Agree	
1	2	3	4	5	DK/NA

25. The leader's emotional maturity—self-control, responsibility for actions, lack of egotism—is consistent.

Disagree				Agree	
1	2	3	4	5	DK/NA

LEADER SKILLS

26. The leader's oral communication skills are exceptional.

Disagree				Agree	
1	2	3	4	5	DK/NA

27. The leader's written communication skills are exceptional.

Disagree				Agree	
1	2	3	4	5	DK/NA

28. The leader's mastery of social and interpersonal skills (e.g., listening and empathy) is exceptional.

Disagree				Agree	
1	2	3	4	5	DK/NA

29. The leader is able to use influence and negotiation skills deftly to the good of the organization, without being perceived to be manipulative or excessively coercive.

Disagree				Agree	
1	2	3	4	5	DK/NA

30. The leader has the analytic skills—memory, ability to handle cognitive complexity, ability to make fine distinctions—necessary to do the job well.

Disagree				Agree	
1	2	3	4	5	DK/NA

31. The leader has technical credibility in the core responsibilities required by the unit entrusted to him/her.

    Disagree   Agree
       1   2   3   4   5   DK/NA

32. The leader demonstrates continual learning on a personal level.

    Disagree   Agree
       1   2   3   4   5   DK/NA

LEADER BEHAVIORS

Rate the leader in these behavior areas.

Task-Oriented

33. Monitoring and assessing tasks of subordinates.

    Poor   Excellent
       1   2   3   4   5   DK/NA

34. Planning and organization of work processes.

    Poor   Excellent
       1   2   3   4   5   DK/NA

35. Clarifying roles and objectives of subordinates.

    Poor   Excellent
       1   2   3   4   5   DK/NA

36. Informing.

    Poor   Excellent
       1   2   3   4   5   DK/NA

37. Delegating work appropriately.

    Poor   Excellent
       1   2   3   4   5   DK/NA

38. Problem solving related to routine work issues.

    Poor   Excellent
       1   2   3   4   5   DK/NA

39. Managing technical innovation and creativity.
Poor   Excellent
    1   2   3   4   5   DK/NA

40. Overall, how would you rate the leader's task-oriented behaviors?
Poor   Excellent
    1   2   3   4   5   DK/NA

People-Oriented

41. Consulting (with employees in their area of responsibility).
Poor   Excellent
    1   2   3   4   5   DK/NA

42. Planning and organizing personnel (e.g., deployment of the right people for the right jobs).
Poor   Excellent
    1   2   3   4   5   DK/NA

43. Developing staff (e.g., training and mentoring).
Poor   Excellent
    1   2   3   4   5   DK/NA

44. Motivating.
Poor   Excellent
    1   2   3   4   5   DK/NA

45. Building and managing teams.
Poor   Excellent
    1   2   3   4   5   DK/NA

46. Managing conflict.
Poor   Excellent
    1   2   3   4   5   DK/NA

47. Managing personnel changes (e.g., redeployment, getting personnel to adopt new standards).
Poor   Excellent
    1   2   3   4   5   DK/NA

48. Overall, how would you rate the leader's people-oriented behaviors?
    Poor   Excellent
    1   2   3   4   5   DK/NA

Organization-Oriented

49. Scanning the environment.
    Poor   Excellent
    1   2   3   4   5   DK/NA

50. Strategic planning and organizing issues related to organizational alignment
    (e.g., introducing a new service or taking steps to eliminate a service that is an
    inefficient use of resources).
    Poor   Excellent
    1   2   3   4   5   DK/NA

51. Articulating the mission and vision of the organization clearly.
    Poor   Excellent
    1   2   3   4   5   DK/NA

52. Networking and partnering (outside the organization).
    Poor   Excellent
    1   2   3   4   5   DK/NA

53. Performing general management functions (human resources, budget, informa-
    tion management, spokesperson responsibilities, etc.).
    Poor   Excellent
    1   2   3   4   5   DK/NA

54. Decision making that is timely, effective, and well articulated (regarding major
    issues).
    Poor   Excellent
    1   2   3   4   5   DK/NA

55. Managing major organizational change and organizational culture over the long
    term.
    Poor   Excellent
    1   2   3   4   5   DK/NA

56. Overall, how would you rate the leader's organization oriented behaviors?
    Poor   Excellent
    1   2   3   4   5   DK/NA

LEADER STYLE

57. How would your rate the leader's style range (whether that style is appropriate or not)? Does the leader change styles in different situations—sometimes being more participative, sometimes more consultative, and sometimes more directive. (The next question will consider style appropriateness.)

Limited				Broad	
1	2	3	4	5	DK/NA

58. How would you rate the leader's style appropriateness? For example, does the leader only use a directive style when speed or discipline are priorities and only use a participative or delegated style when subordinates are equipped and prepared to handle the responsibility?

Not appropriate				Appropriate	
1	2	3	4	5	DK/NA

OVERALL

59. What is the key leadership weakness or organizational issue that is especially important for the leader to deal with, in your opinion?

60. Finally, how would you rate the leader's overall performance, taking into consideration the current level of organizational performance and the leader's effect on it through his/her traits, skills, and management behaviors, and also taking into consideration the constraints the leader faces and his/her time in the position?

Poor				Excellent
1	2	3	4	5

General Instructions for the Assessment of Organizational Conditions and Leader Performance

The assessment form can be used as a part of an organizational activity, a training program, or by an individual manager. The form should be accompanied by a cover letter stipulating the terms of confidentiality, the return address, and a timeline. The terms of confidentiality include: (a) whether the person reviewed will have the forms collected by a third party or collect them personally, perhaps by mail, (b) whether the person reviewed will personally see the forms when they are tabulating them or whether the forms will be tabulated by a third party, and (c) assurances that at least three people are part of the assessment pool for a category (except superior). Confidentiality is increased when a third party collects and tabulates the forms, as well as when more numbers of respondents are requested. A lower level of confidentiality is acceptable; however, the respondents should be informed of the process. Inform superiors that their form is not confidential. If there are not enough subordinates or peers for a category, combine these two categories. **Always fill in the demographic data yourself:** *your name* **and the appropriate box such as "subordinate."** It is common for respondents to neglect to fill these in.

When the forms are sent or handed out, the person reviewed should also fill in his/her assessment form. This must be done prior to seeing the assessment of others.

There are four types of information that can be gathered: self, subordinates, superiors, peers. Subordinate and peer categories need to be averaged. Simply add up the scores and divide by the number of responses. There is a tabulation sheet for the subordinate/peer categories if necessary.

The information is displayed on the profile sheet. It is recommended that different colors be used for different respondents. You can use the following:

> Black: self
> Red: subordinates
> Dashed black: superior
> Green or blue: peers

Make small Xs for each data point; do only one subgroup at a time. Estimate the location of fractions. Connect the Xs to get a better picture and to compare the subprofiles.

Study the profiles for comparative perspectives of the organizational capacity and your leadership strengths and weaknesses. (See the questions provided below.)

SAMPLE LETTER TO ACCOMPANY THE ASSESSMENT FORMS (ASSESSEE TO RESPONDENTS)

Date

Dear Respondent:

I would appreciate your assistance in my management development. Good feedback helps enormously in understanding one's strengths and opportunities for improvement. The following form asks for your perceptions of both the strengths and weaknesses of the organization as well as my leadership skills and styles. The form takes about twenty-five minutes to complete.

Please return the forms to Michelle Ortiz in our Human Resource Department (Box 1020). An addressed envelope is enclosed for your convenience. Michelle has agreed to tabulate these forms for me. I have requested that six subordinates and three peers respond in order to ensure confidentiality. I will not see the original forms. Of course, the superior form is not anonymous.

The forms must be received by Michelle Ortiz by *October 10* at noon to be used in the tabulation. I will receive the tabulated results soon thereafter.

Thank you in advance for assisting me in improving myself!

Sincerely,

John Doe

GUIDELINES FOR UTILIZING FEEDBACK

There are a number of important issues to remember when you begin to review your feedback.

- A positive attitude about getting feedback increases the likelihood of positive improvement enormously.
- Look for similarity and dissimilarity of patterns. If the subordinates and superior agree on an item, but you disagree, you probably have an unidentified weakness.
- Be sure to examine your assessment form by areas as well as items. Note that if organizational effectiveness is low, it tends to lower individual performance somewhat.

- Everyone's perception has equal validity. However, it is up to the person being reviewed to decide what weight to give data. For example, if a manager just gave tough reviews to a number of low-performing employees, then tougher evaluations of the manager are also likely.
- Not all weaknesses need to be addressed now. You may have perceived weaknesses that do not fit with your current priorities. Only the person being assessed can decide what priorities to give to the data. In fact, you may decide to work on an area that is not considered your weakest by respondents.
- It is nearly impossible to improve in numerous areas simultaneously. Therefore, it is best to pinpoint just a few areas to work on, but to be conscientious in doing so. *Remember that the form is keyed to the book. Therefore, when you decide what areas you want to work on, read the appropriate sections of the book with the accompanying guidelines.*
- Be sure to decide on what concrete actions you want to pursue in order to improve. Vague resolutions to do better are rarely effective at changing ingrained behavior.

SUGGESTED QUESTIONS TO USE IN ANALYZING THE ASSESSMENT PROFILE

An assessment profile with all four perspectives involves 240 data points, which have been consolidated from 480 to over 1,000 pieces of data. It takes time to appreciate and understand the complexity of so much data. By asking yourself a series of twelve questions, you are more likely to improve your understanding. Some of the basic questions to ask are:

- What was the strongest area of organizational performance? What was the weakest?
- How do perceptions of constraints agree with or vary from your own?
- What were the different views about your best and worst traits?
- What were the different views about your best and worst skills?
- What were the different views about your best and worst task-oriented behaviors?
- What were the different views about your best and worst people-oriented behaviors?
- What were the different views about your best and worst organization-oriented behaviors?
- How do your perceptions of your style range and appropriateness differ from others'?
- What commonality is there among respondents' perceptions of areas to focus on (item 59)?
- Ultimately, what two or three areas do you want to work on over the next year or so?
- What guidelines does the book recommend for effective leadership in this area?
- What concrete steps are you going to take in order to become more effective in these areas?

RECOMMENDATIONS FOR DEBRIEFING WITH RESPONDENTS

Sometimes individuals want to have a debriefing with respondents either to clarify issues or to assist in a plan of improvement. The following guidelines are recommended:

- Debriefing can occur productively only if the person being reviewed is comfortable with the data. If feelings of anger, hostility, or disbelief are present, it is quite possible to make a situation *worse.*
- Start any debriefing with comments of appreciation to the respondents. It is often good to mention a few of the strengths that were generally agreed upon next. This balances the picture insofar as the debriefing is likely to focus on weaknesses.
- If the debriefing is with your superior and you received some "low marks," consider it an opportunity to fix these problems prior to the next formal assessment.
- Avoid open-ended questions at first unless it is your boss. Provide debriefers with alternatives initially.

COPYRIGHT PERMISSION TO USE THE ASSESSMENT OF ORGANIZATIONAL CONDITIONS AND LEADER PERFORMANCE

Tabulation Form

Question Number	Response					= Average	Question Number	Response					= Average
	1	2	3	4	5			1	2	3	4	5	
1							31						
2							32						
3							33						
4							34						
5							35						
6							36						
7							37						
8							38						
9							39						
10							40						
11							41						
12							42						
13							43						
14							44						
15							45						
16							46						
17							47						
18							48						
19							49						
20							50						
21							51						
22							52						
23							53						
24							54						
25							55						
26							56						
27							57						
28							58						
29							59						
30							60						

Profile

		1	2	3	4	5	
1	Technical focus						Overall Organizational Effectiveness
2	People focus						
3	Change focus						
4	Circle one:						
5	Task skills						Organizational Factors Affecting Success
6	Role clarity						
7	Creativity and innovation						
8	Resources						
9	Subordinate effort						
10	Intergroup cooperation						
11	Performance strategies						
12	External cooperation						
13	Overall organizational effectiveness						
14	Legal contractual constraints						Constraints on Leadership
15	Position constraints						
16	Resource constraints						
17	Self-confidence						Leader Traits
18	Decisiveness						
19	Resilience						

Appendix B.2 *(continued)*

		1	2	3	4	5	
20	High energy						Leader Traits
21	Regard for excellence						
22	Flexibility						
23	Public service motivation						
24	Integrity						
25	Emotional maturity						
26	Oral communication						Leader Skills
27	Written communication						
28	Social and interpersonal skills						
29	Influence and negotiation						
30	Analytic skills						
31	Technical credibility						
32	Continual learning						
33	Assessing and monitoring tasks						Task-Oriented Behaviors
34	Operations planning						
35	Clarifying roles and objectives						
36	Informing						
37	Delegating						
38	Problem solving						
39	Managing innovation and creativity						
40	Overall: Task-oriented behaviors						

Appendix B.2 *(continued)*

		1	2	3	4	5	
41	Consulting						People-Oriented Behavior
42	Planning and organizing personnel						
43	Developing staff						
44	Motivating						
45	Building and managing teams						
46	Managing conflict						
47	Managing personal change						
48	Overall: People-oriented behaviors						
49	Scanning the environment						Organization-Oriented Behavior
50	Planning and organizing alignment						
51	Articulating the mission and vision						
52	Networking and partnering						
53	Performing general management functions						
54	Decision making (major issues)						
55	Major organizational change						
56	Overall: Organization-oriented behaviors						
57	Style range						Leader Style
58	Style appropriateness						
59	Item to focus on:						Overall Performance
60	Overall leader performance						

Study of Federal Managers (2002): Synopsis

The study of federal managers was performed in 2002 using data collected by the Office of Personnel Management (OPM). Their data set was published in 1997 in *Occupational Study of Federal Executives, Managers, and Supervisors: An Application of the Multipurpose Occupational Systems Analysis Inventory—Closed Ended (MOSAIC)*. The data were actually collected in 1991. The survey population consisted of 20,664 federal executives, managers, supervisors, and lead workers. A total of 10,061 usable surveys were returned, of which 7,938 respondents were in supervisory through executive positions. Respondents were asked about the Leadership Excellence Profile—22 overarching competencies that the OPM used for various purposes until it was superseded in the 1999 OPM Leadership Competency Model. They were also asked determine the degree of importance of 151 discrete management/leadership competencies.

This extraordinary data set has strengths and weaknesses. One strength is its breadth and articulation. A survey of 8,000 managers of all descriptions from all types of agencies provides an extremely broad database, even though it is from a single level of government. Further, the data set is fully disaggregated by supervisors, managers, and executives, which provides important insight into which competencies are hierarchically most sensitive. Second, the data set provides both metacompetency perspectives and microcompetencies, which can be reconfigured for a study such as this one. The major weakness of the study is that the data were collected in late 1991 and many researchers, including the author, would contend that the world of leadership has shifted slightly since then. For example, in 1999, the OPM moved to a more decentralized model, which included five more competencies and emphasized change management, entrepreneurial skills, and customer focus more than in the early research. Nonetheless, on balance, it is an extraordinary resource that has been woefully underutilized.

This study linked the data of the OPM study with the Leadership Action Cycle (LAC) used in this book. Linking the twenty-two OPM metacompetencies with the LAC was relatively straightforward, even if the fit was frequently askew. Some of the competencies such as oral and written communication translated easily and neatly from one model to the other. Other competencies such as "interpersonal skill" had to be divided up ambiguously among both "social skills" and numerous people-oriented behaviors in the LAC with its more precise approach.

The reananalysis of the 151 microcompetencies required placing all of them into one or more of the twenty-one behavioral leadership competencies (task, people, and organization oriented) in the LAC. Two OPM microcompetencies were disqualified as being more like value traits than behaviors. In over 50 percent of cases, OPM microcompetencies were placed in a single LAC competency; in less than 10 percent of cases an OPM competency was placed in three LAC competencies. For example, in analyzing the importance of operations planning, the following microcompetencies were included:

- establish organizational objectives to provide for assignment of resources
- determine specific projects of actions to accomplish the goals of the organization
- develop strategies with contingency plans to implement goals
- determine resource requirements to allocate funds to projects
- interpret broad policies and guidelines for program execution
- establish program planning activities to develop fiscal year operation agenda
- set deadlines for project completion
- review strategic plans on a regular basis and integrate into program and policy plans
- work with different parts of the organization to develop operational plans
- estimate costs of resource requirements
- design processes and structures for doing work

The ranking of all the OPM competencies was tracked in terms of the top 20 and top 100 out of the 151 total. For example, establish organizational objectives was 13th for executives and 37th for supervisors. Determine resource requirements to allocate funds to projects was ranked 59th by executives but was unranked by supervisors because more than 50 percent do not even perform this function. However, "set deadlines for project completion" was ranked 91st by executives but 44th by supervisors. These rankings could be used not only to determine the relative importance of various competency subcomponents, but also to aggregate into behavioral categories for comparison.

Exhibit 13.1 (p. 320) displays the most global comparative findings of this study. As expected, supervisors think that their most critical competencies are task and people oriented, while organizational competencies are far less crucial. In terms of criticality, executives believe that organizational competencies are the most important, task-oriented competencies second, and people a distant third. Yet, when one broadens the question to significant competencies (the top 100), supervisors place more emphasis on organizational competencies than either task- or people-oriented behaviors. Their emphasis on organizational-oriented behaviors jumps from only 17 percent of their focus in the short term to 40 percent of their focus in the longer term. Executives also place even more importance on organization-oriented competencies. Three chapters (13, 14, and 15) show similar comparisons among the competencies of the respective behavioral domains.

Study of Local Government Managers

As a part of this project, in 2001, I used the Leadership Action Cycle using students in two classes who were also leaders holding positions in local government: city manager, department head, senior manager, county judge (who functions in Texas as the chief administrative officer), and so forth. In addition to field-testing the instrument, I asked a series of questions based on the Leadership Action Cycle to integrate with my review of the literature and my study of federal managers, as well as Bhatta's international perspective. The full group that field-tested the instrument numbered fifty-five; however, the group that answered a questionnaire used in this ministudy numbered forty-five. Such a small *N* for a leadership study means that it is more demonstrative of illustrative than authoritative leadership trends. However, averages homogenize a wealth of detail and sometimes even damage our appreciation of important variation. Having conducted thousands of leadership assessments over the past fifteen years, I am confident that this was a good sampling of leaders—albeit local leaders in rural and moderately urban settings. I present the findings here as I would a series of focus groups, without arithmetic averages.

What were the findings of the self-reports (after being given feedback from others)? The top traits were decisiveness, assumption of responsibility, energy, and integrity. The weakest traits were flexibility (by far), decisiveness (again), and toleration of stress. The top skills identified were communications, technical skills, and continual learning. The worst self-identified skills were communications and technical skills. The best task-oriented behaviors were problem solving, technical innovations and, creativity; the worst were delegation and clarification of roles and objectives. The best people-oriented skills were managing conflict, consulting, and motivating; the worst were consulting, developing staff, and motivating. The best organizational-oriented behaviors were decision making and performing general management functions; the worst were articulating the mission and vision, and managing organizational change. Furthermore, two-thirds of the respondents reported that their rankings were lower than expected.

In addition to the specific findings, I think three general observations can be gleaned from this study. First, the study reinforces the intuitive understanding that leaders have very different strengths and weaknesses. Indeed, in some cases the strength most noted by some members of the group is also the weakness most noted by others (e.g., decisiveness, communications, technical skills, consulting, and motivating). Second, because addressing weaknesses is so important for leadership development, we get a useful list of competency candidates: flexibility, decisiveness, communication skills, delegation, consulting, developing staff, articulating mission and vision, and managing organizational change. This certainly rings true with my many years of leadership research. I would add that these particular competencies are remarkably hard to teach (as opposed to just preaching about). Just how do you teach flexibility? And just how do you teach it in concert with decisiveness without being contradictory? Of course, it can be done and it is done all the time, for example, in teaching detailed decision analysis (e.g., the normative decision model), but it is not easy to do. Third, it is my contention that leadership is more difficult to do well today than it was in the past (Van Wart and Berman 1999). One reason is that the environment calls for more decentralized leadership models that translate into the expectation that all leaders be able to do many things, hence, that they have more competency strengths. The second reason is that in the more competitive environment with more resource constraints, people generally feel that more is expected of them and there is more pressure to perform. Therefore, they expect more of leaders, too. Although I did not collect empirical data, it was my distinct impression that many more participants were surprised by the higher than expected ratings than I observed ten to fifteen years ago. In sum, although many seek leadership positions, fewer may be prepared today because of greater demands, higher expectations, and the difficulty of teaching/learning many of the complex leadership competencies.

References

Abramson, M.A.; Breul, J.D.; and Kamensky, J.M. 2006. *Six Trends Transforming Government*. Washington, DC: IBM Center for the Business of Government.

Adler, N.J. 1996. "Global Women Political Leaders: An Invisible History, and Increasingly Important Future." *Leadership Quarterly* 7(1): 133–161.

Adler, N.J., and Bartholomew, S. 1992. "Managing Globally Competent People." *Academy of Management Executives* 6: 52–65.

Adler, N.J.; Doktor, R.; and Redding, S.G. 1986. "From Atlantic to the Pacific Century: Cross-cultural Management Reviewed." *Journal of Management* 12(2): 295–318.

Agranoff, R. 2007. *Managing with Networks: Adding Value to Public Organizations*. Washington, DC: Georgetown University Press.

———. 2008a. "Enhancing Performance through Public Sector Networks: Mobilizing Human Capital in Communities of Practice." *Public Performance and Management Review* 31(3): 320–347.

———. 2008b. "Intergovernmental and Network Administration, Accountability, and Performance" (Symposium introduction). *Public Performance and Management Review* 31(3): 315–319.

Alimo-Metcalfe, B., and Alban-Metcalfe, J. 2005. "Leadership: Time for a New Direction?" *Leadership* 1(1): 51–71.

Allison, G., and Zelikow, P. 1999. *Essence of Decision: Explaining the Cuban Missile Crisis*. 2d ed. New York: Addison-Wesley.

Alonso, P., and Lewis, G. 2001. "Public Service Motivation and Job Performance: Evidence from the Federal Sector." *American Review of Public Administration* 31(4): 363–380.

Altshular, A. 1965. "Rationality and Influence in Public Service." *Public Administration Review* 25(3): 226–233.

Alvesson, M., and Sveningsson, S. 2003. "Managers Doing Leadership: The Extra Ordinarization of the Mundane." *Human Relations* 56(12): 1435–1459.

Amit, K.; Popper, M.; Gal, R.; Mamane-Levy, L.; and Lisak, A. 2009. "Leadership-Shaping Experiences: A Comparative Study of Leaders and Non-leaders." *Leadership and Organization Development Journal* 30(4): 302–318.

Ammons, D.N. 2001. *Municipal Benchmarks: Assessing Local Performance and Establishing Community Stands*. 2d ed. Thousand Oaks, CA: Sage.

Ancona, D.G., and Nadler, D.A. 1989. "Top Hats and Executive Tales: Designing the Senior Team." *Sloan Management Review* (Fall): 19–28.

Anderson, C., and Kilduff, G.J. 2009. "Why Do Dominant Personalities Attain Influence in Face-to-Face Groups? The Competence-Signaling Effects of Trait Competence." *Journal of Personality and Social Psychology* 96: 491–503.

Ansoff, I. 1980. "Strategic Issue Management." *Strategic Management Journal* 1(2): 131–148.

Archer, David, and Cameron, Alex. 2008. *Collaborative Leadership—How to Succeed in an Interconnected World*. Oxford, UK: Butterworth Heinemann.

Argyris, C. 1957. *Personality and Organization*. New York: Harper.

———. 1993. *Knowledge for Action*. San Francisco: Jossey-Bass.

Aristotle. 1953. *The Ethics of Aristotle*. Trans. J.A.K. Thomson. New York: Viking Penguin.

Aronson, E. 2001. "Integrating Leadership Styles and Ethical Perspectives." *Canadian Journal of Administrative Sciences* 18(4): 244–256.

Arvey, R.D.; Zhang, Z.; Avolio, B.J.; and Krueger, R.F. 2007. "Developmental and Genetic Determinants of Leadership Role Occupancy among Women." *Journal of Applied Psychology* 92(3): 693–706.

Arvey, R.; Rotundo, M.: Johnson, W.: Zhang, Z.; and McGue, M. 2006. "The Determinants of Leadership Role Occupancy: Genetic and Personality Factors." *Leadership Quarterly* 17(1): 1–20.

Atwater, L., and Carmeli, A. 2009. "Leader-member Exchange, Feelings of Energy, and Involvement in Creative Work." *Leadership Quarterly* 20: 264–275.

Avolio, B.J. 2007. "Promoting More Integrative Strategies for Leadership Theory-building." *American Psychologist* 62(1): 25–33.

Avolio, B.J., and Gardner, W.L. 2005. "Authentic Leadership Development: Getting to the Root of Positive Forms of Leadership." *Leadership Quarterly* 16: 315–338.

Baldwin, T.T., and Ford, J.K. 1988. "Transfer of Training: A Review and Directions for Future Research." *Personnel Psychology* 41(1): 63–105.

Baliga, B.R., and Hunt, J.G. 1988. "An Organizational Life Cycle Approach to Leadership." In *Emerging Leadership Vistas,* ed. J.G. Hunt, B.R. Baliga, H.P. Dachler, and C.A. Schriesheim, 129–149. Lexington, MA: Lexington Books.

Bandura, A. 1977. *Social Learning Theory.* Englewood Cliffs, NJ: Prentice Hall.

———. 1986. *Social Foundations of Thought and Action: A Social Cognition Theory.* Englewood Cliffs, NJ: Prentice Hall.

Barber, H.F. 1990. "Some Personality Characteristics of Senior Military Officers." In *Measures of Leadership,* ed. K. Clark and M.B. Clark, 441–448. West Orange, NJ: Leadership Library of America.

Barker, R.A. 1997. "How can we train leaders if we don't know what leadership is?" *Human Relations* 50(3): 343–62.

———. 2001. "The nature of leadership." *Human Relations* 54(4), 469–494.

Barnard, C.I. 1938/1987. *The Functions of the Executive. Excerpt in Classics of Public Administration,* ed. J.M. Shafritz and A.C. Hyde. Chicago: Dorsey Press.

Bartone, P.T.; Eid, J.; Johnsen, B.; Laberg, J.; and Snook, S.A. 2009. "Big Personality Factors, Hardiness, and Social Judgment as Predictors of Leader Performance." *Leadership and Organizational Development Journal* 30(6): 498–521.

Bartunek, J.M., and Necochea, R. 2000. "Old Insights and New Times: Kairos, Inca Cosmology and Their Contributions to Contemporary Management Inquiry." *Journal of Management Inquiry* 9(2): 103–113.

Barzelay, M. 1992. *Breaking Through Bureaucracy: A New Vision for Managing in Government.* Berkeley: University of California Press.

Bass, B.M. 1985. *Leadership and Performance Beyond Expectations.* New York: Free Press.

———. 1990. *Bass & Stogdill's Handbook of Leadership.* New York: Free Press.

———. 1996. *A New Paradigm of Leadership: An Inquiry into Transformational Leadership.* Alexandria, VA: U.S. Army Research Institute for the Behavioral and Social Sciences.

Bass, B.M. (with R. Bass). 2008. *The Bass Handbook of Leadership: Theory, Research, and Managerial Applications.* New York: Free Press.

Bass, B.M., and Avolio, B.J. 1990. "The Implications of Transactional and Transformational Leadership for Individual, Team, and Organizational Development." In *Research in Organizational Change and Development,* vol. 1, ed. W. Pasmore and R.W. Woodman, 231–272. Greenwich, CT: JAI Press.

Bass, B.M., and Steidlmeier, P. 1999. "Ethics, Character, and Authentic Transformational Leadership." *Leadership Quarterly* 10: 181–217.

Beard, R. 1970. *Teaching and Learning.* New York: Viking Penguin.

Beckhard, R. 1969. *Organizational Development: Strategies and Models.* Reading, MA: Addison-Wesley.

Beinecke, R.H., and Spencer, J. 2009. "Examination of Mental Health Leadership Competencies Across IIMHL Countries." In *Public Sector Leadership: International Challenges and Perspectives,* ed. J.A. Raffel, P. Leisink, and A.E. Middlebrooks. Northampton, MA: Edward Elgar.

Bellone, C.J., and Goerl, G.F. 1992. "Reconciling Public Entrepreneurship and Democracy." *Public Administration Review* 52(12): 130–134.

Bennis, W. 1969. *Organizational Development: Its Nature, Origins, and Prospects.* Reading, MA: Addison-Wesley.

———. 2007. "The Challenges of Leadership in the Modern World." *American Psychologist* 62(1): 2–5.

Bennis, W., and Nanus, B. 1985. *Leaders: Strategies for Taking Charge.* New York: Harper and Row.

Bennis, W.; Parikh, J.; and Lessem, R. 1994. *Beyond Leadership: Balancing Economics, Ethics and Ecology.* Oxford, UK: Blackwell.

Bernstein, M.H. 1958. *The Job of the Federal Executive.* Washington, DC: Brookings Institution.

Berson, Y.; Nemanich, L.A.; Waldman, D.A.; Galvin, B.M.; and Keller, R.T. 2006. "Leadership and Organizational Learning: A Multiple Levels Perspective." *Leadership Quarterly* 17: 577–594.

Bevir, M. 2006. "Democratic Governance: Systems and Radical Perspective." *Public Administration Review* 66(3): 426–436.

Bhatta, G. 2001. "Enabling the Cream to Rise to the Top: A Cross-Jurisdictional Comparison of Competencies for Senior Public Managers in the Public Sector." *Public Performance and Management Review* 25(2): 194–207.

Bird, C. 1940. *Social Psychology.* New York: Appleton-Century.

Blake, R.R., and Mouton, J.S. 1964. *The Managerial Grid.* Houston, TX: Gulf.

———. 1965. "A 9,9 Approach for Increasing Organizational Productivity." In *Personal and Organizational Change through Group Methods,* ed. E.H. Schein and W.G. Bennis. New York: Wiley.

———. 1982. "Management by Grid Principles or Situationalism: Which?" *Group and Organization Studies* 7: 207–210.

———. 1985. *The Managerial Grid III.* Houston, TX: Gulf.

Bligh, D.A. 1972. *What's the Use of Lectures?* New York: Viking Penguin.

Block, P. 1993. *Stewardship: Choosing Service over Self-Interest.* San Francisco: Berrett-Koehler.

Blum, M.L. 1968. *Industrial Psychology and Its Social Foundations.* New York: Harper and Row.

Boal, K.B., and Hooijberg, R. 2000. "Strategic Leadership Research: Moving On." *Leadership Quarterly* 11: 515–549.

Boin, A., and 't Hart, P. 2003. "Public Leadership in Times of Crisis: Mission Impossible?" *Public Administration Review* 63(5): 544–553.

Boin, R.A., and Otten, M.H.P. 1996. "Beyond the Crisis Window of Reform: Some Ramifications for Implementation." *Journal of Contingencies and Crisis Management* 4(3): 149–161.

Bono, J.E., and Ilies, R. 2006. "Charisma, Positive Emotions and Mood Contagion." *Leadership Quarterly* 17: 317–334.

Borins, S. 2000. "Loose Cannons and Rule Breakers? . . . Some Evidence About Innovative Public Managers." *Public Administration Review* 60(6): 498–507.

Bourne, L.E. 1970. "Knowing and Using Concepts." *Psychology Review* 77(6): 546–556.

Bowers, D.G., and Seashore, S.E. 1966. "Predicting Organizational Effectiveness with a Four-Factor Theory of Leadership." *Administrative Science Quarterly* 11: 238–263.

Boyatzis, R.E. 1982. *The Competent Manager.* New York: Wiley.

Brown, M.E., and Trevino, L.K. 2006. "Ethical Leadership: A Review and Future Directions." *Leadership Quarterly* 17: 595–616.

Bryman, A. 1992. *Charisma and Leadership in Organizations.* London: Sage.

Bryson, J.M., and Crosby, B.C. 1992. *Leadership for the Common Good: Tackling Problems in a Shared-Power World.* San Francisco: Jossey-Bass.

Buckingham, M., and Coffman, C. 1999. *First, Break All the Rules: What the World's Greatest Managers Do Differently.* New York: Simon and Schuster.

Burke, C.S.; Sims, D.E.; Lazzara, E.H.; and Salas, E. 2007. "Trust in Leadership: A Multi-Level Review and Integration." *Leadership Quarterly* 18: 606–632.

Burke, C.S.; Stagel, K.C.; Klein, C.; Goodwin, G.F.; Salas, E.; and Halpin, S.M. 2006. "What Type of Leadership Behaviors Are Functional in Teams? A Meta-Analysis." *Leadership Quarterly* 17: 288–307.

Burke, R.J., Weitzel, W., and Weir, J. 1978. "Characteristics of Effective Employee Performance Review and Development Interviews: Replication and Extension". *Personnel Psychology* 31: 903–919.

Burns, J.M. 1978. *Leadership*. New York: Harper and Row.

———. 2003. *Transforming Leadership*. New York: Grove Press.

Butler, C. 2009. "Leadership in a Multicultural Arab Organisation." *Leadership and Development* 30(2): 139–151.

Callahan, K. 2006. "Elmer Boyd Staats and the Pursuit of Good Government." *Public Administration Review* 66(2): 159–167.

Callahan, R. 2007. "Governance: The Collision of Politics and Cooperation." *Public Administration Review* 67(2): 291–301.

Carmeli, A., and Schaubroeck, J. 2007. "The Influence of Leaders' and Other Referents' Normative Expectations on Individual Involvement in Creative Work." *Leadership Quarterly* 18: 35–48.

Carnevale, D.G. 1995. *Trustworthy Government: Leadership and Management Strategies for Building Trust and High Performance*. San Francisco: Jossey-Bass.

Carnevale, A.P.; Gainer, L.J.; and Schulz, E.R. 1990. *Training the Technical Workforce*. San Francisco: Jossey-Bass.

Caro, R.A. 1974. *The Power Broker: Robert Moses and the Fall of New York*. New York: Vintage Books.

Carroll, B.; Levy, L.; and Richmond, D. 2008. "Leadership as Practice: Challenging the Competency Paradigm." *Leadership* 4(4): 363–379.

Cayer, N.J., and Weschler, L. 1988. *Social Change and Adaptive Management*. New York: St Martin's Press.

Cayer, N.J.; Baker, D.; and Weschler, L.F. 2010. *Social Change and Adaptive Management*. San Diego, CA: Birkdale.

Cha, S.E., and Edmondson, A.C. 2006. "When Values Backfire: Leadership, Attribution, and Disenchantment in a Values-driven Organization." *Leadership Quarterly* 17: 57–78.

Champy, J. 1995. *Reengineering Management: The Mandate for New Leadership*. New York: HarperBusiness.

Chemers, M.M. 1997. *An Integrative Theory of Leadership*. Mahwah, NJ: Erlbaum.

Chen, B. 2008. "Assessing Intergovernmental Networks for Public Service Delivery." *Public Performance and Management Review* 31(3): 348–363.

Chen, L. 2008. "Leaders or Leadership: Alternative Approaches to Leadership Studies." *Management Communication Quarterly* 21(4): 547–555.

Chin, J.L.; Lott, B.; Rice, J.; and Sanchez-Hucles, J. (eds.). 2007. *Women and Leadership: Transforming Visions and Diverse Voices*. Boston: Blackwell.

Chrislip, D.D., and Larson, C.E. 1994. *Collaborative Leadership: How Citizens and Civil Leaders Can Make a Difference*. San Francisco: Jossey-Bass.

Ciulla, J.B. (ed.). 2004. *Ethics: The Heart of Leadership*. 2nd ed. Westport, CT: Praeger.

Ciulla. J.B.; Price, T.; and Murphy, S. 2005. *The Quest for Moral Leaders: Essays on Leadership, Ethics*. Northampton, MA: Edward Elgar.

Clarke, M. 2006. "A Study of the Role of 'Representative Leadership in Stimulating Organization Democracy." *Leadership* 2(4): 427–450.

Cleveland, H. 1985. *The Knowledge Executive: Leadership in an Information Society*. New York: E.P. Dutton.

Cohen, M.D.; March, J.G.; and Olsen, J.P. 1972. "A Garbage Can Model of Organizational Choice." *Administrative Science Quarterly* 17(2): 1–25.

Cohen, S.G., and Bailey, D.E. 1997. "What Makes Teams Work: Group Effectiveness Research from the Shop Floor to the Executive Suite." *Journal of Management* 23: 239–290.

Cohen, W.A. 2010. *Drucker on Leadership*. San Francisco: Jossey-Bass.

Collins, J. 2009. "Core Values: Align Your Actions with Them." *Leadership Excellence* 26(3): 5.

Collinson, D. 2005. "Dialectics of Leadership." *Human Relations* 58(11): 1419–1442.

———. 2006. "Rethinking Followership: A Poststructuralist Analysis of Follower Identities." *Leadership Quarterly* 17: 179–189.

Conger, J.A. 1989. *The Charismatic Leader: Behind the Mystique of Exceptional Leadership*. San Francisco: Jossey-Bass.

Conger, J.A., and Kanungo, R.N. 1987. "Toward a Behavioral Theory of Charismatic Leadership in Organizational Settings." *Academy of Management Review* 12: 637–647.

———. 1998. *Charismatic Leadership in Organizations*. Thousand Oaks, CA: Sage.

Conger, J.A., and Pearce, C.L. 2003. "A Landscape of Opportunities: Future Research on Shared Leadership." In *Reframing the Hows and Whys of Leadership,* ed. Pearce and Conger, 285–303. Thousand Oaks, CA: Sage.

Considine, M., and Lewis, J.M. 1999. "Governance at Ground Level: The Frontline Bureaucrat in the Age of Markets and Networks." *Public Administration Review* 59(6): 467–480.

Cooper, D.; Scandura, T.A.; and Schriesheim, C.A. 2005. "Looking Forward but Learning from Our Past: Potential Challenges to Developing Authentic Leadership Theory and Authentic Leaders." *Leadership Quarterly* 16: 475–493.

Cooper, T.L. 1990. *The Responsible Administrator*. San Francisco: Jossey-Bass.

Cooper, T.L., and Wright, D.N. (eds.). 1992. *Exemplary Public Administrators: Character and Leadership in Government*. San Francisco: Jossey-Bass.

Corsino, L. 1982. "Malcolm X and the Black Muslim Movement: A Social Psychology of Charisma." *Psychohistory Review* 10: 165–184.

Corson, J.J., and Shale, P.R. 1966. *Men Near the Top: Filling Key Posts in the Federal Service*. Baltimore: Johns Hopkins University Press.

Cortada, J.W.; Dijkstra, S.; Mooney, G.M.; and Ramsey, T. 2008. *Government and the Perpetual Collaboration Mandate: Six Worldwide Drivers Demand Customized Strategies*. Somers, NY: IBM Institute for Business Value.

Couto, R.A. 1988. "TVA's Old and New Grass Roots: A Reexamination of Cooptation." *Administration and Society* 19(4): 453–478.

Covey, S.R. 1989. *The Seven Habits of Highly Effective People*. New York: Simon and Schuster.

———. 1990. *Principle-Centered Leadership*. New York: Fireside.

———. 2010. "Building Trust: How Leaders Do It." *Leadership Excellence* 26(1): 15.

Cox, T.H. 1993. *Cultural Diversity in Organizations: Theory, Research and Practice*. San Francisco: Berrett-Koehler.

Crafts, L.W. 1934. "Transfer as Related to Number of Common Elements." *Journal of General Psychology* 13: 147–158.

Crosby, B.C., and Bryson, J.M. 2005. *Leadership for the Common Good: Tackling Public Problems in a Shared-Power World*. San Francisco: Jossey-Bass.

———. 2010. "Integrative Leadership and the Creation of Cross-Sector Collaborations." *Leadership Quarterly* 21: 211–230.

Crosby, B.C., and Kiedrowski, J. 2008. "Integrative Leadership: Observations from a University of Minnesota Seminar Series." *Integral Leadership Review* 8(3): 1–14. http://www.integralleadershipreview.com/

Dahl, R.A. 1947. "The Science of Public Administration: Three Problems." *Public Administration Review* 7(1): 1–11.

Dalla Costa, J. 1998. *The Ethical Imperative: Why Moral Leadership Is Good Business*. Reading, MA: Addison-Wesley.

Davis, K. 1953. "Management Communication and the Grapevine." *Harvard Business Review* 31: 43–49.

Dawson, P. 2003. *Understanding Organizational Change: The Contemporary Experience of People at Work*. Thousand Oaks, CA: Sage.

Day, D.V. 2000. Leadership Development: A Review in Context." *Leadership Quarterly* 11(4): 581–613.

Day, D.V., and Lord, R.G. 1988. "Executive Leadership and Organizational Performance: Suggestions for a New Theory and Methodology." *Journal of Management* 14(3): 453–464.

Day, D.V.; Gronn, P.; and Salas, E. 2006. "Leadership in Team-Based Organizations: On the Threshold of a New Era." *Leadership Quarterly* 17: 211–216.

Day, D.V.; Sin, H.; and Chen, T.T. 2004. "Assessing the Burdens of Leadership: Effects of Formal Leadership Roles on Individual Performance over Time." *Personnel Psychology* 57(3): 573–605.

De Bono, E. 1985. *Six Thinking Hats*. Boston: Little, Brown.

Deci, E.L. 1975. *Intrinsic Motivation*. New York: Plenum.

Decker, P.J. 1982. "The Enhancement of Behavior Modeling Training of Supervisory Skills by the Inclusion of Retention Processes." *Personnel Psychology* 35: 323–332.

De Hoogh, A.H.B.; Den Hartog, D.N., Koopman, P.L.; Thierry, H.; Van den Berg, P.T.; Van der Weide, J.G.; and Wilderom, C.P.M. 2005. "Leader Motives, Charismatic Leadership, and Subordinates' Work Attitude in the Profit and Voluntary Sector." *Leadership Quarterly* 16: 17–38.

Denhardt, R. 1992. *The Pursuit of Significance*. Belmont, CA: Wadsworth.

Denhardt, R.B., and Denhardt, J.V. 2006. *The Dance of Leadership: The Art of Leading Business, Government, and Society*. Armonk, NY: M.E. Sharpe.

DePree, M. 1989. *Leadership Is an Art*. New York: Doubleday.

DiIulio, J.J., Jr. 1989. "Recovering the Public Management Variable: Lessons from Schools, Prisons, and Armies." *Public Administration Review* 49(2): 127–133.

Dimock, M.E. 1958. "Executive Development After Ten Years." *Public Administration Review* 18(2): 91–97.

———. 1986. "Creativity." *Public Administration Review* 46(1): 3–7.

Dionne, S.D.; Yammarino, F.J.; Howell, J.P.; and Villa, J. 2005. "Substitutes for Leadership, or Not." *Leadership Quarterly* 16: 169–193.

Dlouhy, J.A. 2010. "Offshore Drilling Agency to be Split in Two." *Houston Chronicle,* May 11. Available at www.chron.com/disp/story.mpl/business/7001009.html.

Dobbins, G., and Platz, S. 1986. "Sex Differences in Leadership." *Academy of Management Review* 11: 118–127.

Doig, J.W., and Hargrove, E.C. 1987. *Leadership and Innovation: A Biographical Perspective on Entrepreneurs in Government*. Baltimore: Johns Hopkins University Press.

Donahue, A. 2006. "The Space Shuttle Columbia Recovery Operation: How Collaboration Enabled Disaster Response." *Public Administration Review* 66 (Supplement): 141–142.

Donnell, S., and Hall, J. 1980. "Men and Women as Managers: A Significant Case of No Significant Difference." *Organizational Dynamics* 8 (Spring): 60–77.

Dow, T. 1969. "The Theory of Charisma." *Sociological Quarterly* 10: 306–318.

Downs, A. 1967. *Inside Bureaucracy*. Boston: Little, Brown.

Downton, J.V. 1973. *Rebel Leadership: Commitment and Charisma in the Revolutionary Process*. New York: Free Press.

Drath, W.H.; McCauley, C.D.; Palus, C.J.; Van Velsor, W.; O'Connor, P.M.G.; and McGuire, J.B. 2008. "Direction, Alignment, Commitment: Toward a More Integrative Ontology of Leadership." *Leadership Quarterly* 19: 635–653.

Drucker, P.F. 1974. *Management: Tasks, Responsibilities, Practices*. New York: Harper and Row.

Dull, M. 2008. "Results-Model Reform Leadership: Questions of Credible Commitment." *Journal of Public Administration Research and Theory* 19(2): 255–284.

Dunbar, R., and Goldberg, W.H. 1978. "Crisis Development and Strategic Response in European Corporations." In *Studies on Crisis Management,* ed. C.F. Smart and W.T. Stansbury. Toronto: Butterworth.

Duncan, C.P. 1958. "Transfer After Training with Single Versus Multiple Tasks." *Journal of Experimental Psychology* 55(1): 63–72.

Dunoon, D. 2002. "Rethinking Leadership for the Public Sector." *Australian Journal of Public Administration* 61(3): 3–18.

Eagly, A., and Johnson, B. 1990. "Gender and the Emergence of Leaders: A Meta-Analysis." *Psychological Bulletin* 108: 233–256.

Eagly, A.A., and Carli, L.L. 2007. *Through the Labyrinth: The Truth about How Women Become Leaders.* Boston: Harvard Business School Press.

Earley, P.C.; Wojnaroski, P.; and Prest, W. 1987. "Task Planning and Energy Expended: Exploration of How Goals Influence Performance." *Journal of Applied Psychology* 72: 107–114.

Eden, D., and Ravid, G. 1982. "Pygmalion Versus Self-Expectancy: Effects of Instructor and Self-Expectancy on Trainee Performance." *Organizational Behavior and Human Performance* 30: 351–364.

Edwards, M. 2009. "Seeing Integral Leadership Through Three Important Lenses: Developmental, Ecological and Governance." *Integral Leadership Review* 9(1): 1–13.

Einarsen, S.; Aasland, M.S.; and Skogstad, A. 2007. "Destructive Leadership Behaviour: A Definition and Conceptual Model." *Leadership Quarterly* 18: 207–216.

Ensley, M.D.; Hmieleski, K.M.; and Pearce, C.L. 2006. "The Importance of Vertical and Shared Leadership Within New Venture Top Management Teams: Implications for Performance of Startups." *Leadership Quarterly* 17: 217–231.

Epstein, P.D. 1992. "Get Ready: The Time for Performance Measurement Is Coming." *Public Administration Review* 52(5): 513–519.

Ernst, C.; Hannum, K.M.; and Ruderman, M.R. 2010. "Developing Intergroup Leadership." In *Handbook of Leadership Development,* 3d ed., ed. E. Van Velsor, C. McCauley, and M. Ruderman. San Francisco: Jossey-Bass.

Etzioni, A. 1967. "Mixed Scanning: A Third Approach to Decision Making." *Public Administration Review* 27: 385–392.

Faerman, S.R.; Quinn, R.E.; and Thompson, M.P. 1987. "Bridging Management Practice and Theory: New York State's Public Service Training Program." *Public Administration Review* 47(4): 310–319.

Fairholm, G. 1991. *Values Leadership: Toward a New Philosophy of Leadership.* New York: Praeger.

Fairholm, M.R. 2004. "Perspectives on the Practice of Leadership." *Public Administration Review* 64(5): 577–590.

Fairholm, M.R., and Fairholm, G. 2009. *Understanding Leadership Perspectives: Theoretical and Practical Approaches.* New York: Springer.

Fairhurst, G.T. 2007. *Discursive Leadership: In Conversation with Leadership Psychology.* Thousand Oaks, CA: Sage.

Farazmand, A. 2001. "Crisis and Emergency Management." In *Handbook of Crisis and Emergency Management,* ed. Farazmand. New York: Marcel Dekker.

Fayol, H. 1949. *General and Industrial Management.* London: Pitman.

Fernandez, C.F., and Vecchio, R.P. 1997. "Situational Leadership Theory Revisited: A Test of an Across-Jobs Perspective." *Leadership Quarterly* 8(1): 67–84.

Fernandez, S. 2005. "Developing and Testing an Integrative Framework of Public Sector Leadership: Evidence from the Public Education Arena." *Journal of Public Administration Research and Theory* 15(2): 197–217.

Fernandez, S., and Pitts, D.W. 2007. "Under What Conditions Do Public Managers Favor and Pursue Organizational Change?" *American Review of Public Administration* 37(3): 324–341.

Fernandez, S.; Cho, Y.J.; and Perry, J.L. 2010. "Exploring the Link between Integrated Leadership and Public Sector Performance." *Leadership Quarterly* 21: 308–323.

Fesler, J.W. 1960. "Leadership and Its Context" (editorial). *Public Administration Review* 20(2): 122.

Fiedler, F.E. 1967. *A Theory of Leadership Effectiveness.* New York: McGraw-Hill.

Fiedler, F.E.; Chemers, M.M.; and Mahar, L. 1976. *Improving Leadership Effectiveness: The Leader Match Concept.* New York: Wiley.

Field, R.H.G. 1979. "A Crtique of the Vroom-Yetton Normative Model of Leadership." *Academy of Management Review* 4: 249–257.

Finer, H. 1941. "Administrative Responsibility in Democratic Government." *Public Administration Review* 1(4): 335–350.

Fisher, J. 1962. "Do Federal Managers Manage?" *Public Administration Review* 22(2): 59–64.

Fisher, R., and Ury, W. 1981. *Getting to Yes: Negotiating Agreement Without Giving In.* New York: Houghton Mifflin.

Flanders, L.R., and Utterback, D. 1985. "The Management Excellence Inventory: A Tool for Management Development." *Public Administration Review* 45(3): 403–410.

Fleishman, E.A. 1953. "The Description of Supervisory Behavior." *Journal of Applied Psychology* 37: 1–6.

Fleishman, E.A.; Mumford, M.D.; Zaccaro, S.J.; Levin, K.Y.; Korotkin, A.L.; and Hein, M.B. 1991. "Taxonomic Efforts in the Description of Leader Behavior." *Leadership Quarterly* 2: 245–287.

Fletcher, B.R., and Cooke, A.L. 2008. "Self-Awareness and Leadership Success." In *The Trusted Leader: Building the Relationships that Make Government Work,* ed. T. Newell, G. Reeher, and P. Ronnyne. Washington, DC: CQ Press.

Follett, M.P. 1933/1996. "The Essentials of Leadership." In *Mary Parker Follett: Prophet of Management,* ed. P. Graham. Boston: Harvard Business School Press.

Ford, J. 2006. "Discourses of Leadership: Gender, Identity and Contradiction in a UK Public Sector Organization." *Leadership* 2(1): 77–99.

Foucault, M. 1970. *The Order of Things.* New York: Pantheon.

———. 1972. *Archaeology of Knowledge.* New York: Pantheon.

Franke, R.H., and Kaul, J.D. 1978. "Hawthorne Experiments: First Statistical Interpretation." *American Sociological Review* 43(5): 623–643.

Freeman, R.E. 1984. *Strategic Management: A Stakeholder Approach.* Boston: Pitman.

French, J., and Raven, B.H. 1959. "The Bases of Social Power." In *Studies in Social Power,* ed. D. Cartwright. Ann Arbor: University of Michigan.

French, W.L., and Bell, C.H., Jr. 1999. *Organization Development: Behavioral Science Interventions for Organization Improvement.* 6th ed. Upper Saddle River, NJ: Prentice Hall.

Friedman, H.S., and Riggio, R.E. 1981. "Effect of Individual Differences in Nonverbal Expressiveness on Transmissions of Emotions." *Journal of Nonverbal Behavior* 6: 96–104.

Friedman, M. 1970. "The Social Responsibility of Business Is to Increase Its Profits." *New York Times Magazine,* September 13.

Friedrich, T.L.; Vessey, W.B.; Schuelke, M.J.; Ruark, G.A.; and Mumford, M.D. 2009. "A Framework for Understanding Collective Leadership: The Selective Utilization of Leader and Team Expertise Within Networks." *Leadership Quarterly* 20: 933–958.

Fry, L.W. 2003. "Toward a Theory of Spiritual Leadership." *Leadership Quarterly* 14: 693–727.

Fry, L.W.; Vitucci, S.; and Cedillo, M. 2005. "Spiritual Leadership and Army Transformation: Theory, Measurement, and Establishing a Baseline." *Leadership Quarterly* 16: 835–862.

Gagné, R.M. 1962. "Military Training and Principles of Learning." *American Psychologist* 17: 83–91.

Galanter, M. 1982. "Charismatic Religious Sects and Psychiatry: An Overview." *American Journal of Psychiatry* 139: 1539–1548.

Gantt, H.L. 1916. *Industrial Leadership.* New Haven, CT: Yale University Press.

Gardner, J.W. 1989. *On Leadership.* New York: Free Press.

Gardner, W.L.; Fischer, D.; and Hunt, J.G. 2009. "Emotional Labor and Leadership: A Threat to Authenticity?" *Leadership Quarterly* 20: 466–482.

Garvin, D.A. 1993. "Building a Learning Organization." *Harvard Business Review* (July–August): 78–91.

Garrett, T.M. 2004. "Whither Challenger, Wither Columbia: Management Decision Making and the Knowledge Analytic." *American Review of Public Administration* 34(4): 389–402.

Gauthier, A. 2008. "Developing Generative Leaders Across Sectors: An Exploration of Integral Approaches." Integral Leadership Review 6 (June). Available at www.integralleadershipreview.com.

George, W. 2003. *Authentic Leadership: Rediscovering the Secrets to Creating Lasting Value.* San Francisco: Jossey-Bass.

Gerencser, M.; Van Lee, R.; Napolitano, F.; and Kelly, C. 2008. *How Leaders of Government, Business and Non-Profits Can Tackle Today's Global Challenges Together.* New York: Palgrave Macmillan.

Ghiselli, E.E. 1963. "Intelligence and Managerial Success." *Psychological Reports* 12: 898–899.

Gilbert, G.R., and Hyde, A. 1988. "Followership and the Federal Worker." *Public Administration Review* 48(6): 962–968.

Gilbreth, F.B., and Gilbreth, L.M. 1917. *Applied Motion Study.* New York: Sturgis and Walton.

Gilligan, C. 1982. *In a Different Voice: Psychological Theory and Women's Development.* Cambridge: Harvard University Press.

Gilman, S.C. 2005. *Ethics Codes and Codes of Conduct as Tools for Promoting an Ethical and Professional Public Service: Comparative Successes and Lessons.* Washington, DC: World Bank (PREM).

Ginter, P.M., and Duncan, W.J. 1990. "Macroenvironmental Analysis for Strategic Management." *Long Range Planning* 23: 91–100.

Gitter, A.G.; Black, H.; and Fishman, J.E. 1975. "Effect of Race, Sex, Nonverbal Communication and Verbal Communication on Perception of Leadership." *Sociological and Social Research* 60: 46–57.

Goffee, R., and Jones, G. 2009. "Authentic Leadership." *Leadership Excellence* 26(7): 17.

Goldsmith, M.; Greenberg, C.L.; Robertson, A.; and HuChan, M. (eds.). 2003. *Global Leadership: The Next Generation.* Upper Saddle River, NJ: Financial Times-Prentice Hall.

Goldsmith, S., and Eggers, W.D. 2004. *Governing by Network: The New Shape of the Public Sector.* Washington, DC: Brookings Institution Press.

Goldstein, A.P., and Sorcher, M. 1974. *Changing Supervisor Behavior.* Elmsford, NY: Pergamon Press.

Goleman, D. 1998. *Working with Emotional Intelligence.* New York: Bantam.

Golembiewski, R.T. 1959. "The Small Group and Public Administration." *Public Administration Review* 19(3): 149–156.

Graeff, C.L. 1997. "Evolution of Situational Leadership Theory: A Critical Review." *Leadership Quarterly* 8(2): 153–170.

Graen, G. 2007. "Asking the Wrong Questions About Leadership." *American Psychologist* 62(6): 604–618.

Graen, G., and Cashman, J.F. 1975. "A Role-Making Model of Leadership in Formal Organizations: A Developmental Approach." In *Leadership Frontiers,* ed. J.G. Hunt and L.L. Larson, 143–165. Kent, OH: Kent State University Press.

Graen, G., and Graen, J.A. (eds.). 2006. *Sharing Network Leadership.* Charlotte, NC: IAP.

———. 2007. *New Multinational Network Sharing.* Charlotte, NC: IAP.

Graen, G., and Uhl-Bien, M. 1995. "Relationship-based Approach to Leadership: Development of Leader-Member Exchange (LMX) Theory of Leadership over 25 Years: Applying a Multi-level Multi-Domain Approach." *Leadership Quarterly* 6(2): 219–247.

Graen, G.; Cashman, J.F.; Ginsburgh, S.; and Schiemann, W. 1977. "Effects of Linking-Pin Quality on the Quality of Working Life of Lower Participants." *Administrative Science Quarterly* 22(3): 491–504.

Graham, J.W. 1991. "Servant Leadership in Organizations: Inspirational and Moral. *Leadership Quarterly* 2: 105–119.

Graham, P. (ed.). 1996. *Mary Parker Follett: Prophet of Management.* Boston: Harvard Business School Press.

Grant, J. 1988. "Women as Managers: What They Can Offer to Organizations." *Organizational Dynamics* 6: 219–247.

Graubard, S.R., and Holton, G. (eds.). 1962. *Excellence and Leadership in a Democracy.* New York: Columbia University Press.

Grayson, C., and Baldwin, D. 2007. *Leadership Networking: Connect, Collaborate, Create.* Greensboro, NC: Center for Creative Leadership.

Greenleaf, R.K. 1977. *Servant Leadership: A Journey into the Nature of Legitimate Power and Greatness.* New York: Paulist Press.

Grinyer, P.H.; Mayes, D.; and McKiernan, P. 1990. "The Sharpbenders: Achieving a Sustained Improvement in Performance." *Long Range Planning* 23: 116–125.

Gronn, P. 2002. "Distributed Leadership as a Unit of Analysis." *Leadership Quarterly* 13: 481–490.

Gulick, L. 1937. "Notes on the Theory of Organization." In *Papers on the Science of Administration,* ed. L. Gulick and L. Urwick. New York: Institute of Public Administration.

Gulick, L., and Urwick, L. (eds.). 1937. *Papers on the Science of Administration.* New York: Institute of Public Administration.

Guy, M.E., and Newman, M.A. 1998. "Toward Diversity in the Workplace." In *Handbook of Human Resource Management in Government,* ed. S.E. Condrey, 75–92. San Francisco: Jossey-Bass.

Guyot, J.F. 1962. "Government Bureaucrats Are Different." *Public Administration Review* 22(4): 195–202.

Haas, P.J. 2003. "The Use of Performance Indicators in State Administration." In *Encyclopedia of Public Administration and Public Policy,* ed. Jack Rabin, 898–900. New York: Marcel Dekker.

Hackman, J.R. (ed.). 1990. *Groups That Work and Those That Don't.* San Francisco: Jossey-Bass.

Halachmi, A. 2003. "Strategic Management and Productivity." In *Encyclopedia of Public Administration and Public Policy,* ed. Jack Rabin, 1157–1164. New York: Marcel Dekker.

Hall, E.T. 1976. *Beyond Culture.* New York, NY: Doubleday.

Hambleton, R.K., and Gumpert, R. 1982. "The Validity of Hersey and Blanchard's Theory of Leader Effectiveness." *Group and Organization Studies* 7: 225–242.

Hambrick, D.C., and Fukutomi, G.D.S. 1991. "The Seasons of a CEO's Tenure." *Academy of Management Review* 16: 719–742.

Hammer, M., and Champy, J. 1993. *Reengineering the Corporation: A Manifesto for Business Revolution.* New York: HarperCollins.

Hannah, S.T., and Lester, P. 2009. "A Multilevel Approach to Building and Leading Learning Organizations." *Leadership Quarterly* 20: 34–48.

Hannah, S.T.; Avolio, B.J.; Luthans, F.; and Harms, P.D. 2008. "Leadership Efficacy: Review and Future Directions." *Leadership Quarterly* 19: 669–692.

Harari, O. 2002. *The Leadership Secrets of Colin Powell.* New York: McGraw-Hill.

Hart, D.K. 1992. "The Moral Exemplar in an Organizational Society." In *Exemplary Public Administrators: Character and Leadership in Government,* ed. T.L. Cooper and D.N. Wright, 9–29. San Francisco: Jossey-Bass.

Hatry, H.P. 1999. *Performance Measurement: Getting Results.* Washington, DC: Urban Institute.

Heclo, H. 1977. *A Government of Strangers: Executive Politics in Washington.* Washington, DC: Brookings Institution.

Heidensohn, F. 1995. *Women in Control? The Role of Women in Law Enforcement.* Oxford, UK: Clarendon Oxford Press.

Heifetz, R.A. 1994. *Leadership Without Easy Answers.* Cambridge, MA: Belknap Press.

Heilman, M.E. 2001. "Description and Prescription: How Gender Stereotypes Prevent Women's Ascent up the Organizational Ladder." *Journal of Social Issues* 57: 657–674.

Heilman, M.E., and Okimoto, T.G. 2007. "Why Are Women Penalized for Success at Male Tasks? The Implied Communality Deficit." *Journal of Applied Psychology* 92: 81–92.

Hejka-Ekins, A. 1992. "Moral Courage in Exposing Corruption." In *Exemplary Public Administrators: Character and Leadership in Government,* ed. T.L. Cooper and D.N. Wright, ch. 12. San Francisco: Jossey-Bass.

Helms, J.D. 1998. "Natural Resources Conservation Service." In *A Historical Guide to the U.S. Government,* ed. G.T. Kurian, 434–439. New York: Oxford University Press.

Hempill, J.K. 1950. *Leader Behavior Description*. Columbus: Ohio State University, Personnel Research Board.

Hempill, J.K., and Coons, A.E. 1957. "Development of the Leader Behavior Questionnaire." In *Leader Behavior: Its Description and Measurement,* ed. R.M. Stogdill and A.E. Coons. Columbus: Ohio State University, Bureau of Business Research.

Hennan, D.A., and Bennis, W. 1999. *Co-Leadership: The Power of Great Partnerships*. New York: Wiley.

Hennessey, J.T. 1998. "Reinventing Government: Does Leadership Make the Difference?" *Public Administration Review* 58(6): 522–532.

Henry, N. 2003. *Public Administration and Public Affairs*. 9th ed. Upper Saddle River, NJ: Prentice Hall.

Henton, D.; Melville, J.; and Walesh, K. 1997. *Grassroots Leaders for a New Economy: How Civic Entrepreneurs Are Building Prosperous Communities*. San Francisco: Jossey-Bass.

Hersey, P., and Blanchard, K.H. 1969. "Life Cycle Theory of Leadership." *Training and Development Journal* 23(1): 26–34.

———. 1972. "The Management of Change." *Training and Development Journal* 26(2): 20–24.

Hinkin, T.R., and Schriesheim, C.A. 1989. "Development and Application of New Scales to Measure the French and Raven Bases of Social Power." *Journal of Applied Psychology* 74: 561–567.

Hodgetts, R.M.; Luthans, F.; and Doh, J.P. 2006. *International Management: Culture, Strategy, and Behavior*. 6th ed. New York, NY: McGraw-Hill/Irwin.

Hofstede, G. 1980. *Culture's Consequences: International Differences in Work-Related Values*. Beverly Hills, CA: Sage.

———. 2001. *Culture's Consequences: Comparing Values, Behaviors, Institutions, and Organizations across Nations*. Thousand Oaks, CA: Sage.

Hogue, M., and Lord, R.G. 2007. "A Multilevel, Complexity Theory Approach to Understanding Gender Bias in Leadership." *Leadership Quarterly* 18: 370–390.

Hollander, E.P. 1958. "Conformity, Status, and Idiosyncrasy Credit." *Psychological Review* 65: 117–127.

Hollenbeck, G.P.; McCall, M.W.; and Silzer, R.F. 2006. "Leadership Competency Models." *Leadership Quarterly* 17(4): 398–413.

Hollingworth, L.S. 1926. *Gifted Children*. New York: Macmillan.

Holzer, M. 2008. "Culture and Leadership." In *Innovations in Public Leadership Development,* ed. R.S. Morse and T.F. Buss. Armonk, NY: M.E. Sharpe.

Holzer, M., and Illiash, I. 2009. "Russian Bureaucracy as an Alternative Model of Leadership." In *Public Sector Leadership: International Challenges and Perspectives,* ed. J.A. Raffel, P. Leisink, and A.E. Middlebrooks. Northampton, MA: Edward Elgar.

Holzer, M., and Lee, S.H. 2004. *Public Productivity Handbook*. 2d ed. New York: Marcel Dekker.

Homans, G. 1958. "Social Behavior as Exchange." *American Journal of Sociology* 63: 597–606.

Hook, S. 1943. *The Hero in History*. New York: John Day.

Hoppe, M. 2006. *Active Listening*. Greensboro, NC: Center for Creative Leadership.

Houghton, J.D.; Neck, C.P.; and Manz, C.C. 2003. "Self-Leadership and Superleadership: The Heart and Art of Creating Shared Leadership in Teams." In *Reframing the Hows and Whys of Leadership,* ed. C.L. Pearce and J.A. Conger, 123–140. Thousand Oaks, CA: Sage.

House, R.J. 1971. "A Path-Goal Theory of Leadership Effectiveness." *Administrative Science Quarterly* 16: 321–339.

———. 1977. "A 1976 Theory of Charismatic Leadership." In *Leadership: The Cutting Edge,* ed. J.G. Hunt and L.L. Larson. Carbondale: Southern Illinois Press.

———. 1996. "Path-Goal Theory of Leadership: Lessons, Legacy, and a Reformulated Theory." *Leadership Quarterly* 7: 323–352.

House, R.J., and Mitchell, T.R. 1974. "Path-Goal Theory of Leadership." *Contemporary Business* 3 (Fall): 81–98.

House, R.J.; Spangler, W.D.; and Woycke, J. 1991. "Personality and Charisma in the U.S. Presidency: A Psychological Theory of Leadership Effectiveness." *Administrative Science Quarterly* 36: 364–396.

House, R.J.; Hanges, P.J.; Javidian, M.; Dorfman, P.W.; Gupta, V.; et al. (eds.). 2004. *Culture, Leadership, and Organizations: The GLOBE Study of 62 Societies.* Thousand Oaks, CA: Sage.

Howard, A., and Bray, D.W. 1988. *Managerial Lives in Transition: Advancing Age and Changing Times.* New York: Guilford Press.

Howell, J.P.; Dorfman, P.W.; and Kerr, S. 1986. "Moderator Variables in Leadership Research." *Academy of Management Review* 11: 88–102.

Huczynski, A.A., and Lewis, J.W. 1980. "An Empirical Study into the Learning Transfer Process in Management Training." *Journal of Management* Studies 17: 542–552.

Hui, C.H.; Chiu, W.; Yu, P.; Cheng, K.; and Tse, H. H. M. 2007. "The Effects of Service Climate and the Effective Leadership Behaviour of Supervisors on Frontline Employee Service Quality: A Multilevel Analysis." *Journal of Occupational and Organizational Psychology* 80(1): 151-172.

Hunt, J.G. 1996. *Leadership: A New Synthesis.* Newbury Park, CA: Sage.

Hunt, J.G.; Dodge, G.E.; and Wong, L. (eds.). 1999. *Out-of-the-Box Leadership: Transforming the Twenty-First Century Army and Other Top-Performing Organizations.* Stamford, CT: JAI Press.

Iacocca, L. 1984. *Iacocca: An Autobiography.* New York: Bantam.

Ilies, R.; Nahrgang, J.D.; and Morgeson, F.P. 2007. "Leader-Member Exchange and Citizenship Behaviors: A Meta-Analysis." *Journal of Applied Psychology* 92(1): 269–277.

Jackson, P.M., and Stainsby, L. 2000. "Managing Public Sector Networked Organizations." *Public Money and Management* 20(1): 11–16,

Jacobs, T.O., and Jaques, E. 1987. "Leadership in Complex Systems." In *Human Productivity Enhancement: Organizations, Personnel, and Decision Making,* vol. 2, ed. J. Zeidner, 7–65. New York: Praeger.

Jaques, E. 1989. *Requisite Organization.* Arlington, VA: Cason Hall.

Javidan, M., and Waldman, D.A. 2003. Exploring Charismatic Leadership in the Public Sector: Measurement and Consequences." *Public Administration Review* 63(2): 229–242.

Jenkins, W.O. 1947. "A Review of Leadership Studies with Particular Reference to Military Problems." *Psychological Bulletin* 44: 54–79.

Jennings, E.E. 1960. *An Anatomy of Leadership: Princes, Heroes, and Supermen.* New York: Harper.

Jennings, H.H. 1943. *Leadership and Isolation.* New York: Longmans, Green.

Jermier, J.M., and Berkes, L.J. 1979. "Leader Behavior in a Police Command Bureaucracy: A Closer Look at the Quasi-Military Model." *Administrative Science Quarterly* 24: 1–23.

Johnson, C.R. 2005. *Meeting the Ethical Challenge of Leadership.* 2d ed. Thousand Oaks, CA: Sage.

Johnston, J. 1998. "Agency Mission." In *The International Encyclopedia of Public Policy and Administration,* ed. Jay Shafritz, 96–98. Boulder, CO: Westview.

Jones, A.M. 2005. "The Anthropology of Leadership: Culture and Corporate Leadership in the American South." *Leadership* 1(3): 259–278.

Jones, S.R.G. 1990. "Worker Interdependence and Output: The Hawthorne Studies Reevaluated." *American Sociological Review* 55(2): 176–190.

Judge, T.A.; Piccolo, R.F.; and Kosalka, T. 2009. "The Bright and Dark Sides of Leader Traits: A Review and Theoretical Extension." *Leadership Quarterly* 20: 855–875.

Kaiser, R.B.; Hogan, R.; and Craig, S.B. 2008. "Leadership and the Fate of Organizations." *American Psychologist* 63(2): 96–110.

Kanfer, E.H. 1970. "Self-Regulation: Research, Issues, and Speculations." In *Behavioral Modification in Clinical Psychology,* ed. C. Neuringer and J.L. Michael, 178–220. New York: Appleton-Century-Crofts.

Kant, I. 1787/1996. *Critique of Pure Reason.* (Werner S. Pluher, Trans.) Indianapolis, IN: Hackett Publishing Co.

Kanter, R.M. 1983. *The Change Masters.* New York: Simon and Schuster.

———. 1994. "Collaborative Advantage: The Art of Alliances." *Harvard Business Review* 72(4): 96–108.

Kanter, R.M.; Stein, B.A.; and Jick, T.D. 1992. *The Challenges of Organizational Change: How Companies Experience It and Leaders Guide It.* New York: Free Press.

Kaplan. R.E. 1984. "Trade Routes: The Manager's Network of Relationships." *Organizational Dynamics* 13 (Spring): 37–52.

Kaplan, R.S., and Norton, D.K. 1996. *The Balanced Scorecard.* Boston: Harvard Business School Press.

Kapucu, N., and Van Wart, M. 2006. "The Evolving Role of the Public Sector in Managing Catastrophic Disasters: Lessons Learned." *Administration and Society* 38(3): 1–30.

———. 2008. "Making Matters Worse: Anatomy of Leadership Failures in Catastrophic Events." *Administration and Society* 40(7): 711–740.

Katz, D., and Kahn, R.L. 1978. *The Social Psychology of Organizations.* 2d ed. New York: Wiley.

Katz, R.L. 1955. "Skills of an Effective Administrator." *Harvard Business Review* 33: 33–42.

Katzenbach, J.R., and Smith, D.K. 1993. *The Wisdom of Teams: Creating the High Performance Organization.* Boston: Harvard Business School Press.

Kaufman, H. 1976. *Are Government Organizations Immortal?* Washington, DC: Brookings Institution.

———. 1981. *The Administrative Behavior of Federal Bureau Chiefs.* Washington, DC: Brookings Institution.

Kearns, K.P. 1998. "Mission Statement." In *The International Encyclopedia of Public Policy and Administration,* ed. Jay Shafritz, 1412–1414. Boulder, CO: Westview.

Kee, J.E.; Newcomer, K.; and Davis, S.M. 2008. "A New Vision for Public Leadership: The Case for Developing Transformational Stewards." In *Innovations in Public Leadership Development,* ed. R.S. Morse and T.F. Buss. Armonk, NY: M.E. Sharpe.

Kellerman, B. 2007. "What Every Leader Needs to Know about Followers." *Harvard Business Review* 85(12): 84–91.

———. 2008. *Followership: How Followers Are Creating Change and Changing Leaders.* Boston: Harvard Business Press.

Kellerman, B., and Rhode, D.L. (eds.). 2007. *Women and Leadership: The State of Play and Strategies for Change.* San Francisco: Jossey-Bass.

Kelly, E.; Davis, B.; Nelson, J.; and Mendoza, J. 2008. "Leader Emergence in an Internet Environment." *Computers in Human Behavior* 24: 2372–2383.

Kelly, S. 2008. "Leadership: A Categorical Mistake?" *Human Relations* 61(6): 763–782.

Kerr, S. 1977. "Substitutes for Leadership: Some Implications for Organizational Design." *Organization and Administrative Sciences* 8: 135–146.

Kerr, S., and Jermier, J.M. 1978. "Substitutes for Leadership: Their Meaning and Measurement." *Organizational Behavior and Human Performance* 22: 375–403.

Kets de Vries, M.F.R. 1985. "Narcissism and Leadership: An Object Relations Perspective." *Human Relations* 38: 583–601.

———. 1988. "Prisoners of Leadership." *Human Relations* 41(3): 261–280.

Kets de Vries, M.F.R., and Miller, D. 1984. *The Neurotic Organization: Diagnosing and Changing Counter-Productive Styles of Management.* San Francisco: Jossey-Bass.

Kettl, D.F. 1994. "Managing on the Frontiers of Knowledge: The Learning Organization." In *New Paradigms for Government: Issues for the Changing Public Service,* ed. P.W. Ingraham and B.S. Romzek, 19–40. San Francisco: Jossey-Bass.

———. 2006. "Managing Boundaries in American Administration: The Collaboration Imperative." *Public Administration Review* 66 (Supplement): 10–19.

Khan, A. 1998. "Strategic Budgeting." In *The International Encyclopedia of Public Policy and Administration,* ed. Jay Shafritz, 2145–2150. Boulder, CO: Westview.

Kiel, L.D. 1994. *Managing Chaos and Complexity in Government.* San Francisco: Jossey-Bass.

Kim, H., and Yukl, G. 1995. "Relationships of Management Games and Simulation in Education and Research." *Journal of Management* 16: 307–336.

Kim, J.S., and Hammer, W.C. 1976. "Effects of Performance Feedback and Goal Setting on Productivity and Satisfaction in an Organizational Setting." *Journal of Applied Psychology* 61(1): 48–57.

King, S. 1981. *Danse Macbre*. New York: Berkley Books.

Kingdon, J. 1984. *Agendas, Alternatives, and Public Policies*. Boston: Little, Brown.

Kinslaw, D.C. 1990. "Improving the Use of Behavior Modeling in Communication and Coaching Skills Training." *Annual Developing Human Resources*: 241–248.

Kirkman, B.L., and Rosen, B. 1999. "Beyond Self-Management: Antecedents and Consequences of Team Empowerment." *Academy of Management Journal* 42: 58–74.

Klauss, R., and Bass, B.M. 1982. *Interpersonal Communication*. New York: Academic Press.

Klijn, E.H.; Koopenjan, J.F.M.; and Termeer, C.J.A.M. 1995. "Managing Networks in the Public Sector." *Public Administration Review* 23(3): 437–454.

Kluckhohn, R., and Strodtbeck, F.L. 1961. *Variations in Value Orientations*. New York: HarperCollins.

Kohlberg, L. 1981. *The Philosophy of Moral Development: Moral Stages and the Idea of Justice*. Vol. 1. New York: Simon and Schuster.

Komaki, J. 1986. "Toward Effective Supervision: An Operant Analysis and Comparison of Managers at Work." *Journal of Applied Psychology* 71: 270–278.

Kort, E.D. 2008. "What, After All Is Leadership? 'Leadership' and Plural Action." *Leadership Quarterly* 19: 409–425.

Kotter, J.P. 1982. *The General Managers*. New York: Free Press.

———. 1990. *A Force for Change: How Leadership Differs from Management*. New York: Free Press.

Kouzes, J.M., and Posner, B.Z. 1987. *The Leadership Challenge: How to Get Extraordinary Things Done in Organizations*. San Francisco: Jossey-Bass.

———. 1993. *Credibility: How Leaders Gain and Lose It, Why People Demand It*. San Francisco: Jossey-Bass.

Kraut, A.I.; Pedigo, P.R.; McKenna, D.D.; and Dunnette, M.D. 1989. "The Role of the Manager: What's Really Important in Different Management Jobs." *Academy of Management Executive* 3(4): 286–293.

Kuhn, T. 1962. *The Structure of Scientific Revolutions*. Chicago: University of Chicago Press.

Lambright, W.H. 2008. "Leadership and Change at NASA: Sean O'Keefe as Administrator." *Public Administration Review* 68(2): 230–240.

Larson, J.R., and Callahan, C. 1990. "Performance Monitoring: How It Affects Productivity." *Journal of Applied Psychology* 75: 530–538.

Latham, G.P., and Baldes, J.J. 1975. "The 'Practical Significance' of Locke's Theory of Goal Setting." *Journal of Applied Psychology* 60(1): 122–124.

Latham, G.P., and Saari, L.M. 1979. "Application of Social Learning Theory to Training Supervisors Through Behavioral Modeling." *Journal of Applied Psychology* 64(3): 239–246.

Latham, G.P., and Yukl, G.A. 1975. "A Review of the Research on the Application of Goal Setting in Organizations." *Academy of Management Journal* 18(4): 824–846.

Latham, G.P.; Wexley, K.N.; and Pursell, E.D. 1975. "Training Managers to Minimize Rating Errors in the Observation of Behavior." *Journal of Applied Psychology* 60(5): 500–555.

Lawler, J. 2008. "Individualization and Public Sector Leadership." *Public Administration* 86(1): 21–34.

Lawrence, K.A.; Lenk, P.; and Quinn, R.E. 2009. "Behavioral Complexity in Leadership: The Psychometric Properties of a New Instrument to Measure Behavioral Repertoire." *Leadership Quarterly* 20: 87–102.

Lawton, F.J. 1954. "The Role of the Administrator in the Federal Government." *Public Administration Review* 14(2): 112–118.

Lefkowitz, J. 1994. "Sex-Related Differences in Job Attitudes and Dispositional Variables: Now You See Them. . . ." *Academy of Management Journal* 37: 323–349.

Lehman, H.C. 1937. "The Creative Years in Science and Literature." *Science Monitor* 45: 65–75.

———. 1942. "Optimum Ages for Eminent Leadership." *Science Monitor* 54: 162–175.

———. 1953. *Age and Achievement.* Princeton, NJ: Princeton University Press.

Lemay, L. 2009. "The Practice of Collective and Strategic Leadership in the Public Sector." *Innovation Journal: Public Sector Innovation Journal* 14(1): 1–19.

Lewin, K. 1951. *Field Theory in Social Science.* New York: Harper.

Lewis, E. 1980. *Public Entrepreneurship: Toward a Theory of Bureaucratic Political Power.* Bloomington: Indiana University Press.

Leys, W.A.R. 1943. "Ethics and Administrative Discretion." *Public Administration Review* 3(1): 10–23.

Lichtenstein, B.B., and Plowman, D.A. 2009. "The Leadership of Emergence: A Complex Systems Leadership Theory of Emergence at Successive Organizational Levels." *Leadership Quarterly* 20: 617–630.

Liden, R.C.; Wayne, S.J.; Zhao, H.; and Henderson, D. 2008. "Servant Leadership: Development of a Multidimensional Measure and Multilevel Assessment." *Leadership Quarterly* 19: 161–177.

Light, P.C. 2008. "A Government Ill Executed: The Depletion of the Federal Service." *Public Administration Review* 68(3): 413–419.

Likert, R. 1959. "Motivational Approach to Management Development." *Harvard Business Review* 37: 75–82.

———. 1961. *New Patterns of Management.* New York: McGraw-Hill.

———. 1967. *The Human Organization: Its Management and Value.* New York: McGraw-Hill.

———. 1981. "System 4: A Resource for Improving Public Administration." *Public Administration Review* 41(6): 674–678.

Lindblom, C.E. 1959. "The Science of Muddling Through." *Public Administration Review* 19(3): 79–88.

Lindholm, C. 1988. "Lovers and Leaders: Comparative Models of Romance and Charisma." *Social Science Information* 27(1): 3–45.

Lipman-Blumen, J. 2000. *Connective Leadership: Managing in a Changing World.* New York: Oxford University Press.

Locke, E.A. 1980. "Latham Versus Komaki: A Tale of Two Paradigms." *Journal of Applied Psychology* 65(1): 16–23.

———. 2003. "Leadership: Starting at the Top." In *Shared Leadership: Reframing the Hows and Whys of Leadership,* ed. C.L. Pearce and J.A. Conger, 271–284. Thousand Oaks, CA: Sage.

Locke, E.A., and Latham, G. P. 1990. *A Theory of Goal Setting and Task Performance.* Englewood Cliffs, NJ: Prentice Hall.

Logan, D.; King, J.; and Fischer-Wright, H. 2008. *Tribal Leadership.* New York: Collins.

Lombardo, M.M., and McCauley, C.D. 1988. *The Dynamics of Management Derailment.* Greensboro, NC: Center for Creative Leadership.

Lorange, P. 1980. *Corporate Planning: An Executive Viewpoint.* Englewood Cliffs, NJ: Prentice Hall.

Lord, R.G., and Hall, R.J. 2005. "Identity, Deep Structure and the Development of Leadership Skill." *Leadership Quarterly* 16: 591–615.

Lord, R.G., and Maher, K.J. 1991. *Leadership and Information Processing: Linking Perceptions and Performance.* Boston: Unwin-Hyman.

Lord, R.G.; DeVader, C.L.; and Alliger, G.M. 1986. "A Meta-Analysis of the Relation Between Personality Traits and Leadership Perceptions: An Application of Validity Generalization Procedures." *Journal of Applied Psychology* 71: 402–410.

Loveday, B. 2008. "Performance Management and the Decline of Leadership within Public Services in the United Kingdom." *Policing* 2(1): 120–130.

Luke, J.S. 1998. *Catalytic Leadership: Strategies for an Interconnected World*. San Francisco: Jossey-Bass.

Lundstedt, S. 1965. "Administrative Leadership and Use of Social Power." *Public Administration Review* 25(2): 156–160.

Luthans, F. 2007. "Emerging Positive Organizational Behavior." *Journal of Management* 33(3): 321–349.

Luthans, F., and Davis, T. 1979. "Behavioral Self-Management (BSM): The Missing Link in Managerial Effectiveness." *Organizational Dynamics* 8: 42–60.

Luthans, F.; Rosenkrantz, S.A.; and Hennessey, H.W. 1985. "What Do Successful Managers Really Do? An Observational Study of Managerial Activities." *Journal of Applied Behavioral Science* 21: 255–270.

Luthans, F.; Vogelgesang, G.R.; and Lester, P.B. 2006. "Developing the Psychological Capital of Resiliency." *Human Resource Development Review* 5(1): 25–44.

Lyon, A.J. 2006/07. "Moral Motives and Policy Actions: The Case of Dag Hammarskjold at the United Nations." *Public Integrity* 9(1): 70–95.

Lynn, L. 1996. *Public Management as Art, Science and Profession*. Chatham, NJ: Chatham House Publishers.

Maak, T., and Pless, N.M. (eds.). 2006. *Responsible Leadership: A Relational Approach*. London: Routledge.

Machiavelli, N. 1998. *The Prince*. Oxford: Oxford University Press.

MacKenzie, R.A. 1969. "The Management Process in 3-D. *Harvard Business Review* 47(6): 80–87.

Macmahon, A.W., and Millett, J.D. 1939. *Federal Administrators: A Biographical Approach to the Problem of Departmental Management*. New York: Columbia University Press.

Mahoney, M.J., and Arnkoff, D.B. 1978. "Cognitive and Self-Control Therapies." In *Handbook of Psychotherapy and Therapy Change*, ed. S.L. Garfield and A.E. Borgin, 689–722. New York: Wiley.

Mahoney, T.A.; Jerdee, T.H.; and Carroll, S.J., Jr. 1965. "The Jobs of Management." *Industrial Relations* 4: 97–110.

Mainiero, L. 1994. "Getting Anointed for Advancement: The Case of Executive Women." *Academy of Management Executive* 8(2): 53–67.

Makri, M., and Scandura, T.A. 2010. "Exploring the Effects of Creative CEO Leadership on Innovation in High-Technology Firms." *Leadership Quarterly* 21: 75–88.

Mann, R.D. 1959. "A Review of the Relationship Between Personality and Performance in Small Groups." *Psychological Bulletin* 56: 241–270.

Manz, C.C. 1986. "Self-Leadership: Toward an Expanded Theory of Self-Influence Processes in Organizations." *Academy of Management Review* 11: 585–600.

———. 1992. *Mastering Self-Leadership: Empowering Yourself for Personal Excellence*. Englewood Cliffs, NJ: Prentice Hall.

Manz, C.C., and Sims, H.P., Jr. 1980. "Self-Management as a Substitute for Leadership: A Social Learning Perspective." *Academy of Management Review* 5: 105–128.

———. 1987. "Leading Workers to Lead Themselves: The External Leadership of Self-Managing Work Teams." *Administrative Science Quarterly* 32: 106–128.

———. 1989. *Superleadership: Leading Others to Lead Themselves*. Englewood Cliffs, NJ: Prentice Hall.

———. 1991. "Superleadership: Beyond the Myth of Heroic Leadership." *Organizational Dynamics* 19: 18–35.

———. 1993. *Business Without Bosses: How Self-Managing Teams Are Building High-Performing Companies*. New York: Wiley.

Manz, C.C.; Adsit, D.J.; Dennis, J.; Campbell, S.; and Mathison-Hance, M. 1988. "Managerial Thought Patterns and Performance: A Study of Perceptual Patterns of Performance Hindrances for Higher and Lower Performing Managers." *Human Relations* 41: 447–465.

Manz, C.C.; Anand, V.; Joshi, M.; and Manz, K. 2008. "Emerging Paradoxes in Executive Leadership: A Theoretical Interpretation of the Tensions Between Corruption and Virtuous Values." *Leadership Quarterly* 19: 385–392.

Marshall, J. 1953. "Spirit and Function of Organizations." In *Freedom and Authority in Our Times.* New York: Conference on Science, Philosophy, and Religion.

Maslow, A. 1967. *Eupsychian Management.* Homewood, IL: Dorsey.

Maslow, A.H. 1954. *Motivation and Personality.* New York: Harper.

Matthews, D.R. 1954. *The Social Background of Political Decision-Makers.* New York: Random House.

Mau, T.A. 2009. "Is Public Sector Leadership Distinct? A Comparative Analysis of Core Competencies in the Senior Executive Service." In *Public Sector Leadership: International Challenges and Perspectives,* ed. J.A. Raffel, P. Leisink, and A.E. Middlebrooks. Northampton, MA: Edward Elgar.

Maxwell, J. 2008. "Charismatic Leadership: Develop Seven Qualities." *Leadership Excellence* 25(11): 13.

McCall, M.; Lombardo, M.M.; and Morrison, A.M. 1988. *The Lessons of Experience: How Successful Executives Develop on the Job.* New York: Lexington Books.

McCauley, C.D., and Lombardo, M.M. 1990. "Benchmarks: An Instrument for Diagnosing Strengths and Weaknesses." In *Measures of Leadership,* ed. K. Clark and M.B. Clark, 535–547. West Orange, NJ: Leadership Library of America.

McClelland, D.C. 1961. *The Achieving Society.* Princeton, NJ: Van Nostrand.

———. 1965. "N-Achievement and Entrepreneurship: A Longitudinal Study." *Journal of Personality and Social Psychology* 1: 389–392.

———. 1985. *Human Motivation.* Glenview, IL: Scott Foresman.

McCrimmon, M. 2007. "Reframing Leadership for a Modern Age." *Integral Leadership Review* 7(2): 1–6.

McGregor, D. 1960. *The Human Side of Enterprise.* New York: McGraw-Hill.

McGuire, M. 2006. "Collaborative Public Management: Assessing What We Know and How We Know It." *Public Administration Review* 66 (Supplement): 33–43.

McKenna, B.; Rooney, D.; and Boal, K.B. 2009. "Wisdom Principles as a Meta-Theoretical Basis for Evaluating Leadership." *Leadership Quarterly* 20: 177–190.

Meindl, J.R. 1990. "On Leadership: An Alternative to the Conventional Wisdom." *Research in Organizational Behavior* 12: 159–203.

Menzel, D.C. 2007. *Ethics Management for Public Administrators: Building Organizations of Integrity.* Armonk, NY: M.E. Sharpe.

Merton, R.K. 1940. "Bureaucratic Structure and Personality." *Social Forces* 18: 560–568.

Miller, D.; Kets de Vries, M.F.R.; and Toulouse, J. 1982. "Locus of Control and Its Relationship to Strategy, Environment, and Structure." *Academy of Management Journal* 25: 237–253.

Miner, J.B. 1978. "Twenty Years of Research on Role-Motivation Theory of Managerial Effectiveness." *Personnel Psychology* 31: 739–760.

———. 1982. "The Uncertain Future of the Leadership Concept: Revisions and Clarifications." *Journal of Behavioral Science* 18: 293–307.

Minerals Management Service. 2010. www.mms.gov.

Mintzberg, H. 1973. *The Nature of Managerial Work.* New York: Harper and Row.

———. 1979. *The Structuring of Organizations.* Englewood Cliffs, NJ: Prentice Hall.

———. 1994. *The Rise and Fall of Strategic Planning.* New York: Free Press.

Mintzberg, H., and Quinn, J. 1991. *The Strategy Process.* 2d ed. Englewood Cliffs, NJ: Prentice Hall.

Moon, M.J. 1999. "The Pursuit of Managerial Entrepreneurship: Does Organization Matter?" *Public Administration Review* 59(1): 31–43.

Mooney, J.D., and Reiley, A.C. 1939. *The Principles of Organization.* New York: Harper and Row.

Morales, A., ed. 2007. *The Business of Government.* Washington, DC: IBM Global Business Services.

Morey, D.; Maybury, M.; and Thuraisingham, B. 2002. *Knowledge Management: Classic and Contemporary Works*. Cambridge, MA: MIT Press.

Morgeson, F.P.; Lindoerfer, D.; and Loring, D.J. 2010. "Developing Team Leadership Capability." In *Handbook of Leadership Development*, 3r ed., ed. E. Van Velsor, C. McCauley, and M. Ruderman. San Francisco: Jossey-Bass.

Morison, E.E. 1968. *Admiral Sims and the Modern American Navy*. New York: Russell and Russell.

Morrow, I.J., and Stern, J. 1990. "Stars, Adversaries, Producers, and Phantoms at Work: A New Leadership Typology." In *Measures of Leadership*, ed. K. Clark and M.B. Clark, 419–439. West Orange, NJ: Leadership Library of America.

Morse, J.J., and Wagner, F.R. 1978. "Measuring the Process of Managerial Effectiveness." *Academy of Management Journal* 21: 23–35.

Morse, R.S. 2008. "Developing Public Leaders in an Age of Collaborative Governance." In *Innovations in Public Leadership Development*, ed. R.S. Morse and T.F. Buss. Armonk, NY: M.E. Sharpe.

Morse, R.S., and Buss, T.F. (eds.). 2008. *Innovations in Public Leadership Development*. Armonk, NY: M.E. Sharpe.

Morse, R.S.; Buss, T.F.; and Kinghorn, C.M. (eds.). 2007. *Transforming Public Leadership for the 21st Century*. Armonk, NY: M.E. Sharpe.

Moses, J.L., and Ritchie, R.J. 1976. "Supervisory Relationships Training: A Behavioral Evaluation of a Behavioral Modeling Program." *Personnel Psychology* 29: 337–343.

Moss, S.A.; Dowling, N.; and Callanan, J. 2009. "Towards an Integrated Model of Leadership and Self Regulation." *Leadership Quarterly* 20: 162–176.

Moynihan, D.P., and Pandey, S.K. 2007. "The Role of Organizations in Fostering Public Service Motivation." *Public Administration Review* 67(1): 40–53.

Mulder, M., and Stemerding, A. 1963. "Threat, Attraction to Group, and Need for Strong Leadership." *Human Relations* 16: 317–334.

Mulder, M.; deJong, R.D.; Koppelaar, L.; and Verhage, J. 1986. "Power, Situation, and Leader's Effectiveness: An Organizational Study." *Journal of Applied Psychology* 71: 566–570.

Mumford, M.D.; Fleishman, E.A.; Levin, K.Y.; Korotkin, A.L.; and Hein, M.B. 1988. *Taxonomic Efforts in the Description of Leadership Behavior: A Synthesis and Cognitive Interpretation*. Fairfax, VA: George Mason University Center for Behavioral and Cognitive Studies.

Murphy, A.J. 1941. "A Study of the Leadership Process." *American Sociological Review* 6: 674–687.

Neider, L.L., and Schriesheim, C.A. 1988. "Making Leadership Effective: A Three-Stage Model." *Journal of Management Development* 7(5): 10–20.

Newcomb, T.M. 1961. *The Acquaintance Process*. New York: Holt, Rinehart and Winston.

Newcomer, K.E. 1996. "Evaluating Public Programs." In *Handbook of Public Administration*, 2d ed., ed. James L. Perry, 555–573. San Francisco: Jossey-Bass.

Newell, T.; Reeher, G.; and Ronayne, P. 2008. *The Trusted Leader: Building the Relationships that Make Government Work*. Washington, DC: CQ Press.

Newman, M.A.; Guy, M.E.; and Mastracci, S.H. 2009. "Affective Leadership and Emotional Labor." *Public Administration Review* 69(1): 6–20.

Niven, P.R. 2003. *Balanced Scorecard: Step-by-Step for Government and Nonprofit Agencies*. Hoboken, NJ: Wiley.

Nutt, P., and Backoff, R.W. 1993. "A Strategic Management Process for Public and Third-Sector Organizations." *Journal of the American Planning Association* 53: 44–57.

Nutt, P., and Hogan, M. 2008. "Downsizing Guidelines Found in a Success Story." *Public Performance and Management Review* 32(1): 103–131.

Oakley, E., and Krug, D. 1991. *Enlightened Leadership: Getting to the Heart of Change*. New York: Simon and Schuster.

O'Leary, R.; Gerard, C.; and Bingham, L.B. 2006. "Introduction to the Symposium on Collaborative Public Management." *Public Administration Review* 66 (Supplement): 6–9.

Olivero, G.; Bane, D.K.; and Kopelman, R.E. 1997. "Executive Coaching as a Transfer of Training Tool: Effects on Productivity in a Public Agency." *Public Personnel Management* 26: 461–469.

Osborn, R. . and Hunt, J. G. 2007. "Leadership and the Choice of Order: Complexity and Hierarchical Perspectives Near the Edge of Chaos." *Leadership Quarterly* 18: 319–340.

O'Shea, P.G.; Foti, R.J.; Hauenstein, N.M.A.; and Bycio, P. 2009. "Are the Best Leaders Both Transformational and Transactional? A Pattern Analysis." *Leadership* 5(2): 237–259.

Padilla, A.; Hogan, R.; and Kaiser, R.B. 2007. "The Toxic Triangle: Destructive Leaders, Susceptible Followers, and Conducive Environments." *Leadership Quarterly* 18: 176–194.

Page, R. 1987. "The Position Description Questionnaire." In *Handbook of Job Analysis,* ed. S. Gael. New York: Wiley.

Pajunen, K. 2006. "The More Things Change, the More They Remain the Same? Evaluating Strategic Leadership in Organizational Transformations." *Leadership* 2(3): 341–366.

Palanski, M.E., and Yammarino, F.J. 2009. "Integrity and Leadership: A Multi-level Conceptual Framework." *Leadership Quarterly* 20: 405–420.

Parks, S. D. 2005. *Leadership Can Be Taught.* Boston: Harvard Business School Press.

Parolini, J.; Patterson, K.; and Winston, B. 2009. "Distinguishing Between Transformational and Servant Leadership." *Leadership and Organizational Development Journal* 30(3): 274–291.

Parry, K.W., and Proctor-Thomson, S.B. 2002. "Perceived Integrity of Transformational Leaders in Organisational Settings." *Journal of Business Ethics* 35: 76–96.

Parson, H.M. 1978. "What Caused the Hawthorne Effect?" *Administration and Society* 10(3): 259–283.

Paunonen, S.V.; Lönnqvist, J.; Verkasolo, M.; Leikas, S.; and Nissinen, V. 2006. "Narcissism and Emergent Leadership in Military Cadets." *Leadership Quarterly* 17: 475–486.

Pavett, C., and Lau, A. 1983. "Managerial Work: The Influence of Hierarchical Level and Functional Specialty." *Academy of Management Journal* 26: 170–177.

Peale, N.V. 1956. *The Power of Positive Thinking.* New York: Spire Books.

———. 1959. *The Amazing Results of Positive Thinking.* New York: Fawcett Crest Books.

Pearce, C.L., and Conger, J.A. (eds.). 2003a. *Shared Leadership: Reframing the Hows and Whys of Leadership.* Thousand Oaks, CA: Sage.

———. 2003b. "All Those Years Ago: The Historical Underpinnings of Shared Leadership." In *Shared Leadership: Reframing the Hows and Whys of Leadership,* ed. C.L. Pearce and J.A. Conger, 1–18. Thousand Oaks, CA: Sage.

Pearce, C.L.; Conger, J.A.; and Locke, E. 2008. "Shared Leadership Theory." *Leadership Quarterly* 19: 622–628.

Pelletier, G. 1966. "Business Management in French Canada." *Business Quarterly—Canada Management Journal* (Fall): 56–62.

Perry, J.L. 1996. "Measuring Public Service Motivation: An Assessment of Construct Reliability and Validity." *Journal of Public Administration Research and Theory* 6(1): 5–22.

———. 1997. "Antecedents of Public Service Motivation." *Journal of Public Administration Research and Theory* 7(2): 181–197.

Perry, J.L., and Hondeghem, A. 2008. "Building Theory and Empirical Evidence about Public Service Motivation." *International Public Management Journal* 11(1): 3–12.

Pescosolido, A.T. 2001. "Informal Leaders and the Development of Group Efficacy." *Small Group Research* 32(1): 74–93.

Peters, T. 1992. *Liberation Management: Necessary Disorganization for the Nanosecond Nineties.* New York: Fawcett Columbine.

———. 1994. *The Pursuit of WOW! Every Person's Guide to Topsy-Turvy Times.* New York: Vintage Books.

Peters, T., and Austin, N. 1985. *A Passion for Excellence: The Leadership Difference.* New York: Random House.

Pfiffner, J.P. 2003. "Elliot L. Richardson: Exemplar of Integrity and Public Service." *Public Integrity* 5(3): 251–270.

Phillips, D.T., and Loy, J.M. 2003. *Character in Action: The U.S. Coast Guard in Action.* Annapolis, MD: Naval Institute Press.

Pick, K. 2009. "First Among Equals: How Board Leaders Lead." *Corporate Board* 30(176): 21–26.

Pielstick, C.D. 2000. "Formal vs. Informal Leading: A Comparative Analysis." *Journal of Leadership and Organizational Studies* 7(3): 99–114.

Pinchot, G. 1947. *Breaking New Ground.* New York: Harcourt, Brace.

Pittinsky, T.D., and Simon, S. 2007. "Intergroup Leadership." *Leadership Quarterly* 18: 586–605.

Pittinsky, T.D., and Zhu, C. 2005. "Contemporary Public Leadership in China: A Research Review and Consideration." *Leadership Quarterly* 16: 921–939.

Pooley, E. 1991. "Reality 101: Young Prosecutors Get a Dose of the City's Mean Streets." *New York Magazine,* October 21: 36–42.

Pops, G. 2006. "The Ethical Leadership of George C. Marshall." *Public Integrity* 8(2): 165–185.

Porter, A. 1965. "Validity of Socioeconomic Origin as a Predictor of Executive Success." *Journal of Applied Psychology* 49: 11–13.

Porter, M. 1980. *Competitive Strategy: Techniques for Analyzing Industries and Competitors.* New York: Free Press.

———. 1994. *Competitive Strategies for Changing Industries.* Boston: Harvard Business School Press.

Powell, G.N. 1990. "One More Time: Do Female and Male Managers Differ?" *Academy of Management Executive* 4: 68–75.

———. 1993. *Women and Men in Management.* Newbury Park, CA: Sage.

Powell, G.N., and Graves, L.M. 2003. *Women and Men in Management.* 3d ed. Thousand Oaks, CA: Sage.

Powell, G.N.; Butterfield, D.A.; and Parent, J.D. 2002. "Gender and Managerial Stereotypes: Have the Times Changed?" *Journal of Management* 28: 177–193.

Powers, R.G. 1987. *Secrecy and Power: The Life of J. Edgar Hoover.* New York: Free Press.

Prahalad, C.K., and Hamel, G. 1990. "The Core Competence of the Corporation." *Harvard Business Review* 68: 79–91.

Priem, R.L. 1990. "Top Management Team Group Factors, Consensus, and Firm Performance." *Strategic Management Journal* 11: 469–478.

Purvanova, R.K., and Bono, J. E. 2009. "Transformational Leadership in Context: Face-to-Face and Virtual Teams." *Leadership Quarterly* 20: 343–357.

Putnam, R.D. 2007. "E Pluribus Unum: Diversity and Community in the Twenty-First Century—The 2006 Johan Skytte Prize." *Scandinavian Political Studies* 30(2), 137–174.

Quinn, L., and Van Velsor, E. 2010. "Global Responsibility: What It Take to Get It Right." *Leadership in Action* 29(6): 8–13.

Quinn, R.E., and Cameron, K. 1983. "Organizational Life Cycles and the Criteria of Effectiveness." *Management Science* 29: 63–77.

Raffel, J.A.; Leisink, P.; and Middlebrooks, A.E. (eds.). 2009. *Public Sector Leadership: International Challenges and Perspectives.* Northampton, MA: Edward Elgar.

Ragins, B.R.; Townsend, B.; and Mattis, M. 1998. "Perceptions of Mentoring Roles in Cross-Gender Mentoring Relationships." *Journal of Vocational Behavior* 37: 321–339.

Rahim, M.A. 1992. *Managing Conflict in Organizations.* Westport, CT: Praeger.

Rankin, N. 2001. "Raising Performance Through People: The Eighth Competency Survey." *Competency and Emotional Intelligence* 2: 2–23.

Raskin, R.; Novacek, J.; and Hogan, R. 1991. "Narcissistic Self-Esteem Management." *Journal of Personality and Social Psychology* 60: 911–918.

Rauch, C.F., and Behling, O. 1984. "Functionalism: Basis for an Alternative Approach to the Study of Leadership." In *Leaders and Managers: International Perspectives on Managerial Behavior and Leadership,* ed. J.G. Hunt, D.J. Hosking, C.A. Schriesheim, and R. Stewart. Elmsford, NY: Pergamon Press.

Reber, R.A., and Wallin, J.A. 1984. "The Effects of Training, Goal Setting, and Knowledge of Results on Safe Behavior: A Component Analysis." *Academy of Management Journal* 27(3): 544–560.

Reiter-Palmon, R., and Illies, J.J. 2004. "Leadership and Creativity: Understanding Leadership from a Creative Problem-Solving Perspective." *Leadership Quarterly* 15: 55–77.

Remland, M. 1981. "Developing Leadership Skills in Nonverbal Communication: A Situational Perspective." *Journal of Business Communication* 18(3): 17–29.

Revell, K.D. 2008. "Leadership Cannot Be Taught: Teaching Leadership to MPA Students." *Journal of Public Affairs Education* 14(1): 91–110.

Riccucci, N.T. 1995. *Unsung Heroes: Federal Execucrats Making a Difference.* Washington, DC: Georgetown University Press.

Roberts, N.C. 1985. "Transforming Leadership: A Process of Collective Action." *Human Relations* 38: 1023–1046.

Roberts, N.C., and Bradley, R.T. 1988. "Limits of Charisma." In *Charismatic Leadership: The Elusive Factor in Organizational Effectiveness,* ed. J.A. Conger and R.N. Kanungo, 253–275. San Francisco: Jossey-Bass.

Roethlisberger, F.J. 1941. *Management and Morale.* Cambridge, MA: Harvard University Press.

Rohr, J.A. 1989. *Ethics for Bureaucrats.* New York: Marcel Dekker.

Romero, E.J. 2005. "The Effects of Hispanic Ethnicity on the Leadership Process." *International Journal of Leadership Studies* 1(1): 28–43.

Ronen, S., and Shenkar, O. 1985. "Clustering Countries on Attitudinal Dimensions: A Review and Synthesis." *Academy of Management Review* 10(3): 435–454.

Rosenbloom, D.H. 1998. *Public Administration: Understanding Management, Politics, and Law in the Public Sector.* 4th ed. New York: McGraw-Hill.

———. 2000. *Building a Legislative-Centered Public Administration.* Tuscaloosa: University of Alabama Press.

Rosener, J. 1990. "Ways Women Lead." *Harvard Business Review* 6 (November–December): 119–125.

Rosenthal, S.A., and Pittinsky, T.L. 2006. "Narcissistic Leadership." *Leadership Quarterly* 17: 617–633.

Rost, J.C. 1990. *Leadership for the Twenty-First Century.* Westport, CT: Praeger.

Rotter, J.B. 1966. "Generalized Expectancies for Internal Versus External Control of Reinforcement." *Psychological Monographs* 80(Whole no. 609).

Rowold, J., and Heinitz, K. 2007. "Transformational and Charismatic Leadership: Assessing the Convergent, Divergent and Criterion Validity of the MLK and the CKS." *Leadership Quarterly* 18: 121–133.

Rugeley, C., and Van Wart, M. 2006. "Everyday Moral Exemplars: The Case of Sam Medina." *Public Integrity* 8(4): 381–394.

Runde, C.E., and Flanagan, T.A. 2010. *Developing Your Conflict Competence: A Hands-On Guide for Leaders, Managers, Facilitators, and Teams.* San Francisco: Jossey-Bass.

Rusaw, A.C. 2001. *Leading Public Organizations: An Integrative Approach.* Orlando, FL: Harcourt.

Russell, R.F., and Stone, A.G. 2002. "A Review of Servant Leadership Attributes: Developing a Practical Model." *Leadership and Organization Development* 23(3): 145–157.

Sandowsky, D. 1995. "The Charismatic Leader as Narcissist: Understanding the Abuse of Power." *Organizational Dynamics* 24(4): 57–71.

Sarkar, S. 1992. "Models of Reduction and Categories of Reductionism." *Synthese* 91: 167–194.

Savage, C. 2008. "Sex, Drug Use and Graft Cited in Interior Department." *New York Times,* September 10. Available at www.nytimes.com/2008/09/11/washington/11royalty.html.

Schaubroeck, J.; Lam, S. S. K.; and Cha, S.E. 2007. "Embracing Transformational Leadership: Team Values and the Impact of Leader Behavior on Team Performance." *Journal of Applied Psychology* 92(4): 1020–1030.

Schein, E.H. 1985. *Organizational Culture and Leadership: A Dynamic View*. San Francisco: Jossey-Bass.

———. 1988. *Process Consultation*, Vol. 1: *Its Role in Organization Development*. Reading, MA: Addison-Wesley.

Schilling. J. 2009. "From Ineffectiveness to Destruction: A Qualitative Study on the Meaning of Negative Leadership." *Leadership* 5(1): 102–128.

Schneider, M., and Somers, M. 2006. "Organizations as Complex Adaptive Systems: Implications of Complexity Theory for Leadership Research." *Leadership Quarterly* 17: 351–365.

Scholtes, P.R. 1988. *The Team Handbook*. Madison, WI: Joiner.

Schriesheim, C.A.; Castro, S.L.; Zhou, X.; and DeChurch, L.A. 2006. "An Investigation of Path-Goal and Transformational Leadership Theory Predictions at the Individual Level of Analysis." *Leadership Quarterly* 17: 21–38.

Schultz, J.D. 1998. "Tennessee Valley Authority." In *A Historical Guide to the U.S. Government,* ed. G.T. Kurian, 567–569. New York: Oxford University Press.

Schwarz, R. 2002. *The Skilled Facilitator*. 2d ed. San Francisco: Jossey-Bass.

Schweigert, F.J. 2007. "Learning to Lead: Strengthening the Practice of Community Leadership." *Leadership* 3(3): 325–342.

Segil, L.; Goldsmith, M.; and Belasco, J. (eds.) 2003. *Partnering: The New Face of Leadership*. New York: Anacom.

Selznick, P. 1949. *TVA and the Grass Roots*. Berkeley: University of California Press.

———. 1957. *Leadership in Administration*. New York: Row, Peterson.

Sendjaya, S.; Sarros, J.C.; and Santora, J.C. 2008. "Defining and Measuring Servant Leadership Behaviour in Organizations." *Journal of Management Studies* 45(2): 402–424.

Senge, P. 1990. *The Fifth Discipline: The Art and Practice of the Learning Organization*. New York: Doubleday Currency.

Shamir, B.; House, R.J.; and Arthur, M.B. 1993. "The Motivational Effects of Charismatic Leadership: A Self-Concept Based Theory." *Organizational Science* 4(4): 577–594.

Shamir, B.; Pillai, R.; Bligh, M.C.; and Uhl-Bien, M. (eds.). 2007. *Follower-Centered Perspectives on Leadership*. Charlotte, NC: IAP.

Shartle, C.L. 1950. "Studies in Leadership by Interdisciplinary Methods." In *Leadership in American Education,* ed. A.G. Grace. Chicago: University of Chicago Press.

Shipper, F., and Wilson, C.L. 1992. "The Impact of Managerial Behaviors on Group Performance, Stress, and Commitment." In *Impact for Leadership,* ed. K. Clark, M.B. Clark, and D.P. Campbell, 119–129. Greensboro, NC: Center for Creative Leadership.

Silva, C., and McGuire, M. 2010. "Leading Public Sector Networks: An Empirical Examination of Integrative Behaviors." *Leadership Quarterly* 21: 264–277.

Simon, H.A. 1947. *Administrative Behavior: A Study of Decision-Making Processes in Administrative Organization*. New York: Macmillan.

Simonsen, W. 1998. "Municipal Bonds: Policy and Strategy." In *The International Encyclopedia of Public Policy and Administration,* ed. Jay Shafritz, 1453–1458. Boulder, CO: Westview.

Sinclair, A. 2005. "Body Possibilities in Leadership." *Leadership* 1(4): 387–406.

Sinha, D., and Chowdry, G.P. 1981. "Perception of Subordinates as a Moderator of Leadership Effectiveness in India." *Journal of Social Psychology* 113: 115–121.

Skinner, B.F. 1953. *Science and Human Behavior*. New York: Macmillan.

———. 1971. *Beyond Freedom and Dignity*. New York: Knopf.

———. 1974. *About Behaviorism*. New York: Knopf.

Slackman, M. 2006. "Iranian 101: A Lesson for Americans. The Fine Art of Hiding What You Mean to Say." *New York Times*, Week in Review, August 6.

Slocum, J.W. 1984. "Problems with Contingency Models of Leader Participation." In *Leaders and Managers: International Perspective on Managerial Behavior and Leadership,* ed. J.G. Hunt, D. Hosking, C.A. Schriesheim, and R. Stewart. New York: Pergamon.

Sorenson, T.C. 1963. *Decision Making in the White House*. New York: Columbia University Press.

Sosik, J.J. 2005. "The Role of Personal Values in the Charismatic Leadership of Corporate Managers: A Model and Preliminary Field Study." *Leadership Quarterly* 16: 221–244.

Spencer, L.M., and Spencer, S.M. 1993. *Competence at Work: Models for Superior Performance*. New York: Wiley.

Standard and Poor's. 1967. *Register of Corporations, Directors and Executives*. New York.

Stein, R.T. 1975. "Identifying Emergent Leaders from Verbal and Nonverbal Communications." *Journal of Personality and Social Psychology* 32: 125–135.

Sternberg, R.J. 2003. "WICS: A Model of Leadership in Organizations." *Academy of Learning and Education* 2(4): 386–401.

———. 2007. "A Systems Model of Leadership." *American Psychologist* 62(1): 34–42.

Stewart, R. 1967. *Managers and Their Jobs*. London: Macmillan.

———. 1976. *Contrasts in Management*. Berkshire: McGraw-Hill UK.

———. 1982. *Choices for the Manager: A Guide to Understanding Managerial Work*. Englewood Cliffs, NJ: Prentice Hall.

St. John, W.D. 1983. "Successful Communication Between Supervisors and Employees." *Personnel Journal* 62(1): 71–77.

Stogdill, R.M. 1948. "Personal Factors Associated with Leadership: A Survey of the Literature." *Journal of Psychology* 25: 35–71.

———. 1959. *Individual Behavior and Group Achievement*. New York: Oxford University Press.

———. 1974. *Handbook of Leadership*. 1st ed. New York: Free Press.

Stohl, C. 1986. "The Role of Memorable Messages in the Process of Organizational Socialization." *Communication Quarterly* 34: 231–249.

Stone, D.C. 1945. "Notes on the Government Executive: His Role and His Methods." *Public Administration Review* 5(3): 210–225.

———. 1981. "Innovative Organizations Require Innovative Managers." *Public Administration Review* 41(5): 507–513.

Strange, J.M., and Mumford, M.D. 2005. "The Origins of Vision: Effects of Reflection, Models, and Analysis." *Leadership Quarterly* 16: 121–148.

Streufert, S., and Swezey, R.W. 1986. *Complexity, Managers, and Organizations*. Orlando, FL: Academic Press.

Svara, J. 2007. *Ethics Primer for Public Administrators in Government and Nonprofit Organizations*. Sudbury, MA: Jones and Bartlett.

Svara, J.H. (ed.). 1994. *Facilitative Leadership in Local Government: Lessons from Successful Mayors and Chairpersons*. San Francisco: Jossey-Bass.

Sy, T.; Cote, S.; and Saavedra, R. 2005. "The Contagious Leader: Impact of the Leader's Mood on the Mood of Group Members, Group Affective Tone, and Group Processes." *Journal of Applied Psychology* 90(2): 295–305.

Taylor, F.W. 1911. *Principles of Scientific Management*. New York: Harper and Row.

Taylor, R.L., and Rosenback, W.E. (eds.) 1984. *Military Leadership: In Pursuit of Excellence*. Boulder, CO: Westview Press.

Terry, L.D. 1995. *Leadership of Public Bureaucracies: The Administrator as Conservator*. Thousand Oaks, CA: Sage.

———. 1998. "Administrative Leadership, Neo-Managerialism and the Public Management Movement." *Public Administration Review* 58(3): 194–200.

Terry, R. 1993. *Authentic Leadership: Courage in Action*. San Francisco: Jossey-Bass.

Thach, E., and Thompson, K.J. 2007. "Trading Places: Examining Leadership Competencies Between For-profit vs. Public and Non-profit Leaders." *Leadership and Organization Development Journal* 28(4): 356–375.

Thibaut, J.W., and Kelley, H.H. 1959. *The Social Psychology of Groups*. New York: Wiley.

Thomas, K.W. 1992. "Conflict and Negotiation Processes in Organizations." In *Handbook of Industrial and Organizational Psychology,* vol. 3, ed. M.D. Dunnette and L.M. Hough. Palo Alto: Consulting Psychologists Press.

Thompson, A.M., and Perry, J.L. 2006. "Collaboration Processes: Inside the Black Box." *Public Administration Review* 66 (Supplement): 20–32.

Thompson, G., and Vecchio, R.P. 2009. "Situational Leadership Theory: A Test of Three Versions." *Leadership Quarterly* 20: 837–848.

Thompson, J.R. 2000. "Reinventing as Reform: Assessing the National Performance Review." *Public Administration Review* 60(6): 508–521.

Tichy, N.M., and Bennis, W.G. 2007. *Judgment: How Winning Leaders Make Great Calls.* New York: Penguin.

Tichy, N.M., and Devanna, M.A. 1986. *The Transformational Leader.* New York: Wiley.

———. 1990. *The Transformational Leader* (with updated preface). New York: Wiley.

Tilly, C. 1978. *From Mobilization to Revolution.* Reading, MA: Addison-Wesley.

———. 2004. *Social Movements, 1768–2004.* Boulder, CO: Paradigm.

Tjosvold, D.; Wedley, W.C.; and Field, R.H.G. 1986. "Constructive Controversy: The Vroom-Yetton Model and Managerial Decision Making." *Journal of Occupational Behavior* 7: 125–138.

Tourish, D., and Vatcha, N. 2005. "Charismatic Leadership and Corporate Cultism at Enron: The Elimination of Dissent, the Promotion of Conformity and Organizational Collapse." *Leadership* 1(4): 455–480.

Trevino, L.K. 1992. "The Social Effects of Punishment in Organizations: A Justice Perspective." *Academy of Management Review* 17(4): 647–676.

Trevino, L.K.; Weaver, G.R.; and Reynolds, S.J. 2006. "Behavioral Ethics in Organizations: A Review." *Journal of Management* 32: 951–990.

Trottier, T.; Van Wart, M.; and Wang, X. 2008. "Examining the Nature and Significance of Leadership in Government Organizations." *Public Administration Review* 68(2): 319–333.

Trump, D.J. 2009: "Bottom-Line Leaders." *Leadership Excellence* 26(7): 11.

Tushman, M.L., and Romanelli, E. 1985. "Organizational Evolution: A Metamorphosis of Convergence and Reorientation." *Research in Organizational Behavior* 7: 171–222.

Tushman, M.L.; Newman, W.H.; and Romanelli, E. 1986. "Convergence and Upheaval: Managing the Unsteady Pace of Organizational Evolution." *California Management Review* 29: 29–44.

Twohig, D. 2001. "George Washington." In *The Oxford Companion to United States History,* ed. P.S. Boyer, 816–817. New York: Oxford University Press.

Uhl-Bien, M. 2006. "Relational Leadership Theory: Exploring the Social Processes of Leadership and Organizing." *Leadership Quarterly* 17: 654–676.

Uhl-Bien, M.; Marion, R.; and McKelvey, B. 2007. "Complexity Leadership Theory: Shifting Leadership from the Industrial Age to the Knowledge Era." *Leadership Quarterly* 18: 298–318.

Ungar, B. (ed.). 1989. *Senior Executive Service: Training and Development of Senior Executives.* GAO-GGD-89–127. Washington, DC: U.S. Government Accounting Office.

U.S. Office of Personnel Management (OPM). 1992. *Dimensions of Effective Behavior: Executives, Managers, and Supervisors.* Drafted by D. Corts and M. Gowing. Washington, DC: Office of Personnel Research and Development, Report no. PRD-92–05.

———. 1997. *Occupational Study of Federal Executives, Managers, and Supervisors: An Application of the Multipurpose Occupational Systems Analysis Inventory-Closed Ended (MOSAIC).* Drafted by D.J. Gregory and R.K. Park. Washington, DC: Office of Personnel Research and Development, Report no. PRD-92–21.

———. 1999. *High Performance Leaders—A Competency Model.* Drafted by L.D. Eyde, D.J. Gregory, T.W. Muldrow, and P.K. Mergen. Washington, DC: Employment Service-Personnel Resources and Development Center, Report no. PRDC-99–02.

———. 2006. "Guide to Senior Executive Service Qualifications." Available at www.opm.gov/ses/references/ses_quals_guide_2006.pdf.

———. 2010. Official website, http://www.opm.gov/index.asp.

Van Fleet, D.D., and Yukl, G. 1986. *Military Leadership: An Organizational Perspective.* Greenwich, CT: JAI Press.

Vanmullem, K., and Hondeghem, A. 2009. "Leadership Diversity in an Ageing Workforce." In *Public Sector Leadership: International Challenges and Perspectives,* ed. J.A. Raffel, P. Leisink, and A.E. Middlebrooks. Northampton, MA: Edward Elgar.

Van Slyke, D.M., and Alexander, R.W. 2006. "Public Service Leadership: Opportunities for Clarity and Coherence." *American Review of Public Administration* 36(4), 362–374.

Van Vugt, M.; Hogan, R.; and Kaiser, R. B. 2008. "Leadership, Followership, and Evolution." *American Psychologist* 63(3): 182–196.

Van Wart, M. 1995. "The First Step in the Reinvention Process: Assessment." *Public Administration Review* 55(5): 429–438.

———. 1998a. *Changing Public Sector Values.* New York: Garland.

———. 1998b. "Organizational Investment in Employee Development." In *Handbook of Human Resource Management in Government,* ed. S.E. Condrey, 276–297. San Francisco: Jossey-Bass.

———. 2001. "A Study of the Leadership Profile of Managers in Local Government." Unpublished paper. Texas Tech University.

———. 2002. "A Reanalysis of OPM's 1997 Occupational Study: Examining 150 Discrete Competencies at Different Levels of Management." Unpublished paper. Texas Tech University.

———. 2003. "Public Sector Leadership Theory: An Assessment." *Public Administration Review* 63(2): 214–228.

———. 2004. "A Comprehensive Model of Organizational Leadership: The Leadership Action Cycle." *International Journal of Organization Theory and Behavior* 6(4): 173–208.

Van Wart, M., and Berman, E. 1999. "Contemporary Public Sector Productivity Values: Narrower Scope, Tougher Standards, and New Rules of the Game." *Public Productivity and Management Review* 22(3): 326–347.

Van Wart, M., and Denhardt, K. 2001. "Organizational Structures as a Context for Organizational Ethics." In *Handbook of Administrative Ethics,* 2d ed., ed. T. Cooper, 227–241. New York: Marcel Dekker.

Van Wart, M., and Dicke, L. (eds.). 2007. *Administrative Leadership in the Public Sector: An ASPA Classics Volume.* Armonk, NY: M.E. Sharpe.

Van Wart, M., and Kapucu, N. Forthcoming. "Crisis Management Competencies: The Case of Emergency Managers in the U.S." *Public Management Review.*

Van Wart, M., and O'Farrell, O. 2007. "Organizational Leadership and the Challenges in Teaching It." *Journal of Public Affairs Education* 13(2), 427–438.

Van Wart, M., with Suino, P. 2008. *Leadership in Public Organizations: An Introduction.* Armonk, NY: M.E. Sharpe.

Van Wart, M.; Cayer, N.J.; and Cook, S. 1993. *Handbook of Training and Development in the Public Sector.* San Francisco: Jossey-Bass.

Vecchio, R.P.; Justin, J.E.; and Pearce, C.L. 2008. "The Utility of Transactional and Transformational Leadership for Predicting Performance and Satisfaction with a Path-Goal Theory Framework." *Journal of Occupational and Organizational Psychology* 81(1): 71–82.

Vera, D., and Crossan, M. 2004. "Strategic Leadership and Organizational Learning." *Academy of Management Review* 29: 222–240.

Vinzant, J.C., and Crothers, L. 1998. *Street-Level Leadership: Discretion and Legitimacy in Front-Line Public Service.* Washington, DC: Georgetown University Press.

Vroom, V.H. 1964. *Work and Motivation.* New York: Wiley.

Vroom, V.H., and Jago, A.G. 1988. *The New Leadership: Managing Participation in Organizations.* Englewood Cliffs, NJ: Prentice Hall.

———. 2007. "The Role of the Situation in Leadership." *American Psychologist* 62(1): 17–24.

Vroom, V.H., and Yetton, P.W. 1973. *Leadership and Decision-making.* Pittsburgh: University of Pittsburgh Press.

Wageman, R.; Nunes, D.N.; Burruss, J.A.; and Hackman, J.R. 2008. *Senior Leadership Teams: What It Takes to Make Them Great*. Boston, MA: Harvard Business School Press.

Waldman, D.A., and Siegel, D. 2008. "Defining Social Responsibility." *Leadership Quarterly* 19: 117–131.

Waldman, D.A.; Berson, Y.; and Keller, R.T. 2009. "Leadership and Organizational Learning." *Leadership Quarterly* 20: 1–3.

Waldo, D. 1948. *The Administrative State*. New York: Ronald.

Wallenstein, S. 2009. "The Roots of the Financial Crisis." *Capital Markets Law Journal* 4(1): 8–30.

Walters, J. 2001. *Understanding Innovation*. Arlington, VA: The PricewaterhouseCoopers Endowment for the Business of Government.

Walton, M. 1986. *The Deming Management Method*. New York, NY: Perigee.

Wang, X., and Van Wart, M. 2007. "When Public Participation in Administration Leads to Trust: An Empirical Assessment of Managers' Perceptions." *Public Administration Review* 67(2): 265–278.

Warner, L.S., and Grint, K. 2007. "American Indian Ways of Leading and Knowing." *Leadership* 3(1): 5–27.

Washington, M., and Hacker, M. 2005. "Why Change Fails: Knowledge Counts." *Leadership and Organizational Development Journal* 26(5): 400–411.

Weber, E.P., and Khademain, A.M. 2008. "Wicked Problems, Knowledge Challenges, and Collaborative Capacity Builders in Network Settings." *Public Administration Review* 68(2): 334–349.

Weber, M. 1930. *The Protestant Ethic and the Spirit of Capitalism*. Trans. T. Parsons. New York: Allen and Unwin.

———. 1947. *The Theory of Social and Economic Organizations*. Trans. T. Parsons. New York: Free Press.

———. 1992/1963. *The Sociology of Religion*. Beacon, NY: Beacon Press.

Weed, S.E.; Mitchell, T.R.; and Moffitt, W. 1976. "Leadership Style, Subordinate Personality, and Task Type as Predictors of Performance and Satisfaction with Supervision." *Journal of Applied Psychology* 61: 58–66.

Weick, K.E.; Sutcliffe, K.M.; and Obstfeld, D. 1999. "Organizing for High Reliability: Processes of Collective Mindfulness." *Research in Organization Behavior* 21: 81–123.

Wexley, K.N., and Latham, G.P. 1981. *Developing and Training Human Resources in Organizations*. Glenview, IL: Scott Foresman.

Wheatley, M.J. 1992. *Leadership and the New Science: Learning About Organizations from an Orderly Universe*. San Francisco: Berrett-Koehler.

Wheelan, S.A., and Johnston, F. 1996. "The Role of the Informal Member Leaders in a System Containing Formal Leaders." *Small Group Research* 27(1): 33–55.

Wiggam, A.E. 1931. "The Biology of Leadership." In *Business Leadership,* ed. H.C. Metcalf. New York: Pitman.

Wilkinson, D. 2006. *The Ambiguity Advantage: What Great Leaders Are Great At*. London: Palgrave Macmillan.

Willner, A.R. 1968. *The Spellbinders: Charismatic Political Leadership*. New Haven, CT: Yale University Press.

Wind, Y., and Mahajan, V. 1981. "Designing Product and Business Portfolios." *Harvard Business Review* 59: 155–165.

Winter, D.G. 1979. *Navy Leadership and Management Competencies: Convergence Among Tests, Interviews and Performance Ratings*. Boston: McBer.

Woodward, H., and Bucholz, S. 1987. *Aftershock*. New York: Wiley.

Wright, B.E., and Pandey, S.K. 2010. "Transformational Leadership in the Public Sector: Does Structure Matter?" *Journal of Public Administration Research and Theory* 20(1): 75–89.

Yammarino, F.J., and Dansereau, F. 2008. "Multi-level Nature of and Multi-level Approaches to Leadership." *Leadership Quarterly* 19: 135–141.

Yammarino, F.J.; Dionne, S.D.; Chun, J.U.; and Dansereau, F. 2005. "Leadership and Levels of Analysis: A State-of-the-Science Review." *Leadership Quarterly* 16: 879–919.

Young, F., and Norris, J. 1988. "Leadership Challenge and Action Planning: A Case Study." *Public Administration Review* 48(1): 564–570.

Yukl, G. 1971. *Leadership in Organizations*. Englewood Cliffs, NJ: Prentice Hall.

———. 1998. *Leadership in Organizations*. 4th ed. Englewood Cliffs, NJ: Prentice Hall.

———. 1999. "An Evaluative Essay on Current Conceptions of Effective Leadership." *European Journal of Work and Organizational Psychology* 8: 33–48.

———. 2002. *Leadership in Organizations*. 5th ed. Englewood Cliffs, NJ: Prentice Hall.

———. 2008. "How Leaders Influence Organizational Effectiveness." *Leadership Quarterly* 19: 708–722.

———. 2009. "Leading Organization Learning: Reflections on Theory and Research." *Leadership Quarterly* 20: 49–53.

Yukl, G.; Gordon, A.; and Taber, T. 2002. "A Hierarchical Taxonomy of Leadership Behavior: Integrating a Half Century of Behavior Research." *Journal of Leadership and Organizational Studies* 9(1): 15–32.

Yukl, G.A., and Latham, G.P. 1975. "Consequences of Reinforcement Schedules and Incentive Magnitudes for Employee Performance: Problems Encountered in an Industrial Setting." *Journal of Applied Psychology* 60(3): 294–298.

Yukl, G.A.; Wall, S.; and Lepsinger, R. 1990. "Preliminary Report on Validation of the Managerial Practices Survey." In *Measures of Leadership,* ed. K.E. Clark and M.B. Clark. West Orange, NJ: Leadership Library of America.

Yun, S.; Faraj, S.; and Sims, H.P., 2005. "Contingent Leadership and Effectiveness of Trauma Resuscitation Teams." *Journal of Applied Psychology* 90(6): 1288–1296.

Zaccaro, S.J. 2007. "Trait-Based Perspectives of Leadership." *American Psychologist* 62(1): 6–16.

Zaleznik, A. 1977. "Managers and Leaders: Are They Different?" *Harvard Business Review* 55(5): 67–78.

———. 2008. *Hedgehogs and Foxes: Character, Leadership, and Command in Organizations*. New York: Palgrave Macmillan.

Zand, D.E. 1997. *The Leadership Triad: Knowledge, Trust, and Power*. New York: Oxford University Press.

Zullow, H.M.; Oettingen, G.; Peterson, C.; and Seligman, M.E.P. 1988. "Pessimistic Explanatory Style in the Historical Record." *American Psychologist* 43: 673–682.

Index

About the Author

Montgomery Van Wart is a professor in the Department of Public Administration and currently Dean of the College of Business and Public Administration at California State University, San Bernardino. He has worked in higher education in various capacities for thirty years, nearly always in an administrative role. Some of his other books are *Leadership in Public Organizations: An Introduction; Administrative Leadership in the Public Sector: An ASPA Classics Volume; Changing Public Sector Values;* and *Handbook of Training and Development for the Public Sector*. Among his awards is the 2005 *Choice* award for the first edition of this book as an Outstanding Academic Title. He has done extensive training of leaders at all levels of governments and internationally.